SPEECH CRITICISM

THE DEVELOPMENT OF STANDARDS
FOR RHETORICAL APPRAISAL

By

LESTER THONSSEN

COLLEGE OF THE CITY OF NEW YORK

and

A. CRAIG BAIRD

STATE UNIVERSITY OF IOWA

THE RONALD PRESS COMPANY ⟁ **NEW YORK**

Library of Congress Catalog Card Number: 48-6420

... I will not hesitate to affirm, that whether it [eloquence] is acquired by art or practice, or the mere powers of nature, it is the most difficult of all attainments; for each of the five branches of which it is said to consist is of itself a very important art; from whence it may easily be conjectured how great and arduous must be the profession which unites and comprehends them all.—Cicero, *Brutus*

PREFACE

"There are plenty of opportunities for criticism," said Lucian, "if one has captious ears." But it is important that our critical evaluations be more than just censorious. We live in a world of talk—talk that influences our lives, from the minor acts of a local club to the policy-making decisions of our government. In a democracy such as ours, this implies a very real obligation upon the citizenry to appraise intelligently what its representatives say; thus is the criticism of speeches made necessary by the nature of our political and social environment.

Believing that this time-honored discipline of criticism should be as closely and definitely related to speechcraft as it has been to literature, history, and art, we offer this volume. There exists a well-developed body of theory for public speaking; here we seek to articulate critical standards *with* the theory. Although designed as a text for a college course in speech criticism, we believe that this book should prove of comparable value in courses dealing with rhetorical theory, advanced speech composition, and the history or philosophy of public address. The extensive scope, the analytical consideration of authorities in speechcraft from the ancients down to our own time, and the wide use of citation that characterize this book should also establish its value as correlative reading in more general introductory courses. It should prove its worth in libraries, whether general or educational, and especially in the personal libraries of speech instructors and speech majors, both undergraduate and postgraduate.

The undertaking is ambitious, and attempting to define it in a prefatory note is most difficult. In simplest form, the critic's objective should be an intelligently critical evaluation and judgment. This task involves (1) investigating the facts relating to the speech, (2) formulating the criteria by which the speech is to be judged, and (3) making the evaluation.

As steps one and three define themselves with relative clarity, we will briefly indicate typical constituents of the second as they are presented in Part I. The criteria derive from the fundamental principles of rhetoric, philosophy, psychology, history, and logic. Sampling these, we note the importance of the psychological factor when

v

we consider the influence of beliefs, attitudes, suggestion, and other emotional manifestations on crowd behavior. The importance of the historical element becomes equally clear in weighing the social, political, and economic factors that form the background of the speech and help to give it meaning. Again, any validity achieved in the evaluation of a speech will depend largely upon the ability of the critic's material to withstand the usual tests of logic.

But most basic is the critic's evaluation of the speaker's ability to adjust his argument to the four factors of rhetoric as developed by the ancients: himself, his audience, his subject, and the occasion. Of these, most important is the audience, for the success of a speech lies not in its well-turned phrases, but in its achieving a desired effect upon the hearers. Thus the primary concept is that of speech as communication, i.e., the degree to which it achieves an end consistent with the speaker's intention. Parts II and III present historical surveys of the development of these principles and of the methods of outstanding critics, while Part IV is devoted to the peculiar and difficult problems of research faced by the speech critic.

It is after establishing this background that, in Part V, we define and illustrate our standards of judgment: Integrity of Ideas, Emotion, Character of the Speaker, Structure of the Discourse, Style, Delivery, and Measures of Effectiveness. The book closes with a brief discussion of a philosophy of rhetoric.

The reader should understand that we offer no set formula for critical evaluation. When it is considered that a speech may be devoted to practically any subject of man's experience, that the background or setting of the speech is equally variable and possibly even more influential in determining its effectiveness, and, finally, that speeches in themselves are of many different types and have greatly varying objectives, it is apparent that no formula can be fitted into even a majority of speech situations. What we do offer is a starting point, a conception of rhetorical criticism as an intellectual enterprise: announced principles are simply statements of theory to be applied to particular cases and are designed to aid the critic in discharging his obligation to relate his criticism to the larger pattern of ideas and ideals in oratorical history.

Every effort consistent with accuracy has been made to avoid detailed argument over definitions. The reader will find the word "rhetoric" used in the broad sense of communication of ideas through speech and writing, but with emphasis upon the former. We do not argue the possible differences between "rhetoric" and "oratory," or between "eloquence" and "public speaking." Instead, we have

PREFACE   vii

drawn freely upon these and related terms, and—unless the specific context reveals a distinction—have used them as synonymous, or at least reliably analogous, expressions.

Two appendixes are included, both arranged according to chapters. The first presents a list of selected correlative readings and exercises. The second includes note material consisting almost exclusively of citation of sources for matter quoted in the text.

Many of our colleagues have given us permission to use passages from their writings. For this courtesy, we express our gratitude to Professors Wilbur S. Howell, Orville A. Hitchcock, Irving J. Lee, Wayland M. Parrish, Roy C. McCall, Everett Lee Hunt, Herbert A. Wichelns, Edward Z. Rowell, Edward L. Pross, Carroll C. Arnold, Carroll P. Lahman, W. Norwood Brigance, W. Hayes Yeager, Forest Whan, Russell H. Wagner, Donald C. Bryant, Karl R. Wallace, Theodore F. Nelson, H. Clay Harshbarger, Wilbur E. Gilman, and John W. Black. For the manner in which we have used their material, and for its interpretation, we are of course solely responsible.

We wish to express our special thanks to Professor Loren D. Reid. With his permission, we have quoted extensively from his dissertation on *Charles James Fox*.

We acknowledge gratefully our debt to the theorists of the past, at the same time accepting accountability for our exposition and adaptation to present usage of their theories. With the deep conviction that the encouragement of intellectual effort in the field of rhetorical criticism will help to reveal the significant role of speechmaking in the historical process, we offer this preliminary treatise.

LESTER THONSSEN
A. CRAIG BAIRD

New York
January, 1948

ACKNOWLEDGMENTS

We acknowledge our indebtedness to a host of scholars. Among the many men from whose writings we have derived substantial assistance are Charles S. Baldwin, Richard C. Jebb, J. F. D'Alton, J. W. H. Atkins, W. Rhys Roberts, and Myron F. Brightfield. Furthermore, works in the Loeb Classical Library and other translations have been of inestimable value.

We wish to express our thanks to the following publishers and individuals for permission to reprint passages from the specified sources:

The Macmillan Company: J. E. C. Welldon (translator), *The Rhetoric of Aristotle* and *The Politics of Aristotle;* R. C. Jebb, *The Attic Orators;* Charles S. Baldwin, *Ancient Rhetoric and Poetic* and *Medieval Rhetoric and Poetic;* George W. Botsford, *Hellenic History;* A. Croiset and M. Croiset, *Abridged History of Greek Literature;* C. T. Winchester, *Some Principles of Literary Criticism;* J. B. Bury, *The Ancient Greek Historians;* Brand Blanshard, *The Nature of Thought;* W. Rhys Roberts (translator), *Dionysius of Halicarnassus on Literary Composition, Longinus on the Sublime,* and *Dionysius of Halicarnassus: The Three Literary Letters* (Cambridge University Press); Louis Cazamian, *Criticism in the Making;* John Morley, *Life of William Ewart Gladstone;* Lord Curzon, *Modern Parliamentary Eloquence;* J. W. H. Atkins, *Literary Criticism in Antiquity* (Cambridge University Press); F. H. Colson, *M. Fabii Quintiliani Institutionis Oratoriae Liber I* (Cambridge University Press); W. A. Edward (translator), *The Suasoriae of Seneca the Elder* (Cambridge University Press); S. F. Bonner, *The Literary Treatises of Dionysius of Halicarnassus* (Cambridge University Press); and *The Cambridge History of American Literature* (Cambridge University Press).

The Harvard University Press (Loeb Classical Library): J. W. Cohoon (translator), *Dio Chrysostom;* R. D. Hicks (translator), *Diogenes Laertius—Lives of Eminent Philosophers;* George Norlin (translator), *Isocrates;* Charles F. Smith (translator), *Thucydides;* W. C. Wright (translator), *Philostratus and Eunapius: The Lives of the Sophists;* A. M. Harmon (translator), *Lucian;* C. R. Haines (translator), *The Correspondence of Marcus Cornelius Fronto;* and William Melmoth (translator), *Pliny: Letters.*

Harper and Brothers: *Essays in Intellectual History;* E. A. Burtt, *Principles and Problems of Right Thinking;* J. P. Mahaffy, *A History of Classical Greek Literature;* Adams S. Hill, *The Principles of Rhetoric;* George R. Collins and John S. Morris, *Persuasion and Debate;* Philo Buck, *Literary Criticism;* Stella Benson, *Pull Devil, Pull Baker;* and John A. Broadus, *Preparation and Delivery of Sermons.*

D. Appleton-Century Company, Inc.: *Studies in Rhetoric and Public Speaking;* W. E. H. Lecky, *A History of England in the Eighteenth Century;* Alexander Bain, *The Senses and the Intellect;* and James Bryce, *William Ewart Gladstone.*

Harcourt, Brace and Company, Inc.: I. A. Richards, *Principles of Literary Criticism.*

Yale University Press: Gertrude Buck, *The Social Criticism of Literature.*

McGraw-Hill Book Company, Inc.: William Norwood Brigance (editor), *History and Criticism of American Public Address.*

Henry Holt and Company, Inc.: Albert E. Avey, *The Function and Forms of Thought;* and *Essays in Honor of John Dewey.*

The University of Chicago Press: Richard G. Moulton, *The Modern Study of Literature;* F. I. Carpenter (editor), *The Arte or Crafte of Rhethoryke by Leonard Cox; International Journal of Ethics;* and *Ethics.*

The University of California Press: Myron F. Brightfield, *The Issue in Literary Criticism;* Robert J. Bonner, *Aspects of Athenian Democracy;* Torsten Petersson, *Cicero: A Biography;* and Frederick J. Teggart, *Theory and Processes of History.*

Charles Scribner's Sons: W. C. Brownell, *Criticism;* Barrett Wendell, *The Traditions of European Literature;* J. Wight Duff, *A Literary History of Rome in the Silver Age* and *A Literary History of Rome from the Origins to the Close of the Golden Age;* Thomas Davidson, *Aristotle and Ancient Educational Ideals;* and John K. Gardiner, *The Forms of Prose Literature.*

Columbia University Press: James T. Shotwell, *The History of History.*

G. P. Putnam's Sons: Albert von Ruville, *William Pitt, Earl of Chatham,* and Henry Hardwicke, *History of Oratory and Orators.*

American Book Company: H. L. Hollingworth, *The Psychology of the Audience.*

Longmans, Green and Company, Inc.: J. F. D'Alton, *Roman Literary Theory and Criticism,* and W. E. H. Lecky, *Historical and Political Essays.*

Little, Brown and Company: W. W. Goodwin (editor), *Plutarch's Miscellanies and Essays.*

Little, Brown and Company and the Atlantic Monthly Press: James Truslow Adams, *The Epic of America.*

E. P. Dutton and Company, Inc.: T. A. Moxon (translator), *Aristotle's Poetics: Demetrius on Style* (Everyman's Library), and J. M. Mitchell (translator), *Petronius: The Satyricon.*

Ginn and Company: John F. Genung, *The Practical Elements of Rhetoric* and *The Working Principles of Rhetoric.*

Alfred A. Knopf: John Morley, *Edmund Burke,* and George E. C. Catlin, *Science and Method of Politics.*

Houghton Mifflin Company: Edward W. Emerson and Waldo E. Forbes, *Journals of Ralph Waldo Emerson.*

The Johns Hopkins Press: *American Journal of Philology.*

J. B. Lippincott Company: Lester Thonssen and Ross Scanlan, *Speech Preparation and Delivery.*

New York World-Telegram: Heywood Broun, "It Seems to Me."

Saturday Review of Literature: Selected passages.

Quarterly Journal of Speech: Selected passages.

Dr. W. P. Sandford: *English Theories of Public Address, 1530-1828.*

Curtis Brown, Ltd.: Hugh Walpole, *Semantics.*

Papers of the Bibliographical Society of America: Selected passages.

University Libraries, State University of Iowa: Selected passages from doctoral theses.

Speech Monographs: Selected passages.

Connecticut Academy of Arts and Sciences: Harry M. Hubbell (translator), *The Rhetoric of Philodemus.*

Donald C. Bryant: *Papers in Rhetoric.*

University of Pennsylvania Library and Alan F. Herr: *The Elizabethan Sermon.*

Transradio Press Service: A news dispatch.

Oxford University Press: Edward Lascelles, *The Life of Charles James Fox.*

John Murray: Theodor Gomperz, *Greek Thinkers.*

Constable and Company and George M. Trevelyan: *The Life of John Bright.*

Methuen and Company: John F. Dobson, *The Greek Orators.*

The Clarendon Press: G. H. Mair (editor), *Arte of Rhetorique* (Thomas Wilson); W. R. Sorley, *Herbert Spencer Lectures,* Second Series; and S. V. Makower and B. H. Blackwell (editors), *A Book of English Essays, 1600-1900.*

Cambridge University Press: John E. Sandys, *M. Tulli Ciceronis ad M. Brutum Orator.*

CONTENTS

PART I

The Nature of Rhetorical Criticism

PART II

The Development of Rhetorical Theory

PART III

The Methods of the Critics

PART IV

Preliminary Aspects of Rhetorical Criticism

PART V

The Standards of Judgment

PART VI

Postscript to an Inquiry

APPENDICES

PART I
THE NATURE OF RHETORICAL CRITICISM

Chapter 1

INTRODUCTORY PRINCIPLES

The Problem of Criticism

Criticism is a much abused word. It has come to mean many things, from discerning appraisal to irresponsible faultfinding. Its locus of meaning probably will never be fixed for, like matters of taste from which it is not wholly dissociated, it often makes excursions into subjectivity, running from honest predisposition to forthright caprice. Small wonder, then, that criticism itself, to quote W. C. Brownell, "is much criticized,—which logically establishes its title." [1]

Despite the fact that criticism is not completely free from a certain "odour of unsanctity," it is an important and necessary business. It is, however, a sadly neglected activity. Of carping objection to what is said and done in public life, there is no shortage; of sentimentalized affirmation and approval, there is no want. But of intelligently critical evaluation and judgment there is not, cannot be, enough.

How does this problem relate to speechmaking, or rhetorical criticism? The criticism of speeches is old; and yet it is in its infancy. It is old in that Plato, Cicero, Quintilian, and a host of other scholars of antiquity practiced the art. It is young in that relatively little systematic effort has been put forth to formulate a working doctrine of rhetorical evaluation. Except for the work of a group of scholars in Speech during the past few decades, a mere handful of substantial contributions to rhetorical criticism is all that the field can claim.

Much of contemporary speech criticism is of an incidental character. The speaking accomplishments of a public figure are often interwoven with the story of his life. This biographical approach, however admirable in its own sphere, usually fails to throw the meaning of a man's speaking efforts into the right focus; the emphasis remains on the sequence of events in the biography, rather than upon the social pattern in which the speaker's thoughts were expressed or upon the responses which the speaker sought to secure from particular audiences. Praiseworthy exceptions to this general rule may be found, however, in such readable contributions as G. M. Trevelyan's

Life of John Bright and, to a somewhat lesser extent, in Bernard Dyer's *The Public Career of William Maxwell Evarts.*

In addition to incidental rhetorical criticism in biography, we find scattered, and usually highly unsatisfactory, segments of speech appraisal in historical surveys and treatises. However, the real stature of Daniel Webster or of Franklin D. Roosevelt, as a speaker, probably will not be revealed in history books until competent rhetorical critics complete studies having sufficient objective discernment and logical integrity to justify the inclusion of the findings in historical analyses.

Newspapers and periodicals furnish a certain amount of speech criticism. The editorial writer or the popular columnist, neither of whom is necessarily skilled in rhetorical investigation, appraises the more important speechmaking of the day. Much of this reviewing— for such it usually is—amounts to little more than highly colored praise or blame of a detail or aspect of a speech. Seldom do we find such a report embracing the many constituents which properly deserve consideration, if a speech *as a whole* is to be evaluated fairly and meaningfully.

But where, it may be asked, does this interest in criticism, however faultily pursued in popular circles, have its origin? The source of any critical inquiry is the recognition of some *problem.* Speech criticism is no exception. Obviously, an intellectual curiosity alone will prompt certain scholars to appraise the written texts of speakers. But, in the main, such critical investigation derives from an outside stimulus, from a problem in the environment. This problem arises from two conditions. In the first place, we live in a world of talk. To paraphrase Frederic Harrison, we are witnesses to the "remorseless cataract" of daily speech. Speechmaking is a natural and wholesome consequent of the form of polity under which we live. In deliberation and decision, the democratic way provides for the exchange of views; the oral transmission of ideas is a rightful prerogative of the man who enjoys the estate of free discussion. There is, then, much speechmaking in our everyday world.

But that alone would not necessarily serve as an impulse to critical inquiry, were it not for a second condition in the environment. Abundance of speechmaking becomes a problem because of the necessity of appraising some of the speeches. A semblance of order, a means of determining goodness and badness, a guide to action must be found if the pattern of talk is to be more than an indiscriminate gnarling of points of view. It is at this moment that the role of the critic takes on meaning. Criticism serves to bridge the gap between external stimulus and internal compulsion to belief and action.

Whether the speeches in question were delivered in the age of William Pitt and Charles James Fox, of John Bright and Richard Cobden, or of Franklin D. Roosevelt and Winston Churchill, is of little concern to us here. In the following pages, we shall attempt to point out a course which the careful critic may follow in arriving at his judgment respecting the character and effectiveness of a speech in any period.

Nature of the Rhetorical Medium

Like other creative workers, the public speaker achieves the end of his art through the resourceful use of reason, memory, imagination, and emotion. In other words, he relies upon the same psychological equipment to realize his purpose as does the sculptor, the painter, or the literary craftsman. There is nothing unique about the mental functioning of the speaker which sets his efforts off sharply from those of skilled individuals in other fields. However, we recognize that the end-products of the speaker's art differ, for example, from those of the novelist or the essayist. The same critical yardstick cannot be applied appropriately and meaningfully both to a novel and to a speech. Some criteria would be similar; but, in the main, either the novel or the speech, depending upon the character of the critique, would suffer through such common appraisal. This circumstance argues the necessity of looking to the medium in which speech operates before considering the criteria by which a particular speaking performance is evaluated. Consequently, we must first examine the basic nature of the rhetorical art.

Ancient and modern authorities on rhetoric agree that the fundamental purpose of oral discourse is social coordination or control. This implies the use of speech as an instrument of communication, as a tool by which ideas and feelings are conveyed from one person to another. Basic to all analyses of the theory and practice of rhetoric, this concept postulates *purpose* in all speaking performances. Men use speech, not simply to hear themselves talk, but to achieve certain responses from hearers.

Every situation in which a speaker performs involves, therefore, at least three essential elements: the communicator or speaker, the medium of expression, and the recipient of the message. These constituents make up the equation of communication. Without any one of them, the process of social control through the instrumentality of rhetoric is destroyed.

The medium through which the communicative function is fulfilled is language. In other words, the coordination and control of social efforts depends upon the use of symbols. Effective in giving formulation and design to oral expression, these symbols are of both audible and visible types. Each of the several sounds of the language is an audible symbol. Each of the many possible movements of the body may have symbolic significance, visually, in the total process of communication. Hence the phonetic and gestural symbols we call language are the external aspects of a highly complex and not too well-known psychological phenomenon, namely, the conception and transference of meaning.

The simple mention of language as the medium of communication, therefore, fails to reveal fully the intricate process of translation which every speaking act involves. Briefly, the process is a two-way affair. The speaker first translates his ideas and feelings into phonetic and gestural symbols. Then, through physical control, he transmits these symbols to the listener, impressing them upon his consciousness as something heard and seen. Immediately the process of retranslation begins, only this time the listener, rather than the speaker, is the active participant. He must now convert the symbols into meaningful, articulated units of thought bearing a faithful resemblance to the original conception of the speaker.

But let us be more specific about the nature of a *speech situation* in which this process of symbolic formulation and translation takes place. In its broadest sense, a speech situation may be regarded as a complex social relationship in which a speaker attempts to secure a particular response from a group of listeners. Except in certain radio setups, the situation usually involves face-to-face engagement. What, then, are the distinguishing characteristics of this social pattern in which rhetoric functions?

The speech situation has certain distinctive features, all interrelated:

(1) It admits of unconfined choice as to subject matter. Any subject properly adapted to the specific audience and occasion can be used; it may deal with geometry, music, political science, or any other topic of inquiry. This is another way of saying that rhetoric confines its service to no special class of material; that it is, as Aristotle remarked, the "faculty of discovering all the possible means of persuasion in any subject." Accordingly, speakers use the tools of rhetoric and the speech situation to carry out their communicative ambitions in all subjects.

Although rhetoric may be employed to develop a point on any subject, it is, because of its practical nature, devoted mainly to a small number of considerations. This seeming paradox arises from the fact that the majority of speech situations involve attempts by speakers (a) to establish the justice or injustice, the true or the false, of an action or a condition; (b) to praise or blame someone or something; or (c) to urge that a course of action be or not be followed. Even the last division, dealing with deliberative speaking, is more sharply limited as to the principal matters of discussion than we might surmise. According to Aristotle, and experience requires our agreement, there are five main topics of deliberation: ways and means, war and peace, national defense, imports and exports, and legislation. Hence we see that a speech situation is confined, not as to *possible subject matter,* but as to the *range of effective choice* within the various fields of thought.

(2) The speech situation is severely controlled by time limitations. Whereas a person may elect to spend a full evening, or a week of evenings, or an entire winter reading a novel, he is obliged to devote his entire attention for a short, continuous period to the hearing of a speech. This circumstance decisively influences the character of oral discourse. The necessity of foreshortening the oral material requires the listener to perceive the import of a subject with maximum speed and minimum detail.

(3) The speech situation is always specific in its point of direction. It aims at achieving something. The very nature of any communicative undertaking in which a speaker tries to elicit a response from hearers makes for *purposiveness.* Speaker and listeners come together, not to rejoice in each other's presence, but to realize an end, be it of entertainment, explanation, information, persuasion, or conviction.

(4) Speech situations are of a transitory character. They contain many elements of an evanescent sort, elements that are effective and significant while the speech is being delivered but irretrievably lost once the speaker leaves the platform. Certain subtle reactions of the listeners, adjustments of the speaker to changes in audience behavior, and momentarily pervasive but subsequently irredeemable moods of the occasion are facts which, to some extent at least, disappear with the event.

(5) Speech situations involve direct social interaction among a plurality of persons. Obviously, this statement is subject to some qualification since radio speech does not always establish face-to-face

contact. Like all other speaking situations, however, such indirect contact groups are held together by bonds of common language and interest.

Every public speech is an experience in audience adjustment. The speech situation provides give-and-take between speaker and hearer. This interaction makes for spirited, effective discourse. The speaker stimulates his hearers who in turn respond with visible or audible symbols, or both. To these responses the speaker then makes such adjustments as may be proper and necessary. Thus a speech situation involves circular response, the flow of stimulation running in both directions, from speaker to hearer and from hearer to speaker.

(6) A speech situation embraces a unique attitudinal relationship because the thought, feeling, and purpose of the communicative venture are *directly* controlled by the personal force of the speaker himself. The speaker has full opportunity to create and maintain a certain tone or attitude through the impress of his character and personality. Whereas a writer can only offer *more words* to command attention at a point where words themselves are already discouraging a reader, a speaker can couple words with vocal and bodily action and ethical appeal to keep the theme of his discourse in the field of interest. Thus, he is able to control more directly and consequently to maintain the proper relation between himself and the audience, and between his subject and the audience.

(7) Finally, and this is essentially a result of the interaction of the foregoing characteristics, a speech situation evokes a distinctive language pattern. True, substantially the same words are used in writing as in speaking, just as the same words are used to mould our censure and our praise. But the external facts of time limitation, reciprocal social stimulation, audience adjustment, and personal appeal through the speaker combine to mould the words into a somewhat different configuration. Hence we find that oral and written material dealing with the same unit of thought often differ as to content, idiom, grammatical structure, and arrangement of parts.

Constituents of the Rhetorical Judgment

A valid judgment of a speech is essentially the same as a valid judgment of any other art form. True, it results from a particular training and appreciation on the part of the critic; it relies upon a special set of criteria; and it derives sanction from a body of its own literature. But, qualitatively, it is simply a *good judgment,* and as such contains no elements peculiar to its own field of inquiry. It makes approximately the same demands on the critic, intellectually, as would a comparable pronouncement upon a novel or a personal essay. In the criticism of speeches, as elsewhere, the formulation of a valid judgment results from the orderly fulfillment of certain requirements inherent in the critical process.

There are three principal stages in the critical process: (a) A searching examination of the facts relating to the particular speech. This is primarily a research undertaking, requiring the use of the standard tools of systematic investigation. (b) The formulation of the principles, or criteria, by which the speech is to be appraised. This is largely a theoretical inquiry into the bases of judgment— the fundamentals derived from accepted works on rhetoric and from the critic's interpretation of their contents as applied to the social sphere of public address. (c) The critical evaluation of the data. The speech is appraised in the light of the findings from the two foregoing stages to determine the degree of merit which may be assigned to the performance.

As in other comparable fields, the judgment of a speech derives much of its substance from facts lying outside its own area. A rhetorical judgment is a composite of data and interpretation that is intended to reveal the *effect* of a given speech upon a particular group of listeners. The word *effect,* or *response,* is all-important. It suggests the central reason for rhetorical criticism. Since speaking is a communicative venture, and since a speaker seeks to communicate a particular set of ideas and feelings to a specific audience, it must follow that the rhetorical critic is concerned with the method employed by a speaker to achieve the response consistent with his purpose. In his essay on "The Literary Criticism of Oratory," Herbert A. Wichelns comments at considerable length on the differences between literary and rhetorical criticism, and he observes that the point of view of the latter is "patently single." "It is not concerned," he remarks, "with permanence, nor yet with beauty. It is concerned with effect." [2] Accepting this conclusion, we may properly ask, What are the constituents of the judgment by which relative merits and eventual effect of a speech are determined?

Speeches occur in social settings. Consequently, their interpretation and criticism must stem from a knowledge of the forces and conditions operative in the social situation at the particular time. In the broadest sense, therefore, the constituents of the rhetorical judgment are without limit as to number and scope; everything that impinges upon the environment plays a part in shaping a speech, and therefore in determining the criticism of it. In short, a rhetorical judgment embraces all the knowledge in the critic's possession; it draws upon his total resources.

But critics, however discerning, cannot embrace a study of the universe, of the total pattern of learning, in the evaluation of a speech. They must rely chiefly upon assumptions, hypotheses, and fixed points of reference derived from *principal* areas of inquiry; and then they must examine available and germane facts in the light of these conceptions. In addition to the purely rhetorical element, the essential constituents of the judgment of a speech derive from philosophy, history, and logic.

The simple concept of criticism suggests a philosophical approach. A given event—in this case, a speech—is surveyed as a functional unity. Systematically, the critic proposes to look at the larger question of social reality as it relates to a speech—or, more accurately, as the speech relates to it—and to investigate not only the means by which the address was accomplished, but also the ends and purposes which it was intended to serve. In short, the critical process presupposes a search for the larger, the comprehensive view of a problem. The critic is engaged in an exploratory venture; he seeks to make an ordered whole of events having an infinity of interrelationships. Philosophically, therefore, he must concern himself with the factors of causation in the social medium. Criticism deals not alone with the facts of a special subject, but with those of the related subjects as well. It formulates from these many data a principle of explanation having "universal" significance.

The philosophical constituent of rhetorical criticism also is evident when we reflect on the nature of the medium in which oral communication functions. A speech is the product of a complex of social events in which human beings and their problems are equated—at least, attempts are made to equate them—with their environment. The purposive character of public speaking tends, therefore, to make a speech more than a superficial happening, more than the mere expression of an individual's fancy. Instead, it makes it a conditioning factor in both individual and collective behavior. The realization of a particular purpose in a speech may actually affect the structure of men's thoughts and actions, and, consequently, may influence the destiny of a community, a nation, a society. The critic of speeches must, accordingly, recognize the patent fact that communication takes place in a social sphere—that it relates men to their environment; he must also acknowledge as a hypothesis the possibility that the communicative intent of a speaker may have *consequential* influence upon the behavior of listeners. These two philosophic considerations are essential elements of any critic's judgment of a public speech.

Finally, the criticism of a speech implies philosophic judgment in that it requires candid recognition of personal attitudes toward certain materials. The critic should hold to the facts as he finds them, and the responsible critic will. But in order to have what James Truslow Adams once called a "delicate intuition" in interweaving the data of history with fidelity to the scientist's love of truth, the critic of speeches must acknowledge his possible prejudices, predispositions, and weaknesses. The rhetorical judgment, therefore, must contain such insight as may be necessary to preserve the objectivity of the evaluation.

A derivative of this line of thinking is the obvious conclusion that the rhetorical judgment contains a psychological and a literary constituent. The former is apparent from the fact that the analyst is deeply concerned with such determining factors of speech effectiveness as intellectual and emotional behavior of listeners, personality manifestations, social incentives, attitudes, suggestion, crowd behavior, propaganda techniques, leadership phenomena, and related matters. That the rhetorical judgment contains a literary component also, is plainly evident. Even though the critic looks upon speechmaking as a useful art, he uses many of the tools and bases many of his conclusions upon the principles of literary craftsmanship. This is particularly true in the assessment of a speaker's style and, to a somewhat lesser extent, of oratorical structure.

Now, let us turn to another, and in many respects the most important, constituent of the rhetorical judgment, namely, the historical. It is a truism that speeches are meaningful only when examined in the social settings of which they are a part. Yet that important fact must be emphasized because it constitutes the core of any satisfactory method of rhetorical analysis. Any event, and a speech is a social event, must be examined in perspective; it must be viewed from afar as well as from the nearest point of vantage, if its full significance is to be understood. "The trouble with so many of our critics," comments an editorial writer in *The Saturday Review of Literature,* "is that they know no history." [3] The critic of oratory is no less subject to such a charge than is the critic of literature. Both must regard the present as the logical result of the past; both must have the inclination and the leisure "to turn from the exciting incidents of the hour to the no less portentous events of bygone times," [4] if they are to appreciate and understand the complex forces with which the problem of criticism deals. The fact that "the past consists of events that have finished happening," as R. G. Collingwood once remarked, is not to be interpreted as meaning that it is dead, and of no consequence.

Whether or not the historian and critic can be united in the same person has been a matter of considerable discussion. Louis Cazamian, commenting on the circumstance that they are "complementary and indispensable to each other," believes they are rarely combined in the same person. According to him, "their efforts will never be entirely reconciled, because they are not on the same plane." [5] In any case, the critic of oratory must have a historical sense as well as skill in historical research if his job is to be done responsibly and comprehensively.

Each public speech is a study in social forces, complex in the extreme. The historical element in the criticism of such a speech includes not only facts which pass under the narrow heading of the data of history, but also related materials from politics, economics, religion, sociology, literature, and law. The Lincoln-Douglas debates, for example, can scarcely be appraised satisfactorily if no account is taken of forces other than the immediate historical details prevailing at the time of each particular speech. There were many other facts—social, economic, and political—which helped to shape the debates and gave them significance; but the discovery of those items of information necessitates a study of forces not immediately discernible in a bare historical account relating only the names and character of the participants, the dates, the number of hearers present, and the length of the speeches. Consequently, the critic of speaking must delve deeply into the past if he is to understand the present. Criticism based upon such research will help establish the "corrective balance" to which Donald C. Bryant refers when he observes that it has been "the fault of the history of literature and oratory, to let the study of figures obscure or blot out the study of forces and social movements." [6]

The rhetorical judgment, then, contains historical constituents because it requires the reconstruction of the speaker's social setting. The critic must, in effect, put on the garment of the past if he would understand fully the forces that shaped a speaker's thinking, the circumstances that prompted a particular speech, and the conditions that modified or determined the outcome of the address. He must, to use the words of George E. Woodberry, conduct all those studies "which assist in the representation of the past, and amplify and clarify historical knowledge."

The critic of oratory probably will never be able to secure all relevant historical facts concerning a particular speech. This should not necessarily invalidate his judgment. The facts of an event are "as innumerable as the grains of sand on a stretch of beach." But by connecting known facts, a critic can reconstruct an occasion or incident with sufficient completeness to make valid judgment possible. That some gaps in the information will be present is almost inevitable. But, to quote Myron F. Brightfield, they "are openly confessed and are allowed to remain as genuine elements of the situation, qualifying all judgments drawn therefrom." [7]

We mentioned above that the critic must connect the available facts. Here, again, we notice his identity with the historian whose task, according to Brightfield, may be said "to consist of the establishment of successive series of *liaisons,* both of the facts within the incident, and of the incident itself with other incidents and, possibly, with more extensive subjects involving other divisions of human knowledge." [8] To a singular degree, the critic of speeches must articulate the findings from many fields—history, economics, politics, etc.—to show how they affect the outcome of a particular address.

The acquisition of an adequate body of the present knowledge concerning a given speech requires the establishment of certain hypotheses. The critic must decide which facts to use, which to discard as unimportant or irrelevant. This is a difficult job, for ways of testing these hypotheses are not always immediately available to check the accuracy of judgment. But it is a vital part of the critic's work. It makes a difference whether a critic decides that the revival meetings in a particular community are more relevant to the understanding of a certain speech than the current price of cotton fiber. The example may be far-fetched, but the point it illustrates in rhetorical criticism is important. From the available totality of facts surrounding a speech event, the critic must select those which are most significant to achieve a full appreciation and understanding of the communicative effort. This cannot be determined by rule. It is but one of the several indispensable aspects of the historical judgment which contribute to the criticism of oratory.

We have now discussed briefly the philosophical and historical constituents of the rhetorical judgment. One more essential consideration remains, namely, the logical component in the critical process.

William T. Brewster once referred to criticism as "a form of argumentation . . ." In the main, the appraisal of a speech is an assignment in argumentative discourse, involving both deductive and inductive forms. The criteria, even if determined originally through induction, are employed by the critic, in greater or lesser measure, as general truths. From them he proceeds to a particular conclusion, thus completing the deductive process. For example, the statement that the audience determines in large part the end and object of a speech is a general principle—one of the fundamental hypotheses—in the light of which a particular speech is evaluated. On the other hand, much of the work of the critic falls under the inductive method. Search is made for facts relating to a speech; the social, political, and economic forces having a presumed bearing upon the address are examined; causal relations among the many items of information are established. And so from a body of particular data the critic draws a general conclusion covering the speech as a complete unit.

The importance of the logical element in rhetorical judgment is further revealed when we remember that historical data figure prominently in the criticism. Historical thinking is, as has been indicated before, selective. In making use of the data of history, the rhetorical critic must, therefore, deal continually with causal explanations. As a temporary historian, to quote E. A. Burtt, he is "trying to find the cause of an event which never happens twice and whose totality ... transcends scientific law and method." [9] But the critic not only selects certain facts as causally significant, to the exclusion of others; he also deals with documents and sources the trustworthiness of which is anything but uniform and the completeness of which is often open to question. Consequently, he must test his evidence and determine its degree of validity.

So the question of "whether there is any other sanction than personality for critical opinion" must be referred to the critic himself. Is he prepared and disposed to subject his data to the tests of verification? To what extent is he willing to look upon his critical function through the eyes of the logician, as well as of the philosopher and of the historian?

The valid judgment of a speech results in large part from the ability of the critic's materials to withstand the usual tests of logic. Accordingly, the critic must test the basic assumptions of his inquiry, assess the evidence which serves as the raw material of his proof, check the deductive principles of his argumentation, and appraise the inductions arising from his use of specific examples, causal relations, and analogies. Here in abundant measure is the source of the logical element in the criticism of oratory. Here is the avenue of approach to the critical method "external to the vagaries of a temperament ..."

Sources of Certain Canons of Rhetorical Criticism

The critic of speeches, like the critic of plays and novels, always faces the problem of steering an intelligent course between two extremes of critical method. He must avoid adoption of a procrustean system into which all speeches are forced according to rule; and, on the other hand, he must not rely solely upon his own judgment, unsupported by outside authority, to determine the worth of a speaking effort.

The canons of rhetorical criticism must of necessity be relative. "Holding the critic's opinions to be obligatory upon other readers," remarks Gertrude Buck, "is very like 'fiat money'—easy to issue but sometimes harder to realize upon." [10] Speeches are highly variable social events; no two are exactly alike. Consequently, the same critical yardstick cannot be applied to all speeches, as the discussion of the standards of judgment in Part V of this book will indicate.

Without suggesting that the dicta of Aristotle be regarded as the unalterable conditions of oratorical achievement, we may nevertheless look upon certain Aristotelian conceptions as safe points of departure in criticism. The canons of rhetorical criticism derive from a classical concept. Rhetoric, to quote Aristotle, is "the faculty of discovering all the possible means of persuasion in any subject." In other words, rhetoric is an instrument by which a speaker can, through the apt use of certain "lines of argument," make an adjustment to a situation composed of himself, his audience, his subject, and the occasion. The impact of these four forces in a social setting gives rise to a certain effect or outcome, the understanding of which concerns the critic. Consequently, to know and evaluate the outcome of a speech necessitates knowing as much as can be determined about each of the constituents of the speech situation. So canons of oratorical criticism cannot properly be divorced from considerations relating to speaker, audience, subject, and occasion. These are indispensable to critical inquiry.

Another concept in Aristotle's *Rhetoric* serves as a determinant of the canons of judgment. Aristotle believed, and practically all writers since his time have concurred, that the audience determines the speech's end and object. In other words, the important aspect of the speech situation is the speaker-audience relationship. Implicit in this idea is the very core of a theory of rhetoric. It embraces the doctrine of speech as communication, purposiveness in discourse, social interaction, and realization of an end or effect consistent with intention. Here, surely, is another concept which the critic of speeches must take fully into account when determining his canons of judgment.

Relation of Criticism to Theory and Practice

Practice, theory, and criticism are, in the broadest sense, indivisible elements of an art. Each influences the other, with the result that all are modified by the circular action.

The effect of these three elements on each other follows a certain chronology. Undoubtedly there was speechmaking—practice—before there was an *art* of speaking. But once an art is systematized, the theory serves as the basis for further practical application. Subsequently, both practice and theory are modified by critical inquiry. In fact, new formulations of theory may even result from this interaction. This is a natural circumstance, occasioned by the fact that the theoretical principles are often inconsistent with or in open violation of the natural and easy practice of the art; criticism then serves to readjust the theory to the practice. Thus a study of the fundamental tenets of rhetorical criticism is also an investigation into the theoretical and practical aspects of public speaking.

Definition of Rhetorical Criticism

Rhetorical criticism contains both a process or method and a declaration of judgment. It involves, first, a process by which unsupported individual preference moves toward rationally defined and systematically determined choice. This movement results from a composite of judgments, not only in rhetoric, but in related fields—particularly philosophy, history, and logic. In the second place, rhetorical criticism embraces a declaration of judgment. It represents an evaluation or appraisal of an oratorical effort with reference to its ultimate effect.

Rhetorical criticism can thus be defined as a comparative study in which standards of judgment deriving from the social interaction of a speech situation are applied to public addresses to determine the immediate or delayed effect of the speeches upon specific audiences, and, ultimately, upon society.

Types of Rhetorical Criticism

As previously indicated, the bases of judgment in rhetoric are not absolute. Consequently, the several types of criticism may enjoy varying measures of acceptance at different times. This may not be unwholesome, for, as Gertrude Buck observes, "Each type of criticism, arising to supplement the inadequacies of previous types, has enriched our conception of the critical process." If this is true in literature, it should be no less true in rhetoric.

In his essay, "The Literary Criticism of Oratory," Wichelns examines three types of criticism which modern writers employ in dealing with public speakers. The first is largely biographical, dealing with the general conduct and character of the man rather than with his speaking activities. The second provides a judgment by balancing the biographical and literary points of interest with the work of the speaker. The third concentrates on the oratorical productions rather than on straight biographical details. Each of these types contributes to an understanding of oratory; none of them can be wholly effective unless the critic approaches his problem with an appreciation of rhetoric and a lively conception of its function in the social structure.

Our classification of the types of criticism is drawn in large part from the literary craftsman, but is adapted to the problems and needs of the field of speech. Not all of these types are consistent with the definition set forth in the preceding section, but they are currently employed and therefore deserve notice.

Classified according to type, the criticism of speeches falls under four main heads, all of which overlap to a certain extent. These types are the impressionistic, analytic, synthetic, and judicial.

The impressionistic criticism of speeches, least systematic and scientific of all, simply records a judgment based upon personal preference and predisposition. It is, indeed, criticism by "idle exclamation." The critic likes or dislikes a certain speech, not necessarily because it conforms or fails to conform to traditional criteria nor because it achieved or failed to achieve the end for which it was intended, but because he entertained a particular attitude toward the speaker, or the subject, or the purpose of the talk. Subjectivity characterizes the appraisal. It should be noted, of course, that in many cases the judgments may be valid; however, such results might almost be considered accidental, for analytical and methodical examination of the facts has not made them so. Such criticism is at the mercy of whim and temperament. (Some criticisms presented by popular columnists are of this type.) Since oratory deals with communication in the area of public affairs, it deserves more exacting analysis.

The second type may be called analytic, despite the fact that, in a larger sense, all criticism is analytical in nature. In this approach the critic makes a methodical examination of all available facts relating to the speech itself. He effects, by "an exact anatomy," an exhaustive structural analysis of the text. This may take the form of word counts, classifications of arguments, ratios of exposition to argumentation or of description to narration, surveys of sentences according to length and structure, listings of figurative elements, itemizations of pronoun usage, and many other classificatory arrangements. The objective of such criticism is not a revelation of the nature of a speech in its social setting, but an understanding of the speech in its own right. Thus analytic criticism is devoted to the collection of facts relating to the speech alone; there is little evaluation.

Synthetic criticism is the third general type. Here, as in the analytic, the critic collects an abundance of facts; but he goes further. He gathers the data which deal not with the speech alone but with the other elements in the total situation, with the speaker, the audience, and the occasion. His principal aim is to collect and arrange these facts so that a faithful reconstruction of the original situation can be achieved. As far as he goes, the critic employing the synthetic method may conduct an effective piece of work. He falls short of the ideal in criticism by failing to interpret his results.

The last type of criticism may be called the judicial. It combines the aims of analytic and synthetic inquiry with the all-important element of evaluation and interpretation of results. Thus it reconstructs a speech situation with fidelity to fact; it examines this situation carefully in the light of the interaction of speaker, audience, subject, and occasion; it interprets the data with an eye to determining the *effect* of the speech; it formulates a judgment in the light of the philosophical-historical-logical constituents of the inquiry; and it appraises the entire event by assigning it comparative rank in the total enterprise of speaking. The material of this book is directed toward the development of criticism of this type.

Qualifications of the Rhetorical Critic

"The fact that there is no royal road to achievement in any branch of human knowledge," Brightfield remarks, "is a most fortunate and necessary circumstance." Fortunate, perhaps, in the sense that the aspirations of the human intellect are never in want of challenges; necessary, no doubt, in that the loftiest of attainments never quite solve the perplexing problems in the realm of thought. It is with recognition of these limitations that we begin our discussion of the essentials of critical inquiry. This treatment cannot prescribe an

absolute formula for success in the criticism of speeches; it can, however, point to a few personal characteristics which should increase
the critic's likelihood of achieving acceptable competence in this field.

It is a painful but nonetheless important truth that the faults of
criticism are the faults of critics. In commenting on this problem
in its relation to literature, John M. Robertson once said "the snares
of criticism . . . may be classed as those set up by defect of real knowledge, defect of aesthetic percipience, defect of logical discipline, and
defect of judicial sense or scruple; and it is hard to say which is the
more serious." [11] Paraphrase this remark as we please, the conclusion remains that a critic must possess certain accomplishments if
he is to carry out his function with propriety and effectiveness. We
shall list a few of the qualifications.

(1) The rhetorical critic must have an appreciation of oratory—
an effective knowledge of what he is judging. He must be sensitive
to the appeal of the spoken word. This sensitivity must be more
than perfunctory respect for a few great orations of the past; it must
embrace a regard for the influence of oral communication, from the
lips of the less important figures as well as from those of acknowledged renown, in the shaping and controlling of man's destiny. In
short, the critic of oratory must have what Gertrude Buck once called
"an intelligent hospitality of mind" for the spoken word.

(2) An intelligent familiarity with the background of rhetoric
is essential to the critic. He must be able to interpret contemporary
theory with reference to its antecedents in more remote times. This
does not mean, to paraphrase Chesterfield, that he must look upon
the moderns with contempt and upon the ancients with idolatry. It
simply suggests that, since the present is the logical result of the past,
the critic must be sufficiently familiar with what has preceded to understand what he is dealing with now. Such a knowledge of the past
gives him added perspective, enables his critical faculty to operate
within the framework of his subject, and affords a measure of traditional sanction for his interpretations and judgments.

(3) An inquiring state of mind is essential to the rhetorical critic.
Since a large part of the critic's job is of an investigative nature, he
must possess a lively respect both for the facts themselves and for
the method of research through which the data are accumulated. A
certain spirit of inquiry, a sense of satisfaction growing out of the
pursuit of causes and effects—these are indispensable.

Furthermore, the critic must be temperamentally disposed to withhold judgment until the area of investigative study has been examined thoroughly. As Richard G. Moulton once remarked, "The

mind cannot commence its work of assaying and judging until it has concluded its work of investigating and interpreting . . ."

(4) A dispassionate, objective attitude toward the object of investigation is a further qualification without which the critic works at a disadvantage. Obviously, the critic should derive personal satisfaction from hearing and reading speeches; but his critical inquiries should be characterized by a certain impersonality of treatment, a detachment, which enables him to view facts and arrive at judgments with a minimum of emotional predisposition. He must be able to do what Wendell Phillips claimed most men were incapable of, namely, view facts with the eyes instead of the prejudices.

The objectivity of which we are speaking is the product of a certain universality of mind. Possessed of it, the critic can project himself into other periods of time; he can examine and evaluate the works of the past as well as of the present, without operating under the influence or within the framework of contemporary prejudices.

The substance of these qualifications may be resolved to simple terms: The rhetorical critic must be an intelligent man, well-versed in his subject. The tools of his craft are appreciation, knowledge, intellectual curiosity, investigative skill, a sense of emotional detachment, and good judgment.

The Functions of Rhetorical Criticism

It may be well to indicate at the outset what the function of rhetorical criticism is *not*. The necessity of approaching the problem negatively arises from the unhappy circumstance that the word "criticism" has, in popular usage, been buffeted about with reckless abandon.

The intelligent criticism of speeches is not a form of censorship. It is not the critic's job to impose checks on ideas and attitudes, even if he were able, simply because they are incompatible with his way of thinking, or because they are contrary to the *status quo*. It does not fall within the province of the critic to discourage the utterance of so-called "rebellious" material, or to dismiss a speech of the past as inconsequential or unworthy of analysis because it was considered "inflammatory" or "reactionary." Perhaps a given speech was "inflammatory." But it is the critic's job to determine that fact in the light of exhaustive investigation of the social situation and the consequences; it is not his prerogative to pre-judge the case or to dismiss the utterance on the ground that it failed to conform to the established political, economic, and social *mores*. The accomplished rhetorical

critic must be able to appraise the speech of a Republican, a Demo-
crat, or a Socialist with the same objective detachment and with the
same criteria. Upon careful examination, the critic may find that
the ideas of one or more of them are logically untenable; he may
find any number of departures from sound rhetorical practice in a
given speech; he may find that the speech failed to achieve the end
which the speaker set for it. These matters the critic may reveal,
interpret, and appraise. A valid judgment, however disapproving,
may still be a good criticism.

What, then, is the province of his service? Generally speaking,
rhetorical criticism serves four major functions.

(1) It helps to clarify and define the theoretical basis of public
address. It does so without proposing to teach the speaker how to
manage his art. The didactic element in criticism is not of first importance; undoubtedly interested students could master the principles
of speaking more efficiently and rapidly through a study of textbooks
devoted to the subject than through an examination of a comparable
body of critical literature. However, criticism helps to reveal the
operation of theory in practice, thus clarifying its meaning and perhaps in some instances even formulating new theory.

(2) Rhetorical criticism helps to set up a standard of excellence.
Naturally, speech situations are highly variable; each one produces
a unique interaction of speaker, audience, subject, and occasion.
Fortunately, critical inquiry does not establish dogmatic principles
by which all addresses must be appraised. Instead, it provides insight into methods of evaluation which help to free the critic from
the rule of whim, thus affording a certain corrective for unfounded
and hasty judgment.

(3) Rhetorical criticism helps to interpret the function of oral
communication in society. It serves as an effective link between the
theory of public address and the outside world. Devoted largely as
it is to a determination of the *effect* or outcome of a speech, it reveals
the nature of the process by which a communicative intent finally
implements, or fails to implement, social action. A study of theory
alone cannot reveal the complete process since it is concerned largely
with methodology. But criticism traces the major steps in oral communication straight through to the *effect,* immediate or delayed, of
the spoken discourse upon society.

(4) As a field of scholarly inquiry, rhetorical criticism indicates
the limits of present knowledge in the field of public speaking. It
points out the areas in which valid judgments cannot now be made,
either because of an insufficiency of evidence or because of an in-

ability to establish substantially the causal relations among ascertainable facts, especially with respect to the effectiveness of speeches in the past.

Speech as a Useful Art

Since the earliest formulations of a theory of speaking, rhetoric has been regarded generally as a useful art. It is largely an instrument of social control. However, some oratory—even though only a fractional part of the total output—seems to go quite beyond the province of sheer utility. It takes on aesthetic characteristics and, in some instances, becomes an object of beauty, permanence, and penetrating insight into human experience. In short, it approaches a fine art. Furthermore, some of our oratorical judgments—as in the case of Burke's speech "On Conciliation"—derive to a considerable extent from aesthetic as well as from practical considerations. While holding to the thesis that speech is a useful art, we must yet allow that there may be a point in rhetorical craftsmanship at which oratory as an instrument of power (utility) meets oratory as a manifestation of aesthetic creation (beauty).

The Ultimate Goal of Rhetorical Criticism

The rhetorical critic operates within a system or hierarchy of values. The nature of his work requires it. He must make judgments based upon interpretative analyses; he must arrive at certain conclusions despite the fact that a totality of information cannot be secured. But the careful critic bases his value judgments upon reliable data, meticulously tested and checked. In other words, he strives for responsibility of statement.

The world of practical affairs is the field of operation for the rhetorical critic. The substance with which he deals is the public speech. The principal end which he seeks to interpret is the result or effect of the utterance. His judgments derive, therefore, from practical, not ideal, considerations. He functions at all times within the realm of the probable. Although, as Brightfield remarks, man's ambitions sometimes may "outrun the existing circumstances in which they are placed," the rhetorical critic is constantly dealing with conditions falling within the limits set by the particular speech situation. That is to say, the goals which serious speakers set for their addresses are usually attainable, though obviously not always attained. And so the critic of oratory, working within the framework of this probability, never deals with the element of make-believe; unlike the literary critic, he does not regard a work as having satisfied the conditions of his art if it goes beyond the limits set by the environment. Accordingly, in his final judgments, the rhetorical critic does not pronounce a "counsel of unattainable perfection." He deals with things as they are, or, in the light of the best available information, as they seem to have been.

This does not mean that the critic of speeches deals only in mundane considerations. On the contrary, he is guided by lofty aspiration since the ultimate goal of his efforts is the realization of truth. Robertson once said of the literary critic that if he "attains to what is new, it is well; if he but attains to what is true, it is still well." So it is with the rhetorical critic. It is indeed well if he gets at and makes known the truth about the speeches with which he deals.

General Summary

Rhetorical criticism is a logical extension of the theory and practice of public speaking. Accordingly, an understanding of its principles requires a familiarity with the nature of the medium in which speech operates; it requires a full recognition of the fact that the basic function of speech, as carried out through the use of symbols, is communication. The communicative activity with which the rhetorical critic is concerned takes place in a speech situation which is characterized by: (1) relative freedom in the use of subject matter; (2) limitation as to time; (3) specificity of purpose; (4) transitoriness; (5) direct social interaction; (6) personal relationships growing out of the presence of a speaker, and (7) peculiarities of idiom, structure, content, and arrangement.

The criticism of oratory involves three stages: the examination of the facts, the formulation of criteria, and the application of the standards to the facts for purposes of general evaluation. The essential constituents of the rhetorical judgment derive mainly from the fields of philosophy, history, and logic. The source of the basic canon of rhetorical criticism is found in the formula: A speech is the result of an interaction of speaker, subject, audience, and occasion. The end toward which the critic's efforts are directed largely is the determination of the *effect* of the speech.

The principal types of criticism are the impressionistic, analytic, synthetic, and judicial. It is to the latter type that the major part of the discussion in this book will be directed.

The able critic will have (1) an appreciation of oratory, (2) a familiarity with rhetorical theory and practice, (3) an intellectual curiosity, and (4) an objective attitude toward his data.

The ultimate goal of the critic's efforts is the attainment of truth regarding a particular speech event. The specific functions of his art are (1) to clarify the theory of speaking, (2) to help formulate a standard of excellence, (3) to interpret the influence of oral communication in society, and (4) to indicate the present limits of knowledge in the field of speaking.

Thus we see that the criticism of speeches is a complex undertaking. It draws upon many fields of knowledge, requires much original research, and imposes heavy demands upon reasoning and judgment. In short, it offers a stern but inviting challenge to the serious student of public address.

PART II

THE DEVELOPMENT OF RHETORICAL THEORY

Chapter 2

FOUNDATIONS OF THE ART OF SPEAKING

The Value of Tradition

The art of rhetoric is old, very old. Its roots reach deep into the past, into an antiquity which is one with poetry, ethics, politics, and law. By indissoluble ties it is linked with remote times and distant places. Indeed, its tradition wears the proverbial snowy beard.[1]

It is satisfying to know that rhetoric derives from an extensive literature. This written tradition provides an unbroken record of intellectual probing into the operation of an ancient art. It helps to give continuity to our efforts. We are mindful of the labors of our predecessors in the field; we realize, as Barrett Wendell once said apropos of the great figures in literature,

> that the names and the works which have survived have done so largely because, though each originally came to light in historical conditions as distinct as those which surround us now, each has proved, when its original surroundings have faded, to appeal for one reason or another to generations widely different from that which it chanced to address in the flesh.[2]

The force of tradition unites the great names and works in a common core of theory, thus linking "generation to generation in the realm of mind, so that, in Pascal's figure, we may regard the whole procession of the ages as one man always living and always learning." [3]

By paying respect to our tradition, by acknowledging the "long sequence of humanized culture" and judgment in the contributions to the art of rhetoric, we do not necessarily commit ourselves to a static conception of the subject. It is possible to appreciate the dignity and worth of a tradition without binding ourselves to the authority of the past. The acceptance of tradition does not imply unthinking obedience to standards based "upon the faults of eminent men." Tradition is not the final criterion of certitude. It is a beacon, however, which helps to light the way to a fuller understanding of the nature of speechcraft.

The alliance of tradition and criticism is a fortunate one. Without the latter, errors and ill-formed conceptions might be perpetuated through the inertia of custom. Criticism, however, as an active force constantly subjects tradition to the searching analysis that should naturally accompany the enlargement of understanding and appreciation. Criticism tends to keep tradition in step with time, and in line with newly formed truth. As W. R. Sorley says, it protects the individual from the harmful aspects of tradition, "so that the truth and social values that have been handed down from the past may continue to be the inspiration of each man.

"He only earns his freedom, owns existence,
Who every day must conquer her anew." [4]

The following chapters present briefly the nature of the tradition upon which the art of rhetoric rests; they review the contributions of men whose conceptions helped to form and sustain the theoretical framework of the subject. In short, they represent a pageant of abiding ideas on speechcraft. These are the ideas that form the substructure of the art. They contribute substantially to a true prolegomenon for the criticism of speeches.

Early Rhetorical Theory in Homeric Expression

In a sermon against long extempore prayers, Robert South once remarked that "the reason of things lies in a little compass." He insisted upon the necessity of gathering "the general natures of things out of a heap of numberless particulars," thus making large units of material "portable to the memory." We take heart from such an observation; we are reminded that, although the sources available on the history of rhetorical theory are almost beyond number, all need not be reviewed to afford a true representation of the stream of ideas in this field of knowledge. More important for our purpose than an exhaustive summary of the contributions of all rhetoricians from earliest times to the present, is the perception of common elements in the progression of ideas. Once revealed, those elements will throw light upon the unity of the theory of speaking.

As indicated in the preceding chapter, the practice, theory, and criticism of public address are closely interrelated. Each is the function and derivative of the others. Hence, before we have trustworthy records of a theory of speaking, we have testimony of the approved *practice* of competent orators. Perhaps the latter presupposes the existence, in oral or written tradition, of some notion of the former, but our reference at this point should be to authenticated records. George Campbell remarked that "speakers existed before grammarians, and reasoners before logicians, so, doubtless, there were orators before there were rhetoricians, and poets before critics. The first impulse towards the attainment of every art is from nature." [5]

Accordingly, the earliest history of rhetorical theory derives from a study of the social organization which made persuasive speaking, as John F. Dobson points out, one of the first necessities of a society. As soon as "men were organized on terms of equality for corporate action, there must have been occasions when opinions might differ as to the best course to be pursued..." Under such circumstances, discussion developed, and that side prevailed "which could state its views most convincingly..." [6]

The ancient Greeks were the first to accord oratorical expression a place of distinction among the cultivated arts. Dobson remarks that with the Greeks "oratory was instinctive"; skill in speaking was no less highly prized "than valour in battle..." We would therefore expect speech to have some sort of representation in their early literature. The epic poems of Homer fulfill this expectation.

As epic poems, the *Iliad* and the *Odyssey* depend largely upon narration. However, the characters in the poems are always in the forefront, and they command attention through the speeches they deliver. Alfred Croiset remarks that these speeches, and particularly the ones in the *Iliad,* "form an element of the poem almost as important as the narrations and descriptions." [7] The speeches help to portray character, especially as they reveal the thought and feeling of the orators who deliver addresses of a deliberative sort before the assembly, or of exhortation to renewed effort on the battlefield, or of simple supplication to a single person.[8] Thus, Achilles and Nestor— to mention only two—assume great literary stature through their oratorical presentations. The "specimens of their persuasive speaking in the poems," says J. P. Mahaffy, "show how keenly the rhapsodists and their audiences appreciated this high quality."

The Homeric epics reveal an elementary art of rhetoric. The speeches uttered by the several characters in the *Iliad,* for example, are not without artistic design calculated to secure certain responses. Croiset observes that the characters "well know what words to begin with, and they know how to make men listen—how to win their attention." Indeed, "they set forth their arguments in the order that seems best and in the form most appropriate to gain acceptance from those whom they address. If they have definite conclusions, they formulate them and sum them up in striking terms. All this is the work of reflection, method, and experience." No less an authority than Quintilian remarked that Homer provided "a model and an origin for every species of eloquence." He indicated that Homer's epics displayed ably the arts of legal pleading and deliberation, established and applied "the laws of oratorical exordia," stated the facts of cases with admirable perspicuity, employed stylistic expressions with consummate skill, and developed faultless perorations. Relative to the last point, Quintilian inquired: "What peroration of a speech will ever be thought equal to the entreaties of Priam beseeching Achilles for the body of his son?" Richard C. Jebb believes no oratory of the ancient world approaches "so nearly as the Homeric to the modern ideal."

However significant the rhetoric in the *Iliad* and the *Odyssey* may be, it must not be considered mature and developed. The system is patently elementary, embryonic; it results in an oratory which is simply part of the larger literary device of the epic. The speeches are weak in argumentation, a point which Croiset makes with telling emphasis when he shows that they seldom develop reasons, seldom, if ever, anticipate objections, and usually overdraw the pathetic element.

Through the addresses of the principal characters, however, the *Iliad* furnishes one of the first semi-organized fragments of speech theory. Dating about 1000 years before the Christian era, deriving from Homer's genius and the collective inventions of a succession of poets, depicting a life that was a "mingling of the traditional and the ideal with contemporary facts," [9] and expressing ethical and religious motives without open preachment of doctrine, these epics open the way to a fuller understanding of the art of speaking.

The Influence of Athenian Democracy upon Speechmaking

The form of government in ancient Greece encouraged public speaking. Men were permitted to voice their opinions and to share in the making of political decisions. The popular Assembly at Athens during the fifth century B.C. included virtually every male citizen "with the leisure and inclination to attend." This Assembly deliberated on questions suggested by the Committee of Five Hundred, which in turn often acted on the recommendations of a prominent statesman, and the Athenian courts offered citizens an opportunity to participate in the administration of justice. Under these conditions there developed a respect for the spoken word unequalled by any other people at any time. Liberty of expression, "the Nurse of all Arts and Sciences," to quote John Lawson, became "in a particular manner the Parent of Eloquence. . . ."

Democratization of the courts during Pericles' time enabled nearly any Athenian citizen over 30 years of age to act as a juror in the courts. Juries were large; "pleaders addressed the jurors as citizens and democrats, and in truth the courts were the stronghold of popular government." [10] George W. Botsford observes that these large gatherings of Athenian citizens "made possible the development of a judicial oratory of universal and eternal literary value." Further, the courts were juries without a judge. Every man was his own pleader; consequently, each case provided a natural stimulus to effective oratorical presentation.

It is of more than passing interest that in this democracy in which free discussion enjoyed a unique position, responsibility of public statement was urgently requested and properly safeguarded. As Robert J. Bonner observes, in Athens "an orator suspected of not giving the best advice to the people could be impeached in the assembly." [11] Callistratus was so impeached, and Demosthenes spoke of a threat by Aeschines to impeach him. Furthermore, Bonner reports that the Athenian system "provided still another means of depriving unworthy citizens of the right to speak in the assembly. It was known as a scrutiny . . . of orators." Evidently, if "one of the regular speakers in the assembly was suspected of certain dishonorable acts, he could be prosecuted, not for the offense, but for continuing to speak in the assembly after committing the offense. The penalty was disqualification." [12] These provisions bespeak a tempered regard for responsibility of utterance and suggest the truly democratic character of the Athenian system.

The man under whom Athens reached this summit of achievement was Pericles, a statesman of unusual vision and an orator on whose lips, according to Cicero, the "graces of persuasion" so dwelt that even when he contradicted the favorites of the people his words "became popular and agreeable to all men . . ." Like Themistocles, Pericles was an orator-patriot whose "deep reflection on and clear perception of what was needful for Athens" gave to his speeches a profound power and solidity. Plato also comments on Pericles' "loftiness of thought and perfect mastery over every subject."

Regrettably, we have no texts of Pericles' speeches. Despite that fact, he is regarded as the first recorded Greek orator. In his history of the war between the Athenians and the Peloponnesians, Thucydides introduces—as was the practice in early Greek historiography—many speeches into his account of the conflict. Among them are several addresses by Pericles, including the celebrated Funeral Oration delivered in 431 B.C. on the occasion of the ceremony for the men who fell in the first year of the war.

Whether or not the speeches in Thucydides represent substantially what the characters said in real life is a question beyond the province of this discussion. It is perhaps sufficient to observe that many scholars believe that they do, although the artistic form in which they are cast is manifestly Thucydides'. K. O. Müller remarks that the speeches contain "a sum of the motives and causes which led to the principal transactions" and hence summarize "much that was really spoken on various occasions"; [13] A. W. Gomme introduces evidence to show that Thucydides made a sincere effort to find out what words were spoken in the original settings; [14] and Harold N. Fowler asserts that the speeches were more than inventions introduced for the sole purpose of imparting vigor to the story. [15]

In the early part of the narrative, Thucydides himself remarks:

> As to the speeches of particular persons either at the commencement or at the prosecution of the war, whether such as I heard myself or such as were repeated to me by others, I will not pretend to recite them in all their exactness. It ... [has] been my method to consider principally what might be pertinently said upon every occasion to the points in debate, and to keep as near as possible to what would pass for genuine by universal consent. [16]

Both for what they tell about Periclean eloquence and what they reveal about the speechmaking of other individuals, Thucydides' narratives offer valuable material to the student of rhetorical theory. The speeches in the history reveal artistry in conception, appreciation of rhetorical forms, and full understanding of the different types of oratory. Among the representative speeches which reveal Thucydides' mastery of speech reporting and writing are the deliberative addresses before the assembly at which the Corcyraeans and Corinthians pleaded their causes, Archidamus' speech before the generals and chief officers of the various states, and Nicias' speech to his depressed men during the dark hours of the campaign.

Three of Pericles' speeches dominate the narrative. In the first, he addressed the Athenians shortly after the Lacedaemonians had made a final request for the restoration of the Hellenes' independence. The assembly had been called at Athens to consider this issue. There was considerable discussion, with some members favoring war and others suggesting that Athens yield to the demand. Pericles began his patriotic discourse by saying:

I firmly persevere, Athenians, in the same opinion that I have ever
avowed—to make no concessions to the Lacedaemonians—though at
the same time sensible that men never execute a war with that warmth
of spirit through which they are impelled to undertake it, but sink in
their ardour as difficulties increase.... Their allegations against us
they are determined to support by arms, and not by evidence; and here
they come no longer to remonstrate but actually to give us law.... I
exhort you therefore to form a resolution, either timely to make your
submission before you begin to suffer; or, if we shall determine for
war, which to me...[seems] most expedient, without regarding the
pretext of it, be it important or be it trifling, to refuse ever the least
concession, nor to render the tenure of what we now possess precarious
and uncertain.

He then went on to show that the Athenians were in a better position to win the war; the Lacedaemonians were poor, unused to wag-
ing great wars, and divided in race. "For in truth," he declared,
"I am more afraid of our own indiscretions than the schemes of the
enemy." He concluded by saying:

It was thus that our fathers withstood the Medes, and rushing to arms
with resources far inferior to ours, nay abandoning all their substance,
by resolution more than fortune, by courage more than real strength,
beat back the Barbarian, and advanced this state to its present summit
of grandeur. From them we ought not to degenerate, but by every
effort within our ability avenge it on our foes, and deliver it down
to posterity, unblemished and unimpaired.[17]

Compton Mackenzie doubts that this speech does justice to Pericles' effort, although it unquestionably reveals "the lucid policy and
clearly defined strategy at the back of it."[18]

In the *Funeral Oration,* Pericles pronounced a eulogy upon the
causes of Athenian greatness. Fervidly patriotic and proudly jealous
of Athenian grandeur, this speech, in the opinion of Botsford, is
"one of the most precious documents in the history of civilization."

Finally, mention should be made of Pericles' speech to the Assembly after the second Peloponnesian invasion and after Attica had
been ravaged by conquest and plague. In this address, important
alike for the technique devised by Thucydides and the statesmanlike
resolution displayed by the orator, Pericles tries to bolster the spirit
and ardor of the Athenians. His speech closes with words which,
in substance, have been the frequent resort of orators through the
ages:

"... They whose minds are least sensitive to calamity, and whose
hands are most quick to meet it, are the greatest men and the greatest
communities."[19]

The Early Sicilian Rhetoricians

The speechmaking of Pericles and Themistocles developed from the recognition of certain problems in the world of practical affairs. There were wars to be waged, men to be inspired, and civic affairs to be administered. Spoken discourse served to bring people together; once together, it helped to consolidate their hopes, ambitions, and desires. An art or system of rhetoric, or speechcraft, was a natural outgrowth of the realization that men could govern themselves through persuasive talk.

The development of the first "system" of rhetoric is generally attributed to Corax and to his pupil, Tisias, both Sicilian Greeks. Quintilian refers to them as the "most ancient composers of rules on the art," with the possible exception of the earliest poets and of Empedocles. Cicero also observes that before Corax and Tisias "no one spoke by prescribed method, conformably to rules of art, though many discoursed very sensibly . . ."

The circumstances surrounding the "birth" of rhetoric in Sicily were chiefly political and legal. Perhaps the temperament of the people contributed, however, to the formulation of rhetorical theory, for Cicero remarks that the Sicilians were "very quick and acute, and had a natural turn for disputation." Following the expulsion of Thrasydaeus by the Agrigentines about 472 B.C. and of Thrasybulus by the Syracusans about 466 B.C., when the reign of Gelon, Hieron, and Thrasybulus ended, the "establishment of a democratical constitution and the requirements of the new order of things gave rise to a special demand for instruction in oratory." [20] Because of the change in the form of government, many people returning from exile demanded restitution of property previously confiscated by the tyrants. Accordingly, "rights that under the stress of despotism had, in the case of Syracuse, remained dormant for some twenty years, would be revived; lands that had been arbitrarily assigned to the favourites of the court would be claimed, by the original owners or their representatives; rival suitors would present themselves to contest the succession to the property in dispute, and intricate cases would thus require to be disentangled by the newly constituted courts of law." [21] Jebb indicates that if a disinterested person were to survey this condition, he would see that the affected "people must be assisted to deal with an array of complex facts; they must be taught method." Furthermore, he would see that "they must be assisted to dispense with documentary or circumstantial evidence; they must be given hints as to the best mode of arguing from general probabilities." [22] Evidently Corax observed what was going on in the courts; meditated over it; and eventually formulated his ideas on the proceedings into a systematic plan. The result was an "art of rhetoric" particularly adapted to forensic speaking, but also usable in deliberative and ceremonial address. Jebb has pronounced the work "the earliest theoretical Greek book, not merely on Rhetoric, but in any branch of art."

Corax's system of rhetoric [23] had three distinctive features, each of which contributed materially to the modern conception of speech theory: (1) It defined rhetoric as an art of persuasion, thus making it a practical art designed to elicit responses from hearers—responses consistent with the speaker's purpose. (2) Arrangement of materials received the first formal consideration. Speeches of persuasion were divided into five parts: a proem or opening, narration, argument, subsidiary remarks, and peroration. (3) Corax showed how *probability* applied to rhetorical invention. He demonstrated that it could be used in either of two ways. For example, "if a physically weak man is accused of an assault, he is to ask, 'Is it probable that *I* should have attacked *him?*' if a strong man is accused, he is to ask, 'Is it probable that I should have committed an assault in a case where there was sure to be a presumption against me?'" [24] Aristotle refers specifically to Corax's *Art of Rhetoric* when he takes up the role of probability in spurious syllogisms, observing that this sort of argument shows what is meant "by making the worse argument seem the better." Bromley Smith believes Aristotle misinterpreted Corax's idea. It is certain, however, that in developing the doctrine of probability, Corax contributed an important idea to rhetorical theory: the principle that "likelihood of truth must always be present in order to be convincing." [25]

The name of Tisias is associated with Corax in this early work on rhetoric. In his independent treatise on the subject, Tisias continued the inquiry initiated by his teacher, especially on the theme of probability. Plato satirically refers to Tisias as one who "found out that probabilities were more to be valued than truths, and who by force of words made small things appear great, and great things small, and new things old, and the contrary new, and who discovered a concise method of speaking and an infinite prolixity on all subjects." [26]

Bonner reminds us that with the development of rhetoric in Sicily, about the middle of the fifth century B.C., oratory became a democratic tool. "Eloquence ceased to be a gift of the favored few; it became an art that could be taught."

The Influence of the Sophists and the Rhetors

The development of a strong Attic prose resulted largely from the "movement of ideas" known as rhetoric and sophistry. Croiset maintains that Corax, Tisias, and the Greek sophists gave a practical and clever turn to oral expression, and that the writing of speeches followed as a natural consequence. Nascent rhetoric's "influence would probably have been small, if it had not met, at this very moment, with nascent sophistry, which took possession of it and increased its power for action tenfold." [27] Jebb also speaks of the interacting influence of rhetoric and sophistry upon the development of Attic oratory. He speaks of these as ideas from the "East" and the "West," the former being the "Practical Culture of Ionia," and the latter, the "Rhetoric of Sicily." The Ionian contributors, including Protagoras, Prodicus, Thrasymachus, and Hippias—properly called Sophists—were most directly concerned in their teaching with dialectic, grammar, and even literary criticism; the Sicilian contributors, especially Corax and Tisias and, in a qualified sense, Gorgias, were more deeply engrossed in Rhetoric.

Jebb believes these men were really Rhetors, rather than Sophists. Gorgias' place in this classification is less clear because he represented an intermediate position, "differing from the Eastern Sophists in laying more stress on expression than on management of argument, and from the Sicilian Rhetoricians in cultivating this faculty empirically, not theoretically." [28]

It should be further noted that some scholars have seen dangers in the Sophist point of view, citing its "indifference to truth, its aversion to all patient, sincere research, its great fondness for the jingle of words, its anxiety for persuasion rather than knowledge, its attachment to appearance . . ." [29] Others, including George Grote and Henry Sidgwick, have contested the view that the Sophists were charlatans who taught an "art of fallacious discourse," regarding them instead as a profession without any "agreement as to doctrines." [30] Obviously, the word Sophist was indeterminate in meaning. Wilmer Wright points out that the name had been applied formerly "not only to orators whose surpassing eloquence won them a brilliant reputation, but also to philosophers who expounded their theories with ease and fluency." [31] Whether the Sophist position was good or bad matters little in this discussion; what is important is that the Sophists and Rhetors contributed to the art of discourse. In this, even the critics of the Sophists agree.

Protagoras and the Development of Debate.—Protagoras, who flourished between 481 and 411 B.C., was the earliest of the Sophists. None of his writings is extant and so his style can be judged only through a study of Plato's dialogue. He was presumably the first to charge a fee for lectures, a practice which, in the words of Wilmer Wright, "is not to be despised, since the pursuits on which we spend money we prize more than those for which no money is charged."

Protagoras contributed to the development of forensic speaking through the use of commonplaces as bases for affirmative and negative argumentation, inventing "themes on which his pupils were to argue the *pros* and *cons.*" This led Bromley Smith to call him the "father of debate." While such rhetorical dialectic as Protagoras developed makes possible the charge that its purpose was to enable the user "to get the better of an opponent in any sort of debate," reliable commentary confirms the judgment that the Sophist intended it otherwise. Theodor Gomperz observes that Protagoras

> ...was evidently unpractised in the interchange of question and answer which was founded by Zeno, and developed by Socrates,...His own favourite dialectic was obviously of a more rhetorical kind. He did not try to confuse his antagonist nor to goad him to contradiction by the method of curt interrogation. The chief weapon in his armoury was that of long speeches delivered successively to refute one another.[32]

Protagoras also was responsible for introducing grammar into the curriculum. He constantly stressed the importance of an eloquence based upon correct thinking and speaking. In this sense, he tried to articulate ethics, dialectic, and rhetoric into a common philosophical inquiry. He believed that through eloquence man could govern both himself and others, and hence become virtuous.

The Gorgian Influence on Style.—Jebb comments on the difficulty of estimating Gorgias' contributions to rhetorical theory that "he was an inventor whose originality it is hard for us to realize, but an artist whose faults are to us peculiarly glaring." However, his place in the rhetorical continuum is assured. As Bromley Smith indicates, Corax laid the substructure of rhetoric, resting it upon orderly arrangement and persuasion by probability. Protagoras brought out the importance of debate, showing that every question has two sides, and that truth is a matter for each individual to decide. Then came Gorgias, gifted with the ability to weave words into artistic form, to create a style in prose. As "one of the founders of the art of Greek prose," Gorgias made a sound contribution to speech-craft, even though Plato's revelations of him in the dialogue bearing the same name might make us suspicious of the Sophists' craft.

Gorgias embraced a culture which, according to Jebb, "was founded neither upon Dialectic nor upon a systematic Rhetoric. Its basis was Oratory considered as a faculty to be developed empirically." Instead of devoting his attention to rhetorical invention, he concentrated his efforts on a study of language, for which he presumably had a brilliant gift.

In 427 B.C. Gorgias came to Athens from Sicily at the head of a Leontinian embassy to secure aid in the struggle against Syracuse. Evidently, the great teacher of rhetoric astounded the Athenians by his elegant language. Although the Greeks had always liked parallelism and other literary flourishes, Gorgias, "by his exaggerated use of these figures and his deliberate adoption for prose of effects that had been held to be the property of poetry . . . set a fashion that was never quite discarded in Greek prose, though it was often condemned as frigid and precious." [33]

In addition to his use of rhythmical movements in prose, Gorgias set an example, as Philostratus observed, "with his virile and energetic style, his daring and unusual expressions, his inspired impressiveness, and his use of the grand style for great themes"; also "with his habit of breaking off his clauses and making sudden transitions, by which a speech gains in sweetness and sublimity; and he also clothed his style with poetic words for the sake of ornament and dignity." [34] Gorgias' name is associated chiefly with panegyric oratory, although even here his writing has been condemned for its "emptiness" of thought. "He very properly directed Attic prose into the path of nobility, precision, and oratorical harmony; but he could not follow along the path, because he had only the appearance of the force necessary—had nothing serious to say." [35]

Despite Gorgias' desire to be what Croiset called a "virtuoso in discourse," some critics offer reasonable extenuation for the Sophist's excesses. Gomperz suggests that in times of great reforms in style, artificiality often creeps in—not only true in Gorgias' time, but during the Renaissance as well. He attributes this to two causes:

> The first is the natural desire at the beginning of a great literary epoch to strike out new modes of expression, the novelty of which is at first taken as the measure of their value. The second is the streaming and unbridled vitality of an age in which the young blood leaps with a wayward pulse, and the mind's activity is in excess of the matter at its disposal.[36]

On the other hand, Jebb maintains that if a style "is new and forcible, extravagances will not hinder it from being received with immense applause on its first appearance. Then it is imitated until its originality is forgotten and its defects brought into relief." Since "Gorgias was the founder of artistic prose . . . his faults are the more excusable because they were extravagant."

Minor Contributors.—Prodicus, one of the so-called teachers of "an encyclopaedic culture," offers, according to Jebb, one point of contact with early rhetoric, namely, "his effort to discriminate words which express slight modifications of the same idea . . ." This influence asserted itself in the oratory of Antiphon. Bromley Smith remarks that the writers on philosophy refer to Prodicus only incidentally as the "sire of synonymy." But, adds Smith, it "is doubtful whether he himself would have posed as a philosopher, for he seemed rather to be a teacher of speech who employed in his lessons ethical illustrations and philosophical reasonings for the purpose of training his pupils to become good homekeepers and good citizens." [37]

Hippias of Elis probably dealt with grammar and prosody in his teaching, but his main contribution to rhetorical theory centers about his promotion of the canon of memory. Tradition has it that Simonides discovered the memory, but undoubtedly Hippias was the first man who "considered the training of the memory as essential discipline in the education of an orator." [38]

Thrasymachus of Chalcedon gave, in the opinion of Jebb, "a new turn to the progress of Attic prose." He made his contribution in the realm of style, founding a form of expression known as the "middle" style which was intermediate "between the Gorgian, or poetical, and the colloquial." Presumably, he was also skilled at representing the pathetic elements of discourse, as his utterances in Plato's *Republic* demonstrate. According to Jebb, Thrasymachus is noteworthy for two reasons:

> In respect to rhythm and to his 'conception' of a middle style, he may be considered as the forerunner of Isocrates. In respect to his development of the terse period, to his training in the forensic Rhetoric, and to the practical bent of his work, he is the pioneer of Lysias and of those orators, whether forensic or deliberative, who are in contrast with Gorgians and Isocratics.[39]

Early Masters of Expression

Canon of the Attic Orators.—The Canon of the Ten Attic Orators is essentially a critical yardstick. It reflects the attempt by several critics to set up a standard of excellence in oratory, and to provide distinguished models to justify the criteria.

The exact origin of the Canon is difficult to determine. Its emergence is associated, however, with the issue of Asianism vs. Atticism, and the attempt by zealous Atticists to establish their models of oratorical excellence as approved standards of artistic prose. The question of Asianism vs. Atticism is succinctly expressed by Jebb in these words:

> This controversy involved principles by which every artistic creation must be judged; but, as it then came forward, it referred to the standard of merit in prose literature, and, first of all, in oratory. Are the true models those Attic writers of the fifth and fourth centuries, from Thucydides to Demosthenes, whose most general characteristics are, the subordination of the form to the thought, and the avoidance of such faults as come from a misuse of ornament? Or have these been surpassed in brilliancy, in freshness of fancy, in effective force, by those writers, belonging sometimes to the schools or cities of Asia Minor, sometimes to Athens itself or to Sicily, but collectively called 'Asiatics,' who flourished between Demosthenes and Cicero? [40]

This, briefly, was the issue. But what of the names associated with the authorship of the Canon? Evidently Caecilius of Calacte, then living in Rome, was the first man to mention the Decade. His work, now lost, on the *Style of the Ten Orators* dealt with the prose distinctions of Antiphon, Isocrates, Lysias, Andocides, Deinarchus, Isaeus, Lycurgus, Hyperides, Aeschines, and Demosthenes. Interestingly enough, Dionysius of Halicarnassus, a friend and devotee of the same Atticist convictions as Caecilius, also at that time a resident at Rome, paid no heed to the Decade; and his own critical work listed only Hyperides, Lysias, Aeschines, Isocrates, Isaeus, and Demosthenes. Jebb believes that Dionysius knew of the Canon "but disregarded it, because it was not a help, but a hindrance, to the purpose with which he studied the Attic orators." In any event, Jebb asserts that "from the first century A.D. onwards the decade is established." Charles S. Baldwin comments on the tendency if not the "preoccupation" among ancient critics (also found among moderns) to effect "criticism by labels," as the classification of "ten canonical Attic orators" suggests. [41]

Contributions of the Attic Orators.—How, specifically, do the early Greek orators contribute to our understanding of rhetorical theory? Largely in the sense of developing a truly conscious art of speech. As Jebb remarks:

The least gifted people, in the earliest stage of intellectual or political growth, will always or usually have the idea, however rude, of a natural oratory. But oratory first begins to have a history, of which the development can be traced, when two conditions have been fulfilled. First, that oratory should be conceived, no longer subjectively, but objectively also, and from having been a mere faculty, should have become an art. Secondly, that an oration should have been written in accordance with the theory of that art. The history of Greek oratory begins with Gorgias. The history of Attic oratory, properly so called, begins with Antiphon.[42]

The distinction between Athenian and Greek oratory, it should be added, is of some importance. In 353 B.C., Isocrates referred to this difference when defending his theory of culture:

> You must not forget that our city is regarded as the established teacher of all who can speak or teach others to speak. And naturally so, since men see that our city offers the greatest prizes to those who possess this faculty,—provides the most numerous and most various schools for those who, having resolved to enter the real contests, desire a preparatory discipline,—and, further, afford to all men that experience which is the main secret of success in speaking. Besides, men hold that the general diffusion and the happy temperament of Attic speech, the Attic flexibility of intelligence and taste for letters, contribute not a little to literary culture; and hence they not unjustly deem that all masters of expression are disciples of Athens. See, then, lest it be folly indeed to cast a slur on this name which you have among the Greeks ... that unjust judgment will be nothing else than your open condemnation of yourselves. You will have done as the Lacedaemonians would do if they introduced a penalty for attention to military exercises, or the Thessalians, if they instituted proceedings at law against men who seek to make themselves good riders.[43]

The Attic orators—and especially Antiphon, Andocides, Isocrates, Lysias, and Isaeus—were responsible for moulding, according to rules of art, a high type of literary prose; they were pioneers in refining techniques for use in forensic speaking. Most of these men were professional speech writers, and unusually successful ones. Lysias, for example, had a wide variety of people as his clients. He was highly skilled in adapting his speeches to the demands of the causes, occasions, and characters for whom they were intended. As Jebb observes, he was "a discoverer when he perceived that a purveyor of words for others, if he would serve his customers in the best way, must give the words the air of being their own."

The Attic orators established, or at least provided, patterns of style in oratory. Antiphon became a lively representative of the austere, dignified style of expression, which Dionysius described as follows:

> It wishes its separate words to be planted firmly and to have strong positions, so that each word may be seen conspicuously; it wishes its several clauses to be well divided from each other by sensible pauses. It is willing to admit frequently rough and direct clashings of sounds, meeting like the bases of stones in loose wallwork, which have not been squared or smoothed to fit each other, but which show a certain negligence and absence of forethought. It loves, as a rule, to prolong itself by large words of portly breadth. Compression by short syllables is a thing which it shuns when not absolutely driven to it.
>
> As regards separate words, these are the objects of its pursuit and craving. In whole clauses it shows these tendencies no less strongly; especially it chooses the most dignified and majestic rhythms. It does not wish the clauses to be like each other in length of structure, or enslaved to a severe syntax, but noble, simple, free. It wishes them to bear the stamp of nature rather than that of art, and to stir feeling rather than to reflect character. It does not usually aim at composing periods as a compact framework for its thought; but, if it should ever drift undesignedly into the periodic style, it desires to set on this the mark of spontaneity and plainness. It does not employ, in order to round a sentence, supplementary words which do not help the sense; it does not care that the march of its phrase should have stage-glitter or an artificial smoothness; nor that the clauses should be separately adapted to the length of the speaker's breath. No indeed. Of all such industry it is innocent.... It is fanciful in imagery, sparing of copulas, anything but florid; it is haughty, straightforward, disdainful of prettiness, with its antique air and its negligence for its beauty.[44]

Antiphon's style was somewhat too stately for forensic oratory and so other orators attempted to find a more flexible mode of expression.

In addition to contributing ideas on audience adjustment, Lysias became the representative of the plain style of oratory, according to the traditional division of grand, plain, and middle modes of expression. "The grand style aims constantly at rising above the common idiom; it seeks ornament of every kind, and rejects nothing as too artificial if it is striking. The plain style may, like the first, employ the utmost efforts of art, but the art is concealed; and, instead of avoiding it, imitates the language of ordinary life."[45]

Jebb holds that Andocides' value is largely historical, although his power of graphic description was noteworthy. Isocrates is by far the most important figure of the group. We shall discuss his contributions in some detail later.

Isaeus represents "the final period of transition" from forensic to deliberative address. While trying, in his preparation of speeches for others in the law court, to hold more or less closely to the Lysian "plainness," he found that an oratory of "technical mastery" had developed in full force. According to Jebb, Isaeus vacillated between the two methods and hence became

> ...an able compromise—the first advocate who was at once morally persuasive and logically powerful, without either entrancing by the grace of his ethical charm or constraining by the imperious brilliancy of his art; one from whom Demosthenes learned the best technical lessons that Antiphon or Thucydides could teach, in a form, at once strict and animated, serviceable under conditions which they had not known... [46]

Isaeus thus bridges the gap in style and method between forensic speaking and the deliberative oratory which achieved such striking distinction at the hands of Deinarchus, Lycurgus, Hyperides, Aeschines, and, most illustriously, Demosthenes.

Relation of Deliberative to Forensic Speaking.—Deliberative oratory in Greece, according to Jebb, did not enjoy an artistic development comparable with and independent of forensic speaking. On the contrary, the great deliberative speakers "are found to owe their several excellences as artists to models taken from the other two departments, to a Thucydides or an Isocrates, to a Lysias or an Isaeus." Jebb states three causes which help to explain this unexpected circumstance. First, the Greeks were disposed to connect their practice of an art with a theory. It is believed that the earliest rules "could be applied with more precision and more effect in a speech for the law courts than in a speech for the ecclesia," a circumstance resulting from the fact that in forensic speaking the subject is fully and accurately known by the speaker beforehand. Furthermore, "the utmost clearness of division is imperative, and is obtainable by a uniform method; and the problem is, how best to use all the resources of persuasion in a limited space of time." [47] And it is to be recalled that the earliest formulation of rhetorical theory dealt primarily with arrangement and probabilities.

Another possible reason derived from the Greek view that "the citizen was at once general and statesman. So long as this identity lasted, the men at the head of the State neither had leisure for the laborious training necessary to eminence in artistic oratory, nor felt its attainment to be of paramount importance." [48]

Lastly, with the exception of the issues involved in the crises over Philip of Macedon and the restoration of Athens to leadership in the Naval League, there were no "moments favourable to a great political eloquence."

Lycurgus, Hyperides, Demosthenes, and less importantly, Deinarchus and Aeschines were the representatives of what Jebb calls a mature civil eloquence. Their fervid patriotism, practiced skill in speaking, and facility in applying artistic principles of rhetoric to speechmaking stamp them as the most finished performers of the period. They "continued, combined and perfected," to use Jebb's words, the best aspects of forensic speaking.

> The Lysian tradition, which Isaeus had striven to ally with the frank strength of technical mastery, is joined by Hyperides to the Isocratic. The Isocratic manner is united, in Lycurgus, to that of the long-neglected school of Antiphon. That same archaic style, studied in a greater master, Thucydides, reaches, in Demosthenes, a final harmony with both the Lysian and the Isocratic; while Aeschines, the clever and diligent amateur, shows, by his failures, how much patient science was needed to bring a faultless music out of all the tones which had now made themselves clear in Attic speech. But, among these various elements, one is dominant. The Isocratic style has become the basis of the rest. That style, in its essential characteristics of rhythm and period, passed into the prose of Cicero; modern prose has been modelled on the Roman; and thus, in forming the literary rhetoric of Attica, Isocrates founded that of all literatures. [49]

The Union of Oratory and Citizenship:
Isocrates' Theory of Culture

"Then behold Isocrates arose, from whose school, as from the Trojan horse, none but real heroes proceeded..." This declaration by Cicero is no literary exaggeration, for few men in the history of rhetoric exercised such a pervasive influence over so many people for so many years as did Isocrates. In his comparison of the teachings of Aristotle and Isocrates, such an authority as Jebb clearly gives the advantage to the latter, not on the ground that Aristotle had an inferior grasp of the basic principles, but because Isocrates "was greatly superior in the practical department of teaching," as the host of orators and writers showing the imprint of his influence demonstrates. Jebb goes so far as to say, and George Norlin supports him, that as far as prose style is concerned the Isocratic pattern became the basis of all others.[50] Müller agrees that without Isocrates' "reconstruction of the style of Attic oratory," there could not have been a Demosthenes or a Cicero.

This man whom Cicero called the "father of eloquence" lived almost a hundred years—a century, as Norlin says, "of extraordinary vicissitudes and disenchantments." He was born in 436 B.C. and died in 338 B.C. Throughout that period he entertained a fixed devotion to Athens and to Hellenism "as a way of life." He was under the literary influence of Gorgias and probably had some personal association with him during later years. Although influences of this sort are difficult to trace, Norlin believes that Isocrates owed to Gorgias' teaching and example "the idea which he later made peculiarly his own, namely, that the highest oratory should concern itself with broad, pan-Hellenic themes, and that the style of oratory should be as artistic as that of poetry and afford the same degree of pleasure." Isocrates avoided, however, the "Gorgian excesses of style." He did not rely for effect upon striking words and phrases, but, instead, subordinated "the individual words and clauses to a larger unity." [51] Furthermore, he exercised greater care in preparing the transitions and other parts of his discourses, severely subordinating them "to the design of an organic whole." Thus Jebb and Norlin agree that Isocrates made the artificially constructed Gorgian style artistic.

Unable to participate in Athenian life because of a weak voice, Isocrates spent about ten years writing forensic speeches for the law courts. In later life, however, he virtually renounced this phase of his oratorical activity.

It is through his work as an educator and political thinker that his fame became established. About 392 B.C., he opened what Cicero calls the house which "stood open to all Greece as the *school* of eloquence." From the beginning he was successful; his pupils and others whom he influenced indirectly through his teachings and writings gave testimony of his skill in instruction. Unlike most teachers, he became surprisingly wealthy, despite the fact that he apparently gave instruction to Athenian pupils free of charge and exacted fees only from foreigners.

Isocrates called his written works "orations" but they qualify as orations only in form and atmosphere. Isocrates never delivered a speech, and few of his discourses were written for delivery. Among his writings, six are definitely political: the *Panegyricus,* the *Philip,* the *Plataicus,* the *Peace,* the *Archidamus,* and the *Areopagiti-*

cus. Two other works are largely educational in character: *Against the Sophists* and the *Antidosis.* Isocrates' theory of culture derives largely from these two contributions. In them he sets forth, as Jebb views them, the "manifesto" and "apologia," respectively, of his professional life. In *Against the Sophists,* he decries those "sophists" who teach Eristic—"a debased form of Dialectic, which consisted of disputation for disputation's sake in the field of ethics";[52] he condemns the teachers of rhetoric who ascribe too much importance to mere techniques; and he berates those writers who deal almost exclusively with the least elevated branch of rhetoric, namely, the forensic.

The *Antidosis* was prepared near the close of his life. To understand it fully, we must consider briefly the meaning of the title. Norlin tells us that the

... wealthier citizens of Athens were required by law to bear the expense of public services known as 'liturgies.' One of these was the 'trierarchy'—that of fitting out a ship of war. Anyone allotted to such a duty might challenge another to accept the alternative of either undertaking this burden in his stead or of exchanging property with him. Such a challenge was called an 'antidosis.' If the challenged party objected, the issue was adjudicated by a court.[53]

Evidently, Isocrates had just faced such a trial. In the *Antidosis* he adopts a factitious charge against his teachings and then presents the defense. The form of the production is, accordingly, similar to the Socratic *Apology.*

On the negative side, the *Antidosis* is, according to Norlin,

... a sharp attack upon the Athenian populace for confusing him with the other sophists... and it is... a criticism... of the narrowness or the impracticableness of the teaching of his rivals and of their failure to appreciate at its full value the broad and useful culture for which he himself stood. On its positive side, it is a definition of the culture or 'philosophy' which Isocrates professed.[54]

In the *Panegyricus,* Isocrates declares:

... if it were possible to present the same subject matter in one form and in no other, one might have reason to think it gratuitous to weary one's hearers by speaking again in the same manner as his predecessors; but since oratory is of such a nature that it is possible to discourse on the same subject matter in many different ways,—to represent the great as lowly or invest the little with grandeur, to recount the things of old in a new manner or set forth events of recent date in an old fashion—it follows that one must not shun the subjects upon which others have spoken before, but must try to speak better than they.[55]

And that is precisely what he attempted to do. As J. W. H. Atkins remarks, "It is in the new direction, the fresh impulse he gave to the study of rhetoric, that the influence of Isocrates in criticism is perhaps most clearly seen." Unlike the Sophists who were mainly concerned with forensic speaking, Isocrates formulated a new "cultural study" in which "fitting expression was sought for elevated themes, and the art of speaking or writing on large political topics was inculcated as a practical training for the active duties of a citizen." [56] In fact, his "philosophy" was, as Jebb says, "the Art of speaking and of writing on large political subjects, considered as a preparation for advising or acting in political affairs." He proposed, in short, to link oratorical ability and statesmanship.

In Isocrates' theory of culture, speech is recognized as an indispensable skill. In the *Nicocles or the Cyprians,* he says:

> ... for if they [critics of eloquence] are really hostile to eloquence because there are men who do wrong and speak falsehood, they ought to disparage as well all other good things; for there will be found also among men who possess these [wealth and strength and courage] some who do wrong and use these advantages to the injury of many. Nevertheless, it is not fair to decry strength because there are persons who assault people whom they encounter, nor to traduce courage because there are those who slay men wantonly, nor in general to transfer to things the depravity of men, but rather to put the blame on the men themselves who misuse the good things, and who, by the very powers which help their fellow-countrymen, endeavour to do them harm.[57]

Later in the same speech—and this passage also appears in the *Antidosis*—he remarks:

> For in the other powers which we possess we are in no respect superior to other living creatures; nay, we are inferior to many in swiftness and in strength and in other resources; but, because there has been implanted in us the power to persuade each other and to make clear to each other whatever we desire, not only have we escaped the life of wild beasts, but we have come together and founded cities and made laws and invented arts; and, generally speaking, there is no institution devised by man which the power of speech has not helped us to establish. For this it is which has laid down laws concerning things just and unjust, and things base and honorable; and if it were not for these ordinances we should not be able to live with one another. It is by this also that we confute the bad and extol the good. Through this we educate the ignorant and appraise the wise; for the power to speak well is taken as the surest index of a sound understanding, and discourse which is true and lawful and just is the outward image of a good and faithful soul. With this faculty we both contend against

others on matters which are open to dispute and seek light for ourselves on things which are unknown; for the same arguments which we use in persuading others when we speak in public, we employ also when we deliberate in our own thoughts ... [58]

Not only did Isocrates postulate a high function for speech; he also recognized the importance of the trinity of nature, art, and practice. "I do hold," he observed,

that people can become better and worthier if they conceive an ambition to speak well.... [And] if they are to excel in oratory or in managing affairs or in any line of work, they must, first of all, have a natural aptitude for that which they have elected to do; secondly, they must submit to training and master the knowledge of their particular subject.... and finally, they must become versed and practised in the use and application of their arts ... [59]

Accordingly, we agree with Jebb that it was Isocrates' intention to be practical—to avoid "barren subtleties."

A note of high ethical resolve is sounded in the Isocratic system. "I, myself," he indicates, "welcome all forms of discourses which are capable of benefitting us even in a small degree; however, I regard those as the best and most worthy of a king, and most appropriate to me, which give directions on good morals and good government ..." [60] In the *Antidosis,* he states that

... the man who wishes to persuade people will not be negligent as to the matter of character ... for who does not know that words carry greater conviction when spoken by men of good repute than when spoken by men who live under a cloud, and that the argument which is made by a man's life is of more weight than that which is furnished by words. Therefore, the stronger a man's desire to persuade his hearers, the more zealously will he strive to be honourable and to have the esteem of his fellow-citizens.[61]

In short, he would direct his instruction to the training of "men who take advantage of the good and not the evil things of life."

Isocrates was also one of the first rhetoricians to enunciate the doctrine of propriety in speech, as this passage from *Against the Sophists* reveals:

For what has been said by one speaker is not equally useful for the speaker who comes after him; on the contrary, he is accounted most skilled in this art who speaks in a manner worthy of his subject and yet is able to discover in it topics which are nowise the same as those used by others. But the greatest proof of the difference between these two arts is that oratory is good only if it has the qualities of fitness

for the occasion, propriety of style, and originality of treatment, while
in the case of letters there is no such need whatsoever.[62]

Next to his refinement of an effective prose style, the most important aspect of his theory of culture dealt with the type of subject
matter recommended for orators. Isocrates insisted upon the use of
broad, noble themes—"discourses, not for private disputes, but which
deal with the world of Hellas, with affairs of State, and are appropriate to be delivered at the Pan-Hellenic assemblies—discourses
which . . . are more akin to works composed in rhythm and set to
music than to the speeches which are made in court."[63] He remarks
that when

> . . . anyone elects to speak or write discourses which are worthy of
> praise and honour, it is not conceivable that he will support causes
> which are unjust or petty or devoted to private quarrels, and not rather
> those which are great and honourable, devoted to the welfare of man
> and our common good. . . . In the second place, he will select from all
> the actions of men which bear upon his subject those examples which
> are the most illustrious and the most edifying. . . . It follows, then, that
> the power to speak well and think right will reward the man who ap-
> proaches the art of discourse with the love of wisdom and love of
> honour.[64]

This aspect of the Isocratic conception affected not only rhetoric,
but history as well. By stressing the idea of Greek unity, he altered
the historical point of view, which previously had emphasized such
sectional matters as the histories of particular states. Isocrates exercised this influence chiefly through two of his admirers and students, Ephorus and Theopompus, who, according to Cicero, "applied
themselves to history by the persuasion of their master . . . and never
attended to pleading at all."

An interesting note on the Isocratic method of teaching relates to
the saying of Isocrates, as told by Cicero,

> . . . that he used to apply the spur to Ephorus, but to put the rein on
> Theopompus; for the one, who overleaped all bounds in the boldness
> of his expressions, he restrained; the other, who hesitated and was
> bashful, as it were, he stimulated: nor did he produce in them any
> resemblances to each other, but gave to the one such an addition, and
> retrenched from the other so much superfluity, as to form in both that
> excellence of which the natural genius of each was susceptible.[65]

These, then, are some of the things for which Isocrates stood and
which he taught. Although admittedly not a man of genius, he
made significant contributions toward the establishment of a literary

rhetoric designed to improve both the individual and the state. "In his school," Jebb concludes, "he did a service peculiarly valuable to that age by raising the tone and widening the circle of the popular education, by bringing high aims and large sympathies into the preparation for active life, and by making good citizens of many who perhaps would not have aspired to become philosophers." [66]

Plato's Inquiry into the Nature of Rhetoric

Cicero relates an anecdote concerning the poet Antimachus who, when rehearsing a long selection before a special audience, was deserted by all except Plato. Undiscouraged, the poet cried out: "*I shall proceed notwithstanding; for Plato alone is of more consequence to me than many thousands.*" [67] The remark, adds Cicero, "was very just."

Plato's reputation in contemporary thinking equals the high esteem accorded him by Antimachus. However, Plato's attitudes toward a technique of speechcraft present a seeming paradox; while satirizing and condemning the art as it appeared to him during his age, he also contributed to its development so materially as to lead such an eminent scholar as W. H. Thompson to call Aristotle's epochal *Rhetoric* in effect an expanded *Phaedrus*.

Plato and Isocrates were contemporaries. The one was, as Jebb points out, the great speculative thinker and seeker after truth; the other, "the great popular educator." "On the one side stands the true philosopher; on the other, the graceless anti-Plato who is continually insisting that his political rhetoric is philosophy." [68] Despite their differences, they probably were not in open hostility.

It was plain that Plato could not follow the doctrines of Isocrates, of the rhetoricians generally, and of the Sophists—particularly Gorgias, Protagoras, Hippias, and Prodicus. "The art of rhetoric," says Everett Hunt, "offered to the Athenian of the fifth century B.C. a method of higher education and, beyond that, a way of life. Plato attacked both. He gave rhetoric a conspicuous place in his dialogues because it represented in Athenian life that which he most disliked." [69] His reasons for disliking it no doubt were numerous. He evidently opposed the Sophists' practice of charging fees, and he opposed whatever part rhetoric had in influencing public opinion in Athenian life. As Hunt says, he "despised mere opinion almost as much as he did the public"—for even right opinion, in Plato's judgment, "fell far short of philosophic knowledge." [70] He opposed a form of government not controlled by philosopher-kings, and, consequently, any government in which rhetoric was employed by merchants and others not possessed of "true wisdom" to decide questions of public policy; he opposed any discipline which, like rhetoric, attempted to get at true virtue by something short of true knowledge; and he opposed rhetoric for its very practical nature—for attempting to train citizens to function in a governmental system which was too faulty, so he thought, to warrant preservation. In short, Plato's indictment of rhetoric is incidental to his condemnation of the civilization he knew.

We are principally concerned with two of Plato's writings, the *Gorgias* and the *Phaedrus*. Like his other works, they are in dialogue form, with Socrates serving as the key spokesman and reflecting Plato's ideas with greatest fidelity. That the dialogue form makes the ready systematization of his point of view difficult is no doubt true. In the opinion of Alfred Weber and Ralph Barton Perry, however, Plato employs this form precisely because he has no finished system. The dialogue might be considered an unsuitable method of exposition if it concealed the philosopher's thoughts. But it hides nothing; form and content are here the same, and the dialogues of Plato present his philosophy in its psychological development.[71] This note on the dialogue form is of passing concern since a goodly number of rhetoricians, including Cicero, Tacitus, Alcuin, and Fénelon, employed the same method.

The Gorgias.—The participants in the *Gorgias* are Callicles, Chaerephon, Socrates, Polus, and Gorgias. Despite the fact that the dialogue bears his name, Gorgias does not play an important part; he seems, instead, to be "the destined victim of the philosopher's dialectical prowess." In the strictest sense, the *Gorgias* is not a critical treatise on rhetoric; rather, its aim "is to discuss the ethical principles which conduce to political well-being."[72] However, in his indictment of the Sophists' teachings Plato brings out an important distinction, as he sees it, between true and false rhetoric. Expressing high admiration for the dialogue, Cicero believed it revealed Plato as an "eminent orator" while he was in the very act of ridiculing orators.

In the *Gorgias,* Plato attacks rhetoric as a way of life, in contrast with philosophy. He doubts that rhetoric is an art since it does not have its roots in universal principles. It deals in words, as do many other arts, and has no specific field of its own. Socrates inquires wherein rhetoric has its peculiar efficiency as contrasted, for example, with arithmetic:

Just as if anyone should ask me respecting any of the arts which I but now mentioned: Socrates, what is the arithmetical art? I should say to him, as you did just now, That it is one of the arts that have their efficiency in words. And if he should further ask me, In reference to what? I should answer, In reference to the knowledge of even and odd, how many there may be of each. But if again he should ask me, What do you mean by the art of computation? I should answer, that this also is one of those arts whose whole efficiency consists in words. And if he should further ask me, In reference to what? I should answer, as they do who draw up motions in the assemblies of the people, That in other respects computation is the same as arithmetic, for it has reference to the same object, that is to say, the even and the odd; but it differs in this respect, that computation considers what relation even and odd have to themselves and to each other in regard to quantity.[73]

Later in the discourse, Socrates remarks:

It appears to me ... to be a certain study, that does not belong to art, but to a soul that is sagacious and manly, and naturally powerful in its intercourse with men. The sum of it I call flattery. Of this study there appear to me to be many other divisions, and one of them is that of cookery; which, indeed, appears to be an art, but, as I maintain, is not an art, but skill and practice. I also call rhetoric a division of this, and personal decoration, and sophistry, these four divisions relating to four particulars. If, therefore, Polus wishes to enquire, let him enquire, for he has not yet heard what division of flattery I assert rhetoric to be....

For rhetoric, in my opinion, is a semblance of a division of the political art.... [74]

...I wish to tell you, after the manner of geometricians, ... that what personal decoration is to gymnastics, that is cookery to medicine: or rather thus, that what personal decoration is to gymnastics, that is sophistry to legislation, and that what cookery is to medicine, that is rhetoric to justice.[75]

Plato also doubts that rhetoric can be an actual good to a person. Rhetoricians presumably attempt through words to achieve the good, but they lack insight and wisdom. Consequently, the supposed power of rhetoric goes for nought. Returning to the dialogue between Socrates and Callicles, we note:

Socr. Do the rhetoricians appear to you always to speak with a view to what is best, aiming at this, that the citizens may be made as good as possible by their discourses? or do they, too, endeavour to gratify the citizens, and neglecting the public interest for the sake of their own private advantage, do they treat the people as children, trying only to gratify them, without being in the least concerned whether they shall become better or worse by these means?

Cal. This is not a simple question that you ask me. For there are some who, looking to the interest of the citizens, say what they do; but others are such as you describe.

Socr. That is enough. For, if this also is twofold, one part of it will be flattery, and a base popular speaking, but the other will be honourable, namely, that which endeavours to make the souls of the citizens as good as possible, and strives to speak what is best, whether it be pleasant or unpleasant to the hearers. But you have never yet seen this kind of rhetoric.[76]

Furthermore, the use of rhetoric in forensic situations is open to suspicion, as the conversation between Socrates and Polus suggests:

Socr. .... Polus, what is the great utility of rhetoric? For, from what has been now agreed on, every one ought especially to beware of acting unjustly, for that, *if he does so act,* he will sustain great evil. Is it not so?

Pol. Certainly.

Socr. And if a man has committed injustice, either himself, or any one else for whom he has regard, he ought of his own accord to betake himself thither, where as soon as possible he will be punished, to a judge as to a physician, taking every pains lest the disease of injustice becoming inveterate should render the soul corrupt and incurable; or what must we say, Polus, if our former admissions are to stand? Do not these things necessarily harmonize with the former in this, but in no other way?

Pol. For what else can we say, Socrates?

Socr. For the purpose, then, of excusing injustice, our own, or that of our parents, or friends, or children, or country, when it acts unjustly, rhetoric is of no use to us at all, Polus, unless on the contrary, any one supposes that he ought especially to accuse himself, and afterwards his relatives, and any other of his friends, who may have acted unjustly, and not conceal the crime, but bring it to light, in order that he may be punished, and restored to health; moreover, that he should compel both himself and the others to lay aside fear, and with eyes shut, and in a manly way, deliver himself up, as to a physician, to be cut and cauterised, pursuing the good and the beautiful, without paying any regard to what is painful; if he has committed a wrong worthy of stripes, delivering himself up to be beaten, if of bonds, to be bound, if of a fine, to pay it, if of exile, to be banished, if of death, to die, being himself the first accuser of himself, and others his relatives, not sparing either himself or them, but employing rhetoric for this very purpose, that, the crimes being exposed, they may be freed from the greatest of evils, injustice. Shall we say thus, Polus, or not?

Pol. These things appear to me, Socrates, to be absurd; but it must be admitted, they accord with what was before said.

Socr. Must not, therefore, either our former conclusions be done away with, or these results necessarily follow?

Pol. Yes; such is the case.

Socr. Contrariwise, if it is requisite to do ill to any one, whether to an enemy, or any other person, provided only that he is not himself injured by his enemy; for this is to be guarded against; but if an enemy injures another, we should endeavour by all possible means, both by actions and words, that he may not be punished, nor brought before a judge: but, if he is brought before him, we should contrive so that our enemy may escape, and not suffer punishment: and if he has robbed us of a great quantity of gold, that he should not restore it, but should retain it and spend it on himself and his associates unjustly and impiously; and if he has committed an injustice worthy of death, we should contrive that he may not die, if possible never, but that he may be immortal in depravity, or if this cannot be, that he may live in this state for as long a period as possible. For such purposes, Polus, rhetoric appears to me to be useful, since to him who does not intend to act unjustly, its utility does not appear to me to be great, if indeed it is of any utility at all,... [77]

The Phaedrus.—The *Phaedrus* has been described by Thompson as "a dramatized treatise on Rhetoric." Like the *Gorgias,* it ridicules the earlier and contemporary rhetoricians; it differs from it in its partial development of a "new and philosophical rhetoric," based partly on dialectic and partly on psychology.

Socrates and Phaedrus are the only participants in this dialogue. The treatment of rhetoric develops from a comparison of three speeches, one of which is represented as the product of Lysias, and the other two, the work of Socrates.

The Platonic conception of rhetoric presented in the *Phaedrus* is based upon the all-important dictum, issuing from Plato's belief that Lysias' speeches were lacking in logical resource, that good speaking derives from a speaker who knows "the truth of the subject on which he is about to speak."

In Hunt's orderly analysis of Plato's "ideal system of rhetoric," this point receives special attention. Hunt remarks, however, that

the above principle "cannot be interpreted as an injunction to speak
the truth at all times. It is rather to *know* the truth in order (a) to
be persuasive by presenting to the audience something which at least
resembles truth, and (b) to avoid being oneself deceived by probabilities. In order to know the truth, the rhetorician must be a philosopher." A second canon, as classified by Hunt, is that the
"rhetorician must define his terms, and see clearly what subjects are
debatable and what are not. He must also be able to classify particulars under a general head, or to break up universals into particulars." [78] In short, he must be a logician. As Socrates remarks in the
Phaedrus:

> The art, then, of arguing on both sides has not only to do with courts
> of justice and popular assemblies, but as it seems, it must be one and
> the same art, if it is an art, with respect to all subjects of discourse,
> by which a man is able to make all things appear similar to each other
> so far as they are capable of being made [to] appear so, and to drag
> them to light, when another attempts to make them appear similar and
> conceals his attempt.[79]

An acceptable rhetoric must also contain principles dealing with
the arrangement of materials. ". . . Every speech," said Socrates,
"ought to be put together like a living creature, with a body of its
own, so as to be neither without head, nor without feet, but to have
both a middle and extremities, described proportionately to each other
and to the whole." [80]
The next feature of the Platonic scheme requires that the rhetorician know the nature of the soul, that he be conversant with psychological data. After setting in order "the different kinds of speech
and of soul, and the different manners in which these are affected,
he will go through the several causes, adapting each to each, and
teaching what kind of soul is necessarily persuaded, and what not
persuaded, by particular kinds of speech, and for what reason." [81]
Socrates adds a note on this and the following consideration:

> Since the power of speech is that of leading the soul, it is necessary
> that he who means to be an orator should know how many kinds of
> soul there are: but they are so many, and of such and such kinds;
> whence some men are of this character and some of that character.
> These then being thus divided, there are again so many kinds of speech,
> each of a certain character. Now men of such a character are for this
> particular reason easily persuaded by certain speeches, and persons of
> a different character are for these reasons with difficulty persuaded.
> It is necessary, therefore, that he, after having sufficiently understood
> all this, when he afterwards perceives these very things taking place

in actions, and being done, should be able to follow them rapidly by perception, otherwise he will know nothing more than the very things which he formerly heard from his preceptor. But when he is sufficiently competent to say, what kind of person is persuaded by what kind of speeches, and is able, when he sees him before him, to point out to himself that this is the person and this the nature for which those speeches were formerly made now actually present before me, and to which these particular speeches are to be addressed, in order to persuade him to these particular things,—when he has acquired all this, and has learnt moreover the proper seasons for speaking and being silent, and again has made himself master of the seasonable and unseasonable occasions for brevity, plaintiveness, and vehemence, and all the other several kinds of speech which he has learnt, then his art will be beautifully and perfectly accomplished, but not before. But whoever is deficient in any of these particulars, either in speaking, or teaching, or writing, and yet asserts that he speaks by art, is overcome by the person who will not be persuaded.[82]

In the fifth place, the rhetorician must, says Hunt in interpreting Plato, know the "instruments" through which the soul is influenced. These instruments are style and delivery.

"The art of writing will not be highly regarded," Hunt comments on the sixth point in his summary of Plato's scheme of rhetoric, "nor will continuous and uninterrupted discourse be regarded as equal to cross examination as a means of instruction." Evidently this is "Plato's way of saying that any method of attempting to persuade multitudes must suffer from the very fact that it is a multitude which is addressed, and that the best of rhetoric is unequal to philosophic discussion." [83]

Lastly, the "rhetorician will have such a high moral purpose in all his work that he will ever be chiefly concerned about saying that which is 'acceptable to God.'" Therefore, rhetoric "is not an instrument for the determination of scientific truth, nor for mere persuasion regardless of the cause; it is an instrument for making the will of God prevail. The perfect rhetorician, as a philosopher, knows the will of God." [84]

Near the close of the dialogue, Phaedrus asks Socrates to repeat the requisites for artful preparation of speeches. Socrates' brief summary serves as the capstone to this section of our study:

Before a man knows the truth of each subject on which he speaks or writes, and is able to define the whole of a thing, and when he has defined it again knows how to divide it into species until he comes to the indivisible; and in like manner, having distinguished the nature of the soul, and having found out what kind of speech is adapted to the nature of each, he so disposes and adorns his speech, applying to a soul of varied powers speeches that are various and all-harmonious, and simple ones to a simple soul, before this is done, he will not be able to manage speech with art, as far as it might be done, either for the purpose of teaching or persuading.... [85]

Aristotle's Systematic Investigation of Rhetoric

General Nature of the *Rhetoric*.—Aristotle (384-322 B.C.) is perhaps the most highly esteemed figure in ancient rhetoric. His *Poetics* and *Rhetoric* compose an analytically thorough treatment of the two phases of writing and speaking which deal respectively with the "art of imaginative appeal" and the "art of daily communication, especially of public address." [86] The *Rhetoric* is generally considered the most important single work in the literature of speechcraft.

Philosophical in its point of view and treatment, the *Rhetoric* nevertheless came late—too late, some would say—in the history of the subject. As contrasted with the school of Isocrates which produced many great orators, the school of Aristotle "in which Rhetoric was both scientifically and assiduously taught" produced but one orator of note, Demetrius Phalereus. This peculiar condition resulted not from a difference in mastery of principles, for Aristotle was clearly the superior in his understanding of the nature of speech. "Aristotle's philosophy of Rhetoric proved comparatively barren, not at all because Rhetoric is incapable of profiting materially by such treatment, but because such treatment can be made fruitful only by laborious attention to the practical side of the discipline." Jebb is not here referring to Aristotle's conception of rhetoric as a useful, practical art; rather, he is suggesting that Isocrates had the advantage because he taught by exercises, using his own writings as models. All in all, Jebb concludes that if Aristotle's *Rhetoric* had "been composed a century earlier, it would have been inestimable to oratory. As it was, the right thing was done too late." [87]

Cicero refers to this difference in the teaching methods of Isocrates and Aristotle, adding that when the latter "saw Isocrates grow remarkable for the number and quality of his scholars ... [Aristotle] changed on a sudden almost his whole system of teaching. ..." Thereafter he evidently "adorned and illustrated all philosophical learning, and associated the knowledge of things with practice in speaking." [88]

There is a legend that Aristotle's *Rhetoric* grew out of a feud between Isocrates and himself. However, Atkins is confident that if such a feud existed, it must have been forgotten with Isocrates' death, for Aristotle relies to some extent upon Isocratic doctrine. If an antagonism had existed, Aristotle probably would not have relied upon the teachings of his foe. It is to be remembered that he virtually ignored Demosthenes, doubtless for political reasons.

In many respects the *Rhetoric* accepts, elaborates, and systematizes doctrines set forth in the *Phaedrus*. Aristotle adopted the typically Platonic principles that the contemporary writers were treating rhetoric in an "unscientific" manner, that rhetoric was closely related to dialectic, and that the orator should be conversant with the laws of human nature as they affected the responses of hearers.

Despite Aristotle's evident reliance upon many of Plato's ideas, the *Rhetoric* reveals, to use Hunt's expression, "certain philosophical and temperamental divergences from Plato." Hunt ventures the generalization that "Plato sought to reform life, while Aristotle was more interested in reorganizing theory about life. For this reason Aristotle's *Rhetoric* is largely detached from both morality and pedagogy. It is neither a manual of rules nor a collection of injunctions. It is an unmoral and scientific analysis of the means of persuasion." [89]

In Baldwin's opinion, the *Rhetoric,* though short, reveals the "full reach" of Aristotle's intelligence. The treatise is in three books, or sections. According to Baldwin's classification Book I deals with the necessities and opportunities of the speaker; Book II, with the audience; and Book III, with the speech itself. In the most general sense, this division is tenable and useful.

It is of interest to indicate, in a preliminary way, that the *Rhetoric* emphasizes deliberative speaking more than the other types. Heretofore the writers on rhetoric had confined their treatments largely to courtroom oratory. Aristotle explained this by saying that forensic oratory offered more inducements to deal in "nonessentials," such as appeals to the feelings of the judges. Furthermore, said he, political oratory "admits less of malicious sophistry than judicial pleading, [and] is more widely interesting...." [90] That his predecessors had stressed forensic oratory and that courtroom speaking as an art had matured somewhat earlier, were manifestly true. Aristotle's explanation of the cause, however, is open to doubt. Jebb's reasons, as set forth on pages 43-44, seem more cogent and plausible.

The Contents of Book I.—Book I opens with a definition: "Rhetoric is the counterpart of Dialectic." It may be described "as a faculty of discovering all the possible means of persuasion in any subject." [91] In other words, it enables a person to find suitable material for achieving persuasion in *any* field of inquiry, for, unlike geometry and certain other disciplines, Rhetoric does not have a subject matter of its own. But, as Baldwin interpolates, it does have subject matter "in every given case." "No less than logic, it is a means of bringing out truth, of making people see what is true and fitting." [92]

The tool which the speaker finds best adapted to effecting persuasion on public questions is the enthymeme, or approximate syllogism. Through its use in rhetoric (1) truth and justice may be guarded against falsehood and wrong; (2) discussion may be conducted where absolute proof through scientific argument is impossible of attainment; (3) both sides of a question may be surveyed; and (4) the self may be defended. [93]

Aristotle draws a distinction between artistic and inartistic, or intrinsic and extrinsic, proofs:

> By 'inartistic' proofs I mean all such as are not provided by our own skill but existed before and independently, e.g. witnesses, tortures, contracts and the like; by 'artistic', such as admit of being constructed systematically and by our own skill; in fine, the former we have only to apply and the latter we have to invent. [94]

As Baldwin indicates, this is "a division of the springs of composition, the sources of effectiveness, into those that lie outside and those that lie inside of utterance, or presentation." [95]

The components of artistic proof—or, as they are more popularly known, the modes of persuasion—constitute the basic pattern for much of the contemporary work in rhetorical criticism. According to Aristotle, the instrumentalities of rhetoric through which proof can be achieved are of three types:

> The instrument of proof is the moral character, when the delivery of the speech is such as to produce an impression of the speaker's credibility; for we yield a more complete and ready credence to persons of high character not only ordinarily and in a general way, but in such matters as do not admit of absolute certainty but necessarily leave room for difference of opinion, without any qualification whatever. (It is requisite however that this result should itself be attained by means of the speech and not of any antecedent conception of the speaker's character.) ... *Secondly,* proof may be conveyed through the audience, when it is worked up by the speech to an emotional state. For there is a wide difference in our manner of pronouncing decisions, according as we feel pleasure or pain, affection or hatred; and indeed *the power of working upon the emotions* is, as we assert, the one end or object to which our present professors of the rhetorical art endeavour to direct their studies. ... *Lastly,* the instrument of proof is the

speech itself, when we have proved a truth or an apparent truth from such means of persuasion as are appropriate to a particular subject.[96]

Aristotle recognizes the importance of the audience in the total speech situation. "For a speech is composed of three elements, viz. the speaker, the subject of the speech, and the persons addressed; and the end *or object* of the speech is determined by the last, viz. by the audience." [97] Since the audience is so essential to an understanding of a speech, Aristotle classifies the types of speeches according to the kinds of audiences to which they are given.

> Audiences are necessarily either critics or judges; and if the latter, they may be judges of things lying either in the past or in the future. A member of the Public Assembly may be taken as an instance of a judge of the future, a member of the Courts of Law as an instance of a judge of the past; while one who judges merely of the ability *displayed in a speech* is the critic. It follows that there must necessarily be three kinds of rhetorical speeches, the deliberative, the forensic and the epideictic.[98]

The remainder of Book I is devoted to an analysis of the topics, or common subjects, such as virtue, happiness, and the like, relating to deliberative, forensic, and epideictic fields. The *topics,* according to Aristotle, were the proper subjects of dialectical and rhetorical syllogisms, *i.e.,*

> ... such as are equally suitable to questions of justice, physics or politics, and to many questions of many different kinds. Such is e.g. the topic of 'the more or less,' or *of degree,* which will serve equally well to construct a syllogism or enthymeme about justice, physics or anything else, although these are subjects differing in kind. Special topics on the other hand are such as spring from the propositions appropriate to a particular species or class of subjects. Thus there are propositions in physics from which it is impossible to form an enthymeme or syllogism upon ethics, ethical propositions again from which it is impossible to form an enthymeme or syllogism upon physics, and so on through the whole range of subjects.[99]

Book II of Aristotle's Contribution.—Whereas Book I dealt with "rhetoric as conceived," Book II of Aristotle's work is devoted to "rhetoric as received." [100] The first part of Book II presents an analysis of the emotions, a study of the division and characteristics of people according as they are young, middle-aged, and old, and a survey of the traits usually observed in people of social preeminence, wealth, power, and good fortune. In this section, says Baldwin, "Aristotle is attempting neither an analysis of mental operations nor a science of human nature, but such a practical classification as may inculcate the habit of adaptation to the feelings of an audience." [101]

Aristotle's approach to the study of audience behavior can best be understood through an examination of his analysis of a typical emotion. Regarding envy, for example, he says:

> Nor is it difficult to see what are the occasions and objects of envy and the conditions under which we feel envious, envy being defined as a species of pain felt at conspicuous prosperity on the part of persons like ourselves in respect of such goods as have been already described, and this not with any view to our own personal advantage but solely because they are prosperous.
>
> For people will be envious, if there are or if they think there are persons like themselves, like, I mean, in race, family, age, habit of mind, reputation or possessions. Or if they only just fall short of having everything *which men can desire;* hence the envious disposition of persons who are engaged in important affairs or who are highly prosperous, as they fancy all the world is robbing them of their due. Or again if they have a permanent reputation for something, and especially for wisdom or happiness. Ambitious persons too are more liable to envy than the unambitious. Pretenders to wisdom are envious, as being ambitious of the credit of wisdom; and in general persons who are eager for reputation in a particular subject are envious in regard to it. Lastly, mean-minded persons are envious; for everything appears important to them. As regards the occasions of envy, the goods which provoke it have been already stated; for all achievements or possessions of which we covet the reputation or are ambitious, all things which arouse in us a longing for reputation, as well as all the various gifts of Fortune are practically without exception natural objects of envy, and of these such especially as we ourselves either desire or imagine we have a right to possess, or as by their acquisition confer a slight superiority or inferiority.
>
> It is clear too who are the natural objects of envy, as they are implied in the statement which has just been made; they are persons who are near to us in time, place, age or reputation. Hence the saying,
>
> 'For to be kin is to be envious.'

We are envious too of people whom we are ambitious of rivalling, i.e. of such people as have been mentioned, but not of those who lived many ages ago or who are yet unborn or dead or at the ends of the world. Nor again, where there are people to whom we think we are far inferior or far superior, whether we depend upon our own opinion only or upon that of the world at large, have we the same feeling of rivalry in regard to them and in cases like theirs. But as this rivalry extends to those who are our antagonists in any competition or in love and indeed to all who aspire to the same things as ourselves, these will necessarily be the principal objects of envy; whence the proverb 'Two of a trade never agree.'

Again, we are envious of people who have attained a rapid success, if we have succeeded with difficulty or have not succeeded at all. Or of people whose possession of a thing or whose success is a reproach to us, such people again being near and similar to ourselves; for as it is evidently our own fault that we fail to obtain the good *which they obtain,* it is the annoyance of this fact which produces in us the feeling of envy. Or again of people who either naturally or by acquisition possess anything which naturally belonged to us or had been acquired by us; this is the reason why seniors are envious of their juniors. Lastly, people who have spent a large sum upon a particular thing are envious of those who have spent little upon it *with an equal result.*

We see now clearly the occasions upon which envious people experience a feeling of pleasure, the persons whose cases give rise to such a feeling and the conditions under which people experience it; for, whatever be the conditions the absence of which produces pain *at certain things,* their presence will produce pleasure at the opposite things. Hence if the audience has been brought to an envious condition of mind and the persons on whose behalf a claim to compassion or to good of any kind is advanced are such as have been described, *i.e. proper objects of envy,* it is evident that they will not meet with compassion at the hands of those who are masters of the position.[102]

Since Aristotle condemned previous writers for giving too much attention to emotional proof, saying it was a "mere accessory," it may seem paradoxical that he then devoted such a large part of his own book to the same consideration. Surely he did discuss at length the ways of producing impressions upon listeners through appeals to sympathy, indignation, and the like. E. M. Cope explains and justifies Aristotle's position. He points to the necessity of using emotional proof in order to meet the inclinations of certain hearers; but more importantly, he shows that its use is "scientific," provided it is regarded as *one of the three modes of proof* which form the art of rhetoric in the strict sense. Emotional proof may, however, be used unscientifically "by the introduction of considerations *ab extra* or beside the real point, arguments *ad hominem* and *ad captandum,* such as *direct* appeals to the feelings, impassioned and exaggerated language... or even, as was often done, the actual production of the widow and orphans or friends of a deceased person to excite compassion and blind the judges to the real merits of the case."[103] Cope concludes, therefore, that to some extent

...the study and analysis of human motives, passions, and feelings belong to rhetoric, and are indeed an essential part of it; and the rules

derived from it may be applied *through the speech* to excite certain
emotions in the audience: this may however be carried a great deal too
far: and the fault that Aristotle finds with the Arts of preceding
Rhetoricians on this point is that they confined themselves to this indirect mode of proving their case, and neglected the more regular and
scientific mode of proof by logical enthymeme.[104]

In the remaining sections of Book II, Aristotle continues his
analysis of the common topics previously mentioned, considering
them largely from the point of view of their availability and of their
effect on listeners. The following analysis will suggest the importance of the topics in Aristotle's scheme:

If there are two opposites, and the existence or production of one of
them is possible, so presumably is the existence or production of the
other. For instance, if a human being can be cured, he can also fall
ill, inasmuch as the potentiality of opposites, *qua* opposites, is identical.
Again, if there are two similar things, and one of them is possible, so
is the other. Or if the more difficult of two things is possible, so is the
easier. Or if the production of a thing in an excellent and noble form
is possible, its production generally is possible, as the making of a fine
house is harder than the making of a house. Again, if the beginning
of a thing is possible, so is the completion of it, as no impossibility
ever comes or begins to come into being; the commensurability e.g. of
the diagonal of a square with its side cannot begin to come, nor ever
does come, into being. Or if the completion of a thing is possible, so is
its beginning; for whatever comes into being originates from a beginning. Or if the posterior in essence or in generation is capable of coming into being, so is the prior; thus if a man can come into being, so can
a boy, the boy being prior in generation, and if a boy can come into
being, so can a man, the man being *essentially* a beginning. Again,
the objects of natural love or desire are possible, as in general nobody
is enamoured or desirous of impossibilities. Again, the existence of
any science or art implies the possibility of the existence or production
of the objects with which it deals. The same is true of anything, if
the origin of its production depends upon things which we can influence by force or persuasion, i.e. upon persons whose superiors or
masters or friends we are. Again, if the parts of a thing are possible,
so is the whole, and if the whole is possible, so in general are the parts;
thus if it is possible to produce an instep, toe-cap and body of a shoe,
it is possible also to produce shoes, and if it is possible to produce shoes,
it is possible also to produce an instep, toe-cap and body. Again, the
possibility of producing the genus as a whole implies the possibility of
producing the species, and *vice versa;* the possibility e.g. of producing
a vessel implies the possibility of producing a trireme, and the possibility of producing a trireme implies the possibility of producing a

vessel. And of two things which are naturally inter-dependent if one is possible, so is the other; if double e.g. is possible, so is half, and if half, so is double. Again, if a thing can be produced without art and preparation, it can *a fortiori* be produced by means of art and careful pains; whence the lines of Agathon

> 'Of some must art be mother, some accrues
> To us of fortune or necessity.'

Lastly, if a thing is possible to inferior, weaker and less intelligent people, it is possible *a fortiori* to their opposites, ...

On the subject of the impossible, it is evident that *the orator* has a stock *of topics* ready to hand in the opposites of those which have been mentioned.

The fact of a thing having occurred or not in the past is to be examined by the light of the following considerations. In the first place, if that which is less likely to have occurred has occurred, it would appear that that which is more likely has also occurred. Or if that which is usually subsequent has occurred, *it may be argued* that that which is usually antecedent has occurred, as e.g., if a person has forgotten something, that he had once learnt it. Or if a person had at once the power and the will to do a certain act, *it may be argued that* he has done it; for everybody acts, when he has the power to do what he wishes, as there is then no impediment to his action. The same is true, if he had the wish and there was no external obstacle, or if he had the power and was in an angry mood, or if he had the power and with it the desire; for it is a general rule that people, when they are eager to do a thing, actually do it, as soon as they have the power, if they are bad people from the lack of self-control, and if they are good, because the objects of their desire are honourable. Again, if it was a person's intention to do a thing, *it may be argued that he did it,* as there is always a probability that the intention was carried out. Or if all the natural preliminaries or means to a thing have occurred, *it may be argued that the thing itself occurred,* as e.g., if it lightened that it thundered too, and if a thing was attempted, that it was done. Similarly, if the natural sequel or end of anything has occurred, *it may be argued that* the preliminaries and means to it have occurred also, as e.g., if it thundered, that it lightened, and if a thing was done, that it was attempted. In all these cases the rule is sometimes one of necessity, and sometimes one of only general validity.

Arguments against the occurrence of an event in the past may evidently be derived from the topics opposite to these.

As to arguments in regard to the future, it is clear *that they may be derived* from the same sources. *It may be argued* that a thing will be done, if there is both the power and the wish to do it or if there is desire, anger and calculation combined with power. Accordingly it will be done, if one has an immediate impulse or an intention to do it;

for what is intended is generally more likely to happen than what is not; or if it has been preceded by all its former natural antecedents; if e.g. the sky is clouded, there is a probability of rain. Finally, if the means to an end have happened, there is a probability of the end itself happening; thus the foundation of a house implies the house itself.

The topic of the greatness and smallness of things, in themselves and in comparison with each other and of great and small things generally, is evident from the remarks we have already made.... Hence as in each of the three kinds of Rhetoric the end proposed is good, whether expediency, honour or justice, it is evident that these must be the means of supplying the materials of amplification in each case. It is idle to look for anything more than this in regard to abstract greatness and superiority, particular facts being more important than general truths to the purpose *which we have now in hand*.[105]

Aristotle said there were two forms of proof common to the three types of oratory, namely, the example and the enthymeme.

It is proper in default of enthymemes to make use of examples as logical proofs, these being the natural means of producing conviction, but otherwise to make use of them as testimonies by way of a supplement to our enthymemes. For if we put them first, they resemble an induction, and induction is something inappropriate to Rhetoric unless in exceptional cases; but if we put them last, they resemble testimonies, and testimony is invariably persuasive. And from this it follows that, if we put them first, it is necessary to employ a considerable number of them, but if last, a single one is sufficient, as even a single credible witness is of service.[106]

Enthymemes are of two species: the demonstrative "which prove that a thing is or is not so," and the refutative, the difference between them being "the same as between a refutation and a syllogism in dialectics. The demonstrative enthymeme consists in drawing conclusions from admitted propositions, the refutative in drawing conclusions which are inconsistent *with the conclusions of one's adversary*."[107]

The materials of enthymemes, said Aristotle, are probabilities, examples, demonstrations, and signs.

They are probabilities, when the conclusion is derived from such facts as either are or are supposed to be generally true; examples, when it is reached by induction from an analogy of one or several instances, the universal rule being first ascertained and the particulars afterwards inferred from it; demonstrations, when it depends upon a rule which is necessary and absolute; signs, when upon general or particular statements which may be either true or false.[108]

Among the topics of enthymemes are the following:

(1) One topic of demonstrative enthymemes may be derived from a consideration of opposites. *If we take any two things, of which one is said to be predicable of the other,* we have to consider whether the opposite of the one is predicable of the opposite of the other, upsetting *the original proposition,* if it is not predicable, and confirming *the original proposition,* if it is, as, e.g., arguing that self-restraint is expedient on the ground that licentiousness is injurious.

(2) A second topic is derived from the inflexions of the same stem, as that which is or is not predicable of one is or is not predicable of another. Thus *we may argue* that justice is not always good; else the word 'justly' would always have a good sense, whereas to be justly put to death is the reverse of desirable.

(3) There is another arising from relative terms. *It may be argued that,* if 'honourably' and 'justly' are terms which are predicable of the action of the agent, they are predicable also of the suffering of the patient, and that if they are predicable of the command, they are predicable of its execution.

(4) Another topic is the argument from degree. Thus *it may be argued that,* if the Gods themselves are not omniscient, much less are men, meaning that if a condition is not realized, where it would be more natural, it will evidently not be realized, where it would be less so.

(5) There is another topic depending upon a consideration of the time. Thus Iphicrates in defending himself against Harmodius said, 'Suppose that before the action I had demanded the statue in case of doing it, you would have granted it; now that the action has been done, will you refuse it? Do not then make a promise in anticipation, and defraud me of it, when you have received the benefit.'

(6) Another topic consists in applying to our adversary's case anything that he has said about ourselves.

(7) There is another topic arising from definition, as, e.g., the *argument* that the supernatural must be either God or the work of God; but anybody who believes in the existence of a work of God necessarily believes also in the existence of Gods.

(8) Another topic springs from the various senses of a word....

(9) Another [arises] from division, as, e.g., if there are three possible causes of a crime, and while two of these are out of the question, the third is not alleged even by the prosecution.

(10) Another topic depends upon induction....

(11) There is another topic derivable from a judgment already pronounced upon the same or similar or an opposite question, especially if it is the judgment of all men and all times, or, failing that, of a large majority or of all or nearly all the wise or good or again of the judges themselves or of those whose authority they admit or whose judgment admits of no contradiction....

(12) Another topic consists in *taking separately* the parts *of a subject, in considering* e.g. .... what sort of motion the soul is, as it must be this or that.

(13) Also, as it happens in the great majority of cases that the same thing has consequences partly good and partly bad, another topic consists in using the attendant circumstances as means of exhortation or dissuasion, accusation, or defence, eulogy or censure.

(14) There is another topic when in reference to two opposite things it is necessary to employ exhortation or dissuasion and to apply to both the method already described, the difference being that, whereas in the last case it was any two things, it is here two opposites that are contrasted.

(15) Again, as there is a difference between the objects which people praise in public and in secrecy, and, while they make a show of lauding justice and honour above everything else, they prefer expediency in their hearts, another topic consists in trying to use *an adversary's premisses, whichever mode of sentiment he adopts,* to infer the opposite *of his conclusion;* for there is no topic of paradoxes so entirely effective as this.

(16) Another topic is derived from analogy of results. Iphicrates, for instance, resisted an effort to impose a public burden upon his son because of his size, although he was under the legal age, by saying, 'If you reckon tall boys men, you will have to vote short men boys.'

(17) Another topic consists in arguing identity of cause from identity of effect.

(18) There is another topic depending upon the fact that people do not always make the same choice at a later as at an earlier time, but often reverse it.

(19) Another topic consists in treating the conceivable as the actual reason of a thing existing or having come into existence, as in the supposition that a person would make a present in order to inflict the pain of taking it away.

(20) There is another topic common to forensic and deliberative oratory, viz. to consider the inducements and discouragements and the motives of acting or abstaining from action; for these are the conditions, the presence or the absence of which renders action desirable or the reverse.

(21) There is yet another topic in the case of things which are supposed to happen but are difficult to believe.

(22) Another topic, which is proper to refutation, consists in examining whether there is any contradiction in the series of dates, actions or words....

(23) Another topic, where there is or appears to be a prejudice against particular persons or things, is to state the explanation of the circumstance which is unaccountable, as there is always something which accounts for the appearance.

(24) Another topic consists in arguing from the presence or absence of the cause the existence or non-existence of the effect; for cause and effect go always hand in hand, and there is nothing which has not a cause.

(25) Another topic is to consider whether it was or is possible to take a better course than that which the person either recommends or takes or has taken in action; for if this course has not been taken, it is evident that he has not done the deed, as nobody voluntarily and intentionally chooses what is bad.

(26) Again, if an intended action is inconsistent with some action already performed, there is another topic which consists in viewing them side by side.

(27) Another topic is to discover a ground of accusation or defence in any mistake that has been made.

(28) [And, finally] another topic is derivable from a play on names. . . . [109]

Refutative argument may be carried to successful completion through the use of counter-syllogism or through the introduction of an objection.

It is clear that the counter-syllogisms may be constructed out of the same topics as the syllogisms of which we have spoken; for it is the common opinions of the world which form the materials of syllogisms, and opinions are often contradictory. Objections on the other hand . . . may be adduced in four different ways, viz., either from the enthymeme of your adversary himself, or from analogy, or from antithesis, or from a previous decision.[110]

Thus Aristotle devotes a large part of Book II to the logical mode of persuasion. At the same time he urges the speaker to analyze carefully the audience for which the arguments are intended.

It should be borne in mind that, whereas Plato "held that the rhetorician must know the Truth, because probability was engendered by a likeness to Truth," [111] Aristotle made probability the essential substructure of his rhetorical system. The topics mentioned in Books I and II were statements designed chiefly to bring to mind quickly the several arguments usable for either side of a case. They constituted, in Hunt's estimation, a "sort of rhetorician's first aid. They were to assist him in producing immediately, and perhaps without any special knowledge of the subject, a plausible argument upon either side of a debatable proposition." [112]

Aristotle's substitution of the enthymeme for the formal syllogism, and the example for the induction—made necessary by the failure of audiences to follow close reasoning—was additional evidence, according to Hunt, that Aristotle recognized the "merely contingent and probable nature of rhetoric." "The enthymeme was a rhetorical syllogism; that is, a syllogism drawn, not from universal principles belonging to a particular science, but from probabilities in the sphere of human affairs." [113]

The Broad Outline of Book III.—In Book III, Aristotle deals first with delivery, linking it in a general way with style. The concept receives only brief examination. He indicates somewhat apologetically that delivery is not popularly considered an elevated topic of inquiry.

> Still as the entire study of Rhetoric has regard to appearance, it is necessary to pay due attention to declamation, not that it is right to do so but because it is inevitable. Strict justice, indeed, if applicable to Rhetoric, would confine itself to seeking such a delivery as would cause neither pain nor pleasure. For the right condition is that the battle should be fought out on the facts of the case alone; and therefore everything outside the *direct* proof is *really* superfluous; although extraneous matters are highly effective, ... owing to the depraved character of the audience.[114]

The art of delivery, as Aristotle sees it, "consists in understanding (1) the proper use of the voice for the expression of the several emotions, *i.e.,* when it should be loud or low or intermediate, (2) the proper use of the accents, *i.e.,* when the tone should be acute or grave or intermediate, and (3) the rhythms suitable to each emotion." [115] Although some perceive in Aristotle's treatment a certain philosophic contempt for delivery, Baldwin doubts that such an impression can be confirmed.[116]

Style should be characterized by perspicuity, purity, dignity, and propriety. Aristotle analyzes each of these elements. As for the stylistic structure, it should be "neither metrical nor wholly unrhythmical. If it is the former, it lacks persuasiveness from its appearance of artificiality, and at the same time diverts the minds of the audience from the subject by fixing their attention upon the return of the similar cadence. ..." [117]

With an eye to adapting style, in the broad sense, to the demands of oratory, Aristotle remarks:

> The style of political oratory is precisely similar to scene-painting. For the greater the crowd, the more distant is the view: hence it is that in both a finished style appears superfluous and unsuccessful. The forensic style on the other hand is more finished, especially when addressed to a single judge; for he is least subject to rhetori-

cal influences, as he can take a more comprehensive view of what is germane to the case or alien to it and, as there is no actual contest, is not prejudiced in his judgment. Accordingly it is not the same orators who succeed in all the different styles of Rhetoric; but, where there is most opportunity for declamation, there is the least possibility of finish. And this is the case where voice, and especially where a loud voice, is required.

The epideictic style is best suited to literary purposes, as its proper function is to be read; and next to it the forensic style.[118]

Book III closes with a brief analysis of oratorical structure. "A speech has two parts. It is necessary first to state the case and then to prove it." [119] These are the so-called "indispensable" parts, but if more are added, Aristotle indicates, "they must not exceed four, viz. exordium, exposition, proof and peroration." [120] As for the functions of the exordium, they correspond to those of the prologue in poetry and prepare the way for what is to follow. The peroration has four objects: "to inspire the audience with a favourable opinion of yourself and an unfavourable one of your adversary, to amplify or depreciate the subject, to excite the emotions of the audience and to recall the facts to their memory." [121]

The Philosophical Significance of the *Rhetoric*.—We have presented this detailed digest because Aristotle's *Rhetoric* is the true pioneer in the field, the one upon which practically all subsequent treatises rely to a considerable extent. It is for us the first orderly, systematic attempt to set down the principles of the art of public speaking. The *Rhetoric* provides a philosophically sound *rationale* of the subject. It embraces a philosophy of discourse relatively free from pedantry and deeply rooted in the basic tenets of the speaking art. Its peculiar distinction, apart from the body of principles which it classifies, derives from four fundamental postulates upon which the work rests:

The first of Aristotle's basic postulates deals with the nature of rhetoric. He assumed that it was a useful art, operating in the social medium for the purpose of *doing* something. He conceived of the art in purely functional terms. This is in keeping with Aristotle's general point of view, confirming John MacCunn's interpretation that "He who would win the harper's skill must win it by harping; he who would write, by writing; he would heal the sick, by healing them. In these, as indeed in all the arts, *faculty is begotten of function,* and definite proclivity comes of determinate acts." [122] As it relates to the subject of our discussion, rhetoric enables a person (1) to maintain truth against falsehood; (2) to advance discussion where definitive proofs are impossible of attainment; (3) to expose irregularities in argument as well as see both sides of a controversy; and (4) to defend himself with reason as well as with physical strength. In other words, speech is an instrument of social adaptation.

The postulate that rhetoric is a useful social tool has an important implication. A rhetoric of simple display, of hollow ostentation, is definitely foreign to this concept. There is no glorification of form to the neglect of substance. Speaking is not declamatory utterance divorced of social consequences. It is, instead, a practical skill serving as a direct link between the individual and his immediate social environment on the one hand and the larger political pattern of the state on the other. Logically, such a position argues for a close relation between the speaking art and the allied fields of social inquiry. The Aristotelian system provides for precisely such an interrelation.

Aristotle also held that rhetoric could be taught. In making this assumption, he believed, first, that rhetoric was composed of a body of material yielding to systematic treatment, and second, that it was possible through practice to develop speaking skills. He observed that all men use speech "either at random or through practice and from acquired habit." Since both ways were possible, the subject could be handled systematically, thus permitting an inquiry into "the reason why some speakers succeed through practice and others spontaneously. . . ." Taking a body of more or less unrelated facts, Aristotle moulded it into a system the essential pattern of which may be found in practically every contribution worthy of the name published since that time.

The *Rhetoric* presents unmistakable evidence of the inquiring nature of Aristotle's mind. Everywhere we perceive the attempt to determine the causes of things. Aristotle realized that some speakers got favorable responses while others did not. He recognized the necessity of systematizing the discoverable principles in order that they might be applied to practice. While Plato had, in a very general way, shown *how* the rhetorician could do certain things, Aristotle gave orderly direction to the principles and observations relevant to the art. According to W. Rhys Roberts, no one has, either before or since, "enriched the subject with so great a store of acute observations on the workings of the ordinary mind and heart." [123]

Charles Woolbert used to say that there is only one rule in public speaking and that is that there are no rules. While Aristotle referred to the systematic principles of rhetoric and to the means and methods of succeeding in speech, he, too, doubted the advisability of setting up formal rules. His emphasis upon the variable nature of the speaker, subject, and audience is adequate evidence to reveal this point of view. He did not conceive of the speaking art as a stereotyped system. He saw in it an instrument for making many and diverse adjustments to a multitude of social conditions.

Aristotle was convinced that the random performances of speakers could be improved through the study and application of orderly principles. In this he was reflecting the spirit of Greek education. Thomas Davidson tells us that "to the realization of their ideal in any individual the Greeks conceived three conditions to be necessary, (1) a noble nature, (2) persistent exercise or training in right action, (3) careful instruction. If any one of these was lacking, the highest result could not be attained." [124] The primary function of imposing habit or exercise upon original nature and finally crowning it with instruction was twofold: first, "to make action free, by making it rational," and second, "to make possible an advance to original action." [125]

Aristotle's "unmistakable emphasis upon habituation" needs no discussion. Whether he was concerned with the formation of moral character or the refinement of a technique in speaking, he was alike convinced, especially during the later years of his teaching, that there was no substitute for exercise or practice. In fact, there are responsible authorities who believe that the value of exercise was "far better understood by the ancients than by the moderns."

The importance of Aristotle's assumption that rhetorical refinements result from practice can scarcely be overemphasized. Modern pedagogical method rests squarely upon that base. Like our contemporaries, Aristotle saw certain shortcomings in the original nature of many speakers. And as John MacCunn has said, "it is precisely the shortcomings of nature that are the educator's opportunity. Here, as elsewhere, art must remedy the imperfections of nature...." [126] By demonstrating that rhetoric was a teachable art, Aristotle established a tenet upon which all subsequent systems of speech instruction depend and from which present training derives much of its just claim to dignity in the scheme of learning.

The two foregoing postulates refer chiefly to the purpose and the scope of rhetoric. The third basic assumption involves both purpose and method. Aristotle believed that a sound projection of rhetorical

theory was based upon the doctrine of the Mean. This concept reveals the true value of practice and instruction in speech by providing
a standard of artistic excellence. The Greek mind sought *proportion*
in all human manifestations. Aristotle urged an avoidance of both
excess and deficiency. Although not stated as plainly as in the
Nicomachean Ethics, the doctrine of the Mean permeates the
Rhetoric and gives it an artistic as well as a practical point of view.
Concretely stated, the doctrine asserts itself in the speech proper;
the quality of an address is directly related to its quantitative proportions. Certain quantitative relations must exist if a product par-
taking of perfection is to develop. In the words of W. D. Ross,
"there is a right amount of each, a right time, a right manner, right
objects for each." [127] What these right amounts are, will depend
upon the speaker and the social circumstances.

Aristotle states the doctrine of the Mean when he says:

> . . . now people tell us, ridiculously enough, that the narration should
> be rapid. And yet I would say, as did one to a baker, who inquired
> 'whether he should knead his bread hard or soft,'—'What,' said he, 'is
> it then impossible to knead it properly?' And so here [in rhetoric a
> mean is to be observed]. For one should not narrate at too great length,
> just as he should not make too long an exordium, nor state his proofs
> [too fully]. For neither in this case does propriety consist either in
> rapidity or conciseness, but in a mean betwixt both: and this is the
> stating just so much as will make the matter clear. . . . [128]

This standard, however difficult to define because of the varying conditions in different speech situations, makes balance, proportion, and
freedom from extremes the ideals toward which practice and instruction should lead. In a general sense, the current practice of
adapting speech programs to the individual needs and capacities of
students is essentially a corollary of Aristotle's Relative Mean. This
Mean, with relation to ourselves, said Aristotle,

> . . . is neither too much nor too little for us. But this is not one and
> the same to all; as, for example, if ten is too many, and two too few,
> six is taken for the absolute mean, for it exceeds two as much as it is
> exceeded by ten. But this is the mean according to arithmetical pro-
> portion. But the relative mean is not to be taken in this manner; for
> it does not follow, that if ten pounds are too much for any person to
> eat, and two pounds too little, the training-master will prescribe six
> pounds; for perhaps this is too much or too little for the person who
> is to eat it. For it is too little for Milo, but too much for one just com-
> mencing gymnastics; and the case is similar in running and wrestling.
> Thus, then, every person who has knowledge shuns the excess and the

defect, but seeks for the mean, and chooses it; not the absolute mean,
but the relative one.[129]

Speech teachers point out today that much of their instruction
applies with reference to *particular cases*. Too much and too little
are purely relative considerations. Hence our modern instruction
rests upon what in reality amounts to a doctrine of the Mean.

The last assumption or postulate of the Aristotelian system deals
with the function of rhetoric in the body politic. While any set of
rhetorical principles may be open to the charge of being partly inconsistent with the best interests of an enlightened state because un-
principled speakers will always be able to use legitimate techniques
in an irregular way, Aristotle came as near giving a true ethic of
discourse as any writer, including Isocrates.

Aristotle assumed that the logical mode of persuasion was the
only true constituent of the art of rhetoric. In his system the appeal
to reason or rational conduct receives primary emphasis. Being a
discerning analyst, however, he knew the elements of rhetorical effectiveness. So it is quite natural that the so-called "accessories"—
the emotional proofs—are given reasonable prominence in the *Rhetoric*. The inescapable conclusion, however, is that, by and large,
Aristotle was concerned with giving effectiveness to truth.

This conclusion agrees with Aristotle's conception of the social
order in which the speaker performed. He believed that man was
a social being with definite relations to the political community.
Hence his idea of the field of Politics was fairly comprehensive.
"Politics" was virtually an omnibus term, embracing Economics
and, as its groundwork, Ethics. The ideal community was a society
held together by moral and rational principles. Moral virtue in the
individual was indispensable to the establishment of reasonable institutions in the body politic.

Aristotle's basic philosophy did not tolerate compromise with the
moral integrity and design of the speaker. Perhaps when Aristotle
enters upon his analysis of arguments, he becomes at times more
concerned, as Everett Hunt suggests, with "rhetorical effectiveness"
than with "moral justifiability."[130] That is the point, however, at
which we encounter what may be the internal contradiction of any
ethics of discourse. If rhetoric is concerned with securing responses,
however enlightened in purpose, it is evident that techniques and
devices capable equally of honorable and evil use will receive systematic treatment. Certain of the "accessories" will creep in. The
truth, if that word may be used, must sometimes be made more

palatable; and an increase in palatability may mean a decrease in rigidly rational content. Aristotle recognized this fact fully when he discussed delivery. It is right, he said, "that the contest be carried on by means of the facts themselves. . . ." But a defect in the art of rhetoric and in the hearers made such a condition impossible. Rhetoric aimed at ends different from those of geometry, for example, and it often dealt with individuals whose intellectual accomplishments were limited. Consequently, emotional flourishes were sometimes necessary. This does not mean that Aristotle either condoned or recommended the use of guile and suspiciously crafty artifice in speaking situations. It would seem that a fair reading of the *Rhetoric* reveals no significant departures from the high moral principles enunciated in the *Nicomachean Ethics*.

That the man who follows Aristotle's suggestions regarding the speaking art will be shrewd and perhaps artfully adroit in manipulating rhetorical instruments, is certainly true; that he will be culpably crafty, cannot be fully demonstrated. The Aristotelian position is clearly revealed in the sixth book of the *Ethics*. Aristotle refers to the faculty of cleverness "the nature of which is to be able to do, and to attain, those things which conduce to the aim proposed." He then goes on to say that "if . . . the aim be good, the cleverness is praiseworthy; but if it be bad, it becomes craft." [131] In other words, the Aristotelian thesis postulates that "cleverness and character must *strike alliance*." [132]

It would seem, therefore, that Aristotle's emphasis upon logical proof as the essential mode of persuasion, together with his insistence upon the prudent use of the instruments by means of which ends are attained, constitutes the basis of an acceptable standard for a twentieth century philosophy of rhetoric. Aristotle's principal contribution lies not alone in his development of rhetorical details, important as they are, but also in his broad, philosophic conception of the place of rhetoric in the scheme of learning. His *Rhetoric* continues to impress students as a succinct, timelessly relevant treatise. It represents a dignified and intellectually respectable statement of the place of Speech in the field of knowledge.

General Summary

The tradition of rhetoric is rich in names and deeds of distinguished men from the earliest period of recorded history. A part of that tradition rests upon oral testimony communicated from generation to generation by people who cherished the dignity and the value of an art of rhetoric. But, in the main, the sources of the subject are fairly specific, traceable in writing, and open to investigative study. Many valuable writings, regrettably, are not extant; others have unquestionably suffered from what Samuel Johnson once called the "pest of speech"—frequency of translation. These shortcomings notwithstanding, we can view the history of the subject over the span of centuries and observe the signal contributions that have illuminated the way for speakers and critics. Only with this historical perspective can we hope to understand and appreciate the theory upon which the art of speaking rests today, and from which the critic gets both his point of view and his methodology.

Long before there was a system of speechcraft, there were speakers. Ideas had to be communicated, either for reasons of practical necessity or of primitive artistic desire. The first systematic art of speaking dates from the period when Corax devised his scheme to meet the needs of the dispossessed people who returned to Sicily to reclaim their lands following the expulsion of the tyrants. The Sophists and the Rhetors of ancient Greece, the great orators of the Attic canon, and the writings of Isocrates on a newer conception of rhetoric—all contributed to the refinement of the art and to the development of an effective prose style.

In Plato we find one of the most acute critics of rhetorical theory, as well as one of the most brilliant contributors to the art. In his ideal system—never as completely developed as we should like, but still sufficiently clear to make the way easier for later theorists—he postulates the quest for truth and familiarity with the souls of men as cardinal features of an enlightened speechcraft. The influence of these tenets upon subsequent contributions was incalculably large.

With the production of Aristotle's *Rhetoric,* the subject of speechmaking achieved genuine maturity and dignity. In three short books, Aristotle stated the principles of the art with a succinctness and accuracy which even today elicit the unqualified respect of scholars everywhere. The *Rhetoric* is the most literate and forthright analysis of the art of speaking in print. Knowing it, one knows much of what was written on the subject after Aristotle's time, and is in a favored position to appraise the theory and criticism of public address to this very hour.

Chapter 3

ELABORATIONS OF ARISTOTELIAN PRINCIPLES

Interrelation of Greek and Roman Thinking

The Greeks gave us the basic principles of rhetoric. But the Romans and Graeco-Romans were highly skilled students whose penchant for organization and refinement of traditional lore asserted itself in their treatment of speechcraft. They may not have added much that was new, but they elaborated upon the previously determined tenets and placed them in patterns of somewhat sharper outline. Furthermore, the practical turn of the Roman mind insured the likelihood of certain departures from the philosophical point of view regarding rhetoric, to a more purely pragmatic, pedagogical development. This is most clearly shown in the treatises of Cicero, the orator speaking on his art, and in the writings of Quintilian, the teacher discoursing on methods of instruction.

Despite certain differences in emphasis and point of view between early Greek and Graeco-Roman writings on rhetoric, the latter quite naturally and uninterruptedly grows out of and blends with the former, so that the tradition of the subject is sustained in unbroken continuity. The following sections show how the basic postulates of Greek inquiry served as the substructure of Roman thinking.

The *ad Herennium*

The *Rhetorica ad Herennium,* sometimes ascribed to Cicero (106-43 B.C.), provides a pattern of the rhetorical system taught at Rome during the early days of Cicero. Perhaps published about 86 B.C., this treatise in four books is, according to Atkins, "the first work of real significance belonging to the first century B.C. . . ." [1]

Book I deals with the kinds of oratory and the parts of rhetoric. [2] Demonstrative, deliberative, and judicial oratory represent the types of causes that a speaker may consider. In order to carry out his assignment, an orator must deal with five aspects or parts of rhetoric: *inventio, dispositio, elocutio, memoria,* and *pronuntiatio.* Each of these five parts can be acquired by an orator through art, imitation, and practice.

An orator's invention is revealed in six sections of an address: *exordium, narratio, divisio, confirmatio, confutatio,* and *conclusio.*

Three kinds of causes, or *constitutio causae,* are mentioned: those of fact (*coniecturalis*), interpretation (*legitima*), and right or wrong (*iuridicialis*). Under the heading of the *status,* or *state,* these concepts are discussed in a later section.

Book II treats of invention as it relates to forensic oratory; Book III, as it relates to deliberative and demonstrative speaking. *Dispositio, memoria,* and *pronuntiatio* also receive consideration.

The last book of the *ad Herennium* is devoted to *elocutio,* or style, and takes up about half of the entire treatise. A. S. Wilkins remarks that this section is of interest, not only because it is the first work on the subject in Latin, but also because it provides an abundance and excellence of illustration.

The author lists three kinds of style—*gravis, mediocris,* and *attenuata.* The general requirements of the speaker's language are elegance, or word choice; composition, or the union of words; and dignity, or adornment. To further the realization of the last requisite, the *ad Herennium* provides a long list of figures (*verborum exornatio* and *sententiarum exornatio*).

The Classical Divisions of Rhetoric

The parts or canons of rhetoric set forth in the *ad Herennium* represent the broad divisions of the whole subject; in many respects, they constitute the basic pattern of all theoretical and critical investigations into the art and practice of speaking.

According to the classical tradition, all rhetoric is divided into five parts: invention, disposition, elocution, memory, and delivery. This fivefold division is fairly standard in all major works after Aristotle until the eighteenth century. Minor changes in the meaning of the terms are developed in various treatises, but the pattern remains the same until the time of George Campbell, when *memory* practically drops out of the analysis.

These parts have distinctive functions. They are not only the concepts with which an orator must deal and which he must master in order to deliver an effective speech; they are also the aspects of the delivered oration which the critic, viewing the finished speech as a creative product, examines and evaluates.

The exact origin of the fivefold plan is in doubt. The first division of speech materials was probably into substance and form; next, into invention and arrangement. But the fivefold division is hard to trace.

The Inventive Aspect.—Invention involves the attempt on the part of the orator, as Cicero says, "to find out what he should say. . . ." It is an investigative undertaking, embracing a survey and forecast of the subject and a search for the arguments suitable to the given rhetorical effort. As Baldwin remarks in his commentary, it refers to "the investigation, analysis, and grasp of the subject matter." [3] Thus certain writers—Aristotle among them—give more attention to invention than to the other parts of rhetoric. This is done on the ground, and perhaps properly, that the content is the most important part of a speech.

Without proposing to categorize the constituents of rhetorical theory, we may say in general that the concept of invention includes the entire investigative undertaking, the idea of the *status,* and the modes of persuasion—logical, emotional, and ethical—in all of their complex interrelations.

Disposition of Materials.—Disposition covers the concept of arrangement, of orderly planning and movement of the whole idea. Although the treatment of it differs within a narrow range among the several treatises, the general meaning is twofold: the appreciation of a plan for the speech as a whole, and the development of the specific parts of the speech, such as the exordium, narration, proof, peroration, and whatever other divisions the authors specify. Baldwin is correct in saying that what is noticeably missing, not only in Aristotle's treatment of disposition, but in the other works of the classical tradition as well, "is some definite inculcation of consecutiveness." [4]

In some treatises, ancient and modern, invention and disposition are treated under a common head—the assumption being that the orderly arrangement of the materials constitutes an essential part of the inventive process.

The Stylistic Feature.—The third part of rhetoric was originally called *elocutio,* and it referred specifically to style. It embraced the concept of expression in language, resulting, basically, from the choice of words and their arrangement or composition. Among the ancient rhetoricians, the study of words and composition led to an analysis of the distinguishing marks of the kinds of style. Accordingly, in Cicero's *Orator,* to name but one treatise, the plain, the moderate, and the grand style are described and analyzed.

The Memory in Rhetoric.—*Memoria,* the fourth part of rhetoric, does not receive systematic treatment in Aristotle's *Rhetoric.* Cicero, Quintilian, and other rhetoricians give it consideration. However, when we come to the major works of the eighteenth century, we note that this canon has been dropped. In recent volumes it receives only incidental treatment, although Lionel Crocker's *Public Speaking for College Students* devotes a complete chapter to "The Memory in Speech."

In the older sense, memory was a fairly comprehensive concept, embracing the speaker's mastery of all his material in sequential order. "Why should I remark," says Cicero,

> ... how excellent a thing it is to retain the instructions which you have received with the cause, and the opinion which you have formed upon it? to keep all your thoughts upon it fixed in your mind, all your arrangement of language marked out there? to listen to him from whom you receive any information, or to him to whom you have to reply, with such power of retention, that they seem not to have poured their discourse into your ears, but to have engraven it on your mental tablet? [5]

That Cicero regarded memory as an important part of the orator's equipment is further revealed in his criticism of the eminent speakers. He censures Curio for his "extremely treacherous" memory, saying

> ... after he had divided his subject into three general heads, he would sometimes, in the course of speaking, either add a fourth, or omit the third. In a capital trial, in which I had pleaded for Titinia, the daughter of Cotta, when he attempted to reply to me in defense of Servius Naevius, he suddenly forgot every thing he intended to say, and attributed it to the pretended witchcraft and magic artifices of Titinia. [6]

In commenting on Hippias' contribution to rhetoric, and on the subsequent disappearance of the canon of memory, Bromley Smith says:

> With the passing of the years ... the notion that the memory of orators can be trained by systematic devices has almost disappeared. Memory itself remains and is highly esteemed, yet it has lost its ancient importance. Long ago Plato foresaw this when he remarked that the invention of writing by the Egyptian God, Theuth, caused learners to trust external written characters rather than themselves. That he was right may be judged from the number of speakers who read their

addresses. Hippias, however, belonged to the old school; he believed he could train the memories of the future statesmen. His labors must have had a measure of success, sufficient indeed to encourage others. Since his days thousands have followed his idea, like a will-o'-the-wisp, through the bogs of discipline. At last sinking below their depth, they have disappeared, leaving only a few bubbles to remind the world that Memory, 'the warder of the mind,' was once a canon of rhetoric.[7]

Delivery.—The last part of rhetoric—*pronuntiatio*—is the art of delivery. Its constituent elements are vocal utterance and bodily action. From Aristotle to the present day all systematic treatises on rhetoric have given some space to this canon.

A Great Orator's Conception of His Art

A Functional Approach to Speechmaking.—"The Romans," said W. S. Teuffel, "were naturally well qualified for oratory by their acute intellect, their love of order and their Italian vivacity, tempered with Roman gravity." [8] They were practical people; so it is natural that their works on speaking should emphasize the functional aspects of the art. Cicero represented this practical inclination at its best. "The most eminent orator of Roman civilization, he wrote more than any other orator has ever written on rhetoric; and historically he has been more than any other an ideal and model." [9]

While discussing the efforts of the philosophers—Aristotle and Theophrastus included—as writers on rhetoric, Cicero inquires whether it would not be advantageous to consider the art of speaking from the point of view of the practicing orator *and* the philosopher. Surely the orator would be able to "set forth with full power and attraction" those same topics of virtue, equity, laws, and the like, with something more than the "tame and bloodless phraseology" of the philosophers. Accordingly, Cicero would interest himself in the development of an orator so "accomplished and complete" that he would be able to "speak on all subjects with variety and copiousness." [10]

Cicero tried, as his works show, to restore rhetoric to something of its earlier scope and vitality. As Atkins indicates,[11] he was "protesting against the narrowing of the province" of the speaking art, hoping to restore rhetoric as a "system of general culture" which would train men to write and speak competently on all possible subjects. In this effort Cicero was influenced and guided by the doctrines of Isocrates whom he regarded as the "father of eloquence."

Cicero was an eclectic. With the possible exception of the *Brutus,* the contents of all his works originate in the contributions of his predecessors and contemporaries. However, he embellished the old, saying it so much better that it took on a character of finality.

The Substance of the *De Oratore.*—*De Oratore* is Cicero's most important book on rhetorical theory. Like many treatises of its kind, it is in dialogue form, with the celebrated orators Crassus and Antonius playing the major roles; and Scaevola, Catulus, Cotta, Sulpicius, Caesar, and Rufus serving in a minor way as interlocutors.

In Book I Crassus comments on the qualifications of the Ideal Orator, while in Book III he develops the Ciceronian conception of oratorical style. Antonius, serving as the protagonist in Book II, discourses on invention and disposition. Incidental remarks on humor are also introduced by Caesar.

Book I of *De Oratore.*—In the first book we find, reminiscent of Isocrates and Aristotle, a development of the theme that to be successful the orator must conform to high and exacting qualifications. He must be a man of great learning.

> A knowledge of a vast number of things is necessary, without which volubility of words is empty and ridiculous; speech itself is to be formed, not merely by choice, but by careful construction of words; and all the emotions of the mind, which nature has given to man, must be intimately known; for all the force and art of speaking must be employed in allaying or exciting the feelings of those who listen. To this must be added a certain portion of grace and wit, learning worthy of a well-bred man, and quickness and brevity in replying as well as attacking, accompanied with a refined decorum and urbanity. Besides, the whole of antiquity and a multitude of examples is to be kept in the memory; nor is the knowledge of laws in general, or of the civil law in particular, to be neglected. And why need I add any remarks on delivery itself, which is to be ordered by action of body, by gesture, by look, and by modulation and variation of the voice, the great power of which, alone and in itself, the comparatively trivial art of actors and the stage proves, on which though all bestow their utmost labor to form their look, voice, and gesture, who knows not how few there are, and have ever been, to whom we can attend with patience? What can I say of that repository for all things, the memory, which, unless it be the keeper of the matter and words that are the fruits of thought and invention, all the talents of the orator, we see, though they be of the highest degree of excellence, will be of no avail? Let us then cease to wonder what is the cause of the scarcity of good speakers, since eloquence results from all those qualifications....[12]

Cicero shortly after sets forth his oft-quoted remark that the "proper concern of an orator, . . . is language of power and elegance accommodated to the feelings and understandings of mankind." [13]

We note, then, that Cicero, through his mouthpiece, Crassus, insists upon the orator's having virtually universal knowledge and skill. In the dialogue, Antonius holds that somewhat less learning is necessary, although he, too, urges broad familiarity with the field of knowledge. But he insists upon a more *intensive* training leading to the acquisition of oratorical excellence. Antonius would develop the orator's natural talents and capacities for oratory, even if his intellectual control over the field of learning were somewhat more moderate than Crassus believed essential. Baldwin feels that, in a sense, both Crassus and Antonius are right. "Normally rhetoric is both extensive and intensive, both a comprehensive study of life and a specific art, even as the means of persuasion are both extrinsic and intrinsic." [14]

In this book Crassus also is made to delineate the five parts of rhetoric when he announces:

> If, therefore, any one desires to define and comprehend the whole and
> peculiar power of an orator, that man, in my opinion, will be an orator,
> worthy of so great a name, who whatever subject comes before him,
> and requires rhetorical elucidation, can speak on it judiciously, in set
> form, elegantly, and from memory, and with a certain dignity of ac-
> tion.[15]

However, the principal reference at this point is to *invention*.

The Second Book.—Book II treats mainly of invention and disposition, and with particular emphasis, of course, upon these concepts in their relation to forensic oratory. Care is taken to point out that the orator's painstaking investigation of the facts is indispensable to inventive skill. The accomplished orator will conduct research before taking the platform, will "take one time for premeditation, and another for speaking."

Though not original, Cicero's treatment of the *status*—determination of the character and issues of the case—is important to the study of rhetorical theory. He remarks:

> There are in all, therefore, three sorts of matters, which may possibly
> fall under doubt and discussion; what is now done, what has been done,
> or what is to be done; what the nature of a thing is, or how it should
> be designated; for as to the question which some Greeks add, whether
> a thing be rightly done, it is wholly included in the inquiry, what the
> nature of the thing is.[16]

These are frequently called states of conjecture, definition, and quality, respectively. Cicero remarks that these considerations apply to all types of oratory in which dispute centers—forensic, deliberative, and panegyric.

The objects of discourse are said to be: "That we prove what we maintain to be true; that we conciliate those who hear; that we produce in their minds whatever feeling our cause may require." [17] The whole business of speaking, Cicero allows, rests upon these things for success in persuasion.

Cicero's treatment of pathetic and ethical proof adds little, if anything, that is new. He indicates that "mankind makes far more determinations through hatred, or love, or desire, or anger, or grief, or joy, or hope, or fear, or error, or some other affection of mind, than from regard to truth, or any settled maxim, or principle of right, or judicial form, or adherence to the laws." [18] He therefore comments on the way to make audience analyses, to move people to various emotional states, and to make the speaker's character aid in the persuasive undertaking.

As to arrangement of speech materials, Cicero offers little that is new. He indicates that two methods may be observed: "one, which the nature of causes dictates; the other, which is suggested by the orator's judgment and prudence." [19] The plan of organization he then describes is more detailed than Aristotle's, the difference resulting largely, however, from the fact that he is making an adjustment to forensic speaking.

Memory, as a distinct part of rhetoric, receives attention in Book II. Cicero opens his discourse by recalling the traditional incident which presumably prompted Simonides to "invent" the art of memory:

> For they relate, that when Simonides was at Crannon in Thessaly, at an entertainment given by Scopas, a man of rank and fortune, and had recited a poem which he had composed in his praise, in which, for the sake of embellishment, after the manner of the poets, there were many particulars introduced concerning Castor and Pollux, Scopas told Simonides, with extraordinary meanness, that he would pay him half the sum which he had agreed to give for the poem, and that he might ask the remainder, if he thought proper, from his Tyndaridae, to whom he had given an equal share of praise. A short time after, they say that a message was brought in to Simonides, to desire him to go out, as two youths were waiting at the gate who earnestly wished him to come forth to them; when he arose, went forth, and found nobody. In the meantime the apartment in which Scopas was feasting fell down, and he himself, and his company, were overwhelmed and buried in the

ruins; and when their friends were desirous to inter their remains, but could not possibly distinguish one from another, so much crushed were the bodies, Simonides is said, from his recollection of the place in which each had sat, to have given satisfactory directions for their interment. Admonished by this occurrence, he is reported to have discovered, that it is chiefly order that gives distinctness to memory; and that by those, therefore, who would improve this part of the understanding, certain places must be fixed upon, and that of the things which they desire to keep in memory, symbols must be conceived in the mind, and ranged, as it were, in those places; thus the order of places would preserve the order of things, and the symbols of the things would denote the things themselves; so that we should use the places as waxen tablets, and the symbols as letters.[20]

Cicero then observes that those things "are the most strongly fixed in our minds, which are communicated to them, and imprinted upon them, by the senses . . ." And for the orator, the "memory of things is the proper business . . ." "This we may be enabled to impress on ourselves by the creation of imaginary figures, aptly arranged, to represent particular heads, so that we may recollect thoughts by images, and their order by place." [21]

The Third Book.—In addition to restating the theme on the union of rhetoric and philosophy, the last book of *De Oratore* considers style and delivery.

The section on style deals chiefly with word choice, composition, and the various ornaments of speech. Cicero's point of view is clearly stated in this passage:

A speech, then, is to be made becoming in its kind, with a sort of complexion and substance of its own; for that it be weighty, agreeable, savoring of erudition and liberal knowledge, worthy of admiration, polished, having feeling and passion in it, as far as is required, are qualities not confined to particular members, but are apparent in the whole body; but that it be, as it were, strewed with flowers of language and thought, is a property which ought not to be equally diffused throughout the whole speech, but at such intervals, that, as in the arrangement of ornaments, there may be certain remarkable and luminous objects disposed here and there.[22]

Baldwin looks upon Cicero's twenty chapters on style as a "brilliant instance of what the ancients meant by amplification. Logically they do little more than iterate the truism that style is inseparable from substance; but actually they make the truism live." [23]

Finally, Book III of the *De Oratore* sets forth a general theory of delivery, that phase of oratory which Cicero said had "the sole and supreme power." Without effective delivery, "a speaker of the highest mental capacity can be held in no esteem, while one of moderate abilities, with this qualification, may surpass even those of the highest talent." [24] Cicero comments on the use of gestures and bodily action, and on the necessity of varying the tones in vocal expression.

It may be said that, while constructing the pattern for the Ideal Orator, Cicero kept constantly in mind the practical requirements of one who proposed to play "the part of a true Roman citizen in the conflicts of the assembly and the law courts."

The *Orator* and a Conception of Style.—Cicero's *Orator* is less comprehensive than the *De Oratore,* being devoted almost wholly to style. John E. Sandys says the purpose of it was to "meet the wishes of Brutus" and "to win over Brutus to his own side in the controversy with the Atticists. . . ." Another purpose, surely, was "to delineate the ideal orator." And it is evident that "the living image of his own oratorical greatness forms the foundation on which he builds his ideal fabric. His own speeches supply him with examples of every variety of oratorical excellence. . . ." [25] Baldwin remarks, apropos of the *Orator,* that few men "writing on style have shown in their own styles so much precision and charm."

The Doctrine of the Three Styles.—In the *Orator,* which Sandys says belongs to the "aesthetics of oratory," Cicero classifies and describes the three kinds of style: the plain, the moderate, and the grand. These types arise from the orator's attempt to prove, to please, and to move; and the skilled orator should be able to do all three.

Regarding the plain style, Cicero says:

> . . . we must give a sketch of the man whom some consider the only orator of the Attic style.
>
> He is a gentle, moderate man, imitating the usual customs, differing from those who are not eloquent in fact rather than in any of his opinions. Therefore those who are his hearers, even though they themselves have no skill in speaking, still feel confident that they could speak in that manner. For the subtlety of his address appears easy of imitation to a person who ventures on an opinion, but nothing is less easy when he comes to try it; for although it is not a style of any extraordinary vigour, still it has some juice, so that even though it is not endowed with the most extreme power, it is still . . . in perfect health. First of all, then, let us release it from the fetters of rhythm. For there is, as you know, a certain rhythm to be observed by an orator, proceeding on a regular system; but though it must be attended to in

another kind of oratory, it must be entirely abandoned in this. This must be a sort of easy style, and yet not utterly without rules, so that it may seem to range at freedom, not to wander about licentiously. He should also guard against appearing to cement his words together; for the hiatus formed by a concourse of open vowels has something soft about it, and indicates a not unpleasing negligence, as if the speaker were anxious more about the matter than the manner of his speech. But as to other points, he must take care, specially as he is allowed more licence in these two,—I mean the rounding of his periods, and the combination of his words; for those narrow and minute details are not to be dealt with carelessly....

The language will be pure and Latin; it will be arranged plainly and clearly, and great care will be taken to see what is becoming....

There will be a moderate use of what I may call oratorical furniture; for there is to a certain degree what I may call our furniture, consisting of ornaments partly of things and partly of words....

He will have besides this, action, not tragic, nor suited to the stage, but he will move his body in a moderate degree, trusting a great deal to his countenance; not in such a way as people call making faces, but in a manner sufficient to show in a gentlemanlike manner in what sense he means what he is saying to be understood.

Now in this kind of speech sallies of wit are admissible, and they carry perhaps only too much weight in an oration. Of them there are two kinds,—facetiousness and raillery,—and the orator will employ both; but he will use the one in relating anything neatly, and the other in darting ridicule on his adversaries.[26]

As for the moderate style, it is

... more fertile, and somewhat more forcible than this simple style of which we have been speaking; but nevertheless tamer than the highest class of oratory... In this kind there is but little vigour, but there is the greatest possible quantity of sweetness; for it is fuller than the plain style, but more plain than that other which is highly ornamented and copious.

Every kind of ornament in speaking is suitable to this style; and in this kind of oratory there is a great deal of sweetness. It is a style in which many men among the Greeks have been eminent; but Demetrius Phalereus, in my opinion, has surpassed all the rest; and while his oratory proceeds in calm and tranquil flow, it receives brilliancy from numerous metaphors and borrowed expressions, like stars....

The same kind of oratory (I am speaking of the moderate and temperate kind) admits of all sorts of figures of expressions, and of many also of ideas. Discussions of wide application and extensive learning are explained in it, and common topics are treated without any impetuosity. In a word, orators of this class usually come from the schools of philosophers, and unless the more vigorous orator, whom

I am going to speak of presently, is at hand to be compared with them, the one whom I am now describing will be approved of.[27]

The orator who uses the grand style

... is the sublime, copious, dignified, ornate speaker, in whom there is the greatest amount of grace. For he it is, out of admiration for whose ornamented style and copiousness of language nations have allowed eloquence to obtain so much influence in states; but it was only this eloquence, which is borne along in an impetuous course, and with a mighty noise, which all men looked up to, and admired, and had no idea that they themselves could possibly attain to. It belongs to this eloquence to deal with men's minds, and to influence them in every imaginable way. This is the style which sometimes forces its way into and sometimes steals into the senses; which implants new opinions in men, and eradicates others which have been long established. But there is a vast difference between this kind of orator and the preceding ones. A man who has laboured at the subtle and acute style, in order to speak cunningly and cleverly, and who has had no higher aim, if he has entirely attained his object, is a great orator, if not a very great one; he is far from standing on slippery ground, and if he once gets a firm footing, is in no danger of falling. But the middle kind of orator, whom I have called moderate and temperate, if he has only arranged all his own forces to his satisfaction, will have no fear of any doubtful or uncertain chances of oratory; and even if at any time he should not be completely successful, which may often be the case, still he will be in no great danger, for he cannot fall far. But this orator of ours, whom we consider the first of orators, dignified, vehement, and earnest, if this is the only thing for which he appears born, or if this is the only kind of oratory to which he applies himself, and if he does not combine his copiousness of diction with those other two kinds of oratory, is very much to be despised. For the one who speaks simply, inasmuch as he speaks with shrewdness and sense, is a wise man; the one who employs the middle style is agreeable; but this most copious speaker, if he is nothing else, appears scarcely in his senses. For a man who can say nothing with calmness, nothing with gentleness; who seems ignorant of all arrangement and definition and distinctness, and regardless of wit, especially when some of his causes require to be treated in that manner entirely, and others in a great degree; if he does not prepare the ears of his hearers before he begins to work up the case in an inflammatory style, he seems like a madman among people in their senses, or like a drunken man among sober men.[28]

Baldwin observes that the philosophy of such a classification, whatever its origin, "has been vicious as pedagogy." "Historically, the trail of the three styles has been baneful. For inculcating style perhaps the least fruitful means is classification." [29]

One of Aristotle's pupils, Theophrastus, is usually credited with being the formulator of the threefold classification of style. In Latin literature, the *ad Herennium* furnishes the first statement of the doctrine. That Aristotle recognized a distinction among types of literary expression is evident from several of his remarks in the *Rhetoric*. In the third book, he remarks that "to each kind of rhetoric is adapted a peculiar style," and goes on to show how written and oral style differ in that the former is more "precise" while the latter "partakes more of declamation." [30] Furthermore, he implies throughout that the different types of speaking—deliberative, forensic, and epideictic—call for different styles. However, he does not classify the styles according to the divisions which we have just discussed. Later theorists, it may be added, sometimes added a fourth kind. Philodemus evidently conceived of a fourfold classification; and Demetrius added the "forcible" type to the original three.

The doctrine of the three styles permeates the literature of rhetoric, either through open statement or through implication. "In the sphere of oratory," J. F. D'Alton remarks,

> ...the division became important, when it was adapted to the theory of the 'officia oratoris,' according to which it was the orator's duty to instruct, delight, and move his audience. The Plain style, with its predominant qualities of clearness and logical subtlety, was best suited to the purposes of instruction. When the Middle style became identified with the 'genus floridum,' with its characteristics of smoothness and charm, it was naturally assigned the task of giving pleasure to, or winning over an audience. The orator, however, could point to his greatest achievements as effected through the medium of the Grand style, which was calculated to play at will upon the feelings of an assembly. Cicero and Quintilian considered this style to be supreme, just as they considered that to stir the emotions was the highest function of the orator.[31]

The necessary qualities of a good style, as Cicero interpreted Theophrastus' teaching, were correctness, clearness, appropriateness, and ornament. Cicero did not, however, ascribe ornamentation to the Plain style, that being reserved in part for the Middle, and wholly for the Grand. Accordingly, we note that the so-called "virtues," or essential qualities, were not necessarily applied to all styles; instead, they were often assigned to particular styles for which they seemed uniquely suitable.

Cicero's Treatment of Rhythm.—Cicero's theory of oratorical rhythm derives largely from Gorgias and Isocrates. Commenting on the nature of his doctrine, he says:

Let oratory then be, ... mingled and regulated with regard to rhythm; not prosaic, nor on the other hand sacrificed wholly to rhythm; composed chiefly of the paeon, ... with many of the other feet which he passes over intermingled with it.

But what feet ought to be mingled with others, like purple, must be now explained; and we must also show to what kind of speech each sort of foot and rhythm is the best adapted. For the iambic is most frequent in those orations which are composed in a humble and lowly style; but the paeon is suited to a more dignified style; and the dactyl to both. Therefore, in a varied and long-continued speech these feet should be mingled together and combined. And in this way the fact of the orator aiming at pleasing the senses, and the careful attempt to round off the speech, will be the less visible, and they will at all times be less apparent if we employ dignified expressions and sentiments. For the hearers observe these two things, and think them agreeable: (I mean, expressions and sentiments.) And while they listen to them with admiring minds, the rhythm escapes their notice; and even if it were wholly wanting they would still be delighted with those other things. ...

Accordingly, if the question is raised as to what is the rhythm of an oration, it is every sort of rhythm; but one sort is better and more suitable than another. If the question is, what is the place of this rhythm? it is in every portion of the words. If you ask where it has arisen; it has arisen from the pleasure of the ears. If the principle is sought on which the words are to be arranged; that will be explained in another place, because that relates to practice, ... If the question is, when; always: if, in what place, it consists in the entire connexion of the words. If we are asked, What is the circumstance which causes pleasure? we reply, that it is the same as in verse; the method of which is determined by art; but the ears themselves define it by their own silent sensations, without any reference to principles of art.[32]

The observations on the preceding pages suggest that, all in all, the *Orator* is to be regarded as one of Cicero's important works. It is, in the opinion of Torsten Petersson, "Cicero's final statement not only of his oratorical idea but also of what he conceived himself to have attained." [33]

Other Rhetorical Treatises.—Among Cicero's other rhetorical works, excluding the *Brutus* and *On the Best Style of Orators* which may more appropriately engage our attention later, are *On Topics, Dialogue Concerning Oratorical Partitions,* and *On Rhetorical Invention.*

On Topics is largely an abstract of Aristotle's treatment of the same subject. Cicero defines a topic as "the seat of an argument, and ... an argument is a reason which causes men to believe a thing which would otherwise be doubtful." [34] The sources and types of topics receive a fairly full measure of analysis.

A Dialogue Concerning Oratorical Partitions includes a brief and superficial discussion between Cicero and his son on the elements of the speaking situation—orator, speech, and subject—and on the parts of an oration—opening, narration, confirmation, and peroration.

On Rhetorical Invention, written when Cicero was about twenty-one years of age, demonstrates the truth of a remark found in the same work: "of those who are worthy of fame or recollection, there is no one who appears either to have said nothing well, or everything admirably." [35] Indeed, this is no consummate statement of the art of rhetoric, although it does reveal Cicero's early enthusiasm for oratory and, in a juvenile sort of way, his early mastery of many of its details. Only two of the four books remain. In later years, Cicero himself renounced the whole work as being "scarcely worthy of my present standing in life." His treatment of what Wilbur S. Howell calls the "Positions of Argument" is, however, important to rhetorical theory. Says Howell:

> Both in *De Inventione* and the *Rhetorica ad Herennium,* analysis and synthesis are specific procedures designed on the one hand to yield, and on the other to employ, arguments and appeals which meet the severest tests of relevance and coherence. Each book is important to us because it gives expression to a precise intellectual method contrived to render purposeful the speaker's search for the natural divisions and the underlying unity of his speech.[36]

Cicero's contributions, in general, are less concise than Aristotle's *Rhetoric;* they are given more fully to the encouragement in the orator of copiousness in language; but they are developed more consistently from the point of view of the orator himself.

Pedagogical Inquiry into Rhetoric

". . . The premier teacher of imperial rhetoric and the greatest Latin authority upon education"—that is J. Wight Duff's [37] estimate of Quintilian who, about 95 A.D., brought out the truly monumental *Institutes of Oratory,* or the Teaching of Rhetoric. Like Cicero, Quintilian was erudite in an eclectic sort of way; in the *Institutes* he reveals a remarkably wide familiarity with and deep appreciation of the Greek and Latin writers. Living during the so-called Silver Age of Latin life, about 14 to 138 A.D., when, as Duff indicates, the "main clue to the literary qualities is to be found in education, and particularly in rhetorical education," Quintilian preserved much of the classical tradition and integrity of rhetoric. He did this at a time when rhetoric was no longer a powerful instrument in public affairs; when it was no longer a severe discipline, devoid of exhibitionism, for training the average man for active citizenship.

The Point of View in the *Institutes*.—On the side of rhetorical theory, there is relatively little in the *Institutes* of an original character. Because most of what Quintilian sets down on the side of systematic rhetoric has been said before, we shall confine our summary to those aspects of the *Institutes* which enlarge the conception of theoretical speechcraft; and we shall omit most of the pedagogical details which, though interesting and significant, are not germane to this inquiry.

Quintilian sets out to form the Perfect Orator who, in his words, "cannot exist unless as a good man." The orator conforming to his standards is, therefore, the good man speaking well.

> Since an orator, then, is a good man, and a good man cannot be conceived to exist without virtuous inclinations, and virtue, though it receives certain impulses from nature, requires notwithstanding to be brought to maturity by instruction, the orator must above all things study *morality,* and must obtain a thorough knowledge of all that is just and honourable, without which no one can either be a good man or an able speaker.[38]

Quintilian's conception of the orator as a good man would alone tend to refute the charge of insincerity against the *Institutes* voiced by a critic who called it a treatise on "Lying as a Fine Art for Those Fully Conscious of Their Own Rectitude." [39]

The formation of this perfect orator is not to be left to the philosophers; instead, the orator shall receive the necessary "excellence of mind" through rhetorical education. "I cannot admit," Quintilian observes, "that the principles of moral and honourable conduct are ... to be left to the philosophers...." Further in the discourse, he remarks:

> As to the objection which some make, that it is the business of *philosophy* to discourse of what is good, useful, and just, it makes nothing against me; for when they say a philosopher, they mean a good man; and why then should I be surprised that an orator, whom I consider also to be a good man, should discourse upon the same subjects? especially when I have shown,... that philosophers have taken possession

of this province because it was abandoned by the orators, a province which had always belonged to oratory, so that the philosophers are rather trespassing upon our ground.[40]

Hence, he voices what Colson calls "the age-long antithesis between rhetoric and philosophy." Colson also indicates that

> Quintilian's view of the superiority of the 'rhetor' to the philosopher is clearly reflected in two events of the time. The first of these is the endowment of rhetoric by Vespasian. The other is the expulsion of the philosophers from Rome about A.D. 94. The latter, whatever its other causes may have been, was certainly from one point of view a triumph for Quintilian's educational views.[41]

The Use of Rules.—While Quintilian respected rules in rhetoric, he did not allow them to interfere with the common-sense principles of speech preparation. He advocated a flexibility of usage, observing that "one great quality in an orator is discretion, because he must turn his thoughts in various directions, according to the different bearings of his subject." [42] A forensic orator, for instance, should, in his pleadings, "keep two things in view, *what is becoming, and what is expedient; but it is frequently expedient,* and sometimes *becoming,* to make some deviations from the regular and settled order...." [43] Quintilian says "rhetoric would be a very easy and small matter, if it could be included in one short body of rules, but rules must generally be altered to suit the nature of each individual case, the time, the occasion, and necessity itself...." [44]

A Conception of the Status.—The plan of the *Institutes* is based upon Quintilian's acceptance of the fivefold division of the art of rhetoric: invention, disposition, elocution, memory, and delivery; [45] of the threefold classification of the types of oratory: deliberative, forensic, and panegyric; [46] and of the threefold analysis of the speaker's object or purpose: to inform, to move, and to please.[47]

A feature of Quintilian's treatment of invention which differs in scope and detail from that of many of his predecessors is that of the *status,* or *state of a cause.* The concept of the *status,* or the location of a center of argument, finds its first formal embodiment in the *ad Herennium* and in Cicero's *On Invention.* This concept is among the most important contributions of the Latin writers to rhetorical theory. By elevating the study of invention, and by providing the speaker with methods by which to find, evaluate, and use his ideas on a given case, this doctrine exercised a profound influence upon subsequent theory and practice in public speaking and debating.

After examining the views adopted by previous writers on the subject, Quintilian thinks it best "to regard that as the *state of the cause* which is the strongest point in it, and on which the whole matter chiefly turns." [48] "Status," Baldwin comments, "meaning the essential character of the case as it appeared to preliminary survey of all the material and all the bearings, had come to denote a uniform system of determining that essential character by leading questions." [49] Through the medium of the status, therefore, the investigator or orator was able to find out what the body of material in the case meant.

Quintilian discusses two general states—the legal and the ratiocinatory. The former has many species, "as laws are numerous, and have various forms." The latter includes the status of conjecture or fact, the status of definition, and the status of quality.

These general states are, then, of two kinds: those depending upon legality, and those depending upon reasoning. The ratiocinatory states are simpler since they consist "merely in the contemplation of the nature of things. . . ." Briefly, they deal with these possible points in a case: whether a thing is—a matter of fact; what it is—a matter of definition; and of what species it is—a matter of quality. Thus, a case in the courtroom might center about the status of conjecture: Brown was either guilty or innocent of the charge of murder. Or, a case might deal with the status of definition: Brown killed a man but it was in self-defense, and hence was not murder. Or the status might concern quality: "Horatius committed a crime, for he killed his sister; he committed no crime, for he had a right to kill her who mourned at the death of an enemy." [50]

Style Treated Conventionally.—Quintilian recommends that the greatest possible care be given to expression,

> . . . provided we bear in mind that nothing is to be done for the sake of words, as words themselves were invented for the sake of things, and as those words are the most to be commended which express our thoughts best, and produce the impression which we desire on the minds of the judges. Such words undoubtedly must make a speech both worthy of admiration and productive of pleasure; but not of that kind of *admiration* with which we wonder at monsters; or of that kind of *pleasure* which is attended with unnatural gratification, but such as is compatible with true merit and worth. [51]

Then follows a long and reasonably conventional discussion of style. The classifications and definitions of the figures and tropes are more systematically handled, however, than in any previous contribution.

Attitude toward Delivery.—It is of interest to note Quintilian's defense of "extempore" speaking:

> But the richest fruit of all our study, and the most ample recompense for the extent of our labour, is *the faculty of speaking extempore;* and he who has not succeeded in acquiring it, will do well, in my opinion, to renounce the occupations of the forum, and devote his solitary talent of writing to some other employment; for it is scarcely consistent with the character of a man of honour to make a public profession of service to others which may fail in the most pressing emergencies, since it is of no more use than to point out a harbour to a vessel, to which it cannot approach unless it be borne along by the gentlest breezes. There arise indeed innumerable occasions where it is absolutely necessary to speak on the instant, as well before magistrates, as on trials that are brought on before the appointed time; and if any of these shall occur, I do not say to any one of our innocent fellow citizens, but to any of our own friends and relatives, is an advocate to stand dumb, and, while they are begging for a voice to save them, and are likely to be undone if succor be not instantly afforded them, is he to ask time for retirement and silent study, till his speech be formed and committed to memory, and his voice and lungs be put in tune? [52]

Practically, this manner of speaking requires a technique differing from the ordinary mode of address.

> Yet if any chance shall give rise to such a sudden necessity for speaking extempore, we shall have need to exert our mind with more than its usual activity; we must fix our whole attention on our matter, and relax, for the time, something of our care about words, if we find it impossible to attend to both. A slower pronunciation, too, and a mode of speaking with suspense and doubt, as it were, gives time for consideration; yet we must manage so that we may seem to deliberate and not to hesitate.[53]

Final Estimate.—Colson has pronounced the *Institutes* "one of the most remarkable and interesting products of Roman common sense." [54] At all points in the twelve books we are impressed by the sanity of the author in refusing to be bound by inflexible rules, and by his insistence upon shaping his doctrine to the varying demands of different speech situations. Eclectic as the treatment is, the contents take on new color and vitality at Quintilian's hands because

he weaves his teaching experience and wise counsel into the fabric
of the old theory.

Excesses in Theory and Practice

Tendencies of the Sophistic.—After Aristotle, oratory declined in
Greece. Whereas in the better days of Greek achievement the virtues
of moderation and balance had been distinguishing marks of creative
effort, now the tendencies toward excess and affectation became apparent. This unhappy circumstance asserted itself in Hellenistic
prose, and particularly in oratory. About 250 B.C., Hegesias of
Magnesia became the leader of the "Asiatic" school of thought. In
violation of Aristotelian and Isocratean standards, this school produced an artificial style which, in the words of Atkins, "depended
for its effects on epigrams, strained metaphors, false antitheses, over-
elaborate rhythms, and the like." This style, which Atkins claims
was "a breakdown of earlier traditions, rather than a fusion of the
Asiatic and Hellenic geniuses," exercised considerable influence
throughout the third and second centuries B.C.[55] A certain reaction
to the degradation of Greek oratory was provided by the rhetorical
system of Hermagoras of Temnos who recaptured some of the spirit
of his distinguished predecessors and who won the praise of Quintilian for his admirable treatise on the art of rhetoric.

During the second century A.D., there was evidence of a new
interest in rhetoric, although the note of artificiality was present.
Greek literature was receiving some patronage at the hand of
Hadrian; exigencies of law courts in the Roman Empire were creating a certain need for forensic speaking; the great Roman writers and
teachers of rhetoric were active; and many of the Rhetors came to
Athens. Some of the Greek rhetoricians travelled from place to
place, declaiming in the temples and elsewhere. Among these men
were Dio Chrysostom and Hermogenes, the latter being the author
of rhetorical works on issues, invention, and the forms and preparation of orations. Baldwin sees in Hermogenes' effort a typical
pattern of the work of the period. "There some of the most characteristic habits of form in sophistic oratory are seen as prolonga-
tions of school exercises." [56]

During the second, third, and fourth centuries A.D., a type of
rhetoric prevailed which is generally referred to as the "second sophistic." While the term is applied chiefly to Greek activity, it is
equally applicable to the Latin. The distinguishing mark of the era
is the separation of speaking from the affairs of the everyday world,

with the consequent emphasis upon themes dealing with the past, or with pure fiction. Accordingly, style came to be cultivated for its own sake, a sad circumstance in the field of oral persuasion. As Baldwin remarks, "Sophistic is the historic demonstration of what oratory becomes when it is removed from urgency of subject matter."

Seeking some inspiration for public occasions, it revives over and over again a dead past. Thus becoming conventionalized in method, it turns from cogency of movement to the cultivation of style. Cogency presupposes a message. It is intellectual ordering for persuasion, the means toward making men believe and act. Style, no longer controlled by such urgencies of subject, tends toward decoration and virtuosity.[57]

In Dio's discourse *On Training for Public Speaking,* we find him saying that statesmen should have training and practice in speechmaking.

For it is true that this will prove of very great help toward making him beloved and influential and esteemed instead of being looked down upon. For when men are afraid, what does more to inspire them than the spoken word? And when they wax insolent and uplifted in spirit, what more effectively brings them down and chastens them? What has greater influence in keeping them from indulging their desires? Whose admonitions do they endure more meekly than the man's whose speech delights them?[58]

During his early years Dio was evidently committed to the sophistic culture. However, he abandoned that interest in later life.

Dio refers to the great orators, mentioning particularly Demosthenes "for the vigour of his style, the impressiveness of thought, and the copiousness of his vocabulary, qualities in which he surpasses all other orators."[59] He also comments on the work of Lysias, Hyperides, Aeschines, and Lycurgus. Furthermore, he suggests that the prospective speaker not remain unacquainted with the modern orators, adding

For the powers they display can be more useful to us because, when we read them, our judgment is not fettered and enslaved, as it is when we approach the ancients. For when we find that we are able to criticize what has been said, we are most encouraged to attempt the same thing ourselves, and we find more pleasure in comparing ourselves with others when we are convinced that in the comparison we should be found to be not inferior to them, with the chance, occasionally, of being even superior.[60]

In addition to Dio and Hermogenes, this period produced such men as Pollux, Apollonius, and Herode Atticus. Most of these orators and rhetoricians were subsequently considered in a semi-critical manner by Philostratus in his *Lives of the Sophists.*

Roman rhetorical history afforded examples of high and low points of development. With the downfall of the Republic, however, oratory declined. This decline was well under way by Quintilian's time. He tried to revive the spirit of Ciceronianism while protesting the false tastes that were taking hold of the age.

The Era of Declamations.—Shortly before as well as after the time Quintilian wrote the *Institutes,* the tendency was to elaborate more and more upon the rules of rhetoric. Many manuals of the art were published and scores of teachers taught the subject, for, in the larger sense, the entire educational plan centered about rhetoric. One of the exercises that enjoyed a fabulously widespread vogue was declamation. Quintilian conjectures that Demetrius Phalereus invented the declamation on fictitious subjects. Originally a school exercise, it soon became little more than a showpiece permitting display and exhibitionism.

Quintilian approved of the declamation, as he understood it, but not as it was practiced about him. He admitted that the "practice has so degenerated through the fault of the teachers, that the license and ignorance of declaimers have been among the chief causes that have corrupted eloquence." But "of that which is good by nature we may surely make a good use." [61] So he recommended its use *as an exercise* having "a very close resemblance to reality," even though admitting that the current practice was out of gear with his intentions. As Baldwin remarks:

> Instead of training youth to lead in public policy and to secure justice for individuals, *declamatio* had become an end in itself, the rhetor's own kind of oratory. As an exhibition of skill it was his easiest means of winning pupils, and of holding them by letting them exhibit themselves. The inherent vice of artificiality, which Quintilian admits by implication, he nevertheless assigns entirely to perverted educational practise. He would recall *declamatio* from invention to actuality, and from display to exercise.[62]

Why was the declamation so popular? The answer probably can be traced in part to the changed political conditions. The Republic was dead and the power of Augustus was established. Assemblies were both infrequent and perfunctory, for their decisions could be altered at any moment "by the Emperor's personal intervention." Pleading in the courts was restricted, and the causes were not of the type that evoked great oratory. There was no longer free outlet in public life for oratorical activity. Consequently, other fields for such endeavor were sought.

One might surmise that under these conditions the interest in oratory would wane. But it did not. According to William A. Edward, the explanation was complex, but it involved certain known elements:

> A decline in the number of successful teachers, a falling-off in interest and in the number of students, a closing down of the schools would have caused no surprise: but it took some time, and Augustus's crafty dissimulation helped this, for the changed conditions to be appreciated. Parents and pupils did not realise all at once that the old prizes were no longer open to success, or that, if open in name, they were empty in substance, and gave only pomp and not the reality of power. By the time the facts of the case were too patent to be ignored the schools were firmly established and had created an interest of their own. The young people of the day had to have their natural and national liking for the beauty of the spoken word satisfied. The declamation as a work of literary art had become an end in itself.[63]

Since the study of expression was virtually the higher education of the period, the declamation offered a convenient instrument to further the instruction. And as time went on, it became a hollow, sterile showpiece, divorced from reality and serving only one purpose fully—that of providing students with a vehicle of display. The mere declaiming became an all-sufficient end in itself.

The Stricture of Petronius.—Petronius' *Satyricon* (meaning, really, a "miscellany," and probably prepared during the middle of the first century A.D.) voices a sharp protest against the rhetoric of the day, declaring that the Asianist influences had destroyed the restraint and dignity of classical Greek and early Roman style. Petronius decried the use of the declamation and inveighed against its false ornamentation.

Commenting on the turgidity of the declaimer, or "tub-thumper," Petronius said: "... the net result of all these high-flown themes and the empty thunder of their platitudes is that, when the pupils make their *début* in the courts, they feel themselves translated into a foreign world." [64] He placed the responsibility for the decay of oratory squarely upon the Asian school whose teachers provided their students with a diet of "sticky rhetorical lollypops," or "honeyed little balls of words." Oratory had degenerated into "inflated, extravagant word-spinning," completely removed from the world of reality.

But the onus of the condition was perhaps not attributable to the teachers alone. In the early part of his work, Petronius remarks through one of the participants in the story that "the professors provide this stupid jargon because they find that in a madhouse they too must be mad." Consequently, "the professor of elocution is in the same position as a fisherman: if he doesn't bait his hook with the particular dainty which he knows will make the little fishes bite, he will hang about on the rock without any hope of sport." [65]

Seneca.—In the *Controversiae* and the *Suasoriae* of Seneca—probably written toward the close of the first half of the century—we find an anthology, as it were, of declamations delivered by celebrated rhetors. The *Controversiae* were fictitious speeches on assumed forensic cases; the *Suasoriae,* fictitious deliberative speeches on historical subjects, designed principally for younger students. In other words, unreal cases were set up, and the students spoke to the point of the themes announced in the exercises. Seneca also provides comparative studies of the cases prepared by different declaimers. Baldwin indicates that Seneca divides the declamations by "a threefold critical classification"—the *sententiae,* implying the high points in leading interpretations; the *divisio,* or analysis of the case; and *colores,* or the imaginative development.[66] Baldwin finds these units "a poor substitute for the five traditional parts of rhetoric," and concludes: "*Elocutio,* thus left to itself, tended inevitably toward an art of display. The history of rhetoric has no more striking proof that style, when cultivated in artificial isolation, goes bad." [67]

Other Contributors to a Rhetoric of Display.—Valerius Maximus, in his *Facta et Dicta Memorabilia,* probably written between 30 and 40 A.D., devoted nine books to various subjects that an orator might wish to discuss. This was an adaptation to the demands of the prevailing rhetorical system. By making his collection of anecdotes and subjects accessible, Valerius Maximus provided, to use Duff's expression, "a serviceable *vade mecum* for speakers or teachers."

The name of Fronto should be included in any consideration of declamations. Not only did he make the writing of controversial themes a part of his scheme of instruction, but he also formulated a partial theory of rhetoric. Fronto, who was born about 100 A.D., assigned *controversiae* to Marcus Aurelius in addition to offering sundry advice on public speaking.

"With me," said Fronto in a letter to Lollianus Avitus, "eloquence holds the most honoured place. . . ." And in a letter to
Caesar:

> Herein lies that supreme excellence of an orator, and one not easily
> attainable, that he should please his hearers without any great sacrifice
> of right eloquence, and should let his blandishments, meant to tickle
> the ears of the people, be coloured indeed, but not along with any great
> or wholesale sacrifice of dignity: rather that in its composition and
> fabric there should be a lapse into a certain softness but no wantonness
> of thought.[68]

Philosophy, he remarked, "will tell you what to say, Eloquence
how to say it. . . ." Eloquence is sovereign: "It inspires fear, wins
love, is a spur to effort, puts shame to silence, exhorts to virtue,
exposes vices, urges, soothes, teaches, consoles."

The eloquence Fronto talked about, however, consisted almost
wholly of stylistic flourishes. Quoting Nepos, he said: *"The su-
premest eloquence is to speak of sublime things in the grand style, of
homely things in simple language. . . ."* [69] His chief interest was in
words. In a letter to Augustus, he said "the distinction between a
first-rate orator and ordinary ones [is] that the others are readily
content with good words, while the first-rate orator is not content
with words merely good if better are to be obtained." After an
orator's words have been examined,

> . . . then from the whole word-population, so to speak, just as in war,
> when a legion has to be enrolled, we not only collect the volunteers but
> also search out the skulkers of military age so when there is need of
> word-reinforcements, we must not only make use of the voluntary re-
> cruits that offer themselves, but fetch out the skulkers and hunt them up
> for service.[70]

He also commented frequently on the importance of similes, on the
necessity of the orator's mastering them, and on the wisdom of returning to the words of the older Latin authors—Ennius, Plautus,
Naevius, and Lucretius, among them.

Fronto's contribution to rhetorical theory is minor, although he
was evidently held in high esteem during his time. In searching for
simplicity of style he merely accentuated certain artificialities which
were already menacing the language. His was an appeal for the use
of archaic words and obsolete expressions. D'Alton remarks, "whatever we may think of Fronto's theories, his attempt to reanimate
Latin prose will at least rank as an interesting experiment." [71]

Appraisal of the Declamation.—A final estimate of the place of the declamation in the rhetorical scheme cannot safely be ventured. However, the view of Edward is temperate and wise:

> As scholarship becomes ignorant and uncritical, as men of genius become rarer, as the world settles into barbarism, it is little wonder that these exercises become more arid, more wearisome, more sterile, and lose all merit until the very name of rhetoric becomes a term of reproach. But this is no more true of the declamation than of all other literary forms. We no longer regard it as a form of fictitious literature worth cultivating. It may be doubted whether we should not do better to cultivate a little more our sense of beauty and propriety in public speaking. If we have the best of matter for eloquent expression it is to be regretted that we do not devote more pains to finding the best expression for our matter. At any rate we should not disparage so much as we have done and still do, these declamations that in Seneca's time were cultivated by the best intellects of the day with an enthusiasm almost too great for pastime.[72]

And Baldwin says:

> Besides Aristotle's conception of rhetoric as the art of giving effectiveness to truth there had persisted the conception of it as the art of giving effectiveness to the speaker. Though the two conceptions are not mutually exclusive, the dominance of the one or of the other tends either to give rhetoric those manifold relations and that constant answer to reality which mark its great ancient achievements, or on the other hand to narrow it toward virtuosity and display. The large pedagogy of Quintilian is animated by the Aristotelian conception. The other conception, brilliant in Gorgias and his like, had already animated not only the *declamatores* at Rome, but that larger 'second sophistic' which became pervasively the rhetoric of the imperial centuries, in Greek and in Latin, throughout the Roman world. Ancient rhetoric offers the historic example, then, of a divergence that has remained typical.[73]

Tacitus Evaluates Oratory.—Just as Quintilian saw a real danger in the undisciplined use of the declamation, so Tacitus, in his *Dialogue Concerning Oratory,* written about 80 A.D., and hence before the *Institutes,* considered the declamation a destructive influence in Roman culture. The *Dialogue* deals chiefly with the decadence of oratory; but it may also be a sort of farewell to public speaking and an explanation of the author's desertion of rhetoric in favor of his endorsement of history. Four eminent men participate in the dialogue: Maternus, the poet, who assumes the role of the idealist; Aper, the advocate, who gives the discussion a practical turn;

Secundus, the historian, who reveals the quiet, refined character; and Messala, the Roman of high birth, who champions the past.

In his analysis of the decline of oratory, Tacitus alleges that the true causes are: "The dissipation of our young men, the inattention of parents, the ignorance of those who pretend to give instruction, and the total neglect of ancient discipline." [74] He claims further that eloquence "has lost her field of glory," that the great theatres of speechcraft—the assemblies and courtrooms—are no longer open to the orators; or, if open, are no longer "kept alive by fresh materials." In other words, changed political and social conditions brought about the decline of oratory.

But, surely, the instruction now offered the youth was largely at fault, Tacitus alleged. No longer did the orator follow a discipline such as made Cicero and Demosthenes celebrated.

> To form that illustrious character, it was not thought necessary to declaim in the schools of rhetoricians, or to make a vain parade in fictitious controversies, which were not only void of all reality, but even of a shadow of probability. Our ancestors pursued a different plan: they stored their minds with just ideas of moral good and evil; with the rules of right and wrong, and the fair and foul in human transactions. These on every controverted point are the orator's province. In courts of law, just and unjust undergo his discussion; in political debate, between what is expedient and honourable, it is his to draw the line; and those questions are so blended in their nature, that they enter into every cause. On such important topics, who can hope to bring variety of matter, and to dignify that matter with style and sentiment, if he has not, beforehand, enlarged his mind with the knowledge of human nature? with the laws of moral obligation? the deformity of vice, the beauty of virtue, and other points which do not immediately belong to the theory of ethics? [75]

Here, then, we have another indictment—not expressed as clearly and directly as others, but nevertheless an indictment—of speaking which glorified *elocutio* to the neglect of the other parts of rhetoric.

Lucian Satirizes Oratory.—The most satirical indictment of the second sophistic period and of its teachings came from Lucian, himself a former devotee of sophistic culture. In his essay entitled *A Professor of Public Speaking,* directed, in the opinion of some scholars, at the lexicographer Pollux—and hence written after 179 A.D.—Lucian satirizes the meretricious methods of acquiring quickly a full measure of skill in speaking. At this time, many speakers felt the need for a short cut to oratorical skill, and it is that idea which Lucian attacks.

The essay opens with a promise: "Do not be daunted, however, and do not be dismayed at the greatness of your expectations, thinking to undergo untold labours before you achieve them. I shall not conduct you by a rough road, or a steep and sweaty one, so that you will turn back halfway out of weariness." He indicates that there are two roads leading to Lady Rhetoric. ". . . One of them is but a path, narrow, briery, and rough, promising great thirstiness and sweat. . . ." "The other . . . is level, flowery, and well-watered. . . ." [76]

At the starting point of the two roads, the lover of Rhetoric will be approached by a man who is the guide to the rough road.

> In exhorting you to follow him, he will point out the footprints of Demosthenes and of Plato. . . . Then he will tell you to imitate those ancient worthies, and will set you fusty models for your speeches. . . . And he will say that hard work, scant sleep, abstention from wine . . . are . . . indispensable. [77]

On the other road, the lover of Rhetoric will find many people, and among them will be a handsome man acting as the guide. "If, then, you go to him and put yourself in his hands, you will at once, without effort, become an orator, the observed of all, and, as he himself calls it, king of the platform, driving the horses of eloquence four-in-hand." [78]

Through the medium of the handsome guide, Lucian states the qualifications of the prospective speaker:

> Bring with you, then, as the principal thing, ignorance; secondly, recklessness, and thereto effrontery and shamelessness. Modesty, respectability, self-restraint, and blushes may be left at home, for they are useless and somewhat of a hindrance to the matter in hand. But you need also a very loud voice, a shameless singing delivery, and a gait like mine. . . . Let your clothing be gaily-coloured. . . . Have also many attendants, and always a book in hand. [79]

As for rules,

> First of all, you must pay especial attention to outward appearance, and to the graceful set of your cloak. Then cull from some source or other fifteen, or anyhow not more than twenty, Attic words, drill yourself carefully in them, and have them ready at the tip of your tongue. . . . Whenever you speak, sprinkle in some of them as a relish. Never mind if the rest is inconsistent with them, unrelated, and discordant. Only let your purple stripe be handsome and bright, even if your cloak is but a blanket of the thickest sort. Hunt up obscure, unfamiliar words, rarely used by the ancients. . . . As for reading the classics, don't you do it—either that twaddling Isocrates or that uncouth

Demosthenes or that tiresome Plato. No, read the speeches of the men who lived only a little before our own time, and these pieces that they call 'exercises,' in order to secure from them a supply of provisions which you can use up as occasion arises. . . .[80]

Furthermore, "When you really must speak, and those present suggest themes and texts for your discussion, carp at all the hard ones and make light of them as not fit . . . for a real man." [81]

Rhetorical disposition comes in for this comment: "Take no pains at all that the first thing, just because it really is first, shall be said at the appropriate time, and the second directly after it, and the third after that, but say first whatever occurs to you first. . . ." [82]

Finally, the prospective speaker should remember that "extemporary readiness goes a long way with the crowd to absolve your mistakes and procure you admiration; so see to it that you never write anything out or appear in public with a prepared speech, for that is sure to show you up." [83]

These quotations throw only incidental light upon the development of rhetorical theory. But they reflect the attitude of a critic toward the speaking practices of his day, and, accordingly, establish at least a partial standard of excellence in critical inquiry for that period.

Critical Investigations into Style

The Work of Dionysius.—Written sometime between 20 and 10 B.C., Dionysius' *On Literary Composition* deals largely with word order, and provides today's student with a lucid analysis of style from the classical point of view.

In practically all speaking, says Dionysius,

. . . two things must have unremitting attention: the ideas and the words. In the former case, the sphere of subject matter is chiefly concerned; in the latter, that of expression; and all who aim at becoming good speakers give equally earnest attention to both these aspects of discourse.[84]

George Ammon's analysis of Dionysius' complete rhetorical system is recast by Baldwin, showing the division indicated in the passage above. It reveals that Dionysius placed invention and disposition under the head of "subject matter" and then devoted the rest of his scheme to style.

The major divisions of Dionysius' works cover the nature of composition, the aims and means of attaining skill in writing, the varieties of composition, and the poetical element in prose as well as the prose elements in poetry. Composition is defined as "a certain arrangement of the parts of speech, or elements of diction...." [85] The processes involved in the art are, first,

> ...that of observing the combinations which are naturally adapted to produce a beautiful and agreeable united effect; the second is that of perceiving how to improve the harmonious appearance of the whole by fashioning properly the several parts which we intend to fit together; the third is that of perceiving what is required in the way of modification of the material—I mean abridgment, expansion and transformation —and of carrying out such changes in a manner appropriate to the end in view. [86]

Those who compose verse and prose should aim at charm and beauty.

> Among the sources of charm and beauty in style there are...four which are paramount and essential,—melody, rhythm, variety, and the appropriateness demanded by these three. Under 'charm' I class freshness, grace, euphony, sweetness, persuasiveness, and all similar qualities; and under 'beauty' grandeur, impressiveness, solemnity, dignity, mellowness, and the like. [87]

Dionysius then describes the three modes of composition. The austere style

> ...requires that the words should be like columns firmly planted and placed in strong positions, so that each word should be seen on every side, and that the parts should be at appreciable distances from one another, being separated by perceptible intervals. It does not in the least shrink from using frequently harsh sound-clashings which jar on the ear; like blocks of building stone that are laid together unworked, blocks that are not square and smooth, but preserve their natural roughness and irregularity. It is prone for the most part to expansion by means of great spacious words. In its clauses it pursues not only these objects but also impressive and stately rhythms, and tries to make its clauses not parallel in structure or sound, nor slaves to a rigid sequence, but noble, brilliant, free. It wishes them to suggest nature rather than art, and to stir emotion rather than to reflect character. [88]

Antiphon's speech illustrates this mode of expression. The smooth composition

> ...does not intend that each word should be seen on every side, nor that all its parts should stand on broad, firm bases, nor that the time intervals between them should be long; nor in general is this slow and deliberate movement congenial to it. It demands free movement in its

diction; it requires words to come sweeping along one on top of another, each supported by that which follows.... It tries ... to give, as
far as possible, the effect of one continuous utterance.... It requires
that all its words shall be melodious, smooth, soft as a maiden's face;
and it shrinks from harsh, clashing syllables, and carefully avoids everything rash and hazardous.[89]

As to figures, it employs "for the most part those which are dainty
and alluring, and contain much that is seductive and fanciful."
Isocrates achieved eminence through the use of this style of composition.

The harmoniously blended or intermediate composition is essentially a union of the other two types. It is a golden mean of
expression, best cultivated by Demosthenes. Thus he assigns to
Demosthenes "the palm for oratorical mastery." In him, Dionysius
finds a "standard alike for choice of words and for beauty in their
arrangement."

Longinus' Analysis of Artistic Sublimity.—A second work which
considers oratory from the point of view of literary craftsmanship
is *On the Sublime,* associated with the name of Longinus but probably not the product of his hand. Although the date of preparation
is also in doubt, it is believed that the work was completed in the
first century A.D.

Devoted solely to style, or to the heightening of effect, *On the
Sublime* links poetical and rhetorical effort in a fairly close union.
It shows at least that they are interdependent. Intellectual and emotional capacities are essential in the orator, as in the poet, if the resulting style is to have imaginative and rhythmic properties. The
author indicates that there are five sources

... from which the Sublimity of eloquence most copiously flows: pre-
supposing as a groundwork common to all these five, a certain power
of elocution without which they are nothing. The first and most effectual of these is, a successful boldness in regard to the sentiments....
The second is, vehement and enthusiastic passion. These two are, for
the most part, natural constituents of Sublimity: the others are chiefly
the result of art. The third is, a suitable combination of figures, which
are of two kinds: those relating to the sentiment (or Metaphors) and
those belonging to the language (or tropes). Next (and in the fourth
place) is majesty of expression, which again may be divided into a
judicious selection of words, and a diction sufficiently elaborate, and
elevated by Tropes. The fifth constituent of Sublimity, which includes
all those that precede it, is a dignified and elevated composition.[90]

Later, a distinction is drawn between sublimity and amplification:

> Sublimity... consists in elevation, and Amplification in quantity: so
> that the former is frequently found in a single thought, whereas the
> latter requires enumeration and circumstantiality. Amplification... is
> the completing of a sentence with all its parts and members; which
> gives a powerful conception of the subject under discussion, by causing
> the mind to dwell upon it.[91]

Near the close of the essay, the author indicates, however, that few
orators ever attain the heights of sublimity, chiefly because they are
too engrossed in the material things of life. Men become petty and
ignoble through their devotion to money, pleasures, and associated
evils. Here, then, we find a treatise in which motive, moral idealism,
dominates the scene.

The short section on imagery points to a truth not so clearly
stated in previous works:

> Every mental conception communicable by language, whencesoever de-
> rived, is known in common discourse by the term *imagery*: but, in a
> more peculiar sense it is used when, through an enthusiastic feeling,
> you seem to see what you describe, and to place it before the eyes of
> your hearers. You must, however, have remarked that there is a differ-
> ence between the imagery of the orator, and that of the poet: the object
> of the latter being surprise, and that of the former, elucidation; al-
> though they both seek to produce emotion....
>
> The imagery of the poet will allow... of an excess of fiction quite
> surpassing credibility: but that of the orator is always the more beauti-
> ful, in proportion to its appearance of feasibility and truth.[92]

On the Sublime contributes certain tenets to a philosophy of
rhetoric, and chiefly through the relation that it establishes between
rhetorical theory and moral standards. More than that, it gives us
a measure of insight into the constituents of artistic creation in literary expression. As Baldwin remarks in his summary of the treatise:

> Aristotle's theory of rhetoric determines its function. Cicero dignifies
> even its conventional tasks as training for leadership. Quintilian sur-
> veys it as a comprehensive pedagogy. Dionysius analyzes its art. But
> the great unknown moves us to share the art ourselves.[93]

General Summary

Based largely upon the work of Aristotle, the contributions discussed in this chapter extend and elaborate upon the early Greek
tenets. They give them more clear-cut form, establish more detailed

classifications, and initiate certain departures respecting the philosophical substructure of the art. But, in the main, they do not go
appreciably beyond the line previously established by the Greeks.

The division of rhetoric into five constituent parts—invention,
disposition, elocution, memory, and delivery—is firmly grounded in
the treatises of this period. Serving as the basis of the *ad Herennium,* it also formed the framework of the theoretical inquiries of
Cicero and Quintilian. Although present in the treatises of the
Greeks, it did not serve quite so mechanically to separate the features
of the systems they developed. The tradition of the five parts of
speaking, however, has been persistent and influential; even to this
day, with some modifications, it serves to divide the essential aspects
of the art, both in theory and in criticism.

With the division of the subject into its component parts, theorists
with certain preferences and interests came soon to develop treatises
dealing almost solely with individual aspects of the art. Thus
Dionysius and Longinus contributed to the subject through their
works on style. Although these contributions did not present balanced accounts of rhetoric as a whole, they afforded additional insight
into the sphere of artistic creation. In this way, they facilitated the
efforts of subsequent writers to provide comprehensive analyses of
the speaking art.

The great names of this period are, of course, Cicero and Quintilian. The former left the most complete set of works on rhetorical
theory and criticism ever assembled by one man. Writing as an
orator of consummate ability, he set forth, in terms more copious
than necessary perhaps, a virtual prolegomena to the whole art of
speaking. Quintilian, on the other hand, spoke as a teacher intent
upon preserving the good in rhetorical education during a period
when the excesses of exhibitionism and declamatory show were
threatening not only this art, but the whole system of culture. His
Institutes represent the most comprehensive contribution in print on
the training of public speakers.

The pedagogical device most frequently associated with the im-
moderate and affected aspects of rhetoric during the decline of oratory was the declamation. Through its injudicious use, artificiality
flourished in speech training, and so eclipsed the true function of
speaking as an instrument of communication. Rhetoric became
divorced from the social reality in which it normally and properly
functions.

Chapter 4

THE CONTRIBUTIONS OF MODERN THEORISTS

Rhetoric in the Middle Period

The long sweep from the period of the second sophistic to the sixteenth century is not distinguished by great effort in the investigation of rhetorical theory. Far from being barren, however, it does afford the names of several men who figure with some prominence in our tradition. Since preaching was the "characteristic form of oratory" during much of the medieval period, it is natural that certain of the contributors to rhetoric should concern themselves with that phase of speech doctrine. Among these was St. Augustine (fifth century) who, in his *De Doctrina Christiana,* applied sound Ciceronian doctrine to the theory of preaching. The school books of the middle period, especially in the separate treatments of the trivium and the quadrivium, also helped to keep the tradition of rhetoric intact.

Other figures of importance in medieval rhetoric include: Martianus Capella whose *Marriage of Philology and Mercury* (c. 430) contained a division of studies in which rhetoric figured rather prominently, with all of the five parts of the classical division receiving attention; Cassiodorus whose *Institutiones* (c. 570) helped to sustain the tradition of the seven arts, although rhetoric was not treated comprehensively; Isidore whose *Etymologiae or Origines* (seventh century) contained summaries of all the seven arts; the Venerable Bede whose considerations of metre and rhythm had wide favor during the eighth century; and Alcuin whose *Rhetoric of Alcuin and Charlemagne* (c. 794) represented a fairly substantial restatement of Cicero's *De Inventione* and Julius Victor's *Ars Rhetorica.*

Christian Preaching and Rhetoric

In some respects, St. Augustine's *On Christian Doctrine* resembles Quintilian's *Institutes of Oratory.* Although it is neither as comprehensive nor as important to the development of rhetorical theory, it has much the same pedagogical flavor. It is intended as a teaching device, supplying both a point of view toward Christian preaching and a small body of general principles for practical use. Augustine's work has historical significance in that it restored rhetoric to the high estate of the best Ciceronian tradition. It ignored sophistic—to the advantage of the cause of rhetoric—and reestablished the pursuit of Truth as the guiding principle of public speaking.

Books I, II, and III of *On Christian Doctrine* were probably written about 397; Book IV, about 426. Book IV deals most directly with rhetorical theory.

Augustine justifies his role as an instructor by saying: "He who reads to an audience pronounces aloud the words he sees before him: he who teaches reading, does it that others may be able to read for themselves. Each, however, communicates to others what he has learnt himself. Just so, the man who explains to an audience the passages of Scripture he understands is like one who reads aloud the words before him. On the other hand, the man who lays down rules for interpretation is like one who teaches reading, that is, shows others how to read for themselves." [1] The interpretation of Scripture depends, according to Augustine, upon "the mode of ascertaining the proper meaning, and the mode of making known the meaning when it is ascertained." [2]

To discover the meaning of Scripture, the preacher must attend both to *things* and *signs*. The former includes things to be *enjoyed* —the triune God; those to be *used;* and those to be *used* and *enjoyed*. *Signs* are symbols—words, for instance. Augustine then discusses at some length the possibilities of obscurity arising from words. He urges the careful use of logical reasoning and definition to keep meanings straight. In short, he asks the preacher to employ logic as a tool of expression. Furthermore, he begs the preacher to curb ambiguities arising from faulty observation of punctuation and from incorrect pronunciation. Words must be appreciated in context; tropes must be fully understood; figurative expressions must not be interpreted literally, or literal expressions figuratively.

Once the meaning is ascertained, it must be made known. This requires expression. And that calls for an elucidation of rhetorical principles. Although Augustine's treatise is not intended as a textbook (he specifically instructs Christian preachers to turn elsewhere for such a body of rules) *On Christian Doctrine* turns out to be a modified manual of instructions.

Like many of his predecessors, Augustine tries to assess the relative value of rules in rhetoric. Rules, he believes, are helpful, provided they are used judiciously. In any event, they must be learned quickly and at an early age. This is but a confirmation of Roman doctrine, especially as set forth by Cicero and Quintilian.

Augustine enters this admonition regarding the use of rhetoric and dialectic for the determination of Scriptural meaning:

> But the art previously spoken of, which deals with inferences, and definitions, and divisions, is of the greatest assistance in the discovery of the meaning, provided only that men do not fall into the error of supposing that when they have learnt these things they have learnt the true secret of a happy life. Still, it sometimes happens that men find less difficulty in attaining the object for the sake of which these sciences are learnt, than in going through the very intricate and thorny discipline of such rules. It is just as if a man wishing to give rules for walking should warn you not to lift the hinder foot before you set down the front one, and then should describe minutely the way you ought to move the hinges of the joints and knees. For what he says is true, and one cannot walk in any other way; but men find it easier to walk by executing these movements than to attend to them while they are going through them, or to understand when they are told about them. . . . And in the same way a clever man often sees that an inference is unsound more quickly than he apprehends the rules for it.[3]

Indeed, "men of quick intellect and glowing temperament find it easier to become eloquent by reading and listening to eloquent speakers than by following rules for eloquence." Furthermore, "I think there are scarcely any who can do both things—that is, speak well, and, in order to do this, think of the rules of speaking while they are speaking." The speeches of eloquent men do not necessarily demonstrate the close observance of rules. "For it is because they are eloquent that they exemplify these rules; it is not that they use them in order to be eloquent."[4]

Insistence upon Truth as the over-all objective of speaking is a cardinal tenet of Augustine's treatise. This is a significant point for it represents a negation of the spurious goals of decadent rhetoric and sophistic. The rules of rhetoric are true, says Augustine, despite the evil use to which they may be put. "There are also rules for a more copious kind of argument, which is called eloquence, and these rules are not the less true that they can be used for persuading men of what is false; but as they can be used to enforce the truth as well, it is not the faculty itself that is to be blamed, but the perversity of those who put it to a bad use."[5]

In all cases, wisdom is to be honored above eloquence. "To speak eloquently, then, and wisely as well, is just to express truths which it is expedient to teach in fit and proper words,—words which in the subdued style are adequate, in the temperate, elegant, and in the majestic, forcible." Consequently, "the man who cannot speak both eloquently and wisely should speak wisely without eloquence, rather than eloquently without wisdom." Indeed, "men who teach lies are the more pitiable if they happen to be eloquent in speech." [6]

All expression should be perspicuous. " . . . the best mode is that which secures that he who hears shall hear the truth, and that what he hears he shall understand." [7] In addition, the expression should display, as far as possible, the merits of beauty and persuasiveness. This is true regardless of whether the style is subdued, temperate, or majestic. In any event, the diction must be appropriate to the subject matter; adapted to the occasion; and sufficiently varied to avoid monotony. Augustine appraises certain passages from Ambrose and Cyprian to illustrate the types of style; and he affirms the value, especially for the young preacher, of imitating the practices of great Christian preachers. Thus he returns to his basic contention that rules, however lucid and however useful to the young student, may be less valuable for the preachers intent upon a great Christian mission than the reading and hearing of truly eloquent models.

Augustine uses the three Ciceronian ends of discourse—to teach, to delight, and to move—as the basis of his instruction. Of these ends, teaching, he believes, is the most essential. It depends on *what* is said, whereas the other two rely on the *way* it is said. However, this analysis does not preclude the use of emotional detail. On the contrary, Augustine recognizes the necessity of moving hearers to action:

> The eloquent divine, then, when he is urging a practical truth, must not only teach so as to give instruction, and please so as to keep up the attention, but he must also sway the mind so as to subdue the will. For if a man be not moved by the force of truth, though it is demonstrated to his own confession, and clothed in beauty of style, nothing remains but to subdue him by the power of eloquence.[8]

On Christian Doctrine is important for setting a high ideal of Truth before the Christian preacher; for avoiding the excesses and obvious falsities of sophistical rhetoric; and for revitalizing the best in Ciceronian doctrine at a time when oratory was largely a showy recital of themes possessing neither public urgency nor motive.

John of Salisbury

Just as Aristotle's *Rhetoric* was in part a protest against the teachers who gave disproportionate emphasis to emotional proof, so John's *Metalogicon* was partially a dissent from the view of one "Cornificius" who had questioned the value of the liberal studies. The *Metalogicon,* probably prepared about 1159, presents a defence of logic, rhetoric, and grammar. More particularly, it is a discourse on the functions of words. Rhetoric, *per se,* does not receive extensive formal treatment; instead, much of the detail relating to composition is articulated with the analysis of *dialectic.*

John's contribution derives largely from his defence of eloquence as a positive good, subordinate only to virtue and wisdom. Despite the claims of the "Cornificians," he holds that eloquence can be learned—that natural aptitude can be defined by theory and practice.

John reveals a thorough familiarity with Aristotle's works on logic. In fact, the *Metalogicon* becomes in substantial part a summary and analysis of the *Organon.* John was not acquainted with Aristotle's *Rhetoric;* but he knew and drew freely upon Quintilian's *Institutes of Oratory.* It is surprising, therefore, that he did not concern himself more fully with rhetoric.

The *Metalogicon* is a fairly vigorous plea for Truth as the end of discourse. It becomes a sort of intellectual prospectus for the attainment of a literary education. The learner begins with grammar —the base of the trivium; proceeds to poetry, which is related to grammatical inquiry; moves on to logic and rhetoric; then to the mathematical studies comprising the quadrivium; next to Natural Philosophy; and, finally, to the pursuit of Moral Philosophy—the capstone of orderly study.

The First Rhetoric in the English Language

The first reasonably complete rhetoric in the English language, Leonard Cox's *Arte or Crafte of Rhethoryke,* helps to sustain the continuity of thinking in the province of oral expression between classical antiquity and the Renaissance. During the sixteenth century in England, says Frederic I. Carpenter, the theory of prose clung "to the traditions of oratory and the classifications and precepts of ancient rhetoric, as modified and interpreted by Medieval and Renaissance thought." [9] The sixteenth century treatises on rhetoric performed a useful service by suggesting an "ordered utterance" and by setting forth a theory of prose. Cox's was the first in the field, coming out before 1530.

Cox's chief service, according to Carpenter, "was that of a translator and commentator."

> [He] served as an intermediary in the transmission to England of the Renaissance and Humanistic influence and literature. He had a reputation of his own among European scholars and men of the new learning, and he helped to carry their work into England. And so the questions of rhetoric and of literary form which deeply concerned all the men of the new learning came to concern Cox also, and to their elucidation . . . he devoted a large share of his attention.[10]

A practical aim guided Cox in his preparation of the *Rhethoryke.* With the spread of education, the establishment of new schools, and the growing recognition of form and style in prose, he sensed the need for a book on rhetoric in English. His book, accordingly, is "little concerned with the theory of rhetoric." "His aim is to tell very plainly the manner of putting together of orations of the several kinds then recognized by the rhetoricians." And he illustrates all his points by citing examples. "The whole method is that of the Ciceronians and the Renaissance educators simplified and put in the vernacular." [11]

The Plan of Cox's Book.—Cox's *Rhethoryke,* a slim volume, deals almost exclusively with invention and disposition as they relate to the preparation of logical, demonstrative, and judicial speeches. Ethical and pathetic proof do not receive systematic treatment. For those of his readers who wished further instruction, Cox recommended a study of the treatises by Hermogenes, Cicero, or Trapesuntius.

Cox discusses the essentials of the art of rhetoric in these words:

> Whosomeuer desyreth to be a good oratour or to dyspute and commune of any maner thynge/hym behoueth to haue foure thynges. The fyrste is called Inuencyon, for he muste fyrste of al imagyne or inuent in his mynde what he shall saye. The ii. is named iudgement/for he muste haue wyt to discerne and iudge whether tho thinges that he hathe founde in his mynde be conuenient to the purpose or nat/for often tymes yf a man lake thys propriete he may as well tell that that is agaynste hym/as with hym/as experience doth dayly shew. The iii. is dysposycyon wherby he maye knowe howe to ordre and set euery thynge in his due place. Leste thoughe his inuencyon and iudgement be neuer so goode he maye happen to be counted as the commune prouerbe sayeth To put the carte afore the horse. The iiii. & is such thynges laste as

(sic) he hathe Inuentid and by iudgement knowen apte to his purpose
when they ar set in theyr ordre so to speke them that it maye be pleasant
and delectable to the audience.[12]

Cox's *Rhethoryke* is largely an adaptation of other works, and
particularly of the 1521 edition of the *Institutiones Rhetoricae* of
Melanchthon, the humanist educator and religious reformer of Ger-
many. A comparison of Melanchthon's section on invention with
Cox's *Rhethoryke,* both of which appear in the Carpenter edition,
reveals a remarkably close textual correspondence. Melanchthon,
in turn, relied chiefly upon Hermogenes, Trapesuntius, Cicero, and
Quintilian. Cox does not, however, refer to Quintilian.

Carpenter believes that Cox's book "served its turn with its own
generation, but any direct influence from it on later English rhetorical
writers can scarcely be traced." [13] Although not a significant figure
in the establishment of an artistic English prose style, which was
then in the making, Cox did, through his straightforward presentation, afford a precept if not a model for subsequent writers.

The Restatement of Classical Doctrines

Thomas Wilson's *Arte of Rhetorique,* issued in 1553 and published eight times during the following thirty years, offers for the
first time in the English Renaissance a comprehensive treatment of
the main divisions of ancient rhetorical theory. Wilson reas-
sembled the many observations and principles derived from ancient
and medieval treatises and put them into an acceptable English prose
pattern. According to Russell Wagner, "Wilson's is the first rhetoric
since Quintilian's to give a full and unified treatment of the best
of the classical doctrines and to make them really useful in the
world of practical affairs." [14]

Cox had devoted his efforts chiefly to invention and partially to
disposition; Richard Sherry, in the *Treatise of Schemes and Tropes*
(1550) and in the *Figures of Grammar and Rhetoric* (1555), had
concentrated on elocution or style; but Wilson embraced *all* five traditional parts of rhetoric in his work, and thus gave the first rounded
account of classical doctrine in the English language.

Essential Features of Wilson's Contribution.—The main features
of Wilson's *Rhetorique* are duplicates of the classical pattern, with
such modifications as a sixteenth-century adaptation necessitated.
His book treats of invention, disposition, elocution, memory, and
delivery; considers demonstrative, deliberative, and judicial oratory;

sets up teaching, delighting, and persuading as the ends of oratory; examines the following as the parts of an oration: entrance or beginning, narration, proposition, division or several parting of things, confirmation, confutation, and conclusion; describes and illustrates the conjectural, legal, and judicial states, or issues; and, through it all, avoids setting up a stereotyped pattern of theoretical detail. For, as Wilson said:

> Rules were therfore giuen, and by muche obseruation gathered together, that those whiche could not see Arte hid in an other mannes dooynges, shold yet see the rules open all in an order set together: and thereby iudge the rather of their dooynges, and by earnest imitation, seeke to resemble suche their inuention.[15]

This observation was followed by the pithy remark: "And I knowe that rules were made first by wisemen, and not wisemen made by rules."

Wagner believes that one of Wilson's specific contributions is his conception of rhetoric as the art of *oral* discourse. Although the *Rhetorique* opens with the definition that "Rhetorique is an Arte to set forthe by vtterance of woordes"—and the reference here is probably to written and oral discourse—the word "orator," as Wagner points out, appears immediately and continuously thereafter. Wagner asserts that the "orators" Wilson had in mind were the lawyers and the preachers. "Rhetoric, then, though it ministers to the needs of writers, is to Wilson, as to the Greeks, the art of the speaker; and so it has remained, consistently in British thought, less so in American." [16]

Another doctrine which distinguishes the Wilsonian treatment of rhetoric concerns the orator's need of getting and holding the attention of his hearers. On the second page of his book, Wilson remarks: ". . . an Orator must labour to tell his tale, that the hearers maie well know what he meaneth, and vnderstand hym wholie, the whiche he shall with ease doe, if he vtter his mynde in plaine woordes, such as are vsuallie receiwed, and tell it orderly, without goyng about the busshe." Again, the orator must "chere his geastes and to make them take pleasure, with hearing of thinges wittely devised, and pleasauntly set foorth." Furthermore, "such quicknesse of witte must be shewed, and such pleasaunt sawes so well applied, that the eares may finde much delite, whereof I will speake largely, when I shall intreate of moving laughter." [17]

Wilson's detailed analysis of amplification also relates to the problem of getting and holding attention. We agree with Wagner that Wilson makes

> ...getting and holding attention the essential principle of effective oral discourse, and, with emotional proof, into which it rapidly fuses, the grand principle of persuasion. This concept and emphasis, differing from that of all his predecessors, is, of course, largely conditioned by the peculiar needs of the times. And whether right or wrong, whether Wilson has been directly influential or not, the principle persists in rhetorical theory today.[18]

Some 40 pages of Wilson's book are devoted to Amplification. Although this figure receives attention in Quintilian's *Institutes,* it gets its first comprehensive analysis at Wilson's hand. "Amplification," he says, "is a figure in *Rhetorique,* whiche consisteth moste in augmentyng, and diminishyng of any matter, and that diuers waies." [19] The kinds and methods of achieving amplification are numerous. Among the important ones are:

> The first kinde of amplification is, when by changyng a worde, in augmentyng we vse a greater, but in diminishyng, we vse a less....
>
> Now in all these kindes, where woordes are amplified thei seeme muche greater, if by correction the sentence be vtterde, and greater wordes compared with them, for whom thei are vtterde. In the which kinde of speeche, we shall seeme as though we went vp by staiers, not onely to the toppe of a thyng, but also aboue the toppe....
>
> There is an othere kinde of Amplification, when vnto the hiest there is added somethyng higher then it is....
>
> Sometyme we amplifie by comparyng, and take our ground vpon the weakest and leaste, the whiche if thei seeme greate, then must that needes appeare greate, which we would amplifie and increase....
>
> By contraries sette together, thynges oftentymes appeare greater....
>
> There is also a notable kinde of amplification, when we would extenuate and make lesse great faultes, whiche before wee did largely increase: to the ende that other faultes might seeme the greatest aboue all other....
>
> There is a kinde of amplifying, whiche in speaking of twoo that fought together, we praise hym muche that hadde the worse, because we would the other to haue more praise.
>
> From the straightnesse of a thyng. Eloquence must nedes be a wonderfull thyng, when so fewe haue attained it. Likewise, notable aduentures doen by a fewe, are more praise worthie, then such as haue been doen by a greate number....
>
> Vehemincie of wordes, full often helpe the matter forwards when more is gathered by cogitation, then if the thyng had bene spoken in plaine woordes....

We encrease our cause, by heapyng of woordes and sentences together, couchyng many reasons into one corner, whiche before were scatterde abroade, to the intent that our talke might appere more vehement. . . .

It is an excellent kinde of amplifiyng, when thinges encreased, and thynges diminished, are bothe sette together, that the one maie the rather beautifie the other. . . .

Likewise, contraries beyng rehearsed, and euill immediately vttered after the good, make muche for encrease.[20]

Related to the theme of amplification and attention, and discussed under the head of the former, is the subject of the Passions. While Wilson did not consider ethical persuasion, he looked upon emotional proof generally as an important aspect of rhetorical theory. He defined the Passions in these terms:

Because the beauty of amplifiyng, standeth moste in apte mouyng of affections: It is nedefull to speake somewhat in this behalfe, that the better it maie be knowen what thei are, and howe it maie bee vsed. Affections therefore (called Passions) are none other thyng, but a stirryng or forcyng of the mynde, either to desire, or els to deteste and lothe any thynge, more vehemently then by nature we are commonly wont to doe. We desire those thynges, we loue theim, like theim earnestly, that appere in our iudgement to be Godly: we hate and abhorre those thynges that seme naught, vngodly, or harmefull vnto vs. Neither onely are we moued with those thinges, whiche we thinke either hurtfull, or profitable for our selues, but also wee reioyse, wee sorie, or wee pittie an other mannes happe.[21]

In moving the affections

. . . and stirring the judges to be greeved, the waight of the matter must be set forth, as though they sawe it plaine before their eyes, the report must be such, and the offence made so hainous, that the like hath not bene seen heretofore, and all the circumstaunce must thus be heaped together: The naughtinesse of his nature that did the dede, the cruell ordering, the wicked dealing, and malicious handling, the tyme, the place, the maner of his doing, and the wickednesse of his will to have done more. The man that sustained the wrong, how little he deserved, how well hee was esteemed among his neighbours, how small cause he gave him, how great lack men have of him. Now, if this be not reformed, no good man shall live saufe, the wicked will overflow all the world, and best it were for saufeguard to be nought also, and so take part with them, for no good man shall go quiet for them if there be not speedie redresse found and this fault punished to the example of all other.[22]

Then follow analyses of pity, laughter, pleasant behavior, and other emotional states.

Carpenter holds that the chief interest of Wilson's *Rhetorique* "is in his discussion of English style and diction," a view generally accepted today. Elocution, said Wilson, reveals invention through words, commending the matter of discourse with such beauty that reason seems clothed in purple.[23] The essential parts of elocution are plainness, aptness, composition, and exornation. These terms are then defined as follows:

> Among all other lessons this should first be learned, that we neuer affect any straunge ynkehorne termes, but to speake as is commonly receiued: neither seking to be ouer fine, nor yet liuyng ouercareless, vsing our speeche as moste men doe, and ordering our wittes as the fewest haue doen....

> Such are thought apt wordes, that properly agree vnto that thyng whiche thei signifie, and plainly expresse the Nature of the same....

> Composition ... is an apte iouynyng together of woordes in suche order, that neither the eare shall espie any gerre, nor yet any man shalbe dulled with ouerlong drawyng out of a sentence, nor yet muche confounded with minglyng of clauses suche as are needeless, beyng heaped together without reason, and vsed without number....

> Exornation, is a gorgious beautifiyng of the tongue with borrowed wordes, and change of sentence or speeche with muche varieties.[24]

On the negative side, Wilson speaks of some of the faults of composition, observing:

> For by such meanes the hearers will be forced to forget full ofte, what was sayd first, before the sentence bee halfe ended: or els be blinded with confounding of many things together. Some againe will be so short, and in such wise curtail their sentences, that they had neede to make a commentary immediately of their meaning, or else the most that heare them shalbe forced to keepe counsaill.

> Some will speake Oracles, that a man can not tell which way to take them, some will bee so fine and so poeticall withall, that to their seeming there shall not stande one haire a misse, and yet every body else shall thinke them meeter for a Ladies chamber, then for an earnest matter in an open assemblie.

> Some will rove so much and bable so farre without order, that a man would thinke they had a greate love to heare them selves speake.

> Some repeate one worde so often, that if such wordes could be eaten, and chopt in so oft as they are uttered out, they would choke the widest

throte in England. . . . Some use overmuch repetition of some one letter, as pitifull povertie for a penie, but puffed presumption passeth not a point, pampering his panch with pestilent pleasure, procuring his passeport to poste it to hell pit, there to bee punished with paines perpetuall. Some will so set their words, they must be faine to gape after every word spoken, ending one word with a vowell, and beginning the next with an other, which undoubtedly maketh the talke to seeme most unpleasaunt. . . . Some end their sentences all alike, making their talke rather to appeare rimed Meeter, then to seeme plaine speeche, the which as it much deliteth being measurably used, so it much offendeth when no meane is regarded. . . .

Some will tell one thing twentie times, nowe in, nowe out, and when a man would thinke they had almost ended, they are ready to beginne againe as fresh as ever they were. . . . Some are so homely in all their doings, and so grosse for their invention, that they use altogether one maner of trade, and seeke no varietie to eschue tediousness.

Some burden their talke with needlesse copie, and will seeme plentifull when they should be short. An other is so curious and so fine of his tongue, that he can not tell in all the world what to speake. Every sentence seemeth common, and every worde generally used, is thought to be foolish in his wise iudgement. Some use so many interpositions . . . that they make their sayings as darke as hell.[25]

Wagner concludes that

Here we have, in embryonic form, a statement of those broad and pervasive qualities of style with which we have become so familiar—unity, coherence, and emphasis,—with clearness and brevity added for good measure. This may be the first statement of the principles of composition, in English, as we today conceive them.[26]

There is reason to believe, then, that Wilson's *Rhetorique* is the most important treatise on public speaking produced by sixteenth-century England. In the words of Wagner,

In re-uniting, selecting and adapting the classical principles of public address, Wilson restored the body and, to some extent, reformed the concepts of rhetorical theory. In recalling rhetoric from the museum to the market-place, he not only re-established the ancient conception of rhetoric as the art of the speaker, but, because of his own self-imposed purpose of adapting old doctrines to new times and new needs, he effected far reaching changes which have greatly influenced the theories of public address we hold today.[27]

Bacon Helps to Revitalize Classical Doctrines

Bacon's Emphasis upon Logical Proof.—Called by one of his biographers [28] a man of "monstrous self-confidence," Francis Bacon left his mark on seventeenth-century rhetorical theory by revitalizing in part the classical doctrines of Greece and Rome. Furthermore, he gave rhetoric a fairly prominent place in his "total enterprise of learning." Deserving most consideration here, however, are his distinct contributions to the concept of speech invention.

Rhetoric, in Bacon's way of thinking, is the application of reason to imagination "for the better moving of the will." Thus the persuasive power of rhetoric acts as an intermediary; it establishes a compact, or a confederacy, between the pictorial representations of the imagination and the impulse to action residing in the will. Affirming the value of ornamentation and imaginative coloring in address, Bacon nevertheless believes that sound reasoning, the "logical integrity of ideas, is the *sine qua non* of rhetorical discourse." Although the "affections themselves carry ever an appetite to good," they "beholdeth merely the present" while reason "beholdeth the future and sum of time." [29]

Pursuant to his interest in logical proof, Bacon concerns himself with the analysis of invention. He doubts that invention of speech or argument is really invention, however, because "to invent is to discover that we know not, and not to recover or resummon that which we already know." Consequently, "the use of this invention is no other but, out of the knowledge whereof our mind is already possessed, to draw forth or call before us that which may be pertinent to the purpose which we take into our consideration." On last analysis, then, invention "is readiness and present use of our knowledge, and not addition or amplification thereof." [30]

Two courses may be followed in procuring this use of knowledge. The first is Preparation, which consists essentially of diligence rather than "of any artificial erudition." Demosthenes, for example, "had ready framed a number of prefaces for orations and speeches" in order that he might be prepared to enter upon and have ready access to causes. The second part or course of invention is Suggestion, which assigns or directs us "to certain marks or places, which may excite our mind to return and produce such knowledge as it hath formerly collected, to the end we may make use thereof." [31]

Bacon's Aids to Invention.—In furtherance of his belief that effective invention required ready access to "certain marks or places" of argument, and in recognition of the shortcomings of the ancient writers in this particular, Bacon brought forth the *Antitheta, Formulae, Apophthegmes,* and *Colours of Good and Evil.*

The *Antitheta* were designed to furnish the speaker with a store of arguments for ánd against certain contentions. Their function was to serve as substructures for argument. Typical examples of the *antitheta* are the following:

> For the letter of the law:
> Interpretation which recedes from the letter is not interpretation, but divination;
> When the judge recedes from the letter, he becomes a legislator.
>
> For the intention of the law:
> We must gather from all the words taken together the sense in which each is to be interpreted.[32]

The *Formulae,* said Bacon,

> ...are but decent and apt passages or conveyances of speech, which may serve indifferently for differing subjects; as of preface, conclusion, digression, transition, excusation, etc. For as in buildings, there is great pleasure and use in the well casting of the staircases, entries, doors, windows, and the like; so in speech, the conveyances and passages are of special ornament and effect.[33]

The following is a typical *formula:*

> A conclusion in a deliberative:
> So may we redeem the faults passed, and prevent the inconveniences future.[34]

Apophthegmes are "pointed speeches" or little "salt pits" from which "you may extract salt out of, and sprinkle it where you will." They may be used in continued speech, or recited by themselves. Bacon's collection included items from previous writers, together with some prepared by himself. Typical of the *apophthegmes* are these two:

> (1) Many men, especially such as affect gravity, have a manner after other men's speech to shake their heads. Sir Lionel Cranfield would say, 'It was as men shake a bottle to see if there were any wit in their head or no?'
>
> (2) One of the Seven was wont to say; 'That laws were like cobwebs; where the small flies were caught, and the great brake through.'[35]

The *Colours of Good and Evil* were sophisms, with their refutations. A representative example of this device for use in the invention of speech materials is the following:

> That which keeps a matter safe and entire is good; but what is destitute and unprovided of retreat is bad: for whereas all ability of acting is good, not to be able to withdraw one's self is a kind of impotency.
>
> Hereof Aesop framed the fable of the two frogs that consulted together in the time of drought, when many plashes that they had repaired to, were dry. What was to be done, and the one propounded to go down into a deep well, because it was like the water would not fail there; but the other answered, yea, but if it do fail, how shall we get up again. And the reason is, that human actions are so uncertain and subject to perils, as seemeth the best course which hath most passages out of it. Appertaining to this persuasion, the forms are, you shall engage yourself, on the other side, 'tantum quantum.' Vales, 'sumes ex fortuna,' etc. You shall keep the matter in your own hand. The reprehension of it is, that proceeding and resolving in all actions is necessary. For as he saith well, not to resolve, is to resolve, and many times it breeds as many necessities, and engageth as far in some other sort, as to resolve. So it is but the covetous—man's disease translated into power; for the covetous man will enjoy nothing, because he will have his full store and possibility to enjoy the more; so by this reason, a man should execute nothing, because he should be still indifferent, and at liberty to execute any thing. Besides necessity and this same 'jacta est alea', hath many times an advantage, because it awaketh the powers of the mind, and strengthened endeavour, 'caeteris paret necessitate certe superiores istes.' [36]

The Doctrine of Audience Adaptation.—Another way in which Bacon contributed to rhetorical theory was through his observation that the materials of speech should be adapted to the particular audience. While this idea was as old as the earliest rhetoricians, it nevertheless received renewed emphasis in Bacon's works. It appears also, he remarked, that logic differs from Rhetoric,

> ... not only as the fist from the palm, the one close the other at large; but much more in this, that logic handleth reason exact and in truth, and rhetoric handleth it as it is planted in popular opinions and manners. And, therefore, Aristotle doth wisely place rhetoric as between logic on the one side, and moral or civil knowledge on the other, as participating of both; for the proofs and demonstrations of logic are toward all men indifferent and the same; but the proofs and persuasions of Rhetoric ought to differ according to the auditors. ... Which application, in perfection of idea, ought to extend so far, that if a man should speak to them all respectively and several ways: though this politic part of eloquence in private speech it is easy for the greatest orators to want. ... [37]

The Influence of Stylistic Rhetoric

The Emphasis on Ornament.—Unquestionably, the treatises that contributed most to the development and refinement of practical and critical standards of speechcraft were those offering a balanced account of *all* the essential parts of the subject, namely, invention, disposition, elocution, memory, and delivery. Certain movements in the history of rhetorical theory, however, prompted able men to advocate theories of speaking that stressed one of the aspects of the subject to the neglect of the others; and from such specialized treatments some good resulted.

Elocutio, for instance, commanded a position of supremacy in several treatises. While their authors were not oblivious of the role of the other phases of rhetorical investigation, they looked upon stylistic embellishment as the matter of first importance. In 1550 Richard Sherry brought out his *Treatise of Schemes and Tropes,* followed in 1555 by his *Figures of Grammar and Rhetoric.* These works plainly presuppose the doctrine that rhetoric is essentially style. Substantially the same view prevailed in other works of the latter half of the sixteenth century, including Talaeus' *Institution Oratores,* Henry Peacham's *Garden of Eloquence,* George Puttenham's *Arte of English Poesie,* and Butler's *Rhetorical Libri Duo.* A cursory examination of Warren Taylor's dictionary of *Tudor Figures of Rhetoric* will suggest the elaborate extent to which the study of *elocutio* went during this period. Taylor's list of figures, incidentally, is drawn from the works mentioned above, and from Angel Day's *The English Secretary,* Dudley Fenner's *The Artes of Logike and Rhetorike,* Abraham Fraunce's *The Arcadian Rhetorike,* John Hoskins' *Directions for Speech and Style,* and Richard Rainolde's *The Foundacion of Rhetorike.*

Thomas Gibbons and John Stirling are the most important eighteenth-century figures to devote their treatises exclusively to the devices of stylistic ornamentation, the former in the *Rhetoric,* and the latter in the *System of Rhetoric.*

The Work of Thomas Gibbons.—Gibbons' *System of Rhetoric* is a good example of the stylistic approach. In the introduction, Gibbons acknowledges reliance upon classical writers, particularly Aristotle, Cicero, Dionysius, Hermogenes, and Tiberius Rhetor. The book contains numerous quotations from the ancients and the moderns to illustrate the embellishments.

Gibbons opens his treatise by distinguishing between a trope and a figure:

> A Trope is a change of a word or sentence from one sense into another, which its very etymology imports; whereas it is the nature of a Figure not to change the sense of words, but to illustrate, enliven, ennoble, or in some manner or another embellish our discourses: and so far, and so far only, as the words are changed into a different meaning from that which they originally signify, the Orator is obliged to the Tropes, and not to the Figures of *Rhetoric*.[38]

His plan, then, is to classify, define, and illustrate the principal tropes and figures. This is carried out with meticulous regard for details, and with an abundance of examples. It is of interest to observe, however, that Gibbons recognized the danger resulting from inept use of the ornaments of rhetoric. With regard to the tropes, he said:

> As Tropes infuse a dignity into our language, and shed a lustre over our expressions, when they are well-chosen and applied; so, on the other hand, when they are mean in themselves, when they are thrown out without judgment, or are in any other respect defective and faulty, they render our discourses mean and contemptible, or in some way or another miserably sink their value.[39]

He then showed how tropes might render a style barren, provided they were excessive in number, too extravagant, too mean, too harsh, too affected, or lacking in delicacy.

> Tropes may be sown too thick, or disgust by being injudiciously and profusely clustered....

> ...an injudicious multitude of Tropes, instead of enlightening and enlivening, in which consists their great service, cloud and obscure, and it may be sometimes even what I might call *strangle* our meaning, and therefore they ought to be discreetly used, and rather sparingly sprinkled, than superfluously lavished upon our discourses....

> Tropes may be blamable for being too extravagant, and beyond the just allowances of nature and reason, and even of the indulgence that may be granted to the most bold and fiery genius....

> Tropes may become faulty by being too mean and low. As Tropes should not swell into a vain and wild extravagance, so neither should they shrivel into a minute and contemptible littleness....

> We should guard against all far-fetched and obscure Tropes. Let the materials out of which our Tropes are formed lie within the reach of every person's understanding, if possible, and not cost the learned pains to investigate their propriety, and leave the unlearned only a company

of hard unintelligible words on which to ruminate, when they should gain from our discourses clear and profitable ideas. . . .

Another fault of Tropes consists in their being harsh and unsuitable to what they would represent. There ought to be care taken that there be an agreement or analogy between the Trope and the proper word for which it stands. . . .

We should guard against every Trope that may appear in the least degree finical and fantastical. Our Tropes should be bold and manly, free and natural, without being stiffened by affectation, or subtilised by a puerile and trifling fancy. . . .

Let us avoid all filthy and impure Tropes. We should take heed that no Tropes we make use of, either as to sound or sense, convey any idea that will not be agreeable to a chaste mind, or make any trespass upon delicacy.[40]

The same warning was coupled to the treatment of figures.

Let our discourses be founded upon reason, and let us establish everything we advance with solid and convincing arguments. We are first to labour to enlighten the understanding, and inform the judgment, and then introduce our *Figures* to affect and engage the passions, and thereby secure a complete triumph over our audience. . . .

Let us be sparing in the use of *Figures*. We should not needlessly multiply them, and seem in our discourses overwrought, and . . . encumbered with *Figures*. . . .

Let not our *Figures* be too much adorned and refined into too nice an exactness. The less art the better.[41]

Emphases on Delivery.—A second movement of ideas in rhetoric that influenced the teaching of the subject and the development of the theory was the one that placed the principal, and in some instances the exclusive, emphasis upon the fifth canon of rhetoric, namely, delivery. As early as 1617 Robert Robinson had brought out his *Art of Pronynciation,* a work devoted to delivery proper. And in 1644 John Bulwer issued his major treatise entitled *Chirologia . . . and Chironomia,* in which the action phase of delivery received exclusive consideration. This detailed work, which served as the basis of many subsequent treatises, including Gilbert Austin's *Chironomia* and Albert M. Bacon's *Manual of Gesture,* represents a highly systematized classification of the many gestures that a speaker may use to convey various shades of meaning. More than that, it is a sort of rationale of the whole subject of gesture, containing notes on the historical antecedents of action in literature

and on the use to which action can be put generally. As Bulwer
stated, both reason and the judgments of the ancients confirm the
"gestures of the Hand to be things of great moment, & the very
Palme and Crown of Eloquence. . . ."

Chirologia contains 64 descriptive analyses of the gestures of the
hand and, under the subdivision of *Dactylogia*, 25 additional analyses
of the gestures of the fingers. *Chironomia*, which is subjoined to
Chirologia, contains 49 canons of the gestures of the hand; and under
the subhead of *Indigitatio*, appear 30 additional canons of the
gestures of the fingers.

Another manifestation of interest in delivery as an important
canon of rhetoric resulted from the criticisms levelled against the
contemporary orators by such eighteenth-century writers as Addison,
Swift, and Chesterfield. "It is certain," wrote Addison, "that proper
gestures and exertions of the voice cannot be too much studied by
a public orator. They are a kind of comment on what he utters;
and enforce everything he says with weak hearers, better than the
strongest arguments he can make use of." [42] And Swift, in his
Letter to a Young Clergyman, imposes a stricture upon the practice
of reading sermons, asserting that it destroys the effectiveness of
the preacher. Chesterfield's *Letters to His Son* reveal clearly his
interest in good enunciation and his belief that delivery is of great moment to the speaker. "A certain degree of good sense and knowledge," he wrote, "is requisite . . . but beyond that, the purity of
diction, the elegancy of style, the harmony of periods, a pleasing
elocution, and a graceful action, are the things which a public speaker
should attend to the most. . . ."

The Elocutionary Movement.—By far the most influential individuals in this movement which gave to delivery a position of prominence were the so-called "elocutionists," including, among others,
Thomas Sheridan, James Burgh, Joshua Steele, John Walker, and
Gilbert Austin. These men are best known as teachers, although
their theorizing about methods of instruction resulted in certain positive contributions to the art of rhetoric.

The men who best illustrate the two schools of thought within the
elocutionary movement are Thomas Sheridan and John Walker.

Sheridan was an advocate of the "natural" manner in delivery.
He was opposed to devices and techniques that interfered in any
way with the spontaneous, conversational expression of the speaker.
In his *Lectures on Elocution* (1763), he deplores the general de-

ficiency of skill in reading and speaking, offering the following observation as a clue to the condition he criticizes:

> When we reflect that the end of public speaking is persuasion ... ; and that in order to persuade others to the belief of any point, it must first appear, that the person who attempts it is firmly persuaded of the truth of it himself; how can we suppose it possible that he should effect this, unless he delivers himself in the manner which is always used by persons who speak in earnest? How shall his words pass for the words of truth, when they bear not its stamp? [43]

The "just" delivery which Sheridan sought

> ... consists in a distinct articulation of words, pronounced in proper tones, suitably varied to the sense, and the emotions of the mind; with due observation of accent; of emphasis, in its several gradations; of rests or pauses of the voice, in proper places and well-measured degrees of time; and the whole accompanied with expressive looks, and significant gesture. [44]

Let the speaker avoid all traces of affectation in delivery. The rule, he remarks,

> ... by which all public speakers are to guide themselves is obvious and easy. Let each, in the first place, avoid all imitation of others; let him give up all pretensions to art, for it is certain that it is better to have none, than not enough; and no man has enough, who has not arrived at such perfection of art, as wholly to conceal his art; a thing not to be compassed but by the united endeavours, of the best instruction, perfect patterns, and constant practice. Let him forget that he ever learned to read; at least, let him wholly forget his reading tones. Let him speak entirely from his feelings; and they will find much truer signs to manifest themselves by, than he could find for them. Let him always have in view, what the chief end of speaking is; and he will see the necessity of the means proposed to answer the end. The chief end of all public speakers is to persuade; and in order to persuade, it is above all things necessary, that the speaker, should at least appear himself to believe, what he utters; but this can never be the case, where there are any evident marks of affectation or art. On the contrary, when a man delivers himself in his usual manner, and with the same tones and gesture, that he is accustomed to use, when he speaks from his heart; however awkward that manner may be, however ill-regulated the tones, he will still have the advantage of being thought sincere; which of all others, is the most necessary article, towards securing attention and belief; as affectation of any kind, is the surest way to destroy both. [45]

Opposed to this point of view was the doctrine set forth by John Walker in the *Elements of Elocution* (1781) and other books. Walker was fond of rules; accordingly, he devised an elocutionary scheme in which they appear with almost unbelievable frequency. ·

In the introduction to his *Elements of Elocution,* Walker states:

Elocution, in the modern sense of the word, seems to signify that pronunciation which is given to words when they are arranged into sentences and form discourse.

Pronunciation, in its largest sense, may signify the utterance of words, either taken separately, or in connection with each other; but the pronunciation of words, connected into a sentence, seems very properly specified by elocution.

Elocution, therefore, according to this definition of it, may have elements or principles distinct from those of pronunciation in its most limited sense; and we may consider the elements of elocution, not as these principles which constitute the utterance of single words, but as those which form the just enunciation of words in dependence on each other for sense: at this point the present work commences. The delivery of words formed into sentences, and these sentences formed into discourse, is the object of it; and as reading is a correct and beautiful picture of speaking; speaking, it is presumed, cannot be more successfully taught, than by referring us to such rules as instruct us in the art of reading.[46]

Furthermore,

The art of reading is that system of rules, which teaches us to pronounce written composition with justness, energy, variety, and ease. Agreeable to this definition, reading may be considered as that species of delivery, which not only expresses the sense of an author, so as barely to be understood, but which, at the same time, gives it all that force, beauty, and variety, of which it is susceptible: the first of these considerations belongs to grammar, and the last to rhetoric.

The sense of an author being the first object of reading, it will be necessary to inquire into those divisions and subdivisions of a sentence which are employed to fix and ascertain its meaning: this leads to a consideration of the doctrine of punctuation.

Punctuation may be considered in two different lights; first, as it clears and preserves the sense of a sentence, by combining those words together which are united in sense, and separating those that are distinct; and secondly, as it directs to such pauses, elevations, and depressions of the voice, as not only mark the sense of the sentence more precisely, but give it a variety and beauty which recommend it to the ear; for in speaking, as in other arts, the useful and the agreeable are almost always found to coincide; and every real embellishment promotes and perfects the principal design.[47]

After setting forth his theory of rhetorical punctuation, Walker establishes the rules for the pauses, inflections, modulations, accent, and emphases. These rules are also applied to the delivery of many types of sentences and passages.

Austin's *Chironomia* and Steele's *Prosodia Rationalis* have much in common with Walker's works in that they propose, respectively, notational systems for indicating the appropriate movements and gestures in delivery, and the various phenomena of vocal action— accent, quantity, emphasis, pause, and force.

The Forerunner of Contemporary Theory

James McCosh once remarked that "the Scottish Metaphysicians following Shaftesbury were fond of speculating about beauty and taste, and that all the Scottish thinkers at this time were anxious to acquire an elegant style." [48] Like the other men to whom McCosh refers—Adam Smith, Lord Kames, and Hugh Blair, among them— George Campbell published his speculations. His was a formal treatise on *The Philosophy of Rhetoric* (1776), a book that exercised a salutary influence on the teaching of public speaking. The style in which Campbell clothed his ideas is itself worthy of notice, although he modestly allowed that since his effort was didactical and addressed only to the understanding, "the style in general admits no higher qualities than purity and perspicuity."

Analysis of the Ends of Oratory.—There is reason to believe that Campbell's greatest contribution to rhetorical theory is set forth in the first chapter of his book, in which he comments on the *ends* or objects of discourse and enlarges the classical doctrine that the primary aim of rhetoric is persuasion. "In speaking," says Campbell,

> ... there is always some end proposed, or some effect which the speaker intends to produce in the hearer. The word *eloquence,* in its greatest latitude, denotes 'that art or talent by which the discourse is adapted to its end.'
> All the ends of speaking are reducible to four; every speech being intended to enlighten the understanding, to please the imagination, to move the passions, or to influence the will.
> Any one discourse admits only one of these ends as the principal. Nevertheless, in discoursing on a subject, many things may be introduced which are more immediately and apparently directed to some of the other ends of speaking, and not to that which is the chief intent of the whole. But then these other and immediate ends are in effect but

means, and must be regarded conducive to that which is the primary intention. Accordingly, the propriety or impropriety of the introduction of such secondary ends will always be inferred from their subserviency or want of subserviency to that end which is, in respect of them, the ultimate. For example, a discourse addressed to the understanding, and calculated to illustrate or evince some point purely speculative, may borrow aid from the imagination, and admit metaphor and comparison, but not the bolder and more striking figures, as that called vision or fiction, prosopopoeia, and the like, which are not so much intended to elucidate a subject as to excite admiration. Still less will it admit an address as to the passions, which, as it never fails to disturb the operation of the intellectual faculty, must be regarded by every intelligent hearer as foreign at least, if not insidious. It is obvious that either of these, far from being subservient to the main design, would distract the attention from it.[49]

Campbell goes on to show that the only form of address in which assistance from the fancy is inappropriate is mathematical demonstration. He continues:

As this doth not, like moral reasoning, admit degrees of evidence, its perfection in point of eloquence, if so uncommon an application of the term may be allowed, consists in perspicuity. Perspicuity here results entirely from propriety and simplicity of diction, and from accuracy of method, where the mind is regularly, step by step, conducted forward in the same track, the attention no way diverted, nothing left to be supplied, no one unnecessary word or idea introduced. On the contrary, an harangue framed for affecting the hearts or influencing the resolves of an assembly, needs greatly the assistance both of intellect and of imagination.

In general, it may be asserted that each preceding species, in the order above exhibited, is preparatory to the subsequent; that each subsequent species is founded on the preceding; and that thus they ascend in a regular progression. Knowledge, the object of the intellect, furnisheth materials for the fancy; the fancy culls, compounds, and by her mimic art, disposes these materials so as to affect the passions; the passions are the natural spurs to volition or action, and so need only to be rightly directed. This connexion and dependency will better appear from the following observations.

When a speaker addresses himself to the understanding, he proposes the *instruction* of his hearers, and that, either by explaining some doctrine unknown, or not distinctly comprehended by them, or by proving some position disbelieved or doubted by them. In other words, he proposes either to dispel ignorance or to vanquish error. In the one, his aim is their *information;* in the other, their *conviction.* Accordingly, the predominant quality of the former is *perspicuity;* of the latter, *argument.* By that we are made to know, by this to believe.

The imagination is addressed by exhibiting to it a lively and beautiful representation of a suitable object. As in this exhibition the task of the orator may, in some sort, be said, like that of the painter, to consist in imitation, the merit of the work results entirely from these two sources: dignity, as well in the subject or thing imitated as in the manner of imitation, and resemblance in the portrait or performance. Now the principal scope for this class being in narration and description, poetry, which is one mode of oratory, especially epic poetry, must be ranked under it. The effect of the dramatic, at least of tragedy, being upon the passions, the drama falls under another species, ... But that kind of address of which I am now treating attains the summit of perfection in the *sublime,* or those great and noble images which, when in suitable colouring presented to the mind, do, as it were, distend the imagination with some vast conception, and quite ravish the soul.

The sublime, it may be urged, as it raiseth imagination, should be considered as one species of address to the passions. But this objection, when examined, will appear superficial. There are few words in any language ... which are strictly univocal. Thus, admiration, when persons are the object, is commonly used for a high degree of esteem; but, when otherwise applied, it denotes solely an internal taste. It is that pleasurable sensation which instantly arises on the perception of magnitude, or of whatever is great and stupendous in its kind; for there is a greatness in the degrees of quality in spiritual subjects analogous to that which subsists in the degrees of quantity in material things. Accordingly, in all tongues, perhaps without exception, the ordinary terms which are considered as literally expressive of the latter, are also used promiscuously to denote the former. Now admiration, when thus applied, doth not require to its production, as the passions generally do, any reflex view of motives or tendencies, or of any relation either to private interest or to the good of others; and ought, therefore, to be numbered among those original feelings of the mind, which are denominated by some the reflex senses, being of the same class with a taste of beauty, an ear for music, or our moral sentiments. Now the ultimate view of whatever is directed to imagination ... terminates in the gratification of some internal taste; as a taste for the wonderful, the fair, the good; for elegance, for novelty, or for grandeur.

But it is evident that this creative faculty, the fancy, frequently lends her aid in promoting still nobler ends. From her exuberant stores most of those tropes and figures are extracted which, when properly employed, have such a marvellous efficacy in rousing the passions, and by some secret, sudden, and inexplicable association, awakening all the tenderest emotions of the heart. In this case, the address of the orator is not ultimately intended to astonish by the loftiness of his images, or to delight by the beauteous resemblance which his painting bears to nature; nay, it will not permit the hearers even a moment's leisure for making the comparison, but, as it were, by some magical spell, hurries them, ere they are aware, into love, pity, grief, terror, desire, aversion, fury, or hatred. It therefore assumes the denomination of *pathetic*, which is the characteristic of the third species of discourse, that addressed to the passions.

Finally, as that kind, the most complex of all, which is calculated to influence the will, and persuade to a certain conduct, is in reality an artful mixture of that which proposes to convince the judgment, and that which interests the passions, its distinguishing excellence results from these two, the argumentative and the pathetic incorporated together. These, acting with united force, and, if I may so express myself, in concert, constitute that passionate eviction, that *vehemence* of contention, which is admirably fitted for persuasion, and hath always been regarded as the supreme qualification in an orator. It is this which bears down every obstacle, and procures the speaker an irresistible power over the thoughts and purposes of his audience. It is this which hath been so justly celebrated as giving one man an ascendant over others, superior even to what despotism itself can bestow; since by the latter the more ignoble parts only, the body and its members, are enslaved; whereas from the dominion of the former nothing is exempted, neither judgment nor affection, not even the inmost recesses, the most latent movements of the soul. What opposition is he not prepared to conquer on whose arms reason hath conferred solidity and weight, and passion such a sharpness as enables them in defiance of every obstruction, to open a speedy passage to the heart?

It is not, however, every kind of pathos which will give the orator so great an ascendency over the minds of his hearers. All passions are not alike capable of producing this effect. Some are naturally inert and torpid; they deject the mind, and indispose it for enterprise. Of this kind are sorrow, fear, shame, humility. Others, on the contrary, elevate the soul, and stimulate to action. Such are hope, patriotism, ambition, emulation, anger. These, with the greatest facility, are made to concur in direction with arguments exciting to resolution and activity; and are, consequently, the fittest for producing what, for want of a better term in our language, I shall henceforth denominate the *vehement*. There is, besides, an intermediate kind of passions, which do not so congenially and directly either restrain us from acting or incite us to act; but, by the art of the speaker, can, in an oblique manner, be made conducive to either. Such are joy, love, esteem, compassion. Nevertheless, all these kinds may find a place in suasory discourses, or such as are intended to operate on the will. The first is properest for dissuading; the second, as hath been already hinted, for persuading; the third is equally accommodated to both.[50]

These passages bring out the ideas essential to an understanding of speech ends. At the same time they throw some light on the distinction between appeals to the understanding and appeals to the

feelings. Campbell's concept of speech ends, so William P. Sandford believes,

> ... with its inevitable corollary that the means by which the orator
> shall accomplish his purpose must differ according to the nature of the
> effect desired, and that whatever material is introduced into the speech
> must be judged according to its 'subserviency or want of subserviency
> to that end' strikes the keynote of modern theories of speech compo-
> sition.[51]

Campbell's analysis of the speech situation, while deriving surely
from the work of his predecessors, is nevertheless a succinct statement directly usable by the critic of oratory. He lists, as the basis
for his consideration of forensic, deliberative, and pulpit speaking,
the following components or particulars: "the speaker, the hearer
or persons addressed, the subject, the occasion, and the end in view, or
the effect intended to be produced by the discourse. . . ."[52] In
terms almost identical with those used today, Campbell thus names
the elements which figure in the interaction of a speech situation.

The Modes of Proof.—The three traditional modes of persuasion
—logical, emotional, and ethical—receive systematic treatment.
     Campbell opens his discussion of logical proof by showing the
relation of logic to eloquence:

> The sole and ultimate end of logic is the eviction of truth; one important
> end of eloquence, though, as appears from the first chapter neither the
> sole, nor always the ultimate, is the conviction of the hearers. Pure
> logic regards only the subject, which is examined solely for the sake
> of information. Truth, as such, is the proper aim of the examiner.
> Eloquence not only considers the subject, but also the speaker and the
> hearers, and both the subject and the speaker for the sake of the hear-
> ers, or, rather, for the sake of the effect intended to be produced in
> them.[53]

Logical proof is of two classes: intuitive evidence and deductive
evidence. The former includes "everything whose evidence results
from the simple contemplation of the ideas or perceptions which form
the proposition under consideration, and requires not the intervention
of any third ideas as a medium of proof." Accordingly, this division
includes "the truths of pure intellection, of consciousness, and of
common sense." On the other hand, "rational or deductive evidence
is derived from one or other of these two sources: from the invariable properties or relations of general ideas; or from the actual,
though perhaps variable connexions, subsisting among things. The

former we call demonstrative; the latter moral." Moral reasoning includes experience, analogy, and testimony. Campbell believes that the "proper province of rhetoric is the second, or moral evidence; for to the second belong all decisions concerning fact, and things without us." [54]

Induction, rather than syllogistic reasoning, meets more fully the demands of the rhetoric Campbell envisages. Agreeing with Locke "that the syllogistic art, with its figures and moods, serves more to display the ingenuity of the inventor, and to exercise the address and fluency of the learner, than to assist the diligent inquirer in his researches after truth," Campbell gives four reasons why the syllogism "bears the manifest indications of an artful and ostentatious parade of learning, calculated for giving the appearance of great profundity to what, in fact, is very shallow." To begin with, "this method of arguing has not the least affinity to moral reasoning, the procedure in the one being the very reverse of that employed in the other." Secondly, "though this manner of arguing has more of the nature of scientific reasoning than of moral, it has, nevertheless, not been thought worthy of being adopted by mathematicians as a proper method of demonstrating their theorems." Next, "in the ordinary application of this art to matters with which we can be made acquainted only by experience, it can be of little or no utility." Finally, "the proper province of the syllogistical science is rather the adjustment of our language, in expressing ourselves on subjects previously known, than the acquisition of knowledge in things themselves." [55]

To emotional proof Campbell gives a treatment that is not fundamentally new, but is more fully conceived in the light of psychological data, and especially of the so-called "faculties" of the mind. He considers hearers from two points of view, "as men in general, and as such men in particular."

In order to evince the truth considered by itself, conclusive arguments alone are requisite; but in order to convince me by these arguments, it is moreover requisite that they be understood, that they be attended to, that they be remembered by me; and, in order to persuade me by them to any particular action or conduct, it is farther requisite that, by interesting me in the subject, they may, as it were, be felt. It is not, therefore, the understanding alone that is here concerned. If the orator would prove successful, it is necessary that he engage in his service all these different powers of the mind, the imagination, the memory, and the passions. These are not the supplanters of reason, or even rivals in her sway; they are her handmaids, they are liable to be seduced by sophistry in the garb of reason, and sometimes are made ignorantly to lend their aid in the introduction of falsehood. But their service is not on this account to be dispensed with; there is even a necessity of employing it founded in our nature.[56]

Campbell therefore analyzes hearers as endowed with understanding, imagination, memory, and passions.

Developing seven circumstances which are instrumental in operating on the passions, Campbell gives a novel turn to this phase of emotional proof.

> The first is *probability,* which is now considered only as an expedient for enlivening passion. Here again there is commonly scope for argument. Probability results from evidence, and begets belief. Belief invigorates our ideas. Belief raised to the highest becomes certainty....
>
> The second circumstance is *plausibility,* a thing totally distinct from the former, as having an effect upon the mind quite independent of faith or probability. It ariseth chiefly from the consistency of the narration, from its being what is commonly called natural and feasible....
>
> The third circumstance I took notice of was *importance,* the appearance of which always tends, by fixing attention more closely, to add brightness and strength to the ideas....
>
> An action may derive importance from its own nature, from those concerned in it as acting or suffering, or from its consequences. It derives importance from its own nature if it be stupendous in its kind, if the result of what is uncommonly great, whether good or bad, passion or invention, virtue or vice, or what in respect of generosity is godlike, what in respect of atrocity is diabolical; it derives importance from those concerned in it when the actors or the sufferers are considerable, on account either of their dignity or of their number, or of both; it derives importance from its consequences when these are remarkable in regard to their greatness, their multitude, their extent, and that either as to the many and distant places affected by them, or as to the future and remote periods to which they may reach, or as to both....
>
> [Fourth], as to *proximity of time,* every one knows that any melancholy incident is the more affecting that it is recent. Hence it is become common with story-tellers, that they may make a deeper impression on their hearers, to introduce remarks like these: that the tale which they relate is not old, that it happened but lately, or in their own time, or that they are yet living who had a part in it or were witnesses of it. Proximity of time regards not only the past, but the future. An event that will probably soon happen hath greater influence upon us than what will probably happen a long time hence....
>
> Local *connexion,* the fifth..., hath a more powerful effect than proximity of time....

Who is not more curious to know the notable transactions which have happened in his own country from the earliest antiquity, than to be acquainted with those which have happened in the remotest regions of the globe, during the century wherein he lives? It must be owned, however, that the former circumstance is more frequently aided by that of personal relation than the latter. Connexion of place not only includes vicinage, but every other local relation, such as being in a province under the same government with us, in a state that is in alliance with us, in a country well known to us, and the like....

Still greater is the power of *relation* to the persons concerned, which was the sixth circumstance mentioned, as this tie is more direct than that which attacheth us to the scene of action. It is the persons, not the place, that are the immediate objects of the passions love or hatred, pity or anger, envy or contempt....

Some have generally greater influence than others; some, again, have greater influence with one person, others with another. They are consanguinity, affinity, friendship, acquaintance, being fellow-citizens, countrymen, of the same surname, language, religion, occupation, and innumerable others....

But of all the connexive circumstances, the most powerful is *interest,* which is the last....

The reason is, a person present with us, whom we see and hear, and who, by words, and looks, and gestures, gives the liveliest signs of his feelings, has the surest and most immediate claim upon our sympathy. We become infected with his passions. We are hurried along by them, and not allowed leisure to distinguish between his relation and our relation, his interest and our interest.[57]

Campbell's treatment of ethical proof centers chiefly about sympathy as the "main engine by which the orator operates on the passions." Whatever weakens sympathy of the hearers toward the speaker militates against the likelihood of his achieving the end consistent with his purpose. Such loss in sympathy may result from (a) a low opinion of the speaker's intellectual abilities, (b) a bad opinion of his moral character, and (c) violent party spirit.

Language in Rhetoric.—Books II and III of *The Philosophy of Rhetoric* deal with style. Campbell remarks:

Eloquence hath always been considered, and very justly, as having a particular connexion with language. It is the intention of eloquence to convey our sentiments into the minds of others, in order to produce a certain effect upon them. Language is the only vehicle by which this conveyance can be made. The art of speaking, then, is not less necessary to the orator than the art of thinking. Without the latter, the former could not have existed; without the former, the latter would be ineffective.[58]

Holding that a sound theory of style requires that the words used be reputable, national, and in present use, he goes on to discuss the canons of good usage. Finally, he treats, and in some detail, the qualities of perspicuity and vivacity as elements of true rhetorical significance. The other elements of importance are purity, elegance, animation, and music.[59]

The Merit of Campbell's Book.—*The Philosophy of Rhetoric* accomplished in part what its author said no moderns had done before, namely, the making of certain improvements on the rules laid down by the Greeks and the Romans. It went even further, by providing a treatise which helped to establish a standard of criticism for public speeches. In Campbell's words, "the artist and the critic are reciprocally subservient and the particular province of each is greatly improved by the assistance of the other."[60]

The over-all dimension of Campbell's contribution to rhetorical theory and criticism is considerable. In the conclusion to his intensive analysis of Campbell's theory of public speaking as derived from a study of the *Philosophy of Rhetoric* and the *Lectures on Systematic Theology and Pulpit Eloquence,* C. W. Edney[61] lists the following distinctive features: (1) Campbell's classification of speech ends in terms of audience response; (2) his conception of audience analysis; (3) his classification of the sources of evidence; and (4) his emphasis upon the use of words to bring out exact meanings.

Whately's Contribution to Argumentative Composition

The Kinds of Argument.—In the introduction to his *Rhetoric,* published in 1828, Richard Whately indicates that in his time the province of rhetoric comprehended two extremes: some looked upon it as "composition in Prose" while others confined it to "Persuasive Speaking." So, he adds, "I propose . . . to adopt a middle course between these two extreme points; and to treat of 'Argumentative Composition,' *generally,* and *exclusively;* considering Rhetoric . . . as an offshoot from Logic."[62] The result is a vigorous and significant restatement of Aristotelian doctrine, with the emphasis placed unmistakably upon the logical mode of proof.

Remarking that the numerous and involved classifications of argument have "contributed so much to lessen the interest and the utility of systems of Rhetoric," Whately proposes to simplify and regularize those divisions. He sets up two principal classes: first, such arguments "as might have been employed—not *as* arguments, but—to *account for* the fact or principle maintained, supposing its truth granted: secondly, such as could *not* be so employed." [63] The former class includes the arguments from probability, such as cause to effect and effect to cause. The latter is of two general types: (a) arguments from sign, including testimony, concurrent circumstance, oaths, negative probabilities, and the like; and (b) arguments from example, including induction, experience and analogy.

The Burden of Proof.—Closely related to the analysis of argument is Whately's discussion of presumption and the burden of proof. He says:

> It is a point of great importance to decide in each case, at the outset, in your own mind, and clearly to point out to the hearer, as occasion may serve, on which side the *Presumption* lies, and to which belongs the (onus probandi) *Burden of Proof.* For though it may often be expedient to bring forward more proofs than can be fairly *demanded* of you, it is always desirable, when this is the case, that it should be *known,* and that the strength of the cause should be estimated accordingly.
>
> According to the most correct use of the term, a 'Presumption' in favor of any supposition, means, not ... a preponderance of probability in its favor, but, such a *preoccupation* of the ground, as implies that it must stand good till some sufficient reason is adduced against it; in short, that the *Burden of proof* lies on the side of him who would dispute it.[64]

Whately goes on to say that a normal measure of common sense

> ... will enable any one to perceive, and to show, on which side the Presumption lies, when once his attention is called to this question; though, for want of attention, it is often overlooked: and on the determination of this question the whole character of a discussion will often very much depend. A body of troops may be perfectly adequate to the defence of a fortress against any attack that may be made on it; and yet, if ignorant of the advantage they possess, they sally forth into the open field to encounter the enemy, they may suffer a repulse. At any rate, even if strong enough to act on the offensive, they ought still to keep possession of their fortress. In like manner, if you have the 'Presumption' on your side, and can but *refute* all the arguments brought against you, you have, for the present at least, gained a victory: but if you abandon this position, by suffering this Presumption to be forgotten, which is in fact *leaving out one of, perhaps, your strongest arguments,* you may appear to be making a feeble attack, instead of a triumphant defence.[65]

As a tentative guide in such a search, Whately offers several suggestions:

There is a Presumption in favor of every *existing* institution. Many of these ... may be susceptible of alteration for the better; but still the 'Burden of Proof' lies with him who proposes an alteration; simply, on the ground that since a change is not a good in itself, he who demands a change should show cause for it. No one is *called on* ... to defend an existing institution, till some argument is adduced against it; and that argument ought in fairness to prove, not merely an actual inconvenience, but the possibility of a change for the better....

There is a 'Presumption' against any thing *paradoxical, i.e.* contrary to the prevailing opinion: it may be true; but the Burden of proof lies with him who maintains it; since men are not to be expected to abandon the prevailing belief till some reason is shown....

A Presumption evidently admits of various degrees of strength, from the very faintest, up to a complete and confident acquiescence.

The person, Body, or book, in favor of whose decisions there is a certain Presumption, is said to have, so far, 'Authority'; in the strict sense of the word. And a recognition of this kind of Authority,—an *habitual* Presumption in favor of such a one's decisions or opinions,—is usually called 'Deference.' ...

Those who are habitually wanting in Deference towards such as we think entitled to it, are usually called 'arrogant;' the word being used as distinguished from self-*conceited, proud, vain,* and other kindred words. Such persons may be described as having an habitual and exclusive 'self-deference.' ...

With some persons, ... Authority seems to act according to the law of Gravitation; inversely as the squares of the *distances*. They are inclined to be of the opinion of the person who is *nearest*. Personal *Affection*, again, in many minds, generates Deference. They form a habit of first, *wishing,* secondly, *hoping,* and thirdly, *believing* a person to be in the right, whom they would be *sorry* to think mistaken....

... though ... questions of *fact* and of *opinion,* ought to be decided on very different grounds, yet, with many persons, a statement of facts is very little attended to when coming from one for whose judgment (though they do not deliberately doubt his veracity) they have little or no Deference....

It is to be observed, that a Presumption may be *rebutted* by an opposite Presumption, so as to shift the Burden of proof to the other side....

Again, there is ... a presumption ... in respect of each question, in favor of the judgment of the most eminent men in the department it pertains to;—of eminent physicians, *e.g.* in respect of medical questions, ...

But there is a counter-presumption, arising from the circumstance that men eminent in any department are likely to regard with jealousy any one who professes to bring to light something unknown to themselves; especially if it promise to *supersede,* if established, much of what they have been accustomed to learn, and teach, and practise.[66]

Whately recognizes a difference between the understanding and the will of the individual, and to this extent he accepts the dichotomy of persuasion and conviction in rhetorical appeal. He also senses the fact, however, that the two processes are interrelated, as these passages reveal:

> The *Conviction* of the understanding ... is an essential *part* of Persuasion; and will generally need to be effected by the Arguments of the Writer or Speaker. For in order that the Will may be influenced, two things are requisite; *viz.* 1. that the proposed *Object* should appear desirable; and 2. that the *Means* suggested should be proved to be conducive to the attainment of that object; and this last, evidently must depend on a process of Reasoning. ...
>
> Persuasion, therefore, depends on first, *Argument,* (to prove the expediency of the Means proposed,) and secondly, what is usually called *Exhortation,* i.e. the excitement of men to adopt those Means, by representing the end as sufficiently desirable.[67]

Advocacy of the Natural Manner in Delivery.—A final distinguishing feature of Whately's *Rhetoric* is his stricture upon the elocutionary methods of delivery, and his recommendation of the Natural Manner. Apropos of the artificial systems of the elocutionists, he remarks that his objection to their emphasis upon *delivery* is not a recommendation for *general inattention* to that aspect of rhetoric.

> But it is evident that if any one wishes to *assume the Speaker* as far as possible, *i.e.,* to deliver a written composition with some degree of the manner and effect of one that is extemporaneous, he will have a considerable difficulty to surmount: since though this may be called, in a certain sense, the Natural Manner, it is far from being what he will naturally, *i.e., spontaneously,* fall into. It is by no means natural for any one to *read* as if he were *not* reading, but speaking. And again, even when any one is reading what he does not wish to deliver as his own composition, ... it is evident that this may be done better or worse, in infinite degrees; and that though ... a studied attention to the sounds uttered, at the time of uttering them, leads to an affected and offensive delivery, yet, on the other hand, an utterly careless reader cannot be a good one.[68]

The practical rule which Whately adopts, then, is

> ... not only to pay no studied attention to the Voice, but studiously to *withdraw* the thoughts from it, and to dwell as intently as possible on

the Sense, trusting to nature to suggest spontaneously the proper emphases and tones.[69]

The orator who follows these suggestions will not attain perfection immediately, but

> ... he may be assured that, while he steadily adheres to this plan, he is in the right road to it; instead of becoming,—as on the other plan,— more and more artificial, the longer he studies. And every advance he makes will produce a proportional effect: it will give him more and more of that hold on the attention, the understanding, and the feelings of the audience, which no studied modulation can ever attain. Others indeed may be more successful in escaping censure, and insuring admiration; but he will far more surpass them, in respect of the proper object of the Orator, which is, *to carry his point.*[70]

Final Appraisal.—Perhaps there is little in Whately's book that is distinctly new. Wayland M. Parrish feels that its chief claim to originality "must consist ... in his novelty of illustration and of arrangement."[71] But the *Rhetoric* has a good Aristotelian flavor. It contains new and refreshing classifications of old facts; and it introduces some material—particularly on presumption and the burden of proof—which students of argumentative discourse should find helpful. Among the other distinctive features of the rhetorical scheme, according to Orville L. Pence,[72] are (1) Whately's clarification of the concepts of *sign, example,* and *probability* in logical proof; (2) his analysis of fallacies, and particularly those arising from ambiguity; (3) his differentiation of analogy and example; and (4) his inquiry into the calculation of probability as affording sufficient reasons for action.

Recent Contributions

A host of scholars, both in Speech and in other divisions of knowledge, have contributed richly to the field of rhetoric and public speaking during the twentieth century. It is plainly impossible to record a full list of the contributors. Many have refined certain of the techniques and theoretical details previously set forth by the classical rhetoricians; some have conducted experimental research into problems having a direct bearing upon our conception of public address; and still others have attempted to articulate the classical and the scientific data into more realistic systems of instruction. All of these varied inquiries have helped to sustain and further the field of Speech.

While acknowledging the numerous contributions of the past fifty years, we might yet single out a specific development which has exercised a profound influence on the theory and teaching of public speaking in America. Relying upon the data of each other's fields, the rhetorician and the psychologist have pooled some of their resources and, accordingly, have enlarged the conception of the speaker-audience relationship. A respected name in this development is that of James A. Winans who, in 1915, published the textbook *Public Speaking* in which a substantially new theory of persuasion was announced. Basing his treatment largely upon the psychological concepts of William James, Winans developed a theory of public address in which *attention* became the focal principle. Persuasion, he said, is a process through which hearers are induced to give attention to the ideas set forth by a speaker. On this premise he established a system which explored the psychological ramifications of the intellectual and emotional processes operative in the act of communicating thought and feeling to an audience.

Although a considerable body of new psychological data has been amassed since 1915, (and especially on the dynamic forces of motives, interests, and desires as they affect the reception of logical propositions), Winans' *Public Speaking* still remains the greatest contribution to rhetorical theory since George Campbell's *Philosophy of Rhetoric*.

General Summary

The three hundred year period between the appearance of the first rhetoric in the English language and the contributions of Richard Whately produced substantial improvements in the adaptation of rhetorical theory to modern conditions. Beginning with Cox and carrying through the mid-nineteenth century, the scholars of the period took the cardinal principles of speechcraft derived from antiquity, gave them current expression, refined some of their outmoded features, added such new ones as would accommodate the art to the new day, and thus established the pattern for much of the theoretical substructure in present day textbooks on speech composition and debate.

Cox, Wilson, Campbell, Bacon, and Whately helped to revitalize the classical tradition in rhetoric. Furthermore, they demonstrated that tradition is not inimical to change; that to be guided by it is not necessarily to violate the laws of progressive adaptation to the changing conditions of cultural growth. Campbell and Whately, especially, show how effectively competent writers can use the wisdom of the past in formulating the principles of an art for the present. They used the basic rhetorical principles of the ancients simply as a springboard to facilitate their movement in the realities of their age. In an uncommonly significant way, their works reveal what can be done by the moderns who are not reluctant to sever certain ties with the past.

PART III

THE METHODS OF THE CRITICS

Chapter 5

THE CRITICS OF ANTIQUITY

Introduction

Establishment of a Point of View.—We have already referred to the manifest interrelation of theory, practice, and criticism. Nearly all writers on rhetorical theory are, in a very real if not a formal sense, critics of speaking. The distinction between theory and criticism is, then, hard to draw, and even the most modest attempt to review the work of the critics of orators will become fabulously detailed unless certain common-sense differentia are established.

It is necessary, therefore, that we distinguish between the critics of *oratory as a subject,* and the critics of *orators per se;* likewise, that we discriminate between the critics who appraise a *general class* or *group of orators,* and those who evaluate *particular members of the class.*

Plato's Analysis of Rhetoric.—Plato was one of the most discerning critics of oratory. His appraisal is, however, more directly concerned with rhetoric as a field of inquiry than it is with the particular excellences or defects of the practitioners of the art. Indeed, Plato directs his indictment against the Sophists and the orators, but behind these attacks is the studied attempt to reveal the inherent weaknesses of rhetoric as a system which trains people for active participation in public life. Because the art of rhetoric admits of separations from truth, often employs questionable techniques in order to achieve persuasion, and hence exercises an unwholesome influence upon the social group, Plato dislikes it; he evaluates it, and finds it wanting, at least in the form which it assumed during his time.

Although it is impossible to determine the absolute beginnings of criticism in any field, many significant doctrines of critical inquiry into rhetoric can be traced back to Plato. Like many of the early Greeks, he was given to philosophizing; and in the recently invented art of rhetoric he found opportunity to apply his intellectual skills. The result was the stricture against a rhetoric which concerned itself

with "nonessentials," and the subsequent development of his own
Ideal Theory which emphasized the importance of subject matter;
recognized the need of natural endowment, knowledge of art, and
practice; stressed the desirability of order and arrangement of materials; and insisted upon the speaker's having a thorough knowledge
of emotional behavior. In postulating an ideal theory of rhetoric,
Plato went far toward establishing critical standards for the art.

It should be noted, of course, that Plato also evaluated the work
of individual orators. Thus, in the *Phaedrus,* he offers a critical
analysis of Lysias' speaking; in the *Protagoras,* he virtually "paro-
dies" the work of Protagoras and Hippias; in the speech of
Pausanias, in the *Symposium,* he criticizes the "unmeaning tricks of
rhythm and the neglect of ordered thought then fashionable"; and so
on through a long list of examples. However, these individual evaluations are subordinate, both in purpose and in value, to the broad
critical investigation of rhetoric as an art. And since rhetoric in
antiquity embraced practically all prose literature, we find in Plato's
work the first solid contribution to a philosophy of expression. By
urging adherence to the *essentials* of the rhetorical art, he placed
criticism "on an exalted plane." [1]

Aristotle's Point of View.—Aristotle's great philosophic contribution to the theory of public address also results from a critical
indictment of what he called a false system of rhetoric. Atkins believes that with the *Poetics* and the *Rhetoric* "we have reached one
of the supreme moments in critical history." [2] In the early part of
the *Rhetoric,* Aristotle expresses his opposition to those writers and
systems which stress the "mere accessories"—the appeals to the emotions—and consequently neglect the logical proofs which are the
"true constituents" of the art. He also criticizes previous writers
for devoting all their attention to forensic oratory, despite the fact
that political speaking "admits less of malicious sophistry than judicial pleading." Then follows his development of a theory of
rhetoric which outlines the practical details of speechcraft and also
sets forth a fairly complete rationale of the subject.

Plan Employed in Examining the Methodology of the Critics.
—Both the Platonic and Aristotelian treatises provide partial yardsticks for the critical evaluation of oratory. The consideration of
these works in previous chapters illustrates the nature of the contributions. The display of theoretical detail also reveals the essential
aspects of the critiques which the authors establish, at least indirectly, for appraising individual speeches. It is to be noted, however,

that neither the *Phaedrus* nor the *Rhetoric* was intended as a treatise on the criticism of speeches, and whatever use we make of them in that regard today is purely incidental and extra-functional to their original design.

In this chapter we shall summarize briefly the methodology employed by a selected group of critics who not only had a philosophy of rhetoric, but also were patently interested in appraising the activities of certain orators; we will consider writers who, directly concerned with the criticism of speeches or speakers, offered at least partially systematic plans for carrying out their purpose. We shall also make incidental reference to a few individuals whose contributions to a critique of speechcraft are not specifically covered in preceding chapters.

The controlling *rationale* for the chapter is twofold: (1) We shall reveal the method which the critic used in the evaluation of speeches; and (2) we shall attempt to isolate the *principle*, or determining point of view, which guided each critic in his evaluative undertaking.

A Necessary Condition for Criticism.—J. E. Spingarn once observed that the purpose of criticism was chiefly the interpretation of finished productions, and that the intellectual processes involved in the effort were vitally akin "to those which first produced the works themselves. . . ." [3] Both creation and criticism presuppose, therefore, a certain degree of cultural progress which permits the free use of the imagination and the intellect.

But critical inquiry needs more than a measure of cultural attainment. It requires, for full expression, what D'Alton calls "a certain advance in self-consciousness." There must be an acknowledgment, a recognition, of the place that the novel or the speech or the play occupies in the continuum of artistic endeavor, and an awareness of the critic's relation to the particular work. Whereas the orator, for example, might fashion an effective speech through his natural instinct for expression, coupled with his awareness of the social significance of the words, the critic, if he were to rely upon the same resources, would doubtless fail to get beyond the boundaries imposed by those limitations, unless he also had a growing consciousness of the philosophy or the *why* of the activity to govern and direct his intellectual efforts.

Correlative to the presupposition that a stage of self-consciousness is a necessary condition of critical inquiry is the all-important necessity of a *standard of comparison.* Evaluative judgments derive their substance from comparisons; and finished criticism results from the reasoned application of a certain production to the criteria of a model or standard of reference. Thus competent criticism of Cicero's oratory is facilitated because the Demosthenean model is available for comparison. Contemporary political oratory yields more easily to intelligent appraisal because the eighteenth century produced a model philosophic speaker in the person of Edmund Burke.

The Atticist-Asianist Controversy

Cicero's distinction as a rhetorical critic derives in large part from his controversy with the men who set up an ideal in Attic oratory and who charged him with Asiatic tendencies. "Asianism" in rhetoric meant all that was florid, luxuriant, even bombastic; Atticism implied tempered restraint and decorum in expression. The declamations on fictitious themes, discussed previously, may well be considered the extremes in Asiatic quality. Cicero did not, of course, live to witness the most pronounced artificialities of declamatory utterance, but he was thoroughly conversant with the Asiatic characteristics. D'Alton asserts that it is one of Cicero's "great merits as a critic that, before he could witness Asianism in its most perverted form, he was able to put his finger on many of its corrupt tendencies." [4]

The Pivotal Position of Style.—The quarrel between the Atticists and the Asianists was largely over matters of style. D'Alton looks upon Atticism as "a movement towards the Ancients," characterized by an attempt to set up the great orators of the past as models of effective prose. On the other hand, Asianism was "more indicative of the modern tendencies in Rhetoric," with its consequent attachment to the living speech and its possible defects. [5]

The true source of Asianism is difficult to trace. Certain aspects of it, however, may go back to the earliest Sophists with whom Plato quarreled because of their stylistic extravagances. The Gorgian influence, with its appeal to rhythmical effect and figurative embellishment, was particularly pervasive. But the greatest excesses in style—those which made the term Asianism offensive to the purists —came with the decline of oratory, the loss of political liberty, and the subsequent declamatory practice divorced from the realities of the everyday world.

Among the Roman orators who favored a revival of the true Attic standards in prose style were Calvus and Calidius, both of whom were active in forensic pleadings about 60 B.C. These men, as the mouthpieces of the Neo-Atticist movement, were staunch advocates of the Plain style. They favored a style characterized by simplicity, restraint, purity, correctness, and clearness. Cicero praises Calvus for his nicety of language and for his good taste, but believes that his exacting concern for refinement of style "suffered all the force and spirit of it to evaporate." Quintilian also remarks on the circumstance of Calvus' imposing such severe criticism upon himself as to diminish his natural force as a speaker. As for Calidius, Cicero commended his precision and nicety of expression, but, as in the case of Calvus, believed that the meticulous regard for Attic simplicity and correctness militated against his oratorical effectiveness. That Calidius was able to *instruct* and to *please* his hearers, Cicero did not doubt. But that he would be able to carry out the third phase of an orator's business, namely, *to move the passions,* Cicero contested. "He had no force, no exertion," Cicero alleged, "and as a result, had no influence over the feelings of his hearers." [6]

Cicero's Place in the Controversy.—Cicero's *De Oratore* does not reveal clearly the presence of the Atticist-Asianist controversy. In all probability, the issues did not enter open dispute until after its publication. However, D'Alton believes "it is more than probable that the treatise was accepted as a challenge by those whose ideal of style differed from that of Cicero, and who felt themselves aggrieved by his exaltation of a style which some of them at least would regard as extravagant and bombastic." D'Alton quotes H. Heck as saying that, upon the publication of the *De Oratore,* Calvus stigmatized the Ciceronian ideal as Asianist. But D'Alton thinks that "Cicero's critics directed their attack quite as much against his practice as against his theory." "At any rate," he continues, "they took up the position that the Plain Style characterized by elegance, restraint, and purity of diction, was the genuine Attic style, and that they alone were the true representatives of the Attic tradition." [7]

In the *De Oratore,* Cicero announces the functions of the orator, saying they are to inform, to conciliate, and to move the listeners. He also comments on the kind of style peculiarly suited to each of these functions. Thus the Grand and the Plain styles are contrasted, the distinctions centering sometimes about changes in delivery and, at other times, about matters of composition and diction. There can be no doubt, however, that Cicero evinces in the *De Oratore* a preference for the Grand style. In fact, the Plain and the Middle styles receive treatment that is far short of systematic; whereas the emphasis upon a rich, impassioned, and moving style immediately attracts

notice. Cicero appeals for copiousness in expression, for, as he saw
it, "the proper concern of an orator . . . is language of power and
elegance accommodated to the feelings and understandings of mankind." [8]

The *De Oratore* does not, however, contain severe strictures on
the Plain style. Surely Cicero expresses a preference for the Grand,
but he speaks temperately of the shortcomings of the other types. He
praises the Stoic conception of style for its subtlety and acuity, but
affirms that it is not well adapted to oratory on great issues before
assembled multitudes. Furthermore, he praises the "extremely keen
and subtle species of oratory" practiced by Cotta who was, as D'Alton
remarks, a true "Atticist in pre-Atticist days at Rome." And Cicero
is free to admit that different orators achieve eminence in their own
ways, without imitating anyone or any standard of excellence. A
pointed observation is made by Cicero in the *Brutus* when he remarks that there are two classes of *good* orators,

> . . . of which the former are distinguished by the simple neatness and
> brevity of their language, and the latter by their copious dignity and
> elevation; but although the preference must always be given to that
> which is great and striking; yet, in speakers of real merit, whatever is
> most perfect of the kind is justly entitled to our commendation. It
> must, however, be observed, that the close and simple orator should be
> careful not to sink into a dryness and poverty of expression; while, on
> the other hand, the copious and more stately speaker should be equally
> on his guard against a swelling and empty parade of words.[9]

The works of Cicero in which evidence of the quarrel with the
Atticists is most pronounced are the *Orator, Brutus,* and *On the Best
Style of the Orators.* In these works, Cicero is not only defending
a thesis; he is also defending his personal reputation. Having for
some time been the great leader and virtual model of oratorical excellence, he resented the move to establish other men as the true representatives of the best style in speaking. The Atticists announced
their preference for the Plain style; accordingly, they regarded
Lysias as their model.

Cicero was not disposed to contest Lysias' claim to eminence. In
fact, in the early part of the *Brutus,* he remarks that one might almost
call Lysias a "complete orator." But, said Cicero, the Atticists were
not sufficiently severe in their critical judgment when they set up
Attic orators as models while at the same time holding that the Plain
style was almost synonymous with Attic oratory.

> But which of them does he mean to fix upon? for they are not all of
> the same cast. Who, for instance, could be more unlike each other

than Demosthenes and Lysias? or than Demosthenes and Hyperides? Or who more different from either of them than Aeschines? Which of them, then, do you propose to imitate? If only *one,* this will be a tacit implication that none of the rest were true masters of Atticism; if *all,* how can you possibly succeed, when their characters are so opposite? Let me farther ask you, whether Demetrius Phalereus spoke in the Attic style? In my opinion, his orations have the very taste of Athens. But he is certainly more florid than either Hyperides or Lysias; partly from the natural turn of his genius, and partly by choice.[10]

Thus Cicero shows that Atticism may mean any one of several things, it being a notorious fact that even Hegesias, a thoroughgoing Asianist, claimed that he followed Attic models and "was so vain of his own taste for Atticism that he considered his predecessors, who were really masters of it, as mere rustics in comparison with himself." [11]

Cicero would not have disapproved of Thucydides as a model of Plain style, provided one were interested in "composing histories instead of pleading causes."

For Thucydides was both an exact and a stately historian; but he never intended to write models for conducting a judicial process. I will even go so far as to add, that I have often commended the speeches which he has inserted in his history in great numbers; though I must frankly own that I neither *could* imitate them if I *would,* nor *would* if I *could.* . . .[12]

In another work, Cicero voices the same sentiment, affirming that Thucydides has no real connection with the orator since "it is one thing to unfold the actions of men in a narration, and quite a different one to accuse and get rid of an accusation by arguing." [13]

To Demosthenes, Cicero grants unconditional recognition as the complete, or supreme orator.

No keen, no artful turns could have been contrived for the pleadings he has left behind him, which he did not readily discover; nothing could have been expressed with greater nicety, or more clearly and poignantly, than it has been already expressed by him; and nothing greater, nothing more rapid and forcible, nothing adorned with a nobler elevation, either of language or sentiment, can be conceived, than what is to be found in his orations.[14]

Cicero attempts to show that Demosthenes was always his model; that the imitation of his excellences was the goal toward which he directed his efforts and his wishes. Thus Cicero tries to harmonize his avowed preference for the Grand style with the Demosthenean idea of Attic simplicity.

This attempted reconciliation is not completely consistent with the generally accepted view that the complete orator, or the ideal model, should be a master of all three styles. Cicero believed, however, that only an impassioned and rich style of oratory could move multitudes to action. Not that he condoned Asianist tendencies of an extreme sort. He condemned the defects present in the orators of the Asian school; and he listed certain faults which Attic speakers should avoid, among them "a dry and lifeless manner." Perhaps a note of the specious is found in Cicero's defense of his position, for in his early speeches he yielded to some of the Asian excesses which he subsequently condemned.

Cicero's position in the Atticist controversy is, therefore, not completely unequivocal. D'Alton's interpretation of a passage in the *Brutus* furnishes a valuable hint of Cicero's view. According to D'Alton, Cicero looked upon Asianism as "an excess of the Grand style. Just as the orator of the Plain style had to beware of becoming bald and jejune (a tendency marked among the Atticists, according to Cicero), so the orator of the Grand style had to guard against passing into tasteless bombast." [15] Despite his respect for the Grand style, Cicero recognized the folly of using it when the minds of the hearers were not properly prepared for it.

> For the man who can say nothing with calmness, nothing with gentleness; who seems ignorant of all arrangement and definition and distinctness, and regardless of wit, especially when some of his causes required to be treated in that manner entirely, and others in a great degree; if he does not prepare the ears of his hearers before he begins to work up the case in an inflammatory style, he seems like a madman among people in their senses, or like a drunken man among sober men.[16]

In the opinion of D'Alton, this "distinction between the Grand style and the excesses to which it might easily lead, is a point of cardinal importance." [17]

Cicero's controversy with the Atticists included critical appraisals of compositional elements and rhythm, as well as of the general features of the kinds of style. The advocates of the Plain style, naturally, were suspicious of rhythmical qualities in prose; they looked upon them as contributing little or nothing to clearness and correctness of speech. Furthermore, rhythmic qualities, openly sought by the speaker, tended to create a certain measure of artificiality; they nurtured a symmetry in form and structure which was removed from the natural expression of plain speech.

In the *Orator,* Cicero discusses rhythm at considerable length, treating its nature, causes, and fields of effective operation. He insists that the prose movement should be pleasing to the ear, this quality resulting largely from the use of symmetrical clauses and the traditional feet employed in poetry. Although Cicero defends vigorously the use of rhythm in speech, he is anxious to assure his readers that oratory chiefly for rhythmical effect is pointless. Those elements which please the ear should not command the attention, to the exclusion of subject matter. Likewise, the orator should be mindful that spontaneity in rhythmic effect is indispensable. Impressiveness of prose movement should be indissolubly linked with impressiveness of sentiment, thought, and language.

All in all, Cicero's defense of rhythm and his announcement of its limitations amount to a defense of his own style of speaking, of his own practice over a long period of years. The Atticists, in their advocacy of the Plain style, were levelling their criticism as much against Cicero's performances as against his critical theory. Cicero's replies served, therefore, both to set up a standard of criticism for oratory and to offer a veiled apology and vindication of his own practice.

The Versatile Genius of Cicero in the Realm of Criticism

Cicero's most important critical works are the *Orator* and the *Brutus.* The purpose of the first was to present a view of the Ideal Orator; it was as Torsten Petersson remarks, "Cicero's final statement not only of his oratorical ideal but also of what he conceived himself to have attained." [18] In one sense, it contained substantially the same content as the *De Oratore,* but the expression of it was fundamentally different. Evidently Cicero tried, though with not too much expectation of success, to win Brutus over to his position in the quarrel with the Atticists. Through the medium of the *Orator,* in which he delineated the character of the ideal speaker, he revealed himself as the master of oratorical excellence, worthy of imitation and support. Since Brutus did not approve of emotional oratory, it seems reasonable to believe that Cicero's argument in the *Orator* failed to draw him away from his Atticist sympathies. It should be borne in mind, however, as G. L. Hendrickson says, that it was "an outgrowth and product of dissenting criticism." Since the *Orator* is, by its nature, critical rather than didactic—there being a positive minimum of precept in it—it seems likely that this work, which Sandys called an "aesthetics of oratory," was intended both as a justification of Cicero's style and as a criticism of those who dissented from his theory of rhetoric.

The Importance of the *Brutus*.—The *Brutus* is the first comprehensive history and criticism of orators and oratory. Written, as was the *Orator,* about 46 B.C., it is Cicero's most original treatise. Devoted almost exclusively to historical exposition and criticism, it contains a didactic note; it involves a veiled attempt to influence Brutus by showing how certain orators had failed to achieve distinction. In the *Brutus,* Cicero directs his argument against the style of oratory which the Atticists encouraged, and of which Calvus was the most distinguished advocate. "Under the appearance of historical objectivity," says Hendrickson; "Cicero seeks to effect an inductive proof in vindication of his own position, showing by appeal to history that the type of emotional discursive oratory which he himself represented had always been the more admired and effective." [19]

Cicero was anxious to reveal in the *Brutus,* as he had in the *De Oratore,* that the attainment of great skill in eloquence was a difficult task, and that few men ever achieved the heights of effectiveness. Whether it was attained by art, nature, or practice, eloquence, he affirmed, "is the most difficult of all attainments. . . ." When in the course of the dialogue, Atticus reminds Cicero that he is discussing some men who were really the "dregs of oratory," Cicero replies: "I wish it to be noticed, that after recounting all who ever ventured to speak in public, we find but few (very few indeed!) whose names are worth recording, and not many who had even the repute of being orators." [20] Without imputing evil design to him, it can be appreciated that the job of making his own oratorical mastery shine forth in a brighter light was made easier by commenting on the arduousness of the assignment, and by contrasting his accomplishments with the shortcomings of many other orators, some relatively insignificant.

In the *Brutus,* we find a fairly large number of short critical appraisals of Greek and Roman speakers with some reputation for eloquence, from earliest times to Cicero's own day. Naturally, however, the treatment of the Greeks is short in Cicero's work. But the fact that he drew upon them for comparative study is important in the development of criticism. It is freely accepted that a critic has a great advantage if he can compare the products of two languages. Without this comparison, George Saintsbury once remarked, "not merely is the diagnosis of qualities mostly guesswork, but even the

discovery of them becomes extremely difficult." [21] Cicero took advantage of this opportunity as fully as the available materials would
permit.

Method Employed in Cicero's Criticism.—Cicero's use of the
historical method in the *Brutus* is particularly noteworthy. Taking
oratory as his theme, he traces the development of speaking achievement from early times to his own period. More than that, he shows
that a principle of growth or improvement operates to heighten the
effectiveness of orators as the years go by, until finally, perhaps in
Cicero's own person, we find the realization of consummate, if not
perfect, skill. A principle of progress is thus enunciated; and the
history of the orators, as Cicero presents it, reveals its operation and
movement toward a mature manner of oral expression.

The dictum upon which Cicero's historical investigation rests derives from a discussion of sculpture and painting. Commenting on
the fact that artistic expression in those fields did not spring into
fullest glory at one time—but, instead, developed and improved
through a process of orderly refinement—Cicero concludes that the
same is true in other arts, including oratory. There "is not one of
them," according to his key remark, "which was invented and carried
to perfection at the same time." This principle suggests two important things: First, it postulates the doctrine of gradual development in the realization of the highest oratorical skill, both in the
individual and in the oratory of a nation; and second, it establishes
the concept of continuity in oratorical literature—the conviction that,
as Atkins suggests, orations "are not isolated phenomena, but products related to one another. . . ." [22]

Precisely what the criteria of progress in oratory are, Cicero does
not express clearly. An interpretation of the text suggests, however,
that he was thinking of the orator's growing facility in emotional
expression, of his attainments in learning and rhetorical skill, of his
development of an effective prose style, and of his power to move
audiences, as well as to instruct and please.

The Ciceronian conception of historical method in criticism includes another tenet which serves the critic of oratory well. In the
Orator, Cicero remarks that the "prudence of the hearers has always
been the regulator of the eloquence of the orators. For all men who
wish to be approved of, regard the inclination of these men who are
their hearers, and form and adapt themselves entirely to their opinions and wishes." [23] He then continues:

. . . in Caria and Phrygia and Mysia, which are nations of no very
great refinement or eloquence, men have adopted a sort of fat and

coarse kind of oratory, as best suited to their ears, which their neighbours the Rhodians, though separated from them by only a narrow sea,
have never approved of; and the Greeks still less; and which the
Athenians have utterly rejected; for they have at all times had a
discerning and accurate judgment, so as to be unable to tolerate anything which was not pure and elegant. And as the orator was bound
to comply with their doctrine on the subject, he never dared to make
use of any unusual or ill-sounding expression.[24]

In other words, Cicero regarded men as moulded by the age in which
they lived; that they were shaped by their environment, and, as far
as oratory was concerned, were to be judged by the criteria or
standards of their period. Thus Cicero recognizes a certain relativity in standards based upon the varying conditions of the environment and culture in which orators participate. "Considering the time
in which he lived," says Cicero of Quintus Pompeius, he was "no
contemptible orator." Admitting that Cato's language had an "anti-
quated air" and that some of his expressions were "harsh and inelegant," Cicero asks us to remember that "this was the language of
the time...." "... only change and modernize it, which it was not
in his [Cato's] power to do; add the improvements of number and
cadence, give an easier turn to his sentences, and regulate the structure and connection of his words, and you will find no one who can
claim the preference to Cato." [25] This indicates Cicero's recognition
of the fact that the standards of criticism must fit the standards of
oratorical achievement at a given period in history. Needless to say,
this is a significant contribution to a philosophy of critical analysis.

The Bases of Cicero's Oratorical Appraisals.—We have observed
that Cicero used the historical method in preparing the studies in the
Brutus. How, specifically, did he apply the method to the several
orators?

The basis of Cicero's work derives from the more or less conventional divisions and classifications of rhetoric. Thus, in the first
place, he appraises speakers according as they conform to his formula
for success in the art. To what extent do the speakers evince natural
endowment, thorough familiarity with the rules of the art, and seasoned practice in the use of the theory? The trinity of nature, art,
and practice serves as a tool for the determination of essential
strength or weakness. The following quotation from Cicero's
analysis of Scaurus' oratory indicates the way in which the critic
used the prerequisites for oratorical success as guides to evaluation:

It will not be amiss to give a short account of Scaurus and Rutilius; neither of whom, indeed, had the reputation of being a first-rate orator, though each of them pleaded a number of causes. But some deserving men, who were not remarkable for their genius, may be justly commended for their industry; not that the persons I am speaking of were really destitute of genius, but only of that particular kind of it which distinguishes the orator. For it is of little consequence to discover what is *proper* to be said, unless you are able to express it in a free and agreeable manner; and even that will be insufficient, if not recommended by the voice, the look, and the gesture. It is needless to add, that much depends upon *art;* for though, even without this, it is possible, by the mere force of nature, to say many striking things; yet, as they will after all be nothing more than so many lucky hits, we shall not be able to repeat them at our pleasure. The style of Scaurus, who was a very sensible and an honest man, was remarkably grave, and commanded the respect of the hearer; so that, when he was speaking for his client, you would rather have thought he was giving evidence in his favor than pleading his cause. This manner of speaking, however, though but indifferently adapted to the bar, was very much so to a calm debate in the senate, of which Scaurus was then esteemed the father; for it not only bespoke his prudence, but, what was still a more important recommendation, his credibility. This advantage, which it is not easy to acquire by art, he derived entirely from nature; though you know that even *here* we have some precepts to assist us.[26]

Another way in which Cicero appraised the orators was through the use of the ends of oratory. In the *De Oratore,* he remarks that persuasion consists of three processes: instructing, conciliating, and moving the listeners.[27] The first duty requires "mildness of address"; the second, "penetration"; and the third, "energy." Cicero believed, it will be recalled, that the great orator was one who could move listeners to action. Consequently, Cicero could not follow the Atticists in their unconditional advocacy of the Plain style.

In comparing the respective skills of Crassus and Scaevola, Cicero turns to the oratorical functions for his guide. Speaking of the trial of Manius Curius, he says:

. . . no man could explain and define, or discuss a point of equity, with a more copious facility than Crassus, as sufficiently appeared upon many other occasions, but particularly in the cause of Manius Curius, which was tried before the centumviri. For he urged a great variety of arguments in the defense of right and equity, against the literal *jubet* of the law; and supported them by such a numerous series of precedents, that he overpowered Quintus Scaevola . . . though the case before them was only a matter of legal right. But the cause was so ably managed by the two advocates, who were nearly of an age, and both of consular rank, that while each endeavored to interpret the law in favor of his client, Crassus was universally allowed to be the best lawyer among the orators, and Scaevola to be the most eloquent civilian of the age; for the latter could not only discover with the nicest precision what was agreeable to law and equity, but had likewise a conciseness and propriety of expression which was admirably adapted to his purpose. In short, he had such a wonderful vein of oratory in commenting, explaining, and discussing, that I never beheld his equal; though in amplifying, embellishing, and refuting, he was rather to be dreaded as a formidable critic, than admired as an eloquent speaker.[28]

Another instance of the use of the ends of speaking as the yardstick of critical measurement is found in Cicero's analysis of Calidius' oratory.

Nothing could be so easy as the turn and compass of his periods; nothing so ductile; nothing more pliable and obsequious to his will; so that he had a greater command of words than any orator whatever. In short, the flow of his language was so pure and limpid that nothing could be clearer, and so free that it was never clogged or obstructed. Every word was exactly in the place where it should be, and disposed . . . with as much nicety as in a curious piece of mosaic work. We may add, that he had not a single expression which was either harsh, unnatural, abject, or far-fetched; and yet he was so far from confining himself to the plain and ordinary mode of speaking, that he abounded greatly in the metaphor—but such metaphors as did not appear to usurp a post that belonged to another, but only to occupy their own. These delicacies were displayed, not in a loose and effeminate style, but in such a one as was strictly *numerous,* without either appearing to be so, or running on with a dull uniformity of sound. He was likewise master of the various ornaments of language and thought which the Greeks call *figures,* whereby he enlivened and embellished his style as with so many forensic decorations. We may add that he readily discovered, upon all occasions, what was the real point of debate, and where the stress of the argument lay; and that his method of ranging his ideas was extremely artful, his action gentlemanly, and his whole manner very engaging and very sensible. In short, if to speak agreeably is the chief merit of an orator, you will find no one who was better qualified than Calidius.

But as we have observed a little before that it is the business of an orator to instruct, to please, and *to move the passions,* he was, indeed, perfectly master of the first two; for no one could better elucidate his subject, or charm the attention of his audience. But as to the third qualification, the moving and alarming the passions, which is of much greater efficacy than the former, he was wholly destitute of it.

He had no force, no exertion; either by his own choice, and from an opinion that those who had a loftier turn of expression, and a more warm and spirited action, were little better than mad men; or because it was contrary to his natural temper and habitual practice; or, lastly, because it was beyond the strength of his abilities. If, indeed, it is a useless quality, his want of it was a real excellence; but if otherwise, it was certainly a defect. I particularly remember, that when he prosecuted Quintus Gallius for an attempt to poison him, and pretended that he had the plainest proofs of it, and could produce many letters, witnesses, information, and other evidences to put the truth of his charge beyond a doubt, interspersing many sensible and ingenious remarks on the nature of the crime—I remember, I say, that when it came to my turn to reply to him, after urging every argument which the case itself suggested, I insisted upon it as a material circumstance in favor of my client that the prosecutor, while he charged him with the design against his life, and assured us that he had the most indubitable proofs of it then in his hands, related his story with as much ease, and as much calmness and indifference, as if nothing had happened. 'Would it have been possible,' said I (addressing myself to Calidius), 'that you should speak with this air of unconcern, unless the charge was purely an invention of your own? And, above all, that you, whose eloquence has often vindicated the wrongs of other people with so much spirit, should speak so coolly of a crime which threatened your life? Where was that expression of resentment which is so natural to the injured? Where that ardor, that eagerness, which extorts the most pathetic language even from men of the dullest capacities? There was no visible disorder in your mind, no emotion in your looks and gesture, no smiting of the thigh or the forehead, nor even a single stamp of the foot. You were, therefore, so far from interesting our feelings in your favor, that we could scarcely keep our eyes open while you were relating the dangers you had so narrowly escaped.' . . . 'But is it possible to doubt,' cried Brutus, 'whether this was a sensible quality or a defect? For as the greatest merit of an orator is to be able to inflame the passions, and give them such a bias as shall best answer his purpose, he who is destitute of this must certainly be deficient in the most capital part of his profession.' 'I am of the same opinion,' said I. . . .[29]

In Cicero's treatises we find full recognition of the five parts of rhetoric. This traditional classification serves also as a framework about which to assemble his critical comments on the orators. Thus, when Cicero appraises Antonius' speaking, he deals specifically with invention—Antonius' comprehension of "everything which could be of service to his cause"; with disposition—"as a skillful general posts the cavalry, the infantry, and the light troops, where each of them can act to most advantage, so Antonius drew up his arguments in those parts of his discourses, where they were likely to have the best effect"; with the "quick and retentive memory"; with elocution—his "language, indeed, was not so refined as to pass for the standard of elegance; for which reason he was thought to be rather a careless speaker; and yet, on the other hand, it was neither vulgar nor incorrect, but of that solid and judicious turn which constitutes the real merit of an orator as to the choice of his words"; and finally, with his delivery, which had a peculiar excellence, both as to voice and to gesture.[30] These excerpts reveal the fidelity with which Cicero adhered to the conventional rhetorical pattern in many of his criticisms. Unvaried adherence to this method would, of course, result in some measure of artificiality. To avoid the plainly stereotyped formula, Cicero sometimes rearranged the parts, considering style or memory before invention. This variation is observable in the criticism of Caius Piso,[31] where he commented first on his style, later on his invention.

Proficiency in all five parts of oratory was deemed indispensable to the accomplished speaker. In fact, a full knowledge of the art of speaking (as embraced in invention, disposition, elocution, memory, and delivery) might even partially compensate for cultural deficiency. Thus Cicero observes that several able orators, including Sulpicius and Antonius, were not well versed in the poets or in law, but those defects were minimized because they had an elaborate knowledge of rhetoric. Furthermore, certain orators excelled in one part of rhetoric, some in others. Antonius, though skilled in all parts, was uncommonly able in delivery; Curio, though weak in invention and disposition, was possessed of a "brilliant and ready flow of expression." However, Curio had both a bad memory and a faulty pronunciation.

Like many of his fellow rhetoricians, Cicero adhered to the threefold classification of deliberative, forensic, and ceremonial oratory. He had a particular fondness for courtroom speaking; accordingly, he devoted considerable attention to the theory affecting that branch of rhetoric. To deliberative speaking, however, he assigned a fair measure of importance; but ceremonial oratory, divorced as it was from practical affairs, received little systematic treatment.

As might be expected of the critic who remained ever close to his theory, Cicero used the types of oratory as an extension of his methodology in criticism. Thus some men were appraised as forensic speakers, others as deliberative speakers. Scaurus' manner of speaking, for instance, is commended for its appropriate adaptation to "debate in the senate." "It not only bespoke his prudence, but, what was a still more important recommendation, his credibility." [32] Numidicus and Silanus are mentioned as being skilled in deliberative speaking. These examples, among many others, suggest the use to which Cicero put his classificatory talents in evaluating the orators.

In the preceding sections we observed that, for Cicero, rhetoric was more than a single art or discipline. It was an all-embracing subject which eventually became an elaborate theory of culture. Like Isocrates, whom he followed in much of his thinking, Cicero conceived of the Ideal Orator as a man of full and ripened wisdom, conversant with the liberal arts, and disciplined in the ways of practical life.

Interestingly enough, Cicero made the cultural achievements of orators a basic indicator of his critical evaluation. Anxious to restore rhetoric to its former position when it had both scope and vitality, he examined the attainments of Roman orators with an eye to improving the taste of his countrymen and with the hope of giving rhetoric unquestioned status as a general theory of culture.

Cicero commends Lepidus for his apparent knowledge of the Grecian masters. Carbo is praised for his application to studies. Caius Sulpicius Gallus was "better acquainted with the Grecian literature than all the rest of the nobility, and to his reputation as a graceful orator, he added the highest accomplishments in every other respect." [33] And Marcus Piso "derived all his talents from his erudition; for he was much better versed in Grecian literature than any of his predecessors." [34] Cicero's regard for Crassus, whom he makes the protagonist of his views in the *De Oratore,* results in large part from the latter's command of the field of learning, his acknowledged versatility, if not genius. Thus we note that Cicero's critical judgments were developed in part from a recognition of cultural attainment in the speakers. An Ideal Orator, possessed of a knowledge and understanding rarely found in human beings, always stood near by, serving as the standard of excellence in speaking achievement.

The Fundamental Standard of Achievement.—The standard of excellence which Cicero sets up for judging the orator is plainly his own oratorical accomplishment and his own theory of speechmaking. In the *De Oratore,* he presented the requirements of the Ideal Orator; in the *Brutus,* he appraised the orators in the light of those essentials; and in the *Orator,* he presented the composite view of the finished orator, with the point of reference always toward himself and his speeches.

Thus it is, as Petersson observes, that the criticisms in the *Brutus* are made from two points of view: an absolute standard, i.e., the contents of the *De Oratore,* and a relative standard, i.e., the orator's own time and culture.[35] The absolute character of the criterion is revealed by a remark that Cicero makes in *The Best Style of the Orators:*

> I do not divide the orator as to class. . . . For I am seeking a perfect one. And of perfection there is only one kind; and those who fall short of it do not differ in kind.[36]

He goes on to say that the differences among orators are ones of degree, not kind, but he is seeking that "perfection which combines every kind of excellence."

Cicero most assuredly believed that he approached or even reached that perfection. As Sandys remarks: "the living image of his [Cicero's] own oratorical greatness forms the foundation on which he builds his ideal fabric. His own speeches supply him with examples of every variety of oratorical excellence." [37] Although he feigned modesty when referring to his own experience, he nevertheless made it clear at every turn that he was himself the criterion by which others were to be judged.

There is a further, and perhaps more fundamental, basis of judgment, however, that stamps Cicero's rhetorical criticism as intelligent, discerning, and relatively free from pedantry. Cicero does not appraise the effectiveness of oratory on the ground of simple adherence to formulated rules of speaking. Interested as he was in theory, he did not permit that predilection to obscure the fact that oratory, to be successful, must affect the individuals to whom it is addressed. Conformity to rules is important only to the extent that it makes possible the acquisition of responses sought by the speaker. Hence, Cicero makes the impression on the public, and on the social group generally, the test of appeal. The effect of the oratory upon people becomes a determining point of judgment; oratory, therefore, requires adaptation to listeners, and its effectiveness is dependent upon the skill with which this adaptation is made. As Cicero remarks, an abstruse poem

> . . . only requires the approbation of the judicious few, but a discourse intended for the people should be perfectly suited to their taste. If Demosthenes, therefore, after being deserted by the rest of his audience, had even Plato left to hear him, and no one else, I will answer for it, he could not have uttered another syllable. Nor could you yourself, my Brutus, if the whole assembly were to leave you, as it once did Curio.[38]

Whereupon Brutus, offering a commentary in the dialogue, replies:

> To open my whole mind to you, I must confess that even in such
> causes as fall under the cognizance of a few select judges, and not
> of the people at large, if I were to be deserted by the casual crowd
> who came to hear the trial, I should not be able to proceed.[39]

Cicero then brings out the cardinal principle to which he gives
heed in his criticism:

> The case, then, is plainly this, . . . as a flute, which will not return its
> proper sound when it is applied to the lips, would be laid aside by the
> musician as useless, so the ears of the people are the instrument upon
> which an orator is to play; and if these refuse to admit the breath he
> bestows upon them, or if the hearer, like a restive horse, will not obey
> the spur, the speaker must cease to exert himself any farther.[40]

Commenting on the likelihood of receiving uniform judgments
of orators both from the common man and the expert critic, Cicero
observes:

> . . . I had rather my *sentiments* on the qualifications of an orator
> should please you and Brutus, than all the world besides; but as to
> my *eloquence,* I should wish *this* to please everyone. For he who
> speaks in such a manner as to please the people, must inevitably
> receive the approbation of the learned. As to the truth and propriety
> of what I hear, I am indeed to judge of this for myself, as well as
> I am able; but the general merit of an orator must and will be de-
> cided by the effects which his eloquence produces. For . . . there
> are three things which an orator should be able to effect; viz., to
> *inform* his hearers, to *please* them, and to *move their passions.* By
> what qualities in the speaker each of these effects may be produced,
> or by what deficiencies they are either lost, or but imperfectly per-
> formed, is an inquiry which none but an artist can resolve; but
> whether an audience is really so affected by an orator as shall best
> answer his purpose, must be left to their own feelings, and the de-
> cision of the public. The learned therefore, and the people at large,
> have never disagreed about who was a good orator, and who was
> otherwise.[41]

It is, Cicero maintains, "the invariable prerogative of an accomplished
orator to be reckoned such in the opinion of the people."

The question might arise, then, as to what advantage, if any, the
trained critic has over the hearer who is not conversant with the
art of rhetoric. Cicero replies that the advantage is considerable and
important, "if it is, indeed, a matter of any consequence to be able to
discover by what means that which is the true and real end of speak-

ing is either obtained or lost." The skilled critic

> . . . has likewise this additional superiority, that when two or more orators, as has frequently happened, have shared the applauses of the public, he can judge, on a careful observation of the principal merits of each, what is the most perfect character of eloquence, since whatever does not meet the approbation of the people must be equally condemned by the more intelligent hearer. For as it is easily understood by the sound of a harp, whether the strings are skillfully touched; so it may likewise be discovered from the manner in which the passions of an audience are affected, how far the speaker is able to command them. A man, therefore, who is a real connoisseur in the art, can sometimes, by a single glance, as he passes through the forum, and without stopping to listen attentively to what is said, form a tolerable judgment of the ability of the speaker. When he observes any of the bench yawning, or speaking to the person who is next to him, or looking carelessly about him, or sending to inquire the time of day, or teasing the quaestor to dismiss the court, he concludes very naturally that the cause upon trial is not pleaded by an orator who understands how to apply the powers of language to the passions of the judges, as a skillful musician applies his fingers to the harp. On the other hand, if, as he passes by, he beholds the judges looking attentively before them, as if they were either receiving some material information, or visibly approved what they had already heard; if he sees them listening to the voice of the pleader with a kind of ecstasy, like a fond bird to some melodious tune; and, above all, if he discovers in their looks any strong indications of pity, abhorrence, or any other emotion of the mind; though he should not be near enough to hear a single word, he immediately discovers that the cause is managed by a real orator, who is either performing, or has already played his part to good purpose.[42]

An Estimate of Cicero's Contributions.—An over-all examination of Cicero's critical work strikes a note of considerable authority. Undoubtedly, his critical estimates would have been more significant if he had made fuller use of the speeches for which the orators were distinguished. This is, indeed, a defect as judged in terms of contemporary evaluation. Likewise, Cicero places what may seem to us a disproportionately heavy emphasis upon delivery as a determinant of success in oratory. Furthermore, no one could claim that Cicero's criticism is characterized by a dispassionate regard for merit, regardless of the school of thought to which the orator was committed. The *Brutus* and the *Orator* both reveal the presence of polemic, of controversy over the Atticist movement; and to that extent both works are intended to show the superiority of the Ciceronian conception of style. Finally, it is obvious that some of

Cicero's critical estimates are superficial and others somewhat un-
inspired in that they fail to reveal the character, the living spirit, of
the particular speakers. Even this battery of possible shortcomings,
however, does not dim the genius of this man whom Duff called "the
supreme index of his age." [43]

Cicero knew the theory of rhetoric, and he was a seasoned practitioner of the art. His criticism reveals the sweep of his intelligence
and the acuity of his observation. Taken as a group, the *De Oratore,*
the *Brutus,* and the *Orator* establish a *rationale* of rhetorical criticism which is at once discerning and ingenious. Cicero's work was
not the product of accident. Essaying, especially in the *Brutus,* to
present a systematic history of orators, he employed a designed
method which revealed complete mastery over the technical details
of rhetorical theory, and full understanding of the influence of history upon the development and refinement of artistic endeavor. He
had constantly before him a point of view regarding the function
of oratory, a method of effecting critical analysis, a criterion of
judgment, and a test for measuring the effectiveness of speeches. If
he failed to become the distinguished critic for which his abilities
so eminently fitted him, it was not because he was confused as to
method or objective. He knew what to do. But, unfortunately, his
quarrel with the Atticists impelled an enthusiasm for both open and
veiled rebuttal which frequently distorted the critical focus so essential to the judge of orators and oratory.

The Lost Works of Caecilius

J. D. Denniston says that one fact about Greek literary criticism
which immediately attracts attention is the important position held
by the prose writers, and especially the orators. It is not surprising,
therefore, that much of the extant criticism "originates in the effort
to purify oratorical style by bringing it back to Attic principles." [44]
Caecilius of Calacte and Dionysius of Halicarnassus, the two principal literary critics of Greece and Rome during the time of Augustus,
confirm this observation.

Caecilius was a Sicilian rhetorician whose works, regrettably,
have not survived. He evidently wrote a treatise on rhetoric and
another on figures of speech; to both of these works Quintilian refers
frequently in the *Institutes.* Caecilius and Dionysius met at Rome,
and there, "united by friendship, by community of labours and by
zeal for the Atticist revival," they became the leading exponents of
the Attic prose style.[45] Baldwin refers to an interpolation of

F. Nassal that the similarity of critical treatment by Dionysius and Cicero argues for a common source, and that this source is probably Caecilius.[46]

The lost work in which we are most interested was entitled *On the Style of the Ten Orators,* and included analyses of Antiphon, Andocides, Lysias, Isocrates, Isaeus, Lycurgus, Aeschines, Hyperides, Demosthenes, and Deinarchus. According to Jebb, Caecilius was one of the earliest writers to be familiar with the canon of the ten orators.

Caecilius was concerned principally with the purification of literary taste, the movement comprehensively known as Atticism. With Longinus, he perceived that what the age needed was not further analysis of rhetoric, but a "better aesthetic criticism" of it. He saw in the florid tendencies of the Asiatic school a *virtual extinction* of the great artistic spirit which had animated true Attic eloquence. In this respect both Caecilius and Dionysius differ from Cicero, for, as Jebb remarks, Cicero "conceives Atticism as an unbroken tradition, which was merely adulterated and debased by those influences which are called Asiatic." [47]

From the fragmentary data on Caecilius' works it is known that he used the comparative method in critical analysis. He compared Demosthenes with Aeschines, and also with Cicero. Furthermore, one of his works dealt with the differences between the Attic and the Asiatic style. Although he favored Lysias as a model, Caecilius criticized him "on the ground that he was less skilful in the arrangement of arguments than in invention." [48]

Regarding the critical work of Caecilius and Dionysius, W. Rhys Roberts says:

> They were true men of letters, not mere masters of technic. Their view of literary criticism was not mechanical, but aesthetic. They had something of the wide outlook and sympathy possessed by the best Roman writers, such as Cicero, for whom the adoption of a pure Attic standard has a living, and not simply an antiquarian interest.[49]

The Critical Efforts of Dionysius

The revival of Atticism, as Jebb wisely observes, did not mean the same thing for Rome as for Greece. "Rome was only developing her artistic literature: Greece had seen hers pass through maturity to decay." Hence, the revival gave "Rome true canons for living work. It gave Greece, not this, but the only thing now possible, a standard for the appreciation of the past." Cicero was the representative of the revival for Rome, while Dionysius, "the greatest critic of the ancient world who was not a philosopher," was the representative for both Greece and Rome.[50]

Associated with Caecilius, Dionysius recommended as models the best Attic orators. Strongly influenced by Isocrates, he believed that rhetoric was subordinate to the broader concept of citizenship, although in his critical analyses he gives little heed to historical details and concentrates chiefly on stylistic considerations.

Dionysius' estimates of the Attic orators constitute, in the opinion of Atkins, "the most considerable body of literary appreciations that has come down from antiquity." [51] These studies were intended to establish a standard for Greek prose, "applicable alike to oratory and to every other branch of composition."

The Principal Critical Works.—Dionysius projected critical judgments of six orators, grouping them into two distinct classes: Lysias, Isocrates, and Isaeus are the "inventors"; Demosthenes, Hyperides, and Aeschines are the "perfecters" of conceptions developed in the history of Attic prose.[52] The studies of the inventors are extant; only the first part of the treatise on Demosthenes has come down to us to represent Dionysius' treatment of the perfecters. It is regrettable that the second part of the criticism of Demosthenes is not preserved. It dealt with the orator's control over subject matter, and might have eased the emphasis which, in the other studies, tends so fully toward stylistic matters.

The pattern of Dionysius' criticisms is a trifle mechanical. It follows, in the main, a set of formulae, tends toward a too liberal use of classifications, and frequently becomes openly pedantic. Each account of an orator contains a limited amount of biographical detail, notes on the orator's style and subject matter, comparative estimates of other masters of prose, and selected quotations from the orator which reveal the critic's bases of judgment.

The *De Lysia,* conforming to the above pattern, provides an exacting scrutiny of the orator's style. Dionysius applies his "system of virtues" as developed in the *De Imitatione:* purity, accuracy, lucidity, brevity, compactness, vividness, character portrayal, appropriateness, and persuasiveness. Each virtue is examined carefully in the light of the Lysian material. S. F. Bonner summarizes by saying that Dionysius, in dealing with the virtues of style, treats the subject from the point of view of inventive power, the selection of arguments, and arrangement; and in selecting his specimen of Lysian style, he follows the "tradition which divided oratory into forensic, deliberative, and epideictic." [53] Finally, Dionysius considers Lysias' powers as revealed in the parts of a speech: proem, narrative, proof, and epilogue.

De Isocrate is similar in design and critical method to *De Lysia,* except that the comparison of Isocrates with Lysias provides additional detail. There is some reason to believe, however, that pure rhetorical theory influences this essay more than it did *De Lysia.* Evidence for this is found in the fact that Dionysius disapproves of Isocrates' style on at least three counts: (a) it is not effective from the point of view of the *hearer;* (b) it lacks the power to inflame and stir the feelings; and (c) it is overloaded in places with figurative expressions. These elements are important in indicating the methodological approach of the critic to the problem of rhetorical effectiveness. [54]

In the *De Isaeo,* there is no departure from the critical pattern set forth in Dionysius' other works. In it, as Bonner says, Dionysius' aim was to offer advice, "for purposes of imitation, on the standard models."

Perhaps the most important work in the list of studies by Dionysius is *De admiranda vi dicendi in Demosthene,* in which the method of the rhetorician is used freely. In this essay, he makes reference to the three styles—plain, middle, and grand—and then sets up the true model of excellence in prose, namely, Demosthenes.

As examples of the grand style, Dionysius turns to Gorgias and Thucydides; of the middle, to Thrasymachus; and of the plain, to Lysias. The style of Thucydides, he says,

> . . . has power to shock the mind, the style of Lysias to gratify it; the one can rally and brace it, the other relax and soothe it; the one can work upon the emotions, the other inspire tranquil sentiment. Moreover, it is a characteristic of Thucydides' style to insist and drive the point home, of Lysias' to mislead and to conceal the facts. Innovation and venturesomeness are inseparable from the historian's character, as are cautiousness and avoidance of risk from the orator's. [55]

Demosthenes is then established as the "all-sufficient model," as the one who combined the virtues and avoided the defects of the various styles. Here we find a true standard of excellence, a model to guide both critic and creative artist in his search for a satisfactory prose form. In order to bring out the superiority of Demosthenes' style, Dionysius compares him with Thucydides, and finds that "Thucydides uses this method [the grand style] of obtaining distinction so unsparingly as to become obscure, whereas Demosthenes always aims at the golden mean and, as a result, does not violate the essential principles of perspicuity and propriety." [56] As for the comparison with Lysias, Dionysius finds some points of similarity. But Demosthenes revealed more vigor in his proof; consequently, he was more effective.

According to Dionysius, Isocrates is definitely inferior to Demosthenes.

> Who would refuse to acknowledge the complete superiority of this style to that of Isocrates? Demosthenes has expressed the subject-matter with greater nobility and magnificence, has clothed the ideas with a finer style, and brought them out in a more concise, compact, and finished fashion; he has shown greater power and a sturdier strength, and avoided those frigid, childish figures in which the other indulges to excess; but it is in movement, action, emotional effect, that he is completely and absolutely superior.

Furthermore,

> . . . when I read a speech of Isocrates, I become serious in spirit, and experience great mental calm, like those who listen to the pipes during libations or to Dorian or enharmonic melodies. But when I take up one of Demosthenes' speeches, I am entranced and borne hither and thither, experiencing one emotion after another, distrust, anxiety, fear, contempt, hatred, pity, benevolence, anger, envy, every emotion in fact that is wont to dominate the human mind. I seem to be no whit different from those who perform rites of initiation. . . . If then we, who are so far removed in time, and are not concerned about the issue, are thus swayed and mastered, and borne whithersoever the speech carries us, how must the Athenians and the Greeks in general have felt when their living interests were at stake, and when the orator himself, at the height of his fame, revealed his own personal experience and laid bare the inmost feelings of his soul? [57]

These and other comparisons establish Dionysius' reasons for assigning to Demosthenes "the palm for oratorical mastery." The achievements of Demosthenes, Dionysius makes clear in his critical inquiries, result from painstaking efforts to attain perfection. "Dionysius more than once reminds us," says Roberts, "of the oft-forgotten truth that the excellence of the ancient authors was the result of ingenious and elaborate art." [58] The Demosthenean speeches, which were like the finest poems and lyrics, did not spring into finished form without the most meticulous observance by the speaker of the details and rules of the rhetorical art. And it was proper that the speaker attend faithfully to those details.

For it appears to me far more reasonable for a man who is composing
public speeches, eternal memorials of his own powers, to attend even
to the slightest details, than it is for the disciples of painters and
workers in relief, who display the dexterity and industry of their hands
in a perishable medium, to expend the finished resources of their
art on veins and down and bloom and similar minutiae.[59]

The essays of Dionysius have an unmistakable rhetorical outlook,
despite the fact that they do not draw fully upon the historical materials relevant to the orator's speechmaking. To the extent that they
indicate the point of view of oratory, and employ the comparative
method, they are significant in the development of rhetorical criticism. In his almost passionate endeavor to delineate stylistic details,
however, Dionysius divorced style from subject matter, and vitiated
partially the integrity of the critical effort. As Jebb remarks,
"Dionysius tends to test the criticism of oratory too much on literary
grounds." [60]

The Critical Standards of Longinus

The great critics of antiquity provide much that the present-day
student searches for in his effort to understand rhetorical theory.
The considered judgments of these critics serve as the bridge between
yesterday and today, for "in art, as in life, it is the part of wisdom
to let the ages instruct the years." [61]

In the preceding chapters we mentioned the contribution made
by the author of *On the Sublime* to rhetorical theory. Now we shall
return briefly to this work to determine its relationship to criticism.
Longinus, or whoever the author may have been, made three contributions, not necessarily original, which helped to establish a critique
of oratory.

The Standard of Excellence.—In the first place, the author
established a fixed standard of excellence in oratory. Since he
adopted a view favoring the return to Greek classical art, he naturally
turned to Demosthenes for his model. Under Demosthenes' approach, oratorical imagery becomes effective, fusing "vehemence and
passion into spoken words" and following trains of reasoning while
at the same time indulging flights of imagination.[62] And when the
author inquires into the value of interrogations, he turns again to
passages from Demosthenes which show that if they had not been
handled by a master, they "would have been altogether weaker." [63]
As in other matters, in the use of metaphors Demosthenes is established as the standard.

Comparative Analyses in Criticism.—A second feature giving *On the Sublime* critical value is its use of the comparative method of appraisal. In comparing Cicero with Demosthenes, the author remarks:

> . . . the latter is characterised by sublimity which is for the most part rugged, Cicero by profusion. Our orator, owing to the fact that in his vehemence,—aye, and in his speed, power, and intensity,—he can as it were consume by fire and carry away all before him, may be compared to a thunderbolt or flash of lightning. Cicero, on the other hand, it seems to me, after the manner of a wide-spread conflagration, rolls on with all-devouring flames, having within him an ample and abiding store of fire, distributed now at this point now at that, and fed by an unceasing succession. This, however, you will be better able to decide; but the great opportunity of Demosthenes' high-pitched elevation comes where intense utterance and vehement passion are in question, and in passages in which the audience is to be utterly en-thralled. The profusion of Cicero is in place where the hearer must be flooded with words; for it is appropriate to the treatment of com-monplaces, and to perorations for the most part and digressions, and to all descriptive and declamatory passages, and to writings on history and natural science, and to many other departments of literature.[64]

Likewise, we may turn to the comparative estimate of Demosthenes and Hyperides:

> If successful writing were to be estimated by number of merits and not by the true criterion, thus judged Hyperides would be altogether superior to Demosthenes. For he has a greater number of accents than Demosthenes and a greater number of excellences, and like the pen-tathlete he falls just below the top in every branch. In all the contests he has to resign the first place to his rivals, while he maintains that place against all ordinary persons.
>
> Now Hyperides not only imitates all the strong points of De-mosthenes with the exception of his composition, but he has embraced in a singular degree the excellences and graces of Lysias as well. For he talks with simplicity, where it is required, and does not adopt like Demosthenes one unvarying tone in all his utterances. He possesses the gift of characterisation in a sweet and pleasant form and with a touch of piquancy. There are innumerable signs of wit in him— the most polished raillery, high-bred ease, supple skill in the contests of irony, jests not tasteless or rude after the well-known Attic manner, but naturally suggested by the subject, clever ridicule, much comic power, biting satire with well-directed fun, and what may be termed an inimitable charm investing the whole. He is excellently fitted by nature to excite pity; in narrating a fable he is facile, and with his pliant spirit he is also most easily turned towards a digression . . . ;

while he has treated his Funeral Oration in the epideictic vein with probably unequalled success. Demosthenes, on the other hand, is not an apt delineator of character, he is not facile, he is anything but pliant or epideictic, he is comparatively lacking in the entire list of excellences just given. Where he forces himself to be jocular and pleasant, he does not excite laughter, but rather becomes the subject of it, and when he wishes to approach the region of charm, he is all the farther removed from it. If he had attempted to write the short speech about Phryne or about Athenogenes, he would have all the more commended Hyperides to our regard. The good points of the latter, however, many though they be, are wanting in elevation; they are the staid utterances of a sober-hearted man and leave the hearer unmoved, no one feeling terror when he reads Hyperides. But Demosthenes draws, as from a store, excellences allied to the highest sublimity and perfected to the utmost, the tone of lofty speech, living passions, copiousness, readiness, speed (where it is legitimate), and that power and vehemence of his which forbid approach. Having, I say, absorbed bodily within himself these mighty gifts which we may deem heaven-sent . . . , he thus with the noble qualities which are his own routs all comers even where the qualities he does not possess are concerned, and overpowers with thunder and with lightning the orators of every age. One could sooner face with unflinching eyes a descending thunderbolt than meet with steady gaze his bursts of passion in their swift succession.[65]

A minor comparison of Plato with Lysias brings out essentially the same method, and reminds us that the author of *On the Sublime* sought the attainment of a certain ideality in the sublime utterance.

The Tests of Excellence.—Finally, *On the Sublime* provides an interesting doctrine which tends to negate Macaulay's contention that Longinus "gives us eloquent sentences, but no principles." The dictum is laid down that *the sublime* and *imitation* of great masters are not incompatible. When we are "elaborating anything which requires lofty expression and elevated conception," we should think of three possible tests: (1) How would Homer "have said this very thing, or how would it have been raised to the sublime by Plato or Demosthenes or by the historian Thucydides"? "If the image of those men were presented to us, our ardor would be inflamed and our path illumined." (2) "What sort of hearing would Homer, had he been present, or Demosthenes have given to this or that when said by me, or how would they have been affected by the other?" (3) "In what spirit will each succeeding age listen to me who have written thus?"[66]

Tacitus on Oratory

The meaning of the *Dialogue Concerning Oratory,* written about
80 A.D., is not always perfectly clear. Varying points of view are
expressed by the several participants, and it is often difficult to determine which one represents Tacitus' convictions. In fact, it is not
improbable that the dialogue reflects a conflict of belief in the author's
mind.

Relativity in Critical Standards.—The critical doctrine of greatest
importance in the *Dialogue* grows out of some remarks Maternus
makes near the end of the treatise. Commenting on the fact that
there is no stability in human affairs, Maternus says:

> We find that the discourse of men always conforms to the temper of
> the times. Among savage nations language is never copious. A few
> words serve the purpose of barbarians, and those are always uncouth
> and harsh, without the artifice of connection; short, abrupt, and nerv-
> ous. In a state of polished society, where a single ruler sways the
> sceptre, the powers of the mind take a softer tone, and language grows
> more refined. But affectation follows, and precision gives way to
> delicacy. The just and natural expression is no longer the fashion.
> Living in ease and luxury, men look for elegance, and hope by novelty
> to give a grace to adulation. In other nations, where the first prin-
> ciples of the civil union are maintained in vigour; where the people
> live under the government of laws, and not the will of man; where
> the spirit of liberty pervades all ranks and orders of the state; where
> every individual holds himself bound, at the hazard of his life, to
> defend the constitution framed by his ancestors; where, without being
> guilty of an impious crime, no man dares to violate the rights of the
> whole community; in such a state, the national eloquence will be prompt,
> bold, and animated. Should internal dissensions shake the public
> peace, or foreign enemies threaten to invade the land, Eloquence
> comes forth arrayed in terror; she wields her thunder, and commands
> all hearts. It is true, that upon those occasions men of ambition en-
> deavour, for their own purposes, to spread the flame of sedition; while
> the good and virtuous combine their force to quell the turbulent, and
> repel the menaces of a foreign enemy. Liberty gains new strength
> by the conflict, and the true patriot has the glory of serving his coun-
> try, distinguished by his valour in the field, and in debate no less
> terrible by his eloquence.[67]

In furtherance of this thesis, Maternus continues:

> The subject, beyond all doubt, lifts the mind above itself; it gives
> vigour to sentiment, and energy to expression. Let the topic be a

paltry theft, a dry form of pleading, or a petty misdemeanor: will not the orator feel himself cramped and chilled by the meanness of the question? Give him a cause of magnitude, such as bribery in the election of magistrates, a charge for plundering the allies of Rome, or the murder of Roman citizens, how different then his emotions! how sublime each sentiment! what dignity of language! The effect, it must be admitted, springs from the disasters of society. It is true, that form of government, in which no such evils occur, must, beyond all question, be allowed to be the best; but since, in the course of human affairs, sudden convulsions must happen, my position is, that they produced, at Rome, that flame of eloquence which at this hour is so admired. The mind of the orator grows and expands with his subject. Without ample materials no splendid oration was ever yet produced.[68]

Thus does Tacitus enunciate the doctrine that standards of style are relative, and that each speaker and each age must work out its own literary salvation. In expounding the variability of standards, Tacitus acknowledges the fact that historical events and tendencies influence speechmaking and that a full understanding of oratory derives from intelligent insight into the age in which it flourished. Atkins says that in Tacitus' hands criticism, "for the first time, ceases to be dogmatic and scholastic in kind; a return is made to the dialectical methods of Plato, so that literature is now approached, not with the object of laying down absolute rules, but in order to inquire, to understand, and thus to explain." [69]

Stylistic Approach to Criticism

Demetrius' Standards of Prose Style.—Both the date and authorship of the work called *On Style* are in doubt. Modern scholars seem to believe, however, that the treatise was not written, as was sometimes claimed, by Demetrius Phalereus; rather, it has been suggested that it might have been prepared by Demetrius of Tarsus, a contemporary of Plutarch. Thus it probably originated sometime during the first century A.D.

As the title indicates, *On Style* is devoted exclusively to the *elocutio* of classical rhetoric, and its chief purpose is to set forth the principles of prose style, rather than to comment on the decline of the art of expression.

The principal sections of Demetrius' work deal with four kinds of style: the plain, the stately, the polished, and the powerful. Demetrius discusses these types with respect to word choice, arrangement of words, and the subject matter appropriate to each. Certain of the excesses or vices to which each is liable are also pointed out.

The stately, or elevated, style requires "idea, expression, and suitable composition." [70] Figures of speech and thought, such as metaphors, hyperboles, word coinages, and the like, receive brief treatment. Through the discussion runs an important theme, namely, that subject matter moulds style, and that style, to be effective, must always preserve propriety. Accordingly, "style must be appropriate to its subject—a modest style to a modest subject, and a grand style to a grand subject." [71]

The polished style—also referred to as the elegant style—possesses "grace and brightness." [72] It is characterized by rhythmical flow and figurative expressions.

The plain style is appropriate to ordinary oral expression. Demetrius alludes to its persuasiveness, adding that its characteristic qualities are clearness and simplicity. "If it is lacking in either of these it fails to persuade. We must aim at a diction which is neither overladen nor ponderous if we wish to persuade; a diction, too, with a steady rhythm and no suggestion of metre." [73] Commenting further, Demetrius remarks:

> Theophrastus adds that every detail must not be described at length, but some points must be left to the intelligence and elaboration of the hearer. When he thinks of the points which you have omitted, he becomes not only a hearer, but a witness and a very partial witness, too. He thinks that he is clever, thanks to your action in giving him an opportunity to use his intelligence. To press home every detail, as though your hearer were a fool, seems like casting a slur on his intelligence.[74]

The last kind of style mentioned by Demetrius is the powerful, or, as Roberts calls it, the forcible. Not completely dissimilar from the stately type, it is characterized by vigorous diction and the liberal use of figures. The proper arrangement of words also conduces to power. Thus he recommends placing the strongest thought at the end; "whatever is buried in the middle of the sentence loses its power." [75] D'Alton believes that the characteristics of the powerful style "were probably in the main derived from a study of the oratory of Demosthenes, whose dominant quality was considered to be his vehemence."

Although it is doubtful whether classifications of style have ever been particularly useful or illuminating, Demetrius' treatment is not without merit. As Atkins observes, "it may fairly be described as forming a part of that first-century movement which had for its object the establishment of classical standards in literature." Concerned chiefly with "the niceties of Greek prose," Demetrius "was instrumental in directing men's attention anew to the models of earlier Greece, by holding up for their imitation the standards of classical art." [76]

The Relation of Philosophy to Rhetoric

Points of View of the Masters.—We have observed in previous sections that many rhetoricians, as well as their critics, were deeply interested in the relation of rhetoric to philosophy. Plato's strictures against the Sophists dealt largely with that theme; Isocrates attempted to join the two fields in his theory of culture; Aristotle, granting rhetoric dignified status, nevertheless joined Plato in calling rhetoric a counterpart of dialectic, and in articulating it with ethics. This controversy over the relative merit and position of philosophy and rhetoric persisted for many years, and eventually became closely associated with the history of education. This developed from the respective claims of the two areas of learning for control over the education of youth.

It has often been said that any intellectually eager man with a broad field of interest will eventually turn to philosophy. Cicero was actively concerned with effecting a union of rhetoric and philosophy, embracing all in a comprehensive culture. Philosophy would be the handmaid of rhetoric; and an end would be put to what Cicero called the "absurd, useless, and reprehensible" division that divorced the "tongue from the heart" and forced acceptance of the belief that "one class of persons should teach us to think, and another to speak, rightly." [77] The controversy over this point led to the establishment of divergent schools of thought.

The Peripatetic school was founded by Aristotle. It emphasized the importance of Dialectic and, since it provided for intensive training in handling both sides of a question, gained Cicero's favor. D'Alton believes, however, that Theophrastus "did much to make the Peripatetic school acceptable in the eyes of Cicero, who was indebted to him for many features in his theory of style." Cicero's own attachment to the Peripatetics is indicated in this remark:

> If, however, we must be indebted for every thing to the philosophers, the Peripatetic discipline is, in my mind, much the most proper to form our language. For which reason, my Brutus, I the more approve your choice, in attaching yourself to a sect (I mean the philosophers of the old Academy) in whose system a just and accurate way of reasoning is enlivened by a perpetual sweetness and fluency of

expression; but even the delicate and flowing style of the Peripatetics and Academics is not sufficient to complete an orator; nor yet can he be complete without it.[78]

Cicero often speaks of the Academics and the Peripatetics in one breath, and considers them the best adapted to the training of the speaker. The Platonic school was once headed by Xenocrates, although as the New Academy its origin stemmed from Arcesilas. Carneades was its best representative.[79]

Cicero has a good deal to say about Stoicism in its relation to the training of speakers. Remarking that the Cynics, afterwards the Stoics, sprung from Antisthenes' "patience and endurance recommended in the discourses of Socrates," he indicates that the Stoics "declared eloquence to be virtue and wisdom." [80] D'Alton ventures the opinion that Cato's well-known description of the orator as "a good man speaking well" probably is of Stoic origin. But Cicero dismisses the teachings of the Stoics for two reasons:

> . . . there are two peculiarities in their doctrine, which are quite un-suitable to that orator whom we are forming; one, that they pronounce all who are not wise, to be slaves, robbers, enemies, and madmen, and yet do not admit that any person is wise (but it would be very absurd to trust the interests of an assembly of the people, or of the senate, or any other body of men, to one to whom none of those present would appear to be in their senses, none to be citizens, none to be freemen); the other, that they have a manner of speaking which is perhaps subtle, and certainly acute, but for an orator, dry, strange, unsuited to the ear of the populace, obscure, barren, jejune, and altogether of that species which a speaker cannot use to a multitude.[81]

In the *Brutus,* Cicero remarks that the language of the Stoics "is too close and contracted to suit the ears of common people." Among the orators of the Stoic school were Q. Mucius Scaevola and Aelius Tubero, both of whom are evaluated in the *Brutus.* Naturally, Cicero found the elaborate analyses, the rigid adherence to dialectical systems, the failure to employ emotional proof, and the insistence of the Stoics upon plain, unadorned language, unsuited to his conception of oratory.

The Stoics' fear that departure from the plain facts would endanger truth finds its counterpart many years later in John Locke's remark in the *Essay Concerning Human Understanding:*

> . . . we must allow that all the art of rhetoric, besides order and clearness, all the artificial and figurative application of words eloquence hath invented, are for nothing else but to insinuate wrong ideas, move the passions, and thereby mislead the judgment; and so indeed

are perfect cheats; and therefore, however laudable or allowable oratory may render them in harangues and popular addresses, they are certainly, in all discourses that pretend to inform or instruct, wholly to be avoided; and, where truth and knowledge are concerned, cannot but be thought a great fault either of the languages or persons that make use of them.[82]

Incidentally, Lord Bolingbroke did not consider Locke's comments on figurative style an indictment of the use of figures. Rather, it was a condemnation of the *abuse* of them.

False eloquence there is, no doubt, and fraudulent eloquence too. Figurative style often causes one, and is often employed by the other; but there is false and fraudulent reasoning too without eloquence: and we may find as much trifling and fallacy in some of the most dry didactic writings, as can be shown in those of poets and orators.[83]

Naturally, then,

Rhetoric may be a powerful instrument of deceit and error, and so may logic too. Both of them are impertinent when they are reduced into arts, and are cultivated and followed as such. But if rhetoric were banished out of the world, and logic with it, eloquence and reason would still remain . . . We may disaffect eloquence as much as we please, or nature may have saved us this trouble by refusing us the talent, but we must cease to speak if we lay figurative speech wholly aside. Figures are so necessary in the communication, at least, of our thoughts, that they are wove into the very constitution of language. . . .[84]

But let us return from our digression. The Stoics, we repeat, were interested in a simple treatment of the facts, and Cicero was committed to the copious style of oratory in which feeling and rhetorical flourish figured importantly.

The last school of thought to which we shall allude is the Epicurean. Founded by Epicurus, this school looked upon science as the servant of life and considered theory important only as it related to practice. The over-all aim of philosophy was to provide men with tranquillity and peace of mind. In general, the Epicureans rejected rhetoric as useless. Perhaps the only branch of the subject which at least two of the disciples of the school, Zeno and Philodemus, would recognize as fit fields of inquiry was the epideictic. The reason for admitting epideictic oratory to fuller status was that its rules could be systematized, a condition not possible in other branches of speaking which depended upon the ability of speakers to gain popular favor.

The Position of Philodemus.—In the *Rhetoric* of Philodemus (first century B.C.), fragments of which have come down to us, we find some of the reasons why Cicero considered the Epicurean point of view unsuited to his conception of oratorical training. It should always be borne in mind, too, that in the *De Oratore* Cicero was not so much concerned with finding out which philosophy was nearest to truth, but rather, which was "the best suited to the orator." [85]

Philodemus supports the claim that sophistic rhetoric is an art. In fact, he devotes considerable space to matters of definition, trying to determine what an "art" is and what "rhetoric" is. He finally decides that an art is a

> . . . state or condition resulting from the observation of certain common and elementary principles, which apply to the majority of cases, accomplishing such a result as cannot be attained by one who has not studied it, and doing this regularly and certainly and not by conjecture.[86]

In the controversy over the relative merits of philosophy and rhetoric, the former is easily the victor. Rhetoric, so Philodemus announces, deals in probabilities and guesses; philosophy, in logic. Rhetoric offers no safeguards as to its use, and so unwise men can employ it craftily; philosophy is in itself a positive good which makes men happy in their state. As Philodemus puts it:

> We do not claim that rhetoric is bad in itself, even if it furnishes weapons for wicked men, but it does not indicate what use is to be made of the power it gives, so as to fit in with our principles of justice and honor. Rhetoricians are like pilots, who have a good training but may be bad men.[87]

The devices of the rhetorician are therefore suspect. "For it is well said that the juryman is not affected by any form of speech as much as by the just and prudent actions of the uneducated, and in trials they fear being misled by the rhetor." [88]

Philodemus berates Aristotle for stepping down from philosophy to rhetoric, and extols Isocrates for stepping up from rhetoric to philosophy. Since rhetoric is associated with an active life in the world of affairs—and that is where rhetors do harm—it is better to turn to philosophy, by which men get away from mundane transactions. "Philosophy shows us how to find and use everything necessary for a happy life." [89]

Unwilling to recommend imitation of the ancients, Philodemus looks to everyday language as the best style of expression. "Much of delivery," he remarks, "is the natural and unconscious bodily ex-

pression of the emotions." And the "formal instruction in delivery
is a product of recent foolishness. . . ." [90]

Here, then, were some of the philosophical doctrines which influenced the course and style of oratory. They were the sects, as
Cicero called them, that presumably had something to offer toward
the training of a speaker. Cicero appraised them all in his *De Oratore* and the *Brutus*.

Pliny's Criticism

His Thoughts on Oratory and Orators.—"I honour and revere
all who discover any talent for oratory," said Pliny the Younger in
a letter to Restitutus, "for the Muse of Eloquence is a coy and
haughty dame, who scorns to reside with those who despise her." [91]
The frequent references to oratory in Pliny's letters attest to his
own interest in the art, as does the fact that he himself attended
lectures by Quintilian and Nicetes, a point which he reveals in his
letter to Fundanus.

Pliny did not commit himself openly in the controversy over the
ancients and the moderns. He tried, in the main, to steer a middle
course, as his letter to Caninus suggests: "Though I acknowledge
myself an admirer of the ancients, yet I am very far from despising
. . . the genius of the moderns. . . ." He seems, however, to get
his principal inspiration from the older models. In a letter to
Voconius Romanus, he indicates specifically that in his own speaking
he tried to emulate Cicero, "and am by no means contented with
taking my example from modern eloquence." And in a communication to Maximus, he intimates that contemporary eloquence is ruined
and extinct, except for certain "unmanly" elocutions. Again, in a
letter to Arrianus, he says that, in a certain composition presented for
criticism, he tried to imitate Demosthenes and Calvus "who is lately
become mine" [model for imitation]. He admits that his imitation
is confined to *manner,* since only a choice few have been able to catch
their "sublime spirit."

Pliny's own style tended toward the elevated or the grand manner
of expression. In a letter to Voconius Romanus, he expresses the
opinion, however, that the lofty and elevated style should not always
be used; for "as shades in a picture best bring out the high lights, so
the plain and simple style in writing is as effective as the sublime."
It is to be noted that Pliny used several styles to please different
groups of hearers, his conviction being that mere variety would have
some effect in recommending the work as a whole. But there can

be no doubt about Pliny's sympathy for the more dazzling and florid type of speaking, as this passage from a letter to Lupercus brings out:

> . . . the true orator should be bold and elevated, and sometimes even flame out and be hurried away with all the warmth and violence of passion, in short, he should frequently soar to great, and even dangerous heights. For precipices are generally near whatever is towering and exalted, whereas the plain affords a safer, but for that reason a more humble and inglorious path; they that run are more likely to stumble than they that creep; but the latter gain no honour by not slipping, while the former fall with glory. It is with eloquence as with some other arts; she is never more pleasing than when she hazards most.[92]

For the actual work at the bar, Pliny urged a style that struck a mean between brevity and reasonable completeness. But, as just mentioned, he favored the majestic in oratory. In a letter to Tacitus, he remarked:

> I have frequent debates with a learned and judicious person of my acquaintance, who admires nothing so much in the eloquence of the bar as conciseness. I admit, where the cause will admit of this matter, it ought to be pursued; but insist, that to omit what is material to be mentioned, or only slightly to touch upon those points which should be repeatedly inculcated, and urged home to the minds of the audience, is, in effect, to betray the cause one has undertaken.[93]

Evidently, he was a bit suspicious of those speeches that "were cut in two by nightfall," while at the same time he insisted upon adequate coverage of a forensic case.

Pliny was interested in the differences between written and spoken style. In the same letter to Tacitus, he remarked:

> But, it is objected, there is a wide difference between a good *spoken* and a good *written* oration. This opinion I acknowledge, has had some favourers; nevertheless I am persuaded . . . that it is possible a speech may be well received by the audience, which has not merit enough to recommend it to the reader; but an oration which is good on paper cannot be bad when delivered; for the oration on paper is, in truth, the original and model of the speech that is to be pronounced. It is for this reason we find in many of the best orations extant numberless extempore figures of rhetoric; and this even where we are sure they were never spoken at all: as for instance in the following passage from the oration against Verres. . . .[94]

It should be noted that in this passage Pliny expresses a regard for the authenticity of texts, allowing that speeches as printed often contain material not used in the oral delivery.

That Pliny was deeply interested in the probable response of the audience is reflected in several of his letters. He believed that the orator "should so adapt himself to his audience as to throw out something to every one of them, that he may receive and approve as his own peculiar thought." [95] As a part of his technique, he urged the method of taking up many points in forensic discourses, saying,

> As in agriculture, it is not my vineyards, or my woods, alone, but my fields also that I cultivate; and as I do not sow those fields with only spelt and winter-wheat, but employ also barley, beans, and the other leguminous plants; so in my pleadings at the bar, I spread at large a variety of matter like so many different seeds, in order to reap from thence whatever may happen to sprout; for the disposition of your jurors is as precarious and as little to be ascertained, as that of soils and seasons.[96]

His defense of this system was clear. "To delight and to persuade requires time," he said, "and a great compass of language; while to leave a *sting* in the minds of his audience is an effect not to be achieved by an orator who slightly pushes, but by him, and him only, who thrusts home and deep." Returning to his conception of elevation in style, he observed "it is not concise and curtailed, it is copious, majestic, and sublime oratory, that with blaze and thunder perturbs and confounds the universe." [97]

Like many other theorists and critics of antiquity, Pliny was interested in the relation between history and oratory. In a letter to Titinius Capito, Pliny commented at length on the relative positions of the two fields, declaring that history "however executed, always pleases, for mankind are naturally inquisitive, and information, however badly presented, has its charm for beings who adore even small talk and anecdote." [98] Oratory and poetry, on the other hand, always require a full measure of eloquence. Asserting that history and oratory possess a number of common features, Pliny remarks

> . . . in these very apparent resemblances, there are several contrasts. Both deal in narrative, but each after a different fashion. Oratory must concern itself as a rule with the low and vulgar facts of every-day life; history treats only of what is recondite, splendid, elevated; a dry, forcible, nervous style befits the one, but embellishments, and what one may call *top-knots,* the other. Oratory pleases most when it is vigorous, biting, and vehement. History, when it is diffusive,

bland, and even dulcet. Lastly, diction, rhythm, and the structure of the periods, are distinctly different in these two arts.[99]

Perhaps the best specimen of Pliny's rhetorical criticism is found in a letter to Nepos, in which he urges the latter to pay heed to Isaeus. Says Pliny:

> He possesses the utmost facility and copiousness of expression, and though always extempore his discourses have all the propriety and elegance of the most studied and elaborate composition. He employs the Greek language, or rather the genuine Attic. His prefatory remarks are terse, easy, and harmonious; and, when occasion requires, serious and majestic. He proposes several questions for discussion, gives his audience liberty to call for any they please, and sometimes even to name what side of it he shall take. . . . He handles every point with almost equal readiness; profound ideas occur to him as he proceeds; his language—but how admirable that is. So choice, so refined! . . . He opens his subject with great propriety; his narration is clear; his controversy ingenious, his logic forcible and his rhetoric sublime. In a word, he at once instructs, entertains, and affects you, and each in so high a degree, that you are at a loss to determine in which of those talents he most excels. He abounds in enthymemes and syllogisms; the latter of a formal exactness, not very easy to attain even in writing. His memory is so extraordinary, that he can recollect what he has before spoken extempore, word for word.[100]

Although Pliny's analysis is short, even perfunctory perhaps, it does reveal his grasp of the problems of rhetoric, the estimate showing, among other things, that he knew what to judge in oratory. If he had elaborated upon his materials, a criticism of genuine merit might very well have resulted.

Criticism from the Point of View of the Theorist-Teacher

Quintilian's Attitude toward the Atticist-Asianist Quarrel.— Distinguished for his sanity and good judgment on educational matters, Quintilian shunned the open espousal of either extreme in the Atticist-Asianist issues. Avoiding the extremists, he urged the study of both ancient and modern orators. In the early part of the *Institutes,* he remarks:

> There are two points in style on which I think that the greatest caution should be used in respect to boys: one is that no master, from being too much an admirer of antiquity, should allow them to harden, as it were, in the reading of the Gracchi, Cato, and other like authors; for they would thus become uncouth and dry; since they cannot, as

yet, understand their force of thought, and, content with adopting their style, which, at the time it was written, was doubtless excellent, but is quite unsuitable to our day, they will appear to themselves to resemble those eminent men. The other point, which is the opposite of the former, is, lest, being captivated with the flowers of modern affectation, they should be so seduced by a corrupt kind of pleasure, as to love that luscious manner of writing which is the more agreeable to the minds of youth in proportion as it has more affinity with them.[101]

Later, he indicates that

... nature has not condemned us to stupidity, but we ourselves have changed our mode of speaking, and have indulged our fancies more than we ought; and thus the ancients did not excel us so much in genius as in severity of manner. It will be possible, therefore, to select from the moderns many qualities for imitation, but care must be taken that they be not contaminated with other qualities with which they are mixed. Yet that there have been recently, and are now, many writers whom we may imitate entirely, I would not only allow, ... but even affirm.[102]

Commenting on stylistic ornamentation, Quintilian says

... ornaments of style are the very eyes, as it were, of eloquence; but I should not wish eyes to be spread over the whole body; lest other members should be obstructed in their functions; and, if I were compelled to make a choice, I should prefer the rudeness of the ancients to the affectation of the moderns. But a middle course is open between them; as, in our mode of living and dress, a certain elegance may be observed which is free from blame. Let us add, therefore, as far as we can, to the merits of our style; but let it be our first care to avoid faults, lest, while we wish to be better than the ancients, we make ourselves merely unlike them.[103]

These quotations illustrate the scope of Quintilian's sympathies; they show him steering a middle course in the controversy over whether the ancients were to be preferred to the moderns as models for imitation.[104] This does not mean that Quintilian had vacillating convictions as to the best style of oratory. Despite his tolerance and his recognition of the need for diversity of style to meet varying conditions, he expressed unqualified preferences which threw light upon his conception of the critical function.

There are some forms of eloquence of a rude nature in agreement with the times in which they appeared, but indicating mental power in the speakers; among whom we may number the Laelli, Africani, Catos, and Gracchi; and these we may call the Polygnoti and Callones of oratory. Of the middle kind Lucius Crassus and Quintus Hortensius may be thought the chief representatives. There may be contemplated a vast multitude of orators, all flourishing about the same time. Among them we find the energy of Caesar, the natural talent of Caelius, the subtlety of Calidius, the accuracy of Polio, the dignity of Messala, the austerity of Calvus, the gravity of Brutus, the acuteness of Sulpicius, and the severity of Cassius. Among those, also, whom we have ourselves seen, we recollect the copiousness of Seneca, the force of Julius Africanus, the mature judgment of Domitius Afer, and agreeableness of Crispus, the sonorous pronunciation of Trachalus, and the elegance of Secundus.[105]

Quintilian follows this analysis with a defence of the Ciceronian style:

But in Cicero we have not merely a Euphranor, distinguished by excellence in several particular departments of art, but eminent in every quality that is commended in any orator whatever. Yet the men of his own time presumed to censure him as tumid, Asiatic, redundant, too fond of repetition, indulging in tasteless jests, loose in the structure of his sentences, tripping in his manner, and . . . almost too effeminate in his general style for a man.[106]

Commenting on the Atticist quarrel, he goes on to say:

But his severest critics were those who desired to be thought imitators of the Attic orators. This band of calumniators, as if they had leagued themselves in a solemn confederacy, attacked Cicero as though he had been quite of another country, neither caring for their customs nor bound by their laws; of which school are our present dry, sapless, and frigid orators.[107]

Quintilian distinguishes between Attic and Asiatic orators by saying the former are regarded as "compressed and energetic" while the latter are "inflated and deficient in force." He also refers to the third type of eloquence, the Rhodian, which was presumably of a middle character. Then he remarks that the

. . . difference in the character of the speakers and their audiences seems to have caused the difference in their styles of oratory; for the people of Attica, being polished and of refined taste, could endure nothing useless or redundant; while the Asiatics, a people in other respects vain and ostentatious, were puffed up with fondness for a showy kind of eloquence.[108]

Recognizing that there was a wide variety of genius within each category, Quintilian openly announced his belief that "of the three styles, that of the Attics is by far the best." But it must be remembered that he saw some good in all types.

His Conception of Style.—Despite Quintilian's temperate stand in the quarrel between the Atticists and the Asianists, he nevertheless reveals throughout the *Institutes* his displeasure with the stylistic abuses of his period. His theory of style clearly reveals his advocacy of a return to the speech of ordinary life, elevated and made impressive as the conditions of speaker, subject, and occasion demand. Thus his conception of style centers about the choice of words, the employment of appropriate ornamentation, and the orderly and artistic arrangements of the selected words.

These essentials of style were always to be studied in relation to existing conditions under which the language flourished. This is a significant point in critical theory. Here we have the reminder that the characteristics of a language at a given time determine in some measure the nature of style. In the Twelfth Book, he remarks:

> He, therefore, that shall require from the Latin the graces of the Attic tongue, must give it a similar sweetness of tone, and a similar abundance of words. If this be impossible, we must adapt our thoughts to the words which we have, and not clothe extremely delicate matter in phraseology which is too strong, not to say too gross, for it, lest the excellences of both be diminished by the union. The less able our language is to assist us, the more efforts we must make in the production of thought. Sublime and varied conceptions must be brought forth. Every feeling must be excited, and our speech illumined by the splendour of metaphor. We cannot be so plain as the Greeks; let us be more forcible. We are excelled by them in refinement; let us surpass them in weight. Exactness of expression is more surely attained by them; let us go beyond them in fulness. The Greek geniuses, even those of inferior degree, have their proper seaports; let us be impelled, in general, with larger sails, and let stronger breezes swell our canvas; but not so that we may always steer out to the deep sea, for we must sometimes coast along the land. The Greeks can easily pass through our shallows; I shall find a port somewhat, though not much deeper, in which my boat may be in no danger of sinking. For if the Greeks succeed better than we in plainer and simpler subjects, so that we are beaten on such ground . . . [we] must cultivate it as far as we can, and we can, at least, rival the Greeks in the temper and judgment with which we treat our subjects; while grace of style, which we have not among us by nature, must be sought from a foreign source.[109]

Quintilian confidently asserted that whereas Latin eloquence was the equal of Greek eloquence in invention, arrangement, judgment, and related matters, it was patently inferior in *elocution,* especially in beauty of diction and agreeableness of sounds.

He also contended that ordinary speech and true eloquence differed in nature.

> . . . for if it were sufficient for an orator to express his thoughts
> plainly, he would have nothing to study beyond mere suitableness of
> words; but since he has to please, to move, and to rouse the minds
> of his audience to various states of feeling, he must have recourse, for
> those purposes, to the means which are afforded us by the same nature
> that supplies us with ordinary speech; just as we are led by nature to
> invigorate our muscles with exercise, to increase our general strength,
> and to acquire a healthy complexion.[110]

This naturally suggested the possible distinction between writing and speaking.

> To me it appears that *to speak well* and *to write well* are but the same
> thing; and that a written oration is nothing else but a record of an
> oration delivered. Written oratory must accordingly, I think, be sus
> ceptible of every species of excellence; I say every species of excel
> lence, not every species of fault, for I know that what is faulty
> sometimes pleases the ignorant. How, then, will what is written and
> what is spoken differ? I reply that if I were to address myself to a
> tribunal composed only of wise men, I would cut off much from the
> speeches, not only of Cicero, but even of Demosthenes, who is much
> less verbose; for, in speaking to such an audience, there will be no
> necessity for exciting the feelings, or for soothing the ear with delight;
> since Aristotle thinks that in such a case even exordia are superfluous,
> as wise men will not be moved by them; and to state the subject in
> proper and significant words, and establish proofs, will be sufficient.
> But when the people, or some of the people, are before us as judges,
> and when illiterate persons, and even ploughmen, are to pass sentence,
> every art which we think likely to conduce to the attainment of the
> object which we have in view, must be employed; and such arts are to
> be displayed not only when we speak, but when we write, that we may
> show how the speech should be spoken. Would Demosthenes have
> spoken badly in speaking exactly as he wrote, or would Cicero? Or do
> we know them to have been excellent orators from any other source
> than from their writings? Did they speak, we may ask, better than
> they wrote; if better, they ought to have written as they spoke?[111]

Shall the orator, therefore, always speak just as he writes? Quintilian says Yes, but recognizes that it is not always possible to do so. For,

> . . . if the time allowed by the judge prevents him from doing so by
> its shortness, much that might have been said will be withheld; but the
> speech, if published, will contain the whole. But what may have been

introduced to suit the capacity of the judges, will not be transmitted unaltered to posterity, lest it be thought to be the offspring of his judgment, and not a concession to circumstances.[112]

In passing judgment upon an orator's style, Quintilian reminds us that since many species of eloquence flourish, it is

. . . extremely foolish to inquire which of them an orator should follow, since every species, if it be but of a genuine character, has its use, and all that people commonly call *ways of speaking* falls under the management of the orator; for he will employ every variety of speech so as to suit, not merely a particular cause, but particular parts of any cause. Thus he will not speak in the same strain in defence of a man who is accused of a capital crime, in a suit respecting an inheritance, and in cases of interdicts, sponsions, and loans; he will observe distinctions between the delivery of opinions in the senate, in the assembly of the people, and in private deliberations; he will vary his style greatly in conformity with the difference of persons, occasions, and places; he will adopt different arts for conciliating, even in the same speech; he will not try to excite anger and pity by dwelling on similar topics; he will employ one style to state his case to the judge, and another to move the judge's feelings. The same colour of diction will not be observable in his exordium, his statement of facts, his arguments, his digressions, and his perorations. He will be able to speak gravely, austerely, sharply, strongly, spiritedly, copiously, bitterly, affably, gently, artfully, soothingly, mildly, agreeably, succinctly, politely; he will not be always alike, yet always consistent with himself. Thus he will not only attain that object for which the use of speech was chiefly intended; I mean, that of speaking to the purpose, and with ability sufficient to establish that which he has in view; but he will also obtain applause, not merely from the learned, but even from the common people.[113]

Thus, what the orator strives for should be

. . . *great* without extravagance; *sublime,* without audacity; *energetic,* without rashness; *severe,* without repulsiveness; *grave,* without dulness; *plenteous,* without exuberance; *pleasing,* without meretriciousness; *grand,* without tumidity. Such judgment will be shown with regard to other qualities; and the path in the middle is generally the safest, because error lies on either side.[114]

Certain Postulates of His Critical Standard.—Like Cicero, for whom he had a deep admiration, Quintilian had a clearly defined conception of the Ideal Orator. His was perhaps more complete than Cicero's. In addition to possessing the characteristics ascribed by Cicero to the perfect speaker, Quintilian's ideal was presumably even more highly qualified as a participant in public life because he had to be a *good* man. Not lacking, to be sure, in the Ciceronian treatments, this attribute was nevertheless discussed at greater length and accorded greater emphasis by Quintilian.

It is probable that Cicero influenced Quintilian in the adoption of the principle of progress in artistic creation. At any rate, Quintilian perceives in the history of oratorical achievement a principle of orderly, gradual growth. His expression of this doctrine, similar in every detail to Cicero's, runs as follows:

> For men of the earliest ages did not speak with our exactness and care, nor had any knowledge of *preparing* an audience with an exordium, *enlightening* them with statements of facts, *convincing* them with arguments, and *exciting* them with appeals to their feelings. They were ignorant of all these arts, and not of composition merely; and if we ought to speak in no respect better than they, huts should never have been relinquished for houses, dresses of skins for decent apparel, or mountains and forests for cities. What art too, we may ask, came to perfection at once? What is not improved by culture? Why do we prune our vines? Why do we dig about them? Why do we root our brambles from our fields, when the ground naturally produces them? But, in truth, a thing is most natural, when nature has allowed it to be brought into the best condition.[115]

As a corollary of this observation, Quintilian suggests that "nature has herself appointed that nothing great is to be accomplished quickly, and has ordained that difficulty should precede every work of excellence";[116] and that "everything great and admirable had some peculiar time at which it was brought to its highest excellence." [117]

Despite the fact that Quintilian had a point of view regarding the basic assumptions of critical inquiry, he remained unquestionably the *theorist* who was trying to check the decline of oratory in his day. His work as a critic is not systematic; neither is it sufficiently complete to enable us to observe the application of the technique, with which he was competently familiar, for the establishing of standards for exacting appraisal of orators.

Quintilian's Critical Estimates.—Scattered criticisms of the orators appear in all of the books of the *Institutes*. In the Tenth Book, however, in which he discusses the improvement of skill in speaking through reading, hearing, and writing, he introduces short critical estimates of a few of the great Greek and Roman speakers, including among others Demosthenes, Lysias, Isocrates, Cicero, Pollio, and Messala.

When he considers Demosthenes, he calls him a most eminent Attic speaker—one who

> . . . has been almost the sole model for oratory; such is his energy, so compact in his whole language, so tense, as it were, with nerves, so free from anything superfluous; and such the general character of his eloquence, that we can neither find anything wanting in it, nor anything superfluous.[118]

And the comparative analysis of Cicero and Demosthenes is effected with this passage:

> But our *orators* may, above all, set the Latin eloquence on an equality with that of Greece; for I would confidently match Cicero against any one of the Greek orators. Nor am I unaware how great an opposition I am raising against myself, especially when it is no part of my design at present to compare him with Demosthenes, for it is not at all necessary, since I think that Demosthenes ought to be read above all other orators, or rather learned by heart. Of their great excellences I consider that most are similar; their method, their order of partition, their manner of preparing the minds of their audience, their mode of proof, and, in a word, everything that depends on invention. In their style of speaking there is some difference; Demosthenes is more compact, Cicero more verbose; Demosthenes argues more closely, Cicero with a wider sweep; Demosthenes always attacks with a sharp-pointed weapon, Cicero often with a weapon both sharp and weighty; from Demosthenes nothing can be taken away, to Cicero nothing can be added; in the one there is more study, in the other more nature. In wit, certainly, and pathos, two stimulants of the mind which have great influence in oratory, we have the advantage. Perhaps the custom of his country did not allow Demosthenes pathetic perorations; but, on the other hand, the different genius of the Latin tongue did not grant to us those beauties which the Attics so much admire. In the epistolary style, indeed, though there are letters written by both, and in that of dialogue, in which Demosthenes wrote nothing, there is no comparison. We must yield the superiority, however, on one point, that Demosthenes lived before Cicero, and made him, in a great measure, the able orator that he was; for Cicero appears to me, after he devoted himself wholly to imitate the Greeks, to have embodied in his style the energy of Demosthenes, the copiousness of Plato, and the sweetness of Isocrates. Nor did he, by zealous effort, attain only what was excellent in each of these, but drew most, or rather all excellences, from himself, by the felicitous exuberance of his immortal genius. He does not, as Pindar says, *collect rain water, but overflows from a living fountain,* having been so endowed at his birth, by the special kindness of Providence, that in him eloquence might make trial of her whole strength. For who can instruct a judge with more exactness, or excite him with more

vehemence? What orator had ever so pleasing a manner? The very points which he wrests from you by force, you would think that he gained from you by entreaty; and when he carries away the judge by his impetuosity, he yet does not seem to be hurried along, but imagines that he is following of his own accord. In all that he says, indeed, there is so much authority, that we are ashamed to dissent from him; he does not bring to a cause the mere zeal of an advocate, but the support of a witness or a judge; and, at the same time, all these excellences, a single one of which any other man could scarcely attain with the utmost exertion, flow from him without effort; and that stream of language, than which nothing is more pleasing to the ear, carries with it the appearance of the happiest facility. It was not without justice, therefore, that he was said by his contemporaries *to reign supreme in the courts;* and he has gained such esteem among his posterity, that Cicero is now less the name of a man than that of eloquence itself. To him, therefore, let us look; let him be kept in view as our great example; and let that student know that he has made some progress to whom Cicero has become an object of admiration.[119]

His Place in the History of Rhetorical Criticism.—Quintilian undoubtedly achieved a measure of success in urging the return to the best Ciceronian standards in oratory. This was a practical result of his careful teaching. He made an eloquent and sincere attempt to restore the classical ideal in Rome at a time when the tides of excess were flowing against such a movement. His contributions to a sound educational philosophy were numerous. In the strict sense, however, his contributions as a critic are of greater importance to the literary craftsman than to the rhetorician. That is, he did more toward developing critical theory—e.g., the elaborate analysis of style—than in applying the doctrines to the judgment of particular speeches. He is a better critic of *oratory* as a form of culture than of individual *orators.*

The Comparative Studies of Plutarch

The Method in Plutarch's Criticism.—Atkins refers to the work of Plutarch (48-120 A.D.) as "another of those cross-currents of doctrine that give to this period its many-sided interest."

In keeping with the plan of his *Lives,* Plutarch presents the parallel accounts of Demosthenes and Cicero and follows them with a comparative study. In the early part of the life of Demosthenes, Plutarch remarks:

    . . . my comparison of their natural dispositions and their characters will be formed upon their actions and their lives as statesmen, and I shall not pretend to criticise their orations one against the other, to show which of the two was the more charming or the more powerful speaker. For there, as Ion says—

'We are but like a fish upon dry land';

a proverb which Caecilius perhaps forgot, when he employed his always adventurous talents in so ambitious an attempt as a comparison of Demosthenes and Cicero; and, possibly, if it were a thing obvious and easy for every man to *know himself,* the precept had not passed for an oracle.[120]

Despite the disclaimer of interest in a comparison of speeches, Plutarch uses the technique in appraising the characteristics of the orators. Thus, in the comparison of Demosthenes and Cicero, following the parallel biographical accounts, Plutarch writes:

But omitting an exact comparison of their respective faculties in speaking, yet thus much seems fit to be said; that Demosthenes, to make himself a master in rhetoric, applied all the faculties he had, natural or acquired, wholly that way that he far surpassed in force and strength of eloquence all his contemporaries in political and judicial speaking, in grandeur and majesty all the panegyrical orators, and in accuracy and science all the logicians and rhetoricians of his day; that Cicero was highly educated, and by his diligent study became a most accomplished general scholar in all these branches, having left behind him numerous philosophical treatises of his own on Academic principles; as, indeed, even in his written speeches, both political and judicial, we see him continually trying to show his learning by the way.[121]

Again, in the same vein, he remarks:

And one may discover the different temper of each of them in their speeches. For Demosthenes's oratory was without all embellishment and jesting, wholly composed for real effect and seriousness; not smelling of the lamp, as Pytheas scoffingly said, but of the temperance, thoughtfulness, austerity, and grave earnestness of his temper. Whereas Cicero's love of mockery often ran him into scurrility; and in his love of laughing away serious arguments in judicial cases by jests and facetious remarks, with a view to the advantage of his clients, he paid too little regard to what was decent. . . .[122]

Later, he observes:

It is necessary, indeed, for a political leader to be an able speaker; but it is an ignoble thing for any man to admire and relish the glory of his own eloquence. And, in this matter, Demosthenes had a more than ordinary gravity and magnificence of mind, accounting his talent in speaking nothing more than a mere accomplishment and matter of practice, the success of which must depend greatly on the good-will and candour of his hearers, and regarding those who pride themselves on such accounts to be men of a low and petty disposition.[123]

Here we find observations that seem to presuppose a method which the author hesitated to use. Whether he willed it or not, Plutarch was comparing speeches, or at least establishing judgments which, if responsible, postulated such comparison.

Incidental Criteria in the *Moralia*: Function of the Listener.— Some of the essays in the *Moralia* shed light upon Plutarch's critical judgment. In "Of Hearing," he discusses the point of view and attitude of the discerning listener, or critic. Commenting on the mistaken notion often held by young men that speaking requires study and attention while "hearing cannot be a thing of any difficulty," he announces some general rules apropos of the observation "that Nature has given every man two ears and but one tongue, as a secret intimation that he ought to speak less than he hears."

The listener should bring with him a "modest and unwearied attention" for then "whatever is beneficial in the discourse he makes his own, . . . he more readily discovers what is false or impertinent. . . ." Furthermore,

> . . . envy and detraction and prejudice are in no case good, but always a great impediment to what is so; yet nowhere worse than when they are made the bosom-friends and counsellors of a hearer, because they represent the best things to him as unpleasant and impertinent, and men in such circumstances are pleased with anything rather than what deserves their applause.[124]

The listener must, accordingly, come "to a kind of truce and accommodation with vainglory, and preserve the same evenness and cheerfulness of humor he would bring with him if he were invited to a festival entertainment or the first-fruits' sacrifice, applauding the orator's power when he speaks to the purpose, and where he fails receiving kindly his readiness to communicate what he knows and to persuade others by what is wrought upon himself." [125]

Plutarch holds that careful listening helps the critic to correct his own mistakes, "For there is nothing in the world more easy than to discover the faults of others; but it is done to no effect if we do not make it useful to ourselves in correcting and avoiding the like failures."

The critic should have a discerningly sensitive ear. Decrying the mood of the fool who, according to Heraclitus, "was put in a flutter at every thing he heard," Plutarch urges tempered consideration.

> We ought indeed to use all the candor imaginable in praising the
> speaker, yet withal as great caution in yielding our assent to what
> he says; to look upon his expression and action with a favorable
> construction, but to inspect the usefulness and truth of his doctrine
> with the nicest and most critical judgment; that speakers may cease
> to be malicious, and that what they say may do no mischief.[126]

The listener must separate "the trash and trumpery of an oration,
that [he] may come at the more fruitful and useful part. . . ."
". . . A well-meaning sincere hearer ought to pass by the flowers of
an oration, leaving the gaudy show and theatrical part to entertain
dronish Sophists; and, diving into the very mind of the speaker and
the sense of his speech, he must draw thence what is necessary for
his own service. . . ."[127]

Expressing his dissatisfaction with the schools that emphasize
the importance of *manner* to the neglect of *matter* in speaking,
Plutarch advises the listener not to make his personal pleasure "the
only end of hearing"; he should not ask for "perfumes and essences"
when "he has need of a poultice and fomentations." "But let him
learn to be thankful to him that purges away the darkness and
stupidity of his mind, though . . . with an offensive or unpalatable
discourse."[128]

> . . . though it lies upon a speaker to take some care that his ex-
> pression be pleasing and plausible, yet a hearer ought not to make that
> the first thing he looks after. Afterward, indeed, when he has satis-
> fied his appetite with the substance and has taken breath, he may be
> allowed the curiosity of examining the style and expression . . . : as
> men quench their thirst first before they have time to admire the
> embossing of the bowl. But now such a one as is not intent on the
> subject-matter, but demands merely that the style shall be plain and
> pure Attic, is much of his foolish humor who refuses an antidote
> unless it be mixed in Attic porcelain, or who will not put on a coat
> in the winter because the cloth is not made of Attic wool. . . .[129]

Plutarch condemns those who "mind nothing but words and jingles,
and express themselves extravagantly upon what they think well
said, without ever understanding or enquiring if it be useful and
necessary, or needless and vain."[130]

The foregoing remarks do not establish Plutarch as a great critic,
but they throw light upon the basis of his judgment. They do reveal
his studied regard for the contextual matter of discourse, as contrasted with style simply for its own sake.

His Oratorical Estimates.—Plutarch's interest in oratory was unquestionably genuine. However, his writings on the orators fail to give us much insight into his critical analysis of speechmaking. His *Lives of the Ten Orators* furnishes additional evidence that the biographical treatment of speakers seldom results in effective rhetorical criticism, unless the total venture is conceived from the point of view of speechcraft and unless the details of the lives are articulated with that theme.

In the *Lives of the Ten Orators,* Plutarch deals briefly with Antiphon, Andocides, Lysias, Isocrates, Isaeus, Aeschines, Lycurgus, Demosthenes, Hyperides, and Dinarchus. His treatment covers chiefly those details relating to the orator's family background, principal activities in the state, and isolated family lore, often of a personal or gossipy nature. Only now and then does he appraise the speaker's skill. Thus, in the biography of Antiphon, he remarks:

> He is most accurate in his orations, in invention subtle; and he would frequently baffle his adversary at unawares, by a covert sort of pleading; in troublesome and intricate matters he was very judicious and sharp; and as he was a great admirer of ornamental speaking, he would always adapt his orations to both law and reason.[131]

Plutarch reminds us that Isocrates "used to tell his scholars that he taught his art for ten minas; but he would give any man ten thousand, that could teach him to be bold and give him a good utterance." Then follows the discerning observation concerning Isocrates: ". . . being once asked how he, who was not very eloquent himself, could make others so . . . he answered, Just as a whetstone cannot cut, yet it will sharpen knives for that purpose."[132] Andocides' style, Plutarch observes, "is plain and easy, without the least affectation or any thing of a figurative ornament."[133] And Lysias was "very cogent in his persuasions, and was always very brief in what he delivered. . . . His style seems plain and easy, though hardly imitable."[134] Hyperides "never affected much action in his orations to the people, his chief aim being to lay down the matter plainly, and make the case as obvious to the judges as he could."[135] And Dinarchus "imitated Hyperides; or, as some incline to judge, rather Demosthenes, because of that vigor and force to move the affections, and the rhetorical ornaments that are evident in his style."[136] Plutarch announces the classic Demosthenic remark that the first, second, and third parts of rhetoric are *action.*

These excerpts, representing much of Plutarch's critical analysis, reveal the treatments to be disappointing. The individuality of the

ten men, as orators, never quite emerges. Plutarch attempts the
difficult if not futile task of energizing biographies of orators, while
neglecting to consider the orations for which the men were distinguished.

His effort is consistent, however, with his recognition of the place
of the orator in public life. Although he was interested in oratory,
he did not consider it as important as military and civic accomplishment. In his essay on "Whether the Athenians Were More Warlike
or Learned," he indicates specifically that, whereas the writings of
the poets are "mere bubbles," the "rhetoricians and orators indeed
have something in them that renders them in some measure fit to be
compared with great captains." [137] But they come off a second best,
it would seem, for greater courage is demanded of the captains.
Thus Isocrates could hardly compare with the heroes of Marathon.
"How would that man have been affrighted at the clattering of
weapons or the routing of a phalanx, who was so afraid of suffering
one vowel to clash with another, or to pronounce a sentence where
but one syllable was wanting!" [138] Plutarch concludes his essay by
comparing Demosthenes and other orators with Miltiades and Alcibiades, the commanders coming off with the greater renown for
their work in defending the honor of the country.

Plutarch formulated no original doctrines in criticism, but offered
a body of suggestive observations sufficiently interesting and revealing to insure him a place in the history of critical thought. His writings throw some light upon Alexandrian learning and upon the
teachings of such significant figures as Gorgias, Isocrates, and
Aristotle.

Philostratus Appraises Declamatory Speech

Proud of the sophistic tradition, anxious "to preserve for all time
a picture of the triumphs of his tribe, when sophists were at the height
of their glory," [139] Philostratus demonstrates in his *Lives of the
Sophists* the type of criticism that naturally derives from an age in
which the conception of rhetoric virtually ignores subject matter and
glorifies stylistic, declamatory utterance. Born about 170 A.D.,
Philostratus falls within the period of the second sophistic, and
accordingly conceives of rhetoric largely in terms of sophistical performance, or of oratory based upon themes—historical and fictitious.

> We must regard the ancient sophistic art as philosophic rhetoric. For
> it discusses the themes that philosophers treat of, but whereas they,
> by their method of questioning, set snares for knowledge, and advance

step by step as they confirm the minor points of their investigations, but assert that they have still no sure knowledge, the sophist of the old school assumes a knowledge of that whereof he speaks.[140]

Philostratus' Critical Standards.—In the *Lives,* written between 230 and 238, Philostratus praises the sophists for their work in declamation. The teaching and practice of the time followed almost identical patterns. As Charles S. Baldwin remarks, "in method, in composition, there was little difference between a teacher's assignments to his amateur pupils and his own professional orations." [141] Philostratus did not consider *declamatio* solely as an exercise; it was "a form of public speaking on a par with any other."

Passages from the *Lives* will reveal Philostratus' studied regard for style as the end of rhetoric. They will confirm Baldwin's belief that the "constant implication of Philostratus probably echoes the ideal of orator and audience alike: behold a great speaker." [142]

In his analysis of the oratory of Dio of Prusa, Philostratus concerns himself chiefly with style:

His style has the ring of Demosthenes and Plato, but Dio has besides a peculiar resonance of his own, which enhances theirs as the bridge enhances the tone of musical instruments; and it was combined with a serious and direct simplicity of expression. . . .

Again, in Dio's orations the elements of his own noble character were admirably displayed. For though he very often rebuked licentious cities, he did not show himself acrimonious or ungracious, but like one who restrains an unruly horse, with the bridle rather than the whip; and when he sets out to praise cities that were well governed, he did not seem to extol them, but rather to guide their attention to the fact that they would be ruined if they should change their ways.[143]

Critias receives Philostratus' praise for substantially the same reasons:

As regards the style of his oratory, Critias abounded in brief and sententious sayings, and he was most skilful in the use of elevated language, but not of the dithyrambic sort, nor did he have recourse to words borrowed from poetry; but his was the kind of elevated language that is composed of the most appropriate words and is not artificial. I observe, moreover, that he was a master of concise eloquence, and that even when he maintained the tone proper to a speech in defence, he used to make vigorous attacks on his opponents; and that he Atticized, but in moderation, nor did he use outlandish words— for bad taste in Atticizing is truly barbarous—but his Attic words shine through his discourse like the gleams of the sun's rays. Critias also secures a charming effect by passing without connectives from one part of his speech to another. Then, too, Critias strives for the daring and unusual both in thought and expression, yet his eloquence is somewhat lacking in virility, though it is agreeable and smooth, like the breath of the west wind.[144]

In Aeschines' orations, Philostratus remarks, "shines the light of perfect lucidity. . . ." Aeschines "is at once sublime and seductive, energetic and delightful, and in a word his sort of eloquence defies the efforts of those who would imitate it." [145]

Isaeus' style was neither "exuberant nor meagre, but simple and natural and suited to the subject matter. Moreover, a concise form of expression and the summing up of every argument into a brief statement was peculiarly an invention of Isaeus. . . ." [146]

It is deserving of note that subject matter, *per se,* receives practically no attention. The charm of speech and of speaker commands the forefront. Dio of Prusa, we are told, had a persuasive charm that captivated "even men who were not versed in Greek letters." When Favorinus delivered speeches in Rome,

> . . . the interest in them was universal, so much so that even those in his audience who did not understand the Greek language shared in the pleasure that he gave; for he fascinated even them by the tones of his voice, [which were evidently shrill], by his expressive glance and the rhythm of his speech.[147]

And Aeschines employed an "inspired manner" that invariably won applause. In Lollianus' oratory, there were brilliant passages that suddenly came to an end "like a flash of lightning." Polemo's utterance "was clear and incisive, and there was a fine ringing sound in the tones of his voice." "Polemo's style of eloquence is passionate, combative, and ringing to the echo. . . . The Demosthenic cast of his thought lends it distinction and a gravity which is not dull or inert but brilliant and inspired, as though delivered from the tripod." [148]

Personal charm in a speaker, Philostratus thus held, should be considered an important element in rhetorical effectiveness. Concerning Hermocrates, he said:

> In his public declamations Hermocrates was aided in the first place by his great-grandfather's renown, since it is human nature to set a higher value on abilities that have been handed down from father to son. . . . But he was also aided by the beauty of his personal appearance, and he was indeed possessed of great charm and looked like a statue with the bloom of early youth. . . . Moreover his easy flow of words and the striking effects of his voice contributed to his success,

and the fact that he could review his themes in the twinkling of an
eye, and that what he recited from a manuscript or declaimed was more
what one expects from hoary old age than from a mere youth to invent
and deliver.[149]

The references to inventive skill are incidental, almost mechanical.
For example, Polemo is defended briefly against the charge that he
was not skilled in defence; that he was unable to establish sustained
arguments but "was forced off the course like a horse for whom the
ground is too rough. . . ." And Herodes' disposition of materials
elicits this comment:

> The structure of his work was suitably restrained, and its strength lay
> in subtlety rather than in vigour of attack. He was impressive in the
> plain style, sonorous after the manner of Critias; his ideas were such
> as would not occur to the mind of another; he had an easy and urbane
> wit which was not dragged in, but inspired by the subjects themselves;
> his diction was pleasing and abounded in figures and had grace and
> beauty; he was skilful in varying his constructions; his tone was not
> vehement but smooth and steady, and, speaking generally, his type
> of eloquence is like gold dust shining beneath the waters of a silvery
> eddying river.[150]

Antiochus, we are told, "handled the emotions more skilfully than
any other sophist, for he did not spin out long monodies or abject
lamentations, but expressed them in a few words and adorned them
with ideas better than I can describe. . . ."[151] Philostratus comments on the fact that Herodes reproached Philagrus of Cilicia for
"not trying to win the good-will of his hearers. . . ."[152] Aristeides'
strength is reputed to have been "in the elaborate cogitation of a
theme; for which reason he refrained from extempore speaking."[153]

The Significance of the *Lives*.—The value of these short biographies, in which the criticism of speaking figures rather prominently,
is perhaps doubtful. At best, the *Lives* represents superficial rhetorical criticism. True, the form of the *Lives* is suggestive of
sounder critical values, for we find data on the speakers' early youth,
training, activities, personal appearance, style, and related details.
Examples from typical speeches illustrate some of the points relative
to the speakers' style. Within narrow ranges, the comparative
method of analysis is employed. But the standards of excellence
that Philostratus sets up presuppose the all-sufficiency of style as the
measure of speaking. Unless speaking well is accepted as an absolute standard, which cannot properly be granted, the *Lives* affords a
type of criticism that is unmistakably capricious.

Philostratus presented, however, a body of semicritical estimates consistent with the spirit and temper of his age. An oratory of themes held sway, and he accepted and defended it. Accordingly, he conceived of rhetoric as an instrument for giving effectiveness to the speaker, rather than to the message. Divorced, as Baldwin expresses it, from "the urgencies of matter and motive," rhetoric thus became empty, ostentatious. Philostratus' criticism is correspondingly deficient. Devoted to the appraisal of exhibitionistic skill, it loses sight of the ideas that normally constitute the reason for speaking.

The Doctrine of Imitation

The literature on rhetoric contains numerous references to imitation—to its necessity, usefulness, and general role in the training of speakers. Indirectly, it concerns the critical functions as well, for some of the greatest orators, in the opinion of the rhetoricians, are imitators. However, they imitated their predecessors with such consummate skill that the critics accredit the actions as artistic refinements.

Quintilian asserts that "a great portion of art consists in *imitation,* since, though to invent was first in order of time, and holds the first place in merit, yet it is of advantage to copy what has been invented with success." Imitation, in itself, is not enough. "When those who had no master in any subject, have transmitted so many discoveries to posterity, shall not the experience which we have in some things assist us to bring to light others, or shall we have nothing but what we derive from other men's bounty, as some painters aim at nothing more than to know how to copy a picture by means of compasses and lines?" In short, it "is dishonourable even to rest satisfied with simply equalling what we imitate." [154]

Quintilian believes it proper to imitate the excellences of several orators, rather than one only. "Of all the Greek orators Demosthenes is by far the most excellent; yet others, on some occasions have expressed themselves better; and he himself has expressed many things better on some occasions than on others. But he who deserves to be imitated most, is not therefore the only author to be imitated." [155]

An orator's artistry can never assert itself wholly through simple imitation. Everything "that is the resemblance of something else, must necessarily be inferior to that of which it is a copy, as the shadow to the substance, the portrait to the natural face, and the acting of the player to the real feeling. The same is the case with regard to oratorical composition; for in the originals, which we take for our models, there is nature and real power, while every imitation, on the contrary, is something counterfeit, and seems adapted to an object not its own." So while the student is asked to make "whatever is excellent in each author his own," he also is warned that borrowing must become more than common plagiarism: ". . . he who shall add to these borrowed qualities excellences of his own, so as to supply what is deficient in his models, and to retrench what is redundant, will be the complete orator whom we desire to see; and such an orator ought now surely to be formed, when so many more examples of eloquence exist than fell to the lot of those who have hitherto been considered the best orators; for to them will belong the praise, not only of surpassing those who preceded them, but of instructing those who followed." [156]

Cicero also believed that the student should seek out good models and, equally important, copy the chief excellences rather than the faults. He remarks that the practice of truly great orators bespeaks the value of imitation: Lysias and Critias "retained the vigorous style of Pericles"; Demosthenes, Hyperides, Aeschines, Lycurgus, and Dinarchus, although unlike in their skills, "all engaged in imitating the same kind of material excellence; and as long as the imitation of their manner lasted, so long did that character and system of eloquence prevail." [157]

One of the more extensive modern treatments of imitation is found in John Ward's *System of Oratory,* published in 1759. Ward shares the view of the ancients that imitation means expressing the best in the chosen models and striving for advantages "above the original." Consequently, it is consistent with the free exercise "and improvement of our abilities." The true art consists in so diversifying "what we take from others, as, if we can, to improve it, or at least not suffer it to receive any detriment by our alteration." This can be done in four ways: (1) Enlarge a thought or expression taken from another. Cicero observed this principle in his orations against Mark Antony, which evidently were copied in part from the Demosthenean pronouncements against Philip. (2) Abridge or take only a part of what others have said. After the battle of Chaeronea, in which the Athenians were defeated by Philip, Demosthenes delivered a funeral oration upon which Cicero drew subsequently for parts of his fourteenth Philippic. (3) Keep the thought but apply it to a different subject, as Cicero, drawing upon Demosthenes' defense of Ctesiphon, did in parts of his oration for

Quinctius. (4) Change the order of thoughts or represent them in a different dress. In his defense of Cluentius, Cicero relied thus upon parts of Demosthenes' oration against Aristogiton.[158]

Many of the best artists, according to Ward, have imitated others. Homer was assisted by writers whose works are no longer extant; Vergil imitated Homer; Terence copied after Menander; Plautus, after Epicharmus; Sulpicius imitated Crassus; and Cicero drew upon the practices of many Greek orators.

It seems, then, that many theorists exercise extreme care in applying the test of originality to oratorical composition. While assigning great importance to original invention, they recognize that the flow of ideas in history is a continuum; and they allow that skilful and improved adaptation of old thoughts and techniques to new conditions may stamp an orator as an accomplished model, rather than as a plagiarist.

General Summary

The evidence shows that the distinguished theorizers on rhetoric were willing to apply their tenets to the criticism of speeches. They used the principles and precepts which they laid down for others; and in so doing, they demonstrated further that the theory and criticism of speaking are common aspects of an indivisible art.

Hence the earliest theorizers were also critics. Beginning with Plato and continuing through the long line of ancient contributors to rhetoric, we note the studied attempt by scholars to hit upon criteria of artistic judgment by which the relative merits of prose forms can be assessed. In this chapter we have seen how patterns of evaluation began to take form; how the comparative method soon came into use; how the impact of historical forces upon speech-making was early recognized as a determinant of rhetorical effectiveness. These critical tenets received their most elaborate embodiment in the efforts of Cicero. Especially in the *Orator* and in the *Brutus* did Cicero establish just claim to distinction as a pioneer in the criticism of speeches, and as the first systematic historian of oratory.

Chapter 6

THE CRITICS OF THE INTERMEDIATE PERIOD
(1600-1850)

Introduction

Perhaps no one has ever considered himself a professional rhetorical critic. For many years, however, men have sought a system by which speeches might intelligently and responsibly be judged. Often, as in the case of the critics of antiquity, these systems were not deliberately established for the purpose of analyzing talks. Instead, they grew out of the general theorizing which was the business of men who probed the operation of an art. Thus Aristotle's *Rhetoric* —however valuable it may be today as a pattern of critical judgment—surely was not designed originally as a yardstick of criticism. In this chapter we shall examine the theories of a selected group of men, some of whom sought to establish, at least for themselves, formal patterns of critical analysis for public speeches.

Rapin Evaluates French Oratory of Seventeenth Century

The Theoretical Basis of His Report.—René Rapin's essay on eloquence [1] is essentially a report on the state of public speaking during the seventeenth century. Specifically, it is an analysis of the major defects evident in the speakers of the period, together with certain suggestions for the correction of faults. Rapin makes no claim of presenting new contributions to rhetorical theory, although his treatment of pulpit eloquence reveals a fair measure of originality. In the main, he relies upon the masters of antiquity for his theory. In the preface to the essay, he pays tribute to the "admirable Memoirs from the Rhetorical Instructions of Aristotle, Cicero, and Quintilian whose Works in this kind are so exact, and their Pourtrait of Eloquence so just, and so accomplish'd, as to leave no Room for our Improvements, nor even for our Wishes." [2] Accordingly, Rapin draws upon those contributors, as well as upon Longinus, for the critical standards by which to appraise the speaking of the day.

Marginal references to the ancients are sprinkled liberally throughout the first part of the essay.

Reflexions on Eloquence, first printed in 1672, is in three parts: "Reflexions upon the Eloquence of the Times in General," "Reflexions upon the Eloquence of the Bar," and "Reflexions upon the Eloquence of the Pulpit." Of the three divisions, the last receives by far the most detailed treatment.

"Reflexions upon the Eloquence of the Times in General" contains, in a negative way, Rapin's standard of effective speaking. The chief sources of eloquence are said to be two: (1) natural talent for speaking, "without which it is not possible to succeed, and with which it is almost impossible to miscarry," and (2) comprehensive knowledge and a severe application. Then follows a long list of the faults found in the speakers of the period. Each of these defects is said to result from the violation of some principle set forth by Aristotle, Cicero, Quintilian, or Longinus. Most of the speakers, Rapin indicates, do not train themselves in composition as they used to do; they pay too little attention to the accurate expression of ideas; they neglect study in pronunciation; they are careless in their use of logic; they do not adapt their styles to the circumstances, and hence fail to get the proper measure of sublimity; they frequently add too much ornamentation to their addresses; they often fail to adhere closely enough to nature; and they sometimes mar the style of their discourses by artificiality and affectation. Furthermore, certain speakers do not have that "just Temperament which ought to be used in mixing Reason with Authority, Comparison and Similitude with Example and Induction"; others amuse only "the Head, without affecting the Heart"; still others fail to arrange and dispose properly the things which they invent. Rapin closes his summary of ills by saying that eloquence must gain admiration, and that it must come from a speaker who is genteel and modest.[3]

In the two subsequent sections of his essay, Rapin relates the foregoing abuses to forensic and pulpit speaking, respectively, and suggests the proper means of avoiding the faults. However, his treatment of forensic eloquence is highly abbreviated, and in general unenlightening.

Rapin deplores the scarcity of good pulpit speakers, especially since Biblical subjects offer unusual opportunities for distinguished effort. He attributes a good share of the failure in this field to the deficiencies of the preachers in learning and study. These shortcomings encourage preachers to copy boldly from one another; "they draw from the Stream, because they are Strangers to the Fountain-head."

Rapin believes that preachers must construct a rhetoric for their own use, since the ancient writers on speechcraft had no idea of the requirements of pulpit speaking.

> For no Man ought to speak of God, and of heavenly Things, without the utmost Dignity of Style, and such *a Voice of great Words* as the Prophet mentions. 'Twould be in vain to seek this Pitch of Eloquence in *Aristotle's* Rhetorick, in the Ideas of *Hermogenes,* or the Institutions of *Quintilian.*[4]

Rapin believes the true standard of preaching "should be taken from the Manner of St. *Peter* and St. *Paul,* in their Sermons to the first Believers."

His Comparative Analysis of the Great Orators.—Rapin's major critical work in rhetoric is "A Comparison of Demosthenes and Cicero," the avowed purpose of which is "no other than to propose to the present Age an accomplished Standard of Eloquence; it being universally agreed, that *Demosthenes* and *Cicero* are the Men who have carried this Art to its utmost Height, and most absolute Per-fection." Intent upon establishing a satisfactory criterion of ora-torical excellence, Rapin establishes a rule by which comparative estimates can be made. Assuming that the critic has a "competent share of Natural Abilities," a "good stock of sound and solid Sense," a recognition of the effect of time and age on artistic creations, and an uncorrupted judgment "gained and improv'd by being well vers'd in Ancient Writers," Rapin concludes, after a survey of controlling rules for the making of comparisons, that Aristotle's doctrines on the nature of eloquence are the most fundamental and practical of all. So he accepts Aristotle's dictum that the end of oratory is persuasion, and that there are "three Things which have the chief Power to persuade, the Merit of the speaker, the Disposition of those to whom he speaks, and his Manner of Speaking." This Aristotelian formula constitutes the basic pattern of Rapin's critical method.[5]

According to the restatement that Rapin makes of Aristotle's rule, three things are essential to comparative estimates of orators: an examination of their personal merits, a fixation of "the Character of Wit and Sense" in the age in which the speaker lived, and a study of the orator's manner of speaking. If we were to make a rough analysis of Rapin's scheme or method of criticism, it would appear as follows:

I. Personal Merit of the Speaker

    A. Abilities
        1. Education
        2. Influence of Parents
        3. Instruction
        4. Reading Activities

    B. Integrity—Sincerity and Honesty

    C. Agreeableness (less important than Ability and Integrity, but still essential)

II. Consideration of the Inclination and Disposition of the Audience

    A. State of Mind of the People Addressed

    B. Temper of the Age

III. Manner of Speaking

    A. Recognition of Natural Inclinations and Their Cultivation
        1. Sprightliness and Vigor
        2. Deep Understanding
        3. Voice, Action, Gestures
        4. Learning and Art
        5. Grace in Doing Things
        6. Sense of Arrangement of Parts; Sense of Proportion
        7. Charm in Delivery
        8. Use of Ornamentation in Speech

    B. Mastery of Subject Matter

    C. Artistic Use of Rhetoric, without Betrayal of the Art

    D. Adaptation of Style to Subject Matter

Using this formula in an almost mechanical way, Rapin appraised the respective merits of the two great models of ancient eloquence. His preference in nearly all departments of judgment inclined toward Cicero, in whose oratory, he believed, there was evidence of more skilful handling of the passions and manners of men. This is in contrast with the conclusion of another French theorist and critic of oratory, Fénelon, whose favorite was Demosthenes. Ignoring some of the minor arguments that Rapin advanced in Cicero's behalf, it is clear that the critic was using the *effect of oratory in influencing people* as the final measure of success. In this respect he was, indeed, applying a canon to which much contemporary criticism adheres. While admitting that Demosthenes' reasoning was closer than Cicero's, Rapin holds that if that man is most eloquent who persuades most, then the Roman was unquestionably the superior. As though he were reluctant to formulate a final judgment, however, Rapin leaves to his readers the query as to whether an appeal to the heart is preferable to an appeal to the mind.

Rapin's method of analysis, it will be observed, was quite comprehensive. If used intensively, and with adequate reliance upon the speeches themselves as well as upon the outcome, it would undoubtedly result in exacting criticism. As used by Rapin, it was only moderately successful, for he neglected to rely adequately upon the speeches for which the orators were distinguished. Despite this shortcoming, he did formulate the most systematic and clearly defined method for criticizing speeches since the time of Cicero. His method is formal and almost stereotyped, but it reveals an intelligent recognition of the nature of rhetorical analysis.

Certain Prose Writers Appraise English Delivery

Incidental rhetorical criticism appeared in the works of certain eighteenth-century prose writers, including Swift, Addison, and Lord Chesterfield. Their chief point of interest is delivery, however, so we do not find here a comprehensive inquiry deserving detailed notice.

Swift's Analysis.—In his "Letter to a Young Clergyman," Jonathan Swift revealed his displeasure with preachers who read their sermons. He frankly admitted "taking some little offence" at this practice, saying there was a difference between reading and speaking which the clergy often overlooked. Furthermore, he remarked,

> . . . you will observe some clergymen with their heads held down from the beginning to the end within an inch of the cushion to read what is hardly legible: which beside the untoward manner, hinders them from making the best advantage of their voice: others again have a trick of popping up and down every moment from their paper to the audience, like an idle school boy on a repetition day.[6]

Addison Also Dissents.—In a similar vein, Joseph Addison protested the oratorical customs of his countrymen. He believed that the British speakers of his time should either "lay aside all kinds of gesture (which seems to be very suitable to the genius of our nation,) or at least to make use of such only as are graceful and expressive." Criticizing the English preachers, debaters, and courtroom speakers for their failure to make proper use of action and gestures, Addison remarks:

> It is certain that proper gestures and vehement exertions of the voice cannot be too much studied by a public orator. They are a kind of comment to what he utters, and enforce everything he says, with weak hearers, better than the strongest arguments he can make use of. They keep the audience awake, and fix their attention to what is delivered to them, at the same time that they show the speaker is in earnest, and affected himself with what he so passionately recommends to others.[7]

Later, he comments:

> We are told that the great Latin orator very much impaired his health . . . by the vehemence of action, with which he used to deliver himself. The Greek orator was likewise so very famous for this particular in rhetoric, that one of his antagonists, whom he had banished from Athens, reading over the oration which had procured his banishment, and seeing his friends admire it, could not forbear asking them, if they were so much affected by the bare reading of it, how much more they would have been alarmed, had they heard him actually throwing out such a storm of eloquence?
>
> How cold and dead a figure, in comparison of these two great men, does an orator often make at the British bar, holding up his head with the most insipid serenity, and stroking the sides of a long wig that reaches down to his middle! The truth of it is, there is often nothing more ridiculous than the gestures of most of our English speakers: you see some of them running their hands into their pockets as far as ever they can thrust them, and others looking with great attention on a piece of paper that has nothing written on it; you may see many a smart rhetorician turning his hat in his hands, moulding it into several different cocks, examining sometimes the lining of it, and sometimes the button, during the whole course of his harangue.[8]

Chesterfield Joins in the Criticism.—Further evidence to suggest that delivery and style were largely the features by which oratory was appraised during this period comes from the *Letters* of Chesterfield to his son. Although the Earl of Chesterfield looked upon Cicero and Demosthenes as good models, and urged his son to study them, he directed most of his advice to the necessity of acquiring an agreeable delivery and manner of expression. In a letter written in 1748, he admonishes his son for rapidity of utterance, adding, "An agreeable and distinct manner of speaking adds greatly to the matter; and I have known many a very good speech unregarded,

upon account of the disagreeable manner in which it has been delivered, and many an indifferent one applauded, from the contrary
reason." [9]

Two months later, Chesterfield urged his son to strive for good
enunciation, asking as he had on previous occasions that the boy
note the stress Cicero and Quintilian "lay upon the gracefulness of
it." "Had Roscius spoken *quick, thick,* and *ungracefully,*" Chesterfield says,

> I will answer for it, that Cicero would not have thought him worth
> the oration which he made in his favor. Words were given us to
> communicate our ideas by: and there must be something inconceivably
> absurd in uttering them, in such a manner as that either people cannot
> understand them, or will not desire to understand them.[10]

Closely associated with accuracy and care in enunciating sounds, a
"graceful manner of presenting yourself"—"a genteel carriage"—
was also essential to effective oral address.

The style of utterance should be cultivated, for "the very first
principle of an orator is to speak his own language . . . with the
utmost purity and elegance." Purity and elegance, he affirmed,
cover many faults in speakers and writers. "For my own part, I
confess . . . that if a speaker should ungracefully mutter or stam-
mer out to me the sense of an angel, deformed by barbarism and
solecisms, or larded with vulgarisms, he should never speak to me
a second time, if I could help it." And, he added, "Gain the heart,
or you gain nothing; the eyes and the ears are the only roads to
the heart. Merit and knowledge will not gain hearts, though they
will secure them when gained." "Engage the eyes by your address,
air, and motions; soothe the ears by the elegance and harmony of
your diction; the heart will certainly follow. . . ." [11]

In his letter of December 5, 1749, Chesterfield appraised the
deliberative speaking then current in England. Believing that the
nature of the British constitution made eloquence more useful than
in any European country, he indicated that a

> . . . certain degree of good sense and knowledge is requisite for that,
> as well as for everything else; but beyond that, the purity of diction,
> the elegance of style, the harmony of periods, a pleasing elocution, and a
> graceful action, are the things which a public speaker should attend to
> the most; because his audience certainly does, and understands them the
> best. . . .[12]

Examples from oratorical history sustain the judgment. Thus, according to Chesterfield, Lord Chancellor Cowper derived his strength

from the "purity and elegance of his style," not from his reasoning, which was frequently weak. Lord Townshend, who excelled in argument but was inelegant in diction, invariably failed to please his hearers. The Duke of Argyll, "though the weakest reasoner, was the most pleasing speaker I ever knew in my life." [13]

Chesterfield advises his son, therefore, to mind his diction and delivery, for they are the important elements in speaking. The complete orator about whom Cicero talks—the man of great learning—is to be regarded as an ideal, virtually impossible of attainment. Accordingly, Chesterfield holds him to be the most complete orator "who speaks the best upon that subject which occurs; whose happy choice of words, whose lively imagination, whose elocution and action adorn and grace his matter, at the same time that they excite the attention and engage the passions of his audience." [14]

On repeated occasions Chesterfield gave this advice to his son. Always the characteristic admonition seemed to be: "Most people have ears, but few have judgment; tickle those ears, and depend upon it, you will catch their judgments, such as they are." [15] Surely this was a cynical, unenlightened conception of the role of oratory in public life. But it was indicative of a trend which subsequently gave rise to the elocutionary movement in rhetorical theory.

Blair's Prolegomena to Criticism

The Basis of Critical Inquiry.—In the first lecture of his treatise, published in 1783, Hugh Blair makes it evident that his undertaking is of an omnibus nature. He is writing a book to appeal to three distinct groups: those whose inclination tends toward a study of composition; those who are interested in public speaking; and, finally, those who "may wish only to improve their taste with respect to writing and discourse, and to acquire principles which will enable them to judge for themselves in that part of literature called the Belles Lettres." [16] Clearly, Blair is concerned with rhetorical criticism; he directs his remarks to the critics, as well as to the students of composition and oratory. "To them," he says, referring to the critics,

> . . . rhetoric is not so much a practical art as a speculative science; and the same instructions which assist others in composing will assist them in discerning and relishing the beauties of composition. Whatever enables genius to execute well, will enable taste to criticize justly.[17]

The criticism with which Blair proposed to deal, however, avoided
the "frigid application of certain technical terms, by means of which
persons are taught to cavil and censure in a learned manner." Instead, he projected a prolegomena to criticism, as it were, which
derived from "good sense and refined taste."

According to Blair, the first topic of inquiry into critical and
creative activity is Taste.   This he defines as the "power of receiving
pleasure from the beauties of nature and of art."   The source of
taste rests basically upon "a certain natural and instinctive sensitivity
to beauty," but *reason* assists and enlarges the operation of the
internal feeling of sense. All men have, in some degree, a sense
of taste, but the range varies widely.   Generally, in "the powers and
pleasures of taste, there is a more remarkable inequality among
men, than is usually found, in point of common sense, reason, and
judgment."   However, frequent exercise and "curious attention to
its proper objects must greatly heighten its power."   Blair indicates
that devotion of attention "to the most approved models, study of
the best authors, comparisons of lower and higher degrees of the
same beauties, operate towards the refinement of Taste."   This
would suggest the validity of Blair's claim that enlarged understanding—the exercise of reason generally—improves taste.[18]

The characters of taste, when richly improved, in Blair's judgment are reducible to two, namely *delicacy* and *correctness*.   The
former "respects principally the perfection of that natural sensi-
bility on which Taste is founded."   Delicacy of taste presupposes
that the person "feels strongly and feels accurately."   Anyone possessing this character is able to see "distinctions and differences where
others see none; the most latent beauty does not escape him, and he
is sensible of the smallest blemish."   Correctness, on the other hand,
results from the application of understanding to the faculty of
taste.[19]

> A man of correct Taste is one who is never imposed on by counter-
> feit beauties; who carries always in his mind that standard of good
> sense which he employs in judging of every thing. He estimates
> with propriety the comparative merit of the several beauties which he
> meets with in any work of genius; refers them to their proper classes;
> assigns the principles, as far as they can be traced, whence their
> power of pleasing flows; and is pleased himself precisely in that degree
> in which he ought, and no more.[20]

This presupposes, however, the existence of a criterion, of a
standard to which critics may appeal in distinguishing between
good and bad artistic endeavor.   Recognizing that there must be a

standard or else all taste will be equally good, Blair indicates that diversity does not necessarily imply corruption. "The Tastes of men may differ very considerably as to their object, and yet none of them be wrong." Hence, it

> . . . is not in matters of Taste, as in questions of mere reason, where there is but one conclusion that can be true, and all the rest erroneous. Truth, which is the object of reason, is one; Beauty, which is the object of Taste, is manifold. Taste, therefore, admits of latitude and diversity of objects, in sufficient consistency with goodness or justness of Taste.[21]

The standard to which Blair appeals when there is opposition of taste is clear. A standard, properly conceived, "signifies that which is of such undoubted authority as to be the test of other things of the same kind." Admitting that nature herself is a partial standard, Blair shows that it is not adequate. So he appeals to the taste of *men in general.* "That which men concur the most in admiring must be held to be beautiful. His Taste must be esteemed just and true, which coincides with the general sentiments of men." Thus he acknowledges the "sense of mankind" as the ultimate basis of judgment. As supplements to the "approbation of the majority," Blair mentions the reason and the sound judgment of the critic. Just as reason and judgment apply in the study of science and philosophy, so they figure in the determination of merit in the arts.[22]

> He who admires or censures any work of genius, is always ready, if his Taste be in any degree improved, to assign some reasons for his decision. He appeals to principles, and points out the grounds on which he proceeds. Taste is a sort of compound power, in which the light of the understanding always mingles, more or less, with the feelings of sentiments.[23]

Blair openly announces his criterion, then, and assures us that the doctrine of universal testimony is valid only if the men involved live in situations which are conducive "to the proper exertions of Taste." The doctrine deals largely with the "sentiments of mankind in polished and flourishing nations; when arts are cultivated and manners refined; when works of genius are subjected to free discussion, and Taste is improved by Science and Philosophy." Time itself becomes the determiner of value; posterity is sure to discern faults where authority or prejudice may, in one age, have afforded temporary repute. In short, "Time overthrows the illusions of opinion, but establishes the decisions of nature." [24]

This is the substructure of Blair's critical system. Criticism for him is the application of taste and good sense to the various artistic productions. The rules by which this critical function is carried out are not derived from abstract reasoning; on the contrary, they grow wholly out of experience—out of the "observations of such beauties as have come nearest to the standard" previously discussed.

As might be expected, Blair devotes a large section of the *Lectures* to style. He treats first the constituents of effective expression, namely words, perspicuity, precision, sentence development, harmony, and figurative forms; and secondly he appraises the style of various writers in the several fields of literary production. His conception of style derives chiefly from Quintilian and Cicero, to whom he turns frequently for precept and illustration.

Blair's Estimates of Orators.—In Lectures XXV through XXX, we find Blair's most direct efforts at rhetorical criticism. Postulating as his definition of Eloquence, "the art of Speaking in such a manner as to attain the end for which we speak," [25] he gives a short history of Grecian and Roman oratory, in which he evaluates chiefly the style of the major speakers. Thus Isocrates' style is pronounced "swelling and full"; and that of Lysias, "pure and Attic in the highest degree." Using Demosthenes and Cicero as his model speakers, Blair crowds out most of the other public figures in order that the truly great may receive proper attention. Demosthenes is praised for the "strength and vehemence" of his style. [26] His orations are strongly animated,

> . . . and full of the impetuosity and fire of public spirit. They proceed in a continued train of inductions, consequences, and demonstrations, founded on sound reason. The figures which he uses, are never sought after; but always rise from the subject. He employs them sparingly indeed; for splendour and ornament are not the distinction of this orator's composition. It is an energy of thought peculiar to himself, which forms his character, and sets him above all others. He appears to attend much more to things than to words. We forget the orator, and think of the business. He warms the mind, and impels to action. He has no parade and ostentation; no methods of insinuation; no laboured introductions; but is like a man full of his subject, who, after preparing his audience by a sentence or two for hearing plain truths, enters directly on business. [27]

Demosthenes uses a style which is

> . . . strong and concise, though sometimes, it must not be dissembled, harsh, and abrupt. His words are very expressive; his arrangement

is firm and manly; and though far from being unmusical, yet it seems difficult to find in him that studied, but concealed number and rhythmus, which some of the ancient critics are fond of attributing to him. Negligent of these lesser graces, one would rather conceive him to have aimed at that Sublime which lies in sentiment.[28]

As contrasted with Aeschines, Demosthenes appears to real advantage. Aeschines "makes much less impression on the mind," whereas Demosthenes "is a torrent, that nothing can resist. He bears down his antagonist with violence; he draws his character in the strongest colours. . . ."

Cicero, "whose name alone suggests every thing that is splendid in Oratory," knew "the power and force of words" better than any other man.

> He rolls them along with the greatest beauty and pomp: and, in the structure of his sentences, is curious and exact to the highest degree. He is always full and flowing, never abrupt. He is a great amplifier of every subject; magnificent, and in his sentiments highly moral. His manner is on the whole diffuse, yet it is often happily varied, and suited to the subject.[29]

But he had certain defects. These shortcomings resulted from his making "too visible a parade of Eloquence." On some occasions,

> . . . he is showy rather than solid; and diffuse, where he ought to have been pressing. His sentences are, at all times, round and sonorous; they cannot be accused of monotony, for they possess variety of cadence; but, from too great a study of magnificence, he is sometimes deficient in strength. On all occasions, where there is the least room for it, he is full of himself. His great actions, and the real services which he had performed to his country, apologize for this in part; ancient manners, too, imposed fewer restraints from the side of decorum; but, even after these allowances [are] made, Cicero's ostentation of himself cannot be wholly palliated; and his orations, indeed all his works, leave on our minds the impression of a good man, but withal, of a vain man.[30]

Blair then compares the oratory of Demosthenes and Cicero:

> The character of Demosthenes is vigour and austerity; that of Cicero is gentleness and insinuation. In the one, you find more manliness; in the other more ornament. The one is more harsh, but more spirited and cogent; the other more agreeable, but withal, looser and weaker.[31]

Blair speculates that the differences in style may result from the types of audiences they addressed. He doubts, however, that that will provide the complete explanation.

Perhaps we shall come nearer the truth, by observing, that to unite all the qualities, without the least exception, that form a perfect orator, and to excel equally in each of those qualities is not to be expected from the limited powers of human genius. The highest degree of strength is, I suspect, never found united with the highest degree of smoothness and ornament; equal attentions to both are incompatible; and the genius that carries ornament to its utmost length, is not of such a kind, as can excel as much in vigour. For there plainly lies the characteristical difference between these two celebrated orators.[32]

On last analysis, Blair gives the palm for greater excellence to Demosthenes. His explanation is both interesting and revealing:

I am of opinion, that were the state in danger, or some great national interest at stake, which drew the serious attention of the public, an oration in the spirit and strain of Demosthenes would have more weight, and produce greater effects, than one in the Ciceronian manner. Were Demosthenes's Philippics spoken in a British assembly, in a similar conjuncture of affairs, they would convince and persuade at this day. The rapid style, the vehement reasoning, the disdain, anger, boldness, freedom, which perpetually animate them, would render their success infallible over any modern assembly. I question whether the same can be said of Cicero's orations; whose eloquence, however beautiful, and however well suited to the Roman taste, yet borders oftener on declamation, and is more remote from the manner in which we now expect to hear real business and causes of importance treated.[33]

In this judgment Blair agrees with the thesis developed by David Hume in the "Essay upon Eloquence." Hume, in his attempt to determine why modern oratory was inferior to that of the ancients, pointed to the "elevated conceptions"—the vehemence of thought, expression, and action—which so signally stamped the efforts of a Demosthenes. Commenting on the moderns' satisfaction with mediocrity, Hume urged a return to the study of true models of sublime eloquence. And, he added, "of all human productions the orations of Demosthenes present to us the models which approach the nearest to perfection." [34]

The Structure of Blair's Critical Method.—Blair's critical investigations reveal a clearly defined method which, though mechanical, is nevertheless systematic and useful. He offers a descriptive analysis of the three kinds of speaking, and illustrates each type by quoting selected passages from a great orator who engaged actively in that field. He recognizes that certain rules apply in common to deliberative, judicial, and demonstrative speaking; at the same time, he wishes to consider the characteristics of spirit and manner peculiar to each type.

Deliberative Speaking.—Since, in Blair's judgment, the eloquence of popular assemblies throws much light upon other types, he opens by indicating that the object of deliberative speaking is, "or always ought to be, Persuasion. There must be some end proposed, some point, most commonly of public utility or good, in favour of which we seek to determine the hearers." [35] Accordingly, the principal constituent of such speaking is *material* that will convince the audience.

> Let it be their first study, in addressing any popular assembly, to be previously master of the business on which they are to speak; to be well provided with matter and argument, and to rest upon these the chief stress. This will always give to their discourse an air of manliness and strength, which is a powerful instrument of persuasion. Ornament, if they have genius for it, will follow of course; at any rate it demands only their secondary study. . . . 'To your expression be attentive, but about your matter be solicitous,' is an advice of Quinctilian, which cannot be too often recollected by all who study oratory.[36]

Furthermore, the deliberative speaker must himself be persuaded of whatever he proposes to his hearers. "Seldom or never will a man be eloquent, but when he is in earnest, and uttering his own sentiments." Of course, the speaker will provide as much time as possible for assembling his thoughts and sentiments, although deliberative speaking—and particularly debate—does not always permit such preliminary investigation. "The arguments must be suited to the course which the debate takes; and as no man can exactly foresee this, one who trusts to a set speech composed in his closet, will, on many occasions, be thrown out of the ground which he had taken." [37]

The style and expression of deliberative speaking should be animated and elevated.

> The very aspect of a large assembly, engaged in some debate of moment, and attentive to the discourse of one man, is sufficient to inspire that man with such elevation and warmth, as both give rise to strong impressions, and give them propriety. Passion easily rises in a great assembly, where the movements are communicated by mutual sympathy between the Orator and the Audience. Those bold figures, of which I treated formerly as the native language of passion, have then their proper place. That ardour of Speech, that vehemence and glow of Sentiment, which arise from a mind animated and inspired by some great and public object, form the peculiar characteristics of Popular Eloquence, in its highest degree of perfection.[38]

The delivery before such groups should be firm and "determined."

> An arrogant and overbearing manner is indeed always disagreeable; and the least appearance of it ought to be shunned: but there is a certain decisive tone, which may be assumed even by a modest man, who is thoroughly persuaded of the sentiments he utters; and which is best calculated for making a general impression. A feeble and hesitating manner bespeaks always some distrust of a man's own opinion; which is by no means, a favourable circumstance for his inducing others to embrace it.[39]

Having examined some of the special characteristics of deliberative speaking, Blair exemplifies the species by quoting passages from Demosthenes' *Philippics* and *Olynthiacs*. Because of the lack of commentary on the passages, the attempt at criticism is somewhat abortive. The preliminary establishment of the criterion tends, however, to give some significance to the effort.

Forensic Oratory.—Following the same method in the next section of his criticism, Blair shows that judicial oratory differs in its object from the deliberative type.

> In Popular Assemblies, the great object is persuasion; the Orator aims at determining the hearers to some choice or conduct, as good, fit, or useful. For accomplishing this end, it is incumbent on him to apply himself to all the principles of action in our nature; to the passions and to the heart, as well as to the understanding. But, at the Bar, conviction is the great object. There, it is not the Speaker's business to persuade the Judges to what is good or useful, but to show them what is just and true; and, of course, it is chiefly, or solely, to the understanding that his Eloquence is addressed. This is a characteristical difference which ought ever to be kept in view.[40]

Furthermore, the audience situation is unique.

> Speakers at the Bar address themselves to one, or to a few Judges, and these, too, persons generally of age, gravity, and authority of character. There they have not those advantages which a mixed and numerous Assembly affords for employing all the arts of Speech, even supposing their subject to admit them. Passion does not rise so easily; the Speaker is heard more coolly; he is watched over more severely; and would expose himself to ridicule, by attempting that high vehement tone, which is only proper in speaking to a multitude.[41]

The nature of the subject matter also differs in judicial pleading. The deliberative speaker has a wide range of action.

He is seldom confined to any precise rule; he can fetch his topics from a great variety of quarters; and employ every illustration which his fancy or imagination suggests. But, at the Bar, the field of speaking is limited to precise law and statute. Imagination is not allowed to take its scope. The Advocate has always lying before him the line, the square, and the compass. These, it is his principal business to be continually applying to the subjects under debate.[42]

Eloquence of the Bar

. . . is of the calm and temperate kind, and connected with close reasoning. Sometimes a little play may be allowed to the Imagination, in order to enliven a dry subject, and to give relief, to the fatigue of attention; but this liberty must be taken with a sparing hand. For a Florid Style, and a sparkling manner, never fail to make the speaker be heard with a jealous ear by the judge. They detract from his weight, and always produce a suspicion of his failing in soundness and strength of argument. It is purity and neatness of expression which is chiefly to be studied: a Style perspicuous and proper, which shall not be needlessly overcharged with the pedantry of law terms, and where, at the same time, no affectation shall appear of avoiding these, when they are suitable and necessary.[43]

Hence, the speaker should eschew verbosity and cultivate distinctness.

Unlike his attempt to exemplify deliberative discourse by quoting passages from Demosthenes, Blair gives a detailed analysis of Cicero's *Pro Cluentio* to illustrate the characteristics of judicial oratory. He reconstructs partially the historical setting of the case; reviews the narrative details of the action; analyzes the parts of the oration; reviews and appraises the argument and reasoning; and introduces occasional quotation to support the critical findings. This represents a serious attempt to find the orator's method of procedure and to evaluate the force and conduct of the arguments used in the case.

Pulpit Speaking.—The last type of speaking Blair examines is that of the pulpit. This type of eloquence has certain advantages over other kinds, a few of which Blair enumerates:

The dignity and importance of its subjects must be acknowledged superior to any other. They are such as ought to interest every one, and can be brought home to every man's heart; and such as admit, at the same time, both the highest embellishments in describing, and the greatest vehemence and warmth in enforcing them. The Preacher has also great advantages in treating his subjects. He speaks not to one or a few Judges, but to a large Assembly. He is secure from all interruption. He is obliged to no replies, or extemporaneous efforts. He chooses his theme at leisure; and comes to the public with all the assistance which the most accurate premeditation can give him.[44]

The preacher should entertain a just view of the end of his speaking. This end is "to persuade men to become good."

Every Sermon therefore, should be a persuasive oration; not but that the Preacher is to instruct and to teach, to reason and to argue. All persuasion . . . is to be founded on conviction. The understanding must always be applied to in the first place, in order to make a lasting impression on the heart; and he who would work on men's passions or influence their practice, without first giving them just principles, and enlightening their minds, is no better than a mere declaimer. He may raise transient emotions, or kindle a passing ardour; but can produce no solid or lasting effect. At the same time, it must be remembered, that the Preacher's instructions are to be of the practical kind; and that persuasion must always be his ultimate object. It is not to discuss some abstruse point, that he ascends the Pulpit. It is not to illustrate some metaphysical truth, or to inform men of something which they never heard before; but it is to make them better men; it is to give them at once, clear views, and persuasive impressions of religious truth. The Eloquence of the Pulpit, then, must be Popular Eloquence. One of the first qualities of preaching is to be popular; not in the sense of accommodation to the humours and prejudices of the people . . . , but in the true sense of the word, calculated to make impression on the people; to strike and seize their hearts. I scruple not therefore to assert, that the abstract and philosophical manner of preaching, however it may have sometimes been admired, is formed upon a very faulty idea, and deviates widely from the just plan of Pulpit Eloquence. Rational, indeed, a Preacher ought always to be; he must give his audience clear ideas on every subject, and entertain them with sense, not with sound; but to be an accurate Reasoner will be small praise, if he be not a persuasive speaker also.[45]

It is unnecessary to remark that Blair expected the preacher to be a good man, as well as a persuasive talker, in order to impart gravity and warmth to his discourses.

Perspicuity is the first requirement of the preacher's style.

As discourses spoken there are calculated for the instruction of all sorts of hearers, plainness and simplicity should reign in them. All unusual, swollen, or high-sounding words, should be avoided; especially all words that are merely poetical, or merely philosophical. Young Preachers are apt to be caught with the glare of these; and in young Composers the error may be excusable; but they may be assured that it is an error, and proceeds from their not having yet acquired a correct Taste. Dignity of expression, indeed, the Pulpit requires in a high degree; nothing that is mean or grovelling, no low or vulgar phrases, ought on any account to be admitted. But this dignity is perfectly consistent with simplicity. The words employed may be all plain words, easily understood, and in common use; and yet the Style may be abundantly dignified, and, at the same time, very lively and animated. For a lively and animated Style is extremely suited to the Pulpit. The earnestness which a Preacher ought to feel, and the grandeur and importance of his subjects, justify and often require warm and glowing expressions. He not only may employ metaphors and comparisons, but, on proper occasions, may apostrophise the saint or the sinner; may personify inanimate objects, break out into bold exclamations, and, in general, has the command of the most passionate figures of Speech.[46]

Blair did not favor the reading of sermons.

No discourse, which is designed to be persuasive, can have the same force when read, as when spoken. The common people all feel this, and their prejudice against this practice is not without foundation in nature. What is gained hereby in point of correctness, is not equal, I apprehend, to what is lost in point of persuasion and force. They, whose memories are not able to retain the whole of a Discourse, might aid themselves considerably by short notes lying before them, which would allow them to preserve, in a great measure, the freedom and ease of one who speaks.[47]

Lecture XXX is devoted exclusively to a critical examination of a sermon entitled "Praise and Thanksgiving" by Bishop Atterbury who, in Blair's opinion, "is deservedly accounted one of our most eloquent writers of sermons." This selection unquestionably is the best critical estimate in Blair's *Lectures*. It amounts to a paragraph by paragraph analysis of the virtues and defects, both of style and matter, in the sermon. The interpolations and commentaries reveal Blair not only as a discriminating analyst of the characteristics of pulpit speaking; they also throw some light upon his sense of word value, his appreciation of religious themes, and his fine discernment of stylistic excellence.

Final Estimate of Blair's Work.—Not concerned with the biographical approach to rhetorical criticism, Blair recognized that sound criticism should rest upon criteria to which various disinterested scholars could appeal. He had the insight to perceive that the social setting—the audience situation generally—had much to do with exact assignment of merit and defect. His liberal use and interpretation of passages from the orators' speeches is an important feature of the work. In spite of his formal adherence to a semifixed pattern as determined by the kinds of oratory under evaluative scrutiny, he contributed richly, especially in the field of style, to critical doctrines of public address.

Barron's Stylistic Approach to Criticism

In his *Lectures on Belles Lettres and Logic,* published in 1806 and originally delivered at the University of St. Andrews, William Barron sets aside a small amount of space for the criticism of orators. Like many writers before and since his time, he turns to Cicero for the standard of excellence. As might be expected from his general approach to oratory, his estimation of speakers derives in large part from stylistic considerations. In terms of contemporary standards, however, his appraisals are not particularly penetrating, chiefly, perhaps, because they lack essential articulation with a speaker-audience situation.

Cicero, Barron remarks, possesses every characteristic of the accomplished orator, although he is not equally great in each department.

He never fails to seize the view of a cause most favourable to the purpose he wishes to support, and displays great art in removing prepossessions, and conciliating the favour of his hearers. His information is pertinent and satisfactory; his illustrations are ingenious, beautiful, and learned; his arguments are solid and convincing. Though he always addresses first the understanding, yet he does not stop there. He often assails the imagination and the passions with vigour and success. Bold metaphors, vivid interrogations, striking antitheses, passionate apostrophes and exclamations are his instruments on such occasions. Sometimes he rises to the Demosthenic fire and thunder, he gets entire command of his hearers, and pours along with a vehemence irresistible. His expression is perspicuous, and in general harmonious. Many of his periods present the most beautiful construction of members, which grow one above another in sound and importance, and exhibit much variety in their length, melody, and arrangement.[48]

Cicero's oratorical virtues, however, are mixed with disfiguring faults.

He is often diffuse in his illustrations, and profuse of his arguments, without resting his cause only upon the best. His orations are sometimes extended to a length that tires the reader, and we cannot easily conceive that the patience of his hearers should not have been exhausted. He is too fond of gay ornaments, which approach the florid style. Many

of his periods are long and involved, devoid of much cadence or harmony, and they are often enfeebled with redundant words.[49]

Barron believes that Cicero's most censurable defect is his vanity.
"Wonderful is the artifice he displays in introducing his own
praise . . ."

Mindful of the value of the comparative method in assessing
oratorical skill, Barron closes his analysis by matching the relative
accomplishments of Cicero and Demosthenes.

> [Demosthenes] totally disappears, and the reader attends to nothing
> but the argument; the latter [Cicero] is always in the fore-ground of
> the picture and one of the principal objects in the eye of the spectator.
> The former seems to speak the language of nature only, the latter never
> fails to mix a portion of that of art. Demosthenes indulges no argument,
> nor illustration, not even word which is not necessary to communicate
> the sense. Cicero is superabundant in all these respects. The leading
> characteristics of the former are gravity, solidity, vehemence; of the
> latter, vivacity, solidity, dignity.[50]

Lord Mansfield's Fragmentary Criticism

Regarded by John Lord Campbell as the first Scotchman ever to
gain distinction "in the profession of the law in England," Lord
Mansfield was singularly adept at investing his legal cases with
logical acuity and literary dignity. It was a common saying that
his *statement* of a case was worth the *argument* of any other man.
Campbell remarks that Mansfield's presentation "seemed to suggest
trains of thinking rather than to draw conclusions; and so skilfully
did he conceal his art, that the hearers thought they formed their
opinion in consequence of the workings of their own minds, when
in truth it was the effect of the most refined dialectics." [51]

Although Mansfield's distinction derives from his conduct as a
lawyer, he made a minor contribution to criticism. During his early
years he prepared a critical analysis of Demosthenes in Latin, and
a fragment of the essay has been preserved. His comparison of
the technique of Cicero and Demosthenes is perhaps the most interesting part of the appraisal:

> Cicero having convinced the understanding of the judges before whom
> he pleads, they, after deliberation, pronounce in his favour the sentence
> which they think just; the eloquence displayed by him, however, being
> so brilliant, that we conceive there is nothing which would not be con-
> ceded to it. Demosthenes does not *ask*—he *seizes*—by an energy almost
> divine, he wrests from the hands of the judges the sentence which he

desires. Being captivated by the witching art of Cicero as by the song
of the Sirens, they are better pleased to go astray with him than to
decide righteously with others. Such authority does Demosthenes carry
along with him, that his hearers are ashamed to differ from him, and,
when struck by the lightning of his eloquence, they do not seem to be
carried away by the art of the orator, but believe themselves to obey
a natural impulse, and to yield to the dictates of right reason.[52]

Rollin's Standard Comparison

The two orators most frequently compared in critical analyses
are, of course, Demosthenes and Cicero. Furthermore, they represent the models or standards of excellence by which much of ancient
and modern eloquence is assessed.

Charles Rollin's criticism of the Greek and Roman masters affords
little, if anything, that is new on the side of methodology. However,
his process of appraisal serves to remind us that Cicero's standards
of judgment exercised a powerful influence upon the ways of the
critics. Rollin seeks the measure of the orators largely by determining their skill in the several kinds of public address—a standard
to which Cicero appealed frequently in the *Brutus*. Asserting that
both Demosthenes and Cicero excelled in all, "as every one must
do who is truly eloquent," Rollin continues: "They know how to
vary their style as their subjects varied; sometimes simple and subtile
in causes of small consequence, in narrations and proofs; and, at
others, adorned and embellished, when there was a necessity of
pleasing; sometimes elevated and sublime, when the dignity of the
subject required it." [53]

Thus Rollin holds to a relative standard. Affirming that orators,
quite different in style and character, may yet be "equally perfect,"
he says Cicero knew the "high merit of Demosthenes' eloquence"
but doubted whether his (Cicero's) audiences always wanted
such austerity and exactness. Consequently, Cicero "believed it necessary to indulge something to the ears and to the delicacy of his
auditors, who required more elegance and graces in orations." [54]

Hazlitt Contrasts Writing and Speaking

Observations on Discourse.—William Hazlitt's essay "On the
Difference between Writing and Speaking" is a highly acid statement which warrants notice because of the cogency of some of its
logic and because of the applicability of certain of its tenets to great
orators.

Hazlitt opens his discourse by announcing that he will illustrate the difference between writing and speaking "by familiar examples, rather than by analytical reasonings. The philosopher of old was not unwise, who defined motion by getting up and walking."

An essential distinction between writing and speaking concerns the time factor. "The chief requisite for the one . . . appears to be quickness and facility of perception—for the other, patience of soul, and a power increasing with the difficulties it has to master." [55] Thus, in speaking, "less is required of you, if you only do it at once, with grace and spirit: in writing, you stipulate for all that you are capable of, but you have the choice of your own time and subject." [56] And there is a further difference:

> Besides habit, and greater or less facility, there is also a certain reach of capacity, a certain depth or shallowness, grossness or refinement of intellect, which marks out the distinction between those whose chief ambition is to shine by producing an immediate effect, or who are thrown back, by a natural bias, on the severer researches of thought and study.[57]

Referring to the popular speaker, Hazlitt comments on the function of the audience:

> [He] is like a vulgar actor off the stage—take away his cue, and he has nothing to say for himself. Or he is so accustomed to the intoxication of popular applause, that without that stimulus he has no motive or power of exertion left—neither imagination, understanding, liveliness, common sense, words nor ideas—he is fairly cleared out; and in the intervals of sober reason, is the dullest and most imbecile of all mortals.[58]

Hazlitt doubts that a speaker can move beyond commonplaces. If he does, he loses his hearers.

> An orator can hardly get beyond *common-places:* if he does, he gets beyond his hearers. The most successful speakers, even in the House of Commons, have not been the best scholars or the finest writers. . . . Those speeches that in general told best at the time, are not now readable. What were the materials of which they were chiefly composed? An imposing detail of passing events, a formal display of official documents, an appeal to established maxims, an echo of popular clamor, some worn-out metaphor newly vamped-up,—some hackneyed argument used for the hundredth, nay thousandth time, to fall in with the interests, the passions, or prejudices of listening and devoted admirers;—some truth or falsehood, repeated as the Shibboleth of party time out of mind, which gathers strength from sympathy as it spreads, because it

is understood or assented to by the million, and finds, in the increased action of the minds of numbers, the weight and force of an instinct.[59]

The commonplace, he holds, "is enshrined in its own unquestioned evidence, and constitutes its own immortal basis." Accordingly, it operates mechanically, "and opens an instantaneous and infallible communication between the hearer and speaker." [60]

The Ways of the Orators.—Edmund Burke "did not often shock the prejudices of the House: he endeavoured to *account for them,* to 'lay the flattering unction' of philosophy 'to their souls.' They could not endure him." The reason Burke emptied the House was that he uttered thoughts requiring time for consideration, of which there was too little. If one reads, one may take his time; but, "in hearing we are . . . in the company of fools; and time presses." Referring to the British government, Hazlitt added: "If we were to wait until Noble Lords and Honorable Gentlemen were inspired with a relish for abstruse thinking, and a taste for the loftier flights of fancy, the business of this great nation would shortly be at a stand." [61] "The impression of anything delivered in a large assembly," Hazlitt continued,

. . . must be comparatively null and void, unless you not only understand and feel its value yourself, but are conscious that it is felt and understood by the meanest capacity present. Till that is the case, the speaker is in your power, not you in his. The eloquence that is effectual and irresistible must stir the inert mass of prejudice, and pierce the opaquest shadows of ignorance.[62]

Unlike Burke whose oratory was "too recondite for his hearers," Chatham was a great debater. "He vanquished because he could not yield." He held fast to strong points in an argument.

He himself evidently had a strong possession of his subject, a thorough conviction, an intense interest; and this communicated itself from his *manner,* from the tones of his voice, from his commanding attitudes, and eager gestures, instinctively and unavoidably to his hearers. . . . He did not wheedle, or palliate, or circumvent, or make a studied appeal to the reason or the passions—he *dictated* his opinions to the House of Commons.[63]

Both Pitt and Fox were speakers, not authors.

There is no thought in them [their speeches] that implies a habit of deep and refined reflection . . . ; there is no knowledge that does not lie within the reach of obvious and mechanical search; and as to the powers of language, the chief miracle is, that a source of words so apt, forcible, and well-arranged, so copious and unfailing, should have been found constantly open to express their ideas without any previous preparation.[64]

Exceedingly critical of the House of Commons, Hazlitt comments on the repetition of material in speech after speech.

Read over the collections of old Debates, twenty, forty, eighty, a hundred years ago; they are the same, *mutatis mutandis,* as those of yesterday. . . . You wonder to see how little has been added; you grieve that so little has been lost. . . . You must serve an apprenticeship to a want of originality, to a suspension of thought and feeling. . . . A man of simplicity and independence of mind cannot easily reconcile himself to all this formality and mummery. . . .[65]

In short, Hazlitt believes the "greatest test of courage" one can conceive "is to speak truth in the House of Commons."

De Quincey Articulates Invention and Style

Basis of His Conception.—Thomas De Quincey is not always lucid in his analyses of the rhetorical process; neither is he completely consistent in his interpretations, unless his readers engage in an inordinate amount of analysis to set the seeming contradictions right. But he is provocative, despite everything, and he is so in a way that furthers critical investigation.

His chief contributions to a study of the theory and criticism of speaking are found in the "Rhetoric," a review of Richard Whately's book of the same title; in the essay called "Style"; and in other studies in which he examines the literature of the ancient Greeks.

De Quincey's most astute rhetorical conception is his formula for the presentation of ideas. In a peculiarly happy way, he brings the processes of rhetorical invention and style together in an indivisible unity. *Matter* and *manner* are thus blended. Ideas are not mechanically clothed with language; being inner manifestations of inventive skill, they still must be embodied in words that reflect accurately the existing mental concept. Says De Quincey:

Ponderable facts and external realities are intelligible in almost any language: they are self-explained and self-sustained. But the more closely any exercise of mind is connected with what is internal and individual in the sensibilities, that is, with what is philosophically termed *subjective,* precisely in that degree, and the more subtly, does the style or the embodying of the thoughts cease to be a mere separable ornament, and in fact the more does the manner . . . become confluent with the matter.[66]

He then refers to the Wordsworthian dictum that "it is in the highest degree unphilosophic to call language or diction 'the *dress* of thoughts.' . . . He would call it 'the *incarnation* of thoughts.'" Commenting further on this idea, De Quincey observes:

> . . . if language were merely a dress, then you could separate the two: you could lay the thoughts on the left hand, the language on the right. But, generally speaking, you can no more deal thus with poetic thoughts, than you can with soul and body. The union is too subtle; the intertexture too ineffable, each co-existing not merely *with* the other, but each *in* and *through* the other. An image, for instance, a single word, often enters into a thought as a constituent part. In short, the two elements are not united as a body with a separable dress, but as a mysterious incarnation. And thus, in what proportion the thoughts are subjective, in that same proportion does their very essence become identical with the expression, and the style become confluent with the matter.[67]

De Quincey recognizes the variable elements in style—the elements that change with the purpose of the speaker and the character of the audience. "That is good rhetoric for the hustings which is bad for a book." Likewise, in the senate, "and for the same reason in a newspaper, it is a virtue to reiterate your meaning: tautology becomes a merit: variation of the words, with a substantial identity of the sense and dilution of the truth, is oftentimes a necessity." [68]

Written discourse has an advantage over oral in permitting a return to a passage upon which subsequent sense depends. Thus the time factor enters again. Both the speaker and the hearer profit by keeping important propositions "before the eye a good deal longer than the chastity of taste or the austerity of logic would tolerate in a book."

> Time must be given for the intellect to eddy about a truth, and to appropriate its bearings. There is a sort of previous lubrication, such as the boa-constrictor applies to any subject of digestion, which is requisite to familiarize the mind with a startling or a complex novelty. And this is obtained for the intellect by varying the modes of presenting it,—now putting it directly before the eye, now obliquely, now in an abstract shape, now in the concrete; all which being the proper technical discipline for dealing with such cases, ought no longer to be viewed as a licentious mode of style, but as the just style in respect to those licentious circumstances. And the true art for such popular display is to contrive the best forms for appearing to say something new, when

in reality you are but echoing yourself; to break up massy chords into running variations; and to mask, by slight differences in the manner, a virtual identity in the substance.[69]

Application of the Doctrine to Oratory.—It is interesting to see how De Quincey applies this doctrine of style to the critical estimate of Burke, "the supreme writer of his century, the man of the largest and finest understanding." Declaring his displeasure with the critics who talked about Burke's "fancy," De Quincey says:

Fancy in your throats, ye miserable twaddlers! as if Edmund Burke were the man to play with his fancy, for the purpose of separable ornament. He was a man of fancy in no other sense than as Lord Bacon was so, and Jeremy Taylor, and as all large and discursive thinkers are and must be: that is to say, the fancy which he had in common with all mankind, and very probably in no eminent degree, in him was urged into unusual activity under the necessities of his capacious understanding.[70]

Then follows more of his remarkable prescription for rhetorical skill:

His great and peculiar distinction was that he viewed all objects of the understanding under more relations than other men, and under more complex relations. According to the multiplicity of these relations, a man is said to have a *large* understanding; according to their subtilty, a *fine* one; and in an angelic understanding, all things would appear to be related to all. Now, to apprehend and detect more relations, or to pursue them steadily, is a process absolutely impossible without the intervention of physical analogies. To say, therefore, that a man is a great thinker, or a fine thinker, is but another expression for saying that he has a *schematizing* (or, to use a plainer but less accurate expression, a figurative) understanding. In that sense, and for that purpose, Burke is figurative. . . .[71]

But De Quincey chides Burke's critics by adding:

. . . understood as he has been understood by the long-eared race of his critics, not as thinking in and by his figures, but as deliberately laying them on by way of enamel or after-ornament,—not as *incarnating,* but simply as *dressing* his thoughts in imagery,—so understood, he is not the Burke of reality, but a poor fictitious Burke, modelled after the poverty of conception which belongs to his critics.[72]

Recapitulation of the Doctrine.—Hoyt Hudson gives a clear summary of the foregoing considerations when he remarks:

De Quincey teaches that the rhetorical process, the process of *presenting an idea attractively,* whether as a display of power, in play, in poetic exuberance, or for a persuasive purpose, involves an inner and an outer activity. The inner activity we may call rhetorical invention; the outer, rhetorical style. The first is a mode of thinking about one's subject, turning the subject over in one's mind, and viewing it in as many relations as possible. The second is the incarnation in speech of the thoughts (or of a selection from the thoughts) engendered by the preceding mental activity. No one has shown so well the organic union of these two.[73]

Brougham Appraises Ancient Oratory

Reappearance of Ancients vs. Moderns Controversy.—One of the several persistent themes in the history of rhetorical criticism is the controversy over the relative merits of the ancients and the moderns. We have already seen how this matter assumed acute polemical proportions in the quarrel of the Atticists and the Asianists. Indeed, nearly every competent theorist and critic has referred to this dualism, either as it relates to the choice of models for imitation or as it concerns the establishment of standards of excellence in criticism.

In the literature on rhetoric and oratory, however, there is probably no more studied and sincere effort to establish the claims of the ancients to superiority than is found in Henry Brougham's *Dissertation on the Eloquence of the Ancients*. Steeped in classical learning himself, and jealously proud of the heritage of antiquity, Brougham tried in a closely reasoned analysis to demonstrate the "immeasurable superiority" of the Greeks and the Romans, and especially the former, over the modern orators.

In his Inaugural Address, Brougham made his preference for the Greeks clearly evident when he said:

> . . . were we to rest satisfied with studying the Roman, we should only be imitating the imperfect copy, instead of the pure original—like him who should endeavour to catch a glimpse of some beauty by her reflection in a glass, that weakened her tints, if it did not distort her features.[74]

And, he added, "if a further reason is required for giving the preference to the Greek orators, we may find it in the greater diversity and importance of the subjects upon which their speeches were delivered."

The central theme of Brougham's argument is that the Athenian audiences were careful critics of oratory, and that the orators accordingly made every possible effort to meet the wishes of the hearers. The audience had what Brougham called a "delicate sense of rhetorical excellence." "No fact in history," he remarked, "is more unquestionable than the union of the two capacities in the Athenian audience,—their exquisite discrimination and high relish of rhetorical beauties, with their susceptibility of the strongest emotions which the orator could desire to excite." The Athenian audience assembled for two purposes: (1) to consider practical matters, and (2) "to enjoy a critical repast." [75] As Brougham observes:

> . . . the orators of Greece and Rome regarded their art as one of eminent display, considered it their province to please as well as to move their audience, and addressed the assembly, not only as hearers who were to be convinced or persuaded, but as critics also who were to judge of rhetorical merit . . . [This] is clear from numberless considerations, some of which must here be adverted to, in order to show that Ancient Oratory held a place among the Fine Arts properly so called, and was, like them, an appeal to the taste, ending in the mere pleasure of contemplation, as well as an appeal to the reason or the passions, leading to practical consequences, and having action for its result. An attention to this subject will explain many things in the structure of ancient orations, which would otherwise be with difficulty apprehended. [76]

Internal Evidence Establishing Ancient Oratory as Fine Art.— Brougham considers the evidence which in his opinion supports the theses set forth in the preceding quotation. Turning to internal evidence, he mentions, first, "the exquisite finish and perfect polish of their [Greek orators'] composition." Furthermore, it is evident

> that the exquisite structure of the sentences, the balanced period, the apt and perfect antithesis, the neat and epigrammatic turn, the finished collocation, all indicate an extreme elaboration, and could hardly have been the suggestion of the moment, because the choice of the earlier expressions is often regulated by those which occur subsequently. [77]

And the well-chosen figures

> . . . with which the ancient speeches are interspersed, and the highly skilful disposition of their materials, do not perhaps furnish more decisive proofs than the diction. But the exemplary temperance with which topics are used, and the conciseness with which ideas of the most important kind are expressed, and images portrayed, certainly can hardly be the effect of any experience or practical skill. [78]

Further evidence develops from the fact that passages

> . . . are very frequently to be found in one oration, sometimes word for word the same with those contained in another by the same speaker,

sometimes varying in certain particulars, and apparently varying because subsequent reflection, perhaps aided by the criticism of others, or by the effects observed to be produced on the audience, had suggested the change, as an improvement upon the earlier composition.[79]

Since the orators often used the same figures in different situations, it follows that they

> . . . had other objects in view than the mere furtherance of the matter actually in hand, and that those passages were repeated, rather because they had been found successful in striking and delighting the audience when first pronounced, and were therefore likely to please in the repetition, than because they conduced materially to carry conviction to their minds, and gain their concurrence to a practical proposition.[80]

And unlike the modern orators, including the illustrious Chatham, the ancient Greeks made sure that *all* parts of their orations, rather than selected "brilliant passages," were "elaborated with extreme art."

Brougham summarizes the internal evidence of his argument by remarking:

> The examination . . . is not more so than was necessary to show the extreme care of composition which guided the workmanship of the Greek orators; to prove that they delivered their orations as finished productions, with the view of satisfying a critical audience; and to illustrate the position, that the audience flocked to hear them, as well for the pleasure of the treat thus afforded to their refined taste, as for the more useful purpose of hearing state affairs practically discussed.[81]

The External Evidence.—Brougham introduces several subordinate theses to reveal the external evidence favoring the ancients. In the first place, the

> . . . number of speeches written, published, and preserved, and which yet never were spoken, is among the most remarkable of these proofs. Nothing can more strikingly illustrate the difference between Ancient and Modern Rhetoric. With us, a speech written at all before delivery, is regarded as something anomalous, and almost ridiculous; because, the proofs of preparation being inconsistent with the inspiration of the moment and the feelings under which the orator is always supposed to speak, we naturally enough feel that it should be carefully concealed from the eye of the audience, and that their being admitted as it were behind the scenes, at once dispels the illusion so necessary to be kept up. But a speech, written and published, which never was spoken at all, is with us at once given over to extreme ridicule; and a speech intended to have been spoken is a kind of by-word for something laughable in itself. . . .[82]

Furthermore, the presence of many Prooemia, or introductions, which were apparently never used, suggests that great care was taken to develop compositional graces and artistic skills. The testimony of historians and other writers indicates "how vast the pains were, and how various, and how unremitting," which the orators took in elaborating their speeches.   Indeed, the accounts reaching us of the "training and study which the ancient orators went through previous to venturing upon the formidable scene of rhetorical display, and even after they had begun their career of eloquence, afford additional proofs of the extreme care bestowed upon their art." [83]

Finally, the "exquisite taste of the Athenian audience both proved their delight in the pleasures of the Forum, or Ecclesia, so to speak, and showed how well they were trained to a nice discernment of oratorical merit." [84]

Further Differentia between Ancient and Modern Oratory.— These, then, are the bodies of evidence and the reasons accounting for the superiority of the ancients, and revealing, particularly, the taste and critical judgment of the Athenian audience. Brougham appends a further comment, however, which we should examine. Admitting that the ancient orations do not compare favorably with the modern ones from the point of view of substance, he says:

> Any merely critical remarks in a modern speech are hardly permitted. It is not a charge which can now-a-days be made against an adversary either at the Bar or in debate, that he has made a bad speech, that his eloquence is defective, that his figures are out of keeping, his tones inharmonious, or his manner awkward. Yet these are topics of ordinary recrimination and abuse between Demosthenes and Aeschines. To have argued inconclusively, to counsel badly, to act corruptly, or feebly, or inconsistently, are the charges to which the combatants in the more close and business-like battles of our Senate must confine themselves. With us it is no matter of attack that an adversary's tropes are in bad taste, or his manners inelegant, or his voice unmusical. So we may perceive the exquisite care taken by the ancient orators to strike and to please their audience, in the attention paid by them to the rhythm or numbers of their periods.[85]

Demosthenes, the Model.—The great model of ancient oratory, the one who was at the head "of all the mighty masters of speech," [86] was Demosthenes. Brougham does not try to establish Demosthenes as a close reasoner; instead, he points to him as a craftsman of words and sentences. Unquestionably, the Greek orator could have excelled in the use of argument, but that would not have pleased his audience; and Demosthenes was a master of the art of adapting discourse to listeners. "What was wanted," Brougham says of the Athenian audience, to move, to rouse, and also to please them,

> . . . was a copious stream of plain intelligible observations upon their interests—appeals to their feelings—recollections of their past, and especially their present history—expositions of the evils to be apprehended from inaction and impolicy of any sort—vindications of the orator's own conduct, upon grounds simple and uncontested—contrasts to show the inconsistency of those who differed from him, or refused to follow his advice—invectives, galling and unmeasured, against all his adversaries abroad and at home. By urging these topics in rapid succession, in the purest language, with a harmony never broken, save where the sense and the ear required a discord, he [Demosthenes] could move and could master the minds of the people, make their enemy quake upon his barbaric throne, and please the exquisite taste of the 'fierce democratie' whom he was chiding and controlling.[87]

His Preference for Stylistic Matters.—Brougham regarded the stylistic features of discourse with strong favor. In the final paragraph of his essay on the ancients, and particularly where he is appraising the greatness of Demosthenes, he leaves the impression that the proper effect of eloquence is to move and to please, but not necessarily to secure the effect through argument. "The two," he says, referring to argument and compositional excellence, "may be well combined, but they differ specifically from each other." Previously, he had shown that modern assemblies were "eminently places of business" where men did not come to have "their fancy charmed with choice figures." In the light of his unqualified preference for the ancient models, the combination of these remarks tends to show that style was his chief concern. An observation from Brougham's review of a French edition of Demosthenes and Aeschines sums up the whole matter concisely. Discussing Demosthenes' skill, Brougham says:

> Let any reader who has been accustomed to hear debates in Parliament, note what passages have struck him most in those works, and he will find that they are the sort of things which have the most instantaneous success in modern speeches; which produce the most sudden and thrilling sensations; and finding in every bosom an echo, occasion the loudest expressions of assent. Now, some speakers may create admiration by careful composition alone, or without sallies; but they do not find their way as the old Greek did to our hearts. Others may find their way thither without the just care of composition; but he united both powers, and concealed, for the time at least, the labour by which the combination was effected. Can we marvel that his success was prodigious—and

that it was equally complete with hearers whom he was to move, and with critics whom he was to please? [88]

Brougham had a profound respect for emotional proofs that were competently presented through graceful composition.

Macaulay's Philosophy of Rhetoric

An examination of Thomas Babington Macaulay's writings on oratory and orators shows a rather clearly formulated theory of public address, as well as a point of view regarding the role of the critic in national life. It is doubtful whether Macaulay contributed directly to rhetorical criticism with respect to method, but his rationale of oratorical judgment has philosophical significance.

The Critic's Knowledge of the Social Milieu.—Like many other critics of eloquence, Macaulay was concerned with the relation between oratory and statesmanship. In his judgment, however, consummate skill in the one field did not necessarily imply great distinction in the other. "Themistocles or Pericles would have been no match for Demosthenes in the assembly, or for Iphicrates in the field. But surely they were incomparably better fitted than either for the direction of affairs." [89] And in his review of the life of William Pitt, Macaulay declares:

> Parliamentary government is government by speaking. In such a government, the power of speaking is the most highly prized of all the qualities which a politician can possess; and that power may exist, in the highest degree, without judgment, without fortitude, without skill in reading the characters of men or the signs of the times, without any knowledge of the principles of legislation or of political economy, and without any skill in diplomacy or in the administration of war. Nay, it may well happen that those very intellectual qualities which give a peculiar charm to the speeches of a public man may be incompatible with the qualities which would fit him to meet a pressing emergency with promptitude and firmness. It was thus with Charles Townshend. It was thus with Windham. It was a privilege to listen to those accomplished and ingenious orators. But in a perilous crisis they would have been found far inferior in all the qualities of rulers to such a man as Oliver Cromwell, who talked nonsense, or as William the Silent, who did not talk at all.[90]

The job of the critic is, then, to pass judgment upon the orators in the light of the social circumstances in which they lived. On this point, Macaulay is specific. He believes that oratory is a venture in adaptation, and that criticism must operate within the province of that adaptive function. Speeches, he goes on to say,

> . . . must be read with the temper of those to whom they are addressed, or they must necessarily appear to offend against the laws of taste and reason. . . . This is perpetually forgotten by those who criticise oratory. Because they are reading at leisure, pausing at every line, reconsidering every argument, they forget that the hearers were hurried from point to point too rapidly to detect the fallacies through which they were conducted; that they had no time to disentangle sophisms, or to notice slight inaccuracies of expression; that elaborate excellence, either of reasoning or of language, would have been absolutely thrown away.[91]

Macaulay then points to the analogy of a sister art, observing that "these connoisseurs examine a panorama through a microscope, and quarrel with a scene-painter because he does not give to his work the exquisite touch of Gerard Dow." In short, the critic will have to divest himself of the modern's "feelings and acquirements" if he is to appreciate the speeches of the past, and especially of antiquity. Emphasizing the necessity of knowing the audience situations, Macaulay indicates that seeming defects in certain Greek orations may actually have been virtues. Consequently, if we acknowledge that assumption, we may find that

> . . . the frequent violation of those excellent rules of evidence by which our courts of law are regulated, the introduction of extraneous matter . . . , the assertions, without proof, the passionate entreaties, the furious invectives, are really proofs of the prudence and address of the speakers.[92]

It is surely time, Macaulay concluded, "that ancient literature should be examined in a different manner, without pedantical prepossessions, but with a just allowance, at the same time, for the difference of circumstances and manners."

The Place of Oratory in Society.—Not only did Macaulay insist upon the critic's understanding the social situation in which an orator performed; he was also convinced that the critic should have a sound point of view relative to the function of oratory. With a mildly satirical touch, he remarks:

> Propositions which are advanced in discourse generally result from a partial view of the question, and cannot be kept under examination long enough to be corrected. Men of great conversational powers almost universally practice a sort of lively sophistry and exaggeration, which deceives, for the moment, both themselves and their auditors.[93]

Later, he suggests that the

> . . . very circumstances which retarded the growth of science were
> peculiarly favorable to the cultivation of eloquence. From the early
> habit of taking a share in animated discussion the intelligent student
> would derive that readiness of resource, that copiousness of language,
> and that knowledge of the temper and understanding of an audience,
> which are far more valuable to an orator than the greatest logical
> powers.[94]

Thus we are led to believe that the rational appeal may not be
as important in speaking as is commonly believed. Whether or not
we accept the doctrine, Macaulay evidently considered it true. He
contended that oratory had to be estimated according to principles
that differed from those used in other artistic productions. "The
object of oratory alone is not truth," he remarked, "but persuasion.
. . ." And then he uttered the oft-quoted statement: "A speaker who
exhausts the whole philosophy of a question, who displays every
grace of style, yet produces no effect on his audience, may be a great
essayist, a great statesman, a great master of composition; but he is
not an orator." [95]

The Tools of the Critic.—These comments make it clear that
Macaulay looked upon rhetoric as a useful tool; that he conceived
the function of oratory to be peculiarly practical, confined to eliciting
responses from hearers.

The critic who evaluates these practical efforts must, indeed, be
intelligent and discerning, but he need not necessarily have the status
of an expert. Commenting on a remark made by Eugene of Savoy,
Macaulay observes

> . . . the greatest generals have commonly been those who have been at
> once raised to command, and introduced to the great operations of war,
> without being employed in the petty calculations and manoeuvres which
> employ the time of an inferior officer. In literature the principle is
> equally sound. The great tactics of criticism will, in general, be best
> understood by those who have not had much practice in drilling syllables
> and particles.[96]

The important requisite was that the critic be able to appreciate
the circumstances and manners of the age whose men he proposed
to appraise.

The Standards of Judgment.—Macaulay holds up a specific
standard of judgment for the critic. In his essay "On the Athenian
Orators," he surely infers, even if he does not openly express the

belief, that certain speakers of antiquity furnish effective models of public address. He has a deep respect for good models, saying it is not "by turning over libraries, but by repeatedly perusing and intently contemplating a few great models, that the mind is best disciplined." Severity should characterize the pattern of imitation; thoroughness should stamp the study habits and practice work of aspiring orators.

> Rumford, it is said, proposed to the Elector of Bavaria a scheme for feeding his soldiers at a much cheaper rate than formerly. His plan was simply to compel them to masticate their food thoroughly. A small quantity, thus eaten, would, according to that famous projector, afford more sustenance than a large meal hastily devoured. I do not know how Rumford's proposition was received; but to the mind, I believe, it will be found more nutritious to digest a page than to devour a library.[97]

Reverting to his analogy of oratory and warfare, Macaulay remarked further:

> There is indeed a remarkable coincidence between the progress of the art of war, and that of the art of oratory, among the Greeks. They both advanced to perfection by contemporaneous steps, and from similar causes. The early speakers, like the early warriors of Greece, were merely a militia. It was found that in both employments practice and discipline gave superiority.[98]

As the great model in eloquence, Demosthenes stands at the head of the list. In the *History,* Macaulay announces that there are speeches, "some speeches of Demosthenes particularly, in which it would be impossible to alter a word without altering it for the worse."

His Critiques.—Macaulay's critical estimates of orators are found chiefly in his reviews and essays. Included among the entries are studies of Chatham, Hastings, Holland, Barère, Mackintosh, and Pitt. In none of these criticisms, however, does he assume the full role of the rhetorical critic; instead, he makes the studies largely biographical-historical, with a sufficiently full measure of material on the oratorical activities of the men to reveal his theory of public speaking.

The most distinctive feature of the criticisms, from the point of view of rhetorical evaluation, is the emphasis Macaulay places upon the early speech training, practice, and capacities of the orators. In his reviews of Chatham and Pitt the Younger, particularly, this professed interest in accounting for the speakers' subsequent proficiency in oratory is patently evident. In the study of Pitt the Younger, Macaulay comments frequently on Pitt's early education, his familiarity with classical literature, his study of the ancient orators, and his early study of parliamentary debates. "His education," Macaulay allows, "was well adapted to form a great parliamentary speaker." Later, he remarks:

> There is . . . abundant evidence that nature had bestowed on Pitt the talents of a great orator; and those talents had been developed in a very peculiar manner, first by his education, and secondly by the high official position to which he rose early, and in which he passed the greater part of his public life.[99]

It should be observed that a considerable body of contemporary research in rhetoric and oratory derives from suggestions offered by Macaulay in his critical reviews. Many theses have been prepared recently which trace the factors accounting for the oratorical abilities of certain speakers. These studies sustain a tradition that traces back, in part at least, to the essays of Macaulay.

General Summary

Although the intermediate period to 1850 produced a number of scholars who devoted a part of their efforts to speech criticism, relatively few major contributions to the critical art were made by these investigators.

Macaulay offered some suggestions as to the method of tracing factors responsible for the development of oratorical skills in individuals, and he was sensibly conscious of the need for understanding the social conditions out of which speeches developed. In general, however, he remained a theorist whose reflections dealt chiefly with the place of oratory in public life, rather than with the critical standards by which such oratory was appraised.

De Quincey and Hazlitt were primarily concerned with stylistic matters, although the latter evaluated the role of the speaker in a democratic society. Brougham revived the persistent theme of the ancients versus the moderns in oratorical achievement. Swift, Addison, and Chesterfield furnished incidental criticism, but chiefly of delivery.

Although Rapin and Blair used critical methods characterized by a certain inflexibility and formality, they are by all odds the most important contributors of this period. Both evinced an intelligent insight into the variables of public address; both had a sound theoretical knowledge of the speech art; and both proceeded methodically in their criticism, working with criteria which, however rigidly employed, gave unmistakable order to their efforts.

Chapter 7

THE MODERN CRITICS

Introduction

The most ambitious attempts at rhetorical criticism, excepting only Cicero's *Brutus,* are products of the past hundred years. In this period, the criticism of speeches has become a more dignified and intellectually challenging art because the subject matter of speech has again become a highly respected curricular discipline in our schools and colleges. It would seem, therefore, that the criticism of rhetoric ebbs and flows with the tides of academic acceptance. It is subject, moreover, to the influence of fads and fashions in thinking, just as are literary criticism and the related arts. In short, it reflects the spirit of the age and the character of its educational philosophy. The past century, it seems clear, has favored the revival of rhetoric. Sharpening of critical faculties in this field, accordingly, is an objective eagerly sought and already in process of realization.

The Master of the Nineteenth Century

The Theoretical Basis of Goodrich's Criticism.—No name in the history of rhetorical criticism has been more favorably received during the recent revival of interest in this field than that of Chauncey Goodrich, Professor of Rhetoric at Yale from 1817 to 1839. For many years Goodrich taught rhetoric to sophomores at Yale and also conducted a combined section in rhetorical theory and criticism for seniors, the latter course including an intensive study of the Demosthenean orations and the masterpieces of English pub-lic address. In addition to these duties, he spent considerable time in lexicographical work, revising and editing Webster's *Dictionary.* In 1852, he published *Select British Eloquence.* Although he planned at a later time to bring out a comparable volume on American ora-tory, the pressure of other duties prevented his finishing the project.

Goodrich was both a theorist and a critic of oratory. Some of the notes recently discovered by John Hoshor, and now in the pos-session of the Yale University Library, throw considerable light upon

Goodrich's conception of public speaking. His theory of address stems directly from the classical pattern, with audience adaptation as its crowning feature. The essential components of his scheme are the traditional types of proof: the logical mode in which *probability,* rather than *exact truth,* is the necessary element; the emotional mode through which the accomplished speaker gains access to the hearer's reason; and ethical persuasion through which a man's character is revealed to the audience. Since an orator's character may be bad and his cause good, Goodrich affirms that whereas virtue is an unquestioned aid to eloquence, it is not a positive essential. This point of view, though subject to certain qualifications, is not without merit. It is perhaps more realistic than that which insists a man cannot be regarded as a real orator unless he is virtuous.

His Critical Method.—We should note that Goodrich approaches the theory of oratory through the criticism of it. Thus he quotes at the beginning of his *Select British Eloquence* a remark of Hume's to the effect that " 'he who would teach eloquence must do it chiefly by example.' " Goodrich then observes that this remark struck him forcibly; and

> . . . in entering on the office of Professor of Rhetoric in Yale College . . . , [I] took Demosthenes' Oration for the Crown as a text-book in the Senior Class. . . . [My object] was not only to awaken in the minds of the class that love of genuine eloquence which is the surest pledge of success, but to aid them in catching the spirit of the authors read, and, by analyzing passages selected for the purpose, to initiate the pupil in those higher principles which . . . have always guided the great masters of the art, till he should learn the *unwritten* rules of oratory, which operate by a kind of instinct upon the mind, and are far more important than any that are found in the books.[1]

Select British Eloquence was the product of that teaching method, articulated with the study of the English orators. Fortunately for the method he adopted, Goodrich chose to include the orations in their entirety. His reason was plain and defensible. "The object is to have each of them studied as a complete system of thought." He then continues:

> Detached passages of extraordinary force and beauty may be useful as exercises in elocution; but, if dwelt upon exclusively as models of style, they are sure to vitiate the taste. It is like taking all one's nutriment from highly seasoned food and stimulating drinks.[2]

What Goodrich calls "the aids afforded for the study of these speeches" represent the method he employs in making his critical estimates. These "aids" include (1) a "memoir of each orator, designed to show his early training in eloquence, the leading events of his public life, the peculiar cast of his genius, and the distinctive characteristics of his oratory"; (2) a historical introduction to each speech, "explaining minutely the circumstances of the case, the state of parties, and the exact point at issue"; (3) an analysis of the longer speeches "in side-notes, giving the divisions and subdivisions of thought"; (4) a body of explanatory notes covering the more minute facts; (5) critical notes "as specimens of the kind of analysis which the author has been accustomed to apply to the several parts of an oration"; (6) translations of passages quoted from foreign languages; and (7) a concluding statement "of the way in which the question was decided, with occasional remarks upon its merits or the results produced by the decision." [3]

His Studies of the Orators.—Goodrich deals with twenty orators, if we include the Letters of Junius, ranging from Sir John Eliot, who was born in the latter part of the sixteenth century, to Lord Brougham, who was still alive when *Select British Eloquence* was written. The larger part of the treatise deals, however, with the key figures of the eighteenth century, including Chatham, Mansfield, Burke, Fox, Pitt, and Erskine.

An examination of Goodrich's estimate of Burke will serve to illustrate the type of appraisal which characterizes *Select British Eloquence*. In an extended passage of some thirty-five pages—the equivalent of about one hundred ordinary octavo pages in Pica type —Goodrich develops the biographical-historical setting for a careful study of Burke's speeches. In no other treatise prior to 1850 is there such an ambitiously detailed account of the social forces which give to oratorical criticism its essential substructure. Scattered throughout the historical section appear hints and collateral critiques of Burke as a speaker, as a literary figure, and as a political philosopher. All of these preliminary guides to an understanding of the orator are supplemented later by specific information concerning each of the occasions or settings of the speeches chosen for criticism, as well as by marginal notes on the texts of the speeches.

Let us consider the final estimate of Burke as an orator. In it we observe a fine expression of Goodrich's method of evaluation.

As an orator he derived little or no advantage from his personal qualifications. He was tall, but not robust; his gait and gesture were awkward; his countenance, though intellectual, was destitute of softness, and rarely relaxed into a smile; and as he always wore spectacles, his eye gave him no command over an audience. 'His enunciation,' says Wraxall, 'was vehement and rapid; and his Irish accent, which was as strong as if he had never quitted the banks of the Shannon, diminished to the ear the effect of his eloquence on the mind.'

The variety and extent of his powers in debate was greater than that of any other orator in ancient or modern times. No one ever poured forth such a flood of thought—so many original combinations of inventive genius; so much knowledge of man and the working of political systems; so many just remarks on the relation of government to the manners, the spirit, and even the prejudices of a people; so many wise maxims as to a change in constitutions and laws; so many beautiful effusions of lofty and generous sentiment; such exuberant stores of illustration, ornament, and apt allusion; all intermingled with the liveliest sallies of wit or the boldest flights of a sublime imagination. In actual debate, as a contemporary informs us, he passed more rapidly from one exercise of his powers to another, than in his printed productions. During the same evening, sometimes in the space of a few moments, he would be pathetic and humorous, acrimonious and conciliating, now giving vent to his indignant feelings in lofty declamation, and again, almost in the same breath, convulsing his audience by the most laughable exhibitions of ridicule or burlesque. In respect to the versatility of Mr. Burke as an orator, Dr. Parr says, 'Who among men of eloquence and learning was ever more profoundly versed in every branch of science? Who is there that can transfer so happily the results of laborious research to the most familiar and popular topics? Who is there that possesses so extensive yet so accurate an acquaintance with every transaction recent or remote? Who is there that can deviate from his subject for the purposes of delight with such engaging ease, and insensibly conduct his hearers or readers from the severity of reasoning to the festivity of wit? Who is there that can melt them, if the occasion requires, with such resistless power to grief or pity? Who is there that combines the charm of inimitable grace and urbanity with such magnificent and boundless expansion?'

A prominent feature in the character of Mr. Burke, which prepared him for this wide exercise of his powers, was *intellectual independence.* He leaned on no other man's understanding, however great. In the true sense of the term, he never borrowed an idea or an image. Like food in a healthy system, every thing from without was perfectly assimilated; it entered by a new combination into the very structure of his thoughts, as when the blood, freshly formed, goes out to the extremities under the strong pulsations of the heart. On most subjects, at the present day, this is all we can expect of *originality;* the thoughts and feelings which a man expresses must be *truly his own.*

In the structure of his mind he had a strong resemblance to Bacon, nor was he greatly his inferior in the leading attributes of his intellect.

In imagination he went far beyond him. He united more perfectly than any other man the discordant qualities of the philosopher and the poet, and this union was equally the source of some of his greatest excellences and faults as an orator.

The first thing that strikes us in a survey of his understanding is its remarkable *comprehensiveness*. He had an amplitude of mind, a power and compass of intellectual vision, beyond that of most men that ever lived. He looked on a subject like a man standing upon an eminence, taking a large and rounded view of it on every side, contemplating each of its parts under a vast variety of relations, and those relations often extremely complex or remote. To this wide grasp of original thought he added every variety of information gathered from abroad. There was no subject on which he had not read, no system relating to the interests of man as a social being which he had not thoroughly explored. All these treasures of acquired knowledge he brought home to amplify and adorn the products of his own genius, as the ancient Romans collected every thing that was beautiful in the spoils of conquered nations, to give new splendour to the seat of empire.

To this largeness of view he added a surprising *subtlety of intellect*. So quick and delicate were his perceptions that he saw his way clearly through the most complicated relations, following out the finest thread of thought without once letting go his hold, or becoming lost or perplexed in the intricacies of the subject. This subtlety, however, did not usually take the form of mere logical acuteness in the detection of fallacies. He was not remarkable for his dexterity as a disputant. He loved rather to build up than to pull down; he dwelt not so much on the differences of things, as on some hidden agreement between them when apparently most dissimilar. The association of *resemblance* was one of the most active principles of his nature. While it filled his mind with all the imagery of the poet, it gave an impulse and direction to his reasoning as a philosopher. It led him, as his favorite employment, to trace out analogies, correspondencies, or contrasts . . ; thus filling up his originally comprehensive mind with a beautiful series of associated thoughts, showing often the identity of things which appeared the most unlike, and binding together in one system what might seem the most unconnected or contradictory phenomena. To this he added another principle of association, still more characteristic of the philosopher, that of *cause and effect*. 'Why?' 'Whence?' 'By what means?' 'For what end?' 'With what results?' these questions from childhood were continually pressing upon his mind. To answer them in respect to *man* in all his multiplied relations as the creature of society, to trace out the working of political institutions, to establish the principles of wise legislation, to lay open the sources of national security and advancement, was the great object of his life; and he here found the widest scope for that extraordinary subtlety of intellect of which we are now

speaking. In these two principles of association, we see the origin of
Mr. Burke's inexhaustible richness of thought. We see, also, how it
was that in his mode of viewing a subject there was never any thing
ordinary or commonplace. If the topic was a trite one, the manner of
presenting it was peculiarly his own. As in the kaleidoscope, the same
object takes a thousand new shapes and colors under a change of light,
so in his mind the most hackneyed theme was transformed and illuminated by the radiance of his genius, or placed in new relations which
gave it all the freshness of original thought.

This amplitude and subtlety of intellect, in connection with his peculiar habits of association, prepared the way for another characteristic
of Mr. Burke, his remarkable *power of generalization.* Without this
he might have been one of the greatest of poets, but not a philosopher
or a scientific statesman. 'To generalize,' says Sir James Mackintosh,
'is to philosophize; and comprehension of mind, joined to the habit of
careful and patient observation, forms the true genius of philosophy.'
But it was not in his case a mere 'habit,' it was a kind of instinct of his
nature, which led him to gather all the results of his thinking, as by
an elective affinity, around their appropriate centers, and, knowing that
truths are valuable just in proportion as they have a wider reach, to
rise from particulars to generals, and so to shape his statements as to
give them the weight and authority of universal propositions. His philosophy, however, was not that of abstract truth; it was confined to
things in the *concrete,* and chiefly to man, society, and government. He
was no metaphysician; he had, in fact, a dislike, amounting to weakness,
of all abstract reasonings in politics, affirming, on one occasion, as to
certain statements touching the rights of man, that just 'in proportion
as they were metaphysically true, they were morally and politically
false!' He was, as he himself said, 'a philosopher in *action;*' his generalizations embraced the great facts of human society and political institutions as affected by all the interests and passions, the prejudices
and frailties of a being like man. The impression he made was owing,
in a great degree, to the remoteness of the ideas which he brought together, the startling novelty and yet justness of his combinations, the
heightening power of contrast, and the striking manner in which he
connected truths of imperishable value with the individual case before
him. It is here that we find the true character and office of Mr. Burke.
He was a *man of principles;* one of the greatest teachers of 'civil prudence' that the world has ever seen. A collection of maxims might be
made from his writings infinitely superior to those of Rochefoucauld;
equally true to nature, and adapted, at the same time, not to produce
selfishness and distrust, but to call into action all that is generous, and
noble, and elevated in the heart of man. His high moral sentiment and
strong sense of religion added greatly to the force of these maxims;
and, as a result of these fine generalizations, Mr. Burke has this pecu-

liarity, which distinguishes him from every other writer, that he is almost equally instructive whether he is right or wrong as to the particular point in debate. He may fail to make out his case; opposing considerations may induce us to decide against him; and yet every argument he uses is full of instruction; it contains great truths, which, if they do not turn the scale here, may do it elsewhere; so that he whose mind is filled with the maxims of Burke has within him not only one of the finest incentives of genius, but a fountain of the richest thought, which may flow forth through a thousand channels in all the efforts of his own intellect, to whatever subject those efforts may be directed.

With these qualities and habits of mind, the oratory of Mr. Burke was of necessity *didactic*. His speeches were *lectures,* and, though often impassioned, enlivened at one time with wit, and rising at another into sublimity or pathos, they usually became wearisome to the House from their minuteness and subtlety, as

'He went on refining,
And thought of convincing when they thought of dining.'

We see, then, in the philosophical habits of his mind . . . why he spoke so often to empty benches, while Fox, by seizing on the strong points of the case, by throwing away intermediate thoughts, and striking at the heart of the subject, never failed to carry the House with him in breathless attention.

His *method* was admirable, in respect at least to his published speeches. No man ever bestowed more care on the arrangement of his thoughts. The exceptions to this remark are apparent, not real. There is now and then a slight irregularity in his mode of transition, which seems purposely thrown in to avoid an air of sameness; and the subordinate heads sometimes spread out so widely, that their connection with the main topic is not always obvious. But there is reigning throughout the whole a massive unity of design like that of a great cathedral, whatever may be the intricacy of its details.

In his *reasonings* (for he was one of the greatest masters of reason in our language . . .) Mr. Burke did not usually adopt the outward forms of logic. He has left us, indeed, some beautiful specimens of dialectical ability, but his arguments, in most instances, consisted of the amplest enumeration and the clearest display of all the facts and principles, the analogies, relations, or tendencies which were applicable to the case, and were adapted to settle it on the immutable basis of the nature and constitution of things. Here again he appeared, of necessity, more as a teacher than a logician, and hence many were led to underrate his argumentative powers. The exuberance of his fancy was likewise prejudicial to him in this respect. Men are apt to doubt the solidity of a structure which is covered all over with flowers. As to this peculiarity of his eloquence, Mr. Fox truly said, 'It injures his reputation; it casts a veil over his wisdom. Reduce his language, withdraw his images, and you will find that he is more wise than eloquent; you will have your full weight of metal though you melt down the chasing.'

In respect to Mr. Burke's *imagery*, however, it may be proper to remark, that a large part of it is not liable to any censure of this kind; many of his figures are so finely wrought into the texture of his style, that we hardly think of them as figures at all. His great fault in other cases is that of giving them too bold a relief, or dwelling on them too long, so that the primary idea is lost sight of in the image. Sometimes the prurience of his fancy makes him low and even filthy. He is like a man depicting the scenes of nature, who is not content to give us those features of the landscape that delight the eye, but fills out his canvas with objects which are coarse, disgusting, or noisome. Hence no writer in any language has such extremes of imagery as Mr. Burke. . . .

His *language*, though copious, was not verbose. Every word had its peculiar force and application. His chief fault was that of overloading his sentences with secondary thoughts, which weakened the blow by dividing it. His style is, at times, more careless and inaccurate than might be expected in so great a writer. But his mind was on higher things. His idea of a truly fine sentence, as once stated to a friend, is worthy of being remembered. It consists, said he, in a union of thought, feeling, and imagery—of a striking truth and a corresponding sentiment, rendered doubly striking by the force and beauty of figurative language. There are more sentences of this kind in the pages of Mr. Burke than of any other writer.

In conclusion, we may say, without paradox, since oratory is only one branch of the quality we are now considering, that while Mr. Burke was inferior as an orator to Lord Chatham and Mr. Fox, he has been surpassed by no one in the richness and splendor of his eloquence; and that he has left us something greater and better than all eloquence in his countless lessons of moral and civil wisdom.[4]

Use of the Comparative Method.—In common with many of the better critics of oratory, Goodrich relied upon comparisons or contrasts to delineate the characteristic style and method of certain speakers. Two passages will illustrate the use to which he put this method. The first is from his analysis of Charles James Fox:

Sir James Mackintosh has remarked that 'Fox was the most Demosthenean speaker since Demosthenes,' while Lord Brougham says, in commenting on this passage, 'There never was a greater mistake than the fancying a close resemblance between his eloquence and that of Demosthenes.' When two such men differ on a point like this, we may safely say that both are in the right and in the wrong. As to certain qualities, Fox was the very reverse of the great Athenian; as to others, they had much in common. In whatever relates to the forms of oratory—symmetry, dignity, grace, the working up of thought and language to their most perfect expression—Mr. Fox was not only inferior to Demosthenes, but wholly unlike him, having no rhetoric and no ideality; while, at the same time, in the structure of his understanding, the modes of its operation, the soul and spirit which breathes throughout his eloquence, there was a striking resemblance. This will appear as we dwell for a moment on his leading peculiarities.

(1.) He had a luminous simplicity, which gave his speeches the most absolute unity of impression, however irregular might be their arrangement. No man ever kept the great points of his case more steadily and vividly before the minds of his audience.

(2.) He took everything in the concrete. If he discussed principles, it was always in direct connection with the subject before him. Usually, however, he did not even discuss a subject—he grappled with an antagonist. Nothing gives such life and interest to a speech, or so delights an audience, as a direct contest of man with man.

(3.) He struck instantly at the heart of his subject. He was eager to meet his opponent at once on the real points at issue; and the moment of his greatest power was when he stated the argument against himself, with more force than his adversary or any other man could give it, and then seized it with the hand of a giant, tore it in pieces, and trampled it under foot.

(4.) His mode of enforcing a subject on the minds of his audience was to come back again and again to the strong points of his case. Mr. Pitt *amplified* when he wished to impress, Mr. Fox *repeated*. Demosthenes also repeated, but he had more adroitness in varying the mode of doing it.

(5.) He had rarely any preconceived method or arrangement of his thoughts. This was one of his greatest faults, in which he differed most from the Athenian artist. If it had not been for the unity of impression and feeling mentioned above, his strength would have been wasted in disconnected efforts.

(6.) Reasoning was his forte and his passion. But he was not a regular reasoner. In his eagerness to press forward, he threw away everything he could part with, and compacted the rest into a single mass. Facts, principles, analogies, were all wrought together like the strands of a cable, and intermingled with wit, ridicule, or impassioned feeling. His arguments were usually personal in their nature, *ad hominem,* &c., and were brought home to his antagonist with stinging severity and force.

(7.) He abounded in *hits*—those abrupt and startling turns of thought which rouse an audience, and give them more delight than the loftiest strains of eloquence.

(8.) He was equally distinguished for his *side blows,* for keen and pungent remarks flashed out upon his antagonist in passing, as he pressed on with his argument.

(9.) He was often dramatic, personating the character of his opponents or others, and carrying on a dialogue between them, which added greatly to the liveliness and force of his oratory.

(10.) He had astonishing dexterity in evading difficulties, and turning to his own advantage every thing that occurred in debate.

In nearly all these qualities he had a close resemblance to Demosthenes.[5]

The second passage is not original with Goodrich. He quotes a contemporary of Lord Brougham and George Canning to show how the qualities of the two orators are the more clearly revealed through juxtaposition of their characteristics:

'Canning was airy, open, and prepossessing; Brougham seemed stern, hard, lowering, and almost repulsive. Canning's features were handsome, and his eye, though deeply ensconced under his eyebrows, was full of sparkle and gayety; the features of Brougham were harsh in the extreme: while his forehead shot up to a great elevation, his chin was long and square; his mouth, nose, and eyes seemed huddled together in the center of his face, the eyes absolutely lost amid folds and corrugations; and while he sat listening, they seemed to retire inward or to be veiled by a filmy curtain, which not only concealed the appalling glare which shot from them when he was aroused, but rendered his mind and his purpose a sealed book to the keenest scrutiny of man. Canning's passions appeared upon the open champaign of his face, drawn up in ready array, and moved to and fro at every turn of his own oration and every retort in that of his antagonist. Those of Brougham remained within, as in a citadel which no artillery could batter and no mine blow up; and even when he was putting forth all the power of his eloquence, when every ear was tingling at what he said, and while the immediate object of his invective was writhing in helpless and indescribable agony, his visage retained its cold and brassy hue; and he triumphed over the passions of other men by seeming to be without passion himself. When Canning rose to speak, he elevated his countenance, and seemed to look round for applause as a thing dear to his feelings; while Brougham stood coiled and concentrated, reckless of all but the power that was within himself.

'From Canning there was expected the glitter of wit and the glow of spirit—something showy and elegant; Brougham stood up as a being whose powers and intentions were all a mystery—whose aim and effect no living man could divine. You bent forward to catch the first sentence of the one, and felt human nature elevated in the specimen before you; you crouched and shrunk back from the other, and dreams of ruin and annihilation darted across your mind. The one seemed to dwell among men, to join in their joys, and to live upon their praise; the other appeared a son of the desert, who had deigned to visit the human race merely to make it tremble at his strength.

'The style of their eloquence and the structure of their orations were just as different. Canning arranged his words like one who could play skillfully upon that sweetest of all instruments, the human voice; Brougham proceeded like a master of every power of reasoning and the understanding. The modes and allusions of the one were always quadrable by the classical formulae; those of the other could be squared only by the higher analysis of the mind; and they soared, and ran, and pealed, and swelled on and on, till a single sentence was often a complete oration within itself; but still, so clear was the logic, and so close the connection, that every member carried the weight of all that went before, and opened the way for all that was to follow after. The style of Canning was like the convex mirror, which scatters every ray of light that falls upon it, and shines and sparkles in whatever position it is viewed; that of Brougham was like the concave speculum, scattering no indiscriminate radiance, but having its light concentrated into one intense and tremendous focus. Canning marched forward in a straight and clear track; every paragraph was perfect in itself, and every coruscation of wit and of genius was brilliant and delightful; it was all felt, and it was felt all at once: Brougham twined round and round in a spiral, sweeping the contents of a vast circumference before him, and uniting and pouring them onward to the main point of attack.' [6]

Postscript on Goodrich's Method.—Goodrich's analyses of the several orators are not of equal merit. The studies of Fox and Burke are no doubt the best. But in all of them there is a sense of direction, a point of view that keeps the audience and the age clearly in focus. Unlike many of his predecessors, Goodrich prepared his critiques with an eye to capturing the rhetorical, rather than the strictly literary, mood. His method was adapted to the realization of that end. Goodrich was an uncommonly successful critic of public address.

Jebb Evaluates the Attic Orators

Jebb's Method of Analysis.—For more than fifty years the name of Richard C. Jebb has been closely associated in the minds of rhetoricians with all that is scholarly and exacting in the study of ancient oratory. Jebb's *Attic Orators* [7] is unquestionably the most readable and penetrating analysis in print of the great ancient figures in oratory.

Originally published in 1876, Jebb's study deals chiefly with the Attic orators before Demosthenes. Thus, instead of covering the complete Attic decade, Jebb offers a systematic and detailed account of Antiphon, Andocides, Lysias, Isocrates, and Isaeus. In a concluding chapter, he includes, however, a section on the "mature civil eloquence" best exemplified in the activities of Lycurgus, Hyperides, Aeschines, and Demosthenes.

The purpose of Jebb's work transcends straight rhetorical criticism. Not content simply with appraising the relative merits of a few orators of antiquity, he proposed to reveal the essential relation between oratorical expression and Greek prose generally. Accordingly, through the lives and works of the great figures, he shows how Greek oratory developed, and in turn how Greek prose was influenced by refinements in that branch of expression. This is an assignment of no mean proportions, requiring as it does a thorough command of the historical, literary, and social facts that contributed to the formation of a style of utterance.

The *Attic Orators* is, then, several projects in one—and all competently handled. It is a history of rhetoric from earliest times to the Rome of Augustus; it is a commentary on the social and political forces that helped to mould the artistic expression of ancient Greece; it is a careful textual study of the speeches of the first five great orators before Demosthenes; and, finally, it is a critical estimate of the stylistic excellences of the Attic orators who were actively responsible for shaping their language into artistic form.

In our previous discussion of the "Antecedents of Contemporary Rhetorical Theory," we referred frequently to conclusions and judgments derived by Jebb from his painstaking researches. It remains now to examine the methods he employed in his rhetorical criticism.

Jebb says he is not interested in adopting a "uniform scale" for analyzing the orations; instead, he prefers to make the studies "more or less full according to the interest of the subject matter or the nature of its difficulties." In keeping with this dictum, he gives a relatively short analysis of Andocides; but to Isocrates he accords more than half of the second volume of his treatise.

Despite the fact that the spatial distributions of the work vary widely with the orators, Jebb uses a strictly uniform pattern for the divisions of study within each analysis. Thus his studies are divided into three sections, dealing with the life, the style, and the works of each orator. To this scheme he adheres with the single deviation of Isocrates, to whose study he adds a chapter on the celebrated Theory of Culture.

Perhaps more fully than any earlier critic with the exception of Goodrich, Jebb recognized the importance of historical study in making critical estimates of orators. Remarking that an oration from Antiphon or Isocrates "will often be poor food for the mind if it is read alone," he goes on:

> What is necessary to make it profitable is some idea of the world in which it was spoken. These orators who were not conspicuous actors in history must be read, not fragmentarily or in the light of notes which confine themselves to explaining what are termed 'allusions,' but more systematically, and with some general comprehension of the author and the age.[8]

Jebb observes that Brougham, distinguished critic that he was, found Isaeus hard to read. But, counters Jebb, if Brougham

> . . . had considered Isaeus, not as merely a writer on a series of will-cases, but as the oldest and most vivid witness for the working of inchoate testation in a primitive society, and, on the other hand, as the man who, alone, marks a critical phase in the growth of Attic prose, it is conceivable that Brougham should have thought Isaeus worthy of the most attentive perusal.[9]

The analyses Jebb makes of the orators furnish abundant testimony to his conviction that history is an essential constituent of the critical judgment of oratory.

Another distinguishing feature of Jebb's analyses is the way he interlaces critical comment on political and artistic events with biographical details. Indeed, Jebb gives biography considerable prominence in his studies; but, unlike many critics who were similarly convinced of its importance, he confines the biographical elements to a frame of reference in which the literary and rhetorical point of view constantly shines forth. He is interested in the biography of the orator only to the extent that it enlarges the understanding of the character as a user and moulder of prose expression. Thus in his summation of the life of Antiphon, Jebb says:

> It was the power of a subtle and quick mind backed by a thorough command of the new rhetoric. He was masterly in device and in utterance. Fertility of expedient, ingenuity in making points in debate, were the qualities which the oligarchs most needed; and it was in these that the strength of Antiphon lay. In promptness of invention where difficulties were to be met on the instant he probably bore some like-

ness to Themistocles; but there is no reason for crediting him with that largeness of view, or with any share of that wonderful foresight, which made Themistocles a statesman as well as a diplomatist.[10]

Here the emphasis is plainly upon the relation of words to the destiny of states. As Jebb observes:

> Antiphon's first and strongest claim to eminence was his mastery over the weapons now indispensable in the ecclesia and the lawcourts; it was this accomplishment, no less fashionable than useful, which recommended him to the young men of his party whom he had no other pretension to influence. . . . In his person the practical branch of the new culture for the first time takes a distinct place among the qualifications for political rank. The Art of Words had its definite share in bringing in the Four Hundred: it was a curious nemesis when seven years later it was banished from Athens by the Thirty.[11]

Jebb is more deeply concerned with the analysis of the orator's style than are most present-day critics. In this regard, he is, perhaps, less the rhetorical and more the literary critic. However, this emphasis is consistent with the plan of his work. He was tracing the development of Greek prose expression; since oratory was the principal form of utterance at that time, he naturally found it necessary to examine its structure with care, to the end that he might determine its influence upon Attic prose generally.

Jebb's analyses conform to a fairly conventional pattern. He reconstructs briefly the setting of the speech; outlines the logical points developed by the speaker; inspects the evidence used in establishing the case; appraises the arrangement of speech materials; and analyzes the style of the oration as a whole. He relies, therefore, upon the usual divisions of rhetoric for the basic scheme of his critical undertakings.

Selections from Jebb's Criticisms.—Short passages from the studies of certain orations will illustrate the procedure. In the summary of Antiphon's speech "On the Murder of Herodes," Jebb remarks:

> In reviewing the whole speech as an argument, the first thing which strikes us is the notable contrast between the line of defence taken here and that traced for a case essentially similar in the model-speeches of the First Tetralogy. There, the defendant employs all his ingenuity in suggesting explanations of the mysterious crime which shall make the hypothesis of his own guilt unnecessary. Here, the defendant pointedly refuses to do anything of the kind. It is enough if he can show that

he was not the murderer; it is not his business to show who was or
might have been. On this broad, plain ground the defence takes a
firm stand. The arguments are presented in a natural order, as they
arise out of the facts narrated, and are drawn out at a length proportionate to their consequence,—by far the greatest stress being laid on
the worthlessness of the slave's evidence; in discussing which, indeed,
the speaker is not very consistent. One apparent omission is curious.
The prisoner incidentally says that he never left the vessel on the night
when Herodes went on shore and disappeared; but he does not dwell
upon, or attempt to prove, this all-essential *alibi*. If the numerous commonplaces and general sentiments seem to us a source of weakness
rather than strength, allowance must be made for the taste and fashion
of the time; and every one must recognise the effectiveness of the appeal
to divine signs in which the argument finds its rhetorical climax.

As a composition, the speech has great merits. The ethos, indeed,
is not artistic; a style so dignified and so sententious is scarcely suitable
to a speaker who is constantly apologising for his youth and inexperience. Nor, except in the passage which touches on the ruin of Mytilene,
is there even an attempt at pathos. But there is variety and versatility;
the opening passage is artistically elaborate, the concluding, impressive
in a higher way; while the purely argumentative part of the speech is
not encumbered with any stiff dignity, but is clear, simple and sufficiently animated. Altogether the style has less sustained elevation, but
shows more flexibility, greater maturity and mastery, than that of the
Tetralogies.[12]

In the summary of his criticism of Andocides' speech "On the
Mysteries," Jebb reveals other features of his rhetorical judgment:

It is impossible to read the speech On the Mysteries without feeling
that, as a whole, it is powerful in spite of some evident defects. The
arrangement is best in what we have called the first division . . . ,
which deals with two distinct groups of facts, those relating to the
Mysteries case and those relating to the Hermae case. These facts
are stated in an order which is, on the whole, clear and natural, though
not free from the parentheses of which Andocides was so fond. . . .
Less praise is due to the second part of the speech . . . , devoted to the
various enactments which had made the decree of Isotimides obsolete.
It is at once full and obscure, giving needless, and withholding necessary, details. The third part . . . is a mere string of topics, unconnected with each other, and but slightly connected with the case. This
confused appendix to the real defence is, however, insignificant. It
shows the anxiety of Andocides to make the judges understand the
rancorous personal feeling of his enemies; an anxiety natural in a man
who for sixteen years had been pursued by unproved accusations. The

passages about Callias and Agyrrhius probably had a stronger effect upon the court than any conventional appeal to compassion would have produced.

As regards style, the language of the speech is thoroughly unaffected and easy, plain without studied avoidance of ornament, and rising at the right places—as when he speaks of the old victories of freedom . . . , and in the peroration. . . . But the great merit of the composition is its picturesqueness, its variety and life. The scene in the prison . . . and the description of the panic at Athens . . . are perhaps the best passages in this respect. If Andocides had not many rhetorical accomplishments, he certainly had perception of character, and the knack of describing it. Diocleides bargaining with Euphemus . . .—Charmides exhorting Andocides to save the prisoners . . .—Peisander urging that Mantitheus and Aphepsion should be put on the rack . . . —are well given in a few vivid touches.[13]

His Regard for Texts.—Finally Jebb's criticism rests upon a deep regard for authenticity of texts. Through appeals to authorities and to research he establishes the speeches as genuine before concerning himself with their evaluation. And, once established, parts of the text are quoted freely to illustrate the points in his critical survey.

Studies Similar to Jebb's.—In many particulars, Jebb's studies coincide in methodology and substance with those of other scholars who have studied the orations of ancient Greece. For instance, J. P. Mahaffy's [14] analysis of Demosthenes' oratory follows substantially the same line of thinking. John F. Dobson, in *The Greek Orators*,[15] does about the same thing, and in some respects does as good a job as Jebb.

Dobson's chapter on Demosthenes merits separate notice. In addition to dealing with the usual features of the orator's biography, the historical background of the speeches, the logical and emotional contents, the arrangement, and the style, Dobson introduces particularly acute comments on audience behavior and on the measures of oratorical effectiveness.

Commenting on the fact that Demosthenes was not completely free from sophistry, Dobson says:

Like many good orators in good or bad causes he laboured from time to time to make a weak case appear strong, and in this effort was often absolutely disingenuous. The whole of the de Corona is an attempt to throw the judges off the scent by leading them on to false trails.[16]

And further on, he remarks:

> . . . a study of other speeches results in the discovery of many minor
> points in which, accurately gauging the intelligence of his audience,
> he has intentionally misled them. Thus, his own knowledge of history
> was profound; but experience has proved that the knowledge possessed
> by any audience of the history of its own generation is likely to be
> sketchy and inaccurate. . . . This gives the politician his opportunity
> of so grouping or misrepresenting facts as to give a wrong impression.[17]

Despite these assertions, Dobson was nevertheless convinced that
Demosthenes was motivated by noble aspirations. "Until the end
he had hopes for Greek freedom, freedom for Athens, not based on
any unworthy compromise, but dependent on a new birth of the old
Athenian spirit."

Dobson's conception of the function of rhetoric is sound. He
looks upon the orator as a communicator of ideas, not as an exhi-
bitionist who is anxious to display his skills. Persuasion is acknowledged to be the end of rhetoric. Referring again to Demosthenes'
speeches, Dobson says:

> A good speech was to him a successful speech, not one which might be
> admired by critics as a piece of literature. It is only incidental that
> his speeches have a literary quality which ranks him among the fore-
> most writers of Attic prose; as an orator he was independent of this
> quality.[18]

In summary we may say that Jebb, as well as Mahaffy, Dobson,
and other scholars, contributed to the art of rhetorical criticism by
stressing the importance of accurate texts—even though that does
not mean the same thing in a study of ancient orators as it does in
the analysis of contemporary oratory; by reaffirming the doctrine
that speeches can best be studied in the light of the social pattern
in which they were originally set; and by articulating (particularly
in the studies of antiquity where facts are scattered and often fragmentary) the oratorical efforts with the audience responses in the
world of practical action. Although Jebb's studies give too much
attention to style to permit us to consider them comprehensively
balanced criticisms, they represent mature investigations into the
art of expression.

The Historian's Approach to Oratory

Lecky's Conception of the Role of Oratory.—Among the distinguished historians of the recent past who held a clear conception
constantly before them of the place of oratory in the social process

was William Edward Hartpole Lecky. It is not necessary to find in his works a separate section on the orators to justify our giving him a place in the history of rhetorical criticism. By showing an interested concern in the relation between oratory and statesmanship, by formulating a point of view respecting the function of discourse in the political process, and by presenting portraits of certain orators while developing the continuity of his historical narrative, Lecky established his right to representation in the field of rhetorical analysis.

In the first volume of his study, Lecky makes an observation pertinent to our inquiry:

> It is the custom of some writers to decry parliamentary institutions as being simply government by talking, and to assert that when they exist mere rhetorical skill will always be more valued than judgment, knowledge, or character. The exaggeration of such charges may be easily established. It is, no doubt, inevitable that where business is transacted chiefly by debate, the talent of a debater should be highly prized; but it is not true that British Legislatures have shown less skill than ordinary sovereigns in distinguishing solid talent from mere showy accomplishments, or that parliamentary weight has in England been usually proportioned to oratorical power. St. John was a far greater orator than Harley; Pulteney was probably a greater orator than Walpole; Stanley in mere rhetorical skill was undoubtedly the superior of Peel. Godolphin, Pelham, Castlereagh, Liverpool, Melbourne, Althorp, Wellington, Russell, and Palmerston are all examples of men who, either as statesmen or as successful leaders of the House of Commons, have taken a foremost place in English politics without any oratorical brilliancy. Sheridan, Plunket, and Brougham, though orators of almost the highest class, left no deep impression on English public life; the ascendency of Grey and Canning was very transient, and no Opposition since the early Hanoverian period sank so low as that which was guided by Fox. The two Pitts are the only examples before our own generation, of speakers of transcendent power exercising for a considerable time a commanding influence over English politics. It is, I believe, quite true that the amazing eloquence and debating skill of the younger Pitt concealed defects in statesmanship which in a less brilliant orator would have been clearly seen, but it would be a grave error to attribute solely to these gifts the long ascendency which he enjoyed. Much was due to his conspicuous ability in managing the finances and commercial interests of the country; to the well-founded confidence of the nation in the purity, loftiness, and strength of his character; to the discredit which had fallen on his opponents; to the inherited lustre of a great name; to the steady support of the King. The case of his father is less disputable. He was

guilty of many faults and of some foibles, but the pinnacle of glory to which he raised his country is surely a sufficient proof that if he was the greatest orator he was also the greatest war minister that England has ever known.[19]

This statement reveals the point of view which unmistakably guides Lecky in his subsequent analyses of social movements during the eighteenth century. He accords to the orators the praise and credit they deserve, but there is no disposition to over-assess their importance, or to underestimate their influence. This is a difficult balance to achieve.

Analysis of Burke.—Since Lecky appraises the eloquence of many key figures of the eighteenth century, we shall consider some of his observations concerning Burke, for they suggest the method employed in dealing with other speakers. Of Burke, Lecky said:

. . . no other politician or writer has thrown the light of so penetrating a genius on the nature and working of the British Constitution, has impressed his principles so deeply on both of the great parties in the State, and has left behind him a richer treasure of political wisdom applicable to all countries and to all times.[20]

The appeal is evidently to the reader as well as to the listener, for Lecky remarks that the "time may come when they [Burke's works] will be no longer read. The time will never come in which men would not grow the wiser by reading them." This is in keeping with the remark once made by Grattan that Burke's speeches "were far better suited to a patient reader than an impatient hearer." [21]
Lecky follows with the statement that

. . . there is scarcely a perceptible difference between the style of his essays and the style of his published speeches; and if the reader selects from his works the few passages which possess to an eminent degree the flash and movement of spoken rhetoric, he will be quite as likely to find them in the former as in the latter.[22]

Lecky's final estimate of Burke's speaking is thus expressed:

He far surpassed every other speaker in the copiousness and correctness of his diction, in the range of knowledge he brought to bear on every subject of debate, in the richness and variety of his imagination, in the gorgeous beauty of his descriptive passages, in the depth of the philosophical reflections and the felicity of the personal sketches which he delighted in scattering over his speeches.[23]

These short quotations cannot capture the spirit of Lecky's complete appraisal. They suggest, however, the strictly rhetorical outlook that characterizes much of his investigation into the activities of the central figures of the century. In addition to such remarks as we have examined, note should be made of the fact that Lecky quotes other authorities relative to Burke's oratorical skills; investigates fully the historical factors with which Burke and others had to deal; and probes searchingly into Burke's thinking, basic premises, mental qualities, and personal characteristics. In short, Lecky provides a tolerably complete portrait of an orator. In their endeavor to appraise the ideas and premises of great public speakers, contemporary critics have relied heavily upon the suggestions afforded by Lecky's example.

Biographical Approaches to Speech Criticism

The Relation of Rhetoric to Biography.—Few historians and biographers have written their treatises with an eye to revealing the role of speechmaking in the affairs of state. This is true even of those studies dealing primarily with public figures whose principal claim to distinction rests upon oratorical activity. The reason for this neglect or avoidance of the rhetorical point of view in historiography is not clear. In some cases, no doubt, it arises from deliberate disregard of the importance of speechcraft in the historical process; in others it may suggest an inability on the part of the writers to incorporate the details of speaking performances into the historical narrative so as to reveal the proper rhetorical perspective.

Morley's Life of Cobden.—Among the exceptions to the general observation that historians and biographers do not provide serious appraisals of oratory, is the work of John Morley. In the *Life of Richard Cobden,* Morley establishes his talents for criticism by revealing a thorough understanding of the dynamics of speech situations and by evincing an intelligent appreciation of the place of the spoken word in society.

The biography of Cobden is also a partial study of John Bright, since an alliance existed between them which "far more than doubled the power that either could have exerted without the other." Morley relies heavily upon the speeches of these two men to bring out the story of their lives. And he always makes sure that the speeches are examined and judged in the light of the historical circumstances that prompted their delivery.

Cobden and Bright became orators, Morley says, "because they had something to say, which they were intent on bringing their hearers to believe, and which happened to be true, wise, and just."

Probing further into Cobden's endowments, Morley indicates that he offered "the glow of a thoroughly convinced reason, of intellectual ingenuity, of argumentative keenness. It came from transparent honesty, thoroughly clear ideas, and a very definite purpose." [24]

Relying frequently upon the comparative method to sharpen the focus of his study, Morley characterizes them thus:

> If in Mr. Bright there was a deeper austerity, in both there was the same homeliness of allusion, and the same graphic plainness. Both avoided the stilted abstractions of rhetoric, and neither was ever afraid of the vulgarity of details. In Cobden as in Bright, we feel that there was nothing personal or small, and that what they cared for so vehemently were great causes. [25]

While Bright had all the "resources of passion," Cobden had, in addition, an engaging persuasiveness. In short, where "knowledge and logic were the proper instruments, Cobden was a master."

Morley reveals Cobden as a facile user of exposition and a skilful framer of arguments.

> [Cobden] always seemed to have made exactly the right degree of allowance for the difficulty with which men follow a speech, as compared with the ease of following the same argument on a printed page which they may con and ponder until their apprehension is complete. [26]

Like other political agitators who were always ready to restate their theses, Cobden was never afraid "of repeating his formula, his principles, his illustrations, his phrases, with untiring reiteration." He had commendable skill in shaping his subject matter to the needs of the occasion. He had

> . . . inexhaustible patience in dealing with the mental infirmities of those whom it was his business to persuade. He was wholly free from the unmeasured anger against human stupidity. . . . Cobden was not without the faculty of intellectual contempt, and he had the gift of irony; but in the contempt was no presumption, and it was irony without truculence. [27]

The elements of ethical persuasion in Cobden's efforts were also examined by Morley. Cobden, it is said, evinced "personal friendliness and undisguised cordiality." Although his speaking was businesslike, it was never dull.

> It was not according to the old definition of oratory, reason fused in passion, but reason fused by the warmth of personal geniality. . . . [His style] seldom went beyond the vigorous and animated conversation of a bright and companionable spirit. [28]

Since tropes and perorations alone do not make the popular speaker, Morley found the key to Cobden's power in the "whole impression of his personality." Cobden had a "peculiar respect for his great popular audiences, and they instinctively felt the presence of it, making a claim to their good-will and their attention."

Through all of Morley's analysis runs the thought that speech-craft, under scrupulous control, can be the handmaid of statesman-ship. Oratory can produce effects that contribute to the public good. Even when the orator fails to achieve his end, he may still be exer-cising a salutary influence, provided the principles for which he stands are praiseworthy. Thus Cobden and Bright were rebuked and reviled for their attitude toward the Crimean War, but they held to their positions. To the point of this conviction, Morley remarks:

> The moral fortitude, like the political wisdom of these two strong men, begins to stand out with a splendour that already recalls the great historic types of statesmanship and patriotism. Even now our heart-felt admiration and gratitude goes out to them as it goes out to Burke for his lofty and manful protests against the war with America and the oppression of Ireland, and to Charles Fox for his bold and strenu-ous resistance to the war with the first French Republic.[29]

Why were Bright and Cobden unsuccessful in their efforts to change public opinion on the Crimean War? Morley believes that the

> . . . public had worked itself into a mood in which the most solid reasoning, the most careful tenderness of prejudice, the most unan-swerable expostulations were all alike unavailing. The incompetency of one part of the Ministry, and the recklessness of the other part, pushed us over the edge.[30]

Brief as these excerpts are, they give a bit of the flavor of Morley's analysis. Prompted by the conviction that the great orator must have "unerring guiding principles," Morley delineates the character of Cobden as a political agitator. And at all times the speeches of Cobden, as well as Morley's evaluation of them, occupy the forefront of attention.

The Method in Morley's Life of Gladstone.—Actuated by the same desire to portray the orators in relation to their speeches, John Morley carried his method even further in the *Life of William Ewart Gladstone*. In tracing the early biographical details, he considers the factors accounting for Gladstone's abilities as a speaker; comments on his methods of speech preparation; and, in short, conforms closely to a pattern of study much used today by students who trace the speech education of great orators.

The treatment of Gladstone's Midlothian speeches of 1879 illustrates Morley's attitude toward oratory and its place in society. On the occasion of these speeches, Gladstone addressed the people just as he would the House of Commons, that is, "with the same breadth and accuracy of knowledge, the same sincerity of interest, the same scruple in right reasoning, and the same appeal to the gravity and responsibility of public life." And, Morley reminds us, the Midlothian speeches "were rallying cries, not sermons. . . ." Morley knew that these speeches, like others, could be understood and judged only through a knowledge of their settings. "To think of the campaign without the scene, is as who should read a play by candle-light among the ghosts of an empty theatre." [31]

At this point, Morley restates his concept of the orator-statesman:

Oratory ever since the days of Socrates, and perhaps long before, has been suspected as one of the black arts; and both at the time and afterwards Mr. Gladstone's speeches in his first Midlothian campaign were disparaged . . . , as sentiment rather than politics, as sophistry not sound reason, as illusory enchantment not solid and subsisting truth. We are challenged to show passages destined to immortality. With all admiration for the effulgent catalogue of British orators, and not forgetting Pitt on the slave trade, or Fox on the Westminster scrutiny, or Sheridan on the Beguns of Oude, or Plunket on the Catholic question, or Grattan, or Canning, or Brougham, we may perhaps ask whether all the passages that have arrived at this degree of fame and grandeur, with the exception of Burke, may not be comprised in an extremely slender volume. The statesman who makes or dominates a crisis, who has to rouse and mould the mind of senate or nation, has something else to think about than the production of literary masterpieces. The great political speech, which for that matter is a sort of drama, is not made by passages for elegant extract or anthologies, but by personality, movement, climax, spectacle, and the action of the time. All these elements Midlothian witnessed to perfection.[32]

The Midlothian speeches were "in groundwork and in essence strictly on the plane and in the tongue of statesmanship."

Bryce's Analysis of the Same Orator.—A digression may be permitted here to refer to a comparable analysis by James Bryce. In his biography of Gladstone, Bryce comments on the interrelation of oratory and statesmanship. By oratory, he remarks, Gladstone

. . . rose to fame and power, as, indeed, by it most English statesmen have risen, save those to whom wealth and rank and family connections have given a sort of presumptive claim to high office, like the Cavendishes and the Russells, the Cecils and the Bentincks. . . . for many years . . . [Gladstone's] eloquence was the main, one might almost say the sole, source of his influence. Oratory was a power in English politics even a century and a half ago, as the career of the elder Pitt shows. But within the last fifty years, years which have seen the power of rank and family connections decline, it has continued to be essential to the highest success although much less cultivated as a fine art, and brings a man quickly to the front, though it will not keep him there should he prove to want the other branches of statesmanlike capacity.[33]

Continuing, Bryce says:

The permanent reputation of an orator depends upon two things, the witness of contemporaries to the impression produced upon them, and the written or printed—we may, perhaps, be soon able to say the phonographed—record of his speeches. Few are the famous speakers who would be famous if they were tried by this latter test alone, and Mr. Gladstone was not one of them.[34]

As to the future of these orations, Bryce believes that twenty years hence Gladstone's speeches

. . . will not be read, except, of course, by historians. They are too long, too diffuse, too minute in their handling of details, too elaborately qualified in their enunciation of general principles. . . . The style, in short, is not sufficiently rich or finished to give a perpetual interest to matters whose practical importance has vanished.[35]

Morley's Conception of Oratory.—Morley holds that Gladstone's oratory bears the stamp of dignity, high vision, and, possibly, permanence.

It was the orator of concrete detail, of inductive instances, of energetic and immediate object; the orator confidently and by sure touch startling into watchfulness the whole spirit of civil duty in a man; elastic and supple, pressing fact and figure with a fervid insistence that was known from his career and character to be neither forced nor feigned, but to be himself. In a word, it was a man—a man impressing himself upon the kindled throngs by the breadth of his survey of great affairs of life and nations, by the depth of his vision, by the power of his stroke.[36]

This is in keeping with Morley's belief that political oratory "is action, not words,—action, character, will, conviction, purpose, personality." [37]

Anyone who would disparage eloquence, then, would "depreciate mankind." And when men remark

> . . . that Mr. Gladstone and Midlothian were no better than a resplendent mistake, they forget how many objects of our reverence stand condemned by implication in their verdict; they have not thought out how many of the faiths and principles that have been the brightest lamps in the track of human advance they are extinguishing by the same unkind and freezing breath. One should take care lest in quenching the spirit of Midlothian, we leave sovereign mastery of the world to Machiavelli.[38]

Morley was, indeed, both the critic and the philosopher of oratory.

Oratory Guides a Biographer's Method

Trevelyan's Analysis of John Bright's Oratory.—No scholar of recent years has been more successful in using rhetorical criticism to enforce biographical portrayal than George M. Trevelyan. In his *Life of John Bright,* Trevelyan unmistakably keeps oratory and speeches constantly in view; and to an extent uncommon in studies of its type, he reveals the true character of his subject by examining what the man spoke from the public platform.

Deliberate Emphasis upon Oratory.—At the beginning of the book, Trevelyan makes clear that he will emphasize speechmaking as the symbol of Bright's activities. No sooner is the introduction begun than we come across references to the "bell-like clearness" of Bright's voice, and the "absence of gestures" in his platform performances. Bright is at once considered an orator whose speechmaking must be dealt with if his character is to be revealed. "His oncoming," says Trevelyan, "was as the surge of the full swollen tide, not of the sea in storm; he awed his listeners by the calm of his passion, a terrible steed restrained by a yet stronger hand."

Lest his biography be misinterpreted, Trevelyan explains his liberal use of materials from Bright's speeches:

> It will, perhaps, be remarked by some readers that this work contains more numerous quotations from speeches than is usual in a political biography. If so, there is reason enough. Not only were Bright's speeches his one form of perfect achievement, but they were his one great political weapon. Not by administration or legislation, not by arguing in the Cabinet or sharing in the counsels of the party, but by his public orations as a private citizen he profoundly modified English politics and the relations and balance of English classes. He himself,

when consulted as to a biography, used to put the question aside by saying 'My life is in my speeches.' But after two generations have gone by, not even the greatest speeches can be widely read or completely understood, except with the help of historical comment, and of such reproduction of a great personality as the biographer, by aid of private letters and recollections, can all too feebly accomplish.[39]

It should be noted that Trevelyan worked with an abundance of source material. He had the necessary facts relating to Bright's oratorical achievements. In his possession were notes and clippings of Bright's speeches from 1860 onward, to say nothing of the letters and documents that threw further light upon the addresses. Bright had kept a diary for fifty years; those observations, together with other papers, were at Trevelyan's disposal. Other historians, indeed, have had comparable data with which to construct their biographical studies, but few have used those materials as fully as Trevelyan to bring out the importance of public speaking in the life of a man, and in the destiny of a nation.

Trevelyan's Method.—The biography of Bright is, therefore, a study of first importance to the rhetorician. Without using the terminology of the present-day critic of speeches and speakers, Trevelyan traces the biographical and historical details against a background of speaking achievement. He comments on the early influences of home, religion, and education that tended to form the speaker; he traces the sources of Bright's ideas and reveals the premises of his thinking; he establishes the background of the many speech occasions; he quotes freely from the speeches to illustrate the man's accomplishments; and, throughout the work, he keeps in view the bearing of oratory upon public affairs. On numerous occasions, he comes back to the thought that Bright helped bring about the repeal of the Corn Laws; that he helped to keep England from casting her lot with the Confederates during the American Civil War; that he figured responsibly in the establishment of the Reform Measures of 1867; and that he assisted materially in disestablishing the Church of England in Ireland. These were concrete accomplishments, realized in large part through Bright's speaking campaigns during a long and active life. Here, indeed, were tangible measures of speech effectiveness.

Trevelyan relies heavily upon comparative analyses to reveal the nature of Bright's oratory. Gladstone and Cobden, particularly, are involved in the comparisons. The following passage illustrates his method:

John Bright had the merits and defects of simplicity, Gladstone of complexity. Gladstone—even in the whirlwind of his own oratory, arms
overhead and eyes flashing—was always a debater, meeting his opponent's every argument, instructing his audience, often exciting them
over the details of some financial or legislative measure. Bright, on the
other hand, for all that he never gave the rein to his passion, never
swung his arm and scarcely raised his voice—was first and foremost a
preacher of broad principles in their moral and poetic force, a speaker
less instructive but even more moving than Gladstone. He has himself
described the difference between them thus: 'When I speak, I strike
across from headland to headland. Mr. Gladstone follows the coast-
line; and when he comes to a navigable river he is unable to resist the
temptation of tracing it to its source.'

Of the two, it is Bright whose speeches can be read with greatest
pleasure, though that, perhaps, is no test of oratory. Gladstone's orations suffer in the reading from a quality which make them delightful
to hear, their dependence on the skill of the speaker to effect his escape
with grammar intact from the maze of parentheses—an operation safely
sustained on that magnificent voice and by those dramatic gestures.
Bright's voice, too, was a gift of heaven; he had never to shout in order
that it might thrill with its music the farthest corner of the largest
hall. But he had no gesture except to raise his hand, and that not above
the level of his breast. Gladstone was everything at once—actor,
missionary, debater, exponent of legislative detail—such an one as
never before or since rose to address an audience; Bright excelled in
pure oratory in its stricter sense.[40]

Trevelyan appraises the temper of the age in his effort to provide additional insight into the role of speechmaking in a well-
organized state:

In the 'fifties and 'sixties a political meeting was a noticeable event,
and wherever a politician of the first rank made a long speech, he was
reported and read at full, not merely in excerpts and headlines. Full
reports of great speeches were eagerly awaited and read by a political
nation that had very little else in the way of politics brought to its door.
For the same reason parliamentary debates were better reported and
more closely followed than they are in our own time, although the
general level of political interest and understanding is higher today, if
all ranks of society are taken into account.

This state of things set a premium on careful oratory that would
not only move the audience but would read well in the paper next
morning and in the pamphlet next month. For all these purposes
Bright's art was supreme. He moved his audiences more than Gladstone, though he instructed them less; and yet his speeches formed a

body of literature which spread his ideas among students of all classes. Since quality rather than quantity in speaking was then required to make an effective politician, Bright was able to indulge his natural preference for leisurely prepared speeches, which stand the test of literature as well as those of oratory.[41]

Not only does Trevelyan make each chapter of his book a virtual analysis of a nineteenth-century speaker; he also includes a separate chapter on "Bright's Oratory." In it he appraises Bright's delivery; discusses his methods of speech preparation (and includes, incidentally, facsimiles of some of the notes used by Bright) ; evaluates the style and language of the speaker; mentions Bright's mannerisms in speaking; comments on the general and specific effects of the oratory; and considers Bright's philosophy of utterance, both as determined from the orator's letters and from a study of his speeches over a fifty-year span.

In short, *The Life of John Bright* is, perhaps, the best modern example of a biography in which oratory is allowed to function as the determinant of a man's claim to distinction. Trevelyan has shown rhetorical critics how letters and speeches, together with the intelligent interweaving of historical narrative and interpretation, can reveal the true stature of an orator.

Minor Contributors to Method in Criticism

The Work of Mathews.—In his *Oratory and Orators*,[42] William Mathews evaluates some of the great speakers of the past. The first section of the book is a sort of anthology of theory, containing pertinent and helpful advice on oratory. But in the critical estimates of the orators, Mathews offers little of real importance. His treatment of Burke, for example, is sketchily general, with little reliance upon the social-historical facts of the period or upon the speeches themselves. The critical findings are really tabulated conclusions in which the reader can share only indirectly since he does not learn from the critic how they were reached. It is a type of "capsuled" criticism, with everything so abbreviated as to destroy the sense of perspective. We never see the orators in social settings.

Moore's Anthology.—Frank Moore's *American Eloquence*,[43] however useful as a collection of speeches, contains only short biographical notes on the orators—with no real attempt at criticism.

Magoon's Method.—In the preface to his *Living Orators in America*, E. L. Magoon refers to his previous work, *Orators of the*

American Revolution, and indicates that critics had expressed the hope that he would, in subsequent efforts, quote more freely from the speeches and that he would try to secure more authentic specimens of the oratory. Accordingly, Magoon claims that his new book rectifies the shortcomings of the previous volume.

The *Living Orators* includes sections on Webster, the logician; Everett, the rhetorician; Clay, the politician; Calhoun, the metaphysician; McDuffie, the impetuous; Cass, the courteous; Benton, the magisterial; Preston, the inspired declaimer, and Corwin, the natural orator. In the handling of Webster, which is typical of the series, the author's plan is to consider circumstances of the orator's youth; "trace the progress of his preparatory discipline; sketch his professional career; and portray the chief features of his eloquence." [44]

Apropos of the last point, Magoon lists the following as Webster's chief oratorical characteristics, and quotes from speeches to illustrate his analyses: (1) "distinctness of mental perception"; (2) sense of "accurate combination" of details; (3) severe deduction; (4) "forcible illustration." He concludes that Webster had three styles: (1) There was the narrative type which was "a slow, deliberate manner employed in stating simple facts, or plain argument. . . . This is exceedingly beautiful because it is the nearest approach to sublimity of character, expressed in pure form, independent of all passion or emotion"; (2) next, he used a senatorial style, which was distinguished by warmth and animation; and, finally, he could use the impassioned style which is "exceedingly rapid in utterance, and violent in action; pours forth a torrent of words, on a high key, and with sharp, shrill emphasis, like the percussion of small arms." [45]

Magoon's analyses are not severely critical. They are so general that characteristics of the orators' styles are often confused with mental and physical traits; there is little reference to the historical patterns of which the speeches were but a part; they are a trifle rhapsodic, despite Magoon's intention to "maintain the strictest impartiality"; and they are so stereotyped that the pattern is substantially the same for all the studies.

Harsha's Treatise.—David Harsha's method of criticism in his *Most Eminent Orators and Statesmen of Ancient and Modern Times* [46] is to incorporate in each chapter a small body of historical and "critical" notes relating to the orator, to include "copious extracts" from the best speeches, to offer testimony from others regarding the speaker's eminence, and to comment on the man's style.

On the whole, the work is definitely uncritical, given too fully to the use of glowing superlatives. Harsha is himself too much influenced by the "bewitching strains" of eloquence and the "beautiful specimens" of style often found in the "wonderful" men about whom he is writing.

In the liberal use of superlatives, Harsha's book is not unlike Vicomte de Cormenin's *The Orators of France*.[47] But the latter contains a more comprehensive coverage of the features with which today's critics are concerned, i.e., training of the speaker, interplay of political forces, types of speaking, methods of preparation, structure of speeches, style, and delivery. Rather than being a criticism of the orators, however, these studies are really informal political pamphlets dealing with the speakers of the Constituent Assembly, the Convention, the Empire, the Restoration, and the Revolution of July. The best study in the group is the one of Mirabeau.

Hardwicke's Brief Accounts of the Orators.—Henry Hardwicke indicates in the early part of his *History of Oratory and Orators* that it is difficult to strike a balance between biographical and historical details. He sets forth his belief

> . . . that the biographer never ought to introduce public events except so far as they are necessary to the illustration of character, and that the historian should rarely digress in biographical particulars except as far as they contribute to the clearness of his narrative of occurrences.[48]

Although Hardwicke's intention undoubtedly was constructive, the result of his investigations is disappointing. His treatment of the orators from ancient times to the twentieth century is highly episodic; everything is treated sketchily—the whole study becoming a series of extracts and quotations, rather than a running commentary.

Sears' History.—Lorenzo Sears' *History of Oratory*[49] fails to capture the spirit of audiences and, therefore, the whole spirit of public performances.

Shaw's Volume.—Warren C. Shaw's *History of American Oratory*[50] contains only a small amount of critical detail. Its essential purpose is to provide an over-all view, historically, of the speechmaking of America's premier performers. Some attempt is made to reconstruct the backdrop against which the speeches were set.[51]

Literary Approaches to Speech Criticism

The histories of literature do not, in the main, provide illuminating estimates of the great orators. Interested chiefly in the personality and style of the speakers, the literary historians give either inadequate or begrudging attention to the strictly rhetorical aspects of the speakers' art. An examination of the method of certain historians will, however, reveal some of the differentia between the purely rhetorical and the literary patterns of critical inquiry.

Lodge's Study of Webster.—In his essay on Webster, Henry Cabot Lodge asserts, with seeming reluctance, that Webster's right to a place in literary history "rests and must rest upon his speeches, for speeches and addresses are all that Webster has left to us to prove his literary quality, and it very rarely happens that a literary reputation can be based upon speeches actually spoken and delivered." [52] The reason for Lodge's disinclination to rely upon speeches as the measure of merit lies, so he remarks, in the nature of the speech itself. Quoting and agreeing with Charles James Fox's statement that "no good speech ever read well," Lodge proceeds to disclose the ramifications of the dictum.

Fox, presumably, lived up to his own principle. "What he actually said has faded from the minds of men despite its enchanting, its enormous effect at the moment." On the other hand, "the speech which is literature before it is spoken is ineffective or only partially effective at the moment, and if it is read afterwards, however much we may enjoy the essay, we never mistake it for the genuine eloquence of the spoken word." Macaulay, for example, never really delivered speeches; he prepared essays. Accordingly, Lodge observes, the highest oratory "must combine in exact balance the living force and freshness of the spoken word with the literary qualities which alone can ensure endurance." Interestingly enough, Lodge finds the best representation of this balance, not in the speeches of reality, but in the "world of imagination." Speeches in literature, and especially those of Brutus and Mark Antony following the death of Caesar, achieve virtual perfection.

> They are speeches, and nothing else—one cool, stately, reasonable; the other a passionate, revolutionary appeal hot from the heart and pouring from the lips with unpremeditated art, and yet they both have the literary quality absolutely supreme in this instance, because Shakespeare wrote them.[53]

The important thing, then, is the achievement of balance between the literary and the rhetorical ingredients. And a speech loses "when the literary quality becomes predominant." In antiquity, Demosthenes and Isocrates succeeded in mixing the two ingredients with precision. Cicero achieved a fairly perfect balance. Among the English orators, Burke came nearest to realizing the ideal, although he erred "on the literary side." [54]

The first test which Lodge postulates for the speech, therefore, is that it reveal properly balanced relations between literary and rhetorical qualities. The second test grows out of a question which he poses thus: "How many speeches to a jury in a criminal trial possessing neither political nor public interest survive in fresh remembrance seventy years after their delivery?" Perhaps a few of Erskine's have lived, but they dealt with political and constitutional questions of the time. And here is where Webster, the object of Lodge's study, really makes his first entrance.

One of Webster's forensic speeches which was completely without political or historical interest has survived—a crucial test, indeed. This is the speech in the White murder case. Why has it lived? Because it possesses an imperishable "literary value and quality." Although Lodge does not stress the point, mention should surely be made of the strict logical reasoning which characterizes and gives abiding value to the speech.

Lodge shows that the White murder trial speech, as well as the Plymouth oration of 1820, stamps Webster as a master of prose style. In the latter discourse, for instance, there is an easy mastery of subject matter, a striking conciseness, a studied regard for philosophic considerations investing it with "weight, seriousness, and the permanence which lasts far beyond the moment of speech." Thus, Lodge says, the distinction between literary and rhetorical qualities is narrow. But when rhetoric is given the "literary touch," it is elevated and illuminated. Just the right word here, or the proper imagery there, may so enhance the style as to give it just claim to the discriminating verdict of posterity.

Other Literary Studies.—In Herbert J. C. Grierson's study of Burke, we find a point of view similar in many respects to Lodge's. The first sentence of the essay suggests a literary approach to the critical evaluation: "Edmund Burke, the greatest of English orators, if we measure greatness not by immediate effect alone but by the durability and the diffusive power of that effect. . . ." Grierson is obviously interested in making a personal estimate of the orator and

in appraising his style according to literary standards. His analysis
of Burke's early biography, of his philosophical tenets, and of his
logical premises is penetrating; his respect for Burke's speeches is
measured by his ranking of some with Shakespeare's plays and Milton's poems. But Burke as an orator who dealt with audiences never
quite emerges, as this passage indicates:

> The successful orator moves most safely among the topics familiar to
> his audience, trusting for success to the art with which he adapts and
> adorns them. But Burke combined the qualities of the orator with
> those of the seer, the logical architecture of western oratory with quali-
> ties which we find in the Hebrew prophets—moral exaltation, the union
> of dignity with trenchancy of language, vehemence, imagery that ranges
> from the sublime to the degrading.[55]

Clearly, Grierson is looking to the qualities of permanence and
beauty, rather than to the patently rhetorical considerations of response, or effect.

In a similar vein, though with considerably less thoroughness,
C. W. Previté-Orton [56] offers short appraisals of Fox, Pitt, Sheridan, and Grattan; while Sir A. W. Ward [57] evaluates Erskine,
Canning, Brougham, Macaulay, O'Connell, Disraeli, Bright, Gladstone, and others. All these criticisms are, however, too brief to
be significant; in none of them does the portrait of an *orator,* rather
than of the writer of prose selections, dominate the scene. To a
somewhat lesser extent, this same failure to deal with orators as
participants in audience situations characterizes Oliver Elton's [58]
evaluation of Burke, and A. C. McLaughlin's [59] study of the well-
known American orators of the first half of the nineteenth century.
Although McLaughlin recognizes the importance of the large themes
which present "alluring opportunity" for oratory, he does not give
us insight into the orators' ways of dealing with audiences in the
controversies over democracy, slavery, free labor, expansion, States'
rights, nationalism, and tariffs. It would seem that his estimates of
the orations fail to take adequate account of the existing social milieu.
"Much of the oratory of the time," he remarks, "was of a kind
which appeals but little to the reader of the present day. The speeches
that have come down to us are often diffuse and occasionally florid."

The Criticism of Parliamentary Oratory

Lord Curzon's Study.—Revealing a thorough familiarity with the
theory of rhetoric, Lord Curzon offers a penetrating analysis of
speech criticism in his monograph entitled *Modern Parliamentary*

Eloquence.[60]   Although his critiques of the orators fall short of what
we might expect, Curzon approaches the job of criticism from the
point of view of oratory.

Anxious to make such distinctions in terminology as will enable
him to develop his thesis appropriately, Curzon announces his intention of using "eloquence" instead of "oratory" to delineate contemporary speaking from that of previous periods. This choice is
justified, he says, because the term "oratory" connotes "a very high
and superlative degree of excellence, to which speakers under modern
conditions only rarely attain"; and, secondly, because, "while Eloquence, irrespective of age or clime, is a part of the continuous though
rare endowment of man, Oratory in the classical sense of the term,
as an art taught, studied, and pursued, has practically ceased to
exist. . . ." [61]

Curzon considers the immediate effect of oratory, or eloquence,
upon audiences as the basic criterion of effectiveness. Looking upon
eloquence as an instrument of persuasion, he says that "of the three
audiences whom the speaker has to face—the hearers of the moment,
the readers of the morrow, and a remote posterity—the first are those
in whose hands his fame as an orator really lies." Consequently,
Curzon limits his critical estimates to those men whom he himself
heard, or for whom he can quote trustworthy evidence from others
who did hear them. He openly announces that he will study the
speakers "as men who produced, by the exercise of certain talents of
speech, a definite impression upon contemporary audiences, and whose
reputation for eloquence must be judged by that test, and that test
alone."

Curzon supports the thesis that the immediate impression upon
hearers is the basic test of eloquence. He believed that speechmaking,
although it exercised greater influence over men during the early part
of the nineteenth century, still functioned effectively to change votes
in the House of Commons. As an example, he points to a speech by
Gladstone on moving a vote of credit in the Russo-Afghan crisis of
1885—a speech which patently changed votes.

As an analyst of the differences between eighteenth- and twen-
tieth-century oratory, Curzon is both shrewd and penetrating. But
when he turns to the individual studies of the orators—such as Lloyd
George, Gladstone, Bright, Disraeli, and others—he does not quite
fulfill the expectations of his readers.

His criticisms are abbreviated; more than that, however, they fail
to reveal fully the "oratorical point of view" which he so clearly
postulates in the opening sections of his essay.

The Analysis by Butler.—Although Henry Montagu Butler [62] spends less time than Curzon in discussing a philosophy of speech criticism, he does manage in his essay on Chatham to capture quite fully the spirit of the orator in his relation to particular audiences.

Criticism through Indictment

Von Ruville's Stricture of Political Speaking.—It is not a common circumstance to find an author and the person who prepares an introduction to his volume entering into formal debate as to the accuracy of the former's thesis. Such, however, is the case in Albert von Ruville's *William Pitt, Earl of Chatham,* for which Hugh Egerton wrote the introductory essay.

Von Ruville presents a scathing denunciation of Chatham's oratory; but his indictment is levelled, in the main, against political speaking, *per se,* rather than against Chatham or any other orator. Convinced that *matter* and *manner* are the principal constituents of oratory, von Ruville often finds Chatham's *matter* inferior. Whereupon he submits his stricture of political speaking in general:

A political speech . . . which is something more than a mere piece of rhetoric produced upon a special occasion, must always keep one object in view, that of exciting other persons to political action. . . . His intention is to make others subserve his own ideas, to strengthen his own scanty forces by means of the power others possess, and this, whatever the character of his efforts, be they selfish or unselfish, be they directed to securing the advantage of an individual, of a party, or of a state. A political speech is distinguished from a pamphlet, from expert advice, from a memorial or a dissertation, by the special fact that it seeks to bring about a comparatively rapid result, and to prevent a close and detailed examination of the subject under discussion. Vigorous, attractive, and even sweeping language, followed by a decision as rapid as possible before the flame of enthusiasm dies away, such is the course of events invariably most desirable to the great orator. This definition does not imply that oratory pursues some reprehensible or perverted aim which cannot stand strict investigation. The consent of the masses can by this means be extorted to the most desirable and the most moral measures, and brilliant oratory is particularly valuable in cases where courage must be inspired. Moreover, the intellectual constitution of an assembly necessitates a procedure of this nature. A crowd of people is in most cases disinclined, and little competent to undertake, an accurate examination of the questions at issue, and the more incompetent it is the greater will be the influence exerted upon it by clever oratory. Where the influence of oratory is supreme we have to suppose a general decay of intellectual force, or an unsound ex-

tension of democratic principles throughout the state. When this is
the case, despotism is usually not far distant, whether it appears openly
or lurks behind the scenes.

To my thinking, the greatest danger of oratory consists in the fact
that it forms an intellectual weapon, the efficacy of which is in no way
dependent upon the purity of the aims pursued. Egoist, party leader
and patriot, all can use this weapon with equal success. If the compelling power of enthusiastic conviction gives one side an advantage,
effrontery and falsehood can enable the opposition to restore the balance. A further element of evil lies in the fact that the keen desire of
holding his audience leads the orator to abandon a clear and unprejudiced point of view, and makes less demand upon his knowledge of
fact, whereas written exposition makes the greatest possible demand
upon such knowledge. I have never been able to understand why a
statesman of the character most chiefly in demand in republics, is bound
to be a great orator. In fact, this necessity seems to me to be a great
constitutional mistake, for the reason that several outstanding capacities
are but rarely united in one and the same person. At the present day
parliamentary orators as such are of infinitely less importance. The
government representatives, who borrow many a suggestion and idea
from them, are not amenable to oratorical persuasions, and cannot be
carried away by eloquence. The members of Parliament follow their
party leaders, who have previously examined every question, and found
a solution in accordance with the interests of the party. In their case
again fine oratory is purposeless. On the other hand, speeches are now
published and made accessible to the nation at large, a circumstance
which makes the orator more careful of the nature of his assertions.
Speeches thus become rather of the character of spoken pamphlets or
electioneering addresses; they are intended to make proselytes in the
nation and to secure suffrages, to show the efforts of the party as
serving the national interests and general welfare. Thus the real art
of oratory, the personal influence upon an audience, and the power to
compel and inspire enthusiasm, loses all its importance, for the reason
that the masses for whom this art is intended are not present. It is indeed still employed, but more from personal inclination or a certain
pride, and without any expectation of definite result.[63]

To this charge, and to the related one that Chatham's oratory
produced no significant or worthy results, Egerton enters his reply.
Claiming that the substance of Chatham's speeches has come down to
us in questionable condition because of the inaccuracy of reporting,
Egerton affirms that the critics must be careful in appraising the
matter of public orations. Furthermore, the evidence tends to support the view that Chatham was a successful speaker. Surely, says
Egerton, it "is idle to ask of oratory more than that it should

influence the immediate hearers, and of the effect of Pitt's speeches all who heard him are agreed." The audience which a speaker faces must not be overlooked in passing judgment upon the speaker's influence. Indeed, it would be a hard measure, Egerton concludes, "to ask of an orator that he should make actual converts by his arguments of a hostile majority." [64]

While the von Ruville-Egerton clash does not enlarge our understanding of critical method, it does reveal the pattern of thinking used by certain of the opponents of oral discussion and expression in political assembly. It also reminds us that the *time factor,* discussed by William Hazlitt and here reiterated by von Ruville, is one of the fundamental differentia between writing and speaking. As the latter critic puts it, the orator, in contradistinction to the pamphleteer, tries to bring about "a comparatively rapid result, and to prevent a close and detailed examination of the subject under discussion." Spurious as that distinction is because of its failure to describe the conditions and aims of the two forms of expression, it nevertheless persists as one of the controversial themes in rhetorical theory and criticism.

Social Criticism

V. L. Parrington [65] offers a provocative and inviting approach to oratorical criticism. His analyses, though not sharply at variance with those of most other critics, chiefly contemporary, are engagingly novel and uncommonly acute. In his brief account of Wendell Phillips, Parrington shows how the speaker's conscience reveals itself in public address. Dealing with Phillips' activities after the Civil War, he appraises the orator's labors in behalf of the workingman: his fight against capitalistic exploitation, against the bankers' control of the national currency, against a host of injustices and malpractices which endangered the economic well-being and personal happiness of the common laborer. Parrington quotes freely from Phillips' speeches to show how the orator gave vent to his moral and social indignation; and how important he regarded the spoken word as a medium for the correction of a nation's ills. Here, indeed, we have a type of social criticism which places oratory in its natural and rightful milieu—the historical urgencies of the moment—and looks to *effect,* or influence, as a measure of effectiveness. It values speech in its larger relation to social process and social movement, thus going well beyond the superficial application of canons of goodness or badness in oratorical composition.

The Conception of Oratory as Propaganda

The Growing Importance of Sociological Approaches to Speaking.—Ever since the first World War, the term "propaganda" has been gaining in currency. Today it is virtually a household word; the grade-school boy uses it with an abandon that would have seemed shocking to his father. What is more, the term has taken on omnibus characteristics. According to some definitions, it is made to embrace practically all persuasive efforts from advertising to the teaching of history. But common-sense interpretations necessitate our confining the term, in this context, to such persuasive efforts through speech as are intended to influence the attitudes and, subsequently, the actions of individuals on controversial matters affecting the body politic. According to this definition, it is apparent that a considerable body of contemporary speech criticism is steeped in the sociological criteria governing the use of propaganda.

To the critics who look upon certain speeches as instances of propaganda, the important standard of judgment is the effectiveness of the addresses in exercising influence upon the political and social environment of the period. A speech is regarded as an instrument of control over collective opinion; it is an attempt at mass management of the public mind. It is not surprising, therefore, that the analysis of speech as propaganda involves careful scrutiny of the *devices,* or the *strategy,* employed by the speaker to secure his objective. In this respect, the evaluation does not differ from other methods, except in the point of emphasis. Instead of throwing the light of investigation upon the several aspects of a speech—including content, structure, style, and the like—the critic who looks for the propagandistic constituents of an address concentrates largely on the methodology employed by the speaker in gaining his end. The principal question is: How did the speaker manipulate the words and concepts in his address so as to establish presumptive evidence in behalf of the desired attitude? In short, how successful was the speaker in getting the group to think and feel alike with respect to the theme of his talk? And will the persuasive effect spread to other groups beyond the range of the immediate audience?

Instances of Sociological Criticism.—An example of this type of oratorical analysis is F. W. Lambertson's study of Hitler as a mob psychologist. In his paper, Lambertson shows how Hitler marshaled his knowledge of group action, showmanship, and public speaking so as to bring his audiences under direct control; how he

attended to every psychological detail that was helpful in inducing
a form of mob hysteria; how he concentrated upon emotional
manipulation to dull the people's impulse to think.[66]

In *World Revolutionary Propaganda*,[67] by Harold D. Lasswell
and Dorothy Blumenstock, we find an analysis of the manipulative
symbols used and elaborated upon in several of the Communist
speeches delivered at a meeting in Chicago during the early part of
1931. Selected passages are quoted to show how the speakers, performing against a backdrop of national depression and insecurity,
touched upon themes and events that would heighten enthusiasm
for the political cause to which a large part of the audience was
already presumably committed. By praising the working class and
condemning the "profiteers," by contrasting the work opportunities
in Russia with those in America, by setting off the ideology of
production for use with that for profit under the "hypocrisy of
capitalism," and by using statistics, anecdotes, and "enemy admissions," the speakers built up their case against the *status quo*. The
techniques employed by the speakers tend to confirm Lasswell and
Blumenstock's contention that a speaker who takes advantage of
the "high tension level" of an audience, can achieve an intemperate-
ness of expression unsuitable for publication.[68]

The *Institute for Propaganda Analysis*, discontinued during the
war, dealt largely with the common devices employed by propagandists in their attempt to direct the attitudes of people. These
devices included such well-known instruments as (1) name-calling,
(2) glittering generalities, (3) transfer of the confirmed sanctions to
something the propagandist wishes his hearers to accept, (4) testi-
monials, (5) "plain folks" device of making the recipients feel the
propagandist is very much like themselves, (6) card-stacking through
omission or distortion of data, and (7) the bandwagon technique of
conveying the notion of universal acceptance. In its analyses of some
of Father Coughlin's speeches, the *Institute* used this classification of
devices to point out the method of the speaker and to expose his
motives.

The Future Possibilities of Such Research.—Whether or not
we are able to set up hard and fast lines between criticism of speech as
propaganda and speech as an ordinary communicative-control device
is unimportant. What matters is that public speaking, generally, is
intended to elicit responses; that it is an instrument of social control.
That the propaganda techniques, *per se,* differ sharply from the conventional devices of oral persuasion is doubtful. Surely the "propa-

ganda speaker" employs certain techniques more freely, and probably
less responsibly on occasion, but his tools are not unknown to the
rhetorician, either of this age or of more remote times. Since the
propagandists or public relations experts—if the first term seems
harsh and mildly sinister—will in all probability exert increasing influence upon national and international life, an assessment of their
efforts will become both a necessity and a desirable undertaking for
the rhetoricians. Sociological criticism of oratory may very well be
one of the fruitful fields for exploration.

Criticism through Analysis of Meaning

The Approach of the Semanticist.—During recent years, increasing attention has been devoted by critics and teachers to the problem
of semantic analysis. Guided by the investigations of Alfred
Korzybski, C. K. Ogden, I. A. Richards, and others, critics have
approached the task of speech appraisal by asking: "What does this
speech mean? Am I taking the speaker's words to mean what he
intends them to convey?" Unlike the student who emphasizes primarily the literary values of the speech, the semanticist tries to find
out whether the language reflects with fidelity the meaning that the
speaker hopes to transmit. This is a challenging venture, requiring not only a thorough familiarity with the way language works,
but also an unusual ability to interpret the meaning of words in
context.

The critic whose interest is largely semantic will be on guard to
detect ambiguities arising from the metaphorical use of language,
from generalities growing out of statements that embrace broad
areas of inquiry, and from such abstractions as "mankind," whose
referents are indeterminate, if not indeterminable.

In his discussion of the semanticist's way of looking at a speech,
Irving J. Lee lists a few of the procedures used by the critic in determining the meaning of discourse. Among the more important
methods of fixing these areas of reference are: (1) the investigation
of "the key terms in their setting and context as the ground of
meaning"; (2) the analysis of metaphorical usage into what Richards [69] calls its tenor and vehicle; (3) the listing of "modes of definition which were used in the speech and those which may be applied
in further clarification and explanation"; (4) the attachment of
"observed entities" to the abstractions or "fictions" in language;
(5) the making of paraphrases, in the restricted vocabulary of Basic
English, of the original materials used in the speech.[70]

In the appendix to his popular book entitled *The Tyranny of Words,* Stuart Chase provides several examples of prose material which, when subjected to semantic analysis, fall a trifle short of being meaningful. As the criteria for evaluation, Chase suggests that the critic translate the passages into sense, keeping constantly in mind such points as clarifying high-order abstractions, the position and accessibility of referents, and the simple inquiry: "Does the speaker appear to know what he is saying?" [71]

That the development of critical technique in semantic analysis will continue to contribute to the fuller understanding and more penetrating appraisal of speeches is generally acknowledged. But that it provides something distinctly new, something which has not heretofore been operative in the work of the critic, is open to serious question.[72] Surely, previous investigations into the logical and emotional proof of speeches have dealt with the problems of meaning, of definition, and of contextual implication. Like the semanticists, the rhetoricians have been concerned with the vagaries of language and with the necessity of remarks making sense.

The Upsurge of Interest in Criticism Today

Recent decades have witnessed a major revival of interest in the criticism of speeches. Encouraged by the directors of advanced rhetorical study in our graduate schools of Speech, many scholars have carried on extensive research into the theory and practice of great British and American speakers. Since most of these studies are in the form of theses prepared for the advanced academic degrees, they are not generally accessible to the public. Many of the critical estimates, however, have been printed—in whole or in part—in books and journals devoted to speech education. Among the complete papers are W. Norwood Brigance's *Jeremiah Sullivan Black,*[73] Loren Reid's *Charles James Fox,*[74] Bower Aly's *Rhetoric of Alexander Hamilton,*[75] Wilbur E. Gilman's *Milton's Rhetoric,*[76] and Dallas C. Dickey's *Sergeant S. Prentiss.*[77]

Critical inquiry into oratory was furthered importantly when the Speech Association of America authorized the preparation of a cooperative study on the *History and Criticism of American Public Address.* This two-volume work, published in 1943, contains introductory historical details and critical appraisals of twenty-eight men whose influence through speechmaking affected the American scene. It is by far the most ambitious and comprehensive project ever completed in this field, Cicero's *Brutus* and Chauncey Goodrich's *Select British Eloquence*—its nearest competitors—not excepted.

Besides the introductory studies which deal with the historical background of American public address, the two volumes contain critical essays on the speechmaking of representative leaders in religion (Jonathan Edwards, Theodore S. Parker, Henry Ward Beecher, and Phillips Brooks); in reform (Wendell Phillips, Robert G. Ingersoll, Henry W. Grady, and Booker T. Washington); in law (Rufus Choate, Jeremiah S. Black, and William M. Evarts); in general culture (Ralph Waldo Emerson); in education (Charles W. Eliot and Edwin A. Alderman); in labor (Samuel Gompers); and in statecraft (Patrick Henry, Henry Clay, John C. Calhoun, Daniel Webster, William L. Yancey, Charles Sumner, Stephen A. Douglas, Abraham Lincoln, James G. Blaine, William Jennings Bryan, Albert J. Beveridge, Robert M. La Follette, and Woodrow Wilson).

A variety of approaches to critical inquiry may be found in the *History and Criticism of American Public Address.* Some of the studies deal largely with the developmental history of the particular orators, their methods of speech preparation, their ways of handling audiences, and their successes in the various branches of oratory. Others concentrate more fully upon the traditional topics of rhetoric: the speaker's invention, plan of arrangement, kinds of proof, style, and delivery. Certain contributors limit their studies to specific aspects of the total rhetorical process: to the audiences a speaker dealt with, or to a particular kind of oratory. Throughout the work, however, there is evidence that Aristotelian standards of criticism are not only highly regarded by the scholars in the field, but are also uncommonly useful as general yardsticks of rhetorical evaluation.

General Summary

The period covered by this chapter produced several important contributions to the literature of speech criticism. These additions to our subject represent various points of view. Goodrich was the teacher whose lectures at Yale College finally resulted in *Select British Eloquence,* one of the three most valuable critical works in print. Jebb was the classical scholar whose interest in the development of prose expression eventually took form in the profound analyses of the *Attic Orators.* Morley, Lecky, and Trevelyan wrote as historians. They demonstrated most ably that the biographical study can also be a rhetorical investigation, provided the historian has a tenable point of view respecting the place of oratory in the social process. And the semanticists, students of propaganda, and literary historians made further suggestions toward a critique of oratorical excellence.

With the development of extensive course offerings in Speech during the past few decades, impetus has been given to critical inquiry. This has resulted in the preparation of exacting studies of the orators and their times. Apart from the many excellent graduate studies completed by American scholars, the most note-worthy contribution of the twentieth century is the *History and Criticism of American Public Address,* edited by W. Norwood Brigance. Setting a high standard of scholarship in rhetoric, this work signalizes a public recognition of the validity of critical inquiry into the work of the orators.

PART IV

PRELIMINARY ASPECTS OF RHETORICAL CRITICISM

Chapter 8

DETERMINING THE AREAS OF INVESTIGATION

Necessity of Defining Limits of Critical Investigation

On first thought, any attempt to prescribe the legitimate areas within which critical functions shall operate may seem arbitrary, if not patently presumptuous. It seems to smatter of an attempt to reduce the critic's intellectual quest to rule, to fixed system. It reminds us of a remark by Thomas Carlyle:

> The Orator persuades and carries all with him, he knows not how; the Rhetorician can prove that he ought to have persuaded and carried all with him! the one is in a state of healthy unconsciousness, as if he 'had no system;' the other in virtue of regimen and dietetic punctuality, feels at best that 'his system is in high order.' [1]

Oftentimes it is thus with the critic and the academician. The former does his work, achieves his end—perhaps without direct recourse to the rules governing the province of his expression; the other, mindful of the facts which academically control the field, appeals to system, to a pattern—which the critic may have followed, whether he willed it so or not. Accordingly, just claim can no doubt be made that criticism, like other products of the intellect, achieves rightness through a "certain spontaneity" or "unconsciousness," as Carlyle puts it. "The healthy know not of their health, but only the sick." [2]

But it is possible, as well as useful, to consider the areas within which critical efforts in rhetoric are peculiarly active and fruitful, without stultifying the critics' endeavors or circumscribing unduly the province within which their work will be most rewarding. Indicating the boundaries within which speech criticism has flourished in the past, and is now operating, can in no way be regarded as a curb upon free intellectual inquiry. Its only purpose is to outline the field—to find out where the critic may direct his investigations with the greatest expectation of success and with the greatest likelihood of increasing our understanding of speakers and speechmaking.

The Two Principal Areas.—There are two main areas of inquiry in rhetorical criticism. The first embraces all those studies which fall within the system of rhetorical art and practice; the second, those which pursue aims external to the field of operative rhetoric. Each of these categories requires further explanation.

Studies within the Framework of the System

An examination of the literature on rhetorical criticism discloses that most scholars have confined their efforts to the first division. They have operated within the framework of the subject, seeking answers to problems closely associated with the theory and practice of speaking. Systematically considered, these studies have usually evaluated orators with reference to one or more, or a combination of all, the following concepts: (1) the nature of oratory; (2) the constituents of the speaking situation; (3) the offices or duties of the orator; (4) the types of oratory; (5) the traditional parts of the art of rhetoric, and (6) the effect of the oratory.

Criticism may thus be confined, as it unquestionably was in certain of Plato's works, to a philosophical determination of the role of speechcraft in a well organized society. Individual appraisals of the orators, in Plato's case, were almost incidental to the enforcement of the thesis that speech, without full knowledge and moral virtue in the speaker, may exercise a deleterious influence on society.

Other critical investigations have approached the evaluative function through a formal recognition and analysis of one or more of the constituents of the speech situation. Assuming the elements to be the speaker, the subject, the audience, and the occasion, critics have found it consistent with their creative intention to examine an orator's right to high rank by studying the orator as a man, the audiences he faced, the topics he developed, and the circumstances under which he appeared. Many investigators have used this pattern as the over-all plan for making their critical estimates.

Oratory and orators have also been viewed in the light of the objectives in audience response sought by the speaker. Thus an estimate of a speaker's merit might derive from his ability to teach, to conciliate, and to arouse. It will be remembered that Cicero applied this test to many of the men about whom he wrote in the *Brutus*.

The base for critical effort has sometimes been the type of oratory in which the speaker interested himself. Cicero, for instance, applied a certain yardstick of measurement to a forensic speaker's effectiveness, and another to the deliberative orator. Accordingly, the classification of oratory into deliberative, forensic, ceremonial, and possibly pulpit types serves as an end in criticism as well as in theory.

Much of the critical literature has developed from the use of the conventional parts of rhetoric, i.e., invention, disposition, elocution, memory, and delivery. For example, a speaker's merit is investigated in the light of his skill at inventing arguments, or of clothing his ideas in appropriate language, or in a combination of all the elements.

Finally, critics seek to answer the questions—as all must eventually do if they prepare comprehensive appraisals of the speakers—"What was the immediate effect of this speech upon the audience? What was the long-range effect upon the flow of historical events?"

The foregoing subdivisions are, of course, interrelated, and the ideal criticism probably affords a balanced treatment of the totality. But whether a critic evaluates only a speaker's invention in a selected group of speeches, or makes a penetrating analysis only of the audiences he faced, the studies are alike directed toward a common objective. Each one seeks the revelation of an orator as an effective agent in the presence of hearers.

This brief survey is not intended to oversimplify the problems of criticism. It serves only to point out how critical studies in oratory can, and in most cases do, operate within the framework of the art with which the critic is concerned. That is to say, the classifications and subdivisions of rhetoric furnish the patterns for most of the dissertations and essays in which the merits of orators are appraised.

Cicero was the first critic to make full use of these categories for critical purposes. A substantial part of his treatment of the Greek and Roman speakers is criticism by formula. He estimates orators' merits with reference to their accomplishments as men; their use of the kinds or types of oratory; their skill in invention, style, and the other parts of rhetoric; their relative talents for the ends of oratory (to teach, to please, and to arouse); and their conformity to the cultural patterns established for the ideal speaker. It is doubtful whether any critic of antiquity confined his efforts as severely within the framework of the art of speaking as did Cicero in the *Brutus,* in the *Orator,* and, to a lesser extent, in *De Oratore.*

An Outline of Studies in This Area.—In order to illustrate the implications and ramifications of this broad area of critical inquiry, consider the following tabular analysis which indicates the various types of studies suggested by the divisions and classifications of the art of rhetoric.

I. The Nature of Oratory
  A. Oratory and Statesmanship
  B. The Orator's Role in the Social Process
  C. Political and Social Conditions Favoring the Development of
     Oratory
II. Constituents of the Speaking Situation
  A. The Speaker
    1. Qualifications
    2. Factors Accounting for His Skill
    3. His Theory of Discourse
    4. Theory in Relation to His Practice in Discourse
  B. The Audience
    1. Nature of the Audience; Its Composition
    2. Its Relation to the Subject
    3. Its Relation to the Speaker
  C. The Subject
    1. Its Relation to the Audience
    2. Its Relation to the Speaker
  D. The Occasion
    1. Social Setting of the Speech: Its Place in the Historical
       Continuum
    2. Its Immediate Nature
III. The Services of the Orator
  A. The Ends of Discourse
    1. To Teach
    2. To Convince
    3. To Actuate
  B. The Orator's Skill in Each of the Duties
IV. The Types of Speaking
  A. Deliberative
  B. Forensic
  C. Ceremonial
  D. Pulpit
V. The Parts of Rhetoric
  A. Invention
    1. The Speaker's Stock of Ideas
    2. The Premises of His Thinking
    3. The "Status" of His Discourses
    4. His Arguments
      a. Logical
      b. Pathetic
      c. Ethical
    5. Adaptation of His Arguments to Hearers
  B. Disposition
    1. Conception of Speech Plan in General
    2. The Specific Parts of the Speech

C. Elocution
   1. Word Choice
   2. Composition
   3. Ornamentation
   4. General Categories of Style
D. Memory
   1. Memorial Conception of the Speech Plan as a Whole
   2. Control in Memory over the Outline
E. Delivery
   1. Voice
   2. Bodily Action
VI. The Effect of the Oratory
   A. Immediate
   B. Delayed

Typical Investigations.—Many recent studies of rhetoric have been based upon one or more of these classifications or single items within a category. Some of these inquiries have stressed the analysis and interpretation of rhetorical principles. Characteristic investigations have included Ota Thomas' *The Theory and Practice of Disputation at Yale, Harvard, and Dartmouth from 1750 to 1800;*[3] Elaine Pagel Paden's *The Theory and Practice of Disputation at Princeton, Columbia, and University of Pennsylvania from 1750 to 1800;*[4] Warren A. Guthrie's *The Development of Rhetorical Theory in America, 1635 to 1850;*[5] Anthony F. Blanks' *An Introductory Study in the History of the Teaching of Public Speaking in the United States;*[6] Porter Gale Perrin's *The Teaching of Rhetoric in the American Colleges before 1750;*[7] David Potter's *Debating in the Colonial Chartered Colleges: A Historical Survey, 1642 to 1900;*[8] W. P. Sandford's *English Theories of Public Address, 1530 to 1828;*[9] Lionel Crocker's *Henry Ward Beecher's Art of Preaching;*[10] M. F. Evans' *Study of the Development of a Theory of Homiletics in England, 1534-1692;*[11] Dorothy Anderson's *Edward T. Channing's Philosophy and Teaching of Rhetoric;*[12] Karl Wallace's *Bacon's Conception of Rhetoric;*[13] and Elton Abernathy's *Trends in American Homiletic Theory Since 1860.*[14]

These analyses and criticisms range from concentration on one speaker or teacher of rhetoric to the survey of a period.

Sometimes the investigator traces the significance of a single rhetorical concept through a period, as illustrated by Orville Pence's *Study of the Principles of Pathetic Appeal in the Works of Certain Classical Rhetoricians*[15] and James H. McBurney's *The Place of the Enthymeme in Rhetorical Theory.*[16]

A second line of inquiry comprehends both the theory and practice of an individual speaker or group of speakers. Recent studies embracing this synthesis include Horace Rahskopf's *John Quincy Adams' Theory and Practice of Public Speaking;* [17] Wilson Paul's *John Witherspoon's Theory and Practice of Public Speaking;* [18] Clyde Yarbrough's *The Homiletic Theory and Practice of Ebenezer Porter;* [19] Kenneth Hance's *The Elements of the Rhetorical Theory of Phillips Brooks.* [20]

A third group of researchers has dealt with the total speaking career of a single orator. Illustrations from this group include Herold T. Ross' *The Oratorical Career of Albert Jeremiah Beveridge;* [21] Orville A. Hitchcock's *Critical Study of the Oratorical Technique of Jonathan Edwards;* [22] Elbert Harrington's *The Public Speaking Career of Albert B. Cummins;* [23] W. Norwood Brigance's *A History and Critical Study of the Life and Speeches of Jeremiah Sullivan Black;* [24] and Rahskopf's *The Oratory of James Wilson of Pennsylvania.* [25]

Occasionally the scope has been limited to one phase of the speaker's career, to one type of his public address, or to one phase of his rhetorical processes. Typical studies from this approach include Orvin P. Larson's *Invention in Ingersoll's Lectures on Religion;* [26] Waldo Braden's *Rhetorical Criticism of William E. Borah's Speeches on the League of Nations, 1918-20;* [27] Howard Bradley's *Study of the Structure of a Selected Group of Webster's Speeches;* [28] Harold F. Harding's *Burke's Leading Ideas;* [29] Junella Teeter's *Study of the Homely Figures of Speech Used by Abraham Lincoln in His Speeches;* [30] Loren D. Reid's *Factors in the Training and Education of Charles James Fox Accounting for His Ability as a Parliamentary Speaker;* [31] and Clair Henderlider's *Evaluation of the Persuasive Techniques of Woodrow Wilson in His League of Nations Speeches, September 4-25, 1919.* [32]

The public speaking trends of a period, including the historical background, have also been studied. Typical investigations of this sort appear in Part I of the *History and Criticism of American Public Address.* And during recent years considerable research has been directed toward analyses of public speaking as practiced in various states and regions of America.

The foregoing are but a few of the many recent studies in rhetoric; for a complete list the reader is invited to examine Franklin H. Knower's "Index of Graduate Work in Speech and Drama," appearing annually in *Speech Monographs.*

The Second General Area of Study

The second area of study, drawing upon substantially the same scholarly resources, deals chiefly with research that is *related to* rhetorical theory and criticism, rather than with that which evaluates oratory and orators. Equally important to the total critical enterprise, it often serves as the substructure for criticism proper. Among the common contributions in this area are the commentaries, translations and editions, and bibliographies.

The significance, essential functions, and general character of the commentaries and translations are so clear as to make discussion of them unnecessary. Suffice it that commentaries such as E. M. Cope's *Introduction to Aristotle's Rhetoric* [33] and Charles S. Baldwin's *Ancient Rhetoric and Poetic* [34] and *Medieval Rhetoric and Poetic* [35] assist the critic by enlarging his understanding of the concepts of speechcraft. On the other hand, the translations and editions make accessible the texts and bodies of theory upon which the critical functions rest. Mention may be made here of such recent contributions as Otto Dieter's translation of Notker's *Rhetoric* [36] and Wilbur S. Howell's translation and commentary on the *Rhetoric of Alcuin and Charlemagne.* [37]

Bibliography opens a challenging field of research in rhetoric. Carefully conducted investigations into some of the areas now inadequately covered would undoubtedly lighten the task of the critics, and eventually add luster and distinction to their criticisms.

Studies in bibliography might follow any one of several lines: (1) compilation of exhaustive listings of printed matter on a particular orator, or movement, or concept in rhetoric; (2) preparation of annotated guides to the genuinely significant literature on a person or concept; (3) determination of textual authenticity of extant speeches; (4) the making of comparative analyses and collations of available texts; (5) preparation of wholly satisfactory editions of the work of the orators; and (6) investigations into the publication and sale of variant editions of great speeches and debates.

General Summary

Critical inquiry into rhetoric does not differ fundamentally from similar intellectual quests in other fields. It flourishes in the atmosphere of free, spontaneous effort; and, while not defiant of rule, it does not necessarily function by formula. However, the very nature of a specific investigation—as into the qualities of a public address—

requires that the critic conceive his undertaking within a certain frame of reference. A speech is always a *speech,* and never a chemical formula. Hence, it can be evaluated only through proper recognition of the field within which speeches, rather than chemical formulae, function. To this extent, if no more, areas of investigation into rhetorical criticism can be delimited. These areas are chiefly the ones which fall within the framework of rhetorical theory and practice, *per se,* and the ones which lie within the province of intellectual aims related to, or forming the substructure of, the field of rhetoric.

We have described some of the areas within which critical analysis of rhetoric is particularly fruitful. These are surely not the only ones, and we have no desire to leave that impression. The ingenuity and vision of discerning critics will carry the projects far beyond the lines indicated by this chapter. The nature of speechcraft, however, makes the areas to which we refer useful points of orientation.

Chapter 9

ESTABLISHING THE AUTHENTICITY OF TEXTS

The Difficulty in Getting Reliable Speech Texts

In an Elizabethan sermon given at Bletsoe, in 1586, Edward
Bulkeley is reported to have said:

> I have never published any thing in print, but one other sermon
> preached about 14. or 15. years past at Paules Crosse. . . . But that
> simple & short sermon was so handled in printing, above 60. faultes
> being committed in it . . . that I have bene ever since more moved to
> continue Platoes safe course of not writing, but learning.[1]

This remark strikes at one of the most difficult problems in rhetorical
criticism, namely, determination of the authenticity of speech texts.

From antiquity to the present day, critics have concerned themselves with establishing the accuracy of the texts upon which their
analyses rest. Always a difficult problem, textual criticism becomes,
in some instances, as challenging an aspect of the critic's work as
the making of the final estimate of the speaker's merit. The distinction between purely literary and rhetorical criticism may be
traced in part to the variable nature of speech texts. Thus, in his
analysis of Daniel Webster, Henry Cabot Lodge observes that the
nature of the oral material, *per se,* renders difficult the establishment of any man's claim to literary fame upon speeches alone. C. W.
Previté-Orton points to the advantages which the pamphlet, for
instance, holds over the speech, since evaluation of the latter requires reconstruction of social settings and the use of texts which
are often incomplete, if not actually unlike the original.

It would be folly to contest the force of these arguments. Unquestionably, it is difficult to get completely satisfactory texts of
speeches. While true today when our facilities for getting authentic
records are fairly good, this indictment has even greater cogency
and pertinence when we turn to the speech texts of a century or more
ago.

Alan E. Herr's comments on the problem of getting texts of
Elizabethan sermons illustrate the nature of the difficulty faced by

critics of later speakers. Observing that the sermons were not written in full, Herr shows how widely the final texts often departed
from the original. Oftentimes the preacher composed the finished
sermon after its original delivery; and the printer revised the copy
to make it a more fit piece for publication. Referring to a certain
John Manningham, whose penchant for taking sermon notes was
evidently noteworthy, Herr reports:

> When Dr. King, afterwards Bishop of London, preached at Paul's
> Cross, Manningham took notes that fill nine printed pages. He begins
> by analysing the structure of the sermon and then notes concisely every
> point that Dr. King made. Any person with any imagination could
> expand these nine pages to twenty, which was the average length of a
> sermon, and publish Dr. King's sermon; with no notice to the contrary,
> one would accept it as a true copy.[2]

We may infer from this statement that the possibility of our being
deceived on textual matters approaches the realm of the probable.

Even the great speeches of the eighteenth century—models upon
which we rely heavily—are without doubt inaccurate, incomplete,
and, occasionally, misleading. In many cases the deft hand of a
Samuel Johnson or some other reporter figured prominently in the
preparation of the texts. Says Chauncey Goodrich relative to the
texts of Chatham's speeches:

> The style and language of Lord Chatham are not to be judged of by the
> early speeches in this volume, down to 1743. Reporters at that day
> made little or no attempt to give the exact words of a speaker. They
> sought only to convey his sentiments, though they might occasionally
> be led, in writing out his speeches, to catch some of his marked pe-
> culiarities of thought or expression. In 1766, his speech against the
> American Stamp Act was reported, with a considerable degree of verbal
> accuracy, by Sir Robert Dean, aided by Lord Charlemont. Much, how-
> ever, was obviously omitted; and passages having an admirable felicity
> of expression were strangely intermingled with tame and broken sen-
> tences showing how imperfectly they had succeeded in giving the pre-
> cise language of the speaker. Five speeches . . . were written out,
> from notes taken on the spot by Sir Philip Francis and Mr. Hugh
> Boyd. One of them is said to have been revised by Lord Chatham
> himself.[3]

So we must deal with these texts in the full knowledge that they
leave something to be desired in authenticity.

In deliberative assemblies, we would expect the recording of
speech texts to be fairly accurate. But this is not necessarily true.
Reporters of speeches were not provided space in the House of

Commons until 1834; and nothing approaching accurate reporting was authorized in the United States Congress until 1873. Even with the lifting of these restrictions, accurate reporting did not follow automatically. To this day, the *Congressional Record* does not serve as a completely faithful recorder of the speakers' words; revisions modify the original utterances.

Commenting on the inaccuracy of reporting during Chatham's time, and also upon the fact that orators were freer "to let themselves go" when there were no reporters in the House to set down what they said, Lord Curzon concludes that the contemporary speaker's reluctance to "frisk and frolic in the flowery meads of rhetoric" results from the current omnipresence of reporters. As Lord Rosebery once remarked epigrammatically, "eloquence and stenography are not of congenial growth."

The experience of the early reporters of English eloquence emphasizes the foregoing remarks. And it must be remembered that the role of the reporter is of considerable consequence in the history of oratory. Frederic Hudson called the reporter "the amanuensis of the public. Through him statesmen speak to the people; through him Congress [or Parliament] is heard; through him orators become celebrated." [4] In 1731, Edward Cave hit upon the idea of distributing reports of the parliamentary debates. Accordingly, he established the *Gentleman's Magazine* as the medium through which to publicize the talks of the members. The practice of giving circulation to the speakers' remarks met with strong opposition, however, and in 1738 the House resolved it an indignity to publish reports of the debates. It affirmed that it would "proceed with the utmost severity against such offenders." [5] Cave got around these provisions, however, by giving the speakers fictitious names, or by referring to the proceedings as the "Debates in the Senate of Magna Lilliputia." He managed to get into the House secretly, took such notes as he could without being apprehended, and then retired to a tavern, there to compare copies with his accomplices and friends. Eventually William Guthrie or Samuel Johnson prepared the draft for *Gentleman's Magazine*. Guthrie did many of the parliamentary debates for Cave's publication between 1735 and 1740; and Samuel Johnson continued the work between 1740 and 1743.

Clearly, these reports were not historically accurate, despite their literary graces. Cave himself admitted their shortcomings. Alluding to the danger of publishing parliamentary debates, he hoped the reader would conceive "that it is impossible to do it in the very words of the Speakers. With regard to the major part, we pretend only to represent the sense, as near as may be expected in a summary way. . . ." [6]

That Samuel Johnson wrote speeches of high quality, no one will deny. Arthur Murphy reports a meeting in 1741 attended by several distinguished men, including Dr. Francis and Johnson, at which Francis spoke glowingly of Pitt's rhetorical skill as evidenced in the reply to Walpole. Whereupon Johnson remarked: "I wrote it in Exeter Street." Much surprised by this remark Francis said: "You have exceeded Demosthenes himself. . . ." [7] Another biographer says Johnson "had the art to give different colours to the several speeches, so that some appear to be declamatory and energetic, resembling the orations of Demosthenes; others like those of Cicero, calm, persuasive; others, more particularly those attributed to such country-gentlemen, merchants, and seamen as had seats in parliament, bear the characteristic of plainness, bluntness, and an affected honesty, as opposed to the plausibility of such as were understood or suspected to be courtiers: the artifice had its effect; Voltaire was betrayed by it into a declaration, that the eloquence of ancient Greece and Rome was revived in the British senate . . . and we are further told of a person in a high office under the government, who being at breakfast at a gentleman's chambers in Gray's Inn, Johnson being also there, declared, that by the style alone of the speeches in the debates, he could severally assign them to the persons by whom they were delivered." [8]

Such remarks indicate only too clearly that the speeches prepared by Johnson constitute a serious problem for the rhetorical critic. Manifestly, the debates are not genuine. In fact, Johnson knew little about debate, and seldom, if ever, attended the meetings. If, as he asserted, he always "took care not to let the Whig dogs have the best of it" in the debates, there may even be a question as to whether these texts are better than none.

How many of the public speeches delivered from the platform or published in the papers bear the marks of hands and minds other than those of the speakers to whom they are attributed, is hard to find out. The number is probably large.

Other reporters undoubtedly complicated the critics' problems in substantially the same way Johnson did. The story is told [9] of a parliamentary reporter named Tyas who, while covering one of Brougham's speeches, decided that a certain quotation from Cicero would strengthen an argument then being developed by the speaker. So he put it in. Subsequently, Brougham adopted the insertion and approved it for publication in his collected speeches. Coleridge reported some of Pitt's speeches in 1800. With pride in his own work and petulance toward the speaker, he asserted that Pitt had never talked that eloquently in his lifetime.[10] Charles Dickens, a renowned reporter in the 1830's, admitted that certain pathetic appeals in Daniel O'Connell's speech on the Coercion Bill affected him so deeply that he put his pen down, forgetting to record the words.[11] Indeed, a reporter without pen in hand is not likely to prepare a faithful copy of the proceedings of the day.

John Lord Campbell reports an incident which shows how easily a casual reader might be deceived in matters of textual accuracy.[12] On November 29, 1759, Bishop Johnson of Worcester preached a sermon at Westminster Abbey. Evidently he was given but a short time to make preparation. So Lord Mansfield, an unquestioned master of classical expression, wrote the sermon for his friend and protégé. Church officials and others pronounced the sermon unusually good, and requested that it be published. In print, it appeared as the composition of "James, by Divine Providence Lord Bishop of Worcester."

Other speeches have suffered at the hands of those who objected to what the orators said. This is no doubt true of Robert Emmet's final address to the special court on September 19, 1803. Enemies of the orator have, it is claimed, removed certain parts of the speech which they did not wish to preserve. On the other hand, Emmet's friends probably inserted items congenial to their way of thinking. At any rate, the available texts are numerous and at variance. Richard R. Madden, the historian of the United Irishmen, found eleven different versions; and later scholars say the number may be as high as twenty.[13]

So in many cases there may be grave doubt as to whether the text which the critic establishes as authentic is really the original work, in full, of the particular speaker. Reporters, "ghost-writers," and professional speech composers have prepared or have helped to prepare many of the talks that have appeared in the daily record of public affairs. As we have seen, this practice of writing speeches for others, apart from regular reporting, is an old profession. Some of the greatest Attic orators, notably Antiphon, Lysias, and Isaeus, were professional writers of forensic speeches, and very good ones, too. From days of antiquity there have been men whose services as writers of addresses were for hire.

During recent times there have been instances in which two speakers in a deliberative assembly have come up with practically the same talk on a legislative matter. Surely the evidence would suggest the influence of common assistance in the preparation of the manuscripts. However, in most cases where internal evidence furnished by the text does not make possible a definitive determination of authorship, we are obliged to turn to the testimony of the speaker and of such of his associates as may be competent to furnish information on the matter.

Critics today, in considering relatively recent American speakers, note with regret that many of the available texts are faulty. In his study of Henry Clay, Ernest J. Wrage [14] observes that most of the copies of Clay's addresses are reporters' accounts—faithful as to the general ideas but unsatisfactory on the side of stylistic expression. Wilbur S. Howell and Hoyt H. Hudson [15] discuss at some length the differences between a reporter's summary and Webster's official text of a speech delivered in New York in 1837; and they conclude that while both versions are fairly persuasive they express noticeably different purposes and methods. W. Hayes Yeager [16] finds after careful study of the sources of Wendell Phillips' speech texts that they evidently do not mirror with complete fidelity the form in which they were originally delivered.

The textual accuracy of Webster's "Reply to Hayne" is also in doubt. The full record of the speech in the Boston Public Library reveals that at least three people had a hand in the preparation of the copy that was eventually published. Joseph Gales, an editor of the *National Intelligencer* and one of the first reporters in Congress, submitted a fourteen-page shorthand report; his wife's transcription of it ran to about one hundred pages; and Webster's copy, which was finally given to the press, was eighty-five pages in length. There were evidently many revisions so that the final draft differs sharply from Gales' report.[17]

What is true concerning the problems of recording deliberative speeches is even more true of the forensic pleas. John W. Black, evaluating Rufus Choate as a forensic speaker in mid-nineteenth century America, noted the difficulty of securing accurate reports of Choate's courtroom speeches. Although this Massachusetts lawyer practiced law from 1825 until 1859, except for some eight years during his career in the United States Congress, practically none of his legal arguments are preserved. Concludes Black:

> It is not difficult to surmise why Choate is represented in American oratory as a deliberative and demonstrative speaker and his forensic speeches are given merely praise. This has been determined partially

by the availability of speeches. The demonstrative speeches usually
were written before delivery and published subsequently in pamphlet
editions; likewise, his important deliberative speeches were recorded,
at least partially, and often put into pamphlet editions. The courtroom
speeches, however, existed only as notes and pleas, no court stenographer
recording the addresses. Choate's lament on John Adams, 'Of that
series of spoken eloquence all is perished; not one reported sentence
has come down to us,' is nearly true of his own legal speeches—'The
Eloquence of Revolutionary Periods.' Only Parker's excerpts from
pleas and a few cases reported by newspapers remain. Also, it is likely
that subject matter has contributed to determining what speeches should
be preserved. Brown, Choate's biographer and the most extensive col-
lector of his speeches, was aided by members of Choate's immediate
family, and it is possible that the lofty themes of the occasional speeches,
e.g., the eulogies on Webster, made them much easier to include than
the few available forensic speeches, all scandalous in nature. Finally,
the great length of the courtroom speeches prohibits extensive reprint-
ings. Even Snyder's *Legal Masterpieces* and *American State Trials*
reproduce only portions of the plea in the Dalton trial. So complete
has been the dominance of his deliberative and demonstrative speeches
that today no complete forensic speech is available to the general
reader.[18]

Pulpit speech, by comparison, is more abundantly recorded, partly
because many sermons were carefully prepared and read from
the pulpit. The need for continual adjustment at the moment, typical
of the demands imposed upon a speaker in Congressional debate or
courtroom argument, has been largely absent. As we have noted,
however, the preachers habitually practicing the purely extempore
style have not been so accurately or frequently recorded. Theodore
F. Nelson, investigating Charles Haddon Spurgeon's *Theory and
Practice of Preaching,* cites this British clergyman as practicing
extempore speaking. "There is no evidence that the Metropolitan
Tabernacle preacher ever read his sermons at the time of presentation, nor that he engaged in writing as a step in preparation." Of
the recording and printing of these sermons Nelson observed, "Beginning in 1855, Spurgeon published weekly sermons. These were
the sermons he preached either on Sunday morning or evening of
that week. These sermons were taken down in shorthand by re-
corders, transcribed by them, and submitted to Mr. Spurgeon for
editing. Monday morning was devoted every week to this task.
These revisions brought the speaker benefits which are ascribed to
writing in preparation for speaking." [19]

Recent Investigations into Textual Accuracy

The reason for the earlier disregard of authentic reporting is complex. In his enlightening study of the "Factors Contributing to Inaccuracy in the Texts of Speeches," Loren D. Reid clarifies certain aspects of the problem. His analysis is threefold:[20]

(1) Inaccuracy has resulted from the lack of "official insistence upon the verbatim reporting of the speeches made by the legislative branch of government." As previously indicated, the English Parliament for many years forbade the publication of debates, and reporters who managed to stay in the galleries worked under baffling handicaps. They were subject to expulsion at any moment, and they had difficulty in hearing what was going on. Consequently, reporters as well as printers operated at some personal risk since members of Parliament had no desire to report to the outside world what they said before the House. During the nineteenth century, however, there is evidence to suggest that the people of England wished full texts of important speeches. George M. Trevelyan indicates that during the 1850's and 1860's political meetings were important events; speeches delivered by the ablest orators "were eagerly awaited and read by a political nation that had very little else in the way of politics brought to its door." Trevelyan also believes that parliamentary debates were reported better then than during the early part of the twentieth century.[21]

(2) The second factor, according to Reid, which accounts for inaccuracy of speech texts "is the strong, almost instinctive desire of speakers to make their speeches read as well as possible." It is obvious that corrections, deletions, and revisions designed by the speaker to improve the readability of the text divorce the finished product more and more from the original utterance.

(3) Finally, Reid points to "the mechanical possibilities for error" which result from shorthand reporting, dictation, editorial revision, and printing. He concludes by observing:

> . . . the very awareness of these factors of inaccuracy should suggest the need for and the possibility of a new type of speech reporting which will be more accurate than that of the *Congressional Record* and at the same time more vivid and useful than that of the present day metropolitan press.

A recent study by Zon Robinson [22] bears out the general conclusion that, whereas congressional reporting today is infinitely more accurate and complete than it was in either England or America a hundred and fifty years ago, it is still not verbatim reporting and probably never will be "until Congress abandons the practices of editing, revision, and extension." Recently the printing of the permanent edition of the *Congressional Record* was postponed for thirty days to give a certain Senator opportunity to establish the "authenticity" of copy entered by him in the *Record* relative to anti-inflationary legislation.[23]

A study by Robert King [24] of a radio speech delivered by Franklin D. Roosevelt confirms the point that so-called "authentic copy" of a speaker's manuscript does not always conform to the words spoken over the air. King checked the manuscript of Roosevelt's "Second Inaugural" of January 20, 1937, with a radio recording of what the President said. The manuscript with which King worked was furnished by the President's secretary, and conformed exactly with the texts printed in the papers, "save for several minor composing room errors." The study revealed that the President "followed his text closely, but not exactly." King concludes that we must remember

> . . . as we read the speeches of the day that they are, after all, what the speaker intended to say, though not necessarily what he said. Similarly, the speeches made over the air represent not what the speaker necessarily has written, fully intending to say, but what he actually says.

Kinds of Textual Investigations

Investigations into the authenticity of texts are of two principal types. The first attempts to answer the question, "Did the specified orator actually deliver this speech, or is it spurious?" The second searches out the answer to this query, "Admitting that the speaker gave the speech, is this the way he said it?" Contemporary critics are less concerned with the former type since in practically all cases earlier scholars have established satisfactory answers, if the historical record is not already completely adequate to establish the facts. In judging the speeches of antiquity, however, the critic had to concern himself with this type of textual analysis. Thus Richard C. Jebb must examine, as he did, the evidence as to whether the speech "On the Peace" was really the work of Andocides, or was, instead, as Dionysius and Harpocration alleged, spurious. Modern critics are concerned, in the main, with the second type of investigation, seeking to answer the question as to whether the available text mirrors faithfully the words originally spoken by the orator.

A study by Paul M. Angle [25] of the available texts of four of
Lincoln's speeches (Subtreasury Speech of December 26, 1839; the
House-Divided Speech, the Cooper Union Address, and the Gettysburg Address) reveals some of the difficulties and barriers with
which the scholar is confronted in his attempt to establish accurate
texts. In considering the Cooper Union Address, Angle reports
that the New York *Tribune* published the speech in pamphlet form
eight days after its delivery, and many other publishers also brought
out editions. Referring to the accuracy of the texts, Angle concludes:

> According to Lincoln's own statement, Tribune Tract No. 4 was pub-
> lished without supervision on his part, but Journal Campaign Document
> No. 1—the Springfield publication—had the benefit of his own 'hasty
> supervising.' The text of the latter, however, is identical with the
> former; the only differences are in spelling and capitalization. How-
> ever, the Nott-Brainerd edition, published by The Young Men's Re-
> publican Union of New York, differs from all earlier editions in one
> important respect—the correction of a factual statement—and in sev-
> eral minor matters of phraseology. Because Lincoln read the proofs
> of this edition, and carried on a correspondence with one of its editors,
> this is the authoritative text. [26]

Similarly, in the case of the Gettysburg Address, Angle points
to the difficulty of determining the best text. He observes that
collectors have been largely of one opinion, "that the Gettysburg
Address was first put into print, aside from the newspapers, in a
48-page booklet entitled *An Oration Delivered on the Battlefield of
Gettysburg . . .* , by Edward Everett. . . ." However, a recent
discovery in the Lincoln collection, entitled *The Gettysburg Solemnities,* reveals this item to have been printed before the previously
mentioned booklet. But, Angle goes on to say, "the text to be found
in *The Gettysburg Solemnities* is a faulty one." It is as follows:

> Four score and seven years ago our fathers brought forth on this con-
> tinent a new nation, conceived in liberty, and dedicated to the proposi-
> tion that all men are equal. Now we are engaged in a great civil war,
> testing whether that nation, or any nation so conceived and so dedicated,
> can long endure. We are now on a great battle-field of that war. We
> are met to dedicate a portion of that field as the final resting-place of
> those who have given their last life-blood that that nation might live.
> But in a larger sense we cannot dedicate, we cannot consecrate, we can-
> not hallow this ground. The brave men living and dead who struggled
> here have consecrated it far above our poor power to add to or detract.
> [Applause.] The world will little know nor long remember what we
> say; but it can never forget what they did here. [Applause.] And it

is for us living to be dedicated here to the unfinished work that they have thus far so nobly carried forward. [Applause.] It is rather for us here to be dedicated to the great task remaining before us, that from this honored day we take increased devotion to that cause for which they here gave the last full measure of devotion. That we here highly resolve that these dead shall not have died in vain; that the nation shall, under God, have a new birth of freedom. [Applause.] And that government of the people, by the people, and for the people, shall not perish from the earth. [Applause.] [27]

Angle observes that among the differences between this and the accepted text is the omission of the sentence "It is altogether fitting and proper that we should do this."

Difficult as the task of finding the correct text is, Angle believes the answer is known.

Actually, I think we do know exactly how Lincoln wanted his speech preserved. In February, 1864, George Bancroft asked for a copy of the address in order that it might be included in a volume of facsimiles entitled, *Autograph Leaves of our Country's Authors.* Lincoln complied, but because he wrote on both sides of the paper, his manuscript was not suitable for reproduction. At Bancroft's request he sent a second copy on March 11, 1864, this time writing only on one side of the sheets. This copy was duly reproduced in the book for which it was intended, which was published by Cushings & Bailey, Baltimore, 1864. As far as is known, this was Lincoln's final revision.[28]

We have considered at some length this reference to the Lincoln texts because it brings two matters clearly into focus. In the first place, it throws light upon the exacting assignment of determining textual authenticity—even for revised, rather than for original copy; and secondly, it suggests the important service that bibliographical research can perform for the rhetorical critic. In their search for possible editions of written materials, and in their solicitous regard for textual accuracy, bibliographers contribute to the enrichment of our subject by verifying and establishing some of the copy from which our speech criticisms derive. In a sense, each critic of oratory is also a bibliographer; he must find the most authentic texts before he proceeds to an evaluation of the speaker's merit.

The Need for Exact Texts

The question may not yet be answered, Why attach so much importance to seemingly minor details of textual accuracy? Cannot the critic evaluate an orator's speechmaking without carrying out such exacting research into authenticity?

Clearly, the critic needs genuine materials, if he is to appraise oratory without prejudice and folly. If a speaker is to be judged by what he said, it would seem proper that his words be quoted with as much fidelity to original utterance as possible. Undoubtedly, a speaker's general train of thought can be evaluated, and with discernment, even though the critic works with inaccurate texts. Minor changes in expression, such as the omission or inclusion of certain words, may not militate irreparably against a full understanding of the speaker's ideas, although such inaccuracies make the critical assignment treacherous and liable to error. It has been said that, whereas the texts of Chatham's speeches are sufficiently accurate to enable us to examine his ways of thinking, attachment of heavy reliance upon any single statement to reveal his point of view would be open to grave suspicion. However, in the case of Chatham, and many other speakers before and after him, we try to work with the best available texts.

Important as textual authenticity is in the evaluation of rhetorical invention and disposition, it is even more essential to the study of a speaker's style. Word choice, compositional elements, and ornamental flourishes must be as near the original as possible, if we are to appraise the speaker rather than the editors who prepared his copy for subsequent publication.

But wishing texts to be unequivocally accurate will not make them so. One of the limitations under which the critic works, and which he must recognize frankly, is that few, if any, speeches not electrically transcribed are exactly as the orator gave them. Such excellent publications as J. E. Thorold Rogers' [29] edition of John Bright's speeches, or Sherman Evarts' [30] edition of his father's (William Maxwell Evarts') speeches, are still inaccurate in the strictest sense; they are the best copies, without doubt, but they have undergone editorial revision, both by the editor, and, in the former case, by Bright himself.

The best method of getting an authentic text is, of course, to make a recording of the speech while it is being delivered. Since recording is a recent development, and even now often unfeasible because of the equipment and financial resources necessary for its successful use, we must turn to the next best way of finding the most accurate version. That method is one of matching, or comparison. Thus the critic who deals with texts that appear in Hansard's *Parliamentary Debates,* the London *Times,* and other publications has an opportunity to compare versions, check obvious mechanical errors, and secure composite estimates as to the wording of the original utterance. It is admitted, of course, that there is danger in comparing reports of texts. If all embrace a common error, the collation will be meaningless. Comparison of separate and independent texts is therefore preferable.

Specimen Texts Matched for Accuracy

For illustrative purposes, consider the following parallel texts of selected sections from John Bright's speech of June 30, 1863, to see how widely, if at all, the copy varies from source to source. The first text is from the volume of Bright's collected speeches, revised by himself and edited by J. E. Thorold Rogers; [31] the second is from the reporter's version as printed in the London *Times*; [32] and the final copy is from Hansard's *Parliamentary Debates*. [33] From the body of the speech:

> The point that I am about to argue is this: I believe that the war which is now raging in America is more likely to abolish slavery than not, and more likely to abolish it than any other thing that can be proposed in the world. I regret very much that the pride and passion of men are such as to justify me in making this statement. The supply of cotton under slavery must always be insecure. The House felt so in past years; for at my recommendation they appointed a committee, and but for the folly of a foolish Minister they would have appointed a special commission to India at my request. Is there any gentleman in this House who will not agree with me in this,—that it would be far better for our great Lancashire industry that our supply of cotton should be grown by free labour than by slave labour?

The conclusion:

> We know the cause of this revolt, its purposes, and its aims. Those who made it have not left us in darkness respecting their intentions, but what they are to accomplish is still hidden from our sight; and I will abstain now, as I have always abstained with regard to it, from predicting what is to come. I know what I hope for,—and what I shall rejoice in,—but I know nothing of future facts that will enable me to express a confident opinion. Whether it will give freedom to the race which white men have trampled in the dust, and whether the issue will purify a nation steeped in crimes committed against that race, is known only to the Supreme. In His hands are alike the breath of man and the life of States. I am willing to commit to Him the issue of this dreaded contest; but I implore of Him, and I beseech this House, that my country may lift nor hand nor voice in aid of the most stupendous act of guilt that history has recorded in the annals of mankind.

The *Times* version reads as follows:

> I believe that the war now raging is more likely to abolish slavery than
> not, and more likely to abolish it than any other thing that could be
> proposed in the world. I regret that the pride and the passions of men
> are such as to justify me in making that statement. The supply of
> cotton under slavery must always be insecure, and the House felt this
> to be the case in past years, for on my recommendation it appointed a
> committee on the subject, and but for a very foolish minister the House
> would have appointed a commission to go to India. Is there any gentle-
> man in this House who will not agree that it would be far better for
> our great Lancashire industry if the supply of cotton were grown by
> free labour rather than by slave labour?
>
> We know the cause of this revolt. We know its purpose and its end.
> Those who have made it have not left the world in darkness with re-
> spect to their intentions. But what the revolt is to accomplish is still
> hidden from our sight, and I will abstain now—as I have always ab-
> stained—from predicting what is to come. I know what I hope for,
> what I shall rejoice in, but I know nothing of future events that will
> enable me to express a confident opinion. Whether the revolt will give
> freedom to the race which the white man for centuries has trampled
> in the dust, or whether, to use the expression of my hon. friend, it will
> purify a nation steeped in crime in connexion with its conduct to that
> race, is known only to the Supreme. In His Hand are alike the breath
> of men and the life of States. I am willing to commit to Him the issue
> of this dread contest; but I implore Him, and I beseech this House, that
> my country may lift nor hand nor voice in aid of the most stupendous
> act of guilt recorded in the annals of mankind.

Finally, we have this version from Hansard's *Debates:*

> I believe that the war that is now raging in America is more likely to
> abolish slavery than not, and more likely to abolish it than any other
> thing that can be proposed in the world. I regret very much that the
> pride and passion of men are such as to justify me in making such a
> statement. The supply of cotton under slavery must always be in-
> secure. The House felt so in past years; for at my recommendation
> they appointed a Committee, and but for a foolish Minister they would
> have appointed a special Commission to India at my request, and I feel
> the deepest regret that they did not do so. Is there any Gentleman in
> this House who will not agree with me in this matter—that it would be
> far better for our great Lancashire industry that our supply of cotton
> should be grown by free labour rather than by slave labour?
>
> Sir, we know the cause of this revolt, its purposes, and its aims. Those
> who made it have not left us in darkness respecting their intentions—
> but what it is to accomplish is still hidden from our sight, and I will
> abstain now, as I have always abstained with regard to it, from pre-

dicting what is to come. I know what I hope for and what I shall rejoice in—but I know nothing of the future that will enable me to
express a confident opinion. Whether it will give freedom to the race
which, for generations past, white men have trampled in the dust, and
whether it will purify a nation steeped in crime in connexion with its
conduct to that race, is known only to the Supreme. In His hands are
alike the breath of man and the life of States. I am willing to commit
to Him the issue of this dread contest; but I implore of Him, and I
beseech this House, that my country may lift nor hand nor voice in aid
of the most stupendous act of guilt that history has recorded in the
annals of mankind.

An examination of these texts shows that although there is variation, all are agreed as to the ideas expressed by the speaker, and
fairly consistent as to his style. A copy of what Bright *really said,*
however, might show still other differences.

It should be borne in mind that punctuation and paragraph struc-
ture influence the impression the material makes upon the *reader.*
These are evidently minor matters, but they make a difference.
To the critic of style, the visual appeal may have significance.

The foregoing and similar collations will not necessarily give us
the exact truth as to how the speaker expressed his thoughts. But
if we collate the texts carefully, and articulate the collation with
other evidence deriving from our knowledge of the orator and his
way of thinking, we should at least be able to approximate the establishment of a text adequate for purposes of critical analysis. If
the critic recognizes the limitations of his textual inquiry and makes
intelligent allowance for them, he is doing the best he can with the
available resources. No one can reasonably be expected to do more.

General Summary

In practically all cases, critics are obliged to work with speech
texts of questionable accuracy. Texts often suffer with time. From
the moment the words issue from the mouth of the speaker to the
day, often distantly removed, when the critic assays the spirit, meaning, and effect of those words, many opportunities for error and
change in transcription occur. It is the critic's obligation to determine textual authenticity—to establish the best possible text through
such processes of investigation and collation as may be open to him.
At best, his research may produce a copy not wholly faithful to
the original. However, it will at least reveal the degree of fidelity
achieved in a given text, and thus indicate the limitations imposed
upon critical effort.

Chapter 10

RECONSTRUCTING THE SOCIAL SETTINGS

The Historical Setting as the Framework of Oratorical Criticism

The story is told of a cub reporter who was sent out by a metropolitan newspaper to cover an assignment in an eastern area where flood waters were doing considerable damage. Hours went by; competing newspapers were printing lengthy and dramatic reports of the flood, but still no word came from the young newspaperman. Finally, in a state of frenzy, the city editor wired the reporter, asking why the stories were not being sent. Immediately came the reply: "Can't send reports now; too much excitement."

This anecdote serves to remind us that not all events happening at a moment of crisis or momentous public occasion are likely to be recorded; and that those which do receive tangible expression are selective, that they are dependent upon the judgment of the witnesses or historians who make the decisions as to what shall be included and what omitted from the reports.

Since every judgment of a public speech contains a historical constituent, the critic is peculiarly concerned with determining the nature of the setting in which the speaker operated. Although almost a truism, it cannot be overemphasized that speeches are events occurring in highly complex situations; that responsibility of critical appraisal depends heavily upon the critic's ability to effect faithful reconstructions of social settings long since dissolved. No task is more challenging, none more essential to the successful prosecution of the task. In a restricted sense, it may be possible to evaluate a speaker's written style through a simple examination of the text, without regard to the events which gave rise to the delivery of the speech. But even if possible, such an appraisal would be superficial; the evidence derived from the literature of speech education and criticism attests to the sterility of rhetoric when divorced from the urgency of matter and the imperatives of the particular historical moment.

The circumstances under which great speechmaking flourishes will alone affirm the importance of historical narrative in the process of criticism. Distinguished oratory and social crisis are closely interrelated. Ralph Waldo Emerson once remarked: "Times of eloquence are times of terror." [1] The stress of events associated with man's quest for freedom in civil and political life, the upsurges of patriotic fervor occasioned by man's desire to preserve his rights or to extend the influence of his power—these and other manifestations of the human will have always dominated the scene during those periods most productive in public address. Accordingly, we associate the name of Pericles with the ardent, patriotic defence of Athenian life and freedom during the crucial period of the Peloponnesian War; Demosthenes, with the epochal struggle between the Athenians and Philip of Macedon, involving again the question of freedom and personal liberty; Cicero, with the attempt to crush the conspiratorial designs of a Catiline, and thus sustain the integrity of the commonwealth; Chatham, Burke, Fox, and Pitt, with the stirring times and issues of the late eighteenth century; Clay, Webster, Calhoun, and Lincoln, with the inflammatory subjects of slavery, States' rights, and national expansion; Roosevelt and Churchill, with the global problems relating to the affirmation and establishment of the Four Freedoms. These are but a few speakers whose services stemmed from the great issues of history—men whose oratory was prompted by and positively influenced the ebb and flow of major events which have determined the destiny of nations. Whether these men are remembered as orators only because their speeches dealt with matters of great human concern is an academic question. It is enough to recognize that the man and the issue met, and that the issue gave free rein to the man's vision and his skill in the use of the spoken word.

During the nineteenth century, writers frequently asserted that modern speakers, as contrasted with those of antiquity, no longer exercised great influence over men and issues. Thus Edward Channing concluded that, whereas a momentous issue might bring a competent speaker to the forefront, the nature of democratic society precluded the necessity of keeping him there for any period of time. Instead of looking to a few key men for extraordinary service, societies now entrusted their security to laws and institutions. Consequently, the orator, according to Channing,

> . . . has not escaped the restraints that are thus laid on individual power, nor the circumstances that thus lessen individual importance. He can no longer be a despot, either to save freedom or destroy it. He

is not the important personage he once was. He is fortunately less able to do harm, and less needed to do good.[2]

Returning to Channing's point of view, we note his assertion that the orator is the "creature of the circumstances in which he is placed." Then, he continues, it is

> . . . visionary to suppose, as some have done, that a few great men, by taking advantage of public enthusiasm, during the stormy periods of a free government, might effect an entire revolution in eloquence, and revive it in its ancient spirit and power. Such a revolution might be forwarded by their skilful exertions, but it could only be wrought by those secret and slowly operating causes which change entirely the face of society, the character and, in some degree, the occupations of a whole people. At present, however, we think it one of the happiest, and we trust most permanent distinctions between our state of society and the ancient—and the effect of this distinction is very observable in modern eloquence—that the power of individuals is lessened; we do not encourage any man to aspire after an overwhelming greatness and sway.[3]

The accuracy of Channing's claim is open to question. With the tremendous improvements in communication facilities, especially in radio, able speakers exercise an influence, or at least a potential influence, over audiences the size and complexity of which would have seemed fantastically absurd fifty or a hundred years ago. The crises in public life continue to reveal the mettle of speakers; tend to link anew, and on a wider scale, the men of the hour and the issues which periodically threaten nations.

One of the characters in Tacitus' *Dialogue Concerning Oratory* puts this matter pointedly relative to ancient speechmaking. Observing that the splendor and magnitude of the subjects which engaged the talents of Crassus and Pompey accounted in large part for their claim on the public memory, Tacitus says the subject "lifts the mind above itself; it gives vigour to sentiment, and energy to expression." If the subject be a "paltry theft," the orator will be chilled by the meanness of the question. But if it deals with "a charge for plundering the allies of Rome," the speaker will rise to the dignity and proportions of his inquiry. Thus the speaker's effect "springs from the disasters of society." The "mind of the orator grows and expands with his subject. Without ample materials no splendid oration was ever yet produced." [4] In short, eloquence must have its theatre.

The Relation of Rhetoric to History

The foregoing section reminds us that oratory functions within the framework of public affairs, and that the criticism of it must be soundly based upon a full and penetrating understanding of the meaning of the events from which it issues. Rhetoric and history, age-old partners, cannot be divorced. The critic of speeches knows that their union is indissoluble.

The relationship of rhetoric and history has not always been wholly congenial. This circumstance arises from the conviction that when the historian employs the tools of the rhetorician—i.e., the instruments of effective expression—he may be tempted to depart from the strict presentation of recorded fact, and may venture into the inviting, but often inaccurate, field of narrative embellishment. Thus historians might make history largely an instrument of rhetoric. In the *Brutus,* we observe that Cicero holds Atticus to task for describing the death of Coriolanus in such a manner as to raise questions concerning the justness of the representation. Whereupon Atticus replies: ". . . it is the privilege of rhetoricians to exceed the truth of history, that they may have an opportunity of embellishing the fate of their heroes. . . ." [5] In Cicero's works, as a whole, we find evidence that he believed the historian should be a master of rhetoric. This is precisely the issue which develops when we comment on the relation of rhetoric to historical scholarship.

The ancient historians were unquestioned masters of an *art* of history writing. They invented many speeches, undoubtedly elaborated upon others, and wove them into the fabric of their historical narratives. James T. Shotwell believes that the invention of speeches in history had its origin in primitive storytelling. Thucydides then took over this form of expression, and soon it became "a definite part of the historian's trade." [6] Whether or not the speeches of Thucydides had substantial bases in fact, their inclusion in the narrative added artistic lustre to the history. Even if, as Shotwell remarks, these speeches seem somewhat futile and unreal, they "gave to the antique mind the very reflection of reality." Other historians who introduced speeches into their presentations are Ephorus who probably made up the orations himself; and Livy, in whose extant works can be found scores of speeches, many of them of considerable length.

The historian's suspicion of the art of rhetoric in its relation to the writing of history does not stem from any reluctance to make historical narratives artistically pleasing. Rather, it grows out of the fear that in attempting to secure stylistic excellence, facts may be distorted. Thus, J. B. Bury, who disliked the "rhetorical view" of history, registered his opposition because such history failed to remain fully within the area of facts. Evidently historians would borrow a description of a battle or of a speech event from another writer—just because the account happened to be picturesque. So Bury concluded that as long as history was considered an art, "the sanctions of truth and accuracy could not be severe."[7]

Shotwell's observation reveals a similar point of view. Admitting that history is at best "a poor enough mirror of reality," he says it

> . . . is readily warped by art; and rhetoric is art of the most formal kind. It distorts into ordered arrangement the haphazard, unformed materials which chance produces or preserves. It sets its pieces like an impressario and completes with convincing elegance the abrupt and incomplete dramas of reality. All history writing does this to some degree, since it is art. But rhetoric passes easily over into the sphere of conscious distortion.[8]

Rhetoric and history, however, are not irreconcilable, if, as Shotwell remarks, "by rhetoric we mean the use of language appropriate to the occasion." This brings us to the conception which the rhetorical critic keeps in mind when he speaks of the interrelation of the two subjects. In common with the historian, the critic is not interested in historiography written primarily with an eye to artistic effect. The accuracy and wisdom of rhetorical judgments depend largely upon the historian's making available authenticated records from which social situations can be reconstructed.

With due respect to the historians whose researches into the data of the past make possible our present inquiries into speech criticism, the fact remains, unfortunate though patent, that the available record of past events is fragmentary. This is not the fault of the historian; it is, instead, the necessary circumstance of life that not everything is recorded, and hence, much that has happened is unknown, even to the most astute scholars. As Frederick J. Teggart remarked: "The subject matter of history consists of occurrences, which are unusual and out of the common, of events which for one reason or another compel the attention of men, and which are held worthy of being kept in remembrance." But it follows clearly that every age "has its own criteria for distinguishing between the usual and the unusual, and the conception of what is remarkable and worthy of record is a function of the whole body of ideas current in any generation."[9]

Totality of Historical Data Impossible of Attainment

As indicated in Chapter 1, neither the critic nor the historian can acquire a totality of information which would satisfy completely the demands of present-day thought. Both must deal with statements and testimony which occasionally fall short of the strictest trustworthiness. Whether the historian likes it or not, he must still fill in open spots in historical narrative. Since historians continue to select the data which are presumably most important in revealing the occurrence of events, their work remains, as Teggart puts it, a "personal presentation."

Frequently the historian delves into the motives of men to explain events. And motives are hard to determine. "The ascription of motives, based on the psychology of daily life, is a dubious venture for one who professes to limit his statements to known and documented facts." [10] If, as William Roscoe Thayer once remarked, man has a strong instinct for "certitude," he will unquestionably try to find out, if at all possible, the motives that gave rise to certain actions. The interpretations resulting from such quests make up a part of the available "facts" with which we reconstruct events of the past. In the absence of total and absolute data, we have to do the best we can with what is available. We cannot expect the historian to furnish materials which are beyond the range of the knowable. [11]

Because the historian has had to work with incomplete data, and because he has frequently been unable to set down available facts without traces of bias and passion, the claim has been made that history cannot be a science. Complete impartiality and detachment, complete freedom from emotional and aesthetic predispositions are undoubtedly difficult to achieve. What is true of the historian in this connection is no less, and possibly more, true of the literary and rhetorical critic. But whether or not these branches of research are scientific, in the usual sense of the term, is relatively unimportant. The only thing that really matters is that the method and techniques employed be severely critical. If we proceed along what F. M. Salter calls the "slow and laborious path of Scientific Method," by making painstakingly careful observations of the available facts; by drawing upon sound and workable hypotheses for our inquiries; by drawing logically valid inferences from the findings; and by making such verifications of our conclusions as the conditions will permit—if these things are done, and with appropriate objectivity, our investigations will have "scientific" integrity, whether the Scientific

Method, *per se,* applies to them or is, instead, the "exclusive property of the physical sciences." [12]

The rhetorical critic therefore accepts as one of the limitations of his task the conclusion that he cannot get all facts necessary for complete reconstruction of the social setting in which a speech occurred. Despite that concession, the critic can still get a workable conception of the whole pattern of a social event. In order to appreciate the design of a fabric, it is not necessary to examine every thread.

One of the functions of historical investigation, wrote Dionysius in a letter to Pompeius, "is to determine where to begin and how far to proceed." Difficult as is the determination of the boundaries of original research, the objective sought for is clear and attainable. Like the historian, the rhetorical critic seeks some sort of unity in the pattern of social forces operating at a given moment in history. He seeks to secure a sufficiently large body of reliable data to enable him intelligently to understand a specific event—a speech, for example—in its relation to the larger whole of which it is a part. In keeping with the logical postulates of the organismic and Gestalt schools of thought, this doctrine asserts that the *whole* is primary, and that it governs the operation of the parts. Consequently, the specific occurrence must be explained in terms of the conditions under which it took place. Fox's speech on the Overtures to Napoleon, according to this view, is meaningful only when related to the complex historical continuum of which it is a part; criticism of it in isolation, and without regard for the social forces which prompted it, would be a venture in artistic futility. As Bury remarks, we recognize that past events are relative to their "historical conditions; that they cannot be wrenched out of their chronological context and endowed with an absolute significance." He then goes on to show what we have already referred to, that these events "are parts of a whole, and have no meaning except in relation to that whole. . . ." [13]

Meaning of This Concept

The implications of this thesis are manifold, but two considerations plainly dominate; both relate to the work of the historian and the rhetorical critic.

The first of these is the concept of *causality.* Facts of history must be put into some sort of pattern; they must be articulated so as to suggest continuity, relationship. Both the critic and the historian may have that "supreme virtue" of truthfulness, to which Lecky refers, and yet fail to mould the facts of history into proper form. Both must be able to distinguish between proximate and ultimate causes; both must be able accurately to generalize from available data. In short, they must be mature logicians.

Preserved Smith puts the matter pointedly when he says that, by "explaining" the phenomena of history,

> . . . we mean putting the observed facts in their proper relationships, especially in that causal relationship which . . . has usually been accepted by the human mind as the most illuminating means of grasping reality. . . . For, masses of fact can be grasped only when gathered into bundles under the collective action of some generalization. To describe facts promiscuously, without arrangement or order, is merely to produce the effect of a buzzing strident confusion in the most pluralistic of worlds.[14]

The causal relationships to which Smith refers are "those which lead us to see beneath the surface events of politics and the accidental action of personality and great cosmic forces governing and shaping the development of social forms." [15]

The other conception which derives from the postulate that specific events are meaningful only in relation to the whole of which they are parts, is that of *historical development*. Fundamentally, this idea suggests the truism that history does not exactly repeat itself. More importantly, it points to the necessity of studying the "slow processes of growth" in social forms, and of refraining from judging the actions of the past by the standards of our own times. Hence the critic must view the events of the past, as well as the judgments of men in the past, with an eye to a certain "historical relativity," believing, with Bury, that these judgments are not final. Rather, "their permanent interest lies in the fact that they are judgments pronounced at a given epoch and are characteristic of the tendencies and ideas of that epoch." [16] This will account in part for the circumstances to which Teggart refers:

> In any age the activity of the historian arises from the perception that, judged by his standards, the histories previously written are unreliable and misinformed. The background of historical inquiry is, therefore, the existence of these earlier accounts, and, with implied reference to this background, the historian defines his purpose as being to set forth what it was that actually occurred.[17]

It should be said that certain of the critics of antiquity paid considerable heed to the concept of historical continuity. In unmis-

takable terms, Quintilian announced his acceptance of the principle
when he asked: "What art . . . came to perfection at once?" Impressed with the process of development, he remarked that "a thing
is most natural, when nature has allowed it to be brought into the
best condition." [18] Cicero contended that no art was invented and
carried to perfection at a single stroke. He thus made known his
faith in a growing, enlarging principle of improvement, or at least
change, through time. He carried his doctrine directly into practice when he evaluated the orators of Greece and Rome. Clearly, he
regarded men as moulded by their age. Accordingly, speeches were
to be appraised by the criteria applicable to their time.

Nature of the Critic's Historical Investigation

The question may arise whether the reconstruction of a social
setting for rhetorical criticism involves substantially the same materials and traces the same events as for straight historical narrative. In the main, the two inquiries draw upon common data. Since
the rhetorical critic is concerned, however, with the effect of certain
speeches upon certain people, and upon the flow of public events
generally, it follows that he will be interested in some data which
the historian might ordinarily overlook, or exclude as unnecessary to
his assignment. Basically, the rhetorical critic takes all the historical
narrative as the beginning of his investigation; discards some as not
contributing directly to his project; and searches out other data
having "rhetorical" significance. The differences relate, therefore,
to details, not to fundamental method or facts. Undoubtedly, the
rhetorical critic will seek further data than the historical record usually provides concerning audiences and speech situations generally.
Likewise, he may make different judgments as to what the important
elements in a particular occurrence are. Whereas the historian might
decide that the price of cotton was important to an understanding of
a given moment in history, the rhetorician, keeping a somewhat different objective in view, might conclude that the influence of certain
religious movements was of greater concern. These remarks simply
confirm the previous observations that there cannot be a totality of
information on a given subject; researchers are consequently obliged
to work with the data they have, selecting and interpreting those
which, in their judgment, most demonstrably establish causal con-
tinua. Perhaps all investigators seek truth as the *ultimate* objective.
Since they are not all seeking the same *immediate* ends, however,
differences in their selection of facts will inevitably develop.

It is thus apparent that the rhetorical critic's task is in its primary character a research undertaking. Motivated by the desire to view a particular speech in its larger social setting, he reconstructs as far as the facts will permit the social milieu of the period. This reconstruction centers largely about two considerations: the tracing of the antecedents—historical, economic, political, social, cultural—which impinge upon the ideas set forth in the speech; and the examining of details and circumstances—including the audience—relative to the specific occasion on which the speech was given.

Critic's Use of Historical Materials.—The question arises as to what end is served by bringing together the body of historical materials which presumably shape the speech situation. Assuming that the rhetorical critic has meticulously traced the antecedents of a problem, to what use can he put the data? In no other way can a critic study the total audience situation, for audiences bring with them the composite influence of the happenings of the past. Accordingly, the background of a speech situation furnishes the data which enable the critic to study the speaker's adaptation of ideas to listeners. If, as Aristotle indicated, the hearers are the most important aspects of a speech situation; and if they determine in large measure the speaker's end and object, then, surely, the more the critic learns about them, the more acute will be his analysis of the speech. The critic who knows much about a specific audience is indeed in a better position to understand what the speaker does and says than anyone not possessing comparable knowledge. In no other way can the analyst trace the possible effectiveness of a speech than through (a) familiarity with antecedent trends and happenings, (b) knowledge of the hearers, and (c) study of the subsequent events upon which the speaker might have exercised a causal influence.

Examples of the Use of Historical Data.—A study of Stephen A. Douglas' speeches in the 1858 senatorial campaign, prepared by F. L. Whan,[19] reveals both the extent to which settings can be reconstructed and the use to which the facts can be put in the subsequent criticism. The first two sections of Whan's investigation, dealing respectively with the "Audience" and the "Occasion," trace in minute detail the principal factors which influenced the beliefs and attitudes of the people before whom Douglas appeared. This is chiefly a study of trends, including population changes; new attitudes toward agriculture and economics (according to Whan, the "Honor of extravagance, the new attitude towards tariff, the belief in the dignity of labor, and the experience with unemployment during the panic, all had a vital influence on the 1858 campaign issues") ; the educational movements of the period (the diffusion of learning and the advancement of training and schools "symbolized their [the people's] sincere belief in the manifest destiny of the State, the Union, and democracy") ; the influence of religious movements; the trend of slavery beliefs; and political alignments, especially the shifting of party affiliation and control "from the hands of the long dominant Democrats to the new Republican party." As for the immediate occasion of the speeches, Whan considers more than the simple fact that Douglas was seeking re-election. He shows how the influence of the newspapers, splits in the Democratic party, local political conditions, and issues involved in the contest helped to give the speech situations distinctive character. All in all, Whan's study shows the complexity and interrelation of the many historical facts which affect importantly the outcome of speaking efforts.

Loren D. Reid's study of Charles James Fox also illustrates effectively how a knowledge of the speaker's audiences contributes to the understanding and appraisal of oratory. Apart from the analysis of the specific audiences for the speeches of February 2, 1778; November 16, 1778; June 8, 1784; and February 3, 1800, Reid devotes a separate chapter to Fox's audience in general. To clarify the problems Fox faced, as well as to reveal the way in which he met them, Reid traces the historical data relative to parliamentary audiences in England during the late eighteenth century.

Selected passages from Reid's study will indicate the importance of such a reconstruction of historical facts.

GEORGE THE THIRD AND THE "KING'S FRIENDS"

George the Third assumed the crown of England with the deep-rooted desire that he would be the actual as well as the titular head of the government. An important part of achieving that desire was the creation of a strong party of 'king's friends' in the House of Commons. This was a comparatively simple matter because of the ease with which seats in that house could be bought. Fox himself had secured his seat because his father could buy the right to represent the borough of Midhurst; Chatham had been returned time after time from Old Sarum, that classic example of the rotten borough; Sir Philip Francis was once returned as a member for Appleby by the vote of a single elector. Seats were bought and sold like merchandise, and sometimes even advertised in the newspapers. With seats so easily acquired, the crown could exert a tremendous influence in controlling elections. Letters between the king and Lord North reveal clearly the government's activity in the purchase of seats. So strenuous were North's exertions in building up a strong party of 'king's friends' that when he resigned from office in 1782 he had paid out more than £72,000 for 'election expenses' for the previous three years; and this sum, he insisted, was no larger than customary. Little wonder that John Wilkes declared on the floor of the lower house on April 16, 1777, that the English House of Commons was 'the most corrupt assembly in Europe.'

OTHER METHODS OF PARLIAMENTARY CONTROL

There were other ways of controlling parliament than by outright purchase of seats. George the Third had an elaborate system of rewards to dangle before the eyes of his followers, and these he handed out with a good deal of finesse. Those who held governmental positions and those who had hopes for further favors found it advisable to serve the king's ministers well in matters of parliamentary legislation, because the king was ever on the alert to discover and discipline backsliders.

This alertness appears constantly in the king's correspondence with Lord North. 'I have a right to expect a hearty support from everyone in my Service and shall remember Defaulters,' he wrote in 1772. A few days later he asked for a list of those who had defaulted, noting that 'there would be a Rule for my conduct in the Drawing Room tomorrow.' On the other hand, the surest route to political preference was to be known as a faithful supporter of governmental policies. Those who attended regularly and voted correctly might ask almost any favor for themselves or their friends, with great likelihood of its being granted. Offices, commissions, sinecures, pensions, and even peerages were conferred upon loyal 'friends.'

Moreover, the king was a good manager of parliament in ways which did not burden the treasury. He was a shrewd observer and manipulator, ready to seize upon any advantage and profit by any carelessness of the opposition. Thus in 1772, when the Commons had adjourned for two days, he reminded North that 'two days respite is allways (sic) more favorable to Administration than to Opposition.' Two days later he advised North, with respect to the passage of the Marriage Bill, to seize the floor early in the day and wear out the patience of the house with general speeches covering 'the whole of the business'—so that members would presumably be too tired to listen to the opposition. Always he was cautious. 'Success must not render us inattentive,' he wrote in 1775, 'for Opposition will watch every opportunity to give trouble.'

EXTENT OF KING'S INFLUENCE

The numerical result of these practices was that slightly over thirty per cent (30.6) of the members of the House of Commons of the fourteenth parliament, elected in 1774, held places in some branch of the king's government. Nineteen were elevated to the peerage; 50

had positions in the army; 16 in the navy; 11 in the royal household; and 75 in governmental administration—a total of 171 placeholders. This, of course, makes no allowance for the influence of these members upon other members. The obvious conclusion is that Fox's audience was made up in large part of men actually in the pay of the king's government and subject to his rigorous discipline. Fox and his colleagues were compelled to adapt their speaking to this definite audience situation. While the king quietly dictated policies from the Queen's House, Fox and the Whigs argued with the 'faithful commons' amid the uproar and confusion of old St. Stephen's chapel, where the major problem was not only to get a fair hearing, but to get any sort of hearing at all. . . .

KING'S NEED OF GOOD SPEAKERS

It must be remembered . . . that the House of Commons was not wholly corrupt. Burke believed that many of the members who usually voted with the minister would not follow him to the extreme, and upon many of these a good speech would have some influence. A certain act might be passed despite opposition, yet that very opposition would serve to alter and remodel certain parts of it. Thus the orator, by appealing to these more friendly and more psychologically suggestible elements in the audience, would gradually set in motion the forces of what Allport terms social facilitation. Favorable responses from these hearers gradually aid him in winning over the more hostile. It is significant to note at this point that, even with the power of influence, the king could not control the house without good speakers. Sir Joshua Reynolds, the painter, once asked Burke what would happen if a minister, sure of his majority, should resolve that there should be no speaking at all on his side; and Burke's answer was that such a minister must speedily get out. Again and again North complained to the king of lack of support in the House of Commons; and in one of his gloomiest moments in the fall of 1779 he wrote that though there would be a good majority on the side of the government, yet even this majority, 'unless it is well supported by speakers, will sink in the course of the Sessions.'

CONTROL OF PUBLIC OPINION

The activities of the king's ministers were thus greatly detrimental to the correct reporting of parliamentary debates. Any attempts on the part of opposition orators to educate the public were hampered. But the king's activities in controlling public opinion were positive as well as negative. Through the columns of the London *Gazette,* official publication of the government, he and his ministers managed to supply the sort of misinformation that they wished generally believed. A search through the correspondence of William Knox, for many years editor of the *Gazette,* reveals definite information concerning official doctoring of the news. Evidently Knox was in the habit of consulting the ministers before printing each issue. Thus in 1777 North criticized one of his bulletins, saying: 'It gives a worse colour to Lord Cornwallis's march and retreat, and to the action between Col. Mawhood and the rebels, than they deserve. I hope this account will not (be) published in its present shape.' In 1781 Germaine advised Knox upon one occasion to publish as little as possible, but that since Washington was marching to Virginia, to stress the sailing of the fleet with reenforcements.

Besides the *Gazette* there was the Tory *Morning Chronicle,* equally diligent in the service of the administration. Walpole wrote in 1782 that posterity would not be able to discern a thousandth part of the lies of Bate, its editor, and of Macpherson, an administration pamphleteer. He said: 'Most things are in the newspapers now as soon as they happen, but so are ten thousand things that have not happened, and who can winnow them, but on the spot?' Walpole's distrust of newspapers inspired him to keep a whole series of journals of political events for the benefit of future historians.

Moreover the king had an excellent staff of pamphleteers to supplement the work of his periodicals. He seems to have secured the idea from Lord Bute, who first developed the project of establishing a body of political writers to defend governmental policies. Chief of this group were Dr. Samuel Johnson, dean of literary critics of his day; Edward Gibbon, historian of the decline and fall of Rome; and others, less famous but more prolific, including John Shebbeare, James Macpherson, John Lind, and Adam Ferguson. Each of these men received a pension or other reward in return for his services. Their political agility was commented upon by Fox in 1776; in America, he said, they spoke of 'peace, conciliation, and parental tenderness,' while in England the tune was 'subjugation, unconditioned submission, and a war of conquest.' [20]

Synthesis of Details Necessary.—The rhetorical critic must, then, be able to put together many historical elements and facts; he must search out the relationships among data, making of them all a meaningful pattern which is faithful to the original occurrence in time. He must have what Edwin P. Whipple ascribed to Macaulay: an eye that "is both microscopic and telescopic," conversant at once with the smaller matters as well as "the larger objects of human concern."

Before concluding this discussion, it should be noted that, whereas we have been stressing the necessity of criticizing speeches in their relation to the *whole* historical continuum of which they are but *parts,* practical as well as aesthetic considerations preclude the possibility of our avoiding all traces of analytical dissection. It is undoubtedly true that analysis—i.e., the abstracting of selected features, such as organization or delivery, from the total speech pattern—

tends to a certain extent to falsify the appraisal. But it is possible to analyze the parts, then resynthesize them, and finally produce a composite evaluation which is faithful to the organic whole. This is precisely the critic's assignment.

It is frequently alleged that an atomistic approach to speech criticism militates against competent workmanship. Assuming that the critic does not resort solely to statistical analysis, and that he does not lose sight of the total speech situation in his solicitude over arguments from authority or the nature of special figures of rhetoric, he can conduct a certain amount of analytical inquiry with profit. A driver need not know all about the pistons, cam shaft, and ignition system to run an automobile, but he does have to know about the field of operation encompassed in driving—i.e., the use of the foot pedal, accelerator, and so on. To this extent he is making an atomistic approach to his assignment. Furthermore, a complete knowledge of the technical aspects may enable him the more fully to appreciate the total operation of the vehicle. It is the same with the critic. In order to secure a judgment of the *whole* speech, the critic will have to examine certain parts of it, and be fully conversant with other parts which he does not abstract from the total setting. It is important, however, that he appreciate the parts in their relation to the whole, not in their right as entities having significance out of context.

Rewriting the Criticism of Oratory

The critical estimates of the orators will have to be reexamined and rewritten periodically. This circumstance arises, not from an alleged defect in current scholarship, but from the nature of the data with which the critic works. At no time will he have, as we have just seen, that totality of information, let alone consummate wisdom in interpretation, which will permit the preparation of definitive criticism. At best, he works with fragmentary data, and prepares his evaluations for an audience whose interests may differ sharply from those of a later generation. Just as historians find it necessary to rewrite history because of the extension of knowledge concerning past events, so the rhetorical critic, relying heavily upon historical data, must reshape and reinterpret his findings in the light of the newly discovered facts. Like the historian, the critic of public address must follow the "ever-ascending spiral" of research. However resourceful and competent his present probings into the activities of the great speakers, his work must inevitably bear the mark of preliminary inquiry. His labors will spare equally accomplished critics of tomorrow many false starts, but in no sense will he have given the final word on the complex problems of oratorical effectiveness.   Were it otherwise, the light that guides the intellectually curious to original inquiry would burn dimly, indeed.

General Summary

In this chapter we have reaffirmed the dictum that the historical constituent is of major importance in rhetorical criticism.   Speeches take place in social settings.   Hence their full understanding requires such reconstruction of past events as will help to reveal the meaning of the words used by the speaker.

Much as he might desire it, the critic is unable to accumulate the totality of data which would result in complete and wholly faithful reproduction of a past event.   However, he does the best he can with the available evidence, emphasizing those facts which are peculiarly significant to a study of the effect of the spoken word on public life.

In his attempt to re-create a situation long since dissolved by time, the critic acts both as an analyst and a synthesist.   He assembles discrete data, establishes their interrelations, and thus rebuilds, under the limitations imposed by the nature of his investigation, the pattern in which the speechmaking occurred.   He does this with full recognition of the need for comprehensiveness in research, impartiality and objectivity in the selection of details, and reliability in the establishment of causal relations among the many facts.   He can do no more; he should do no less.

PART V

THE STANDARDS OF JUDGMENT

Chapter 11

THE INTEGRITY OF IDEAS

The organization of this part of the book approximates the conventional framework of rhetorical study.[1] Rhetoricians since Aristotle have generally accepted his concept that the modes of persuasion, depending upon the effect they produce in hearers, "are of three kinds, consisting either in the moral character of the speaker or in the production of a certain disposition in the audience or in the speech itself by means of real or apparent demonstration."[2] These, in the order mentioned by Aristotle, are usually called the ethical, the pathetic or emotional, and the logical. Most rhetorical estimates are based in some degree upon this classification, many being so firmly founded upon it as to become noticeably stereotyped. This and the following two chapters will deal respectively with the logical, the pathetic, and the ethical modes of persuasion. In the conventional rhetorical scheme, these three chapters should be grouped under the general head of Invention; Chapter 14, dealing with "The Structure of Oral Discourse," embraces the idea of Disposition; Chapter 15, on "The Style of Public Address," covers the conceptions originally included under Elocution; and Chapter 16 embodies the data on Delivery. The only part of the conventional scheme not covered by this analysis is Memory, a canon no longer given individual status but usually considered (when its treatment seems relevant) under delivery.

Place of Logical Proof in Rhetoric

Students of speechmaking, whether critic or practitioner, are still divided on the question as to what degree of emphasis the so-called rational appeal should be given in the process of their art. Aristotle was impelled to write his *Rhetoric* because he felt that his predecessors had neglected to give logical materials their deserved place in speechcraft. While the *Rhetoric* surely gives emotional and ethical proof due consideration, Aristotle held to his conviction that the most important ingredient of a speech is rational demonstration through severe argumentation.

And today writers differ in their views concerning the emphasis which logical proof should receive in classroom instruction. While all are convinced of the importance of rational demonstration, there are differences of opinion concerning the chronological order in which analyses of materials, audiences, and personal situations should be undertaken by student speakers. In his essay on "Logic and Public Speaking," Wilbur E. Gilman [3] remarks that the teachers of today fall into three groups "according to which one of the three kinds of Aristotelian modes of persuasion they emphasize." He goes on to say that one group, of which Elwood Murray is a representative, emphasizes the adjustment of the speaker to his own speaking situation; another, of which Alan Monroe is a representative, emphasizes the adaptation of material to listeners; and the last group, of which James A. Winans is an exponent, stresses the speaker's search for the ideas necessary to the effective development of subject matter. Gilman then expresses his view, that the exacting analysis of subject matter should come first and hence facilitate the making of subsequent adjustments to the audience and the speaking situation.

Interrelation of Theory and Criticism.—The foregoing is another reminder that the theory and criticism of public address are inseparable. The processes of original creation and of critical evaluation of the creations of others are fundamentally alike, and interrelated. Each of us is both an originator and a critic, but more often the latter. As Albert E. Avey says:

> Most of us spend more time listening to arguments presented to us than in originating them from our own minds. And even when we have occasion to originate and construct them our own products at once stand before us for review and judgment as to their soundness and perfection.[4]

Importance of Ideas in Speechmaking.—The importance of logical materials in discourse is freely admitted. Surely, as W. T. G. Shedd once remarked, every complete speech is "the evolution of an idea." Each speaker serves as a middleman between a reasonable concept and the world of reality in which that idea can appropriately take root. It follows that a great speech must be more than what Samuel Johnson said about a good conversation, "that of which nothing is distinctly remembered, but a general effect of pleasing impression." In short, oratory to be great must deal with ideas which make a difference in the affairs of men and states.[5] Consequently, a seriousness of design characterizes the overwhelming majority of speeches which commentators and critics pronounce

significant. Most orators share John Bright's opinion that only a
sense of duty should prompt a speaker to take the platform. He
said he would not deliver a speech simply to rejoice with men in
their own good fortune. Evidently, like most great speakers, Bright
agreed with Emerson that the eloquent man is he who "is inwardly
drunk with a certain belief. . . ."

The foregoing implies that important speechmaking must deal
largely with the determination of points of fact, and the determination of expediency in proposed courses of action. In other words,
forensic and deliberative speaking have always been the two favored
branches of oratory since they presumably deal with the urgencies
of the times and hence draw most freely upon the capacities and
ingenuities of speakers. Furthermore, excepting the celebrated forensic speeches of antiquity, the greater share of remembered oratory
is of the deliberative variety.

Why great forensic speeches fail to command the interest of succeeding generations is not completely clear, but that the forensic
speaker is forgotten sooner remains a fact. Edward A. Parry has
remarked that the great lawyer is like the accomplished actor; both
occupy the stage for a brief moment, win applause, and then make
their last bow before the curtain falls. "Nothing is so elusive,"
Parry continued, "as the art of acting, unless indeed it be the sister
art of advocacy." [6] That the forensic speaker is as fully a dealer in
ideas as the deliberative is acknowledged. Severity in logical development characterizes the one as clearly as the other; and, in many
cases, no doubt, the courtroom orator is the superior.

The prominence of deliberative speaking in oratorical literature
probably results from the nature of the subject matter. While the
case at law is important, it usually is of more temporary interest and
has a more limited field of reference and application than the matter
of public expediency with which the orator deals in a deliberative
assembly. Consequently, most of the great forensic speeches remembered today contain broad principles of public conduct which tran-
scend the immediate cause to which the speeches are devoted. Thus
Lord Erskine's address in the case of Lord George Gordon, his defense of John Stockdale in a libel suit, his speech in the case of the
Dean of Asaph involving the rights of juries, and the speech in behalf of Thomas Hardy on a treason charge are all appeals to high
principles of personal and civil liberty, going well beyond the confines of the particular individual's cases. In other words, Erskine is
remembered not only as a user of sound ideas and cogent reasoning,
but as a mouthpiece of liberty and fair play for the common man.

Obviously this explanation does not alone account for the relative eclipse of courtroom as contrasted with deliberative oratory. Daniel Webster's speech in the White murder trial has no important bearing upon any profound governmental or personal doctrine, yet it remains a classic to which students return for the study of seasoned rhetoric and brilliant argument. But, in the main, the ideas which live within the memories of succeeding generations, and the ideas whose integrity is tested and appraised more often in later history, are the ones which deliberative speakers have developed in addresses on the burning issues of their time. Hence, they are ideas directed to expediency of certain conduct or action.

The great demonstrative orations, such as Lincoln's "Gettysburg Address," proclaim broad principles of human conduct which are often closely associated with purely deliberative affairs. They deal, at least in their finest representations, with noble themes, universal doctrines, expressions of man's higher aspirations. Despite this tendency toward what the classical writers would have called sublimity in expression, the truly fine demonstrative speeches grow out of and derive their genuine substance from the practical, matter-of-fact doings of men and women. They are more closely related to deliberative talk than many people suppose.

Method of Determining Integrity of Ideas

With our primary interest now focused upon the evaluation of logical content, our objective will be to determine how fully a given speech enforces an idea; how closely that enforcement conforms to the general rules of argumentative development; and how nearly the totality of the reasoning approaches a measure of truth adequate for purposes of action. As Avey expresses the matter in his consideration of argumentative analysis:

> Critical estimation consists in judging the value of a discussion as an instance of proof, the determination of how far it succeeds in showing the necessity of the truth of the contention offered, on the basis of accepted logical principles.[7]

How does the critic determine the relative integrity of ideas in a speech? The evaluation cannot be made by formula; it is a complex problem and does not yield to mechanical, rule-of-thumb treatment. However, the critic proceeds by method. And he finds that the integrity of ideas can be judged through three principal means: determination (1) of the intellectual resources of the speaker, (2) of the severity and strictness of the argumentative development, and (3) of the "truth" of the idea in functional existence.

Determining the Speaker's Intellectual Stock

While it is not true that great ideas flow only from the minds of men of corresponding intellectual stature, the relationship between cogency of thought and personal resources is sufficiently close to interest the critic. The preparation and background that the speaker brings to the process of logical invention figures strongly in the determination of argumentative soundness and integrity. Cicero believed that genius, method or art, and diligence were the three basic requisites for finding arguments; and of the three, he assigned to genius the chief place.[8]

To ascertain the factors which contribute to individual skill in logical development is admittedly difficult. In fact, John F. Genung believed that the "original discovery of the thought" was too individual to be within the scope of ordinary instruction. We can, however, point to some of the outward manifestations of inventive skill which influence the arguments men compose and deliver. These considerations will indicate, in part at least, the speaker's supply of thought and the adequacy of its support.

Both as critics and as creators of arguments, we look first to the capacity for formulation of ideas. This will contain, to use Genung's words, "a natural ability to grasp facts and ideas not as isolated or vagabond but in combination, as helpers or as goals to other facts or ideas." [9] This implies sound judgment on the part of the speaker; judgment to make fine discriminations between the essential and the nonessential; facility in making analyses of questions, to the end that significant items are held constantly in view; capacity to sense that which lies at the center of issues, rather than to develop what is tangential to them. In short, we are appraising the speaker's powers of observation, alertness, and ability in independent analysis. To the extent to which this matter concerns the preliminary formulation of argument, it may be referred to as the *prospective* aspect of logical invention.

Another closely related consideration in appraising the relative integrity of ideas in the light of personal resources is the speaker's recognition of the pressing problems of his time. After all, the reflective undertakings in which orators engage are essentially ventures in problem-solving. Such great orators of the past as Demosthenes, Burke, Webster, and Calhoun are associated with great movements in history. There were undoubtedly many other competent speakers whose names might now be indelibly inscribed upon the memory, had they been equally skilled in sensing the nature of the problems of their day, and in placing them in the context of a larger social system. One of the marks of the distinguished orator is the facility to direct intellectual energy to the manifestly urgent necessities of the moment. And, as Brand Blanshard states, "the more precisely thought can locate its objective, the less groping, the more quick and neat and effortless will be the manner of reaching for it." [10] Clearly, then, nobility of conception stamps the intellectual effort of the praiseworthy speaker. Great themes derive from momentous events, actual or impending; great speeches translate those themes into catalogues of proposed action.

In a more formal sense, the orator is appraised as a man thinking reflectively. Accordingly, the pattern of thought set forth by John Dewey and others serves as a framework for critical analysis. The presentation of a speech is a good example of a reflective experience. And so, according to the Dewey formula,[11] the speaker's logical capacities are estimated in the light of (1) his recognition of the problem which, at the moment, is disturbing or is about to disturb the *status quo;* (2) his analysis of the nature and bearing of the problem upon the social setting; (3) his fertility of mind in suggesting ideas relevant to the solution of the difficulty; (4) his acuteness in examining, through reasoning, the implications of his suggestions; and (5) the verification of his judgment following the acceptance of the most feasible solution.

Thus the speaker's knowledge and experience figure importantly in any critical estimation of his merit. Rhetoricians generally agree that a sound training—a broad familiarity with the field of knowledge—is essential to the development of an effective speaker. Cicero also used the speaker's knowledge as a criterion in his estimates of the orators; that is, he appraised orators as they conformed to his ideal theory of culture.

Recent studies rest on sound precedent, therefore, in stressing the importance of the orator's background for a full understanding of the speeches subjected to criticism. Hence, a knowledge of what Pitt studied and read, of what he actually knew about history and politics and the classics, is helpful to a fuller appreciation of his thinking. Likewise, the critic will be in a better position to understand an orator's arguments if he knows the practical experience upon which the thinking rests. The student should be interested to learn, for example, that Burke had something to do with the anony-

mous *Account of the European Settlements in America,* published in
1757; that he gained additional familiarity with American affairs
through his work on the *Annual Register;* that he heard many parliamentary speeches on the American situation; that he read many of
the pamphlets of the day; that he conferred with men who were
conversant with colonial affairs. Such data facilitate the study of
sources from which the speaker's arguments issue, and, in general,
throw light upon the developmental course of the orator's reasoning.
By themselves, they will not necessarily enable a critic to estimate
the merit of the speaker's ideas; when considered with the several
other points of judgment, they make possible a readier and more
penetrating critique of logical materials.

The prospective aspect of logical analysis also is furthered by
determining the premises from which the speaker argued. Did the
speaker exercise wisdom in selecting the basic postulates upon which
his reasoned case rests? The critic who searches out these premises
will, of course, find that their isolation can be effected only through
a thoughtful study of the historical pattern in which the speeches are
set. Not only that, but the accuracy with which the fundamental
tenets of a man's reasoning are uncovered will depend upon penetrating insight into the orator himself, his training, social conditioning, and relation to and attitude toward the complex problems
of his time. And in all of this inquiry, the critic must act dispassion-
ately and with detachment. He must survey the thought of others
in the light of conditions operative at the time.[12] Only through such
a measure of impartiality can we get at the roots of a speaker's ideas.

A cursory examination of recent studies of the orators will show
the extent to which this phase of critical inquiry can be taken.

In his careful analysis of Burke's principal speeches, H. Clay
Harshbarger [13] reveals the basic assumptions from which Burke
argued and which he so clearly enunciated and used in the development of his arguments. Harshbarger shows how Burke fortified his
reasoning on the American crisis by articulating his contentions with
these major premises. Burke, it is shown, postulated *happiness* as the
end of government. And to this claim he linked three other assumptions which served as the substructure of much of his reasoning:
(1) The means for attaining the end of happiness was expediency;
"not the narrow furthering of selfish interest, but rather the much
broader adaptation of government to the present circumstances of
the people in the attainment of which the necessity exists for large
and liberal ideas." (2) The most useful criterion for judging the
validity of the means was an appeal to the wisdom of the ancestors.

And (3) the medium in which the means was to be rendered efficacious was the Constitution of the British Empire, or the Empire itself, with the Parliament serving as the residuum of the common authority, together with other and lesser legislatures under it.

Other studies which investigate the sources and nature of the orator's logical premises may be mentioned. In his analysis of Borah's "Invention in the Speeches of the League Controversy," Waldo Braden [14] found the basic premises of thought to be *isolationism* and *nationalism*. These postulates were then traced to their source in certain of Borah's early experiences in Illinois, Kansas, and Idaho.

Roy C. McCall's analysis of the rhetorical training and invention of Theodore Parker throws considerable light upon the set of basic beliefs controlling Parker's homiletic system.

> The only rhetorically significant inheritance of Parker was a philosophical cast of mind from his father and an active religious instinct from his mother. . . . these traits were operative in determining his reading, his religious outlook, the direction of his attempts at reform, and, both directly and indirectly, his rhetorical practice.
>
> Parker himself tells us that as he grew up among the New England hills, where nature so strongly impressed him, he applied his mind early to books far beyond his age, reading 'Homer and Plutarch before I was eight. Rollins' *Ancient History* about the same time, and lots of Histories, with all the poetry I could find, Pope, Milton, Cowley, Dryden, before ten.' The family took great care that his potential powers of observation, memory, and judgment should not fail of their development and at the same time taught him 'to respect the instinctive promptings of conscience as the "voice of God in the soul of man." '
>
> Although Parker's early schooling offers nothing particularly suggestive of his later developments, his total boyhood experience combined with his inherited qualities to prepare him for his later career as ecclesiastical and social reformer.
>
> Until Parker entered Harvard Theological School in 1834, his education was largely a matter of his own reading. Even during his sojourn there books apparently held a larger place in his studies than did the lectures of his professors. Likewise were books his staple throughout life. It is appropriate, therefore, that we should give careful consideration to Parker's reading as influencing his thinking and as a process of preparation for his speaking.
>
> One who has thumbed the 20,000 volumes of the Parker library, now in a special section of the Boston Public Library, will answer the question of what Parker read with one word—everything. Upon the dusty shelves are books in thirty languages; books of history, literature, theology, philosophy, logic, mathematics, zoology, chemistry, physics, law,

biography; books rare and ancient, books that were modern in his day; books of all the great masters. Practically all of them show evidence of use, though few are annotated.

Now as to the portion of this vast array that early affected Parker's thinking: The story is most briefly told by pointing out that with a background of English literature and Greek and Roman classics he began his theological study at Harvard by entering upon a critical study of the Bible, using as authority the leading German and French transcendentalists, the English rationalists, and the English transcendentalists. In addition, he read the early church fathers, the mystics, the humanists, and the scholastic group. In such reading is easily discerned the likely bias toward transcendentalism, the tempering of rationalism, the eclecticism of contact with many schools.

Parker's more specifically rhetorical reading was in the *English State Trials,* the classical orations and books of rhetoric, Campbell's *Philosophy of Rhetoric,* Whately's *Elements of Rhetoric,* and Adams's *Lectures on Rhetoric and Oratory.* 'Here [in the *English State Trials*] and in the Greek and Latin orations I got the best part of my rhetorical culture.' Thus his rhetorical training manifests a definitely classical base, though he appears to have admired greatly some American speakers and recommends them as valuable study.

Concerning the leading ideas that motivated Parker's behavior, our first observation is that his whole philosophy was based upon his renunciation of the prevailing sensational ideology and his complete dependence upon conscience, or intuition, as 'the last standard of appeal' beyond rational processes. He summarizes the matter well thus: 'I often find I can *feel* farther than I can *see,* and accordingly I rest the great doctrines of Christianity not on Reasoning—but Reason on Intuition.'

Out of this rational-intuitive subsoil grew the following beliefs: (1) God is everywhere and always present; (2) God is infinitely powerful and perfect; (3) God reveals himself to man through nature, through reason, but most often, and most clearly, through the conscience; (4) man's purpose upon earth is to improve himself physically, intellectually, morally, spiritually, that is, in 'God-consciousness'; (5) since God operates always by natural law, revealing himself to all through natural channels, it is the preacher's function as a teacher of religion to break down false conceptions of theology and to build from the 'emotional germ' of 'feeling' and the 'Intellectual blade of thought' a rational religion of intellect, conscience, 'good deeds' and 'moral fruits,' which shall not end in the church, but *shall extend to every act of life and to every branch of social relationship.* '. . . he is to promote the application of this consciousness of religion to all the departments of human life,— individual, domestic, social, national, and universal. . . . It is idle to say the minister must not meddle with practical things. . . . he must have an eye to the business of the nation. . . .' [15]

Carroll Arnold's [16] study of "The Parliamentary Oratory of Benjamin Disraeli: 1842-1852," probes with some completeness into the inventive process of the orator. Arnold concludes that

> Experience generally and national experience particularly were the sources from which Disraeli drew the theories of statecraft which he advocated in the House. Political reforms . . . must result from the painstaking selection of the best practices of the past; hence, a State was never the product of mere abstract principles, but it was instead the evolved result of national experience.

Arnold then indicates how these principles applied and what they meant to the issues that came before the House of Commons between 1842 and 1852.

> Applied to the issues which came before the House of Commons during the decade, these principles meant in practical politics, (1) that the forms and responsibilities of the legislative and administrative sections of government must be maintained; (2) that Irish administration must be suited to the taste of social evolution prevailing there, and to the legal unity of Ireland and England; (3) that even uneconomic practices should be retained if they contributed to the strength of the imperial fabric; (4) that legislation must be based on a broad and inclusive appreciation of all social and political motives, for which the economic interpretation alone was inadequate; and (5) that reforms could not be legislated but must evolve, hence legislation to create a status for the new industrial interests was unwise, for these interests should find their privileges and responsibilities within existing social and political institutions.

The importance of such discoveries to the critic need scarcely be mentioned. With them, he is able the more accurately and deeply to probe the thinking of an orator—to push back beyond the commonplace and superficial manifestations of the orator's thought to the basic ideas which not only permeated, but determined, the line of argument used in a given case.

This section, then, simply indicates that the ideas with which an orator deals make a difference in the run of human affairs. His ideas affect other ideas and eventually large segments of the social situation react in one way or another to the impact of the concepts. The critic, searching always for the source of the speaker's reasonings as well as for the reasons themselves, tries to appraise the personal resources of the orator and tries to get at the root of the man's thinking. In that way he may begin the difficult job of determining the integrity of the logical proof. But it should be borne in mind that this step is merely preliminary to the second investigative aspect of logical analysis, namely, judging the severity and strictness of the arguments advanced by the speaker.

Testing the Argumentative Development

In passing judgment upon the logical aspect of a persuasive address, we ask the question: "Did the speaker enforce his point?" As we have previously indicated, proof may be of several kinds; but at this moment we are primarily concerned with the establishment of that measure of assent which indicates a reasonable degree of truth. Fundamentally, the constituents of logical proof are *evidence* and *argument* or reasoning. Each conforms to general rules and admits of rigorous testing.

Examining the Evidence.—Evidence is the raw material used to establish proof. It may include the testimony of individuals, personal experiences, tables of statistics, illustrative examples, or any so-called "factual" items which induce in the mind of the hearer or reader a state of belief—a tendency to affirm the existence of the fact or proposition to which the evidence attaches and in support of which it is introduced. Thus, in his attempt to establish ground for conciliation with the Colonies, Burke introduced comparative data as to the export trade of England to the Colonies in 1704 and in 1772; and he remarked: "The trade with America alone is now within less than £500,000 of being equal to what this great commercial nation, England, carried on at the beginning of this century with the whole world." Previously, he had presented figures to reveal the accuracy of this claim. And then he turned to his conclusion: "This is the relative proportion of the importance of the colonies at these two periods; and all reasoning concerning our mode of treating them must have this proportion as its basis, or it is a reasoning weak, rotten, and sophistical." [17] Likewise, in his speech of May 27, 1941, declaring an unlimited national emergency, Franklin D. Roosevelt relied upon external data when he asserted that "All freedom—meaning freedom to live and not freedom to conquer and subjugate other peoples—depends on freedom of the seas."

> Since 1799, 142 years ago, when our infant Navy made the West Indies and the Caribbean and the Gulf of Mexico safe for American ships; since 1804 and 1805, when we made all peaceful commerce safe from the depredations of the Barbary pirates; since the War of 1812, which was fought for the preservation of sailors' rights; since 1867, when our sea power made it possible for the Mexicans to expel the French Army of Louis Napoleon, we have striven and fought in defense of freedom of

the seas, freedom of the seas for our own shipping, for the commerce of our sister republics, for the right of all nations to use the highways of world trade, and for our own safety.

Here are typical displays of evidence, and upon the relevance and merit of these and allied materials will depend much of the argument's claims to integrity. The critic's chief function at this point is to test the speaker's evidence to determine whether it serves as an adequate and valid substructure of reasoning. Since the principal types of evidence used by the speaker, apart from the reference to his own authority, are statistics and testimony, we shall refer briefly to the criteria governing reliability in those divisions.

Edwin A. Burtt tells us that the problem of statistics, on the critical side, must be approached in the light of two cardinal principles.[18] The statistician must discover, and subsequently the critic must examine, "some quantitative unit in terms of which he can translate the phenomenon he is studying into a magnitude whose variations are mathematical." That is, the task involved deals with *counting;* finding out *"how much* of the phenomenon is present in the locality or under the conditions which determine [the] investigation." The second principle of statistical inquiry "is that the limits of the field within which the measurements hold should be carefully determined and clearly stated." Thus, if an investigator finds that a certain group of men gives ten per cent of its time to political interests, he should not point to general conclusions regarding the public as a whole, unless he has made the necessary checks on the limitations of his study. This brings up the whole problem of sampling, of finding out whether the instances chosen represent a systematically typical segment of the group as a whole. Burtt concludes "Wherever it is possible, each single case within the field to which the conclusion is to apply should be examined. . . ." Obviously, this is not always feasible or possible. In recent years, the public opinion polls have done much to refine statistical inquiries of this sort, so that we no longer regard accuracy of judgment in generalization as an immediate function of numbers. Through systematic sampling, remarkably accurate estimates of the public's thoughts and actions are made weekly, to the end that prediction of political developments is materially facilitated.

It follows, then, that the evaluation of statistical units requires investigation into the methods employed by the statisticians in collecting, classifying, and interpreting the data. The critic of speeches,

however, makes two judgments: one, of the speaker's wisdom in
choosing a certain body of figures; another, of the statistician's severity and accuracy in setting forth the facts from which the inferences are drawn. The tests applied to the statistics will accordingly
fall into the following categories: (1) Are the instances from which
the inference is developed sufficiently numerous to be significant?
(2) Are the units included in the investigation properly and carefully
defined? (3) Is there comparability between the things compared?
(4) Are the instances of such a character as to provide a systematically typical sample of the field as a whole? (5) Are the facts reported and classified accurately? (6) Do the statistics furnish an
index to the information desired, i.e., is the relationship clear between the conclusion derived from the figures and the conclusion
sought in the subject of the discourse? These tests, it should be
noted, relate closely to the ones employed in checking arguments
from specific cases, or generalizations. We shall refer to them later.

Much of the evidence used by speakers in support of their ideas
is of a testimonial nature. In other words, outside authorities often
furnish testimony which the speaker incorporates into his speech,
hoping thereby to give credence to his cause and plausibility to his
claims. Or he may rely mainly on his own reputation for expert-
ness to enforce his propositions. What is the value of such evidence?
How is its validity determined? Several tests serve to orient the
critic in his appraisal.

Although consistency may be the "idol of small minds," it is,
nevertheless, the guiding consideration for the critic when he appraises speech compositions. Addresses must present unified, in-
ternally consistent ideas. The parts must be consonant with one
another, producing, in the end, a composite that is logically harmonious. This means simply that the evidence used by a speaker
must not clash; what is affirmed at one point must not be denied at
another. Nor does this allow any tampering with data to fit them
to the demands of the speaker's thesis. It is assumed that if the evidence does not sustain an argument, the speaker will refrain from
developing the contention. The appeal must clearly be to the truth
of the case, not to the whim of the speaker.

The story is told of a confused witness who was testifying in
his own behalf on a charge brought against him by a neighbor. The
matter at issue involved damages for the destruction of a copper
kettle. The distraught witness presented the following case: "In
the first place, I didn't borrow the kettle. Anyway, it had a hole

in it when I got it; and, finally, it was brand new when I brought it back." Since inconsistencies of statement, or of combined facts, even though not so palpably obvious as the one in the foregoing illustration, cast suspicions upon the integrity of argument, critics will turn to some, if not all, of the following tests of evidence:

(1) Is the testimony or evidence consistent with itself and with the known laws of logical argument? (2) Is the particular authority whose testimony is used to support a contention reliable? (3) Has the authority had an opportunity to examine and observe the data from which he speaks? (4) Does he entertain any prejudices which might influence his judgment on the matter at issue? (5) Is he generally recognized as able and competent in the given field? (6) Are the facts in the testimony causally related one to the other? (7) Is the source citation or the authority specific? That is, does it indicate exactly where the testimony comes from, and whether it is first- or second-hand? (8) Does other evidence corroborate what is introduced? (9) Is the evidence recent? (10) Does the evidence satisfy the listeners?

The last test, while very important, must be considered in a specific light. It does not suggest that the speaker should use evidence, even though inadequate and faulty, provided it satisfies the hearers' demands and prejudices. On the contrary, it reminds us that evidence, however good, must be so adapted to the hearers that they will remain sensibly aware of its essential merit. The speaker alone can provide for such adaptation; he must prepare the minds of the audience for the ready acceptance of the evidence used to support the arguments. A more complete discussion of this aspect of the process of conviction will be reserved for the next two chapters.

Appraising the Argument.—We turn now to the second constituent of logical proof, namely, the argument or reasoning. Assuming that the evidence is at hand, how shall it be woven into a complete pattern? What is the nature of the elements that bind the totality of material together? The process of reasoning or argument serves as the cohesive force; through the relationships it establishes, the mind is led from the recognition of discernible facts to a conclusion.

The principal forms of discourse used by the speaker in the logical development of his ideas are exposition and argument. The distinction between them is not absolute; indeed, the two are complementary in the sense that argument depends heavily upon expository detail. Since all argument, regardless of type, must make certain ideas clear before it can lead to the fixation of belief or attitude, it follows that expositional detail is prerequisite to argumentative development.

Definition and example play important roles in exposition. Both contain power of illustration, of enlarging understanding through sharpening of verbal focus. The critic's concern with their use is limited largely to the simple inquiry: Do these instruments make the idea *clearer?*

Briefly, then, the definitions will be tested in the light of these questions: (1) Do the remarks designed to elucidate points through definition emphasize the distinguishing characteristics of the subject? (2) Do they cover the items properly included in the subject? (3) Do they exclude everything not properly included in them? (4) Do they make clear the meaning of concepts without relying upon the terms themselves or derivatives of them? (5) Do they have instant intelligibility value?

The foregoing tests represent usable instruments for determining areas of meaning. They are not to be applied with such narrow tolerances as to defeat their broader purpose. Fundamentally, definition is a process, not a fixed mould. It undergoes changes as its relationship with the general field of inquiry becomes more complex. Through definition we place a term in a series or a spectrum of meaning, and reveal how, through progressive enlargement of its relations to the field, it becomes meaningful in the unbroken continuity.

This process character of definition makes certain of the special methods of determining meaning peculiarly useful: (1) through explanation of the operational plan (how a thing works); (2) through description of function (what it does); (3) through historical exposition (how it was developed); and (4) through comparison and contrast.

As for the examples, they should conform to the spirit of these questions: (1) Do they belong in the class or form of experience which they are intended to exemplify? In other words, examples must illustrate; failing that, they lose their logical right to a place in discourse. (2) Are they described in sufficient but not too much detail to make for full and easy understanding? (3) Do they fit sensibly into the context of the speech? (4) Are they sufficiently numerous, but not so numerous as to overwhelm the listeners? Both the speaker and the critic should remember that, as a homiletician once remarked, a single lamp is worth a thousand fireflies.

When our object is not only to clarify but also to proceed from premises to conclusions through the use of issues, we use argument as the foundation of our speaking. In such cases we are resorting to inference, a process that explores proof possibilities in cases. The methods by which we conduct this process include induction and deduction.

These forms of argument are present to some extent in all thinking. To arrive at a general principle through the examination of particulars (induction), certain assumptions of a deductive sort must be used as the basis of argument. Conversely, to establish an individual truth through the medium of a universal principle (deduction), recourse must be had to induction in order to establish the universal. Consequently, these forms of argument supplement each other.

The Process of Deduction.—It is generally recognized that reasoning from a general truth to a particular conclusion (deduction) occurs most typically through the syllogism. Composed of three propositions—major premise, minor premise, and conclusion— the syllogism is not only an effective form of argument, but also a practical device for the critic in testing arguments. The principal types of syllogism are the categorical, disjunctive, and hypothetical.

The categorical syllogism defines, classifies, and asserts without qualification. Its form is represented in this example.

> All rhetoricians rely upon the classics.
> Thomas Wilson is a rhetorician.
> Therefore, Thomas Wilson relies upon the classics.

Schematically, this syllogism, with its three propositions and three terms, looks as follows:

Middle Term	Major Term
Major Premise: All rhetoricians	rely upon the classics
Minor Term	Middle Term
Minor Premise: Thomas Wilson	is a rhetorician
Minor Term	Major Term
Conclusion: Thomas Wilson	relies upon the classics.

The validity of these syllogisms can be determined through certain tests or rules which specifically relate to the categorical pattern as set forth above: (1) The syllogism must contain a major premise, a minor premise, and a conclusion. (2) It must contain three terms: major, middle, and minor. The arrangement of these terms in the propositions conforms to the scheme previously outlined. (3) The middle term of the syllogism must be distributed—i.e., used in a universal sense, meaning *all* or *every*—in at least one of the premises.

(4) To be distributed in the conclusion, the term must be distributed in one of the premises. (5) Two negative premises make impossible the drawing of a valid conclusion. (6) If one premise is negative, the conclusion must likewise be negative. (7) Negative conclusions cannot be drawn unless one premise is negative. (8) The facts alleged in the premises should be true.

In a disjunctive syllogism the major premise is a disjunctive proposition, listing alternative possibilities. Its form is as follows:

> Either overproduction or underconsumption was responsible for the postwar depression.
>
> Overproduction was not responsible.
>
> Therefore, underconsumption was responsible for the postwar depression.

When testing such an argument, we usually refer to these criteria: (1) The alternative possibilities mentioned in the major premise should be as exhaustive as the case will permit. (2) The enumerated possibilities should not overlap. (3) If the minor premise affirms one of the alternatives, the conclusion must deny the other. (4) If the minor premise denies one of the alternatives, the conclusion must affirm the other.

The last basic type of syllogism is the hypothetical, in which the principal assertion is conditioned. Complex in structure, the sentence setting forth the major premise contains an antecedent (the conditional clause) and a consequent (the main clause). This illustration brings out its structure and also suggests its relation to causal patterns of reasoning:

> If world peace is to be achieved, an international federation must be established.
>
> World peace must be achieved.
>
> Therefore, an international federation must be established.

In order to test such a syllogism, care must be taken to insure compliance with these rules: (1) If the minor premise affirms the antecedent, the conclusion must affirm the consequent. (2) If the minor premise denies the consequent, the conclusion must deny the antecedent. (3) A denial of the antecedent or an affirmation of the consequent does not make possible the realization of a reliable conclusion.

The foregoing tests, chiefly of deductive reasoning, serve both the speaker and the critic by providing guides to validity in argument. Since most of the arguments used in daily life rest upon basic

assumptions, and since many of the arguments are expressed en-
thymematically—that is, syllogistically, but with one of the premises
or the conclusion suppressed—it becomes necessary and profitable
for the critic, especially, to recast such reasoning in complete syllogistic form and then apply the appropriate tests to the pattern.

By their very nature the syllogisms set up a formal, "absolute"
standard of logical development. Irregularities in reasoning often
result from rigid adherence to such categorical, all-or-none patterns.
Therefore the critic will want to ascertain the *relative,* the *probable*
status of major deductive claims by checking them against deter-
minable criteria of causation, definition, factual verification, attendant circumstance, and related inductive techniques.

The Process of Induction.—This involves movement from particulars to a general conclusion. As a result of his observation of
specific instances or concrete facts, the speaker tries to formulate a
general conclusion or principle deriving from observed data. Chief
among the types of inductive argument are those of causal relation,
specific instance, authority, and analogy.

Arguments from causal relation establish links between particulars—by noting the impact or influence of one event upon another,
or by tracing the cause of an observed event. In the first instance,
the direction of the reasoning is from cause to effect; in the latter,
from effect to cause.

Basically, the concept of causation presupposes an interaction of
phenomena. A given event is part of an unbroken series—cause and
effect operate within a system, with certain forces impinging more
directly upon the event than others, but all occurring within a series
of happenings.

The general rules for testing causal arguments may be summed up
in these questions: (1) Is there a causal connection between the two
events? (2) Is a particular cause adequate to produce an alleged
effect? (3) Is the alleged cause adequate to produce the known
result? (4) Are there any other causes operating in such a way
as to preclude the likelihood of the known cause producing the alleged effect? (5) Have the alleged facts been verified?

Arguments from specific instance, or generalization, arrive at a
general conclusion through the examination of particular cases.
Their validity is tested in much the same way as was previously
mentioned in the discussion of statistical evidence. In other words,
we determine whether the number of instances is sufficiently large
to warrant the generalization; whether there are any negative in-

stances which invalidate the conclusion; whether the instances chosen
are typical; whether the generalizations conform to the demands of
the causal patterns implicit in their development; and whether the
facts are true as set forth.

Argument from authority proposes to establish the speaker's case
by linking an expert's testimony to the allegation contained in the
generalization. The tests of its reliability would be the same as those
for expert testimony, previously discussed.

In testing analogical reasoning, the comparison between objects
or relationships, we inquire, first, whether the points of likeness out-
weigh the points of difference. Granting that the analogy is useful
chiefly as a reinforcer or illustrator of argument, rather than as an
exacting argument in its own right, we should scrutinize penetrat-
ingly the essential features of comparability between the two objects or relationships involved in the comparison. Furthermore, we
determine whether the analogy is valid by checking the related arguments from generalization and causal relation upon which analogical
reasoning draws. And, finally, we ascertain whether the facts as
set forth in the analogy are true.

The orator's thinking is a cardinal feature of the speaking enterprise. One of the most challenging phases of the critic's function, therefore, is to determine accurately and fairly how free the
speaker's reasoning is from error, both logical and psychological. It
is patently impossible to prepare an exhaustive catalog of the many
forms of faulty thinking. But the contents of this chapter, supplemented by other common sense observations, should enable the critic
to classify, for purposes of practical convenience, the major inquiries
which will explore the adequacy and soundness of a speaker's
thinking.

Questions may be put as follows: (1) Does the speaker deal with
an adequate and reliably established body of facts? (2) Does he
proceed from assumptions and hypotheses which are neither biased
nor gratuitous? (3) Does his verbalization of ideas reveal the true
significance of his claims clearly, unequivocally? (4) Does his
analysis of the idea reveal unity of intention, internal consistency,
and a full recognition of the important as against the unimportant
elements in the discourse? (5) Does his reasoning meet the tests
of validity appropriate to the various forms of argumentative development? (6) Does he substitute emotional excitation of the hearers
for logical proof?

To sum up the whole matter, the thinking of the orator must be
characterized by features which, according to Avey,[19] can best be

suggested by this alliteration: clearness in language usage; consistency, in the sense of being free from contradiction; completeness, to the extent of providing conclusions only when adequate facts have been surveyed; consecutiveness in its order of thought presentation; and cogency, in the sense that all of the parts are held together and articulated with the main proposition.

Functional Appraisal of Ideas

Up to this point, we have dealt with two of the means by which we assess the integrity of ideas in a speech: an examination of the intellectual resources of the speaker and the testing of the arguments developed in the speech. We now turn to the last of the means to be considered in this appraisal of logical proof.

In the long run, integrity of ideas depends also upon the accuracy and potency of the intellectual conceptions in functional existence. Did the speaker's ideas take root in society and result in good for the group as a whole? Was the speaker right, as determined by an appeal to historical reality? Obviously, such a test cannot be applied to contemporary address since we do not know the turn of future events. But where time has afforded the critic perspective, where it has given him an opportunity to survey the ebb and flow of human events subsequent to the presentation of a certain speech or speeches, he is in a position to observe the impact of an idea upon the course of history.

Surely, the accuracy of an orator's vision should figure in the critic's final evaluation of the speeches. Acuity of intellect, as revealed through the orator's ability to foresee the consequences of political action, is a possession of real worth. If history confirms an orator's judgment; if future events prove the accuracy of ideas set forth by the speaker, then the critic must be impressed by the weight of such public address. The integrity of an idea can hardly be subjected to a more severe test than the practical fact that it worked, and in conformity with the speaker's predictions. This does not rule out the speech on a contemporarily "unpopular" or minority cause as faulty rhetoric. Such an address can still be evaluated in the light of other criteria. And, possibly, in the even longer run of history, it may be found to be right and true. But critics cannot find the answers to such questions by looking into a crystal ball; they cannot be expected to fold back the years still unrevealed to man.

It would seem highly significant, therefore, in the appraisal of Burke's ideas, to observe the unusual scope of political wisdom which enabled the speaker to foresee the consequences of the American crisis—consequences originally conceived in prophecy and subsequently confirmed in fact. Likewise, the vision of John Bright in anticipating and pleading the causes to which he devoted his life is remarkable in its conformity to later historical occurrence. Not alone, obviously, but to an important degree, Bright developed ideas which resulted in the repeal of the Corn Laws in 1846; the support of the North during the Civil War; the passage of the Reform Bill of 1867, and the disestablishment of the Church of England in Ireland. These are, indeed, practical measures of the worth of ideas.

Appraisal of Refutative Skill

Many great speeches depend for their excellence upon the speakers' skill at adapting arguments to the claims of their opponents. Thus evaluations of certain of Lincoln's speeches in the Illinois campaign or of Fox's addresses before the House of Commons result in large part from an assessment of the speaker's ability in refutation and rebuttal.

The critic is concerned, therefore, with determining how effectively an orator meets objections and defends his own case. Among the factors accounting for competency in this department of argumentative development—and hence serving the critic as general standards for analysis—are the speaker's ability (1) to pick out the relevant and significant points of clash; (2) to resolve the contested issues to their lowest logical denominators; (3) to reveal clearly the relation of the opponent's claims to his own; (4) to meet and overcome the salient contentions with adequate argument and evidence; and (5) through it all, to preserve the structural wholeness of the speech as a constructive enforcement of an idea.

Practical Value of Briefing

The practical task of analyzing a complete argument is often simplified by reducing the logical continuity to an outline, or brief. Whereas a sequence in reasoning may be deeply imbedded in elaborate detail or in excessively involved language, recasting of the fundamental thought in its barest form permits more careful examination of its validity and consecutiveness. Briefing has the effect of revealing the framework of arguments; it brings into sharp focus the underlying analysis upon which the logical case rests.

If we turn to one of Burke's arguments in the "Conciliation" speech, we find its basic pattern to be substantially as follows:

I. Force is an unsatisfactory method of coping with the American problem, for

    A. It is a temporary expedient.

    B. It is uncertain.

    C. It impairs the very object you seek, for

        1. The things you fight for are depreciated by the strife.

        2. It breaks the spirit of a country—and spirit made the American colonies what they are today.

    D. It is out of harmony with English colonial practice.

Such schematic representation assists the critic by laying bare the skeleton of the contention. It returns the argument to the analytical form which it originally assumed in the speaker's thinking. And when an entire speech is so briefed, the critic is in a fair position to judge the consecutiveness of the reasoning. This type of briefing has been used widely as an exercise in rhetorical training. Theodore Parker stated that a study and analysis of the arguments in the English State Trials helped him materially to get clearness of arrangement in his own speeches.

As the example from Burke's speech shows, the system of briefing rests upon a few well-established rules of outline construction. If the scheme is to serve the analyst well, it should (1) include only complete sentences expressing the speaker's judgments; (2) isolate the major points and show the relation of subordinate material to them; (3) develop sequences according to a causal or "for" relationship; (4) employ a uniform system of symbols to make clear the order of ideas in the case; and (5) express one, and only one, point under each head. Constructed thus, a brief becomes a balance sheet of the speaker's thought, and accordingly facilitates a scrutiny of the total argumentative plan of a discourse.

A Specimen Logical Analysis

Loren D. Reid's appraisal of the logical proof in Charles James Fox's speech of February 3, 1800, illustrates the manner in which certain of the foregoing principles are used in rhetorical criticism:

Pitt had presented four contentions leading to the conclusion that Bonaparte's proposals for peace should not be accepted. Briefly stated, they were: first, that France was the original aggressor and thus responsible for the war; second, that France had transgressed upon the rights of every European nation; third, that Napoleon's government, being founded upon the principles of the French revolution, was destructive, dishonest, and unstable; and finally, that England was in an advantageous position to carry on the war and should not grasp at a shadowy peace. Pitt had spoken long and convincingly, and had rooted his argument in fact. It was Fox's tremendous job, as he rose to his feet immediately after Pitt's address, to answer those arguments and to persuade the House of Commons that England should follow the path of peace, not war.

Disregarding for the moment the intellectual feat involved in replying to a five-hour speech, let us see how Fox attacked each of the four contentions. Pitt had supported his first proposition by declaring (in refutation of a previous speech) that the dismissal of the French minister was not the cause of war; that France had committed acts of hostility against the allies, which he proceeded to name; and that she had issued a decree which imperilled the safety of Europe. His method of argument was that of specific instance. Fox's handling of this argument proceeds from a much more comprehensive view of the whole situation. Realizing that the basis of peace should be judged by conditions in 1800, not 1792, he declared that Pitt's detailed descriptions of the origins of the war 'are nothing to the present purpose, and ought not to influence the present feelings of the House.' It is idle employment to consider the origin of the war, since men should contemplate only 'the means of putting an end to it.' But since the argument had been made, and especially since it had been supported by so much evidence, it was necessary to attack it. This Fox did, using the argumentative method of showing that the effect (the beginning of the war) was not due to the alleged cause (aggression by France) but to other causes.

Before showing these other causes, Fox attacks Pitt's alleged causes. As for the decree directed against Europe, Fox declared that Pitt takes this too seriously (alleged cause not capable of producing effect). If you did not like this decree, he said in effect, you should have demanded an explanation; if the explanation was not satisfactory, you should say so at the time. Instead of this you summarily dismissed the French minister. Did you not realize that, according to the terms of a previous treaty with France, this act of dismissal was itself tantamount to a declaration of war? This would show that England was the original aggressor, not France; and thus the cause of the war is shown to be acts of England, rather than of France. Furthermore, England's allies were equally guilty of aggression; they made a public declaration promising to aid the king of France in establishing a monarchical government, agreeing to furnish armed force if necessary. If two powers made such a statement regarding England (argument from analogy) would not the English feel that their peace was threatened? Thus Fox established his point—attacking Pitt's reasoning by showing the war was due not to the alleged cause but to other causes, and, by establishing those other causes, completely refuting the validity of Pitt's conclusion. Argument from authority (reference to documentary material), argument from analogy, and specific instance are all employed in establishing this contention. Fox could indeed speak fluently and effectively on this point because, as has been seen, the belief that France was not the original aggressor was firmly fixed in his mind long before this speech.

Pitt had further shown that France had transgressed upon the rights of European nations, a contention which he supported by enumerating a number of specific instances. But again Fox based his answer upon the implications of Pitt's argument rather than the argument itself. Admitting that France's behavior in these instances was probably unjustifiable (with the exception of the Sardinia affair), he thought that England should not have stood idly by and countenance the behavior without doing anything to prevent it. But he did not believe that this was a valid reason for rejecting Bonaparte's proposals for peace. Pitt's point was really this: England should not enter into a treaty with nations which had behaved badly. To this Fox declared: 'If we must not treat with the French on account of the iniquity of their former transactions, ought we not to be as scrupulous of connecting ourselves with other powers equally criminal?' He then proceeded to cite instances of atrocities committed by England's allies.

Pitt's third contention was directed against the French government and the character of its leader, Bonaparte. The government was dishonest and unstable; Napoleon could not be trusted. He supported this contention by citing facts of general belief, and by enumerating instances of Napoleonic behavior. Fox's answer was weak. He attempted a defense of Bonaparte, pointing out that he had made reforms in the French government. It was to Bonaparte's interest to make peace because, having tasted the glories of war, he should be eager to enjoy the fruits of peace. This, of course, was mere assertion. Finally, he fell back upon his argument that the government of France was no worse than the government of England; that Bonaparte's treatment of European nations was no more despotic than England's treatment of Ireland.

Pitt concluded his speech by declaring that England was in a position to carry on the war, that France was beginning to weaken, and that England should not grasp at a shadow of peace, but wait for the real thing. Fox attacked this contention at the very beginning of his speech—showing his ability to answer argument immediately and on the spot—by declaring that Pitt had told the house this same thing many times before, and that he had always been wrong. Fox returns to this argument later in the speech, when he concludes that there is no good reason for delay; that in the past England has not benefited by postponing peace; and that to continue the war will cost unnecessary men and money and may result in a far less advantageous position to treat for peace. His most effective reply to this contention was, however, through use of pathetic rather than logical proof; it was in this connection that he spoke of the folly of 'pausing,' as pointed out just above.

Both weak and strong factors may be pointed out in Fox's use of logical proof. An important weakness is found in viewing the argumentative structure as a whole. The component parts of the speech are not effectively arranged; Fox tends to present part of one argument, then to take up a second, and later return to the first. From the point of view of refutation the speech is stronger. Fox shows refutative skill in tracing Pitt's arguments back to their fundamental implications, and in showing the weakness of those implications in the light of new evidence, using specific instance, causal relation, authority, and analogy to support his contentions.

Factors of effectiveness in his logical proof—and the speech suffers in comparison with previous speeches discussed—are probably traceable to the fact that he was compelled to make an immediate reply to Pitt, and to his reluctance and unwillingness to speak. 'When one does a thing . . . against one's inclination it must be expected that it will be ill done.' [20]

The Ultimate Objective of Logical Analysis

Our discussion suggests that logical proof should achieve Truth as the final desideratum. As John Lawson said, "Rhetoric must be the Handmaid of Truth." The Emersonian dictate of making the orator "the vehicle of truth" is an ideal state to which we can hopefully aspire, rather than an easily attainable goal. The orator, who deals with social problems and hence with matters involving value judgments and variant interpretations, can do no more than earnestly strive for a logical coherence which in the long run may approximate truth.

Although in testing the arguments for validity we may find them acceptable, we are ever mindful that their validity is no necessary guarantee of their truth. What the orator strives to achieve in reasoning on social and political matters is a high degree of certainty, or at least of probability. The nature of the orator's art and the materials with which he deals require reliance upon the probable. He cannot hope to get all of the evidence, and so his judgments are constantly subject to revision.

Since the orator himself operates under limitations imposed by his subject and his data, the critic must prepare his analysis with full recognition of the limitations. As Avey remarks in *The Function and Forms of Thought,* good judgment demands

. . . no greater certainty of proof in a given case than the data available and the nature of the field of discussion warrant. To be satisfied with little rigor in mathematics would be inferiority in intellectual standards. But equally to demand dogmatic certainty in practical realms bespeaks a bigotry which is reprehensible. A sense of fitness must operate here as elsewhere.[21]

Final Determinant of Logical Criticism

On last analysis, the quality of the criticism resulting from an examination of logical proof is proportionate to the critic's understanding and knowledge of the subject under discussion. Arguments require scrutiny that goes beyond the mere determination of validity. Judgment must operate in the critical function; this implies the necessity of appraising not only the validity of the line of reasoning, but also of the material content—the facts—upon which the speech is based. In the words of Avey:

The best equipment for significant criticism must be thorough knowledge of the principles of logic and methodology together with an extensive acquaintance with the facts of the field under discussion. And that discussion will rank highest under criticism which realizes most fully the requirements of formal validity and uses most significantly the facts which are relevant to the issue and objectively true.[22]

Chapter 12

EMOTION IN SPEECH

The Problem of Emotion in Discourse

Commenting on the purpose of council meetings, a character in a recent novel observes that it is not proper to force decisions through the stultifying influence of emotional appeals. Action so achieved, according to this claim, is won by falsity and trickery. Such observations are both important and provocative, for they suggest another of the persistent problems in rhetoric: the place of emotional appeal in the process of persuasion. Much has been written about it; schools of thought have debated the question; and pedagogical technique since antiquity has been moulded by the relative emphases accorded the concept from period to period. To this day, the matter has not been resolved to the satisfaction of all students, although all realize the significance of emotional appeal in speechmaking.

The problem with which we are now concerned is basically clear. It assumes that at least two forms of expression operate in rhetoric: the one appeals to the intellect while the other addresses the emotions. As John Ward put it: ". . . bare conviction is not sufficient for many persons, to excite them to action. They will acquiesce in the truth of a thing, which they cannot contradict, or will not give themselves the trouble to examine; and at the same time remain unconcerned to prosecute it." [1] Joseph Priestley looked upon emotional proof as an energizer and expediter of conduct: "The genuine and proper use of the passions undoubtedly is to rouze men to just and vigorous action upon every emergency, without the slow intervention of reason." [2]

When we come to analyze the differences between the two types of appeal, we run into difficulties—difficulties both of definition and interpretation. Common sense tells us, of course, that both thought and feeling function in public address; that is, the notion of communication presupposes both an ideational and an emotional state in the speaker. Demonstration of an idea to others has its root in feelings and attitudes which result from the speaker's having, either directly or vicariously, experienced the thought. As John K. Gard-

357

iner says: "When you undertake to explain, you must put into your words the warmth of your personal interest. . . . If you are arguing, you must be not only clear but moving. . . ." [3]

The problem affects the listeners no less than the speaker. They are the respondents in the rhetorical process; their reaction is, to the speaker, an all-important consideration. To affect them as human beings requires more than error-free demonstration; there must also be judicious appeal to the feelings. The achievement of the goal of effective response therefore draws upon the two offices of rhetoric which, though blended, may yet be regarded separately. The first of them, says Thomas De Quincey, is "the literature of *knowledge;* the other, the literature of *power.* The function of the first is—to *teach;* the function of the second is—to *move:* the first is the rudder; the second, an oar or a sail." [4] The metaphor is well chosen; for, indeed, the emotional counterparts of rhetoric may with propriety be said to furnish the dynamic or the energizing force which moves speech and writing toward the goal of readier acceptance. In general, we may agree with George Campbell that when a speaker attains a rational end without the emotional, he is often

> . . . as far from his purpose as before. You have proved beyond contradiction that acting thus is the sure way to procure such an object. I perceive that your reasoning is conclusive, but I am not affected by it. Why? I have no passion for the object. I am indifferent whether I procure it or not. You have demonstrated that such a step will mortify my enemy. I believe it: but I have no resentment, and will not trouble myself to give pain to another. Your arguments evince that it would gratify my vanity. But I prefer my ease. Thus passion is the mover to action, reason is the guide. [5]

The foregoing warns us that the process of persuasion is complex, and that the materials and methods employed to achieve the end of influencing listeners are varied. One of the modes of persuasion, the logical, has already been discussed. But as this discussion indicates it is not enough, by itself, to complete the task of inducing belief or action. So we turn to another mode, traditionally called the pathetic or the emotional. Concerning this, Aristotle reminds us that "proofs may be conveyed through the audience, when it is worked up by the speech to an emotional state." Then follows the essential point, that there is "a wide difference in our manner of pronouncing decisions, according as we feel pleasure or pain, affection or hatred. . . ." [6] Briefly, then, pathetic proof includes all those materials and devices calculated to put the audience in a frame of mind suitable for the reception of the speaker's ideas.

It is of interest to recall that Aristotle acknowledged the value of pathetic proof, while at the same time expressing suspicious concern over its injudicious use; and he was disturbed by the evident stress placed upon it by his predecessors. Thus he says, at the beginning of his treatise, that the only "true constituents" of the rhetorical art are the *logical* proofs; all others are merely accessory.[7]

Much of the adverse criticism of public speaking as an art, from before Aristotle's time up to the present day, has grown out of people's fears of the orator's exercising demagogic influence. Critics have viewed apprehensively the control which an orator can exercise over audiences by appealing to their feelings. It has been held, and with justification, that an irresponsible orator can, through emotional manipulation, induce belief or action—all without the support of factual data or with the data distorted and warped to suit his sinister design. As Plato once charged, orators can deal in words without knowledge. But these strictures do not reject the necessity and ethical wisdom of using emotional proof; rather, they illustrate the need for honest, high-principled reliance upon it as a means of making truth the more palatable, and, accordingly, the more decisive in the social process. Recognizing with A. K. Rogers[8] that the "normal human mind is not content merely to be logical and realistic," and that "it craves food for its emotions also," we shall now turn to a more direct analysis of the constituents of emotional proof as they function in the process of speechmaking.

Analysis of Emotional Mode of Persuasion

Emotional proof, as we have just indicated, is designed to put the listeners in a frame of mind to react favorably and conformably to the speaker's purpose. Assuming the purpose to be scrupulously honorable, to the speaker's best knowledge, we may ask: What is the broad meaning of this concept of emotional proof as a mode of persuasion? The discussion of three related inquiries should throw some light upon the whole matter: (1) the principle of audience adaptation, (2) the practical applications of the principle, and (3) the assumptions underlying the total concept.

Principles of Audience Adaptation and Adjustment

Aristotle observed that a speech was composed, or grew out of the interaction, of three elements: the speaker, the subject, and the persons addressed. He added that of the three elements, it was the last, the audience, that determined a speech's end or object. Never seriously questioned, this pronouncement has almost become a rhetorical axiom. It announces the fact that, for the speaker, the audience is the most important element in the situation and that, if he is to be effective, the speaker must adjust both himself and his ideas to it. The basic consideration, then, is *adaptation,* or adjustment to the variables of human behavior as found in a specific group of hearers. Even though he wished and were able to present the Truth as he saw it in purely logical form, he could not do so, owing, perhaps, to what John Lawson calls "the Imperfection of Mankind." "If our Hearers were always serious, attentive, knowing, and unprejudiced," Lawson went on, "we should have nothing to do but to lay Truth before them in its own genuine Shape; But as Men actually are, we find it necessary, not only to shew them what is right, but to make Use of all the Skill we have, to induce them stedfastly to behold it." [9] Therefore speakers adapt what they have to say to the peculiar audience conditions facing them.

Such adaptation does not imply mechanical or arbitrary orientation simply for the sake of rhetorical expediency. Speakers can make adjustments to hearers without distorting, suppressing, or in any way vitiating the integrity of their ideas; but practical wisdom decrees that they expound their views with forethought of the emotional makeup of the audience, with full recognition of the possible reactions of the group to the presentation. A critic of oratory, writing in the *Edinburgh Review,* once declared there is never a speech "which does not somehow give to its hearers the feeling that the arguments are used not because they are sound but because they fit the understandings of those to whom they are addressed, that the sentiments are not those of the speaker but simply what best suit the emergency. . . ." [10] The imputation here is manifestly false, as the record of distinguished British and American oratory attests, but that speakers attempt to adapt their ideas to hearers is unquestionably true, and thoroughly wholesome. Were it otherwise, critics would find even more to censure in the annals of public address. Whether we like it or not, some truth inheres in Cicero's dictum that "mankind makes far more determinations through hatred, or love, or desire, or anger, or grief, or joy, or hope, or fear, or error, or some other affection of mind, than from regard to truth, or any settled maxim, or principle of right, or judicial form, or adherence to the laws." [11] It is the orator's task to link the truth to man's emotional nature so as to insure the most responsible beliefs and actions consistent with human limitations. This implies, as Alexander Bain remarks, that the course of action "shall be so described, or expressed, as to coincide, or be identified, with the active impulses of the individuals addressed, and thereby command their adoption of it by the force of their own natural dispositions." [12] It is the critic's job to appraise the orator's success in effecting that union.

So far, our discussion has dealt largely with the more general considerations relative to pathetic proof. But the critic, like the speaker himself, must approach this problem in a practical way. The question that arises, therefore, is: How does the speaker make necessary adjustments to his hearers in order to dispose them favorably toward his ideas and purposes? The answer necessarily deals with the factors of audience analysis.

Speech is plainly an instrument of social control whose function is to bring about adjustment and coordination of the social body. In its serious operation in the practical world, it should not be a medium for the realization of personal achievement, exhibition, or development. The range of its effective use is limited to situations in which there are people whose conduct can be controlled or influenced by words and actions.

The critic is interested in determining the extent of the speaker's control over his audience. Recognizing that no one is able to gain complete mastery over listeners, the critic looks to the speaker's facility and competence in handling the two aspects of audience analysis: analysis of the group prior to the delivery of the speech and audience adjustment during the presentation of the address.

The preanalysis of an audience is designed to furnish the speaker with information that will enable him to adapt his material to the hearers. This is a purely investigative undertaking which the speaker conducts prior to his talk, and upon the data of which he relies for guidance in composing the speech. So far as the critic is concerned at this point, the question requiring resolution is: To what extent, and with what measure of success, did the speaker adapt himself and his message to the ascertainable facts relating to the composition of the audience? In other words, did the speaker evince an intelligent understanding of the nature of the problem, and did he apply that insight to the practical task of disposing his hearers in his behalf?

The lines of study bearing relevantly upon this inquiry are manifold. Each speech situation has unique features that demand individual analysis. But, by and large, the critic will try to determine how fully the speaker took the following audience characteristics into account in the preparation and presentation of his speech: (1) age level; (2) sex; (3) intellectual and informational status with regard to the subject; (4) the political, social, religious, and other affiliations; (5) the economic status; (6) known or anticipated attitude toward the subject; (7) known or anticipated prejudices and predispositions; (8) occupational status; (9) known interest in the subject; (10) considerations of self-interest in the subject; and (11) temper and tone of the occasion. The general objective, it will be seen, is to find out how completely the speaker adapts his remarks within the limitations imposed by the particular audience situation.

Another important phase of this matter is the adjustment that the speaker makes to his hearers *during* the speech. Here we are dealing either with the response he makes to such overt behavior as applause or heckling, or to the intangibly tacit reactions indicating degrees of satisfaction or dissatisfaction with the proceedings. Since the critic frequently deals with speeches which he did not hear, he must necessarily rely upon texts which, at their best, serve as unsatisfactory if not wholly unreliable indicators of these subtle reactions. In this particular, therefore, he operates under several restrictive conditions.

Practical Applications of the Foregoing Principles

The foregoing observations have their roots in common soil. They posit the thesis that the speaker must have penetrating insight into the human emotions; that he must be conversant with the motivating elements that energize behavior, be it belief or action. Since antiquity, rhetoricians have regarded a knowledge of the emotions, or of the soul, as an indispensable condition to competency in speaking. As Plato remarks in the *Phaedrus:* "Since the power of speech is that of leading the soul, it is necessary that he who means to be an orator should know how many kinds of soul there are. . . ." [13] Aristotle, whose remarks on the emotions still make eminently good sense after these many years, believed that the only effective way of considering pathetic proof was through an analysis of emotional behavior. So he analyzed the several emotions in the light of (1) the conditions under which people assume the particular emotion; (2) the objects of it; and (3) the causes which induce the state.

As to the practical wisdom that should guide the speaker in his attempts to induce emotional states, the rhetoricians have been generous in their counsel. Cicero was explicit in urging the speaker not to hasten into pathetic portions of the speech before making all points luminously clear. Men are desirous, he remarked, first to learn

... the very point that is to come under their judgment; nor, when you have entered upon that track, are you suddenly to diverge from it; for you are not to suppose that as an argument is understood as soon as it is stated, and a second and a third are then desired, so you can with the same ease move compassion, or envy, or anger, as soon as you make the attempt. Reason itself confirms an argument which fixes itself in the mind as soon as it is delivered; but that sort of eloquence does not aim at instructing the judge, but rather at agitating his mind by excessive emotion, which no one can produce unless by fulness and variety and even copiousness of language, and a proportionate energy of delivery. Those, therefore, who speak either with brevity, or in a low submissive strain, may indeed inform the judge, but can never move him, an effect on which success altogether depends.[14]

John Lawson urged speakers not to attempt pathetic excursions on subjects undeserving of such efforts; to use emotional appeals, not as substitutes for reason, but as adjuncts to it; to make emotional appeals short. "Seek not to keep long in Motion a Spring formed for quick, but short Action." The speaker should conceal the attempt to play upon the feelings, for emotion should be perceived only by its effects; and he should avoid the excessive use of pathetic proof before an audience which is clearly unmoved.[15]

Hugh Blair laid down rules similar to Lawson's. Said Blair:

The first is to consider carefully, whether the subject admit the Pathetic, and render it proper; and if it does, what part of the Discourse is the most proper for attempting it. To determine these points belongs to good sense; for it is evident, that there are many subjects which admit not the Pathetic at all, and that even in those that are susceptible of it, an attempt to excite the passions in the wrong place, may expose an Orator to ridicule. All that can be said in general is, that if we expect any emotion which we raise to have a lasting effect, we must be careful to bring over to our side, in the first place, the understanding and judgment. The hearers must be convinced that there are good and sufficient grounds for their entering with warmth into the cause. They must be able to justify to themselves the passion which they feel; and remain satisfied that they are not carried away by mere delusion. Unless their minds be brought into this state, although they may have been heated by the Orator's discourse, yet, as soon as he ceases to speak, they will resume their ordinary tone of thought; and the emotion which he has raised will die entirely away. . . .

In the second place, Never to set apart a head of a discourse in form, for raising any passion; never give warning that you are about to be pathetic; and call upon your hearers, as is sometimes done, to follow you in the attempt. This almost never fails to prove a refrigerant to passion. It puts the hearers immediately on their guard, and disposes them for criticizing, much more than for being moved. The indirect method of making an impression is likely to be more successful, when you seize the critical moment that is favourable to emotion, in whatever part of the discourse it occurs, and then, after due preparation, throw in such circumstances, and present such glowing images, as may kindle their passions before they are aware. . . .

In the third place, It is necessary to observe, that there is a great difference between showing the hearers that they ought to be moved, and actually moving them. . . .

In the fourth place, The only effectual method is, to be moved yourselves. There are a thousand interesting circumstances suggested by real passion, which no art can imitate, and no refinement can supply. There is obviously a contagion among the passions. . . .

In the fifth place, It is necessary to attend to the proper language of the passions. We should observe in what manner any one expresses himself who is under the power of a real and a strong passion; and we shall always find his language unaffected and simple. It may be animated, indeed, with bold and strong figures, but it will have no ornament or finery. He is not at leisure to follow out the play of Imagination. His mind being wholly seized by one object, which has heated it, he has no other aim, but to represent that in all its circumstances, as strongly as he feels it. . . .

In the sixth place, Avoid interweaving anything of a foreign nature with the Pathetic part of Discourse. Beware of all digressions, which may interrupt or turn aside the natural course of the passion, when once it begins to rise and swell. Sacrifice all beauties, however bright and showy, which would divert the mind from the principal object, and which would amuse the imagination, rather than touch the heart. Hence comparisons are always dangerous, and generally quite improper, in the midst of passion. Beware even of reasoning unseasonably; or at least, of carrying on a long and subtle train of reasoning on occasions when the principal aim is to excite warm emotions. . . .

In the last place, Never attempt prolonging the Pathetic too much. Warm emotions are too violent to be lasting. Study the proper time of making a retreat; of making a transition from the passionate to the calm tone; in such a manner, however, as to descend without falling, by keeping up the same Strain of Sentiment that was carried on before, though now expressing it with more moderation. Above all things, beware of straining passion too far; of attempting to raise it to unnatural heights. Preserve always a due regard to what the hearers will bear; and remember, that he who stops not at the proper point; who attempts to carry them farther in passion, than they will follow him, destroys his whole design.[16]

Although but a few of the practical hints which rhetoricians have set down for the use of speakers, these quotations suggest some of the lines of thinking that must guide the critic in his investigation. Emotional appeal has frequently been linked with the concept of arrangement. Thus it was deemed more appropriate and effective to concentrate the pathetic elements in certain parts of the speech, preferably in the introduction and conclusion. Not that emotional details were to be excluded elsewhere; but the tacit assumption remained that their influence would be greater if used at appropriate times and in strategic places. Cicero remarks that while "solicitation and excitement" produce significant effects in other parts of the speech, "their proper place is chiefly in the exordium and the peroration"; but, he adds, even "to make a digression from what you have proposed and are discussing, for the sake of exciting the passions, is often advantageous." [17] Admitting that pathetic appeals are peculiarly effective in the peroration, Quintilian states that they "are admissible also in other parts." [18] And Blair urges speakers to determine carefully "what part of the Discourse is the most proper" for attempting emotional persuasion. We see, then, that pathetic proof, though properly a division of rhetorical invention, is also considered an aspect of disposition. This reminds us of the indivisibility of the elements of rhetoric; and of the necessity for the critic to look upon a speech in its entirety, a Gestalt, which, though reducible to parts for reasons of practical convenience, is nevertheless to be appraised as a totality.

The speaker is usually considered an interpreter of the mood or emotional state which he proposes to induce in the hearers. "Be yourself possessed with the Passion you would excite," wrote John Lawson. In the main, the observation is plausible. The point nevertheless is highly controversial as the varying opinions of great actors indicate. But that the speaker must competently simulate the emotional state—even though it does not take complete possession of him—is admitted by many writers. Cicero remarks:

> Nor is it possible that the judge should feel concern, or hate, or envy, or fear in any degree, or that he should be moved to compassion and tears, unless all those sensations which the orator would awaken in the judge shall appear to be deeply felt and experienced by the orator himself.[19]

Simulated or feigned emotion is by definition synthetic; only the most accomplished actor can give it a plausibility that induces confidence. But great orators, speaking on significant issues, are not on display as performers. Their histrionics are accessories. Exhibitionism in speech is not a congenial ally of responsibility of statement.

Everything we have said so far points to the patent conclusion that feelings require delicate handling. Rogers once remarked, "it is seldom safe to try to commandeer them"; the record of distinguished oratory testifies to the wisdom of that comment. Excepting the demagogues who arrogate to themselves a monopoly over the emotional states of their subject peoples, and usually find that such high-handed attempts lead to an early reversal—excepting the charlatans, we repeat, the great orators seem wisely to have recognized the extremely delicate balance between the emotional *status quo* and the one they hope to excite.

Assuming the proper conditions, the appeals that speakers can make are manifold. Men are excited to belief or action by different motives at different times. Since the state of affectivity of hearers varies with any number of conditions, ranging from the nearness of a due date for tax payments to the time of day at which an appeal is made, it obviously is impossible to enumerate all the motivating agents. As a part of his psychological analysis, Aristotle postulated happiness as the end of man's efforts; and to facilitate the speaker's task of disposing hearers in his favor, he listed the constituent parts of happiness through which appropriate appeals might be directed. The list included: good birth, plenty of friends, good friends, wealth, good children, plenty of children, happy old age, health, beauty, strength, large stature, athletic prowess, fame, honor, good luck, and virtue.[20] Later, he analyzed the emotions—those states that "are attended by pain and pleasure and produce a change or difference in our attitude as judges."[21] The feelings or emotions which impressed him as being most influential were: anger, calmness, friendship, enmity, hatred, fear, confidence, shame, shamelessness, kindness, unkindness, pity, indignation, envy, and emulation.

Contemporary analyses of the motivating appeals are largely derivatives of the Aristotelian classification. Thus A. E. Phillips[22] speaks of the things that "mankind desires" and calls the inducing agents "impelling motives." He classifies them as self-preservation, property, power, reputation, affections, sentiments, and tastes.

Corollaries of the motives mentioned by Phillips include appeals to patriotism, fear, social responsibility, fair play, expediency, personal honor, family life, self-assertion, social recognition, and social approval.

Examples of the Use of Motivating Materials.—Instances from public speeches in which such or similar appeals figured are found at every turn. In Franklin D. Roosevelt's speech of December 29, 1940, we find a good example of emotional proof directed to the motives of security and self-preservation:

> Some of our people like to believe that wars in Europe and in Asia are of no concern to us. But it is a matter of most vital concern to us that European and Asiatic war-makers should not gain control of the oceans which lead to this hemisphere. . . .
>
> Does anyone seriously believe that we need to fear attack anywhere in the Americas while a free Britain remains our most powerful naval neighbor in the Atlantic? And does anyone seriously believe, on the other hand, that we could rest easy if the Axis powers were our neighbors there? If Great Britain goes down, the Axis powers will control the continents of Europe, Asia, Africa, Australasia, and the high seas—and they will be in a position to bring enormous military and naval resources against this hemisphere. It is no exaggeration to say that all of us in the Americas would be living at the point of a gun—a gun loaded with explosive bullets, economic as well as military. We should enter upon a new and terrible era in which the whole world, our hemisphere included, would be run by threats of brute force, and to survive in such a world, we would have to convert ourselves into a militaristic power on the basis of war economy.

Charles James Fox appealed to the wisdom of expediency and fair play when, in his speech on the rejection of Bonaparte's overtures, he said:

> If this war of reproach and invective is to be countenanced, may not the French with equal reason complain of the outrages and horrors committed by the powers opposed to them? If we must not treat with the French on account of the iniquity of their former transactions, ought we not to be as scrupulous of connecting ourselves with other powers equally criminal? Surely, sir, if we must be thus rigid in scrutinizing the conduct of an enemy, we ought to be equally careful in not committing ourselves, our honor, and our safety, with an ally who has manifested the same want of respect for the rights of other nations. Surely, if it is material to know the character of a power with whom you are about only to treat for peace, it is more material to know the character of allies with whom you are about to enter into the closest connection of friendship, and for whose exertions you are about to pay. Now, sir, what was the conduct of your own allies to Poland? Is there a single atrocity of the French, in Italy, in Switzerland, in Egypt, if you please, more unprincipled and inhuman than that of Russia, Austria, and Prussia, in Poland? [23]

An excellent example of oratorical power which capitalized upon the distinction between logical and emotional presentation is found in the work of Sam Adams. James Truslow Adams calls him "the greatest master (excepting Bryan) in manipulating the masses whom America has ever seen . . ."[24] Commenting on the techniques used by the merchants and by Adams, the historian appraises the "inflammable material" with which the fiery orator worked. Using slogans—the ever popular and effective tool of the propagandist— Adams proceeded to create a state of mind conformable to his beliefs. As our analyst remarks:

> While the merchants were busy pointing out to their London correspondents that the new laws would hurt the business of all alike, Adams at once struck boldly out to inflame the passions of the crowd by threatening that it was to be reduced to the 'miserable state of tributary slaves,' contrasting its freedom and moral virtue with the tyranny and moral degradation of England. He proclaimed that the mother country was bent on bringing her colonies to a condition of 'slavery, poverty and misery,' and on causing their utter ruin, and dinned into the ears of the people the words 'slavery and tyranny' until they assumed a reality from mere reiteration. His political philosophy was eagerly lapped up by a populace smarting under hard times and resentful of colonial even more than imperial conditions of the moment.[25]

Fundamental Assumptions Underlying the Concept of Pathetic Proof

Having dealt with the adaptation of materials to hearers and with the practical applications of the concept to audience situations, we shall now consider the underlying assumptions of both inquiries. It is necessary first to examine the basic postulate that language is capable of performing a dual function of appealing both to the rational and to the emotional nature of man. This is a fundamental distinction, upon the validity of which must inevitably rest much of the traditional theory concerning pathetic proof.

Although rhetoricians have always considered the varying uses of language in different contexts, they have not given the matter as full attention as have the semanticists and their disciples during the past decade. The development of the so-called science of meanings has placed increasing emphasis upon words as multiedged instruments. The effect of words in a particular place varies with the conditions of the moment. Accordingly, words have both *referential* and *emotive* value. While this distinction is not completely adequate, it helps to illustrate the functional bearing of certain words in certain places. I. A. Richards indicates that words may be used for "the sake of the references they promote" or for "the sake of the attitudes and emotions which ensue." [26] He then remarks that in the case of the former (the referential) there is need for precision and clearly established relations—in short, for what we would call logical development. On the other hand, the emotive words may not make up a wholly logical sequence and yet be peculiarly effective. [27] Poetic or emotional language uses words in such relationships as will help to objectify fresh meanings.

Many speeches illustrate how referential and emotive materials overlap. One example will serve to bring out the point. In his speech of May 27, 1941, in which he proclaimed the existence of an unlimited national emergency, Franklin D. Roosevelt outlined the steps which the nation had taken to meet the growing threat of Naziism:

> The first and fundamental fact is that what started as a European war has developed, as the Nazis have always intended it should develop, into a war for world domination.
>
> Adolf Hitler never considered the domination of Europe as an end in itself. European conquest was but a step toward ultimate goals in all the other continents. It is unmistakably apparent to all of us that unless the advance of Hitlerism is forcibly checked now, the Western Hemisphere will be within range of the Nazi weapons of destruction.
>
> For our own defense we have accordingly undertaken certain obvious necessary measures:
>
> First, we have joined in concluding a series of agreements with all the other American republics. This further solidified our hemisphere against the common danger.
>
> And then, a year ago, we launched, and are successfully carrying out, the largest armament production program we have ever undertaken.
>
> We have added substantially to our splendid navy, and we have mustered our manpower to build up a new army which is already worthy of the highest traditions of our military service.
>
> We instituted a policy of aid for the democracies—the nations which have fought for the continuation of human liberties.
>
> This policy had its origin in the first month of the war, when I urged upon the Congress repeal of the arms embargo provisions in the old Neutrality Law. In that message of September, 1939, I said, 'I should like to be able to offer the hope that the shadow over the world might swiftly pass. I cannot. The facts compel my stating, with candor, that darker periods may lie ahead.'
>
> In the subsequent months, the shadows did deepen and lengthen.

And the night spread over Poland, Denmark, Norway, Holland, Belgium, Luxembourg and France.

In June, 1940, Britain stood alone, faced by the same machine of terror which had overwhelmed her allies. Our Government rushed arms to meet her desperate needs.

In September, 1940, an agreement was completed with Great Britain for the trade of fifty destroyers for eight important off-shore bases.

And in March, 1941, this year, the Congress passed the Lend-Lease Bill and an appropriation of $7,000,000,000 to implement it. This law. realistically provided for material aid 'for the government of any country whose defense the President deems vital to the defense of the United States.'

Our whole program of aid for the democracies has been based on hard-headed concern for our own security and for the kind of safe and civilized world in which we wish to live. Every dollar of material that we send helps to keep the dictators away from our own hemisphere. And every day that they are held off gives us time to build more guns and tanks and planes and ships.

Here we see how a straightforward summary of data may take on emotional value. Technically, this is historical background material designed chiefly to acquaint us with the facts. Yet the words in this context and under the conditions of the moment take on affective value as well. The result is that the factual items establish a presumption in favor of Roosevelt's thesis, and predispose the minds of the hearers to the more ready acceptance of his beliefs.

The distinction between referential and emotive material does not necessarily imply that there is such a thing as *the* right word or set of words for a particular statement. In fact, the semanticist would not hold such a thesis. Concerned as he is with the context in which words are set and with the necessity of exercising control over definitions, he is sure that the effect of words will be dependent, as Hugh Walpole [28] observes, "upon our hearers' knowledge of the context." In this sense, the semanticist furnishes a wholesome point of view for the study of orators' language by insisting upon the critic's examining all individual stylistic features, not only in the light of the total written context, but also in the light of the hearers' knowledge and understanding of that context.

The logical-affective dichotomy thus results from the way hearers respond to certain words or combinations of words. And as we have just observed, no particular word is certain to be "loaded," or affectively charged for all people; nor will it necessarily bear the same emotional relevancy at different times or in different configurations. Statements which are purely matter-of-fact—designed to tell something without embellishment—might be highly affective in their influence upon hearers. Thus a report of a daring rescue at sea, told in the simplest possible terms, will in all probability take on emotional coloration, despite the speaker's or writer's attempt to curb it. So the task of drawing distinctions between logical and emotional material is far from easy. Unanimity of judgment among several objectively minded critics may not always result from a common examination of a speech in which certain statements and words are subject to different, though equally plausible, interpretations. This possibility has prompted Walpole to suggest that someone write "A Semantic Study of the Decisive Speeches of History." Then, he remarks, "we would see how man through the ages has listened to emotive words and told himself that they persuaded his reason."

It is evident from what we have said that a consideration of the logical-affective dualism is closely related to style. If word choice and the position words occupy in a sentence have much to do with the distinction—as seems certain—then the totality of compositional effect is of paramount importance. An example or two will exemplify the point.

Some years ago, in an article entitled "Pirates of the Air," [29] Isabelle Keating discussed the differences in technique between the radio reports issued by the Press-Radio Bureau and the Trans-Radio Press Service. To bring out the distinctions, she quoted part of a news release sent out by the former to tell listeners about a fire that was destroying considerable property in the Chicago stockyards area. The first report went somewhat as follows:

> A disastrous fire is raging in Chicago's stockyards tonight. All available apparatus has been summoned by a general alarm. Three firemen are reported killed. Two bank buildings, the Drovers National Bank and the Live Stock National, are destroyed.

Contrasted with this relatively matter-of-fact statement, the Trans-Radio report took on vividness and affective value by announcing:

> Lurid tongues of flame visible for hundreds of miles stabbed the night here as a raging inferno sweeps southeastward through Chicago's stockyards, greatest in the world.
>
> Thousands of persons are streaming from the old tenement houses of Chicago's south side carrying their belongings with them in a frantic exodus from the fire area as a southwest wind sweeps the flames on through miles of stockyards toward the center of Chicago.

> Thousands of firemen from every section of the city, reinforced by other companies from Chicago's suburbs and nearby Illinois towns, are fighting desperately to check the blaze that threatens the entire city.
>
> The odor of burning meat permeates the atmosphere. Smoke hangs like a black fog over the city.

Both reports deal with the same event. Yet the one is more likely to have emotional value than the other because of the word selection and arrangement. The abundance of adjectives, the pictorial effect, and the appeal to imagery contribute in no small measure to its affective construction.

Lincoln's "Gettysburg Address" is no doubt a good example of logical-emotional fusion. There are many people, however, who regard it as chiefly emotional. Contrast the original, then, with the following version prepared some years ago by an advertising agency to illustrate differences in writing, especially as they relate to good and bad advertising copy. The address in the so-called "textbook manner" might read as follows:

> Eighty-seven years ago certain of the British colonies in America revolted and set up an independent democratic government.
>
> This form of government was experimental, and the present Civil War is being fought to determine whether or not it is practical. A great battle of that war was fought on this spot. The men who died here are buried here, and the present assemblage is for the laudable purpose of dedicating the cemetery.
>
> In reality, however, nothing of importance will be accomplished by this ceremony. The dead men buried here have already dedicated this cemetery by their deeds. The address given on this occasion will soon be forgotten, but it will be impossible to forget their exploits. A continuation of their past efforts is now desirable. There is an extensive program still to be carried out—to achieve additional fidelity to the Union cause, to justify by a final victory for humanity the loss of these valuable lives, and to insure the continued existence of democratic government.[30]

As in the previous example, the word choice—especially the use of adjectives and other "coloration" words—and their arrangement contribute to the difference in effect. The lack of rhythmic flow in the textbook version also is noticeable.

The Persuasion-Conviction Dualism

In the first comprehensive analysis of rhetorical processes, Aristotle inquired into the psychological reactions of listeners. He made the term "persuasion" embrace not only the appeals to the emotions of the hearers, but the logical and ethical modes as well. By this token Aristotle made persuasion nearly synonymous with the goal or end of speaking. As previously indicated, he regarded logical proof as the "true constituent" of oratory; but his extensive and penetrating treatment of the emotions demonstrated his recognition of the place of emotional appeal in the attempt to influence hearers. Link these matters with Aristotle's expressed opposition to the schools of thought that placed the primary emphasis upon the ways of disposing hearers in the speakers' behalf, and we observe that the dualism reaches deep into antiquity.

Theoretically, of course, there is no clear-cut dichotomy in the Aristotelian system, such as we find in the persuasion-conviction scheme of later times. And the three modes of proof which he mentions are not treated as sharply separated entities; all apparently unite in greater or lesser measure to induce the end-product of persuasion. These distinctions are, however, purely verbal; the Aristotelian analysis takes into account the differential between the materials that *demonstrate* and those that *predispose* listeners to receive the logical demonstration.

Cicero's rhetorical theory involves a recognition of the different offices of logical and emotional appeal. This is evident from his remark that the proper concern of an orator "is language of power and elegance accommodated to the feelings and understandings of mankind." Like Aristotle, he indicates that persuasion is the objective of the orator's art, asserting that three things contribute to its achievement: "that we prove what we maintain to be true; that we conciliate those who hear; that we produce in their minds whatever feeling our cause may require." [31] Because of possible difficulties in translation, it is hard to tell whether he held consistently to that view. In a later section, he speaks of the necessity of arranging material so as to prove, to inform, and to persuade. Hence there may be some justification for the belief that Cicero compartmentalized the types of appeals somewhat more severely than did Aristotle. Be that as it may, he surely sustained the tradition of separating the appeals according to the basic nature of hearers.

The *Institutes* of Quintilian furnish no new data on the dualism. It is apparent that Quintilian looked upon logic and emotional appeal as playing supporting roles in the rhetorical process. Without declaring either the one or the other to be primary, he proceeded on the assumption that both contributed to the handling of audiences.

The later writers furnish data to support the belief that tradition has fixed the dichotomy securely in the literature of the subject. It

is quite probable, of course, that the more recent investigators—
especially those who were not philosophers themselves—took their
notions not only from empirical observation, but from the classics
and from the thoughts relative to the dualism of mind and matter,
and of the division of the mind into separable faculties.

Thomas Wilson was a disciple of the classical school which elevated logical proof to the position of primacy. The tongue was
ordained to express the mind so that others might grasp the speaker's
meaning, he remarked. But he did not ignore the other phase of
man's makeup, for he assured the readers of his *Arte of Rhetorique*
that people are persuaded through appeals to the affections. By
linking amplification with the moving of the affections, he made the
figure of speech a virtual key to persuasion.

The empirical philosophy of Thomas Hobbes, with its reliance
upon an epistemological dualism, brings forth a clear distinction between persuasion and conviction. Hobbes differentiates between
speech that expresses emotional content and speech that expresses
thought content. He observes that the "forms of speech by which
the passions are expressed, are partly the same, and partly different
from those, by which we express our thoughts." [32] It is to be recognized, however, that there is a "feeling" attached to mere thought
inasmuch as thought involves motion. This division of speech
forms for passion and for thought is, indeed, suggestive of the
dichotomous treatment so prevalent in current speech theory.

Because of his familiarity with the psychology of his time, Campbell gave a new turn to the dualistic concept. He approached the
problem through the medium of speech objectives, observing that
every speech is intended "to enlighten the understanding, to please
the imagination, to move the passions, or to influence the will."
Making the analysis much more atomistic than in the classical tradition, Campbell restricts the field of operation for any one of the
ends. While he allows for the interaction of the appeals, he sets up
one, and only one, as the *principal* motivator:

> . . . a discourse addressed to the understanding, and calculated to
> illustrate or evince some point purely speculative, may borrow aid from
> the imagination, and amid metaphor and comparison, but not the bolder
> and more striking figures. . . . Still less will it admit an address to
> the passions, which, as it never fails to disturb the operation of the
> intellectual faculty, must be regarded by every intelligent hearer as
> foreign at least, if not insidious. [33]

Using the term "conviction" and the term "persuasion" in their
more modern sense, Campbell states that the former is characterized

by the predominant quality of argument. Persuasion, on the other hand, has its "marvellous efficacy in rousing the passions, and by some secret, sudden, and inexplicable association, awakening all the tenderest emotions of the heart." Here we have, indeed, the modern statements of the controversial dualism. Groupings of the powers of the mind according to its faculties are evident in these separations of the basic psychological appeals.

In Blair's work, we also see the evidence of this clear-cut division. Blair attempts to delineate the two processes by indicating that "convincing and persuading, though they are sometimes confounded, import, notwithstanding, different things," which it is necessary for us to distinguish from each other. Conviction affects the understanding only; persuasion, the will and the practice. Therefore, "it is the business of the philosopher to convince me of truth; it is the business of the orator to persuade me to act agreeably to it, by engaging my affections on its side." [34] Blair believes that conviction and persuasion constitute a sort of rhetorical hierarchy, with the former serving as the base. Although the two do not always go together, Blair says they ought to and would "if our inclination regularly followed the dictates of our understanding." "The inclination," he continues,

> may revolt, though the understanding be satisfied; the passions may prevail against the judgment. Conviction is, however, always one avenue to the inclination, or heart; and it is that which an orator must first bend his strength to gain; for no persuasion is likely to be stable which is not founded on conviction.[35]

The persuasive aspects are highly essential, however, and so conviction alone is often insufficient. The orator "must consider man as a creature moved by many different springs, and must act upon them all. He must address himself to the passions; he must paint to the fancy, and touch the heart. . . ." [36]

Richard Whately's point of view is fundamentally similar. He, too, openly admits the division between materials having rational and those having emotive value. After speaking of the proofs that a speaker should introduce to substantiate a proposition, he says:

> This is, of course, what may be called, in the widest sense of the word, Conviction; but under that term are comprehended, *first,* what is strictly called *Instruction;* and, *secondly, Conviction* in the narrower sense; i.e. the Conviction of those who are either of a contrary opinion to the one maintained, or who are *in doubt* whether to admit it or deny it. By instruction, on the other hand, is commonly meant the conviction

376   SPEECH CRITICISM   [Ch. 12

of those who have neither formed an opinion on the subject, nor are deliberating whether to adopt or reject the proposition in question, but are merely desirous of ascertaining *what* is the truth in respect to the case before them.[37]

Having devoted about half of his treatise to conviction, or argument proper, Whately then turns to persuasion, which is "the art of influencing the Will. . . ." However,

. . . the *Conviction* of the understanding . . . is an essential *part* of Persuasion; and will generally need to be effected by the Arguments of the Writer or Speaker. For in order that the Will may be influenced, two things are requisite; *viz.* 1. that the proposed *Object* should appear desirable; and 2. that the *Means* suggested should be proved to be conducive to the attainment of that object; and this last, evidently must depend on the process of Reasoning.[38]

His conclusion is, therefore, that persuasion depends upon argument and exhortation. In its general outline, this point of view is similar to Aristotle's. It emphasizes the logical proof, but recognizes the need for at least modified appeals to the feelings of hearers if their wills are to be moved.

These are some of the more important contributors to the persuasion-conviction duality. In recent times, the work of the pioneers has been sustained or often assumed valid without further investigation. As a result, the classical division persists today, determining not only the pedagogical approach to argumentative speaking, but the critical estimation of speeches as well.

Perhaps the most cogent objections to the uncritical acceptance of persuasion and conviction as the basic constituents of the rhetorical process came from Mary Yost. In 1917, she published an article entitled "Argument from the Point of View of Sociology" in which she vigorously opposed the standard treatment of argumentation. "Almost all of the text-books," she declared,

. . . state that an argument effects its end by means of *conviction* and *persuasion*. With some variation in wording in the different books, the definitions of each term are practically the same: *conviction* and *persuasion* were formulated when the belief held sway that the mind was divided into three compartments, the reason, the emotion, the will —roughly the assumptions of the old faculty psychology. Today, however, the leading psychologists have found these assumptions inadequate to explain the phenomena of the mind.[39]

Miss Yost went on to say, "A conception of the mind as an organic unit performing a particular function—reasoning, feeling, willing—as may be demanded by the situation the individual is meeting, has taken the place of the rigid, formal idea. . . ." In short, Miss Yost adopts a monistic approach to audience behavior and she finds the traditional analysis of appeals to reason and emotions, respectively, invalid.

Stimulated by the Yost pronouncements, Charles Henry Woolbert,[40] a disciple of the behavioristic school of psychology, promptly entered his indictment of the traditional classification. Urging a study of the reactions of hearers rather than disproportionately elaborate analyses of subject matter, Woolbert asserted that behavioral manifestations to stimuli were essentially unitary—that they defied the artificial divisibility into rational and emotional responses. In general, he branded the conventional dualism as useless at best, and pernicious at its worst. Modern psychology—and especially behaviorism—did not sanction the distinction between perceived and nonperceived action which the dualism presupposed.

Other critics of the classical division have entered the field with their particular theses. Gladys Murphy Graham [41] questioned the modern teaching of argumentation on the ground that the true function of logic was being overlooked or ignored; and she advocated the use of a form of argument based largely upon Bernard Bosanquet's process of implication and linear inference.

Among textbooks departing most radically from the traditional method of treating argument is *Persuasion and Debate,* by George R. Collins and John S. Morris. Adopting the Woolbertian point of view, Collins and Morris classify the methods of objective reasoning into explicit and implicit materials. As to the former, two processes are possible:

1. Connecting propositions expressing new beliefs with propositions expressing old beliefs by propositions expressing the relationship of resemblance.

2. Connecting propositions expressing new beliefs with propositions expressing old beliefs by propositions expressing causal relationship.[42]

In order to make the propositions vivid, implicit methods are also used, including such details as exemplification, figurative language, analogies, repetition, parallel construction, effective word selection and sentence construction, euphony, and rhythm. Although the authors treat the explicit and implicit methods separately, they do not regard them as discrete elements. Instead, they insist that " 'reason' and 'feeling' are appealed to, not separately, but together."

Like some of their predecessors, notably Aristotle, they include both appeals under the general head of persuasion.

Validity of the Dichotomy.—The dichotomy is significant to the extent that it emphasizes the role of hearers in determining the object of speeches. It brings into sharp relief the necessity of regarding hearers' reactions as the all-important determinant of success in speechmaking. And the strictures of the critics upon the conventional division of appeals into persuading and convincing constituents, far from being unwholesome, have stimulated inquiry into speech as an instrument for influencing public opinion. Furthermore, the dualism fills a common sense need which simple appeal to experience confirms. We perceive differences in materials, according as they seem to establish proof or excite feelings. Whether we call these constituents by one name or another is of little moment; but that we take them into account when creating or criticizing oratory is important. That such a division is inconsistent even with modern schools of psychology is open to doubt. Considering the duality from the point of view of audience response, Edward Z. Rowell asks just what this "psychological monism" is, and then concludes:

Taken negatively, it is simply a repudiation of the old faculty psychology which talked of reasoning as the work of *a reason,* of willing as the work of *a will,* and so forth. Taken positively, it is a recognition of the functional approach to psychological processes, an approach which views men as unified reaction-systems which can exert the functions called reasoning, feeling, and so forth. Psychological monism makes no denial of the reality of the time-honored distinctions between reasoning, feeling, and willing. All it denies is the idea that these forms of behavior are expressions of individual faculties. This monism is as pluralistic as it is monistic. It talks as easily of reasoning, feeling, and willing as did any psychology before it and as does all commonsense. It does not give the modern psychologist any of the trouble that it seems to have given some of our rhetoricians. It makes room for every aspect of our newly-interpreted duality.[43]

Specimen Appraisals of Emotional Proof

The interacting influence of emotional and logical proof is pointed up by this passage from W. Norwood Brigance's study of Jeremiah S. Black's oratory:

Let us come to the qualities that mark Black's style of speech. Consider first his motivation of ideas. He never appealed to mere passions, yet there was always a powerful emotional drive behind his arguments. Indeed, one of his great sources of power sprang from a rare ability to unite argument with the springs of action in human beings. He could premise logic upon impelling motives—self-preservation, progress, honor—things that men live for and at times are willing to die for. When he had finished, not only had he impelled the mind to accept his logic as true but he had aroused emotions to *want* what the mind proclaimed as true. But this was not *argumentum ad populum*. It was logic surcharged. 'I make no appeal to the passions,' he said scornfully to the Supreme Court in the Civil Rights argument after they had listened to an address of this sort. 'Let the stump and the newspaper do that.'

The argument that followed in this case will illustrate the motivation behind his logic. The issue was whether Kentucky or the Federal government had the right to try a murder case in which a Negro was witness to the crime. Black's propositions were simple: (1) The effect of the Civil Rights bill, passed by Congress in 1866, was to abolish the autonomy of the states. (2) Such an act was a 'sheer, naked, flat breach of the Constitution.' The treatment of these propositions clicks with logical precision, but behind the logic were powerful turbines of emotional drive. He was arguing before the Supreme Court. They were judges, learned in the law; they were high in cultural level, well-versed in history; they were human beings, proud of their country and of its form of government. All these attributes and attitudes he used in applying motivation to his argument. Consider in brief the motivation of argument on the first proposition, that of abolishing the autonomy of states:

The state of Kentucky—and therefore every state of the Union—would be stripped by this law of the power to administer justice, even 'to the smallest and the lowest cases.' State lines would fade into dark shadows, and Federal prosecutors, like the proconsuls of Rome, would rule with a heavy hand. But the prosecutors went further than proconsuls, for the Empire of the Seven Hills in her most vicious days had never interfered with the local tribunals to the degree that the Civil Rights bill empowered Federal courts. Justice, removed to these distant courts, would leave nine-tenths of the lower class of crimes 'unwhipped of justice,' until people 'graduate in crime from the lowest to the highest, and society is altogether broken up.' 'The autonomy of a free State is not a thing to be trifled with,' and out of Megara and Corinth, Thebes and Athens, he lifted examples of disaster that flowed from such triflings; and fitted them in outline to the disaster that hung over Kentucky, and through her, over all states of the union. But one must read the full score to test the logic and sense the full drive behind it.[44]

Orville Hitchcock traces a similar interweaving of emotional and logical proofs in the sermonizing of Jonathan Edwards.

While Edwards uses a great many pathetic arguments, these appeals are, in general, subordinated to the logical elements. Even in those sections in which pathetic proof predominates there is a strong substructure of logic. Seldom do these appeals to duty, fear, jealousy appear alone. They seem to be added 'for good measure.' Overlooking no avenue of conviction, first he appeals to the understanding and then interweaves into this fabric of logic appeals to motives and desires. Emotional arguments, as we should expect, appear principally in the 'applications.' Only when Edwards wishes to apply the thesis does he resort to motivation. Logical proof is used to secure belief and pathetic proof to ensure action. This combination of logic and persuasion partly explains his skill in handling arguments, evidence, and audience factors.

The principal appeals are to fear, shame, desire for happiness, security, and pride. Gratitude, common sense, emulation, greed, and courage receive less emphasis. In appealing to fear, Edwards frequently refers to hell. It is a very real hell that he pictures, a hell of endless burning of the flesh. He is not content with merely describing the nature of hell and eternal punishment. He drives home the horrors of the torment to each of his listeners. He paints a fearful picture and then sets the audience squarely in the middle of it. It is a positive, powerful suggestion. Everyone has read this famous illustration: 'O sinner! Consider the fearful danger you are in: It is a great furnace of wrath, a wide and bottomless pit, full of the fire of wrath, that you are held over in the hand of that God, whose wrath is provoked . . . against you. . . . You hang by a slender thread, with the flames of divine wrath flashing about it, and ready every moment to singe it, and burn it asunder. . . .' [45]

Chauncey Goodrich's evaluation of John P. Curran's emotional proofs compartmentalizes the affective elements in oratory somewhat more severely than do many of the contemporary criticisms.

His power lay in the variety and strength of his emotions. He delighted a jury by his wit; he turned the court-room into a scene of the broadest farce by his humor, mimicry, or fun; he made it 'a place of tears,' by a tenderness and pathos which subdued every heart; he poured out his invective like a stream of lava, and inflamed the minds of his countrymen almost to madness by the recital of their wrongs. His rich and powerful imagination furnished the materials for these appeals, and his instinctive knowledge of the heart taught him how to use them with unfailing success. He relied greatly for effect on his power of painting to the eye; and the actual condition of the country for months during the insurrection, and after it, furnished terrific pictures for his pencil. Speaking of the ignorance which prevailed in England as to the treatment of the Irish, he said, 'If you wished to convey to the mind of an English matron the horrors of that period, when, in defiance of the remonstrances of the ever-to-be-lamented Abercromby, our poor people were surrendered to the brutality of the soldiery by the authority of the state, you would vainly attempt to give her a *general* picture of lust, and rapine, and murder, and conflagration. By endeavoring to comprehend everything, you would convey nothing. When the father of poetry wishes to portray the movements of contending armies and an embattled field, he *exemplifies,* he does not describe. So should your story to her keep clear of generalities. You should take a cottage, and place the affrighted mother with her orphan daughters at the door, the paleness of death in her face, and more than its agonies in her heart—her aching heart, her anxious ear struggling through the mist of closing day to catch the approaches of desolation and dishonor. The ruffian gang arrives—the feast of plunder begins— the cup of madness kindles in its circulation—the wandering glances of the ravisher become concentrated upon the shrinking and devoted victim. You need not dilate—you need not expatiate; the unpolluted matron to whom you tell the story of horror beseeches you not to proceed; she presses her child to her heart—she drowns it in her tears— her fancy catches more than an angel's tongue could describe; at a single view she takes in the whole miserable succession of force, of profanation, of despair, of death. So it is in the question before us.'

The faults of Mr. Curran arose from the same source as his excellences. They lay chiefly on the side of *excess;* intense expressions, strained imagery, overwrought passion, and descriptions carried out into too great minuteness of circumstance.[46]

Emotional Proof: A Point of View

Admittedly, emotion plays a significant role in speech. If, as Rogers declares, the normal mind "is not content merely to be logical and realistic," the critic's first obligation is to equate emotional coloration in oratory with his conception of thorough, objective analysis. This is not easy, but it is an imperative of the obligation which critical inquiry imposes. There can be no doubt that allegiance to "large principles of truth and reason" is the desideratum of oratory, be it political, forensic, or ceremonial speaking. But all men are not completely prepared, intellectually and emotionally, to receive the truth in its boldest and least adorned guise; it must often be articulated or identified with feelings that will conduce to the good of the people themselves, of their party, or of their country. Any critic who fails to recognize this patent fact cannot possibly hope to evaluate the oratory of any period with the acuity and insight that the task requires.

But the recognition of emotional proof—made necessary by a defect in human nature, if you will—places a further and no less challenging obligation upon critics. They are now charged with the responsibility of assaying the relative merits of the appeals, not only in the light of their immediate effect upon hearers, but also as to their long-range impact upon the social organization. Emotional excitation is an instrument of indeterminate power, and when used unscrupulously it may move men to foolish or evil deeds; it may even obscure, if not covertly frustrate, human reason. Without becoming the moral guardian of the spoken word, the critic nevertheless stands between oratory as an art—capable of both good and evil use—and the verdict of a responsible, intelligent interpretation as to its influence upon the society to which persuasion ministers as a coordinating agency.

Finally, we may say that emotional appeals—pathetic proof generally—should be regarded as facts or data of rhetoric, but not as basic principles of the art. With Aristotle, we would say that the proof of cases—the enforcement of ideas through logical means— is the true desideratum of discourse. As human beings, however, we are probably neither prepared for nor desirous of acting solely upon rational demonstration, assuming it to be possible. So we extend the range of the rhetorical process to include what the Greeks called the "accessories" of the art. As H. L. Hollingworth [47] remarks: "the instincts do not always lead men aright, and . . . the emotions are by no means infallible guides to truth."

This is not intended to minimize the importance of emotion in oratory; nor is it designed as an indirect way to hold pathetic proof in contempt. Rather, it is a way of saying that great public speaking should, first of all, be a demonstration of significant ideas. That is a principle of the art. If, however, the ideas require emotional coloration—and they probably will—in order to insure their successful reception by hearers, then that is an auxiliary fact supplementing our conception of the art of oratory. The first, let us repeat, is a *principle;* the other is a *datum* of rhetoric.

Chapter 13

THE CHARACTER OF THE SPEAKER

Ethical Proof in Discourse

Ralph Waldo Emerson defined eloquence as "the art of speaking what you mean and are." [1] On another occasion he supplemented this reflection by saying: "The reason why anyone refuses his assent to your opinion, or his aid to your benevolent design, is in you. He refuses to accept you as a bringer of truth, because, though you think you have it, he feels that you have it not. You have not given him the authentic sign." [2]

Much has been written under various captions about what Emerson calls the "authentic sign." The writers are virtually of one mind, however, in declaring that the force of the speaker's personality or character is instrumental in facilitating the acceptance of belief. Macaulay tells us that a comparison of Pitt the Younger with Charles James Fox reveals how the former inspired respect and confidence because of the correctness of his private life. Conversely, a personal touch which is neither pleasing nor inspiring may, and often does, militate against the speaker's likelihood of achieving his desired response. As John Lawson said in his *Lectures:* "You cannot be much affected by what he [the speaker] says, if you do not look upon him to be a Man of Probity, who is in earnest, and doth himself believe what he endeavoreth to make out as credible to you." [3]

Like so many of the concepts with which the modern student of rhetoric deals, this one received its first fairly specific statement at the hand of Aristotle. It will be recalled that Aristotle believed success in persuasion depended upon three things; or, to put it differently, the proofs provided "through the instrumentality of the speech" were of three kinds: "in the moral character of the speaker or in the production of a certain disposition in the audience or in the speech itself by means of real or apparent demonstration." [4] We have already discussed the last two, namely, emotional or pathetic proof and logical proof. Let us now turn to what is usually called *ethical* proof.

Aristotle's Point of View.—Although Aristotle does not devote much space to the concept of ethical proof, he says enough to enable us to perceive its essential role in the process of persuasion. "The instrument of proof is the moral character," he says,

> . . . when the delivery of the speech is such as to produce an impression of the speaker's credibility; for we yield a more complete and ready credence to persons of high character not only ordinarily and in a general way, but in such matters as do not admit of absolute certainty but necessarily leave room for difference of opinion, without any qualification whatever.[5]

That Aristotle looked upon this mode of persuasion as important and effective is plain. Censuring his predecessors for not regarding high character in the speaker as contributing to effectiveness, Aristotle sets up the general rule "that there is no proof so effective as that of the character." It may be observed, however, that his respect for the efficacy of ethical proof did not argue against the primacy of the logical materials. While recognizing the speaker as a primary factor in persuasion, Aristotle still looked upon logical argument as the most important element in the speech.

The foregoing remarks establish Aristotle's concern for the personal character of speakers. But what are the constituents of ethical proof? What are its signs in the speech proper?

Aristotle answers these queries directly. He holds that there are three sources of personal credibility in orators; "or in other words there are three things, apart from demonstrative proofs, which inspire belief, viz. sagacity, high character, and good will." [6] He then remarks:

> It is *the want* of all these qualities or of one of them that occasions great errors in matters of discussion or deliberation; for either people are so foolish that they entertain erroneous opinions, or, although their opinions are right, they are so corrupt that they do not express their true sentiments, or, although they are persons of sagacity and high character, they are not well-disposed to their audience, and perhaps in consequence do not recommend the best policy, although they understand it.[7]

The inference is that "if a person is supposed to command them all, he will be deserving of credit in the eyes of his audience." [8]

Similar "ethical" requisites are evident in Cicero's remark that character contributes to success in speaking if "the morals, principles, conduct, and lives of those who plead causes, and of those for

whom they plead, [are] such as to merit esteem. . . ." Furthermore, the "feelings of the hearers are conciliated by a person's dignity, by his actions, by the character of his life. . . ." [9] And it is

> . . . of peculiar advantage that indications of good nature, of liberality,
> of gentleness, of piety, of grateful feelings, free from selfishness and
> avarice, should appear in him; and every thing that characterizes men
> of probity and humility, not acrimonious, not pertinacious, nor litigious,
> nor harsh, very much conciliates benevolence, and alienates the affections
> from those in whom such qualities are not apparent.[10]

All these sources of credibility resolve to the essentials set forth by
John Ward in his *System of Oratory:* wisdom, integrity, benevo-
lence, and modesty.

Aristotle hoped to include in his *Rhetoric* the data which would
help the speaker get credit for the three sources of personal credibility. Pursuant to that intention, he stated that sagacity and high
character "must be ascertained from our analysis of the virtues, as
it is by the same means that we shall succeed in establishing our own
character and the character of others. . . ." [11] That is to say, the
speaker is to get his cues from Book I of the *Rhetoric,* and especially from those sections dealing with moral nobility and the human
virtues. As for good will, or a "friendly disposition," it can best
be considered in the light of the speaker's knowledge of human
emotions.

It should be noted that Aristotle confined the operational influence of ethical proof more severely than did his successors. He insisted that the audience's antecedent conception of the speaker's
character should not figure in the determination of the speaker's skill
in establishing credibility through sagacity, high character, and good
will. In other words, what the speaker did *during* the speech was
of primary concern; what people thought of him *before* he spoke
was not in itself directly related to the modes of persuasion. This
distinction is defensible, perhaps, if we conceive of ethical proof
as an artistic creation brought about by the speaker's skill in asserting
his intelligence, revealing his probity, and accommodating himself
to his hearers. It is, however, an artificial restriction, since the attitude of the audience toward the speaker—based upon previous
knowledge of the latter's activities and reputation—cannot accurately
be separated from the reaction the speaker induces through the medium of the speech.

Difference between Emotional and Ethical Proof

It is apparent that the distinction between emotional and ethical proof is not always clear; and in some instances it may be virtually nonexistent. *Ethos* and *pathos* have, indeed, much in common. The speaker who establishes his own moral integrity and imposes strictures upon that of his opponent is unquestionably using both ethical and pathetic proof. He is establishing credence in his own probity and character, and, at the same time, is predisposing the minds of the hearers toward the readier acceptance of his cause. Despite the apparent indivisibility of appeal, this difference seems to stand out: *Ethos* refers chiefly to what the speaker chooses to do; *Pathos*, to what the reaction has done to the listeners.

In the Aristotelian sense, as construed by Irving J. Lee, the difference between ethos and pathos seems to be "the moral states evidenced in the speech and the emotional states aroused in the audience." [12] There may also be a difference in the intensity of the effects induced by the two appeals. This is consistent with Volkmann's belief that "the effect of the *ethos* is a quiet attention and comprehension followed by a willing belief and confidence, quite different from the more powerful torrent-like effect of the *pathos*." [13]

The point of view adopted by Edward L. Pross in his experimental investigation seems to be both sound and workable. He looks upon the logical, emotional, and ethical modes of persuasion as aspects of a continuum, supplementing each other.

> In most cases the skilled speaker, in possession of full knowledge as to the audience and occasion, is able to make a functional differentiation. Students of rhetoric may take a speech delivered by a speaker of another era, and upon securing a thorough insight into the nature of the audience, occasion, and the speaker can make a reasonably good analysis and differentiation of the forms of proof in that address. Nevertheless, it must be recognized that these modes of proof are on a continuum and a continuum that varies from person to person. The only consummately accurate judge as to the forms of proof employed by a speaker is the individual auditor. Up to a certain point the veteran of the platform and the skilled rhetorician can predict that auditor's verdict but their prognostications can never be perfectly reliable.[14]

The Constituents of Ethical Proof

The possibilities for the use of *ethos* in the subject matter of a speech are manifold. Assuming, as Aristotle suggested, that the three constituents of ethical proof are character, sagacity, and good will, a speaker may give credibility to his message in a variety of ways. Any attempt to present an inclusive catalog of ethical attributes or manifestations would be futile. Our summary is therefore purely exploratory.

In general, a speaker focuses attention upon the probity of his character if he (1) associates either himself or his message with what is virtuous and elevated; (2) bestows, with propriety, tempered praise upon himself, his client, and his cause; (3) links the opponent or the opponent's cause with what is not virtuous; (4) removes or minimizes unfavorable impressions of himself or his cause previously established by his opponent; (5) relies upon authority derived from his personal experience; and (6) creates the impression of being completely sincere in his undertaking.

With certain qualifications varying with the circumstances, it may be said that a speaker helps to establish the impression of sagacity if he (1) uses what is popularly called common sense; (2) acts with tact and moderation; (3) displays a sense of good taste; (4) reveals a broad familiarity with the interests of the day; and (5) shows through the way in which he handles speech materials that he is possessed of intellectual integrity and wisdom.

Finally, a speaker's good will generally is revealed through his ability (1) to capture the proper balance between too much and too little praise of his audience; (2) to identify himself properly with the hearers and their problems; (3) to proceed with candor and straightforwardness; (4) to offer necessary rebukes with tact and consideration; (5) to offset any personal reasons he may have for giving the speech; and (6) to reveal, without guile or exhibitionism, his personable qualities as a messenger of the truth.

Instances from Speeches of the Use of Ethical Proof

Examples of the use of ethical proof are numerous. Let us consider two passages from celebrated speeches to illustrate the operation of this mode of persuasion. The first is from the introduction— a not uncommon part of the speech in which to find such appeals— to Thomas Erskine's argument in behalf of Lord George Gordon. After a short opening statement, Erskine said:

Gentlemen, I feel myself entitled to expect, both from you and from the court, the greatest indulgence and attention. I am, indeed, a greater object of your compassion than even my noble friend whom I am defending. He rests secure in conscious innocence, and in the well-placed assurance that it can suffer no stain in your hands. Not so with me. I stand before you a troubled, I am afraid a *guilty* man, in having presumed to accept of the awful task which I am now called upon to perform—a task which my learned friend who spoke before me, though he has justly risen, by extraordinary capacity and experience, to the highest rank in his profession, has spoken of with that distrust and diffidence which becomes every Christian in a cause of blood. If Mr. Kenyon has such feelings, think what mine must be. Alas! gentlemen, who am I? A young man of little experience, unused to the bar of criminal courts, and sinking under the dreadful consciousness of my defects. I have, however, this consolation, that no ignorance nor inattention on my part can possibly prevent you from seeing, under the direction of the Judges, that the Crown has established no case of treason.[15]

The passage is of interest in that it attempts (1) to confirm the innocence, and hence goodness, of his client; and (2) to establish the speaker's sense of modesty, honesty, and candor. Such appeals serve a dual purpose: they help to put the speaker in the proper light as a man conscious of his solemn and challenging responsibility, and they predispose hearers favorably to the cause by establishing preliminary presumption in favor of the client's innocence. Commenting on this passage, Chauncey Goodrich remarks:

. . . the paragraph, though in form a plea for indulgence to himself as a young speaker, is in fact the strongest possible assumption of the prisoner's innocence, since the *guilt* referred to consisted in his venturing to endanger, by his inexperience, the cause of one who stood secure himself 'in conscious innocence.' There is hardly any thing for which Mr. Erskine deserves more to be studied, than his thus making every circumstance conspire to produce the desired impression. All is so easy and natural, that men never think of it as the result of design or premeditation, and here lies his consummate skill as an advocate.[16]

In the introduction to his speech on the White murder case, Daniel Webster also employed ethical proof, although his technique differed from that used by Erskine in the Lord George Gordon case. Said Webster:

I am little accustomed, gentlemen, to the part which I am now attempting to perform. Hardly more than once or twice, has it happened to me to be concerned, on the side of the government, in any criminal prosecution whatever; and never, until the present occasion, in any case affecting life. But I very much regret it should have been thought necessary to suggest to you, that I am brought here to 'hurry you against the law, and beyond the evidence.' I hope I have too much regard for justice, and too much respect for my own character, to attempt either; and were I to make such attempt, I am sure, that in this court, nothing can be carried against the law, and that gentlemen, intelligent and just as you are, are not, by any power, to be hurried beyond the evidence. Though I could well have wished to shun this occasion, I have not felt at liberty to withhold my professional as-sistance, when it is supposed that I might be in some degree useful, in investigating and discovering the truth, respecting this most extraor-dinary murder. It has seemed to be a duty, incumbent on me, as on every other citizen, to do my best, and my utmost, to bring to light the perpetrators of this crime. Against the prisoner at the bar, as an individual, I cannot have the slightest prejudice. I would not do him the smallest injury or injustice. But I do not affect to be indifferent to the discovery, and the punishment of this deep guilt. I cheerfully share in the opprobrium, how much soever it may be, which is cast on those who feel and manifest an anxious concern that all who had a part in planning, or a hand in executing this deed of midnight assassi-nation, may be brought to answer for their enormous crime, at the bar of public justice.[17]

Webster, it will be noted, attempts to reflect the spirit of his good intentions and his high moral principles by disavowing any relish for criminal prosecutions, especially those involving murder; by assuring the jury of his disinclination to hurry the orderly proc-esses of justice; by pointing to his solicitude for preserving his self-respect and character; by indicating his reluctance to take part in the proceedings; by making known his earnest desire to be of service to the cause of decency; by disclaiming any personal antipathy toward the accused; and by indicating his willingness to suffer pos-sible opprobrium, if only the criminals can be brought to answer for their heinous crime. This is a heavily charged passage and, like the previous one, it contains elements of pathetic proof. But, in the main, its purpose is to convey to the jury a favorable impression of the speaker's goodwill and character.

A Critical Analysis of Ethical Proof

Loren D. Reid evaluates Charles James Fox's ethical proof in the speech of February 2, 1778, by remarking:

If Fox still remembered his Aristotle on February 2, he knew that 'persuasion is achieved by the speaker's personal character when the speech is so spoken as to make us think him credible'; that a speaker's character 'may almost be called the most effective means of persuasion he possesses'; that the three factors which inspire confidence in the orator's character are 'good sense, good moral character, and good-will.'

Just before Fox rose to speak, as has been noted, the galleries were cleared of visitors. Fox met the situation by declaring modestly that he was sure he would not have answered the expectations of those who had come. As he continued to speak, it is further evident that his intention was to conciliate his audience by showing his 'good sense, good moral character, and goodwill,' as he insisted that he was simply acting as an instrument of the nation.

Still other statements indicate the good sense and fairmindedness of the speaker. Thus he says he intends to base his arguments upon the facts 'as they appear from the papers on the table'—referring to the documents furnished by the administration. Nothing can be fairer than to use the evidence of one's opponent. He says that, although a radical error has been made in the conduct of the war, 'it is not of itself a proof of the criminality of ministers.' Thus he tells the House that his attack is not personal—not an attempt to incriminate the ministers personally—but directed against policies. Finally, he promises to be brief:

'Sir, I shall not now enter into any more of the proceedings relative to America, than are necessary to shew the immediate steps which have brought us into our present situation. Without discussing the various questions which have been for many years agitated in Parliament, I shall take up the measures relative to America in the year 1774. . . .'

Ethical proof is not used extensively but serves to strike the keynote of the first part of the speech. It is apparent that Fox made conscious, purposeful use of this method of persuasion. Yet this statement is based upon an inference rather than upon direct proof. In none of his earlier speeches is he so conciliatory and so persuasive. Why, then, does he adopt this attitude in this particular speech? The answer is that it was a part of the Whig plan as developed in the Grosvenor Square meetings. Now if it was decided that Fox should be conciliatory in the House of Commons, it must also have been decided that the Duke of Richmond should be conciliatory in the House of Lords. This was exactly the case.[18]

Synthesis Must Result from Analysis

With this chapter on ethical proof we close that section of the book dealing largely with rhetorical invention. We have concerned ourselves with the search for and the analysis and development of arguments suitable to the enforcement of ideas and the establishment of belief in hearers. Our attention has centered chiefly about kinds of proof. Occasionally we found it necessary to consider details relating to disposition or arrangement, to style, and to delivery.

In other words, speeches are totalities made up of several interrelated aspects, and the study of one aspect automatically directs attention to all the others.

The critic's inquiry thus becomes more complex as the number of specific points of investigation increases. It is the critic's job, however, to maintain a conception of rhetorical unity in the midst of his analytical examination of the discrete elements.

Chapter 14

THE STRUCTURE OF ORAL DISCOURSE

Interrelated Character of Disposition

Theophrastus is reported as saying that an "unbridled horse ought to be trusted sooner than a badly arranged discourse." Believing that good organization is essential in a speech, the classical rhetoricians designated it the second part of rhetoric. They called it *dispositio,* and in the broad sense it dealt with the selection, orderly arrangement, and proportion of the parts of an address.

Disposition is almost inextricably interwoven with the data of invention.[1] This fact is even more patent to the critic than to the creator of the speech. The critic seeks to understand an event during or, in a large number of cases, after the occurrence of the speech. And why a speaker arranged his material in a certain way cannot be fully determined until it is known why he chose certain arguments, or why he developed them as he did. Consequently, any distinctions that we may draw between finding and organizing arguments must candidly be accepted as semiarbitrary, as serving the ends of academic convenience almost as much as of theoretical accuracy.

Invention and disposition have often been linked in the manner previously suggested. John F. Genung looked upon the original aspects of discovery in invention as too individual to fall within the scope of ordinary textbook treatment. So he asserted that real invention did not begin

> . . . until to the original conception there is applied a process of organization, that is, of verifying, sifting, and selecting for ulterior disposal. It is in the various stages of organization, of working up thought to a completed form and effect, that invention centres.[2]

The mutual dependence of finding and arranging material is thus clearly indicated. And the distinction between *originative* and *organizing* invention is accordingly specified.

Two additional opinions from homileticians corroborate Genung's view. John A. Broadus held that arrangement reacted directly upon invention. "One has not really studied a subject when he has simply thought it over in a desultory fashion," Broadus remarked. "The attempt to arrange his thoughts upon it suggests other thoughts, and can alone give him just views of the subject as a whole." [3]   And George W. Hervey makes disposition a part of invention—"first, because the proper exercise of invention either proceeds from or results in thinking according to some *method,* good or bad; secondly, because in searching for the best method the most pertinent and useful thoughts are not infrequently suggested to us." [4]

Objectives of Inquiry in This Field.—The critic who evaluates a speaker's finished discourse proceeds with two objectives in view: First, he examines the speech as an instance of rhetorical crafts-manship, *per se.* That is, he considers the speech from the point of view of its basic construction, as an assembly of many parts bound together in an orderly and balanced whole.   Secondly, he appraises the total organizational plan with reference to the peculiar audi-ence conditions to which it was presumably accommodated.   In other words, the critic recognizes the possibility that a speech may be a masterful combination of discrete elements; that it may be a model of unitary cohesion, considered *in vacuo,* and yet be ineffective in its adaptation to the audience for which it is intended.   These two problems are connected, yet distinct.   Let us consider them in order.

Analyzing a Speech for Craftsmanship

In its broadest sense, disposition embraces the following matters: the *emergence of a central theme,* the general *method of arrangement* adopted for the speech, and the *order* in which the parts of the dis-course are developed.

(1) Thematic Emergence.—Little need be said here about the emergence of the central theme.   It is assumed that the speech pos-sesses a clearly defined and easily determined thesis or purpose; that this thesis is unencumbered by collateral theses which interfere with the clear perception of the principal one; and that the develop-ment is of such a character as to provide for the easy and unmis-takable emergence of the thesis through the unfolding of the contents of the speech.   That is to say, the critic is interested in find-ing out whether the speaker's conception of his task—be it to ex-plain, to entertain, to convince, or to persuade—is clear, and whether the selection and arrangement of the ideas conduce to their effec-tiveness.

(2) Method of Division and Arrangement.—In general, *method* here implies the choice of a principle by means of which the materials of a speech are divided. We may call this the search for a basis of division, or the determination of the most suitable major units of the subject. Whether the speaker consciously considers this point or not, he is obliged to effect such divisions of data as will provide ready manageability of details. The oratory of the past reveals that most speeches fall into one or another of the following groups, as far as the basic partition of subject matter is concerned: the historical, the distributive, and the logical.

Historical Method—According to the historical basis of division, material is arranged in chronological order. The order may be, and often is, from past to present to future. However, it may move from present to past to future, or from a prophecy of the future to the past to the present. Instances of the use of the historical order in public speeches are numerous. In the last part of Burke's speech on "American Taxation," we find that he traces the chronology of the American problem through four distinct periods: the Navigation Acts, the efforts to get revenue from America, the Rockingham Ministry and the Stamp Act repeal, and, finally, the taxation imposed by Townshend. Charles James Fox also relied heavily upon this method in his speech on the rejection of Bonaparte's overtures. And Webster's address in the White murder trial illustrates the scheme of using a time order to determine the major divisions of the speech.

Distributive Method—According to the distributive method of arrangement, matters having a common thought center and an obvious connection among themselves are grouped in certain sections. If a certain body of subject matter deals with the political implications of a World Union, and another body of data deals with the economic implications of the plan, an effort may be made to distribute the materials according to the relation they bear to the specified ideas. In Burke's speech to the Bristol electors in 1780, he made use of this method, although the historical order also figures in the development. Asserting that "bad laws are the worst sort of tyranny," Burke set forth his reasons for taking a part in the repeal of certain cruel enactments against the Catholics. "To prove this— to prove that the measure was both clearly and materially proper, I will next lay before you . . . the political grounds and reasons for the repeal of that penal statute, and the motives to its repeal at that particular time." He then broke down the "political" unit of his speech and discussed such distributed considerations as (1) the loyalty of the Roman Catholics, (2) the claims of humanity, (3) the beneficial effects of the repeal on the British Empire, and (4) the beneficial example set for foreign countries.

Logical Method—Finally, the logical order may characterize the basis of division. In such cases, the arrangement of materials is determined by the continuity of the reasoning process; materials are placed at those points where they serve as links in the uninterrupted sequences or chains of thought. Practically all speeches urging a change in the *status quo* rely in greater or lesser measure upon this method. Its use is, of course, not limited to deliberative speaking, as a casual examination of specimen forensic and ceremonial talks will reveal.

Outline of Bases of Division—Since the foregoing methods of arrangement admit of elaboration, the following tabular analysis presents the common bases of division:

I. HISTORICAL ORDER
   A. Material can be divided as to time units
      The arrangement can be from past to present to future; or from present to past to future; or any other reasonable derivative of this pattern

II. DISTRIBUTIVE ORDER
   A. Material can be divided according to the parties involved in the problem
      For example, capital and labor; or the Northerners and the Southerners; etc.

   B. The division can be made according to legal and ethical implications

   C. The nature of the subject matter can determine the division
      1. The material may be specific and general
      2. The material may be familiar and novel
      3. The material may be debatable and undebatable
      4. The material may be admitted and contested

   D. The division can be made according to the fields of inquiry involved in the subject
      These fields may, for example, be the economic, political, social, etc.

   E. The division can be made according to the definitional requirements of the case

III. LOGICAL ORDER

   A. Material can be divided according to proof requirements implicit in the problem-solving technique

      1. Statement dealing with the immediate cause of the controversy

      2. The origin and history of the question

      3. The definition of ambiguous words or terms

      4. The exclusion of granted material

      5. The listing of main heads or issues

      6. The logical development of those issues

   B. The material can be divided according to the framework of a logical pattern for discussion of policy

      1. The definition of terms

      2. The statement of goals in accordance with which the problem is analyzed and solved

      3. The statement of factors involved in the problematic situation (the "felt difficulty," including causes and results)

      4. The weighing of representative solutions for tentative adoption

      5. The analysis of a solution representing the consensus of those engaged in the analysis

      6. The program to implement any formulated judgment

   C. The material can be divided according to issues developed by the *proponents* of a proposed course of action

      1. Present conditions are bad; the proposed plan will correct the difficulties; the proposed plan is practicable

      2. The present system is good; the proposed plan is better

   D. The materials can be divided according to issues developed by the *opponents* of a proposed course of action

      1. There are instances of irregularities in the present system, but they are not numerous or serious

      2. There are some evils in the present system, but they are not inherent in the system

      3. There are evils in the present system, but the proposed plan is not a remedy

      4. Abuses exist; the proposed plan may have some advantages; but it introduces new evils

      5. Abuses exist; the proposed plan has some merit; but a better plan is available

      6. Abuses exist; the proposed plan is just; but it is inexpedient

      7. Abuses exist; the proposed plan is expedient; but it is not just

   E. Material can be divided according to refutative requirements
      inherent in the subject
      1. A speaker may first discuss objections to his plan and
         then give arguments in its favor
      2. It is sometimes possible to show that all methods, save
         one, of correcting present evils will fail
   F. The materials can be divided according to proof requirements
      for developing a proposition of fact (to determine the truth
      or falsity of a proposition or an alleged fact)
      1. The subdivisions may consist of a listing of types of
         evidence, including statistics, testimony of witnesses,
         authorities, circumstantial details
      2. The subdivisions may include the classification of types
         of arguments—causation, analogy, deduction, etc.

These schematic representations are not intended to suggest that
a *single* basis of division necessarily prevails throughout an orator's
complete speech. These principles often work in combination, so
that the historical, distributive, and logical methods may all be in
operation in a given discourse. Assuming that the principles are not
in conflict and that structural consistency is maintained, we may on
occasion find such an interlacing of methods quite satisfactory.
Witness, for instance, the multiple principles of division in Burke's
speech "On Conciliation" or on "American Taxation." Fundamentally, however, the subjects of discourse usually yield to a single
principle of division; and, other things being equal, analyses resulting from the application of one basis of partition are more likely
to be characterized by clarity, relevancy, and economy of style and
effort.

   (3) **Rhetorical Order in Disposition.**—Thus far we have discussed the speech as an instance of craftsmanship in relation to two
concepts : the emergence of a central theme, and the method of arranging the subject matter. We shall turn, finally, to the *order* in
which the parts of a speech are developed.

   Plato remarks that "every speech ought to be put together like a
living creature, with a body of its own, so as to be neither without
head, nor without feet, but to have both a middle and extremities,
described proportionately to each other and to the whole." [5] In other
words, a speech should have a beginning, a middle, and an end. In
furtherance of that expectation, rhetoricians have devised certain
parts that contribute to the formation of a whole artistic piece, and
have given general instructions as to the order in which these parts
shall appear.

The parts of a speech were conceived in terms of function, of operational utility. Consequently, their names are unimportant, so long as the tasks assigned to the units are adequately fulfilled. Because simplicity is a virtue in this instance, many rhetorical critics use the Aristotelian plan of organization as the criterion for evaluating *disposition*. This would seem to be a defensible standard since the critic is not interested in form for its own sake, but rather for the contribution it makes in eliciting a desired response from hearers.

Aristotle believed that "the only indispensable parts *of a speech* are the statement of the case and the proof." [6] He added, however, that if other parts were necessary, the total number should not exceed four: the exordium, exposition or statement of the case, proof, and the peroration. These are the four parts whose functions most critics examine when evaluating the structure of selected orations.

The functions of these parts are almost set forth by their descriptive titles. The *introduction,* which Aristotle said conformed to the prologue in poetry, is intended to enlist the attention and interest of the listeners, to render the audience well disposed toward the speaker, and to prepare the way for the ideas to come. The *statement* of the case sets forth clearly and concisely the nature of the subject presently to be developed. The *proof* contains the elaboration of subject matter through which the idea or ideas are enforced. And the *peroration* or conclusion, to quote Aristotle, proposes "to inspire the audience with a favorable opinion of yourself and an unfavorable one of your adversary, to amplify or depreciate the subject, to excite the emotions of the audience and to recall the facts to their memory." [7]

Example of Aristotelian Analysis of Disposition.—In Reid's study of Charles James Fox, use is made of the Aristotelian pattern of organization. The analysis of Fox's speech of February 2, 1778, illustrates how Reid applied this yardstick:

> Fox was not insensible of his diminished audience as he began his speech, but turned the occasion to his own advantage by declaring that he was sure he would not have answered the great expectations which had brought so many visitors down to the house. This is unusual modesty; in fact, the whole introduction is marked by its quiet modesty and conciliatory manner. Note such statements as these:
>
> > 'I must, however, beg not to be considered as the mover in this momentous concern; it is the nation that calls for this inquiry, and I am only one instrument in the bringing it about . . .
> >
> > 'What I have to beg of the House is not to mix this day's business with any thing that has passed before, but to go plainly and directly to the business to consider what is the actual state of the

country, and how Great Britain can be saved from the critical situation in which she now stands.'

Fox's introduction was quite brief, evidently being less than five minutes in length—indeed a short time especially when compared to the two hours and forty minutes which he spoke. The Statement was equally brief:

> 'Sir: the method I have chalked out to myself, as the most likely way to bring men to a right understanding of the present state of the nation, . . . is to state facts as they appear from the papers on the table; first, with respect to the Army; . . . I shall, secondly, state the impossibility of increasing that army; and, thirdly, the enormous expense that has already been incurred. . . .'

The most important part of the speech to Aristotle was the discussion, or Argument. Rhetoric in the philosophy of Aristotle is essentially the art of giving effectiveness to truth; and it is in the Argument that this is chiefly accomplished. Looking at the speech as a whole, and from the point of view of structure, it is evident that the Argument was welded into an organic whole by the use of topic and transition sentences. For example:

> 'I shall take up the measures relative to America in the year 1774, when the riots at Boston first called for the attention of this House . . .'
>
> 'But, Sir, there was another circumstance which tended to mislead the House, and for which the ministers and not the House were entirely to blame . . .'
>
> 'But, as if all this was not sufficient to irritate and provoke, the Quebec Act was passed, the contents of which every body knows. . . .'
>
> 'Another extraordinary idea, Sir, was at this time taken up, namely, that the coercive Acts passed that session would execute themselves. . . .'
>
> 'But, as if all this was not enough to exasperate, . . . we rejected, before the end of the session of 1775, the Petition from New York . . .'

In the Argument Fox gradually built up a strong case against the King's government by showing a causal relation between the 'absurdity' and 'madness' of administration policies and the state of national affairs. The Conclusion added a dramatic touch to this cumulation of governmental wickedness. Fox had not yet revealed the exact wording of the motion he was about to present. The obvious motion for him to make, and one which the administration expected, was to ask for an inquiry into the causes of the defeat at Saratoga. The motion that Fox did present in the Conclusion (using the method of the dilemma) was to the effect that, considering the present defenseless state of Great

Britain, no more troops should be sent to America. He concluded, in good Aristotelian fashion:

> 'On the whole, Sir, it appears to me that if gentlemen are not blind, they will see that the war is impracticable, and that no good can come from force only; that the lives that have been lost, and the treasures that have been wasted, have been wasted to no purpose; that it is high time we should look to our own situation, and not leave ourselves defenceless upon an idea of strengthening the army in America, when, after all, it will be less strong than it was last year,—a year which produced nothing decisive, nor in the least degree tending to complete conquest.'

Thus in a few brief lines he reviewed the leading arguments of his speech and left his hearers with a very definite impression of the absurdity and madness of governmental policies. Little wonder that not a single person in that crowded house attempted a reply to this speech.[8]

Classifications of Parts of a Speech Vary with Authors.—Other rhetoricians, of course, have set up their own classifications of the parts of a speech. But all are in virtual agreement, the only essential difference being in the number of parts admitted. Thus Cicero and Quintilian include *narration* as a part, and suggest that it come after the exordium, especially in forensic speeches. In it, the speaker tells of the events that lead to the question at issue. Other parts mentioned by classical rhetoricians include *division,* in which the parts of the case are outlined; *refutation,* in which counter-arguments are introduced; *amplification,* in which the key issue of a case is given heightened effect through stylistic embellishment and emotional coloration. A fairly faithful reproduction of the more complex classical division is found in the late nineteenth-century speech plan discussed by Charles Coppens. He says the following parts may appear in an oration: introduction or exordium, narration or explanation, proposition, division, proofs or argumentation, pathetic (or emotional excitement), and conclusion or peroration.[9]

It is apparent from an examination of any typical speech that all, or virtually all, of these parts are still with us. True, we have dropped some units and have subsumed others under the headings of the remaining ones. But, fundamentally, we still retain the divisions announced by the theorists of antiquity.

Use of Brief in Studying Disposition.—To facilitate the task of getting at the organizational plan of a speech, the critic will find it helpful to prepare a brief or outline of the entire address. This will enable him to appreciate more fully the basic divisions of the discourse, the functions they serve, the space allotments accorded them, and the relation of details to the larger rhetorical pattern. The brief is no less useful here than it is in tracing the logical continuities in an argument. There is no better way of viewing the internal makeup of a speech, nor of checking the coherence of the total sequence.

Analyzing Total Speech in Terms of the Audience

At the beginning of this chapter we said that the critic considers rhetorical *disposition* from two related points of view: he examines the speech as an instance of craftsmanship, and he evaluates the total organizational plan with reference to existing audience conditions We are now ready to discuss briefly the second of these consid erations.

A speech conforming to the principles of good organization may be ill-adapted to the specific audience for which it is intended. In other words, so-called natural or logical structure may not coincide with the most effective *sequence* of presentation. It may be necessary to alter the natural order sharply to accommodate the speech to certain people. Coppens calls this the "oratorical" method of arrangement; and he defines it as "that which departs designedly from the natural order to avoid some special difficulty or to gain some special advantage, sacrificing regularity to usefulness." [10]

Accordingly, certain speeches may not contain all parts previously mentioned. Or they may contain the conventional parts but present them in different order. Perhaps no two speeches will be introduced in the same way; yet the introductions may serve substantially the same functions. These are but a few of the many variables. No one can anticipate them in the abstract. They are the direct consequences of real speech situations.

The critic may find here, as elsewhere, that an attempt to reduce rhetoric to a set of rules, either on the creative or the critical side, is a venture in futility. Many effective speeches stand as refutation of the claim that a particular way of organizing materials must be followed.

The position which arguments should occupy in the proof is also subject to variation with changes in audience conditions. Whereas we may favor the order of climax, circumstances may militate against its effective use in certain cases. H. L. Hollingworth points out that there is evidence to show that the reverse order of climax may produce more permanent results, at least in printed appeals. What is true of the uncertainties of appeal regarding the number of points and the order of climax also concerns the position of repeated materials and other devices calculated to impress hearers.

The foregoing remarks stress the importance of the critic's being thoroughly familiar with the audience conditions under which the orator performed. It seems certain that in no other way will he gain the insight necessary to full understanding of *why* an orator disposed his materials as he did. Essential as it is for the critic to know the *craft* of rhetorical disposition, and to be able to appreciate the plan which the speaker chooses, it is even more important that he determine the degree and success of the speaker's accommodation to the variabilities of audience behavior. If there are alleged irregularities in the organization and arrangement of a speech, it is the critic's job, indeed, to point them out, but only after he has examined the social milieu and has found no compelling reason for the speaker's departure from conventional plans. This is not an invitation to rhetorical chaos under the protective guise of artistic deviation or audience requirements. Most speeches will doubtless follow the traditional scheme, for experience has fixed it as fundamentally good. But where there is deviation, it must not be arbitrarily and automatically assigned to the speaker's perversity or ineptitude. Responsibility of judgment requires that the critic's pronouncements issue from the facts of the situation, rather than from the rules of the savants.

A Critical Analysis of Speech Structure

A judicious blending of the data dealing with audience conditions and the ordering of the speaker's thought is found in Karl R. Wallace's fine study of Booker T. Washington:

> Skillful in adapting his lines of argument to attitudes and emotions of his listeners, masterly in sketching his self-portrait, Washington is extraordinarily felicitous in the presentation of his utterances. The pattern of his thought, although simple, appears in ingenious arrangements that gently lead his hearers into his program; and the earnestness and quiet directness of his delivery seem designed to let his ideas and his great purpose speak for themselves.
>
> The rhetorical arrangement of his speeches for the most part shows the modern tripartite division: introduction, discussion, or body, and conclusion. The 15-minute Atlanta Address is representative of such partition. With the introduction and conclusion each about two minutes long, the speech also reflects Washington's preference for brevity in these divisions. Except in one instance, no introduction is longer

than 5 minutes, even though Washington usually spoke for about an hour. Perorations are invariably short.

In moving from the opening remarks to the body of a speech, Washington rarely states his governing idea completely and explicitly in sentence form. The topic, or the purpose, however, is occasionally alluded to unmistakably. To Muchakinock children, for example, he is explicit; they are 'to think what you are going to school for.' To his own students of Tuskegee, he proceeds, almost without preliminaries, to announce that he wants 'to emphasize the importance of teamwork.' At times, as in the Atlanta Address and in the talk to Muchakinock coal miners, he moves from introduction to body by means of a narrative illustration whose point is the governing idea of the speech. Washington's practice, then, is to lead an audience to his theme, without stating it as a proposition.

Similarly, in developing the body of a speech he avoids throwing his program abruptly at a group. In effect he surrounds his hearers before they realize what is happening. Accordingly, to biracial audiences in both North and South—particularly to groups from whom he is seeking support of Tuskegee—Washington's favorite method of disposition in the body proper resembles an expository-inductive process. First comes a short sketch of Tuskegee's growth and an explanation of the methods and aims of manual and industrial training for Negroes, followed by a brief, general description of the poverty and ignorance of the Southern Negro. Then, in a much longer section, emerges the idea that such education will improve the Negro's lowly state and will enable him to determine his own economic status. Finally, with the ground thus laid, comes discussion of industrial education as affording the techniques and attitudes necessary for racial harmony. By such a method, therefore, Washington adduces and applies his theme. Such a sequence, also, constitutes the order of climax, for it is probable that most audiences— even educational groups—were more interested in his solution of the race problem than in a discourse merely upon education at Tuskegee. The expository-inductive plan, it should be observed, may well have been the result of Washington's belief that 'the average audience . . . wants facts rather than generalities or sermonizing. Most people . . . are able to draw proper conclusions if they are given the facts in an interesting form. . . .'

Besides the expository-inductive method of disposition, Washington likes to present the chief parts of the discussion topically, often in this order: material or industrial, educational, moral, religious, and social. Most of his speeches reveal all these heads, but they are not all developed to the same extent. Special heads receive extended treatment according to the group addressed. When, for example, he bids frankly for support of Tuskegee before a receptive Northern group, he devotes most time to education, although the other heads are treated adequately. Or when he faces an audience, Northern or Southern, that has heard of Vardaman's denunciation of Negro education, he passes lightly over education at Tuskegee and amplifies the topic of the salutary industrial and moral results of the limited education vouchsafed his race. Similarly, in his annual addresses to the National Negro Business League, he dwells primarily on the material progress made by businessmen, on the additional opportunities before them, and considers but briefly the other heads. Thus, Washington's method of classification enables him to strike the right notes for a given audience and occasion.

Such topical disposition and classification may be in part responsible for the extraordinary vigor in the movement of Washington's addresses. Since most of his speeches boil down to the same logical content, the scheme, applicable to most of his audiences and yet elastic to allow easy and logical amplification of any part, manifestly encourages great variety of emphasis and subordination. The apparent inclusiveness of the scheme, furthermore, gives the impression of having revealed all the facets of the theme, until the hearer feels that he has been shown not merely the beginning of the subject but its end.

The progression of ideas in Washington's speeches is distinguished, also, by movement from the less interesting to the more interesting. In most instances this does not involve a methodical building up in stair-step fashion from topic to topic until a single climactic point is attained; rather, the more factual, less emotionally charged topics, placed in the first half or two-thirds of an address, are succeeded by the more emotionally charged, intenser lines of argument, and the hearer is thus carried from a lower to a higher tone. In the expository-inductive arrangement the effect is obvious.[11]

Speech Organization Related to Persistent Theme in Rhetoric

Our discussion of disposition has suggested the age-old controversy of *matter vs. form.* We need not labor that question with further remarks. It is enough simply to point out that the most impressive and truthful matter conceivable can lose lustre and attractiveness through faulty organization, and conversely that perfect organization can never transform drivel into shining truth. Form is not a sterile concept. It makes a difference whether material combines into a unified whole or remains an inchoate mass of disjointed particulars; under no circumstances, however, should we regard form as an independent virtue. William Shedd once remarked that mere form is a ghost, "and a ghost possesses neither being nor reality." Disposition, as the rhetorical counterpart of form in its broader sense, must be viewed as a *means;* through it the potency of subject matter asserts itself and makes its purposes evident to the perceiving mind. But it remains a means—not a terminal value.

Chapter 15

THE STYLE OF PUBLIC ADDRESS

The Problem of Style

Joseph Addison once remarked that "there is not so variable a thing in nature as a lady's hairdress." Perhaps he should have added, unless it be the concept of style. Surely no term has been bandied about more freely, or has provoked a fuller measure of controversy. This chapter is intended neither as a refutation of previous claims, nor as a statement of an original thesis. Rather, it represents both a survey and, it is hoped, a common sense point of view which should help to orient the critic in his task of assessing the style of public address.

Style, said Hugh Blair, is "the peculiar manner in which a man expresses his conceptions, by means of Language." This definition affords a useful point of departure because it stresses the relation between thought and language. As Blair observes, "Style has always some reference to an author's manner of thinking. It is a picture of the ideas which rise in his mind, and of the manner in which they rise there; . . ." So "style is nothing else than that sort of expression which our thoughts most readily assume." [1] All of which is an indorsement of Quintilian's dictum that we should bestow great care on expression,

> provided we bear in mind that nothing is to be done for the sake of words, as words themselves were invented for the sake of things, and as those words are the most to be commended which express our thoughts best, and produce the impression which we desire on the minds of the judges. [2]

The functional idea introduced by Quintilian is significant. It postulates style as an indivisible element of the process of persuasion, and focuses attention upon what language *does,* rather than exclusively upon what it *is.* John F. Genung emphasizes this thesis by saying that style is "the skillful adaptation of expression to thought." [3] And the nature of subject matter determines the extent to which style becomes an operative influence. Certain facts such

405

as statistics do not, as Genung indicates, admit of stylistic enhancement; but, when they are expressively translated, they may yield to felicitous statement. Thus, through the concept of style is thought "made to stand out as adapted to act upon men." [4] The writer's or speaker's effort is directed, "not so much to the qualities of style in themselves, as to the demands of his subject, in order to bring out in its fullness what is essentially there." [5] Style is an instrument of communication, inextricably interwoven with the other parts of rhetoric.

Under its older title of *elocutio,* style was regarded as the third part of rhetoric. It referred chiefly to the way in which the speaker clothed his ideas with language. But, like the other parts of rhetoric, it is closely interrelated with its correlative members. Thus style and invention play interacting roles, since the conception of thought and its expression are virtually inseparable. Likewise, the arrangement accorded ideas is in itself a stylistic consideration, for the position an idea occupies in the total discourse may influence materially the way in which language is employed to express it.

Style and Personality.—The relationship between style and ethical proof has given rise to a considerable body of literary comment. It has been alleged, and with demonstrable reason, that personal character is clearly revealed by the speaker's style of expression. While this concept has been considered chiefly in relation to written, rather than oral, expression, the thesis seems equally applicable to the latter. In other words, a man may be said to speak as he does because of what he is. As a speaker, in a face-to-face situation, he is the style. His words reveal his inner character.

That this revelation will always be complete and unalterably exact, whether in speech or writing, cannot be claimed. As John A. Symonds [6] once remarked, the secret of a man's personality is not always revealed by his actions and words. However, it may be said that the qualities of style are closely identified with the qualities and limitations of the man, and accordingly tell us a good deal about him. The analyst of a speaker's or writer's style will undoubtedly be able, as Symonds suggests, to detect broad distinctions of temperament, both moral and emotional, in the productions. He will be able to find evidence linking the speaker with his inborn traits, his training, habits, and general outlook on life. But he cannot expect a man's expression to be an open revelation of his character. The epigrams "style is the man" and "the man is the style" are only conditionally acceptable.

Involved Nature of Style.—With the possible exception of invention, no part of rhetoric is more complex than style. Its ramifications are elaborate, extending, as has just been suggested, deeply into the fundamentals of invention and disposition and losing themselves in them, so that what we arbitrarily call style becomes indistinguishable from the other elements.

The concept of style has enjoyed varying measures of emphasis by analysts ever since Aristotle wrote his *Rhetoric*. The classical works generally accorded it a balanced treatment. But in later years, when the doctrine of exornation began to take root, there was a tendency to make style the *sine qua non* of rhetoric. Paraphrasing Alexander Pope, a time came when

> Others for *language* all their care express,
> And value speech, as women men, for dress.

When schools of declamation held sway in Greece and Rome, style was practically everything. Style and delivery, linked indissolubly, marked the speaker of skill. The essential relation of manner to matter was lost sight of, with the result that cogency of ideas figured for nought. Display was the keynote. Divorced from what Charles S. Baldwin called the "urgencies of subject," style moved toward decoration, exhibitionism, "virtuosity." During the eighteenth century in England, there was a resurgence of interest in the conception of rhetoric as style. Thomas Gibbons' *Rhetoric,* devoted exclusively to tropes and figures, illustrates an extreme in the stylistic approach to the subject. During recent years, rhetoricians have given less emphasis to style; instead, they have regarded language as a functional element, important chiefly for what it *does* rather than for what it *is* in its own right.

Plan of This Treatment.—The purpose of this chapter is twofold: to present a short survey of some ideas persistently associated with the problem of style; and, secondly, to develop a point of view relative to stylistic matters. This conception should afford the critic a convenient and usable yardstick for measuring an orator's skill in expression, by making style a function of the broader consideration of rhetorical adaptation and adjustment to the audience.

Persistent Problem in Style: Classifications

Fruitless and even pernicious as is the effort to classify the types of style, the impulse to do so has the authority of the ages to support it. Sensibly conscious of certain distinguishing marks in the style of selected speakers, rhetoricians have found it convenient to group modes of expression into classes. We have already shown how the three-way classification of style got its first development in Latin in the *ad Herennium*. It was believed that there was a Grand, a Middle, and a Plain style, each with distinctive characteristics. Cicero continued this tradition by describing the three complexions, as he put it, of eloquence. There is one sort, he said, "which has a fulness but is free from tumor; one which is plain, but not without nerve and vigor; and one which, participating of both these kinds, is commended for a certain middle quality." [7] While recognizing the shortcomings of classificatory schemes, Quintilian accepted the standard division: the plain, the grand, and the middle. "Of these," he remarked, "the nature is such that the *first* seems adapted to the duty of *stating facts,* the second to that of *moving the feelings,* and the third, by whichsoever name it be designated, to that of *pleasing,* or *conciliating, . . .*" [8] By linking the types of style to their functional significance, such classifications become somewhat less suspect. Here Quintilian makes the styles conform fairly closely to the so-called "offices" of the orator in explaining, conciliating, and moving. And for the first, he postulates the necessary condition of perspicuity; for the second, gentleness of manner; and for the third, energy. [9]

Quintilian also subdivided styles on another basis. He turned to the distinction between the speaking of the *Attic* and the *Asiatic* orators, observing that the former were "compressed and energetic" in their style while the Asiatics were "inflated and deficient in force." And the Attics were distinguished by their freedom from redundancy; the Asiatics, by their lack of judgment and restraint. [10] Quintilian went on to report that some critics had added a third kind of eloquence, the Rhodian, which had a character intermediate between the other two. It derived its quality from the country itself and from its founder, Aeschines, who, exiled in Rhodes, "carried thither the accomplishments then studied at Athens, which, like certain plants that degenerate when they are removed to a foreign climate and soil, formed a union of the Attic flavour with that of the country to which they were transplanted." The orators of this school were "accounted somewhat deficient in vigour and spirit, though nevertheless not without force, resembling, not pure springs, nor turbid torrents, but calm floods." [11]

It is interesting to note how the doctrine of classes has pervaded the conception of style. During the second half of the nineteenth century, such a widely used textbook as G. F. Quackenbos' *Composition and Rhetoric* [12] resorted to an elaborate division of the types.

There is the *dry* style, said Quackenbos, which excludes ornament
of all kinds and aims only at intelligibility, eschewing everything
manifestly intended to "please either the fancy or the ear." A *plain*
style is one degree above the dry; it strives for perspicuity, first of
all, but also considers precision, purity, and propriety. "Such figures
as are naturally suggested and tend to elucidate [the] meaning, . . .
[the writer] does not reject, while such as merely embellish he avoids
as beneath his notice." The *neat* style employs ornaments, but not
the most elevated or sparkling kinds. "Beauty of composition is
sought to be attained rather by a judicious selection and arrangement of words than by striking efforts of imagination." The sentences are of moderate length, and free from superfluities. *Elegant*
style "possesses all the beauty that ornament can add, without any
of the drawbacks arising from its improper or excessive use." This
was regarded as the perfection of style. A *florid* style employs ornaments everywhere. These may spring

> from a luxuriant imagination and have a solid basis of thought to rest
> upon: or, as is too often the case, the luxuriance may be in words
> alone and not in fancy; the brilliancy may be merely superficial, a
> glittering tinsel, which, however much it may please the shallow-
> minded, cannot fail to disgust the judicious.[13]

It is observed that only those of "transcendent genius" can continuously engage in ornament with any expectation of success. Quackenbos believes, however, that time usually corrects excess in the use
of this style; and he quotes as supporting testimony Quintilian's
dictum that "luxuriance can easily be cured; but for barrenness
there is no remedy."

The *simple* style is characterized by sentence structure that "bears
no marks of art; it seems to be the very language of nature." It aims
always to be consistent with nature. *Labored* style—the exact opposite of the simple—is stamped by "affectation, misplaced ornament, a
preponderance of swelling words, long and involved sentences, and
a constrained tone, neither easy, graceful, nor natural." The *concise* style, aiming at brevity, "rejects as redundant every thing not
material to the sense." It relies upon strong, compact sentences
which suggest more than they express directly. The *diffuse* style
employs repetitions freely; indulges in long sentences "making up
by copiousness what . . . [it] lacks in strength"; and draws often
upon amplification. And, finally, the *nervous* style produces a strong,
and the *feeble* style a slight, impression upon the hearer. They are

often considered synonymous with the diffuse and concise styles, though Quackenbos doubts the wisdom of such an identification.[14]

As illustrations of the various styles, Quackenbos mentions Aristotle for the dry; Locke and Swift for the plain; Addison for the elegant; Ossian for the florid; Homer and Goldsmith for the simple; Markham for the labored; Bacon for the concise; Cicero for the diffuse; and Burke for the nervous style.

These representative classifications suggest the pervasiveness of the effort to compartmentalize kinds of expression according to certain features or qualities. The effects of these classifications persist in recent rhetorical criticism. When Chauncey Goodrich, for instance, calls Thomas Erskine's style "chaste, forcible, and harmonious"; and when, in his appraisal of Curran's oratory, he contrasts it with Erskine's "Attic taste," he is obviously holding close to the line established by the classifiers.[15]

Qualities of Style

For many years it has been the practice of rhetoricians to analyze the concept of style in terms of the qualities that contribute to its excellence. Cicero speaks of Theophrastus' attempt to establish four such features: correctness, clearness, ornateness, and propriety. The classical tradition accepted, generally, such or a variant classification. Any attempt to analyze expression according to its distinguishing qualities reveals traces of arbitrary subdivision, but it is nevertheless helpful in highlighting the elements which manifestly contribute to stylistic excellence. We shall, accordingly, discuss briefly the qualities of correctness, clearness, and propriety. Since ornateness can be considered more appropriately at a later point in this chapter, we shall dwell but lightly upon it here.

Correctness.—Correctness refers chiefly to word choice or usage. At its simplest, it is little more than a study of vocabulary; at its most complex stage, it embraces the whole doctrine of purity and excellence in diction. Aristotle believed correctness of language to be the foundation of all good style. He listed as its constituent elements: (1) proper use of connecting words; (2) use of specific rather than general words for things; (3) avoidance of ambiguity; 4) accurate classification of nouns as to gender; and (5) correct expression of plurality, fewness, and unity.[16]

Approaching the problem from approximately the same point of view, but with a different emphasis, Cicero remarked that all speech was a matter of words, and that the words had to be studied both as individual units and as parts of a compositional whole.[17] Each of these aspects had a peculiar merit. As for word choice, he suggested that the orator use metaphorical words often, new ones sometimes, and very old ones rarely.[18]

One of the most detailed treatments of word choice and usage is found in George Campbell's *Philosophy of Rhetoric*. His analysis has been used widely; it still serves, as a matter of fact, as the standard for many studies in the field. Campbell[19] puts words to a threefold test: (1) Are they reputable? That is, do they enjoy good standing among men of taste? As he puts it, the words must be authorized by the practice of a great number, if not the majority, of distinguished writers or speakers. (2) Are they in national use? In other words, they should be divorced from provincial or foreign attachments. And (3) are they in present use? This simply suggests that time and period affect usage, but it does not imply that words are necessarily the worse for being old or the better for being new.

Recognizing purity of diction as the foundation of excellence in other aspects of style, Campbell sets forth his celebrated canons of usage. These canons are intended to show how purity, or "grammatical truth," may be realized. In their briefest form, the canons state:[20]

The first canon, then, shall be, When use is divided as to any particular word or phrase, and the expression used by one part hath been preoccupied, or is in any instance susceptible of a different signification, and the expression employed by the other part never admits a different sense, both perspicuity and variety require that the form of expression which is in every instance univocal be preferred. . . .

The second canon is, In doubtful cases regard ought to be had in our decisions to the analogy of the language. . . .

The third canon is, When the terms of expression are in other respects equal, that ought to be preferred which is most agreeable to the ear. . . .

The fourth canon is, In cases wherein none of the foregoing rules gives either side a ground of preference, a regard to simplicity (in which I include etymology when manifest) ought to determine our choice. . . .

The fifth and only other canon that occurs to me on the subject of divided use is, In the few cases wherein neither perspicuity nor analogy, neither sound nor simplicity, assists us in fixing our choice, it is safest to prefer that manner which is most conformable to ancient usage.

Note should also be made of these subcanons:

> All words and phrases which are remarkably harsh, and unharmonious, and not absolutely necessary, may justly be judged worthy of this fate [that is, merit degradation]. . . .
> When etymology plainly points to a signification different from that which the word commonly bears, propriety and simplicity both require its dismission. . . .
> When any words become obsolete, or, at least, are never used, except as constituting part of particular phrases, it is better to dispense with their service entirely, and give up the phrases. . . .
> All those phrases which, when analyzed grammatically, include a solecism, and all those to which use hath affixed a particular sense, but which, when explained by the general and established rules of the language, are susceptible either of a different sense or of no sense, ought to be discarded altogether.

The virtue of correctness thus embraces a variety of concepts, including those of words and of their union. But, by and large, it deals with word choice that insures accuracy in developing the speaker's thought—an accuracy that is unimpaired by modish colloquialisms, archaisms, and word coinages. Correctness facilitates the use of language as an effective vehicle for conveying thought.

Clearness.—Closely related to correctness, and no less important in the total process of language usage, is the quality of clearness. ". . . let excellence of style be defined," said Aristotle, "to consist in its being clear; (a sign of this is that the diction, unless it make the sentiment clear, will not effect its purpose. . . .")[21] Like the other qualities of good style, this one concerns both the choice of words and their arrangement. It arises from a certain simplicity and perspicuity which Quintilian considered the first virtue of composition. "Let there be proper words, and a clear order," he observed; "let not the conclusion of the sense be too long protracted; and let there be nothing either deficient or superfluous."[22] The true end of style, Quintilian remarked later, is that the judge not only understand us, "but that he may not be able not to understand us."[23] In the words of Philo Buck, the "highest ends can be reached by the simplest means; and this is one very great secret in style."[24]

Perspicuity is an essential in all types of discourse, regardless of the purpose the speaker tries to realize. A speaker must be understood, or he labors to no avail. And the clearness of the speech must be, as it were, an unrecognized element of its merit. As John Broadus once said: "Style is excellent when, like the atmosphere, it shows the thought, but itself is not seen."[25]

Barriers to Clearness—What, then, are the possible violations against perspicuity which may mar the clarity of discourse? Again we may turn to Campbell [26] for helpful guidance. The first general cause grows out of an obscurity which may take various forms. (1) It may result from a defect in the expression, as when a fairly well established elliptical expression fails to convey meaning to the particular hearers. Or, this defect may result from an overconciseness which carries the thought to a point just short of intelligibility. (2) There may be a faulty arrangement of words, resulting in unclear constructions. As Campbell remarks:

> A discourse . . . excels in perspicuity when the subject engrosses the attention of the hearer, and the diction is so little minded by him that he can scarcely be said to be conscious that it is through this medium he sees into the speaker's thoughts. On the contrary, the least obscurity, ambiguity, or confusion in the style, instantly removes the attention from the sentiment to the expression, and the hearer endeavours, by the aid of reflection, to correct the imperfections of the speaker's language.[27]

(3) Obscurity may arise from using the same word in different senses. (4) Uncertain references in pronouns and relatives may be the cause. (5) Too artificial or complicated sentence structure may militate against perspicuity. This is particularly true where the sense of the statement is too long suspended. (6) The injudicious use of technical words and phrases may prove another "source of darkness" in composition. And (7) extremely long sentences are likely to admit of excesses against the dictates of clearness.

The second violation of perspicuity often arises from double meaning. Here, as Campbell remarks, the "fault is not that the sentence conveys darkly or imperfectly the author's meaning, but that it conveys also some other meaning which is not the author's." [28] There is, then, the possibility of varied and various interpretation of the meaning. When such misinterpretation develops from an expression having more meanings than originally intended for it, it is known as equivocation; when it results from an arrangement of words that renders the whole construction equivocal, it is called ambiguity.

The last general offense against perspicuity is that which results from a speaker's failure to convey his meaning at all. In other words, this is the offence of unintelligibility. It may arise, first, from a confusion of thought on the part of the speaker. And it is evident that no language medium, however perfect, "will suffice for exhibiting a distinct and unvarying image of a confused and unsteady object." [29] Furthermore, unintelligibility may arise from an "affectation of excellence," as when a speaker tampers with an otherwise perspicuous statement by inserting a clause of doubtful meaning, simply for purposes of exhibition. Finally, unintelligibility may arise from a want of meaning. Campbell distinguishes "want of meaning" from that of confusion of thought, by saying:

> When this is the cause of difficulty, the reader will not fail, if he be attentive, to hesitate at certain intervals, and to retrace his progress, finding himself bewildered in the terms, and at a loss for the meaning. Then he will try to construe the sentence, and to ascertain the significations of the words. By these means, and by the help of the context, he will possibly come at last at what the author would have said; whereas, in that species of the unintelligible which proceeds from a vacuity of thought, the reverse commonly happens. The sentence is generally simple in its structure, and the construction easy. When this is the case, provided words glaringly unsuitable are not combined, the reader proceeds without hesitation or doubt. He never suspects that he does not understand a sentence, the terms of which are familiar to him, and of which he perceives distinctly the grammatical order. But if he be by any means induced to think more closely on the subject, and peruse the words a second time more attentively, it is probable that he will then begin to suspect them, and will at length discover that they contain nothing but either an identical proposition, which conveys no knowledge, or a proposition of that kind of which one cannot so much as affirm that it is either true or false.[30]

Granted that all thoughts do not admit of equally clear expression, it is generally agreed that good style preserves the integrity of thoughts while at the same time achieving intelligibility. The fusion of those two elements requires, as John F. Genung observes, that the speaker or writer subdue "language to perfect flexibility and obedience." Thus clearness really becomes "the intellectual quality of style." [31]

Appropriateness.—The quality of appropriateness in style embraces much of what has been said relative to correctness and clearness. This is true because the latter elements derive much of their character from the fact that they are adapted to the circumstances in which the expression is used. What may be correct or clear before a certain group may be decidedly not so to another. These virtues reside partly in their propriety, in their being fitted to the special conditions of the moment. Thus we must look to appropriateness as an important stylistic quality. It is, indeed, the most functional aspect of the whole problem of style; through it we are best able to study language as a tool of adaptive behavior used by the orator to adjust himself to his audience situation.

It is generally recognized that the style of expression should be appropriate to or in correspondence with the subject; that is, the mode of expression should be consistent with the nature of the address. Aristotle holds unmistakably to this doctrine. He affirms that when weighty matters are being discussed, the casual manner of expression should not be used; when trivial topics are being considered, there should not be a manner of solemnity.[32] Cicero accepts substantially the same point of view. Indicating that propriety, or the *becoming* in oratory, is essential, he says

> . . . no single kind of style can be adapted to every cause, . . . For capital causes require one kind of oratory, panegyric another, judicial proceedings another, common conversation another, consolation another, reproof another, disputation another, historical narrative another.[33]

Cicero's conception of copious language springs directly from the doctrine of propriety, his conviction being that "copiousness of matter produces copiousness of language; and, if there be an inherent dignity in the subjects on which he [the orator] speaks, there must be . . . a certain splendor in his expression." [34]

It should be observed that Quintilian formalized this concept by saying that the style should be adapted not only to the cause, but to particular parts of the cause. Thus the orator will rely upon different arts and modes of expression in the exordium, narration, and so on, as his intention is to conciliate, or to inform, or to induce to action.[35] The speaker accommodates himself to the purpose in view; and his style changes with the accommodations.

The doctrine of propriety also governs the use of figurative language. Hugh Blair, for instance, insists that we suit the tropes and figures to the subject; that we avoid forcing subjects into a state of elevation through the use of figures that are not congruous with the content.[36]

The concept of appropriateness goes beyond this point, however. Style must also be appropriate to the type of oratory used and to the particular audience addressed. The style of deliberative oratory, said Aristotle, "is exactly like sketching; for in proportion as the crowd is larger, the view is taken from a greater distance. . . ." [37] He then says that the forensic style is highly finished, as is that addressed to a single judge since there is little room for rhetorical artifice. Ceremonial speaking is the most literary of all, chiefly because it is intended to be read. Cicero agreed in general with this belief. He indicated that it was of consequence to consider "who forms the audience, whether the senate, or the people, or the judges; whether it is a large or a small assembly, or a single person, and of what character. . . ." [38] All these considerations he relates closely to subject matter, remarking that "it is the part of art and nature to be able *to do* what is becoming on every occasion. . . ." [39]

The concept of adapting style to the audience and to the type of oratory has remained essentially unchanged since antiquity. It is still considered important, even though treated less formally today. For instance, we believe that ceremonial oratory, because of its very nature, yields to somewhat different stylistic development than expositional analysis, which is intended simply to enlighten the understanding. In short, we still believe, as Aristotle did centuries ago, that "to each kind of rhetoric is adapted a peculiar style."

Finally, in considering appropriateness in style, it is assumed that the style should be consistent with the speaker himself. In other words, it should help to reveal the character of the speaker; it should not seem to clash with his personality. Thus it is generally agreed that the style should be congruent with the speaker's age. Aristotle regarded this matter as important; [40] Cicero deemed it significant to inquire who the speakers were, of what age, rank, and authority, in order that the *becoming* qualities in oratory might be evaluated. So far as this matter concerns the critic of oratory, it centers largely about one inquiry: Does the speaker's style represent the person employing it; or, does it, instead, seem to cloak the thoughts in language unsuited to him as an individual?

Ornateness.—We have referred to four possible qualities of good style, the last being ornateness. At this point it is sufficient to say that it refers principally to a certain elevation or grandeur in discourse, and results from the full and intelligent use of the constituents of style, presently to be discussed. Hence, ornateness is a distinctive quality that depends upon the artistic handling of words, sentences, and figurative elements. Essentially, it is a manifestation of sublimity in discourse, a heightened effect giving an individual stamp to oratory.

Constituents of Style

The foregoing summary of the qualities of style is by no means exhaustive. Many other qualities can be mentioned, including force, vivacity, vividness, and simplicity. But the terms employed are not important, as long as we recognize the stylistic features which the words are intended to describe. So we need to supplement our analysis of qualities by considering the fundamental constituents of style: choice of words, composition, and embellishment.

(1) The Choice of Words.—Word choice has already been discussed under the qualities of correctness and clearness. Fundamentally, it deals with the selection of the best possible words for the particular task. It is a highly individual matter, the eventual choices varying with a large number of circumstances, including the speaker's knowledge, his language facility, his understanding of the nature of the speaking problem and of the audience, and the character of the response sought through the speech.

(2) Composition.—The second constituent of style is composition, or the orderly arrangement of the words chosen. Under the headings correctness and clearness, we have discussed certain aspects of this concept. In its broad sense, composition embraces a host of topics. Regarded as the medium through which beauty and sense are imparted to language, it includes an extensive range—from the careless, primitive moulding of words into united forms, straight through to the artificially conceived elaborations which aim primarily at nicety, however puerile. For our purposes, composition is regarded as a tool with which the speaker works. Nicety of effect for its own sake need not concern us. Therefore, we may confine our remarks to two aspects of composition: structure and rhythm.

Structure has to do with the way in which words are assembled and related so as to convey thought with economy of effort and effectiveness of purpose. Obviously, this suggests that the laws of grammar must serve as the basis of operation. However, it also implies a further and, for the orator, a very important fact: that the purpose he entertains will mould the materials in a particular way adapted to the requirements of the audience situation. Thus both grammatical and rhetorical principles operate in the finished composition of public address.

Composition is a complex process. It begins with the syntactical principles governing number, mood, case, and tense, and it extends to the construction of the finished paragraph. All these arrangements cannot be considered here; the proper province of their discussion lies in a standard textbook on grammar. Suffice it, however, that critical inquiry looks to these aspects of composition and appraises their usage in the light of the practical requirements of the audience situation in which they are employed. Hence the inquiry deals with matters of syntax; the collocation of qualifying elements in sentences, since force and emphasis may depend upon the position certain parts occupy in the construction; the accuracy and specificity of the antecedents, or, as John F. Genung [41] expresses it, the "retrospective" and the "prospective" references; the precision with which relations are indicated in sentence structure through the use of conjunctions and other correlating devices; the effectiveness with which thoughts are emphasized and expanded consistent with the demands of the speaker's purpose; the presence of comparable facility in securing effectiveness through brevity; the use of repetition, and the employment of devices for securing emphasis.

Extending the discussion of structure, we acknowledge the importance of variety in the finished patterns of sentences. Thus interspersing long with short sentences tends to enhance style, breaking, as it does, the sameness of thought patterns. Conversely, an unbroken sequence of long sentences tends to become monotonous, while a succession of short ones may produce a staccato, choppy effect.

The subject matter, it is true, will determine in some measure the type of sentence to be employed. But, in the main, good style is the result of the judicious use and interaction of three kinds of sentences: the periodic, the loose, and the balanced. A periodic sentence is one in which neither idea nor grammatical structure is completed until the final words; adaptable to the building of a climax, it contains some primary feature that is more effectively carried across to the listener through delay in revelation. A loose sentence, on the other hand, does not follow this principle of suspense. It is so constructed, both in grammar and in the presentation of the idea, that it could be terminated, possibly at several points, before the end is reached without violating grammatical sense. Finally, the balanced sentence is a compound sentence in which the different elements, through similarity of form, answer each other or set each other off.

Naturally, an orator's style is not judged by rule as to the statistical proportion of one sentence type to another. The speaker has certain thoughts to communicate. The language in which he clothes those thoughts is not determined by law; it is suggested by the requirements of himself and of his hearers. He must fulfill more than a simple grammatical function. Accordingly, it would be folly to require that certain thoughts be expressed in certain ways. The variables of rhetorical effectiveness militate unalterably against such a procedure.

The final stage is the assembly of related sentences into paragraphs which should be specific units of the thought structure. Here we have occasion to observe the interweaving of materials which make up single topics. The prime consideration is unity, for the series of sentences in each paragraph must represent an unbroken continuity. On the whole, however, the construction of paragraphs follows the same general lines as the development of a complete discourse.

Rhythm has long been considered a pleasing attribute of prose style. Through it, speech seems to take on added beauty, and to become a more effective instrument for conveying the emotional fervor of the speaker. As it relates to prose, however, rhythm has a special signification. Aristotle believed that prose should be rhythmical to a certain extent, but not metrical.[42] Cicero agreed, but added that an oration should not be inharmonious, "like the conversation of the common people." [43]

The sources of rhythmical prose are manifold. They rest in the structure of the sentences; in their arrangement in the paragraph; in the combination of metrical feet; in the delivery accorded the material by the speaker, and, according to Cicero, in the figures of speech. No doubt what the speaker should strive for, however, is what Genung calls an "unmeasured rhythm, ever varied, yet never neglected. . . ." To achieve an effect pleasing to the ear, the speaker relies chiefly upon "the easy flow of accented and unaccented syllables"; upon the "musical regularity, yet variety, of the natural pauses"; upon the distribution of accented syllables, "in order that the stress may not fall on too many words in succession"; upon variety in the "time" of the speech; upon the gradual suspension of sense, rather than the abrupt termination, at the end of sentences, and upon the measures of volume proportionate to the importance and emphasis of the ideas.[44] Whereas the poet holds to more fixed metrical schemes, the speaker conforms to no such patterns. He uses metre only to serve the larger purpose of achieving oratorical effectiveness.

(3) **Embellishment.**—The third constituent of style is embellishment. Its primary function is to adorn or to elevate through the judicious use of tropes and figures. Both Cicero and Quintilian devote considerable space to an analysis of the devices which add lustre to ordinary expression. It was the rhetoricians of Tudor England and of the late eighteenth century, however, who were most systematic and comprehensive in treating this aspect of style. So it is that

we turn to one of the latter for most of our classifications. Thomas Gibbons' *Rhetoric* provides a usable list of the tropes and figures upon which speakers continue to rely. While it is true that the figures no longer receive the attention they used to, we are perhaps in a better position to assess their value now than were the men of the periods during which figurative forms enjoyed fuller status. We no longer make *elocutio* the primary point of concern in rhetoric; instead, we appraise it in its relation to the larger function of getting responses. But we use tropes and figures regularly, even though we may not assign fancy names to them, as our predecessors did. Figurative language represents a part of the total process of rhetoric and therefore should not be overlooked.

Tropes and Figures.—There is a distinction between tropes and figures. While this distinction is not discussed frequently in the contemporary literature of speechcraft, it seems to be a valid differentiation. A trope, says Thomas Gibbons, *"is the changing a word or sentence with advantage, from its proper signification to another meaning. Thus, for example, God is a Rock."* [45] A figure, on the other hand, *"is the fashioning or Dress of a Composition, or an emphatical manner of speaking different from what is plain and common."* [46] The distinction, then, is that the trope

> . . . is a change of a word or sentence from one sense into another, which its very etymology imports; whereas it is the nature of a Figure not to change the sense of words, but to illustrate, enliven, ennoble, or in some manner or another embellish our discourses. . . . [47]

The following definitions and examples, derived from Gibbons, cover certain of the tropes most frequently used in public address:

> A *Metaphor* is a Trope, by which a word is removed from its proper signification into another meaning upon account of Comparison. . . . Thus our blessed Lord is called *a vine, a lamb, a lion,* &c.

> An *Allegory* is a change or continuation of Tropes, and more generally of Metaphors; and differs from a single Trope in the same manner as a cluster on the vine does from only one or two grapes.

> > Did I but purpose to embark with thee
> > On the smooth surface of a summer's sea,
> > While gentle zephyrs play in prosp'rous gales,
> > And fortune's favour fills the swelling sails;
> > But would forsake the ship, and make the shore,
> > When the winds whistle, and the tempests roar. . . .

A *Metonymy* is a Trope, in which one name is put for another, for which it may be allowed to stand by reason of some relation or coherence between them. . . . Thus Mars among the Heathens is used for *war,* Ceres for *corn.* . . . 'He has a good heart'. . . .

A *Synecdoche* is a Trope, which puts the name of the whole for a part, or the name of a part for the whole; a general name for a particular under that general, or a particular for the general. . . . Put up your *weapon,* that is, your sword.

Under the Synecdoche we may also range the *Autonomasia,* which is a Trope by which we put a proper for a common name, or a common name for a proper. . . . Thus, that man is an Hercules. . . . he is gone to the City, . . . meaning *London.*

An *Irony* is a Trope, in which one contrary is signified by another; or, in which we speak one thing, and design another, in order to give the greater force and vehemence to our meaning. . . . Under the *Irony,* we may include the *Sarcasm,* which may be defined to be an *Irony* in its superlative keenness and asperity.

An *Hyperbole* is a Trope, that in its representation of things either magnifies or diminishes beyond or below the line of strict truth, or to a degree which is disproportioned to the real nature of the subject. . . . *whiter than snow, blacker than a raven.* . . . *deaf as a rock, blind as a mole.* . . .

A *Catachresis* is the most licentious as to language of all the Tropes, as it borrows the name of one thing to express another, which has either no proper name of its own; or if it has, the borrowed name is used either for surprising by novelty, or for the sake of a bold and daring energy. . . . Thus Quintilian allows us to say, that we *dart* a ball or a stake, though darting belongs only to a javelin. . . . Thus Virgil says, 'The goat himself, man of the flock, had stray'd,' by man, evidently intending the father and leader of the flock.[48]

Among the most common figures, the following should be noted:

An *Ecphonesis* is a Figure, that by an exclamation shews some strong and vehement passion.

Aporia, or doubting, is a Figure whereby we express an hesitation where to begin our discourse, or a difficulty what to do in some arduous affair, or what to resolve upon in some critical emergency.

The *Epanorthosis* is a Figure whereby we retract or recall what we have spoken or resolved.

Aposiopesis is a Figure whereby a person, often through the power of some passion, as anger, sorrow, fear, &c. breaks off his speech without finishing the sense.

Apophasis, or denial, is a Figure by which an Orator pretends to conceal or omit what he really and in fact declares.

Anacoenosis is a Figure by which the speaker applies to his hearers or opponents for their opinion upon the point in debate; or when a person excuses his conduct, gives reasons for it, and appeals to those about him whether they are not satisfactory.

Anastrophe, or inversion, is a Figure by which we suspend our sense, and the hearer's expectation; or a Figure by which we place last, and perhaps at a great remove from the beginning of the sentence, what, according to common order, should have been mentioned first.

Erotesis is a Figure by which we express the emotion of our minds, and infuse an ardor and energy into our discourses, by proposing questions.

Prolepsis is a Figure by which a speaker suggests an objection against what he is advancing, and returns an answer to it: or it is a Figure by which a speaker, more especially at the entrance upon his discourse, removes any sort of obstruction that he foresees may be likely to prevent the success of his cause.

Epanaphora is a Figure, in which the same word is gracefully and emphatically repeated; or in which distinct sentences, or the several members of the same sentence, are begun with the same word.

Apostrophe is a Figure in which we interrupt the current of our discourse, and turn to another person, or to some other object, different from that to which our address was first directed.

Periphrasis is a Figure in which we use more words than what are absolutely necessary, and sometimes less plain words, either to avoid some inconvenience and ill-effect which might proceed from expressing ourselves in fewer or clearer words, or in order to give a variety and eloquence to our discourses, and multiply the graces of our composition.

Synchoresis is a Figure whereby we grant or yield up something, in order to gain a point, which we could not so well secure without it.

Asyndeton is a Figure, occasioned by the omission of conjunctive particles, which are dropped either to express vehemence or speed; or sometimes it may be from a noble negligence or nice accuracy, arising from an attention to our ideas. . . . 'There was . . . an horrible spectacle in the open plains, pursuit, flight, slaughter, captivity.'

The very opposite to this Figure is the *Polysyndeton;* for as the *Asyndeton* drops, so the *Polysyndeton* on the contrary abounds with conjunctive particles.

Oxymoron is a Figure, in which the parts of a period or sentence disagree in sound, but perfectly accord with one another in meaning; or

. . . it is sense in the masquerade of folly. . . . *A coward dies often, a brave man but once.*

Enantiosis is a Figure, by which things very different or contrary are compared or placed together, and by which they mutually set off and enhance each other.

Climax, according to Mr. Blackwall's definition, is, 'when the word or expression, which ends the first member of a period, begins the second, and so on; so that every member will make a distinct sentence, taking its rise from the next foregoing, till the argument and period be beautifully finished: or . . . , it is when the word or expression, which was predicate in the first member of a period, is subject in the second, and so on, till the argument and period be brought to a noble conclusion.'

The *Hypotyposis* is a Figure, by which we give such a distinct and lively representation of what we have occasion to describe, as furnishes our hearers with a particular, satisfactory, and complete knowledge of our subject.

The *Prosopopoeia* is a Figure which consists in describing good and bad qualities of the mind, or the passions or appetites of human nature as real and distinct persons; in clothing with corporeal forms, or endowing with speech and action imaginary beings, or general notions and abstracted ideas; in introducing persons silent as speaking, or persons deceased as living; and in making rocks, woods, rivers, temples, and other inanimate beings, assume the powers and properties, and express the emotions of living, and even reasonable creatures.

Parabole is a Figure that compares one thing with another, to which it bears a resemblance.

An *Epiphonema* is a pertinent and instructive remark at the end of a discourse or narration.[49]

Use of Ornamentation.—The practical question with which the critic must deal in appraising the embellishment of a speech is: Do the tropes and figures contribute to the realization of the speaker's aim and object? If, as Emerson [50] believed, "nothing so works on the human mind . . . as a trope," it is necessary to inquire into the sources of its effectiveness.

Rhetoricians agree that figurative forms should not be used as substitutes for reason. Even Gibbons—a disciple of the school of exornation—declared that discourses should first "enlighten the understanding, and inform the judgment" before figures were introduced "to affect and engage the passions. . . ." The figures must help to reinforce thought, but should not be regarded as the real thought, *per se*. Accordingly, illustrative value is their chief virtue. By themselves they may conceivably have decorative value, but that is significant only if the more important service of support to thought is initially rendered.

Figurative forms must, therefore, be used sparingly. "Nothing so quickly tireth," says John Lawson, as the excessive use of figures. By their nature they are likely to attract notice; as illustrators and supporters of thought, they lose their functional significance as soon as they do nothing more than focus attention upon themselves. Under such circumstances, they tend to "*strangle* our meaning," as Gibbons put it.

And, finally, figures and tropes require a development that is economical of detail and of the time necessary for presentation. Failing this standard, they may easily become show-pieces, interesting perhaps, but ineffective in revealing swiftly the point under development. Remembering Herbert Spencer's observation that figures should be used with economy of attention, we may say with him: "To bring the mind more easily to the desired conception, is in many cases solely, and in all cases mainly, their [figures'] object." [51]

Economy of Style

Spencer's popular thesis that good style and economy of effort are indissolubly linked applies not only to figures of speech; indeed, it embraces the whole concept of expression in language. Spencer believed that style, to be good, had to make minimum demands upon the hearer's mechanism of reception—upon interpreting the symbols—in order that it might enlist maximum energy to appreciate the full meaning of the thought. As he put it:

> To so present ideas that they may be apprehended with the least possible mental effort, is the desideratum towards which most of the rules . . . point. When we condemn writing that is wordy, or confused, or intricate—when we praise this style as easy, and blame that as fatiguing, we consciously or unconsciously assume this desideratum as our standard of judgment. Regarding language as an apparatus of symbols for the conveyance of thought, we may say that, as in a mechanical apparatus, the more simple and the better arranged its parts, the greater will be the effect produced. In either case, whatever force is absorbed by the machine is deducted from the result. A reader or listener has at each moment but a limited amount of mental power available. To recognise and interpret the symbols presented to him requires part of this power; to arrange and combine the images suggested requires a further part; and only that part which remains can be used for the

realization of the thought conveyed. Hence, the more time and attention it takes to receive and understand each sentence, the less time and
attention can be given to the contained idea; and the less vividly will
that idea be conceived. How truly language must be regarded as a
hindrance to thought, though the necessary instrument of it, we shall
clearly perceive on remembering the comparative force with which
simple ideas are communicated by mimetic signs. . . . No phrase can convey the idea of surprise so vividly as opening the eyes and raising the
eyebrows. A shrug of the shoulders would lose much by translation into
words. Again, it may be remarked that when oral language is employed, the strongest effects are produced by interjections, which con-
dense entire sentences into syllables. And in other cases, where
custom allows us to express thoughts by single words, as in *Beware,*
Heigho, Fudge, much force would be lost by expanding them into specific verbal propositions. Hence, carrying out the metaphor that language is the vehicle of thought, there seems reason to think that in
all cases the friction and inertia of the vehicle deduct from its efficiency; and that in composition the chief if not the sole thing to be
done is, to reduce this friction and inertia to the smallest possible
amount. Let us then inquire whether economy of the recipient's attention is not the secret of effect, alike in the right choice and collocation of words, in the best arrangement of clauses in a sentence,
in the proper order of its principal and subordinate propositions, in
the judicious use of simile, metaphor, and other figures of speech,
and even in the rhythmical sequences of syllables.[52]

This doctrine draws upon the qualities of correctness of word
choice, perspicuity of statement and arrangement, and wisdom in the
selection of illustrative details and ornamental features. The validity
of Spencer's philosophy is freely accepted, especially in its relation
to speechmaking, where the hearer has no opportunity to back up
for a review of material previously presented. Instant and exact
intelligibility is a prime requisite of the speaker's style. So the less
attention the style attracts to the mechanics of word composition, the
more energy will be available to appreciate the ideas in the discourse.

Sincerity and Style

A derivative of our previous discussion of style as an index of
the speaker's personality is the relation of sincerity to the manner
of expression. Whether or not style can ever serve as a true reflector
of the man is not precisely the question. But that the state of a man's
faith in his cause, and of his devotion to it, may be revealed through
his presentation is no doubt true. Such revelation of the speaker's

character derives not necessarily from the deliberate use of art in composition; rather, it may result from the unstudied, the spontaneous, outpouring of his personal convictions. "Indignation does not require artifice," said Demetrius. ". . . the style should be natural in such denunciations, and the words should be simple." [53]

But even such an observation postulates art as a necessary condition, for it tells the speaker what he *should* do. In reality, however, what he does will probably not be dictated by rule. It will, instead, be a free expression governed only by the nature of the provoking cause for discussion, and by his own natural promptings to express what is most congruent with his thoughts and feelings on the matter.

Oral vs. Written Style

Since antiquity, the rhetoricians and critics have recognized a difference between oral and written style. Aristotle spoke of the written style as being "more finished" and of the oral style as admitting of "dramatic delivery." [54] Although asserting in one place that *"to speak well* and *to write well* are but the same thing," Quintilian [55] nevertheless saw that the two were not identical, and that good writing would have to be altered some if it were translated into the oral medium. He recognized the necessity of suiting materials to the capacities of judges, adding, however, that the speech would probably be "edited" later "lest it be thought to be the offspring of his judgment, and not a concession to circumstances."

Quintilian observed further that the language of ordinary discourse and that of a "truly eloquent man" are of a different nature. Were this not true, and were it sufficient for an orator

> . . . to express his thoughts plainly, he would have nothing to study beyond mere suitableness of words; but since he has to please, to move, and to rouse the minds of his audience to various states of feeling, he must have recourse, for those purposes, to the means which are afforded us by the same nature that supplies us with ordinary speech; just as we are led by nature to invigorate our muscles with exercise, to increase our general strength, and to acquire a healthy complexion. [56]

In his essay "On Familiar Style," William Hazlitt suggested that a familiar style in writing was the approximate equivalent of the expression one used in common conversation. It was like the expression of one "who had a thorough command and choice of words, or who could discourse with ease, force, and perspicuity, setting aside all pedantic and oratorical flourishes." This point of view, applied to speaking proper, seems reasonable since it does not set up artificial distinctions between types of discourse having communication of ideas as the common goal.

Whatever the differences between oral and written style may be —and they are differences of degree rather than of kind—it is evident that they result from the character of the medium in which they operate. The mode of expression is a function of the object the speaker intends to achieve. Hence, in the oral medium the speaker deals with hearers whose needs and capacities will govern much of his behavior. Word choice, arrangement, and embellishment will be controlled by the demands of the occasion, which will vary from audience to audience. The essential marks of oral style must, therefore, be determined in the light of the peculiar medium in which speech functions. Those features have already been discussed in Chapter 1.

Classical Interpretation of Style Still Prevalent

The conception of style deriving from a study of its qualities and constituents, such as we have considered, is essentially classical in nature. It has been widely accepted, and even today serves as a basis for most investigation in this field. Before we turn to a somewhat broader view of style, we should observe how the critics of the past dealt with stylistic matters in their studies of the orators. One of the illustrative analyses to which we shall turn is Chauncey Goodrich's study of Burke.

After discussing Burke's skill in debate, intellectual independence, subtlety and comprehensiveness of intellect, and power of generali· zation, Goodrich says:

> His *method* was admirable, in respect at least to his published speeches. No man ever bestowed more care on the arrangement of his thoughts. The exceptions to this remark are apparent, not real. There is now and then a slight irregularity in his mode of transition, which seems purposely thrown in to avoid an air of sameness; and the subordinate heads sometimes spread out so widely, that their connection with the main topic is not always obvious. But there is reigning throughout the whole a massive unity of design like that of a great cathedral, whatever may be the intricacy of its details.
>
> In his *reasonings* . . . Mr. Burke did not usually adopt the outward forms of logic. He has left us, indeed, some beautiful specimens of dialectical ability, but his arguments, in most instances, consisted of the amplest enumeration and the clearest display of all the facts and principles, the analogies, relations, or tendencies which were applicable to

the case, and were adapted to settle it on the immutable basis of the nature and constitution of things. Here again he appeared, of necessity, more as a teacher than a logician, and hence many were led to underrate his argumentative powers. The exuberance of his fancy was likewise prejudicial to him in this respect. Men are apt to doubt the solidity of a structure which is covered all over with flowers. . . .

In respect to Mr. Burke's *imagery,* however, it may be proper to remark, that a large part of it is not liable to any censure of this kind; many of his figures are so finely wrought into the texture of his style, that we hardly think of them as figures at all. His great fault in other cases is that of giving them too bold a relief, or dwelling on them too long, so that the primary idea is lost sight of in the image. Sometimes the prurience of his fancy makes him low and even filthy. He is like a man depicting the scenes of nature, who is not content to give us those features of the landscape that delight the eye, but fills out his canvas with objects which are coarse, disgusting, or noisome. Hence no writer in any language has such extremes of imagery as Mr. Burke. . . .

His *language,* though copious, was not verbose. Every word had its peculiar force and application. His chief fault was that of overloading his sentences with secondary thoughts, which weakened the blow by dividing it. His style is, at times, more careless and inaccurate than might be expected in so great a writer. But his mind was on higher things. His idea of a truly fine sentence, as once stated to a friend, is worthy of being remembered. It consists, said he, in a union of thought, feeling, and imagery—of a striking truth and a corresponding sentiment, rendered doubly striking by the force and beauty of figurative language.[57]

It will be remembered that Goodrich presents the full texts of the orator's important speeches. His conclusions can, therefore, be checked directly as to fact, and indirectly as to interpretation, by referring to the texts. This is a matter of some importance. Critics who appraise the talks of others are expected to quote sufficiently liberal portions of the speeches to give meaning and literary wholeness to their investigations. Failing to do so, they court the hazard of making their judgments and analyses seem perfunctory, dissociated from the living remarks which made the criticism necessary and significant. While this does not mean that critical estimates should be largely reviews of speeches, supported by extensive quotation, it suggests the advisability of quoting enough to give the reader a fair understanding of what was said and an appreciation of the relation between the critical comments and the text.

A Rhetorical Point of View Regarding Style

We come now to discuss another point of view relative to the role of style in public speaking. It is not entirely new, but it has a different point of focus. It takes us back to the principle of communication, mentioned often in this book and developed specifically in Chapter 1. The nature of the point of view is illustrated by a remark made by Richard Steele in his essay on "Conversational Talent." He says many people attempt to be eloquent before they can speak; they "affect the flowers of rhetoric before they understand the parts of speech" and hence many talk well, but few are understood. "The matter is not to make themselves understood, but admired." The lesson Steele's observation has for us is that we speak to communicate ideas, not to display artifices which may hinder the communicative function.

Throughout the series of operations involved in the preparation of a speech, the speaker uses and works with words. He relies upon a process of symbolic formulation—a process which imposes severe demands of accuracy, specificity, and clarity upon language. The extent to which a speaker's control of meanings through words is successful will be revealed when he finally delivers his speech. The expression which he then gives to his ideas, together with whatever rhetorical devices he uses to enhance effectiveness, may be called his style.

To the critic of public speaking, style should not be regarded as a mysterious quality.[58] It is not a combination of esoteric elements which are added to a speech, or superimposed upon it, in order to give it literary acceptability. According to the broad conception, style or language is important only to the extent that it helps prepare and subsequently open the minds of the hearers to the ideas developed in the speech. Far from regarding style as a static consideration, this view makes it functional, variable, and personal. Whether the speech contains beauty in the formal sense of meeting the requirements of traditional standards of aesthetics is of little direct concern to the speaker; whether the speech is a model of purity in language usage as determined by abstract criteria also is of minor concern to the speaker. If these highly desirable qualities can be achieved without the loss of the more important and immediate consideration—the acquisition of the response for which the speaker is striving—then, surely, the speaker is interested in them. But they are incidental matters, except as they contribute to the basic purpose of style, which is to prepare the minds of the hearers for the speaker's purpose and ideas.

We may look upon style, therefore, as a medium through which a speaker tries to secure a response. Like all other aspects of a speech, this one takes us back to the concept of rhetorical adaptation. There is no such thing as *a* style for a particular speaker. True, the speaker may have certain characteristics which stamp his language pattern from others. But in many cases those marks are related to delivery or speaking mannerisms. Style becomes a function of the elements in the speech situation; thus the language employed in a speech is variable. It will be subject to the influences of the speaker's background, his experience, the end he wishes to achieve, the ability and willingness of the audience to comprehend the ideas, and the peculiar conditions surrounding the occasion.

According to this conception, style is neither a mysterious embellishment added to a speech nor a literary veneer superimposed upon it. Instead, it represents the way in which a language pattern is used, under a given set of conditions, (1) to make ideas acceptable and (2) to get the response sought by the speaker. Style becomes the instrumentality through which ideas are made meaningful; it clothes the reason and emotion of the speaker in such words as will have intelligibility value for the hearers.

Components of Style According to This View.—The essential components of a speaker's style are aspects of the communicative act. An effective style—that is, one capable of preparing and opening the minds of the listeners for a particular subject—depends upon a speaker's having (1) an idea worth presenting, (2) an unmistakably clear conception of the idea, (3) a desire to communicate it, (4) a willingness to adapt it to a particular set of circumstances, and (5) a mastery of language adequate to express the idea in words.

Principal Means of Enhancing Style as Communication.— Broadly interpreted, there are two sets of materials which are more likely to open listeners' minds to the ideas of the speaker: (1) elements that make for clearness, and (2) elements that make for impressiveness in discourse. The line of distinction between these is not always clearly fixed; nor need it be, since the two classes of material admittedly interact. However, these are among the more important rhetorical instruments or devices which, under proper use and appropriate conditions, contribute to the effectiveness of the communicative act.

Elements of Clearness.—The following elements assist in achieving clearness in speech:

A. Thorough knowledge and understanding of the ideas
B. Discerning word selection
    1. Appropriateness of the words
    2. Currency; popular usage of the words
    3. Reputability of the words
    4. Intelligibility of the words
    5. Variety: adequacy of vocabulary
C. Simplicity of sentence structure
D. Use of definitions to clarify ideas
E. Use of examples
F. Use of illustrations
G. Control over details in the speech •
    1. Avoidance of involved elaborations
    2. Proper discrimination between the essential and the less essential materials
H. Orderly sequence of ideas: organizational integrity
I. Proper transition materials designed
    1. To bridge the gap between parts
    2. To suggest the direction in which subsequent material will move
J. Adequacy of logical materials: assumptions, evidence, argument
K. Suitable summaries designed
    1. To refresh the memories of the hearers as to the broad outline of the ideas
    2. To refresh the listeners' memories as to the interrelation of details within individual points

Elements of Impressiveness.—The elements contributing to impressiveness in speech are:

A. The sources of persuasion
    1. Logical materials
    2. Emotional materials
    3. Ethical materials: force of personal character
B. Imagery
C. Variety in sentence structure
    1. As to length
    2. As to complexity
    3. As to form: position of the words
D. Devices for emphasis
    1. Repetition
    2. Climax

E. Rhythm

F. Tropes

G. Figures

Utility the Keynote of This Conception.—The critic's interest in an orator's style is associated, then, with the question of rhetorical utility. Does the expression contribute fully to the communication of ideas and to the acquisition of the intended response? A speaker's words are appraised for their function. Stella Benson once remarked that words "are like citizens in cities; as long as they live in accord with their neighbours, they are beyond outside challenge." Their "neighbors" in this case are the conditions of the speech situation: the speaker himself, his purpose, his subject matter, the audience, the time, and the place. In a sense, this is a return to the classical doctrine of decorum, or propriety, as an essential quality of style. It differs from the older conception, however, in that it makes the other so-called "virtues" of style subordinate to it, rather than correlatives of it.

Golden Mean in Style

The critic will recognize, of course, that a speaker may regard style as a means of opening the minds of hearers to his ideas, and yet run afoul of good practice in the wording of the speech. This occurs when the speaker, intent upon enforcing his point and convinced that certain devices or elements are properly adapted to that end, uses those elements in excess of the requirements for clear understanding. Thus a speaker may use more examples than are necessary or desirable; he may use more epigrammatic statements than can properly be understood by the hearers in a limited time; he may make more appeals to visual imagery than can have any appreciable effect upon the ability of the hearers to comprehend a given thought.

Consequently, the critic will look for proportion in the use of language. There is a point—difficult to determine because of the variable nature of speaking situations—at which the speaker can strike the balance between excess and deficiency; a point at which there is neither too much nor too little, be it of illustrations, long sentences, parables, or any other element of clearness or impressiveness. This is nothing more than a restatement of Aristotle's Golden Mean, applied to the speaker's style of expression. It simply means that in the light of a given set of conditions a speaker must know how much of any material *can* be used without loss of interest and comprehension by the audience, and how much *must* be used to insure the likelihood of getting the intended response. This is a personal matter, varying from speaker to speaker and from situation to situation. Little wonder, then, that the making of stylistic analyses is for the critic one of the most difficult aspects of rhetorical evaluation.

Chapter 16

THE DELIVERY OF THE SPEECH

Importance of Delivery in Rhetoric

Some years ago, after he had delivered a speech at Columbia University, Heywood Broun wrote in his daily column that he had learned one thing about public speaking, even though it had not been of great use to him. "People respond less to ideas," he remarked, "than to particular vocal tones." He added that he was informed a certain note played on a violin could bring down a bridge. On this observation he reflected: "That may not be true, but it is sure that there can be such a thing as a sound within the throat which will bring down a house." [1]

In Broun's comments we find the modern facsimile of an ancient conviction. From the beginning of the art of speaking, there has been a full recognition of the need for effective delivery; but coupled with this acknowledgment has been the suspicion, if not open distrust, of the use of vocal manipulation to induce responses from listeners. Aristotle commented very briefly on delivery, and that only because he believed the imperfections of hearers made it essential. He did not regard delivery as an elevated topic of inquiry; and he would have preferred that ideas be received upon their own demonstrable merit, rather than upon the auxiliary support of vocal management. It is reported that Demosthenes, on an occasion when his voice failed him, and the audience hissed, cried out: "Ye are to judge of players, indeed, by their voice, but of orators by the gravity of their sentences." [2] Admirable as such a condition might be, it has never existed, and probably never will; so we must equate delivery with the total rhetorical process, assessing its value in the light of the support it gives to an orator's effort to elicit defensible responses from an audience.

Delivery has received varying measures of emphasis in the works on public speaking. In some treatises—Aristotle's *Rhetoric*, for instance—it is dismissed with a few sentences; in others—especially those dealing with the elocutionary tradition, such as John Walker's *Elements of Elocution* and Thomas Sheridan's *Lectures on Elocution*

—delivery is the focal point of attention, with the other parts of rhetoric getting little, if any, consideration.

The Critic's Point of View toward Delivery

A broad conception of delivery is helpful to a fuller understanding of orators and oratory. Here considered, delivery embraces: (1) the orator's methods of preparing his speeches, (2) his method of delivery, (3) the physical factors conducing to his effectiveness as a speaker, (4) his bodily action in delivery, and (5) his use of the voice as an instrument of persuasion. We are interested in more than a simple survey of the way a speaker uses gestures and voice; as critics, we wish to get a faithful portrait of the orator. This can be done only by considering all factors which influence the finished speech.

Examining the Orator's Method of Speech Preparation

Here, as elsewhere in rhetorical criticism, we are not necessarily concerned with the development of straight biography. A full knowledge of an orator's life is important, and it is assumed that the critic is familiar with those details. But it is not his obligation to write biography in order to appraise oratory. In fact, to do so usually distorts the focus of scholarly effort, resulting in a type of criticism which concentrates upon the events in the speaker's life, rather than upon the elements which are peculiarly influential in moulding him *as a speaker*. It may be alleged that if a man is preeminently an orator, everything associated with his biography relates pertinently to his oratory. This may be granted. The point to be observed, however, is that the biographical details must be articulated with the study of the man as a *speaker*. If such focus is attained and consistently held, the unfolding story will contribute to an understanding of the man's speechmaking.

Some of the difficulties accompanying research into the orator's method of preparing his speeches are revealed in Forest L. Whan's study of Stephen A. Douglas:

> A second question of importance concerns the method used by Douglas in preparing his speeches. Little positive evidence remains on this point. But it seems certain that he spoke extemporaneously in every instance during the campaign of 1858. Stevens tells us that Douglas frequently admitted that he could not write a speech for delivery. The conclusion is further borne out by the lack of speech notes

found in the Douglas manuscripts. Although the manuscripts contain many personal items, such as receipts for hotel bills, not a single speech outline or page of notes taken during the debates is to be found for the year 1858. One thing is certain; like all local campaigns in which Douglas participated for 25 years, that of 1858 was far too strenuous to allow either contestant to write out his speeches in full, even had he been so inclined. Lincoln claimed that he trusted to the inspiration of the moment; the more experienced Douglas may have done likewise.

More positive evidence that the speeches were not written lies within reported speeches themselves. Douglas was often interrupted by members of his audience or by an opponent on the platform. In every instance he replied to his questioner, and after his reply, worked back smoothly into the stream of thought that had been interrupted. We must conclude that Douglas carried the outline of his speech in mind and delivered that speech extemporaneously.[3]

Fuller appreciation of a speaker and his speeches results from acquiring insight into the way he went about preparing his talks. This is not a simple matter. The problem has its roots in the orator's early training, his home life, possible influence of church and school and various clubs, his reading habits and favorite methods of study, and a host of other factors. For instance, consider John Bright, the nineteenth-century English reformer, whose early training moulded his method of writing speeches. We find that Bright's training in a home of strict Quaker observance, his early associations with English mill hands (especially with Nicholas Nuttall, whom he engaged in political discussions), his lifelong interest in such publications as the *Manchester Guardian,* his participation in the activities of the Rochdale Literary and Philosophical Society—we find that these and other influences helped to determine his way of preparing speeches.

Furthermore, the critic searches out the facts concerning the orator's sources of material. Do they stem directly from his reading, the nature of which is ascertainable? from his public and private experiences? from his consultations and conferences with others? Something already has been said about this point in the chapter on textual authenticity. It is enough to add here that speculations on the sources of speech materials might tend to modify judgments as to the relative merit of speeches. Everyone is agreed that Franklin D. Roosevelt was a speaker of consummate skill. But many have inquired: Did he prepare the talks; and, if so, how? Competent authorities agree that he wrote his own talks. But they also agree that he drew freely upon a selected group of associates and counselors for general suggestions and ideas.

A concise, revealing account of Robert M. La Follette's methods of preparation throws light upon the technique used by the critic in this phase of oratorical appraisal. Says Carroll P. Lahman :

> What was his own method of preparation for speaking? For important messages and political speeches the first step was to call on authoritative sources for accurate information. Often special research was done by someone, usually a young university-trained man, designated for the task. The next step was for him and Mrs. La Follette —for on such occasions they often worked together—to surround themselves with endless stacks of source material and bury themselves in personal research away from interruptions. For ideas to be included he also welcomed and solicited suggestions from trusted friends and advisers. If they seemed good, they were accepted, but not until they were worked over and incorporated in his own way. He wrote out most of his speeches in longhand, although he also dictated to one or two faithful stenographers who were long with him. He was a slow writer, taking great pains to find the right word to express his thought. The first draft, if time allowed, was submitted to a few close advisers for criticism. Of course, he reserved the right to accept or reject such suggestions, but many were accepted. Mrs. La Follette's role was especially important here, for it was she, to a considerable extent, who put the final stamp of approval on the text of both speeches and other campaign documents.
>
> Not only did La Follette solicit suggestions on the ideas and wording of a speech; at least in the early days he sought criticism of his actual speaking. Until his death Sam Harper, his law partner, thus acted as one such critic and counselor.
>
> When time allowed, he liked to have an hour or so to relax and rest at a hotel before his speech, but in the rush of campaigns this, of course, was usually impossible.[4]

Analyzing the Orator's Mode of Delivery

There are probably as many methods of delivery as there are public speakers. Each orator has his own way of going about the business of delivering a talk. Whatever the method, the critic will want to discover it. In general, the critic should find out whether the speech is delivered from memory, from manuscript, or extempore; and, if the latter, whether the man spoke with or without notes. The orator's own reflections on his method, when obtainable, are of real service. John Bright's method of delivery, for instance, was clearly extempore; he neither wrote the speech in full nor committed it to memory, *in toto*. He tells us, however, that he frequently wrote out and memorized his introductions and conclusions, as well as selected illustrations in the body of certain speeches.

The orator's notes, when obtainable, also throw light upon the total portrait of a speaker. They give some hint as to the way in which ideas are integrated; how effectively the orator controls the details; and how he adapts a previously prepared plan to the exigen cies of a particular audience situation.

To clarify the point, let us consider a one-hour speech given by John Bright on January 12, 1878, in the Town Hall of Birmingham, England. Bright's notes for the occasion were written on five half-sheets which he turned over to R. W. Dale at the close of the meeting. A few years later Dale [5] published facsimiles of the two half-sheets covering the introduction and conclusion of the talk. The beginning of the first sheet and the end of the last one appear below, each followed by the reporter's text [6] of the corresponding sections in the complete address. (Although the transcription of the longhand copy to print removes some of the interest value from the notes, all details of spelling, spatial arrangement, and underscoring are reproduced here with fidelity to the original.)

(Sheet 1)

Meeting early. Parl. early—anxiety—consternation
                                        centres of Trade

No confidence in Govt.   crisis—uncertain voice.

Question—Peace or War   —no greater possible.

Same 1854 —same question—then war—its lesson.

advised not dwell in past. Circumstances changed

Men dwell on past—why not nations? & learn?

Then errors. Public mind fed with falsehoods
                            & drunk with passion

Russia—Power—designs—despotism—danger to Europe

(Corresponding Text)

Mr. Mayor and Gentlemen,—This meeting, as you know, has been called some days earlier than was some time ago intended and you know also that Parliament has been summoned about three weeks before the usual time. It is because Parliament has been summoned so early that this meeting has been called so early. In ordinary times the summoning of Parliament creates a considerable interest in the country; but, on the whole, I think it is an interest of rather a pleasurable kind.

On this occasion the announcement that Parliament was to meet on the 17th of January had the effect of creating great anxiety; in some cases I have heard it described as consternation; and in all the centres of trade it has caused a certain depression which has been sensibly felt. I am driven to the conclusion, at which, I think, a large portion of the people have arrived, that the cause of all this is not a fear of Parliament, but a want of confidence in the Administration. We have been passing through something like a crisis, and we have had no decisive voice from the Government. In point of fact, if one body of men has said that the Government has spoken in a particular way, the next body of men you met would tell you that the Government intended something entirely different. Of one thing, however, we may be quite sure—that the question which fills the minds of the people at this hour, and which has filled their minds for a long time past, is the great and solemn question of peace or war; and I doubt whether it would be possible to submit to any people a greater question than that. There are many in this hall who remember a period, about 23 years ago, when the same question was submitted to the people. In 1854 the very same question was put to the people which the nation at this moment is considering, and that is whether peace or war is the true policy and the true interest of this people. At that time the conclusion to which the people came was in favour of war. They followed a Government that unwisely, as I thought then and as most people think now, threw them into war. I think we may learn some lessons from that war. I read a short time ago, in a very influential paper which had supported the war of 1854, that it was a pity to go back at all to the past, that circumstances had entirely changed, and that many who had then been in favour of the war might very justly and properly be against a repetition of it. For my part, I believe the arguments at this moment for war are as strong as they were in 1854; and as I believe that in point of fact the war then had no just arguments in its support, so now I think that no just arguments can be brought forward to induce this people to countenance or enter into the existing conflict. As to not going back to the past, what is common with individuals? Nothing is more common and nothing more wise than to look back to our past years and 'ask them what report they bore to Heaven.' How does a man become wiser as he grows older but by looking back on the past and learning lessons from the mistakes he has made in his earlier years. And that which is true of an individual must surely also be true of a nation with regard to its foreign policy. At that time the public mind was filled with falsehoods; it was in a state which one might describe by saying that it became almost drunk with passion. With regard to Russia, many of you recollect what was said of her power, of her designs, of the despotism which ruled in Russia, of the danger which hung over the freedom of all the countries of Europe.

(Sheet 5)

Some cunning phrase—as the old hobgoblin.   The
      Balance of Power—or the new terror—The
      danger to British interests.

Lord Derby—"The greatest British Interest is Peace"

A Hundred public meetings say the same

Tonight we say amen to this wise Declaration.

This noble Hall—this vast gathering—representing

the countless population aroused in a resolve

that the sanguinary record of the past shall be closed,

& that our future annals shall be inscribed

with the blessed message of mercy & of peace.

(Corresponding Text)

Yes, 'some cunning phrase, by faction caught and spread'—like the
cunning phrase of 'the balance of power,' which has been described
as a ghastly phantom which the Government of this country has been
pursuing for centuries and has never yet overtaken—'some cunning
phrase,' like that we have now of 'British interests.' Lord Derby said
the wisest thing that has been uttered by any member of the Administration during the discussions on this war when he said that the
greatest of British interests is peace. A hundred,—far more than a
hundred—public meetings have lately said the same. Tonight we shall
say amen to this wise declaration. I am delighted to see this grand
meeting in this noble hall. This building is consecrated to peace and to
freedom. You are here in your thousands, representing the countless
multitudes outside. May we not tonight join our voices in this resolution—that, so far as we are concerned, the sanguinary record of the
history of our country shall be closed, that we may open a new page, on
which shall henceforth be inscribed only the blessed message of mercy
and of peace?

Against the background of complete speeches, notes such as these
—supported, of course, by other data—tell the critic a good deal
about a speaker's skill in adaptation and, not less importantly, about
his formulation of ideas from phrases and catchwords. Furthermore, Bright's notes tend to show, as other evidence confirms, that
the perorations were written almost in full, and probably memorized.

Physical Factors in Delivery

A third inquiry which may yield interesting information on the ways of an orator is: Do the speaker's physical characteristics contribute to his effectiveness? There has been some disposition to build up a stereotype of the orator as a large, imposing-looking person. Presumably it is felt that a man of majestic mien has a better chance of success with the fluctuating behavior of audiences than a man of less attractive bearing. Thus we read that certain orators "looked their part"; prominently mentioned among them are Bryan, Chatham, Bright, La Follette, Webster, and Phillips. Chauncey Goodrich attributes some of Lord Chatham's success to "his extraordinary personal advantages." "In his best days . . . his figure was tall and erect; his attitude imposing." Indeed, Goodrich observes, few men "have ever received from the hand of Nature so many of the outward qualifications of an orator." [7]

The uncritical acceptance of striking physical appearance as an index of oratorical excellence is not recommended. The way an orator looks—the way he impresses his hearers as a physical specimen—is an accessory. Stephen Douglas was a short man, but his oratory was not correspondingly diminutive. And Edmund Burke "derived little or no advantage from his personal qualifications. He was tall, but not robust; his gait and gesture were awkward; his countenance, though intellectual, was destitute of softness, and rarely relaxed into a smile; and as he always wore spectacles, his eye gave him no command over an audience." [8] However, the critic who would give his readers a picture of a speaker should consider even the "nonessentials." Oftentimes these "nonessentials" figure prominently in the judgments of men; and it is the critic's job to analyze the reason speeches do or do not take root in the hearers' lives. In all probability, rhetorical effectiveness can be enhanced by the impress of a striking personality.

Bodily Action in Speaking

How does the speaker manage himself while he is on the platform? What of his bodily action, his movement on the stage, and his gestures? Does the orator supplement his words with appropriate action? These and other questions have been asked by critics since antiquity. Cicero found Publius Antistius' delivery blameworthy because of "a few ridiculous gestures, of which he could not entirely break himself." [9] And Curio's action was such as to provoke ridicule: the swaying and reeling of his body from side to side prompted Julius to inquire *"who it was that was speaking from a boat?"* On another occasion when Curio and Octavius, then consuls, had been summoned to the forum, and Curio had given a tiresome harangue, "while Octavius sat silently by him, wrapped up in flannels, and besmeared with ointments, to ease the pain of the gout," Cnaeus Sicinius said: *"Octavius, you are infinitely obliged to your colleague; for if he had not tossed and flung himself about today in the manner he did, you would certainly have been devoured by the flies."* [10]

For an object of praise Cicero looked to the gestures of Antonius. His actions were such as "to correspond to the meaning of every sentence, without beating time to the words." In a singular manner, his "hands, his shoulders, the turn of his body, the stamp of his foot, his posture, his air, and, in short, all his motions, were adapted to his language and sentiments." [11]

In our search for data relating to the bodily action of the orators of the past we turn to the testimony of their contemporaries, or of those who knew contemporaries. Thus N. W. Wraxall comments on Richard Sheridan's manner of speaking:

> His countenance and features had in them something peculiarly pleasing, indicative at once of intellect, humor, and gayety. All these characteristics played about his lips when speaking and operated with inconceivable attraction; for they anticipated, as it were, to the eye the effect produced by his oratory on the ear. . . .[12]

This is properly a part of delivery in the stricter sense. Goodrich refers to the Younger Pitt's harsh features, but observed that they were "lighted up with intelligence by the flashes of eye," and his "gesture was animated, but devoid of grace. . . ." [13] To Thomas Erskine, Goodrich also attributes an "animated gesture." [14] And John P. Curran, the Irish orator, had, Goodrich says, "an eye that glowed like a live coal." [15] Sir James Mackintosh says that Charles Fox gave an initial impression of being awkward, but after a time no one thought of anything except his ideas and the lucid simplicity with which he developed them. [16]

Observers and critics of oratory look, then, to such physical manifestations as grace of movement on the platform, facility in gesticulation, meaningful use of facial expression, and the effective use of the eyes as instruments of audience control. Relative to the latter, it may be observed that the rhetoricians have long considered the action of the eyes important in oratory. Cicero mentioned the eyes, "by whose intense or languid gaze, as well as by their quick glances and gaiety" orators were able to reveal the workings of their mind. Quintilian was of the same opinion, believing that the mind manifested itself through the eyes. Gilbert Austin, emphasizing delivery above all other parts of rhetoric, regarded the eyes as the most expressive part of the countenance:

> As the principal object of every public speaker must be to obtain the attention of his audience; so every circumstance which can contribute to this end must be considered important. In the external demeanour nothing will be found so effectually to attract attention, and detain it, as the direction of the eyes. It is well known the eyes can influence persons at a distance; and that they can select from a multitude a single individual, and turn their looks on him alone, though many lie in the same direction. The whole person seems to be in some measure affected by this influence of another's eyes, but the eyes themselves feel it with the most lively sensibility.[17]

Additional insight into a speaker's ways is afforded through a study of his mannerisms and distinguishing habits of dress. For instance, the picture of John Bright is sharpened when we visualize his manner of taking a position before popular audiences. William Robertson comments on Bright's mild eccentricities as follows:

> . . . he is welcomed with deafening cheers, and waving of hats and handkerchiefs. He walks quietly toward the table, apparently unaffected by the excited reception, but a close observer might detect that it is with difficulty he suppresses his emotion. So anxious are they to hear him speak that the preliminaries of the meeting are hurried through, and at length the orator stands up. He is received with rapturous and sustained applause, and while they are enthusiastically greeting him he quietly arranges his position, places his hat on the table before him, and on the rim of it lays his scanty notes, and then surveys the vast assembly with subdued emotion.[18]

Goldwin Smith [19] tells us that when Bright finished with a note-sheet, he dropped it into the hat, and moved on to the next sheet.

Each orator provides the critic with new and different focuses of investigation. But the foregoing material suggests some of the leads the investigator should pursue. Since visual appeals operate to influence hearers, the critic will want to effect as complete a reconstruction of the original scene as possible.

Voice as a Determinant of Effective Delivery

Finally, the critic must assess the vocal skill of the speaker. And here, admittedly, the task takes a difficult turn. If the critic has not himself heard the speaker, as is more than likely, he must depend upon testimony which, even if trustworthy, is subject to verbal confusion. While one observer may pronounce an orator's speech "flat," another may call it "harsh"; and neither may be too exact in his definition of the terms. Judgments of voice require skill to an extent not ordinarily found in the untrained commentator. The lack of uniformity in nomenclature today attests to the difficulty inherent in the formulation of such opinions.

The nature of the problem is revealed by reference to a few observations by Goodrich in *Select British Eloquence,* a work of uncommon merit in this field. Goodrich quotes Wraxall as saying the tones of Sheridan's voice were "singularly mellifluous" and unaccompanied by an "unpleasant Irish accent" such as Burke had. [20] Apropos of Pitt's voice, Goodrich remarks that it was "full and clear, filling the largest room with the volume of sound." [21] Erskine's voice was "somewhat shrill but beautifully modulated." [22] Curran's speech "was uncommonly distinct and deliberate; the modulations of his voice were varied in a high degree, and perfectly suited to the widest range of his eloquence." [23]

A comparison of ancient and modern criticism reveals that Goodrich, for instance, treated the subject of delivery (as far as it concerns vocal attributes) with no more comprehensiveness or acuity than did Cicero. In the *Brutus,* Cicero speaks of Cnaeus Pompeius' "sonorous and manly" voice; Publius Autronius had a "very clear and strong voice"; Caius Memmius' voice was "sweet and sonorous"; Antonius had a voice that was "strong and firm, though naturally hoarse." Here, as in much of contemporary criticism, loose terminology is a barrier to full understanding.

We do not infer that such observations are irresponsible; indeed, they are the composite judgments derived from careful research into the testimony of men who presumably knew what they were saying. But because the observations are couched in equivocal language, it is seldom easy to determine just what the distinguishing marks of the orator's vocal delivery were. Thanks to the present-day recording equipment, critics of the future will be able to deal more accurately with all phases of vocal delivery.

Testimony relative to articulation and pronunciation is also subject to a variety of vagaries. Omission of details seems to be one of the most conspicuous faults. The writers of memoirs and personal reflections on orators rarely discuss at any length the habits of diction cultivated by the speakers. In consequence, the full account of many orators' speaking accomplishments will remain permanently incomplete.

But some evidence concerning these matters is usually available and the discerning critic will assess its value in relation to the speaker's proper place in the history of public address. In his study of Wendell Phillips, W. Hayes Yeager [24] appraises some of the testimony dealing with Phillips' manner of speaking. He establishes a reasonable claim as to the authorship of certain editorial comments on the matter; evaluates its discriminative character; and quotes selected passages which throw considerable light upon Phillips' delivery, including specific data on pronunciation habits, use of the pause, and the like.

Problem of the Critic in Assaying Delivery

The critic's task is, then, peculiarly taxing. And the more remote the period in which an orator lived, perhaps the greater the difficulties. Hard as the assignment may be, however, it should not preclude the use of such reliable information as may be available. Recalling a remark attributed to St. Jerome, we may say: "Remote as we are from perfect knowledge, we deem it less blameworthy to say too little rather than nothing at all." Surely there are some facts with which the critic can deal, despite the limitations of testimony.

Fundamentally, the critic is desirous of getting data which shed light upon the orator's skill in eliciting the intended response from his hearers. This means an interest in such matters as distinctness and loudness of utterance, the rate of speaking, and the pleasantness or unpleasantness of the vocal quality. In short, the critic asks, Was the delivery clear, intelligible, and pleasing?

While it is claimed—how responsibly no one knows—that George Whitefield could be understood by a crowd of 20,000 in the open fields, it is known that other speakers could not reach the last row of an audience less than one-hundredth that size. In one of his early speeches at Castle Garden in 1850, William Maxwell Evarts is known to have "broken down" so that he was forced to withdraw, and chiefly because a large part of the audience could not hear and, in consequence, whistled and shouted.

Here, as elsewhere, however, the critic is concerned with the delivery of the *particular speech,* not the over-all estimate of the orator's delivery. Important and illuminating as the general estimate of a speaker's vocal skill is, it is subordinate to a penetrating understanding of its effectiveness on a *specific* occasion. After all, delivery is another *means* of achieving a response; it is not a terminal value.

An important public speech is not a satisfactory laboratory for testing a speaker's orotund qualities and pleasing cadences. Once the speaker takes the floor to develop an idea, we have a right to expect a lively enforcement of his thoughts. He is there to communicate something worth passing on. Delivery serves as a tool by which to enhance the impressiveness of the communication; it is not the focus of attention. If it were, it would be a distraction. There are places where men assemble to appreciate vocal artistry *in its own right,* but the platform of the public speaker is not one of them.

So the critic attempts to appraise a speaker's delivery in a given speech, to the end that he may the better understand why the audience responded as it did. He determines its congruency with the nature of the speech; its unobtrusiveness as a vehicle of communication; its intelligibility to the respondents; its agreeableness to the ear, generally. All these facts are not easy to find, but they still are relevant to the critical function. It is not a case of matter *vs* manner; it is not a question of whether *what* is said is more important than *how* it is said. The two are related. It is both *what* and *how* it is said that makes for effectiveness in public address.

Essentials of Inquiry into Delivery.—It is clear that an investigation into the character of an orator's delivery includes the two standard constituents of critical inquiry. First, it requires exacting research. Facts concerning a speaker's delivery are, at best, scattered, if not downright elusive. Only on rare occasions does the biographer or the commentator assemble all his observations on this point in one chapter or section. Instead, he weaves them into the fabric of his story. Furthermore, the sources from which such data stem are numerous—so numerous that the investigator cannot rest in his search until he has examined large portions of contemporary and near-contemporary literature. In his endeavor to reveal the portrait of his chosen orator, he must first scrutinize the portraits of the men with whom the orator lived and worked. He who would know a particular man who participated in the important doings of the social sphere must be conversant with the social milieu in all its ramifications.

Secondly, the critical analysis of an orator's delivery requires severe testing of authorities. If the critic has not heard the orator, he must depend upon the word of those who did or of those who knew someone who did. The possibility of error is considerable, especially in view of the varying judgments as to whether an orator's rate was fast or slow, his articulation sharp or dull, his quality pleas-

ing or unpleasing—and any number of other differences and dis-
parities in definition. Accordingly, the critic must continue his role
as logician, testing the evidence according to criteria discussed in
Chapter 11. Only after he has culled the untenable observations and
has accumulated the concurrent evidence is he in a position to appraise the effect of an orator's delivery on a specific occasion, and
thus present an estimate of the speaker's skill in this phase of the
rhetorical process.

Chapter 17

THE MEASURES OF EFFECTIVENESS

Response the Key to Oratory

"Historians," said W. E. H. Lecky, "will probably always judge men and policies by their net results, by their final consequences, and this judgment is on the whole the most sure that we can obtain. It is not, however, altogether infallible. Apart from the question of the moral character or the methods employed which a good historian should never omit from his consideration, success is not always a decisive proof of sagacity. Chance and the unexpected play a great part in human affairs . . ."[1] This observation is important to the study of rhetoric. It suggests that the men who play roles in the making of history—and this includes the orators—are judged finally by their influence upon people and events. In the eventual reckoning, men will be tested in the light of what they did. Orators will be judged by what they accomplished, either immediately or in the long run of public affairs.

What are the tests we apply to oratory? How measure its effectiveness? By what criteria do we call a speech successful?[2] These and related questions engage our attention in this chapter. Upon the answers rests, in last analysis, the attitude which we assume toward rhetoric as an instrument of social progress.

By its very nature, speaking is a response-getting activity. Conceived as an act of communication, it seeks to realize an end or objective agreeable to the purpose of the orator. Consequently, the speaker himself looks to response as a measure of his success; failing to secure the end he seeks, he must feel that his undertaking is incomplete, his efforts unfruitful.

It is not a simple task to trace the influence of a speaker's words upon the public mind. Influences operating upon the people at a given moment may be manifold and complexly interrelated. To establish the direct causal relation between spoken words and subsequent actions or tendencies requires not patience alone, but facility in understanding the processes of history. The superficial appreciation of a speech as an excellent piece of craftsmanship may leave the critic as far from understanding the effect of the speech on hearers as he was before turning to his critical assignment. Daniel O'Connell is reported to have remarked once that a "good speech is a good thing, but the verdict is *the* thing." And it is the verdict which assumes elusive characteristics, often changing its nature with the position from which it is viewed.

It would not be accurate to assert, or even imply, that authorities are agreed on the standard by which effectiveness of oratory is determined. In fact, some critics shift their opinions on this matter from section to section in their treatises. The reason is not far to seek. The measures of effectiveness undoubtedly vary with the different conditions under which speeches are given. Thus a ceremonial speech may not exercise a profound influence upon the life of a particular community, as far as observable changes in belief or action are concerned, and yet it may be a commendable piece of rhetoric. The judgment of such a speech would have to be made with the type of oratory constantly in mind. While the acquisition of a response would still be the end of the speaking activity, other factors might figure prominently in its analysis—factors which might command only incidental attention in a speech of a deliberative nature on an occasion of great social urgency. But to these matters we shall give further attention later.

Critics of oratory are generally agreed that the effectiveness of oratory is a function of audience adaptation; that it must be regarded in the light of what people *do* as a result of hearing the speech. Some have held that great and extensive changes in audience behavior can be expected from hearing a speech; others are almost apologetically modest in their claims for the efficacy of the spoken word. Emerson believed that the secret of eloquence—be it in a half-hour's discourse or in a few sentences only—was "to persuade a multitude of persons to renounce their opinions, and change the course of life." [3] Through the influence of eloquence, he said, an audience can be made to go forth "not the men they came in, but shriven, convicted, and converted." Plutarch conceived of discourse exercising a purgative function. After listening to a speech, the hearer should "inspect diligently and try faithfully the state and temper of his mind" to see whether or not

> . . . his affections are more moderate, if any afflictions grow lighter, if his constancy and greatness of spirit are confirmed, if he feels any divine emotions or inward workings of virtue and goodness upon his soul. For it becomes us but ill, when we rise from the barber's chair, to be so long in consulting the mirror, or to stroke our heads and ex-

amine so curiously the style in which our hair is trimmed and dressed,
and then, at our return from hearing in the schools, to think it needless to look into ourselves, or examine whether our own mind has
discharged any turbulent or unprofitable affections and is grown more
sedate and serene. For, as Ariston was wont to say, the bath and a
discourse are of no use unless they are purgative.[4]

While acknowledging the operative impact of wise words upon the
social body, Lecky nevertheless believes that the influence is slow to
make itself known. Saying that the wisdom of a teaching or of a
policy is determined by its results, he remarks that "these results
are in most cases very gradually disclosed." [5]

A Specimen Appraisal of Oratorical Effectiveness.—Before
turning to an examination of the methods commonly employed to
determine the impact of speechmaking, let us look at a passage which
assesses the influence of Stephen A. Douglas' efforts. This is from
Forest L. Whan's provocative analysis of Douglas' campaign for the
senatorship in Illinois in 1858:

> Although it is impossible to allot to the speeches the exact part they
> played in determining the results of the election, certain things should
> be noted that tend to support the conclusion that Douglas's speaking
> was extremely important in keeping the Illinois legislature Democratic
> in 1858. As has been noted, reports of applause, cheers, and other
> marks of approval given by an immediate audience cannot be accepted
> as evidence of effectiveness. Not only were newspapers partial and
> biased to the extent of falsifying reports but a small minority of de-
> termined supporters might account for the interruptions and applause
> recorded. It was the day of intense rivalry, staunch support of candi-
> dates, and noisy interruptions. On the other hand the skill shown in the
> use of the various methods of proof and refutation would lead a
> present-day critic to suspect that the speeches were very effective.
>
> In analyzing the campaign, historians have arrived at conflicting
> conclusions in answering the question: Who won the debates? By far
> the majority have noted that the Republicans polled more votes than
> did the Democrats, concluding that this proved that the better speaker,
> Lincoln, was cheated out of a hard-earned victory by an antiquated
> apportionment system. However, others have pointed out that the
> Democrats gained more votes over the 1856 total than did the Republi-
> cans, and Cole had invalidated this argument by pointing out that the
> 1856 vote was not a fair indication of previous Republican strength.
> Still others have concluded that the question is 'still unanswered.'
>
> No attempt will be made here to answer the question conclusively,
> but certain new evidence should be noted. The foregoing description

of trends, affecting the people of Illinois, indicates that the state was rapidly drifting toward Republican-party philosophy. Although the anti-Nebraska vote of 1854 gives an indication of what the Republicans could expect in 1858, a mere comparison of total votes gained gives no indication of the relative effectiveness of the speaking ability of the two candidates. It does not take into account the rapid growth in population and other trends before mentioned. More importantly, it does not take into account the fact that the speeches of these two candidates represented only one element of the campaign. To assume that the speeches of Lincoln and Douglas accounted entirely for the shift in vote is questionable causal reasoning.

However, there is one method of comparing votes that does indicate the relative effectiveness of the two speakers in this campaign. No historian has yet compared the shift in votes in counties in which the two men spoke with the shift in vote in counties in which they did not speak. Assuming that other influencing factors were operative in all counties, such a comparison should give a better basis for judging the effectiveness of the two speakers. Lincoln, in nearly every instance, spoke where Douglas had spoken previously. He had, as he admitted, an advantage in having 'a concluding speech on him'; it 'is the very thing.' The comparison is possible.

Dividing the state arbitrarily, as most historians have divided it, into the north (twenty-three counties), the central (forty-nine counties), and the south (thirty counties), the following gains of 10 per cent or more over the 1854 vote are discovered for the two parties. *In the Republican counties in which the two men spoke in the north, Douglas gained in 4; Lincoln, in 3. In those in which they did not speak, Douglas gained in 1, and Lincoln gained in 7. In the great, doubtful, central section, where the two men spoke, Douglas gained in 18; Lincoln did not gain in a single county. Where they did not speak in this area, Douglas gained in 5 and Lincoln in 4. In the Democratic strongholds of the south, Douglas gained in 2 in which they spoke; Lincoln gained in 2. Where they did not speak, Douglas gained in 2 and Lincoln in 8. For the state as a whole, then, Douglas gained strength of 10 per cent or more in 24 counties in which the two men spoke. Lincoln gained in 5. In counties where they did not speak, Douglas gained in only 8 and Lincoln in 19.*

It must be remembered that Douglas shunned counties that were admittedly Democratic, speaking only twice in those places. He chose to speak nine times in admittedly Republican strongholds. Both men spent the remainder of their time in the doubtful counties of the state. It is also interesting to note that ten counties that had gone anti-Nebraska in 1854 went Democratic in 1858; only three that had been Democratic went Republican in the latter year. This was true in spite of the trends of the decade and the split in the Democratic party. Douglas spoke in eight of the ten Republican counties that became Democratic; Lincoln spoke in but one of the three Democratic counties that became Republican.

The foregoing analysis bears out our earlier conclusion that the state was rapidly drifting toward Republican philosophy. The Republicans seem to have had good reason to believe that Lincoln's election was certain.

It is impossible to conclude that the great difference in shift in vote between counties in which the men spoke and counties in which they did not was entirely due to their respective speaking abilities. But it seems logical to believe that speaking ability played an important part in bringing about this difference. To assume otherwise is to place an unusual reliance on coincidence or to argue that neither man had the ability to determine in which counties speaking would influence the election. Such a large difference in shift in votes in the two types of counties indicates that the oratory of Stephen A. Douglas was one of the sustaining factors in keeping the Democratic legislature in Illinois in 1858. It indicates that Douglas's campaign speeches were very effective.

We may conclude, then, that history has sadly misjudged Douglas as a speaker. The charges of inconsistency, insincerity, trickery, and carelessness have been made in the light of post-Civil War philosophy, after an examination of only a few of the printed speeches. Historians and critics have ignored the need to understand thoroughly the four elements that go into every speaking situation before judgment may be passed; they have failed to realize that it is dangerous to criticize isolated speeches that appear in print until the conditions under which the speeches were given have been reconstructed.

An examination of the individual audiences to whom Douglas spoke, the various influences that accounted for his beliefs, and the total number of campaign speeches now in existence shows conclusively that Douglas was not driven to the defensive by a superior opponent. It shows conclusively that his arguments were basically honest, sincere, and consistent. In fact, many of the things that have drawn the critics' disapproval prove to be masterly techniques of an unusually fine speaker, who was a past master at audience analysis and adaptation. Douglas should be remembered as one of the ablest speakers the United States has produced.[6]

A General Appraisal of an Orator's Influence.—Whereas the foregoing passage assesses an orator's specific effectiveness in a particular campaign, the following quotation from W. Hayes Yeager's study of Wendell Phillips presents a more generalized account of a speaker's influence on his time.

It is very difficult, if not quite impossible, to measure Phillips's influence on his times; so great were his merits as a public figure, so closely were those merits interwoven with his faults, and so great were the controversies raging around him that his contemporaries and present-day students of his influence, alike, differ very greatly.

In the first place, he represented minorities (and sometimes very small minorities) almost all his life. For a brief period of about ten months, in 1861, to January 7, 1862 (in which he had supported the President and the Union), he enjoyed the rare experience—for him— of finding himself acting with the majority; then intermittently from the end of the war to the ratification in 1870 of the Fifteenth Amendment, he enjoyed a considerable following, as one of the leading men who were working to obtain full rights of citizenship for the freedmen; and then from 1870 to his death in 1884 (in the period when his principal interest was labor reform), his views were entirely unacceptable to the majority, and he was as bitterly hated by the so-called 'upper classes' as during the long antislavery struggle.

From 1838 to the early 1840's he had some, although not very great, influence on his times; he was too young and too new to the antislavery movement to build a large following. Nevertheless, he did help to arouse the people of the North to the realization that slavery was an evil. Strangely enough, this was accomplished, in large part, because the whole Abolition movement was the source of great irritation to the South and aroused intense anger toward all abolitionists; this anger was expressed in newspaper attacks, petitions to Congress and the various state legislatures, offers of rewards for the capture of abolitionists, etc.—all of which publicized the Abolition cause better than the abolitionists alone could possibly have done it.

From the early 1840's to the outbreak of the war, his extreme views on nonvoting and holding office, his cursing of the Constitution, and his advocacy of disunion never were accepted by more than a small minority, even of the abolitionists themselves; *his views in this period, therefore, had no direct influence upon the policies of the state and Federal governments.* He was merely one of the very articulate leaders of the small left, or Garrisonian, wing of the Abolition movement.

Although he had no direct influence upon governmental policies on the antislavery issues, *as an agitator—of the very first rank—he helped to keep all phases of the subject alive throughout the country.* His ability as an orator before popular audiences was so great that large crowds came to hear him on almost all occasions. Although he exhibited considerable mastery of more argumentative discourses, particularly before committees of the Massachusetts legislature, it is to his speeches before popular audiences that his chief fame is due.

Although he had very little direct influence on governmental policy throughout most of his life, nevertheless, *no other orator who was active in these reform movements—particularly in the antislavery cause —had the publicity value of Wendell Phillips.* In addition to his reputation as a speaker, interest in him was greatly enhanced by the fact that his bitter attacks on men and measures and the circumstances under which he spoke—very frequently—had great news value; his speeches, therefore, were widely publicized and were used as models for declamation in the schools and colleges. His abusive attacks on friends and foes became so commonplace that his audiences expected them and were disappointed when they were sometimes omitted. Besides, he so often was the object of mob violence or intended mob violence and so often was faced by hostile audiences that *the occasions had certain interest and entertainment values beyond the subject matter itself.*

His chief service to antislavery and to the other reforms in which he was interested, therefore, was in stimulating people to think about the evils of the system he condemned and the methods of bringing it to an end; in short, his influence was principally as an *agitator.*[7]

Approaches in Examining Speech Effectiveness

Measures of effectiveness can be examined from two points of view: individual and societal. According to the former, a speech is regarded as successful if it enables the speaker to realize his fullest potentialities as an individual, or to reveal fully his intellectual and moral character. If it brings out his character, or reveals him as a person endowed with a fine delivery, it is presumably a good speech. This position is patently untenable. It violates the entire doctrine of speech as communication, and places the emphasis upon speech as exhibition, as a form of display. As far as the audience is concerned—and the hearers are the most important part of the equation since it is for them that the speech is designed and given—it is of little importance whether a speaker achieves his *personal* ambition to speak agreeably to his own preconceived notion of individual betterment. Even though he should hit upon materials that enable him to practice his vocal skills successfully, it is of little concern to the listeners. They did not assemble for the purpose of giving the speaker *practice* in his art; they came to hear his ideas—to be informed, or convinced, or whatever the purpose is. Hence we may dismiss *individual* measures of effectiveness as being incidental to a serious consideration of the standards by which a speech is to be appraised.

The societal point of view provides, on the other hand, the proper approach to the study of effectiveness. According to this conception, the success of oratory must be evaluated in terms, not of the speaker alone, but of the larger social sphere within which he functions. Thus the speech is studied in its possible relation to social change.

This is a complex consideration necessitating a recognition of such factors as attitudes toward change—conservatism, liberalism, and the like—the influence of tradition, and the power of the coercive authorities in the state. Social changes involve people in *association*, rather than individual actions, *per se*. In any dynamic social situation, therefore, a particular speech is seldom, if ever, the sole force operating to produce a certain effect. Instead, it is one of many agencies acting as determinants of change. It functions along with natural forces and other social instruments, and must, therefore, be viewed in its interrelated, societal aspects.

Suggested Measures of Effectiveness

What, then, are the genuine standards by which the effectiveness of discourse is determined? There are many, indeed, for each critic brings to the job of appraisal certain personal guides which, even though unsystematic and only partially formulated, assist him in arriving at his verdict. Whether we like it or not, complete objectivity is impossible; even if it were possible, it might be, as someone once suggested, a mark of insanity. Accordingly, certain individual predispositions will assert themselves when the critic assesses influence. Even though confining himself to the facts as he finds them, the critic's judgment will not be completely divorced from subjective elements. The consequence of this circumstance is patent: Though we may wish the critic's caprices to be removed from his evaluation, a residual factor of "I like this because I like it" may possibly remain. This is not an invitation to the cultivation of that attitude; on the contrary, it is a denial of its place in criticism. But a candid recognition of probable conditions makes necessary our considering this factor in the final evaluation of speeches.

Excluding the multifold subjective standards which virtually defy analysis and classification, we may point to the following measures of effectiveness as being most common in contemporary evaluation:

(1) The effectiveness of a speech may be judged by the character of the *immediate,* surface response. If a speaker succeeds in holding the audience's unbroken attention; if he receives a favorable response in the form of applause or cheering; if he does these or other things which relate straightway to the response of the moment, he is presumed to have carried through his communicative attempt competently. This is a superficial, though sometimes accurate, indicator of rhetorical merit. The nature of many speech occasions—a political rally, for instance—is such as to provoke applause and enthusiastic

reception, even though what is said may be conspicuously faulty both on the side of validity and of expression. Such cursory judgments are seldom adequate; they need supplement from other standards. They need such collateral support as will make possible the *interpretation* of the response, rather than the uncritical listing of the fact that people applauded or hissed or just remained silent. And silence may mean either attention or inattention, for as Alice B. Greene remarks, "Applause is lightly given, but not silence." [8] Simple adherence to the aforementioned standard would throw little light upon the *why* of speech effectiveness. Indeed, if a speaker holds the attention of the audience throughout a speech, that is an important fact. But it is a transient criterion of effectiveness in the world of statesmanship.

(2) Charles James Fox once observed: "Did the speech read well when reported? If so, it was a bad one." This test of readability has been widely discussed, and it has come to be considered a possible standard for measuring the effectiveness of a speech. In essence, it declares that there is a sharp difference between oral and written style and that if a speech reads well after it is translated into print, it must not have been agreeable to the ear of the listener. If accepted in its entirety, this would mean, and a good many people would accept it as true, that Burke's speech "On Conciliation" is not an effective oration, despite the fact that according to other standards it is considered a masterpiece of oratorical prose. It reads well today; in fact, it is a virtual preface to political economy. The speech is quotable; its maxims have become the common stock of school boys and of statesmen.

George M. Trevelyan probably had Fox's dictum in mind when he contrasted the oratory of Gladstone and Bright: "Of the two, it is Bright whose speeches can be read with greatest pleasure, though that, perhaps, is no test of oratory." [9] But people do make it a test. The test of readability—be it on the morning following the delivery of the speech, or fifty years later—has a popular appeal. But once again we find our standard inadequate by itself, for it abstracts one quality—the simple appeal to a reader—from the complicated social pattern in which speech functions. Thus it neglects the essential goal of speech—the acquisition of a response from the audience, not from the critic.

(3) Another possible measure of the merit of a speech is its technical perfection. If it is praiseworthy as a model of craftsmanship —that is, if it is superior in structural makeup, stylistic grace, and technical composition—it may be viewed as good speechmaking.

This criterion sets up the speech as something to be viewed from the outside, without necessary regard for the social conditions which prompted it. The speech is viewed as a finished product having certain rhetorical features which conform agreeably to fixed principles or rules. The critic's judgment is thus based upon the speaker's ability to master technique, to construct a speech which has the essential qualities of good rhetoric, as viewed from the printed page.

Important as mastery over the technical details of rhetoric is, it cannot be considered, apart from other criteria, as a satisfactory measure of speech effectiveness. It overlooks the significant fact that departures from accepted norms of composition and structure may be necessitated occasionally by peculiar audience conditions. Technical accuracy, however desirable, is no particular virtue if it militates against the speaker's likelihood of communicating his ideas.

(4) Partially consistent with the doctrine of communication, though not fully adequate as a measure of rhetorical effectiveness, is the criterion which appraises the orator's wisdom in judging the trends of the future. This is essentially a test of the speaker's vision, of his capacity to understand the meaning of current happenings, of his facility for appreciating their probable effect upon the course of history. It is a test such as might be used in evaluating the merit of a Burke, or of any other orator who was not immediately successful, but who foresaw the shape of things to come with more than ordinary perspicacity. The criterion would apply in part, surely, to the labors of a John Bright. During the later years of his life, says Trevelyan, "men began to reflect that John Bright had been right about Free Trade, right about the Crimea, right about the American Civil War, and right about the Franchise. . . ." [10] With such a test, we link the concepts of statesmanship and oratory; we measure a man's greatness as a speaker in terms of his competence in gauging the effects of a contemporary action upon the destinies of men.

(5) Much more significant is the test which measures effectiveness by the substantial responses deriving from possible changes in belief or attitude. Unlike the responses discussed under section (1) of this chapter, these may come hours, days, or possibly weeks after the delivery of the speech. Thus, in an extended debate in the House of Commons or in the American Congress, a vote may not be taken for days after the delivery of certain significant speeches. But the fundamental test will be: Did these speeches have an effect upon the subsequent disposition of the question? Did they help to produce the delayed response?

The unqualified use of this test would, of course, render a manifest disservice to many great speakers. Burke's speech "On Conciliation" failed to carry the question; the resolution with which he closed his celebrated address was lost; on the vote on the previous question Burke's case was rejected by a count of 270 to 78. Similarly, his motion deriving from the speech on "American Taxation" was rejected, 182 to 49. Despite the fact that Fox is regarded by Loren Reid and others as "the most effective orator of the opposition," he failed to get the vote of the House on most of his important speeches. It must be remembered that, with a large segment of the House under the direct control of the king, Fox faced only a small minority of men who were willing—the case being sufficiently cogent—to alter their beliefs. Accordingly, we cannot say that a speech is necessarily unsuccessful if it fails to get the vote. Facing an insuperable task, the orator may still be a great interpreter of truth or justice within the restricted field of effective action.

On the other hand, there are surely some speeches which have a profound effect upon hearers, and upon the votes that subsequently decide the question at issue. Lord Curzon declares that he has often seen votes affected by speeches in the House of Commons. He mentions specifically the addresses of Mr. Fowler in a debate in the House in 1895; and he refers to the unmistakable influence of Gladstone's speech in moving a vote of credit in the Russo-Afghan crisis of 1885. Furthermore, Curzon points to the celebrated instances of divisions turned by the speech of Wilberforce in the Melville case of 1806, by Plunket's speech on Catholic Emancipation in 1807, and by Macaulay's speeches on the Copyright Bill in 1842 and on the proposal of 1853 to make the Master of Rolls incapable of sitting in the House.[11]

(6) Closely related to the last criterion is the one which appraises a speech in terms of its long-range effects upon the social group. Over a period of years, did a particular speech or series of speeches exercise a discernible and significant influence upon the course of events? Lecky, it will be recalled, believed that the wisdom of a policy was usually disclosed "very gradually." He held that the "final consequences" determine the sagacity of a proposal. However, he urged the historian not to overlook the part that "chance and the unexpected" play in human affairs, saying that "success is not always a decisive proof of sagacity."[12]

Unquestionably many speeches have exercised such a long-range effect upon history. A few examples will illustrate the point.

Apropos of the effect of Ebenezer Porter's pulpit speaking, Clyde Yarbrough holds that the sermon on "The Fatal Effects of Ardent Spirits" resulted in the formation of a committee which started the nineteenth-century temperance reformation in America.[13] J. E. Thorold Rogers asserted that there was not a homestead in England in which there was not an added comfort as a result of John Bright's oratory on social reform. He said higher wages, steadier employment, and "more solid independence" were Bright's enduring monument.[14] Trevelyan bears out this testimony by asserting that seldom "has any public man, after labouring long years in the wilderness, seen so many of the reforms which he has urged placed upon the Statute Book." [15] He goes even further, saying that, not by his arguing in the Cabinet or by his sharing in the affairs of a party, "but by his public orations as a private citizen he [Bright] profoundly modified English politics and the relations and balance of English classes." [16] The evidence is specific. Not alone, of course, but nevertheless very effectively, he labored for and realized his aims in the repeal of the Corn Laws in 1846; in his efforts to keep England from turning to a Southern sympathy during the Civil War; in bringing about the Reform Bill in 1867, and in disestablishing the Church of England in Ireland.

The case for Charles James Fox is similar in its essentials Edward Lascelles believes that Fox's "greatness rests on the vindication after his death of those principles and causes for which he lived." Continuing, Lascelles says:

> On that day in 1832 when without revolution or bloodshed the Reform Bill became law; on that day two years later when eight hundred thousand slaves became free; and when, more than a century after his death, Parliament in the greatest of wars met discontent by projects for an extension of the franchise, posterity added its tribute to the immortal memory of Mr. Fox.[17]

A critic may, indeed, turn to such tangible results when appraising an orator and his speeches. The testimony of service to society is no servile guide to oratorical merit. As John Morley put it:

> Is not the highest object of our search in a study of the career of a conspicuous man an estimate of his contributions to the cause of the collective progress of mankind? We have to ask first, what general advance was made by this cause, while he was still a witness of it; and next, what place and part he took as an actor in it.[18]

Combination of Standards Most Desirable

A single measure of oratorical effectiveness is probably neither possible nor desirable. A speech is a complex affair; its evaluation is not likely to be any simpler. A determination of its merit is, then, dependent upon all the foregoing criteria. An effective address should bring out the moral and intellectual character of the speaker; it should elicit an early, favorable response; rhetorically it should conform, within certain limits, to the technical virtues; it should exercise a certain influence upon subsequent events. Perhaps no two speeches will do all, or part, of these things in the same way or in equal measure. That is not important. Most important, and beyond all such attempts at classification we have been concerned with here, stands the doctrine of speech as a venture in the communication of ideas.

Manifestly, *response* is the key determinant of effectiveness. This presupposes the speaker's intelligent recognition of the necessity of adapting his materials to listeners; of his keeping the audience, rather than formal rules, constantly in mind. Unlike the writer who may deliberately prepare his copy for the ages, the orator must direct his remarks to the immediacy of the present occasion. This does not close the door to statesmanlike conduct. But it does require that the speaker adapt himself to conditions as he finds them, and that he communicate his ideas with a view to their taking root in the lives of the hearers, and, either immediately or subsequently, influencing their belief or action.

Clearly, the response to a speech need not be immediate. Speeches may be inadequate to produce a certain effect at once and still be none the less great. But a good idea, initiated by a speaker, may in turn be supplemented by other addresses and writings, and eventually result in wholesome action. This may be referred to as the theory of cumulative effects in oratory. The concept is consistent with the democratic process. Individual pronouncements are important; they contribute to the unfolding of a case as a whole; they stimulate the wholesome exchange of additional views and opinions; they encourage that collision of error with truth to which John Stuart Mill refers in his "Essay on Liberty of Expression." But the final result may derive from many causes, rather than a single one. Great speeches are often important links in a long chain of influencing circumstances.

It is conceivable, therefore, that society profits from the slow-tempo response to public address. If changes of opinion or action could be induced immediately, and without the necessary time for reflection, the effect upon society might be unwholesome. In fact, it might become highly pernicious. Rabble rousers and demagogues hope for instantaneous responses, and often get them. Yet the critic of such oratory will not regard the acquisition of the response as a total measure of speech effectiveness. This is true whether the demagogue happens at the moment to be telling the truth or not, for the critic will also search out the motive for the pronouncement. Recalling William Blake's line, the critic would note that

> A truth that's told with bad intent
> Beats all the lies you can invent.

Effectiveness, in such case, might be simply synonymous with technical mastery of the methods of persuasion. But the techniques of an art are superficial means of achieving ends; their use must always be assessed with regard to the terminal values they help to realize. A speech is effective, therefore, if it achieves an end or response consistent with the speaker's purpose—provided that the purpose is, in turn, consistent with the dictates of responsible judgment and solicitous regard for the positive good of an enlightened society.

PART VI

POSTSCRIPT TO AN INQUIRY

Chapter 18

TOWARD A PHILOSOPHY OF RHETORIC

Systems Require Internal Unity

"There is no philosophy," said T. V. Smith, "only philosophers and their philosophies." Surely there is no final philosophy of discourse. But though there may be no fixed certainties, conceptions of the meaning and function of the field of rhetoric are as numerous as investigators interested in examining it. This chapter is but one of those conceptions. It makes no pretense of offering distinctively new conclusions.

The need for philosophies arises from the complexity resulting from the application of theory to practice. One of the functions of criticism is to provide a certain internal unity of the various, and often conflicting, theories and judgments which make up the area of inquiry. A philosophy, or rationale, helps to bring together the many elements of a subject, thus articulating them with man's other interests in and obligations to the whole field of knowledge. Like all scholars, we seek an intelligent conception of our subject. We attempt to view the many parts in their essential relation to the whole. It is not a matter of our examining emotional proof by itself, or of appraising style by itself, or of viewing any one of the many other elements of the rhetorical art in isolation. As parts, they take on meaning only in their relation to the whole speaking performance in its social setting. Consequently, we feel a need for a set of principles which will bind the many concepts together. We seek what Bernard Bosanquet called a "connected vision of the totality of things."

Statements on the philosophy of our subject need to be rewritten often because the point of view toward oratory changes from period to period, and the known facts pertaining to it increase with the passing of time. Goethe once said that histories should be rewritten occasionally, not only because new facts come to light, "but because new aspects come to view, because the participant in the progress of an age is led to standpoints from which the past can be regarded and judged in a novel manner." The history of rhetoric needs to be rewritten at different periods because criticism also becomes more exacting. Through the eyes of the critic, we come to see how oratory operates in the social organization; what its effects upon men are; where it errs on the side of excess or deficiency. And, generally speaking, it is the critic, rather than the theorist or teacher, who is more likely to bring the elements of an art together, the better to appraise its function in society.

Determinants of a Sound Conception of Rhetoric

What, then, are the lamps by which we are to be guided in our search for a point of view toward rhetoric? They are no doubt numerous, but we shall concern ourselves with the three which seem to us to offer the surest and clearest light.

Recognition of Value of Classical Works.—With Burke, we believe the "past is the best source for the reenforcement of opinion." The emphasis in this book has revealed an abiding faith in the classical treatises as yardsticks of excellence in oratory. This is not accidental; nor is it disrespectful to the moderns. It requires no apology since it gives added lustre to contemporary efforts.

We should, it seems to us, appropriate the wisdom and counsel of the ancients, especially of the Greeks, and use it as a guide to an intelligent understanding of our subject. The older contributions are not error-free, nor are the moderns. Fully mindful of the fact that "in no sense can antiquity *privilege an error* or novelty *prejudice a truth*," [1] we may yet conclude that the classical treatises give a balanced account of the speaking art and articulate it closely with the related fields of politics, ethics, and law. This does not argue for the servile acceptance of ancient doctrines. It simply suggests that "the greatest compliment we can pay to the greatness of the past is to surpass it, but in common courtesy we should doff our hats as we pass." [2]

Oratory As Extension of Democratic Forms: Union of Rhetoric and Politics.—Rhetoric has long been the handmaid of politics. Its association should be made even closer, more direct. While it is not necessary to regard politics as a branch of rhetoric, it is essential that we recognize fully the importance of speechcraft as a means of realizing desirable ends in political action. Nowhere are the relations of men to their constituencies more fraught with social consequence than in the area of political representation. And the politician, seeking to provide programs for the social body, need not, as George Catlin alleges the reformer used to do, play the role of an evangelist.

He can become the social doctor, provided he recognizes his obligation as a speaker to embrace knowledge of the facts, high ethical resolve, and a sense of public good.

Admittedly, rhetoric is a practical art. And the political figure is a practical man. He seeks to realize his ends by bringing people into line with his own will. In so doing, he relies upon the techniques of persuasion. As a practical man, he will frequently gauge the wisdom of proposed actions in the light of expediency. He will find, as a political philosopher once put it, that "the impracticable ideal is, as a guide to action, a false ideal." [3] But it is at this point that the full importance of rhetoric must assert itself. The mere possession of the tools of persuasive manipulation—without a stabilizing ethic to control their usage—is not enough. If politics—and, in its turn, rhetoric—is associated with the means of getting things done, it is imperative that ethics, which deals with ends and the relative values of what is achieved, be reunited with the political art. Rhetoric, as the intermediary between the will to action and the achievement of the result, must accordingly be conceived as both a political and an ethical instrument. This is another way of saying, perhaps, that there must be a *moral principle* supporting and guiding the liberal tradition. While there has been some disposition to resist the inclusion of such a principle in the scheme of learning—a circumstance resulting from our virtual deification of the so-called scientific spirit and method—its return as an active force in the field of knowledge is necessary. A sustained faith in democracy itself depends upon it.

One of the logical implications of an appeal to a closer union between politics and rhetoric is the wisdom of extending training in oratory to every citizen. The practical uses of rhetoric to which Aristotle referred are even more applicable to society today than they were to the Greece of his time. True, the complexity of modern society makes it more difficult for every man to participate directly in the deliberations of assemblies and in the administration of justice. Many of these duties have been delegated to men of professional rank in those callings. But every citizen still needs—in fact, needs more imperatively today—a familiarity with rhetoric, to the end that he may avail himself of its advantages in the true Aristotelian sense: (1) of perceiving the difference between truth and error; (2) of understanding how people are moved to action, despite the absence of compelling argument; (3) of arguing both sides of a question in order to determine the truth; and (4) of being able to defend himself with speech.

Democratic society is based upon the premise that the collective body of the common people is competent to exercise supreme authority in the state. In such a scheme, the power of public address must be a force of no mean proportion. If each citizen is to be—or is *naturally,* as Aristotle put it in his *Politics*—a "political animal," and if speech is to be the instrument by which advantage and disadvantage, truth and justice, are to be sustained, it follows that each man must be something of a statesman and of an advocate in his own right. Each citizen must serve as a balance wheel in an exceedingly complex political mechanism. Only then will Aristotle's remarks regarding the collective wisdom of the masses be correct:

> For it is possible that the Many, of whom each individual is not a virtuous man, are still collectively superior to the few best persons, *i.e.* superior not as individuals but as a body, as picnics are superior to feasts supplied at the expense of a single person. For as the total number is large, it is possible that each has a fractional share of virtue and prudence and that, as the multitude collectively may be compared to an individual with many feet, hands and senses, so the same is true of their character and intelligence. It is thus that the Many are better judges *than the Few* even of musical and poetical compositions; for some judge one part, some another, and all of them collectively the whole.[4]

Democracy lives by talk. It functions through speech. Indeed, "Language is democracy," as Henry N. Wieman observes, "when language carries the full load of a people's most cherished meanings from each to all and back again from all to each."[5] When men have something on their minds, freedom to speak it constitutes the natural outlet for their will to action. But it presupposes literacy on their part, a knowledge of what they express, and a recognition of the responsibility inherent in free expression. Quite properly, the inculcation of such principles of conduct is the task of those who train the citizenry in speechcraft. An enlightened conception of rhetoric as an aid to politics is one of the surest protectors of democratic society. Tyranny cannot flourish where responsible men have the right to say responsible things. But men have that right only if they impose upon themselves certain restraints dictated by their control of facts and by their consideration of the welfare of others. Without that restraint some men will be free, as L. T. Hobhouse remarks, "but others will be unfree." Some will exercise their full will, while the rest will have only such freedom as the powerful allow them.[6] This is not an appeal for silence. It is, instead, an appeal for the free expression of statements for which the speaker is answerable. As a recent release by the Office of War Information indicated: "The enemies of all liberty flourish and grow strong in the dark of enforced silence."

The foregoing remarks suggest that intelligent men will always present noble themes in their discourses. It is evident that this is not completely true. But it is within the province of the rhetorician to insist upon nobility of conception in the expression of topics. Hundreds of years ago, Isocrates developed a theory of culture which urged precisely this thing. The revival of certain features of the Isocratic doctrine is overdue. While holding to a defense of practical knowledge, Isocrates insisted that the individual strive for good conduct—that he be a citizen whose ethical principles shone through his actions. The citizen was to be a cultivated speaker, "for the power to speak well is taken as the surest index of a sound understanding, and discourse which is true and lawful and just is the outward image of a good and faithful soul." [7]

In Isocrates' theory of culture, there was no room for discourses on petty and unjust causes. Instead, the themes were to be grand in their scope and nature, honorable in their motives, and "devoted to the welfare of man and our common good. . . ." [8] The speakers were to embrace subjects of broad, almost universal character. Thus oratory and disciplined statesmanship were linked in common bond.

The closer union of politics and rhetoric will insure for speeches a more permanent place in historical records. Surely this would be desirable. It is regrettable that the great speeches of history today find such inadequate representation in our textbooks. The speech is a document; faithfully reproduced, it presents a trustworthy record of what was said. If a message of moment, it speaks not only for the present, but for the future; and it speaks in terms which defy the hazards of trickery imposed by those who would seek to misinterpret it.

With the attachment of increasing importance to speeches as documents will come a fuller realization of the relation between oratory and practical action. There is a logic of discourse, the goal of which is the attainment and protection of personal liberty. This is its design: to achieve and hold fast to the rights for which men have fought and died since the beginning of history. Rabble rousers and tyrants use speech, indeed, to make secure their own self-contained ambitions. But in making expression their exclusive monopoly; in assuming that audiences were made for public address, rather than the reverse, and that only the rulers can exercise speech as an instrument of control, tyrants misread the history of mankind. There is adequate testimony to disprove their thesis. From the time Corax devised an art of speech to meet the practical demands of people who sought restitution of their property, to the latest pronouncements of a Roosevelt who pleaded the cause of the Four Freedoms—the line is unbroken. It is a continuous, never-yielding search for liberty as the goal of political utterance. That there are frequent setbacks, no one will deny. But that there is an inexorable logic of speechcraft which postulates the freedom of man as the object of its efforts, history proves and man's conscience confirms.

Reunion of Rhetoric and Ethics.—So closely connected with the concept of a union of politics and rhetoric that it would be folly to dissociate them, is the wisdom of linking rhetoric with ethics. This is no new idea. The ancients recognized the necessity of doing precisely this. If man is a political animal; if he uses speech to achieve his ends in deliberative situations, he also needs a guiding ethic, a set of principles which will enable him to judge the right from the wrong and to govern his conduct by appeal to moral standards.

This is simply another way of saying that rhetoric is to be used to give effectiveness to truth. It is not intended to give effectiveness to the speakers, *per se,* or to techniques, *per se.* It is not an instrument, to adapt a remark from Macaulay, by which people are to be maddened by sophistry, calumny, and stimulants, so that in the fulness of bread, they rave as if famine were in the land. Rhetoric must take truth, or a reasonable approximation, as its substance. It must make W. G. T. Shedd's phrase—*"truth clearly perceived, deeply felt, and strongly expressed"* [9]—the principle of all genuine public address.

The cultivation of a sense of responsibility for the uttered statement is a crying imperative for public speakers today—just as it was yesterday and will be tomorrow. We can but hold in contempt those "whose talent consists in language, and who by . . . superior eloquence . . . decorate error with the garb of truth." To deceive through words is no less reprehensible than to cheat through more overt and demonstrable ways. It is still deception. To use rhetoric as an instrument for making promises which he has no intention of keeping, or which involve so many conditions that they cannot possibly be consummated, even though he were willing, is as culpable in a speaker today as it was in ancient Greece centuries ago.

The issue is one involving the reconciliation of the instrumental means of acquiring responses from hearers with the ethical considerations relative to the character of the desired ends. It has been

said that "the consciousness of end must be more than merely intellectual." [10] This is an important truth, although there has been
some tendency to veer away from moral or ethical concepts in rhetorical theory. It has been assumed that the techniques of rhetoric are
amoral, capable of both enlightened and evil use, depending upon
the character of the speaker. While this is unquestionably true, it
does not absolve critics of the responsibility of considering the
ethical implications of public statements. Nor does it release
teachers from the obligation of inculcating moral principles in
speakers, and of advising future citizens of the necessary duty of
holding themselves strictly accountable for what they say.

There is a need for the establishment of a more binding relationship between the instrumental and the ethical components of the
speaking art. Overemphasis of *technique* in speaking; the disposition to regard rhetoric as an instrument of power, by which a speaker
may improve himself, make more money, control people—these are
the snares which beset a sound point of view in contemporary public
speaking. Disproportionate emphasis upon the purely instrumental
means of controlling people through persuasion is likely to nurture
a perfunctory regard for truth in statement and honesty in purpose.
If not held in check by some other instruction, it develops into a
doctrine of self-realization through the crafty use of tested techniques. The speaker who serves his state with scrupulous regard for
trustworthiness of statement and with solicitous concern for the possible good his remarks may do the common cause need not be an
instrument of cold calculation, devoid of vehemence and force. Quite
the contrary. Society needs, and needs desperately, orators who,
working with facts, are also poets and philosophers, men who can
costume truth effectively. Society needs speakers who possess the
intellectual and emotional resources ascribed by Hoyt Hudson [11] to
the liberally educated person: a full body of information, a severe
operative logic, and a sensitive, disciplined imagination. In an age
which is often impatient of deep feeling in public address, there is a
deserved place for speakers who embrace sound ideas with passionate zeal. Society stands to gain if these conceptions are expressed—
not necessarily elegantly—but, surely, carefully, accurately, and with
a show of beauty. The tradition of a free America is richer because
Webster took pains to prepare the "Plymouth Oration"; because
Lincoln conceived the "Gettysburg Address"; and because Phillips
confirmed the rights of man in his speech on the "Murder of Love-
joy." It may be doubted whether any considerable number of men
is willing today to spend the time necessary for the development of

great themes, in dignified and distinctive expression. The need for it is as urgent now as at any time in history. The opportunities for it are multiplied a thousandfold by the extension of the public platform and the radio. The audiences are ready, provided the speakers have the competence, patience, and will to meet the challenge. To paraphrase Cicero, great speakers will, even in our time, be "expected with impatience, and heard with pleasure."

The Prospect

Great orators will unquestionably arise to meet the recurring crises in man's quest for a freedom unfettered both by domestic and foreign foes. The inviolable logic of discourse is to secure, safeguard, and preserve liberty. Its inescapable potency will prevent temporary halts in the movement toward freedom from becoming chronic or sustained. While this is being written, orators are being trained and others are emerging to cope with the problems man creates through association with his neighbors.

The spoken word is eternal. It is a treasured legacy of the ages. Some few men there will always be, when the future of the state is in doubt, who will come forward to express the aspirations of the people in dignified, honest speech. Such words may yet help man to realize the genuinely good life.

APPENDIX A

SUPPLEMENTARY READINGS
AND
EXERCISES

Appendix A

The following readings and exercises suggest further lines of study in the theory and criticism of public address.

CHAPTER 1

READINGS

1. Edwin A. Burtt. "Logical Problems in Historical Explanation." In *Principles and Problems of Right Thinking*, New York, Harper & Bros., 1928. pp. 498-517.
2. Herbert A. Wichelns. "The Literary Criticism of Oratory." In *Studies in Rhetoric and Public Speaking in Honor of James A. Winans*, New York, Century Co., 1925. pp. 181-216.
3. Donald C. Bryant. "Some Problems of Scope and Method in Rhetorical Scholarship." *Quarterly Journal of Speech,* 23:182-189 (April, 1937).
4. Everett Lee Hunt. "Rhetoric and Literary Criticism." *Quarterly Journal of Speech,* 21:564-568 (November, 1935).
5. Hoyt H. Hudson. "Rhetoric and Poetry." *Quarterly Journal of Speech Education,* 10:143-154 (April, 1924).
6. Giles Wilkeson Gray. "Some Differences between Speaking and Writing." In *A Course of Study in Speech Training and Public Speaking for Secondary Schools,* A. M. Drummond, ed., New York, Century Co., 1925. pp. 112-118.
7. Bower Aly. "The Criticism of Oratory." In *The Rhetoric of Alexander Hamilton,* New York, Columbia University Press, 1941, pp. 25-32.
8. ———. "A Rhetorical Theory for a History of Public Speaking in the United States." In *Papers in Rhetoric,* Donald C. Bryant, ed., St. Louis, privately printed, 1940. pp. 34-38.
9. Wayland M. Parrish. "Objective Literary Standards in Interpretation." *Quarterly Journal of Speech,* 22:368-379 (October, 1936).
10. Irving J. Lee. "Four Ways of Looking at a Speech." *Quarterly Journal of Speech,* 28:148-155 (April, 1942).
11. Everett Hunt. "The Rhetorical Mood of World War II." *Quarterly Journal of Speech,* 29:1-5 (February, 1943).
12. Loren Reid. "The Perils of Rhetorical Criticism." *Quarterly Journal of Speech,* 30:416-422 (December, 1944).
13. Stephen C. Pepper. *The Basis of Criticism in the Arts.* Cambridge, Harvard University Press, 1945.
14. Alfred R. Orage. *Selected Essays and Critical Writings.* Herbert Read and Denis Saurat, eds., London, Stanley Nott, 1935.
15. Theodore M. Greene. *The Arts and the Art of Criticism.* Princeton, Princeton University Press, 1940.

EXERCISES

1. What essential differences would you note between a typical political speech and a personal essay?

2. Prepare a paper in which are set forth the fundamental differences between oral and written composition.

3. To what extent should the rhetorical critic aim at social usefulness in the preparation of his criticism? If, in determining the effect of a particular speech, he observes the irregular or unethical use of data or devices, how shall he dispose of such a consideration in his evaluation?

4. For subsequent use in this course, collect specimens of speech criticism found in newspapers and periodicals. Try, especially, to secure a number of reports by editorial writers and columnists on speeches of major importance.

5. Rhetoric is commonly considered a useful art. How does the circumstance of usefulness make its criticism differ from that of a fine art?

6. Discuss the possible relation between the criticism of speeches and the improvement in quality or the enlargement of influence of public addresses.

7. Comment on the more important causes that occasion expressions of criticism in oratory.

8. Comment on the relation between rhetorical criticism and such fields as ethics, psychology, and politics.

9. To what extent should the literary considerations of permanence and beauty enter into the judgment of a speech?

10. Define the following terms: oratory, eloquence, rhetoric, speech, and public speaking.

11. Comment on John Quincy Adams' definition of rhetorical criticism as "the art of appreciating the real merits of a public speaker."

12. Differentiate between *reviewing* and *criticism*.

13. Comment on the following: "Speeches, as a rule, even the best, are as evanescent as fireworks or thistledown. They are explored for untimely quotation during the speaker's life, and when that useful purpose ceases at his death, they cease to be opened at all."—Lord Rosebery.

CHAPTER 2

READINGS

1. Bromley Smith. "Thrasymachus: A Pioneer Rhetorician." *Quarterly Journal of Speech Education*, 13:278-291 (June, 1927).
2. ———. "Corax and Probability." *Quarterly Journal of Speech Education*, 7:13-42 (February, 1921).
3. ———. "Theodorus of Byzantium: Word-Smith." *Quarterly Journal of Speech*, 14:71-81 (February, 1928).
4. ———. "The Father of Debate: Protagoras of Abdera." *Quarterly Journal of Speech Education*, 4:196-215 (March, 1918).
5. ———. "Gorgias: A Study of Oratorical Style." *Quarterly Journal of Speech Education*, 7:335-359 (November, 1921).

6. ———. "Hippias and a Lost Canon of Rhetoric." *Quarterly Journal of Speech Education,* 12:129-145 (June, 1926).
7. ———. "Prodicus of Ceos: The Sire of Synonymy." *Quarterly Journal of Speech Education,* 6:51-68 (April, 1920).
8. Hoyt H. Hudson. "The Tradition of Our Subject." *Quarterly Journal of Speech,* 17:320-329 (June, 1931).
9. Lane Cooper. "The Rhetoric of Aristotle." *Quarterly Journal of Speech,* 21:10-19 (February, 1935).
10. Friedrich Blass. *Die Attische Beredsamkeit.* Leipzig, B. G. Teubner, 1887-1898. (Cf. especially: Antiphon, I, 91-203; Lysias, I, 339-644; Isocrates, II, 9-331.)
11. Robert J. Bonner. "Advocates and Speech-Writers." In *Lawyers and Litigants in Ancient Athens,* Chicago, University of Chicago Press, 1927. pp. 200-243.
12. George W. Botsford. "The Age of Pericles." In *Hellenic History,* New York, Macmillan Co., 1926. pp. 234-299.
13. Richard Jebb. "The Age of Pericles." In *The Greek Genius and Its Influence,* Lane Cooper, ed., New Haven, Yale University Press, 1917. pp. 63-76.
14. ———. "Rhetoric." In *Encyclopedia Britannica.*
15. ———. *The Attic Orators.* London, Macmillan and Co., 1893. 2 v.
16. A. W. Gomme. "The Speeches in Thucydides." In *Essays in Greek History and Literature,* Oxford, Basil Blackwell, 1937. pp. 156-189.
17. G. L. Hendrickson. "The Peripatetic Mean of Style and the Three Stylistic Characters." *American Journal of Philology,* 25:125-146 (Whole No. 98).
18. ———. "The Origin and Meanings of the Ancient Characters of Style." *American Journal of Philology,* 26:249-290 (Whole No. 103).
19. Aristotle. *Topics.*
20. ———. *Poetics.*
21. Alfred E. Zimmern. *The Greek Commonwealth.* 3rd ed. rev., Oxford, Clarendon Press, 1922. pp. 198-209. (Notes on the Ideal of Citizenship.)
22. George A. Simcox and William H. Simcox. *The Orations of Demosthenes and Aeschines on the Crown.* Oxford, Clarendon Press, 1872. (Material on the life of Demosthenes, the oration, the text, nature of the evidence, etc.)
23. Lewis M. Hammond. "Rhetoric and Dialectic." In *Eastern Public Speaking Conference: 1940,* Harold F. Harding, ed., New York, The H. W. Wilson Co., 1940. pp. 173-182.
24. Wilbur S. Howell. "Nathaniel Carpenter's Place in the Controversy between Dialectic and Rhetoric." *Speech Monographs,* 1:20-41 (September, 1934).
25. Francis P. Donnelly. "Ancient Rhetoric and Modern Practice." In *Eastern Public Speaking Conference: 1940,* Harold F. Harding, ed., New York, The H. W. Wilson Co., 1940. pp. 183-190.
26. Everett Lee Hunt. "Plato and Aristotle on Rhetoric and Rhetoricians." In *Studies in Rhetoric and Public Speaking,* New York, Century Co., 1925. pp. 3-60.
27. Bernard W. Kelly. *Famous Advocates and Their Speeches.* London, Sweet and Maxwell, 1921. (Comments on forensic eloquence in England.)
28. A. E. Taylor. *Plato: The Man and His Work.* New York, Dial Press, Inc., 1936. pp. 103-129; 299-319.
29. R. Hackforth. "Sicily." In *The Cambridge Ancient History,* Cambridge, University Press, 1940. V, 145-164. (Establishes the background for the discovery of Corax's material.)
30. *Thucydides.* Charles F. Smith, trans., New York, G. P. Putnam's Sons, 1928. (The Funeral Oration, Book II, sections xxxv-xlvi, pp. 319-341.)
31. Charles Sears Baldwin. "The Elementary Exercises of Hermogenes." In *Medieval Rhetoric and Poetic.* New York, The Macmillan Co., 1928. pp. 23-38.
32. Werner Jaeger. *Paideia.* Gilbert Highet, trans., New York, Oxford University

Press, 1944. (The Rhetoric of Isocrates and Its Cultural Ideal, III, 46-70; Isocrates Defends His Paideia, III, 132-155; Plato's Phaedrus: Philosophy and Rhetoric, III, 182-196.)

33. Paul Shorey. "What Teachers of Speech May Learn from the Theory and Practice of the Greeks." *Quarterly Journal of Speech Education,* 8:105-131 (April, 1922).

34. Lester Thonssen. "A Functional Interpretation of Aristotle's Rhetoric." *Quarterly Journal of Speech,* 16:297-310 (June, 1930).

35. William E. Utterback. "Aristotle's Contribution to the Psychology of Argument." *Quarterly Journal of Speech Education,* 11:218-225 (June, 1925).

36. Russell H. Wagner. "The Rhetorical Theory of Isocrates." *Quarterly Journal of Speech Education,* 8:323-337 (November, 1922).

37. Arthur S. Way. *Thucydides: Speeches and Funeral Orations.* London, Macmillan and Co., 1934.

38. John H. Finley, Jr. *Thucydides.* Cambridge, Mass., Harvard University Press, 1942. pp. 250-288. ("The Style of Thucydides.")

39. Giles Wilkeson Gray. "The Precepts of Kagemni and Ptah-Hotep." *Quarterly Journal of Speech,* 32:446-454 (December, 1946).

EXERCISES

1. Compare and contrast the English term "orator" with the Latin term *orator* and the Greek word *rhetor.*

2. Review the internal and external evidence related to the assertion that "Ancient oratory was a fine art."

3. Comment on this statement by Jebb: "The broadest characteristic of modern oratory, as compared with ancient, is the predominance of a sustained appeal to the understanding."

4. Point out features in an oration of Burke's that suggest the classical type of oratory.

5. Comment on Lord Brougham's observation: "There is hardly one of the political or forensic orations of the Greeks that might not be delivered in similar circumstances before our senate or tribunals."

6. Analyze typical orations of the *Iliad* or the *Odyssey* to illustrate the characteristics of Homeric eloquence.

7. Explain the relation of deliberative to forensic and epideictic oratory in the history of Greek public address.

8. Compare and contrast Demosthenes' and Aeschines' speeches "On the Crown."

9. Compare Plato's *Phaedrus* and Aristotle's *Rhetoric* concerning (1) relationship of rhetoric to truth; (2) relationship of rhetoric to dialectic; (3) relationship of rhetoric to philosophy.

10. Point out the relation of rhetoric, in the classical sense, to the fields of politics and ethics.

11. To what extent can the rhetorician be regarded as representative of the culture of his time? To what extent was Isocrates successful in establishing that concept?

12. There is evidence that some of the classical rhetoricians looked upon medicine as the model for a true rhetoric. Examine the *Phaedrus* and the *Rhetoric,* among others, to ascertain the extent to which medical concepts were used to establish rhetorical principles.

13. Prepare a paper on the concept of the "golden mean."

14. Discuss the relation of history to rhetoric. Assess the reflections of the principal contributors to rhetorical theory apropos of this theme.

15. Read the *Rhetorica ad Alexandrum.* (In *The Works of Aristotle.* Oxford, Clarendon Press, 1924. XI, 1420a-1447b.) This work, often ascribed to Aristotle, was probably written by Anaximenes about 340 B.C.

CHAPTER 3

READINGS

1. Earl W. Wells. "Methods of Memorization for the Speaker and Reader." *Quarterly Journal of Speech,* 14:39-64 (February, 1928).
2. J. P. Ryan. "Quintilian's Message." *Quarterly Journal of Speech,* 15:171-180 (April, 1929).
3. John Emperor. "The Rhetorical Importance of Lucan's *Pharsalia.*" *Quarterly Journal of Speech,* 16:463-471 (November, 1930).
4. Gaston Boissier. "The Schools of Declamation at Rome." In *Tacitus and Other Roman Studies,* W. G. Hutchinson, trans., London, Archibald Constable, 1906. pp. 163-194.
5. Clarence W. Mendell. "Long Speeches." In *Our Seneca,* New Haven, Yale University Press, 1941. pp. 94-115.
6. Russell H. Wagner. "The Meaning of *Dispositio.*" In *Studies in Speech and Drama* in Honor of Alexander M. Drummond, Ithaca, Cornell University Press, 1944. pp. 285-294.
7. Harry Caplan. "The Decay of Eloquence at Rome in the First Century." In *Studies in Speech and Drama* in Honor of Alexander M. Drummond, Ithaca, Cornell University Press, 1944. pp. 295-325.
8. Harold F. Harding. "Quintilian's Witnesses." *Speech Monographs,* 1:1-20 (September, 1934).
9. Lester Thonssen, comp., *Selected Readings in Rhetoric and Public Speaking.* New York, The H. W. Wilson Co., 1942.

EXERCISES

1. Compare and contrast the points of view held by Aristotle, Cicero, and Quintilian relative to the following concepts: (1) function of oratory; (2) ends of oratory; (3) qualifications of the speakers; (4) invention; (5) arrangement; (6) style; (7) memory; (8) delivery.

2. In the light of present-day pedagogical practices, evaluate Quintilian's suggestions concerning (1) the reading of history and speeches; (2) the writing of compositions, and (3) the practice of declamation.

3. Appraise Quintilian's concept of the "perfect" orator. Include a discussion of the orator as a civic leader and as a "good" man.

4. Through a study of typical orations by Cicero, compare and contrast his practice with his theory.

5. What is the full significance of Cicero's statement: "For the proper concern of an orator . . . is language of power and elegance accommodated to the feelings and understandings of mankind"?

6. Compare and contrast the treatments of refutation in Cicero and Quintilian.

7. Many treatises on rhetoric appear in dialogue form (*viz.*, Plato's *Gorgias* and *Phaedrus*, Cicero's *De Oratore*, Tacitus' *Dialogue Concerning Oratory*, etc.). Evaluate the effectiveness of this technique. Make a list of the principal works in which the dialogue pattern is used.

8. Study Erskine's "Defense of Lord George Gordon" as an instance of a case based upon the *status of definition*.

CHAPTER 4

READINGS

1. Hoyt H. Hudson. "Jewel's Oration against Rhetoric: A Translation." *Quarterly Journal of Speech*, 14:374-392 (June, 1928).
2. ———. *"Compendium Rhetorices* by Erasmus: A Translation." In *Studies in Speech and Drama* in Honor of Alexander M. Drummond, Ithaca, Cornell University Press, 1944. pp. 326-340.
3. ———. *The Praise of Folly*, by Desiderius Erasmus. Princeton, Princeton University Press, 1941.
4. Bromley Smith. "A College Oration by John Milton." *Quarterly Journal of Speech*, 14:392-395 (June, 1928).
5. Wayland M. Parrish. "Whately and His Rhetoric." *Quarterly Journal of Speech*, 15:58-79 (February, 1929).
6. William P. Sandford. "English Rhetoric Reverts to Classicism." *Quarterly Journal of Speech*, 15:503-525 (November, 1929).
7. Russell H. Wagner. "Wilson and His Sources." *Quarterly Journal of Speech*, 15:525-537 (November, 1929).
8. ———. "Thomas Wilson's Contributions to Rhetoric." In *Papers in Rhetoric*, Donald C. Bryant, ed., St. Louis, privately printed, 1940. pp. 1-7.
9. C. A. Fritz. "From Sheridan to Rush: The Beginnings of English Elocution." *Quarterly Journal of Speech*, 16:75-88 (February, 1930).
10. Karl R. Wallace. "Rhetorical Exercises in Tudor Education." *Quarterly Journal of Speech*, 22:28-51 (February, 1936).
11. ———. "Early English Rhetoricians on the Structure of Rhetorical Prose." In *Papers in Rhetoric*, Donald C. Bryant, ed., pp. 18-26.
12. ———. *Francis Bacon On Communication and Rhetoric*. Chapel Hill, University of North Carolina Press, 1943.
13. James A. Winans. "Whately on Elocution." *Quarterly Journal of Speech*, 31:1-8 (February, 1945).
14. ———. *Public Speaking*. New York, Century Co., 1915. (Chapters on Attention, Emotion, and Persuasion.)
15. Otto A. L. Dieter. "The Rhetoric of Notker Labeo." In *Papers in Rhetoric*, Donald C. Bryant, ed., pp. 27-33.
16. Clement C. J. Webb. *John of Salisbury*. London, Methuen and Co., 1932. pp 75-101. ("John's Metalogicon and Entheticus.")

17. Lee S. Hultzén. "Charles Butler on Memory." *Speech Monographs,* 6:44-65 (1939).
18. Frederick W. Haberman. "De Quincey's Theory of Rhetoric." In *Eastern Public Speaking Conference: 1940,* Harold F. Harding, ed., New York, The H. W. Wilson Co., 1940. pp. 191-203.
19. Wilbur S. Howell. *The Rhetoric of Alcuin and Charlemagne.* Princeton, Princeton University Press, 1941.
20. William G. Crane. *Wit and Rhetoric in the Renaissance.* New York, Columbia University Press, 1937. ("Rhetoric in the Schools of the Sixteenth Century," pp. 57-79; "English Rhetorics of the Sixteenth Century," pp. 97-112.)
21. Harry Caplan. "A Late Medieval Tractate on Preaching." In *Studies in Rhetoric and Public Speaking* in Honor of James A. Winans, New York, Century Co., 1925. pp. 61-90.
22. Mary Margaret Robb. *Oral Interpretation of Literature in American Colleges and Universities.* New York, The H. W. Wilson Co., 1941.
23. Milton B. Kennedy. *The Oration in Shakespeare.* Chapel Hill, University of North Carolina Press, 1942.
24. William James. *Psychology.* New York, Henry Holt & Co., 1893. pp. 217-238. (Chapter on "Attention.")

EXERCISES

1. What were the Seven Liberal Arts? What significance did Rhetoric have in this curricular program?

2. Compare and contrast Thomas Wilson's *Arte of Rhetorique* with John F. Genung's *Practical Elements of Rhetoric* (Boston, Ginn and Co., 1886) with reference to (1) the treatment of the five traditional parts of rhetoric; (2) the principal types of public speech; (3) the ends of speaking; (4) the several parts of a speech; (5) the forms and methods of proof, and (6) the principles of audience adaptation.

3. Account for the movement in rhetorical theory in England that stressed *elocutio.*

4. Compare and contrast the theories of Thomas Sheridan and John Walker concerning elocution. Indicate how the principles set forth by these writers are reflected in the modern textbooks on the fundamentals of speech.

5. Evaluate the theory of logical proof in Richard Whately's *Rhetoric,* including an analysis of his treatment of propositions, burden of proof, persuasion, and delivery.

6. Point out the relationship between the conventional rhetorical theory and homiletical theory.

7. Appraise the contributions of certain modern teachers to the development of a theory of rhetoric. Include estimates of the contributions of James A. Winans, Charles H. Woolbert, and George P. Baker.

CHAPTER 5

Readings

1. J. W. H. Atkins. "The Critical Revival and Theories of Style of Tacitus and Demetrius." In *Literary Criticism in Antiquity*. London, Cambridge University Press, 1934. II, 175-209.
2. E. M. Cope. *An Introduction to Aristotle's Rhetoric*. London, Macmillan and Co., 1867.
3. Everett Lee Hunt. "Rhetoric and Literary Criticism." *Quarterly Journal of Speech*, 21:564-568 (November, 1935).

Exercises

1. To what extent can the critical standards of the ancients be applied to contemporary speechmaking?

2. Define Asianism; indicate its origins, limitations, tendencies, and alleged defects in contrast to Atticism.

3. Do we have contemporary schools of thought that are roughly analogous to the old Atticist-Asianist division? Justify your answer by presenting illustrative data.

4. Are we justified in applying Cicero's standard of "cultural achievements" of the orators as basic indicators of their merit? Did Cicero's enthusiasm for his own rhetorical tenets vitiate his critical judgments? Are rhetorical critics of today (*e.g.,* the contributors to *History and Criticism of American Public Address*) governed by similar limitations?

5. In the light of Philostratus' assumptions concerning the ends of rhetoric, comment on the place of declamation in present-day school and college education.

6. To what extent does Cicero's method of criticizing the orators conform to the general suggestions set forth in Chapter 1 of this volume?

7. Prepare a paper in which you elaborate upon instances in which teachers of rhetoric addressed advice to rulers of state (*e.g.,* Isocrates to Nicocles, Fronto to Aurelius, etc.).

8. Study the *Brutus* to determine whether or not Cicero used "service to friends" as a subsidiary criterion of oratorical excellence (*e.g.,* his treatment of Caius Caelius, Lucius Gellius, etc.).

CHAPTER 6

Readings

1. Donald C. Bryant. "Burke's Opinion of Orators." *Quarterly Journal of Speech*, 20:241-254 (April, 1934).
2. Harold F. Harding. "The Listener on Eloquence: 1750-1800." In *Studies in Speech and Drama* in Honor of Alexander M. Drummond, Ithaca, Cornell University Press, 1944. pp. 341-353.

3. J. W. H. Atkins. *English Literary Criticism: The Medieval Phase.* New York, The Macmillan Co., 1943. pp. 36-58. ("Early Grammarians: Bede and Alcuin.")
4. Henry Brougham. *Rhetorical Theories and Literary Dissertations and Addresses.* London, R. Griffin and Co., 1856.
5. Hoyt H. Hudson. "De Quincey on Rhetoric and Public Speaking." In *Studies in Rhetoric and Public Speaking* in Honor of James A. Winans, New York, Century Co., 1925. pp. 133-151.
6. Thomas Babington Macaulay. "On the Athenian Orators." In *The Complete Works of Thomas B. Macaulay,* New York, Sully and Kleintech, 1900. VI, 40-56.
7. John Lord Campbell. *The Lives of the Chief Justices of England.* London, John Murray, 1849. II, 302-584. (Lord Mansfield.)
8. Wilbur S. Howell. "De Quincey on Science, Rhetoric, and Poetry." *Speech Monographs,* 13:1-13 (1946).

EXERCISES

1. Apply the Rapin formula to the criticism of a recent speaker.

2. Prepare a report on Fénelon as a critic of rhetorical theory and of French public speakers.

3. Prepare a report on Samuel Johnson as a critic of rhetorical theory and practice.

4. Trace the influence of contemporary psychology, logic, and philosophy on the rhetorical principles and critical tenets of Blair.

5. Construct a tabular analysis of Blair's scheme or method of criticism, as being similar mechanically to that of Rapin's method as outlined in this chapter.

6. Evaluate Hazlitt's observations on the differences between written and oral style by reference to experimental, normative, and other evidence from later studies on this problem. Indicate lines of further investigation concerning oral and written style.

7. Criticize in detail Brougham's argument that ancient oratory has "immeasurable superiority" over that of the moderns.

8. Make a study of Macaulay as a critic of orators. In your analysis refer to his critical opinions in the essays on "William Pitt," "Sir James Mackintosh," "William Pitt, Earl of Chatham," "Warren Hastings," and "On the Athenian Orators."

9. Examine the *Historical and the Posthumous Memoirs of Sir Nathaniel William Wraxall* (ed. by H. B. Wheatley, New York, Scribner and Welford, 1884. 5v.) to determine his attitude toward orators and oratory.

CHAPTER 7

READINGS

1. Everett Lee Hunt. "Matthew Arnold: The Critic as Rhetorician." *Quarterly Journal of Speech,* 20:483-507 (November, 1934).

2. Loren D. Reid. "Did Charles Fox Prepare His Speeches?" *Quarterly Journal of Speech,* 24:17-26 (February, 1938).
3. Laurence B. Goodrich. "Chrysostom, 'King of Preachers.'" *Quarterly Journal of Speech,* 24:27-35 (February, 1938).
4. W. Norwood Brigance. "The Twenty-Eight Foremost American Orators." *Quarterly Journal of Speech,* 24:376-380 (October, 1938).
5. J. Frederick Doering. "David Hume on Oratory." *Quarterly Journal of Speech,* 25:409-416 (October, 1939).
6. Bower Aly. "The Rhetoric of Semantics." *Quarterly Journal of Speech,* 30:23-30 (February, 1944).
7. ———. "The History of American Public Address as a Research Field." *Quarterly Journal of Speech,* 29:308-314 (October, 1943).
8. Elwood Murray. "The Semantics of Rhetoric." *Quarterly Journal of Speech,* 30:31-41 (February, 1944).
9. Kenneth G. Hance. "The Elements of the Rhetorical Theory of Phillips Brooks." *Speech Monographs,* 5:16-39 (1938).
10. Horace G. Rahskopf. "The Oratory of James Wilson of Pennsylvania." *Speech Monographs,* 5:40-61 (1938).
11. *History and Criticism of American Public Address.* Brigance, ed. New York, McGraw-Hill Book Co., Inc., 1943. (Study the following specimens of contemporary rhetorical criticism: Wilbur S. Howell and Hoyt H. Hudson's "Daniel Webster," II, 665-733; Brigance's "Jeremiah S. Black," I, 459-482; and Karl R. Wallace's "Booker T. Washington," I, 407-433.)
12. Chauncey A. Goodrich. *Select British Eloquence.* New York, Harper & Bros., 1852. (Examine the memoir of Lord Chatham, the historical introduction to the speech on the "Right of Taxing America," and the text of the speech.)
13. Harold F. Graves. "Public Speaking in Propaganda." *Quarterly Journal of Speech,* 27:29-38 (February, 1941).
14. Walter Blair. *Manual of Reading.* Chicago, Scott, Foresman & Co., 1943. ("Analyzing Explanatory Writing," pp. 29-98; "Analyzing Rhetorical Writing," pp. 144-221.)
15. Bernard De Voto. "The Easy Chair." *Harper's Magazine,* July, 1945. pp. 33-36. (A criticism of Norman Corwin's "On a Note of Triumph," and of the "rhetoric of radio" generally.)
16. C. Harold King. "God's Dramatist." In *Studies in Speech and Drama* in Honor of Alexander M. Drummond, Ithaca, Cornell University Press, 1944. pp. 369-392. (An appraisal of George Whitefield's speaking.)
17. Theodore F. Nelson. "Charles Haddon Spurgeon's Theory and Practice of Preaching." *Quarterly Journal of Speech,* 32:173-181 (April, 1946).
18. Lionel Crocker. *Henry Ward Beecher's Speaking Art.* New York, Fleming H. Revell Co., 1937.
19. Robert T. Oliver. "Behind the Word: Studies in the Political and Social Views of the Slave-Struggle Orators." *Quarterly Journal of Speech,* 22:413-429 (October, 1936); 23:409-426 (October, 1937); 23:13-32 (February, 1937). (Appraisals of Calhoun, Clay, and Webster.)
20. William F. Mitchell. *English Pulpit Oratory from Andrewes to Tillotson.* London, Society for the Promotion of Christian Knowledge, 1932.
21. Sir Edward Boyle. *Biographical Essays, 1790-1890.* London, Oxford University Press, 1936. pp. 74-99. ("The Oratory of Victor Hugo.")
22. Wilbur E. Gilman. *Milton's Rhetoric: Studies in His Defense of Liberty. University of Missouri Studies,* 14:5-173 (July 1, 1939). pp. 9-44. ("Areopagitica.")
23. John P. Hoshor. "Lectures on Rhetoric and Public Speaking, by Chauncey Allen Goodrich." *Speech Monographs,* 14:1-37 (1947).
24. Warren Guthrie. "The Development of Rhetorical Theory in America." *Speech Monographs,* 13:14-22 (1946).

25. ———. "The Development of Rhetorical Theory in America, 1635-1850." *Speech Monographs,* 14:38-54 (1947).
26. Dorothy I. Anderson. "Edward T. Channing's Definition of Rhetoric." *Speech Monographs,* 14:81-92 (1947).
27. William A. Behl. "Theodore Roosevelt's Principles of Invention." *Speech Monographs,* 14:93-110 (1947).
28. Martin Maloney. "The Forensic Speaking of Clarence Darrow." *Speech Monographs,* 14:111-126 (1947).
29. Carroll C. Arnold. "Invention in the Parliamentary Speaking of Benjamin Disraeli, 1842-1852." *Speech Monographs,* 14:66-80 (1947).

EXERCISES

1. Prepare a research paper on "Chauncey Goodrich as a Critic of the Oratory of Richard B. Sheridan" (or of "Thomas Erskine").

2. Prepare a paper on one of the following: (1) Albert J. Beveridge as a critic of Lincoln; (2) Claude M. Fuess as a critic of Webster; or (3) V. L. Parrington as a critic of speakers.

3. Analyze the procedures for the criticism of oral discourse suggested by S. I. Hayakawa in his *Language in Action* (New York, Harcourt, Brace and Co., 1939).

4. Prepare a paper on the criticism of collegiate debate in the United States.

5. Analyze the influence of John Dewey on the speech philosophy of teachers of public speaking.

6. Prepare a critique of an article in a recent number of the *Quarterly Journal of Speech* dealing with the criticism of a speaker or of the theory of public speaking.

7. Compare and contrast the critical method of Cicero with that of Goodrich; of Jebb; of Brigance (in his study of Jeremiah S. Black in the *History and Criticism of American Public Address,* I, 459-482).

8. Comment on this remark by William Barron (*Lectures on Belles Lettres and Logic,* I, 452) : "The best unpremeditated spoken language would make an indifferent figure when subjected to the eye of a nice reader."

9. Appraise the critical method employed by G. H. Francis in his essays on "Mr. Bright," "Lord Palmerston," and "Mr. Roebuck" (*Orators of the Age.* New York, Harper & Bros., 1847).

10. Prepare a comparative analysis of two contemporary speakers. Does the method of comparison and contrast enable you to delineate the speakers' characteristics more sharply than would be possible in an individual appraisal? Specify.

11. Compare and contrast the following appraisals of Jonathan Edwards: (1) in Charles Angoff's *Literary History of the American People* (Knopf, 1931), I, 289-310; in (2) *History and Criticism of*

American Public Address (McGraw-Hill Book Co., 1943), I, 213-235; and in (3) V. L. Parrington's *Main Currents in American Thought* (Harcourt, Brace, 1927), I, 148-163.

12. Read the introduction to A. Craig Baird's *Representative American Speeches: 1944-1945* (New York, H. W. Wilson Co., 1945), pp. 9-17. Then examine the introductory statements to several of the speeches printed in the volume.

CHAPTER 8

READINGS

1. A. Craig Baird. "A Selected Bibliography of American Oratory." *Quarterly Journal of Speech Education,* 12:352-356 (November, 1926).
2. ———. "Opportunities for Research in State and Sectional Public Speaking." *Quarterly Journal of Speech,* 29:304-308 (October, 1943).
3. A. M. Drummond. "Graduate Work in Public Speaking." *Quarterly Journal of Speech Education,* 9:136-147 (April, 1923).
4. "Some Subjects for Graduate Study." *Quarterly Journal of Speech Education,* 9:147-153 (April, 1923).
5. Hoyt H. Hudson. "The Field of Rhetoric." *Quarterly Journal of Speech Education,* 9:167-180 (April, 1923).
6. Dallas C. Dickey. "What Directions Should Future Research in American Public Address Take?" *Quarterly Journal of Speech,* 29:300-304 (October, 1943).
7. Bower Aly. "The History of American Public Address as a Research Field." *Quarterly Journal of Speech,* 29:308-314 (October, 1943).
8. "The Historical Backgrounds of American Public Address." In *History and Criticism of American Public Address,* W. Norwood Brigance, ed. New York, McGraw-Hill Book Co., Inc., 1943. ("The Colonial Period" by George V. Bohman, pp. 3-54: "The Early National Period" by Bower Aly and Grafton P. Tanquary, pp. 55-110; "The Later National Period" by Kenneth G. Hance, Homer O. Hendrickson, and Edwin W. Schoenberger, pp. 111-152; "Women's Introduction to the American Platform" by Doris G. Yoakam, pp. 153-192; "The Teaching of Rhetoric in the United States during the Classical Period of Education" by Ota Thomas, pp. 193-210.)
9. Dorothy B. Porter. "Early American Negro Writings: A Bibliographical Study." *Papers of the Bibliographical Society of America,* 31:192-268 (Third Quarter, 1945). (Observe how prominently oratory and sermonizing figure in the study. Further research on the nature of the speechmaking in early Negro expression should be rewarding.)
10. Nora E. Cordingley. "Extreme Rarities in the Published Works of Theodore Roosevelt." *Papers of the Bibliographical Society of America,* 39:20-50 (First Quarter, 1945). (The paper suggests opportunities for research in the bibliographic phases of rhetorical criticism.)
11. Carter Good, A. S. Barr, and Douglas E. Scates. *The Methodology of Educational Research.* New York, D. Appleton-Century Co., Inc., 1935. pp. 648-678.
12. Franklin H. Knower. "Graduate Theses—An Index of Graduate Work in the Field of Speech." *Speech Monographs,* 1935 to date. (Excellent source

from which to get an over-all view of the research undertaken in the larger graduate departments of Speech.)

13. Lester Thonssen, Elizabeth Fatherson, and Dorothea Thonssen. *Bibliography of Speech Education*. New York, H. W. Wilson Co., 1939.

EXERCISES

1. What are some of the problems of equipping an investigator for adequacy in the "philosophical determination of the role of speechcraft in a well-organized society"?

2. Analyze in some detail the subtopics to be treated in the investigation of one of the following constituents of the speaking situation: (1) the speaker's theory of discourse; (2) factors accounting for the skill of the speaker; (3) nature of the audience; (4) the deliberative type of speaking, and (5) the speaker's ideas.

3. Outline the chief topics treated in one of the studies of public speakers in the *History and Criticism of American Public Address*. We suggest one of the following studies for examination: Dayton McKean's "Woodrow Wilson," Herold T. Ross' "Albert J. Beveridge," Wilbur S. Howell and Hoyt H. Hudson's "Daniel Webster," W. Norwood Brigance's "Jeremiah S. Black," or Louis Mallory's "Patrick Henry." Comment on the critical approach of the author, the nature and extent of the rhetorical topics covered in the study, and the adequacy with which these topics are treated. (Keep in mind that each of these contributions was limited to about nine thousand words.)

4. Compare and contrast the types of critical materials and rhetorical topics covered in two studies of individual speakers listed in Exercise 3.

5. Prepare a list of bibliographical items on a representative living speaker whom you propose to investigate.

6. Draft a list of rhetorical studies, completed since 1920, on Daniel Webster, or on Edmund Burke. Classify your bibliographical items according to the apparent areas of rhetorical inquiry covered by the studies; suggest further fields of investigation of either of these speakers.

CHAPTER 9

READINGS

1. Robert D. King. "Franklin D. Roosevelt's Second Inaugural Address: A Study in Text Authenticity." *Quarterly Journal of Speech*, 23:439-444 (October, 1937).

2. John W. Black. "Webster's Peroration in the Dartmouth College Case." *Quarterly Journal of Speech*, 23:636-642 (December, 1937).

3. Zon Robinson. "Are Speeches in Congress Accurately Reported?" *Quarterly Journal of Speech,* 28:8-12 (February, 1942).

4. Elizabeth Gregory McPherson. "Reporting the Debates of Congress." *Quarterly Journal of Speech,* 28:141-148 (April, 1942).

5. ———. "Reports of the Debates of the House of Representatives during the First Congress, 1789-1791." *Quarterly Journal of Speech,* 30:64-71 (February, 1944).

6. *History and Criticism of American Public Address.* W. Norwood Brigance, ed., New York, McGraw-Hill Book Co., Inc., 1943. (The following sections deal with studies of text authenticity. Examine for suggestive leads: II, 721-726; I, 353-356; II, 593-594.)

7. Loren D. Reid. "Factors Contributing to Inaccuracy in the Texts of Speeches." In *Papers in Rhetoric,* Donald C. Bryant, ed., St. Louis, privately printed, 1940. pp. 39-45.

8. ———. "The Perils of Rhetorical Criticism." *Quarterly Journal of Speech,* 30:416-422 (December, 1944).

9. Glen E. Mills. "How Webster Revised the 'Reply to Hayne.' " *The Speaker,* 26:4+ (November, 1941).

10. Josef Israels II. "The Saga of Sammy the Rose." *Saturday Evening Post,* 215, No. 23:18+ (December 5, 1942). (An account of Roosevelt's association with Samuel I. Rosenman. Contains some notes on Roosevelt's methods of speech preparation.)

11. Ernest J. Wessen. "Debates of Lincoln and Douglas." *Papers of the Bibliographical Society of America,* 40:91-106 (Second Quarter, 1946). (A bibliographical study. Contains an annotated list of variant editions of the debates.)

12. William E. Barton. *The Life of Abraham Lincoln.* Indianapolis, Bobbs-Merrill Co., 1925. II, 185-226. ("Gettysburg: What He Said There.")

13. Thomas L. Stokes. "Who Writes President's [Roosevelt's] Speeches?" *New York World-Telegram,* March 2, 1944.

14. Robert T. Oliver. *The Psychology of Persuasive Speech.* New York, Longmans, Green & Co., 1942. (Examine the photostatic copies of some revisions of Roosevelt's Victory Dinner speech, March 4, 1937, facing p. 320.)

15. Albert Britt. *Great Indian Chiefs.* New York, Whittlesey House, 1938. pp. 106-110. (Notes on and partial reconstruction of Pontiac's speech at the Council on the Ecorces.)

16. William E. Hall. "How to Report Speeches." In his *Reporting News.* Boston, D. C. Heath & Co., 1936. pp. 328-334.

17. Raymond Moley. *After Seven Years.* New York, Harper & Bros., 1939. (Contains scattered notes on Roosevelt's methods of speech preparation.)

18. Julian Boyd. *The Declaration of Independence.* Princeton, Princeton University Press, 1945. (Assembles reproductions of the known drafts and copies of the Declaration.)

19. Paul M. Angle. "Four Lincoln Firsts." *Papers of the Bibliographical Society of America,* 36:1-17 (First Quarter, 1942). (A careful study dealing with textual accuracy.)

20. R. W. Postgate. *Dear Robert Emmet.* New York, Vanguard Press, Inc., 1932. pp. 224-241. (On his last speech.)

21. Henry L. Dawes. "Has Oratory Declined?" *Forum,* 18:146-160 (October, 1894). (Notes on Seaton's reporting of Webster's "Reply to Hayne.")

22. Alfred Kinnear. "Parliamentary Reporting." *Contemporary Review,* 87:369-375 (April, 1905).

23. Lucy M. Salmon. *The Newspaper and the Historian.* New York, Oxford University Press, 1923. pp. 158-179.

24. Michael Macdonagh. *The Reporters' Gallery.* London, Hodder and Stoughton, 1913.

EXERCISES

1. Make or secure an electrical recording of a speech delivered over the radio by the President of the United States or some other prominent national leader. Secure also an official version of the speech as released by the White House or other authoritative sources. Check the official version with the recording and note the differences.

2. Examine the text of Webster's argument in the Dartmouth College case (*World's Best Orations,* D. J. Brewer, ed., Chicago, F. P. Kaiser Co., 1923. X, 198-203). Read John W. Black's "Webster's Peroration in the Dartmouth College Case" (*Quarterly Journal of Speech,* 23:636-642, December, 1937). What is your conclusion concerning the authenticity of this peroration?

3. Examine the text of Charles Sumner's address on "The True Grandeur of Nations," July 4, 1845, as printed in (a) Charles Sumner, *The True Grandeur of Nations.* Boston, J. H. Eastburn, 1845; (b) Charles Sumner, *Orations and Speeches.* Boston, Ticknor, 1850. I, 1-130; (c) Charles Sumner, *Works.* Boston, Lee, 1870-1883. I, 1-132; (d) Charles Sumner, *Addresses on War.* Boston, Ginn and Co., 1902. pp. 1-132. Then study the conclusions of Carl Dallinger and Elaine Pagel concerning the extensive inconsistencies in the various texts (*History and Criticism of American Public Address,* II, 751-776).

4. Compare and contrast the various versions of Franklin D. Roosevelt's "Yalta Conference Address," March 1, 1945, as given in (a) A. Craig Baird's *Representative American Speeches: 1944-1945* (New York, H. W. Wilson Co., 1945, pp. 40-52); (b) *The New York Times* (March 2, 1945); (c) *The Congressional Record* (March 1, 1945).

5. Report on the problem of establishing authentic texts of an oration by Demosthenes or Cicero.

6. Select a speech or group of speeches of a contemporary orator. As one of the preliminary steps to the full study, secure as accurate texts as possible. Explain the procedure in establishing the authenticity of these texts.

7. Investigate one of the following problems: (a) textual authenticity of the addresses of William Cullen Bryant; (b) the textual accuracy of the occasional speeches of Mark Twain; (c) the textual authenticity of representative speeches of James A. Bryce, delivered in the United States.

CHAPTER 10

READINGS

1. Forest L. Whan. "Stephen A. Douglas." In *History and Criticism of American Public Address,* W. Norwood Brigance, ed. New York, McGraw-Hill Book Co., Inc., 1943. II, 777-824.
2. Chauncey A. Goodrich. "Edmund Burke." In *Select British Eloquence.* New York, Harper & Bros., 1852. pp. 206-240; 265-291.
3. Torsten Petersson. *Cicero: A Biography.* Berkeley, University of California Publications, 1919. pp. 123-170. ("The Prosecution of Verres." A critical estimate of oratory; throws light upon the social milieu in which oratory functioned.)
4. Robert T. Oliver. "A Rhetorician's Criticism of Historiography." In *Eastern Public Speaking Conference: 1940,* Harold F. Harding, ed., New York, The H. W. Wilson Co., 1940. pp. 161-172.
5. Robert P. Tristram Coffin. "Can a Poem Be Explained?" In *The Substance That Is Poetry.* New York, The Macmillan Co., 1942. pp. 79-104.
6. Barbara Deming. "The Library of Congress Film Project: Exposition of a Method." The Library of Congress *Quarterly Journal of Current Acquisitions,* 2:3-36 (July-August-September, 1944). (Offers suggestive hints on selection of the events and facts necessary for subsequent study of historical happenings.)
7. J. B. Black. *The Art of History.* London, Methuen and Co., 1926.
8. C. G. Crump. *History and Historical Research.* London, George Routledge and Sons, 1928.
9. F. H. Giddings. *The Scientific Study of Human Society.* Chapel Hill, University of North Carolina Press, 1924.
10. A. Johnson. *The Historian and Historical Evidence.* New York, Chas. Scribner's Sons, 1926.
11. Vernon Parrington. *Main Currents in American Thought.* New York, Harcourt, Brace and Co., Inc., 1927-1930. I, 292-356.
12. J. T. Shotwell. *Introduction to the Study of History.* New York, Columbia University Press, 1922.

EXERCISES

1. Criticize the ideas, audience appeals, structure, language, and other rhetorical elements of Franklin D. Roosevelt's address "This Nation Will Remain Neutral," delivered September 3, 1939. (For copy, see A. Craig Baird's *Representative American Speeches: 1939-1940.* New York, H. W. Wilson Co., 1940, pp. 21-25). Supply the necessary historical materials to give validity to your criticism.

2. Select an important political speech of the day. Secure abundant historical data and such other economic, political, religious, and social details as may be relevant to the address. Write an appraisal of the address in the light of this historical background. Supply footnotes that conform to the acceptable methods of citation.

3. Carry out a similar project for a great sermon or for a courtroom argument.

4. Study the historical methods and techniques used by the critics of certain orators in American history. Examine especially a few of the studies in the *History and Criticism of American Public Address*.

CHAPTER 11

READINGS

1. Gladys Murphy Graham. "Analogy—A Study in Proof." *Quarterly Journal of Speech*, 14:534-542 (November, 1928).
2. W. Norwood Brigance. "A Genetic Approach to Persuasion." *Quarterly Journal of Speech*, 17:329-339 (June, 1931).
3. ———. "Can We Re-Define the James-Winans Theory of Persuasion?" *Quarterly Journal of Speech*, 21:19-26 (February, 1935).
4. Edward Z. Rowell. "Prolegomena to Argumentation." *Quarterly Journal of Speech*, 18:1-13 (February, 1932); 18:224-248 (April, 1932); 18:381-405 (June, 1932); 18:585-606 (November, 1932).
5. ———. "The Conviction-Persuasion Duality." *Quarterly Journal of Speech*, 20:469-482 (November, 1934).
6. H. B. Gislason. "An Approach to Persuasion." *Quarterly Journal of Speech*, 19:175-186 (April, 1933).
7. Wilbur E. Gilman. "Logic and Public Speaking." *Quarterly Journal of Speech*, 26:667-672 (December, 1940).
8. Wilbur S. Howell. "The Positions of Argument: An Historical Examination." In *Papers in Rhetoric*, Donald C. Bryant, ed., St. Louis, privately printed, 1940. pp. 8-17.
9. ——— and Hoyt H. Hudson. "Daniel Webster." In *The History and Criticism of American Public Address*, Brigance, ed., New York, McGraw-Hill Book Co., Inc., 1943. II, 692-711. (An analysis of the argument in the Webster-Hayne debate.)
10. John W. Black. "Rufus Choate." In *The History and Criticism of American Public Address*. I, 410-453. (Deals with invention in Choate's oratory.)
11. Orville A. Hitchcock. "Jonathan Edwards." In *The History and Criticism of American Public Address*. I, 213-235.
12. Roy C. McCall. "Theodore Parker." In *The History and Criticism of American Public Address*. I, 238-263.
13. Chauncey A. Goodrich. *Select British Eloquence*. New York, Harper & Bros., 1852. pp. 629-655. (Memoir of Lord Erskine, historical introduction to and text of the speech in behalf of Lord George Gordon.)
14. Brand Blanshard. "The Nature of Invention." In *The Nature of Thought*. New York, The Macmillan Co., 1940. II, 130-165.
15. John Dewey. "The Analysis of a Complete Act of Thought." In *How We Think*. Boston, D. C. Heath & Co., 1910. pp. 68-78.
16. ———. *Logic: The Theory of Inquiry*. New York, Henry Holt & Co., Inc., 1938. pp. 419-441.
17. Walter Blair. "Analyzing Lines of Reasoning." In *Manual of Reading*. Chicago, Scott, Foresman & Co., 1943. pp. 99-123.
18. Karl R. Wallace. "On Analogy: Re-definition and Some Implications." In *Studies in Speech and Drama* in Honor of Alexander M. Drummond. Ithaca, Cornell University Press, 1944. pp. 412-426.
19. James Gordon Emerson. "The Case Method in Argumentation." *Quarterly Journal of Speech*, 31:8-15 (February, 1945); 31:282-291 (October, 1945); 32:1-12 (February, 1946).

20. George P. Rice, Jr. "The 'Special Topic,' $EI\Delta H$, in late Tudor and Early Stuart Public Discussion." *Quarterly Journal of Speech,* 32:21-25 (February, 1946).
21. A. Craig Baird. *Discussion: Principles and Types.* New York, McGraw-Hill Book Co., Inc., 1943. pp. 130-182.
22. Edwin A. Burtt. *Right Thinking,* 3rd ed. New York, Harper & Bros., 1946.
23. Graham Wallas. *The Art of Thought.* New York, Harcourt, Brace & Co., Inc., 1926. pp. 108-132; 173-203.
24. Charles H. Woolbert. "The Place of Logic in a System of Persuasion." *Quarterly Journal of Speech Education,* 4:19-39 (January, 1918).
25. Mary Yost. "Argument from the Point of View of Sociology." *Quarterly Journal of Public Speaking,* 3:109-124 (April, 1917).
26. Kenneth Burke. *A Grammar of Motives.* New York, Prentice-Hall, Inc., 1945.

EXERCISES

1. Point out the relative prominence of logical and pathetic proof in a representative (a) debate speech, (b) panel discussion, (c) college oration, (d) classroom lecture, (e) eulogy.

2. Make a careful study of Webster's speech on the White murder case. Appraise the method of using evidence and of framing arguments.

3. Summarize the political and other premises that dominated the thinking of Albert J. Beveridge, of Henry Clay, of Daniel Webster, or of Stephen A. Douglas.

4. Reduce to a brief the argument as presented in a recent debate in the United States Senate. Comment on the methods of logical development.

5. Present a critical appraisal of the logical proof in Quentin Reynolds' "Address to the Democratic National Convention," July 20, 1944. (For a copy of this address, see A. Craig Baird's *Representative American Speeches: 1944-1945.* New York, The H. W. Wilson Co., 1945. pp. 200-213.)

CHAPTER 12

READINGS

1. Norman Mattis. "Robert South." *Quarterly Journal of Speech,* 15:537-560 (November, 1929).
2. Robert T. Oliver. "Human Motivation: Intellectuality, Emotionality, and Rationalization." *Quarterly Journal of Speech,* 22:67-77 (February, 1936).
3. ———. *The Psychology of Persuasive Speech.* New York, Longmans, Green & Co., 1942. ("Basic Factors in Persuasion," "The Avenues of Persuasion," and "Techniques of Persuasion," pp. 33-281.)
4. *History and Criticism of American Public Address.* W. Norwood Brigance, ed., New York, McGraw-Hill Book Co., Inc., 1943. (Examine the following appraisals of emotional proof in public speeches: I, 227-229; II, 676-692; II, 813-818.)

5. Herold T. Ross. "Albert J. Beveridge." In *History and Criticism of American Public Address.* II, 919-941.
6. H. L. Hollingworth. *The Psychology of the Audience.* New York, American Book Co., 1935. ("Types of Audience," pp. 19-32; "Impressing the Audience," pp. 63-108; "The Psychology of Persuasion," pp. 109-139; "Directing Action," pp. 141-159; "Experimental Studies of Audience Effects," pp. 185-203.)
7. Charles Bird. *Social Psychology.* New York, D. Appleton-Century Co., Inc., 1940. ("Motivation," pp. 29-58; "Propaganda," pp. 305-341; "The Behavior of Crowds," pp. 345-368; "Suggestion, Suggestibility, and Stereotypes," pp. 258-300.)
8. Graham Wallas. "Thought and Emotion." In *The Art of Thought.* New York, Harcourt, Brace & Co., Inc., 1926. pp. 108-132.
9. ———. "Non-Rational Inference in Politics." In his *Human Nature in Politics.* Boston, Houghton Mifflin Co., 1919. pp. 98-113.
10. James R. Mock and Cedric Larson. *Words That Won the War.* Princeton, Princeton University Press, 1939.
11. John Dewey. "Affective Thought." In his *Philosophy and Civilization.* New York, Minton, Balch & Co., 1931. pp. 117-125.
12. Peter H. Odegard. "From Conviction to Persuasion." In *Pressure Politics.* New York, Columbia University Press, 1928. pp. 36-77. (An analysis of the persuasive instruments used by American temperance leaders.)
13. Edrita Fried. "Techniques of Persuasion." In *Propaganda by Short Wave,* Harwood L. Childs and John B. Whitton, eds., Princeton, Princeton University Press, 1942. pp. 263-301.
14. Ross Stagner. "How Is Psychology Used in Influencing Other People?" In *Psychology in Use,* by J. Stanley Gray and others. New York, American Book Co., 1941. pp. 547-591.
15. L. L. Bernard. *Social Control.* New York, The Macmillan Co., 1939. pp. 3-50.
16. William Norwood Brigance. *Speech Composition.* New York, F. S. Crofts & Co., 1937. pp. 120-196.
17. Charles H. Woolbert. "A Behavioristic Account of Intellect and Emotions." *Psychological Review,* 31:265-272 (July, 1924).
18. ———. "Persuasion: Principles and Method." *Quarterly Journal of Speech Education,* 5:12-25 (January, 1919); 5:110-119 (March, 1919); 5:211-238 (May, 1919).
19. Richard Whately. *The Elements of Rhetoric.* new ed. rev. New York, Sheldon & Co., 1871. pp. 209-298.
20. Jon Eisenson, Sylvia G. Souther, and Jerome Fisher. "The Affective Value of English Speech Sounds." *Quarterly Journal of Speech,* 26:589-594 (December, 1940).

EXERCISES

1. Analyze a specific audience of the present day to show how a representative speaker on a given occasion adapted himself to his listeners with respect to (a) ideas, (b) forms of proof, and (c) language.

2. Evaluate the emotional proof in one of the following:

    (a) Albert J. Beveridge, "The Republic That Never Retreats,"

    (b) William J. Bryan, "America's Mission,"

    (c) Wendell Phillips, "The Murder of Lovejoy,"

    (d) Henry W. Grady, "The Race Problem in the South."

3. Compare and contrast the emotional appeals made by Franklin D. Roosevelt in his campaign address before the International Teamsters' Union, September 23, 1944, with those made by Thomas E. Dewey in his speech of reply at Oklahoma City, Oklahoma, September 25, 1944. (For copies of these addresses, see A. Craig Baird's *Representative American Speeches: 1944-1945.* New York, The H. W. Wilson Co., 1945. pp. 134-151.)

4. Present examples from recent speechmaking of thoughts that are obviously colored, and perhaps weakened, by an excess of emotional accompaniment.

5. Appraise the critical estimates of a recent speech as reported editorially in newspapers of varying political attachment. To what extent do editorial writers and columnists employ the critical standards discussed in this volume?

6. Study Herbert A. Wichelns' "Ralph Waldo Emerson" (in *History and Criticism of American Public Address.* Ed. by William Norwood Brigance. New York, McGraw-Hill Book Co., Inc., 1943. II, 501-524). Comment on Emerson's apparent desire to achieve independence from his audiences.

7. Evaluate the critical method in V. L. Parrington's study of George William Curtis (*Main Currents in American Thought,* New York, Harcourt, Brace and Co., Inc., 1930. III, 147-154).

CHAPTER 13

READINGS

1. Loren D. Reid. "'Private John' Allen: A Humorist in Politics." *Quarterly Journal of Speech,* 28:414-421 (December, 1942).
2. *History and Criticism of American Public Address.* W. Norwood Brigance, ed., New York, McGraw-Hill Book Co., Inc., 1943. (Examine representative appraisals of ethical proof. See I, 419-423; II, 609-614; II, 813-818.)
3. W. Hayes Yeager. "Wendell Phillips." In *History and Criticism of American Public Address.* I, 329-360.
4. Chauncey A. Goodrich. "Charles James Fox." In *Select British Eloquence.* New York, Harper & Bros., 1852. pp. 437-474.
5. Torsten Petersson. *Cicero: A Biography.* Berkeley, University of California Publications, 1919. pp. 68-122. (Interesting study of beginnings of orator's training and place of oratory in education and public life.)
6. John Stuart Mill. *Autobiography.* New York, Henry Holt & Co., Inc., 1874. (The first three chapters reveal the extent of his reading, parental influence, etc. Helpful to those who propose to trace the early training of orators.)
7. Irving J. Lee. "Some Conceptions of Emotional Appeal in Rhetorical Theory." *Speech Monographs.* 6:66-86 (1939).
8. Robert T. Oliver. "The Speaker and the Occasion." In *Psychology of Persuasive Speech.* New York, Longmans, Green & Co., 1942. pp. 90-105.

9. Norman W. Mattis. "Phillips Brooks and the Problem of Personality in Rhetorical Criticism." In *Eastern Public Speaking Conference: 1940,* Harold F. Harding, ed., New York, The H. W. Wilson Co., 1940. pp. 301-305.
10. William M. Sattler. "Conceptions of *Ethos* in Ancient Rhetoric." *Speech Monographs,* 14:55-65 (1947).

EXERCISES

1. Evaluate the ethical proof in one of the following addresses:
   (a) Henry Ward Beecher's "Address at Liverpool" (S. B. Harding, *Select Orations Illustrating American Political History,* New York, The Macmillan Co., 1924. pp. 392-413),
   (b) The Lincoln-Douglas debate at Ottawa, Illinois (*ibid.,* pp. 309-341),
   (c) The Herbert Hoover-Alfred E. Smith debate on "Government Ownership" (J. M. O'Neill and Floyd K. Riley, *Contemporary Speeches.* New York, Century Co., 1930. pp. 521-555).

2. Evaluate the ethical proof in a representative debate of a recent session of Congress.

3. Evaluate the ethical proof in a typical courtroom plea in a criminal trial. (Suggested sources: J. M. O'Neill, *Classified Models of Speech Composition.* New York, Century Co., 1922; Frederick C. Hicks, *Famous American Jury Speeches.* St. Paul, West Publishing Co., 1925.)

4. What differentia would you establish between ethical and emotional proof?

CHAPTER 14

READINGS

1. Gilbert S. MacVaugh. "Structural Analysis of the Sermons of Dr. Harry Emerson Fosdick." *Quarterly Journal of Speech,* 18:531-546 (November, 1932).
2. Samuel A. Yoder. "*Dispositio in Richard Hooker's* 'Laws of Ecclesiastical Polity.'" *Quarterly Journal of Speech,* 27:90-97 (February, 1941).
3. *History and Criticism of American Public Address.* W. Norwood Brigance, ed. New York, McGraw-Hill Book Co., Inc., 1943.   I, 251-255; I, 315-318; I, 425-428; II, 545-548.
4. Francis P. Donnelly. "A Function of the Classical Exordium." In *Literature: The Leading Educator.* New York, Longmans, Green & Co., 1938. pp. 104-116.
5. Louis A. Mallory. "Patrick Henry." In *History and Criticism of American Public Address.* II, 580-600.
6. John F. Genung. "General Processes in the Ordering of Material." In *Practical Elements of Rhetoric.* Boston, Ginn & Co., 1886. pp. 245-285.
7. Edd Miller. "Speech Introductions and Conclusions." *Quarterly Journal of Speech,* 32:181-183 (April, 1946).

8. Russell H. Wagner. "The Meaning of *Dispositio.*" In *Studies in Speech and Drama* in Honor of Alexander M. Drummond, Ithaca, Cornell University Press, 1944. pp. 285-294.

EXERCISES

1. Compare and contrast the treatment accorded to speech structure by Aristotle, Cicero, and Quintilian.

2. Analyze the method and indicate the relative effectiveness of the organization in one of Douglas' speeches in the Lincoln-Douglas debates.

3. Compare the treatment of arrangement in a contemporary text-book on public speaking with that of Aristotle, Cicero, or Quintilian.

4. Prepare a paper on the "Form vs. Content" problem so frequently mentioned in the literature of the subject.

5. Outline in detail a recent speech published in *Vital Speeches,* or in a daily newspaper. To what extent does the outline conform to the principles and methods of structural planning discussed by the rhetoricians?

6. Make a careful analysis and critical appraisal of a speech from literature (*e.g.,* Othello's speech of defense before the dukes and senators). To what extent can the critic of contemporary speechmaking profit from an examination of orations in literature?

7. Examine and appraise John Quincy Adams' analysis of oratorical disposition: exordium, narration, proposition and partition, confirmation, confutation, digression and transition, and conclusion. (*Lectures,* I, 391-431; II, 3-138.)

CHAPTER 15

READINGS

1. Lionel Crocker. "The Refrain in Oratorical Prose." *Quarterly Journal of Speech,* 15:24-29 (February, 1929).
2. Henry Lee Ewbank. "Four Approaches to the Problem of Speech Style." *Quarterly Journal of Speech,* 17:458-465 (November, 1931).
3. Raymond H. Barnard. "An Objective Study of the Speeches of Wendell Phillips." *Quarterly Journal of Speech,* 18:571-584 (November, 1932).
4. Bromley Smith. "Some Rhetorical Figures." *Quarterly Journal of Speech,* 20:16-29 (February, 1934).
5. Elaine Pagel. "Concepts of Perspicuity as a Factor in Public Speaking." *Quarterly Journal of Speech,* 26:38-44 (February, 1940).
6. Dayton D. McKean. "Woodrow Wilson." In the *History and Criticism of American Public Address,* W. Norwood Brigance, ed., New York, McGraw-Hill Book Co., 1943. II, 968-990.
7. Raymond F. Howes. "The Talked and the Written." *Quarterly Journal of Speech,* 26:229-235 (April, 1940).
8. Henry Alonzo Myers. "The Usefulness of Figurative Language." *Quarterly Journal of Speech,* 26:236-243 (April, 1940).
9. *History and Criticism of American Public Address.* I, 474-480; II, 533-535; II, 848-851; II, 983-985.

10. Arthur Jersild. "Modes of Emphasis in Public Speaking." *Journal of Applied Psychology,* 12:611-620 (December, 1928).
11. Albert R. Chandler. *Elements of Psychological Aesthetics.* New York, D. Appleton-Century Co., Inc., 1934. ("Rhythms of Speech," pp. 238-276; "Language and Literature," pp. 277-300.)
12. Rudolf Flesch. *The Art of Plain Talk.* New York, Harper & Bros., 1946.
13. Francis P. Donnelly. "Allotment of Humor to Oratory." In *Literature: The Leading Educator.* New York, Longmans, Green & Co., 1938, pp. 1-13.
14. Warren Taylor. *Tudor Figures of Rhetoric.* Chicago, University of Chicago Libraries, 1937.
15. Wayland M. Parrish. "The Rhythm of Oratorical Prose." In *Studies in Rhetoric and Public Speaking* in Honor of James A. Winans. New York, Century Co., 1925. pp. 217-231.
16. ———. "The Style of Robert G. Ingersoll." In *Studies in Speech and Drama* in Honor of Alexander M. Drummond. Ithaca, Cornell University Press, 1944. pp. 393-411.
17. William Empson. *Seven Types of Ambiguity.* New York, Harcourt, Brace and Co., Inc., 1931.
18. H. F. Harrington and T. T. Frankenberg. "The Writer and His Readers." In *Essentials in Journalism.* Rev. ed. Boston, Ginn & Co., 1924. Ch. 3.
19. Marjorie Nicholson. "What's Wrong with Scholars?" *The Saturday Review of Literature,* April 15, 1944. p. 18+.
20. Dallas C. Dickey. "Were They Ephemeral and Florid?" *Quarterly Journal of Speech,* 32:16-20 (February, 1946).
21. Ray Ehrensberger. "An Experimental Study of the Relative Effectiveness of Certain Forms of Emphasis in Public Speaking." *Speech Monographs,* 12:94-111 (1945).
22. Gladys Borchers. "An Approach to the Problem of Oral Style." *Quarterly Journal of Speech,* 22:114-117 (February, 1936).
23. Paul P. Bushnell. *An Analytical Contrast of Oral with Written English.* New York, Bureau of Publications, Teachers College, Columbia University, 1930.
24. Lane Cooper, ed. *Theories of Style.* New York, The Macmillan Co., 1907.
25. Howard Runion. "An Objective Study of the Speech Style of Woodrow Wilson." *Speech Monographs,* 3:75-94 (1936).
26. Robert Graves and Alan Hodge. *The Reader Over Your Shoulder.* New York, The Macmillan Co., 1943.

EXERCISES

1. Summarize and comment on Georges-Louis LeClerc de Buffon's "Discourse on Style" (In Rollo W. Brown, *The Writer's Art.* Cambridge, Harvard University Press, 1921. pp. 277-288).

2. Study Thomas De Quincey's "Style as Organic and Mechanic," from his *Essay on Style* (Cf. Brown, pp. 295-301).

3. Evaluate the style in one of the following:
   (a) Charles James Fox's "East India Bill" speech,
   (b) Richard B. Sheridan's "Against Warren Hastings,"
   (c) Abraham Lincoln's "Cooper Union Address,"
   (d) Franklin D. Roosevelt's "Fourth Inaugural."

4. Compare and contrast one of Woodrow Wilson's essays with one of his representative speeches on a similar theme with respect to qualities of style. Suggested examples: Woodrow Wilson's "First Inaugural Ad-

dress," March 5, 1913 (in James M. O'Neill, *Models of Speech Composition,* New York, Century Co., 1922. pp. 488-491) ; and Woodrow Wilson's "The New Freedom," (in Willard Thorp, Merle Curti, and Harold Baker, *American Issues,* Vol. I, *The Social Record.* Chicago, J. B. Lippincott Co., 1941. pp. 873-878).

5. Study and evaluate the figures and tropes in a representative address by Robert G. Ingersoll ("Eulogy at His Brother's Grave," in W. Norwood Brigance's *Classified Speech Models.* New York, F. S. Crofts & Co., 1928. pp. 400-402; or Wendell Phillips' "Eulogy on Daniel O'Connell," in *ibid.,* pp. 373-400).

6. Compare a speech from the Bible with a contemporary orator's address on a similar theme (*e.g.,* a dedicatory speech of today with Solomon's consecration of the temple, *Chronicles* II, 6).

7. Compare and contrast the technique of the dramatic critic with that of the rhetorical critic.

CHAPTER 16

READINGS

1. Floyd K. Riley. "The Conversational Basis of Public Address." *Quarterly Journal of Speech,* 14:233-242 (April, 1928).
2. Fred J. Barton. "The Signification of 'Extempore Speech' in English and American Rhetorics." *Quarterly Journal of Speech,* 27:237-251 (April, 1941).
3. *History and Criticism of American Public Address.* W. Norwood Brigance, ed. New York, McGraw-Hill Book Co., Inc., 1943. I, 279-280; I, 322-323; I, 358-360; I, 428-432; II, 517-518; II, 959-963.
4. William A. Behl. "Theodore Roosevelt's Principles of Speech Preparation and Delivery." *Speech Monographs,* 12:112-122 (1945).
5. Myron G. Phillips. "William Jennings Bryan." In the *History and Criticism of American Public Address.* II, 891-918.

EXERCISES

1. Compare the classical treatment of oratory with that of a present-day textbook on public speaking.

2. To what extent do experimental data on delivery assist the critic in evaluating modern oratory?

3. What tests must the critic apply to testimony concerning the delivery of an orator?

4. From the point of view of the critic, what is the relative importance of delivery in the final assessment of an oration's merit? How does it compare with the other parts of rhetoric, *i.e.,* invention, disposition, style, and memory?

5. Examine and discuss the notes used by Winston Churchill for his secret speech before the House of Commons on June 20, 1940. (See

Winston Churchill's Secret Session Speeches, comp. by Charles Eade. New York, Simon and Schuster, Inc., 1946. pp. 3-12.)

CHAPTER 17

READINGS

1. Newell L. Sims. "How Society Becomes Dynamic." In *The Problem of Social Change.* New York, Thomas Y. Crowell Co., 1939. pp. 241-278.
2. Chauncey A. Goodrich. "William Pitt." In *Select British Eloquence.* New York, Harper & Bros., 1852. pp. 551-578; 604-628.
3. William E. Utterback. "Contemporary Theories of Public Opinion." In *Studies in Speech and Drama* in Honor of Alexander M. Drummond. Ithaca, Cornell University Press, 1944. pp. 427-450.
4. John M. Vorys. "How a Member of Congress Measures the Response of His Constituents." *Quarterly Journal of Speech,* 32:170-172 (April, 1946).
5. A. I. Bryan and W. H. Wilke. "Audience Tendencies in Rating Public Speakers." *Journal of Applied Psychology,* 26:371-381 (June, 1942).
6. W. K. C. Chen. "The Influence of Oral Propaganda Material upon Students' Attitudes." *Archives of Psychology.* 23: No. 150 (1933).
7. L. A. Dexter. "An Attempt to Measure Change of Attitude as a Result of Hearing Speakers." *Sociometry,* 2:76-83 (1939).
8. Franklin H. Knower. "Experimental Studies in Change of Attitude: I. A Study of the Effect of Oral Argument on Changes of Attitude." *Journal of Social Psychology,* 6:315-347 (August, 1935).

EXERCISES

1. Evaluate the speaking effectiveness of a contemporary speaker. What criteria do you use in determining the measure of success?

2. Evaluate the effect of one of the following addresses:

  (a) William E. Borah's "Against the Repeal of the Embargo" (in A. Craig Baird's *Representative American Speeches: 1939-1940.* New York, The H. W. Wilson Co., 1940. pp. 38-52).

  (b) Franklin D. Roosevelt's "Message to Congress," September 21, 1939 (*ibid.,* pp. 26-37).

  (c) Arthur H. Vandenberg's "American Foreign Policy," January 10, 1945 (*ibid., 1944-1945,* pp. 43-55).

3. In what particulars does a successful novel or poem differ from a successful speech?

CHAPTER 18

READINGS

1. William Schrier. "The Ethics of Persuasion." *Quarterly Journal of Speech,* 16:476-486 (November, 1930).
2. Angelo M. Pellegrini. "Public Speaking and Social Obligations." *Quarterly Journal of Speech,* 20:345-351 (June, 1934).

3. Lionel Crocker. "Sinclair Lewis on Public Speaking." *Quarterly Journal of Speech,* 21:232-237 (April, 1935).
4. James H. McBurney. "Some Contributions of Classical Dialectic and Rhetoric to a Philosophy of Discussion." *Quarterly Journal of Speech,* 23:1-13 (February, 1937).
5. A. Craig Baird. "The Educational Philosophy of the Teacher of Speech." *Quarterly Journal of Speech,* 24:545-553 (December, 1938).
6. ———. "Speech and the Democratic Process." *Vital Speeches,* 6:240-242 (February 1, 1940).
7. Arleigh B. Williamson. "Social Standards in Public Speaking Instruction." *Quarterly Journal of Speech,* 25:371-377 (October, 1939).
8. William E. Utterback. "The Appeal to Force in Public Discussion." *Quarterly Journal of Speech,* 26:1-6 (February, 1940).
9. William R. Gondin. "The Field of Speech—A Problem in Definition." *Quarterly Journal of Speech,* 28:91-94 (February, 1942).
10. Paul F. Lazarsfeld. "The Effects of Radio on Public Opinion." In *Print, Radio, and Film in a Democracy,* Douglas Waples, ed., Chicago, University of Chicago Press, 1942. pp. 79-98.
11. "Demosthenes and Abraham Lincoln." In *The New Invitation to Learning,* Mark Van Doren, ed. New York, Random House, 1942. pp. 341-355.
12. J. E. Spingarn. "Politics and the Poet." *Atlantic Monthly,* 170:73-78 (November, 1942).
13. *Freedom: Its Meaning.* Ruth Nanda Anshen, ed. New York, Harcourt, Brace and Co., Inc., 1940. Part I (Freedom Invades History), Part II (Freedom for the Mind), Part III (Freedom in the Body Politic).
14. C. Wright Mills. "The Powerless People: The Social Role of the Intellectual." *Bulletin* of the American Association of University Professors. pp. 231-243 (Summer, 1945).
15. Hoyt H. Hudson. *Educating Liberally.* Stanford University, California, Stanford University Press, 1945. Ch. 2 (Three Foes and Three Arms of Attack), Ch. 3 (The Arm of Information), Ch. 4 (The Arm of Operative Logic), Ch. 5 (The Arm of Imagination).
16. Richard Murphy. "Speech for the Masses." University of Colorado *Studies,* 2:16-26 (October, 1945).
17. Walter Bagehot. "The Age of Discussion." In *Physics and Politics.* New York, D. Appleton Co., 1875. pp. 156-204.
18. Carl Dahlstrom. "A Proposed Preface to a Text on Public Speaking." *Quarterly Journal of Speech,* 24:418-424 (October, 1938).
19. Lyman Bryson. "Discussion in the Democratic Process." In *Principles and Methods of Discussion* by James H. McBurney and Kenneth G. Hance. New York, Harper & Bros., 1939. pp. 425-433.
20. Gladys Murphy Graham. "Speech in the Service of Deliberation." In *A Program of Speech Education in a Democracy,* W. Arthur Cable, ed. Boston, Expression Co., 1932. pp. 242-256.
21. Dayton McKean. "Public Speaking and Public Opinion." *Quarterly Journal of Speech,* 17:510-522 (November, 1931).
22. Andrew T. Weaver. "The Challenge of the Crisis." In *Representative American Speeches: 1944-1945,* A. Craig Baird, comp., New York, The H. W. Wilson Co., 1945. pp. 229-240.
23. John W. Studebaker. *The American Way.* New York, McGraw-Hill Book Co., Inc., 1935.
24. Edward Z. Rowell. "Public Speaking in a New Era." *Quarterly Journal of Speech,* 16:62-69 (February, 1930).

Exercises

1. What are the limitations of classical treatises as yardsticks of excellence in oratory?

2. If oratory has value for all citizens in their political and moral experience, how may training in the art be extended more widely? Or is it sufficient, as was the case in Attica, to encourage only those of superior oratorical gifts and inclinations?

3. What philosophical schools or systems are we to follow if we are to progress in our ability to "perceive the difference between truth and error"?

4. Analyze the forces of political speaking at work in the American Colonies during the 1770's and trace their possible influence on the immediate political changes and results in America up to 1782.

5. Analyze the character of British parliamentary speaking during 1770-1790 and evaluate the contribution of such speaking to the formation of British foreign and domestic policies and programs of the time.

6. Analyze and interpret deliberative speechmaking in America from 1939-1945; gauge the relationship of such speaking to the military and political policies of the period.

7. Frame a philosophy of discussion and of argumentation.

8. Evaluate the strength and weakness of contemporary "government by talk" in the United States.

9. Trace the history of free speech in the United States during the period 1930 to date.

10. With the principles of this chapter for reference, outline and interpret the philosophy of discourse as revealed in the speeches of a contemporary political leader in the United States.

11. Comment on this statement by John Stuart Mill: "In the opinion, not of bad men, but of the best men, no belief which is contrary to truth can be really useful. . . ."

APPENDIX B
NOTES

Appendix B

CHAPTER 1

[1] *Criticism.* New York, 1914. p. 1.
[2] *Studies in Rhetoric and Public Speaking.* New York, 1925. p. 209.
[3] August 11, 1934. p. 44.
[4] *Ibid.*
[5] *Criticism in the Making.* New York, 1929. p. 34.
[6] "Some Problems of Scope and Method in Rhetorical Scholarship." *Quarterly Journal of Speech,* 23:187-188 (April, 1937).
[7] *The Issue in Literary Criticism.* Berkeley, Calif., 1932, p. 11.
[8] *Ibid.,* p. 12.
[9] *Principles and Problems of Right Thinking.* New York, 1928. p. 500.
[10] *The Social Criticism of Literature.* New Haven, 1916. p. 50.
[11] "On Criticism." *The New Criterion,* 4:254 (April, 1926).

CHAPTER 2

[1] Cf. Quintilian. *Institutes of Oratory.* II, 15, for scattered references to early work in the art.
[2] *The Traditions of European Literature.* New York, 1920. p. 2.
[3] W. R. Sorley. *Herbert Spencer Lectures.* 2nd ser. Oxford, 1930. p. 11.
[4] *Ibid.,* p. 24.
[5] *The Philosophy of Rhetoric.* New ed. New York, 1851. p. 19.
[6] *The Greek Orators.* London, 1919. p. 1.
[7] Alfred Croiset and Maurice Croiset. *An Abridged History of Greek Literature.* Trans. by G. F. Heffelbower. New York, 1904. p. 30.
[8] *Ibid.*
[9] George W. Botsford. *Hellenic History.* New York, 1926. p. 43.
[10] *Ibid.,* p. 252.
[11] Robert J. Bonner. *Aspects of Athenian Democracy.* Berkeley, Calif., 1933. p. 80.
[12] *Ibid.,* pp. 81-82.
[13] K. O. Müller. *A History of the Literature of Ancient Greece.* Trans. by J. W. Donaldson. 1858. II, 128.
[14] *Essays in Greek History and Literature.* Oxford, 1937. p. 185.
[15] *A History of Ancient Greek Literature.* Rev. ed. New York, 1923. p. 282.
[16] *History of the Peloponnesian War.* Trans. from Greek of Thucydides by William Smith. Philadelphia, 1836. I, 8.
[17] *Ibid.,* I, 47-50.
[18] *Pericles.* London, 1937. p. 295.
[19] *The History of the Peloponnesian War.* Trans. by Richard Crawley. London, 1876. p. 140.
[20] John Edwin Sandys. *M. Tulli Ciceronis ad M. Brutum Orator.* Rev. ed. Cambridge, 1885. p. iv.
[21] *Ibid.*
[22] R. C. Jebb. *The Attic Orators.* London, 1893. I, cxvii.
[23] Cf. the modern parallel to Sicilian demands in Hiram Motherwell's article, "Hunger, Hatred, and Post-War Europe," *Harper's Magazine,* Dec. 1942. pp. 33-34.

24 Jebb. *Op. cit.*, I, cxix.

25 Bromley Smith. "Corax and Probability." *Quarterly Journal of Speech Education,* 7:38 (February, 1921).

26 *Phaedrus.* Trans. by Henry Cary. In *Works of Plato.* London, 1854. I, 345-346.

27 Croiset. *Op. cit.,* p. 281.

28 Jebb. *Op. cit.,* II, 42.

29 Croiset. *Op. cit.,* pp. 282-283.

30 Henry Sidgwick. *Lectures on the Philosophy of Kant and Other Philosophical Lectures and Essays.* London, 1905. p. 325.

31 Philostratus and Eunapius : *The Lives of the Sophists.* Trans. by Wilmer C. Wright. The Loeb Classical Library, 1922. p. 13.

32 Theodor Gomperz. *Greek Thinkers.* Trans. by Laurie Magnus. London, 1920. I, 465.

33 Wilmer C. Wright. *Op. cit.,* p. xxvi.

34 Philostratus. *The Lives of the Sophists.* p. 31.

35 Croiset. *Op. cit.,* p. 285.

36 *Op. cit.,* I, 479-480.

37 "Prodicus of Ceos : the Sire of Synonymy." *Quarterly Journal of Speech Education,* 6:51 (April, 1920).

38 Bromley Smith. "Hippias and a Lost Canon of Rhetoric." *Quarterly Journal of Speech Education,* 12:138 (June, 1926).

39 *Op. cit.,* II, 426.

40 *Ibid.,* I, lxi-lxii.

41 Charles Sears Baldwin. *Ancient Rhetoric and Poetic.* New York, 1924. pp. 227-228.

42 *Op. cit.,* I, cvi.

43 Jebb. *Op. cit.,* I, cxxx-cxxxi.

44 *Ibid.,* I, 22-23.

45 *Ibid.,* I, 157.

46 *Ibid.,* II, 311.

47 *Ibid.,* II, 371.

48 *Ibid.*

49 *Ibid.,* II, 433-434.

50 Jebb. *Op. cit.,* II, 434; George Norlin, trans., *Isocrates.* 1928. The Loeb Classical Library. I, xvi.

51 Norlin. *Op. cit.,* I, xiii-xv; Cf. Jebb, *op. cit.,* II, 51ff.

52 J. W. H. Atkins. *Literary Criticism in Antiquity.* London, 1934. I, 124.

53 Norlin. *Op. cit.,* II, 181.

54 *Ibid.,* II, 182.

55 *Ibid.,* I, 123-125.

56 Atkins. *Op. cit.,* I, 124.

57 Norlin. *Op. cit.,* I, 79.

58 *Ibid.,* I, 79-81.

59 *Ibid.,* II, 291-293.

60 *Ibid.,* I, 81-83.

61 *Ibid.,* II, 239.

62 *Ibid.,* II, 171.

63 *Ibid.,* II, 213.

64 *Ibid.,* II, 337-339.

65 *De Oratore.* III, 9.

66 *Op. cit.,* II, 33.

67 *Brutus.* LI.

68 *Op. cit.,* II, 36.

69 Everett Lee Hunt. "Plato and Aristotle on Rhetoric and Rhetoricians." *Studies in Rhetoric and Public Speaking.* New York, 1925. p. 3.

[70] *Ibid.,* p. 21.

[71] Alfred Weber and Ralph Barton Perry. *History of Philosophy.* New York, 1925. p. 55.

[72] W. H. Thompson. *The Gorgias of Plato.* London, 1871. p. i-ii.

[73] *Gorgias.* Trans. by Henry Cary. In *Works of Plato.* London, 1854. I Secs. 12-13.

[74] *Ibid.,* 41-42.

[75] *Ibid.,* 46.

[76] *Ibid.,* 125-126.

[77] *Ibid.,* 78-81.

[78] *Op. cit.,* p. 37.

[79] Plato. *Phaedrus.* 97.

[80] *Ibid.,* 105.

[81] *Ibid.,* 124.

[82] *Ibid.,* 125-126.

[83] *Op. cit.,* p. 37-38.

[84] *Ibid.,* p. 38.

[85] *Phaedrus.* 141.

[86] Baldwin. *Op. cit.,* p. 1.

[87] Jebb. *Op. cit.,* II, 433.

[88] *De Oratore.* III, xxxv.

[89] *Op. cit.,* p. 44.

[90] *Aristotle's Treatise on Rhetoric.* Trans. by Theodore Buckley. London, 1883. p. 6.

[91] *Rhetoric.* Trans. by J. E. C. Welldon. London, 1886. pp. 1, 10. (Unless otherwise indicated subsequent references in this chapter are to the Welldon edition.)

[92] *Op. cit.,* p. 9.

[93] *Rhetoric.* pp. 6-8.

[94] *Ibid.,* p. 10.

[95] *Op. cit.,* p. 11.

[96] *Rhetoric.* pp. 10-12.

[97] *Ibid.,* p. 22.

[98] *Ibid.*

[99] *Ibid.,* pp. 20-21.

[100] Baldwin. *Op. cit.,* p. 17.

[101] *Ibid.,* p. 19.

[102] *Rhetoric.* pp. 158-161.

[103] E. M. Cope. *An Introduction to Aristotle's Rhetoric.* London, 1867. p. 5.

[104] *Ibid.,* p. 6.

[105] *Rhetoric.* pp. 176-180.

[106] *Ibid.,* p. 184.

[107] *Ibid.,* p. 194.

[108] *Ibid.,* pp. 220-221.

[109] *Ibid., passim,* 194-211.

[110] *Ibid.,* p. 219.

[111] Hunt. *Op. cit.,* p. 49.

[112] *Ibid.,* p. 50.

[113] *Ibid.*

[114] *Rhetoric.* p. 226.

[115] *Ibid.,* p. 225.

[116] *Op. cit.,* p. 22.

[117] *Rhetoric.* p. 248.

[118] *Ibid.,* p. 273.

[119] *Ibid.,* p. 274.

[120] *Ibid.,* p. 275.

08 APPENDIX B [Ch. 3

121 *Ibid.*, p. 301.

122 "The Ethical Doctrine of Aristotle." *International Journal of Ethics,* 16:301 (April, 1906).

123 "Aristotle on Public Speaking." *Fortnightly Review,* 122:204 (Aug. 1, 1924).

124 *Aristotle and Ancient Educational Ideals.* New York, 1902. p. 9.

125 *Ibid.*, p. 11.

126 MacCunn. *Op. cit.*, p. 300.

127 *Aristotle.* London, 1923. p. 195.

128 *Rhetoric.* Trans. by Theodore Buckley. London. Geo. Bell & Sons, 1883. pp. 258-259.

129 *The Nicomachean Ethics of Aristotle.* Trans. by R. W. Browne. London, 1850. II, VI, 4-5. (pp. 43-44).

130 *Op. cit.*, p. 52.

131 *Ethics.* VI, xii, 8 (p. 173).

132 MacCunn. *Op. cit.*, p. 298; Cf. *Ethics.* VI, xii, 10.

CHAPTER 3

1 J. W. H. Atkins. *Literary Criticism in Antiquity.* London, 1934. II, 16.

2 Cf. Augustus S. Wilkins. *M. Tulli Ciceronis De Oratore.* 3rd ed. Oxford, 1895. I, 56-64.

3 Charles Sears Baldwin. *Ancient Rhetoric and Poetic.* New York, 1924. p. 43.

4 *Ibid.*, p. 34.

5 *De Oratore.* Trans. by J. S. Watson. Philadelphia, 1897. II, lxxxvii.

6 *Brutus.* LX.

7 "Hippias and a Lost Canon of Rhetoric." *Quarterly Journal of Speech Education,* 12:144 (June, 1926).

8 *Teuffel's History of Roman Literature.* Trans. and ed. by George C. W. Warr. London, 1891. I, 64.

9 Baldwin. *Op. cit.*, p. 37.

10 *De Oratore.* I, xiii.

11 Atkins. *Op. cit.*, II, 23.

12 *De Oratore.* I, v.

13 *Ibid.*, I, xii.

14 *Op. cit.*, p. 46.

15 *De Oratore.* I, xv.

16 *Ibid.*, II, xxvi.

17 *Ibid.*, II, xxix.

18 *Ibid.*, II, xlii.

19 *Ibid.*, II, lxxvi.

20 *Ibid.*, II, lxxxvi.

21 *Ibid.*, II, lxxxviii.

22 *Ibid.*, III, xxv.

23 *Op. cit.*, p. 55.

24 *De Oratore.* III, lv.

25 John Edwin Sandys. *M. Tulli Ciceronis ad M. Brutum Orator.* Cambridge, 1885. pp. lviii, lxiv.

26 *Orator.* From *The Orations of Marcus Tullius Cicero.* Trans. by C. D. Yonge. London, 1852. IV, 403-407, *passim.*

27 *Ibid.*, IV, 407-409, *passim.*

28 *Ibid.*, IV, 409-410.

29 *Op. cit.*, pp. 56-57.

30 *Rhetoric.* Trans. by Theodore Buckley. London, 1883. pp. 246-247.

31 J. F. D'Alton. *Roman Literary Theory and Criticism.* London, 1931. pp. 74-75.

32 *Orator.* IV, 442-445, *passim.*

33 Torsten Petersson. *Cicero: A Biography.* Berkeley, Calif., 1919. p. 442.

34 *On Topics.* In *The Orations of Marcus Tullius Cicero.* Trans. by C. D. Yonge. London, 1919. IV, 460.

35 *On Rhetorical Invention.* In *ibid.* IV, 309.

36 Wilbur Samuel Howell. "The Positions of Argument: An Historical Examination." In *Papers in Rhetoric.* Donald C. Bryant, ed. St. Louis, 1940. p. 9.

37 J. Wight Duff. *A Literary History of Rome in the Silver Age.* New York, 1927. p. 387.

38 *Institutes of Oratory.* Trans. by J. S. Watson. London, 1856. XII, ii, 1.

39 F. H. Colson. *M. Fabii Quintiliani Institutionis Oratoriae Liber I.* Cambridge, 1924. p. xxviii.

40 *Institutes.* II, xxi, 12-13.

41 *Op. cit.,* p. xxiv-xxv.

42 *Institutes.* II, xiii, 2.

43 *Ibid.,* II, xiii, 7.

44 *Ibid.,* II, xiii, 2.

45 *Ibid.,* III, iii.

46 *Ibid.,* III, iv.

47 *Ibid.,* III, v.

48 *Ibid.,* III, vi, 21.

49 *Op. cit.,* p. 74.

50 *Institutes.* III, vi, 76.

51 *Ibid.,* VIII, introd., 32-33.

52 *Ibid.,* X, vii, 1-2.

53 *Ibid.,* X, vii, 22.

54 *Op. cit.,* p. xxi.

55 *Op. cit.,* I, 167.

56 Charles Sears Baldwin. *Medieval Rhetoric and Poetic.* New York, 1928. p. 23.

57 *Ibid.,* p. 7.

58 *Dio Chrysostom.* Trans. by J. W. Cohoon. Cambridge, Mass., 1939. The Loeb Classical Library. pp. 213-215.

59 *Ibid.,* p. 223.

60 *Ibid.,* p. 225.

61 *Institutes.* II, x, 3.

62 *Ancient Rhetoric and Poetic.* p. 71.

63 *The Suasoriae of Seneca the Elder.* Trans. and ed. by William A. Edward. London, 1928. pp. xviii-xix.

64 *Petronius: The Satyricon.* Trans. by J. M. Mitchell. London, n.d. p. 1.

65 *Ibid.,* p. 3.

66 *Ancient Rhetoric and Poetic.* p. 97.

67 *Ibid.,* p. 100.

68 *The Correspondence of Marcus Cornelius Fronto.* Ed. and trans. by C. R. Haines. 1919. The Loeb Classical Library. I, 121.

69 *Ibid.,* II, 145.

70 *Ibid.,* II, 53-55.

71 *Op. cit.,* p. 320.

72 *Suasoriae of Seneca the Elder.* p. xxxvi.

73 *Ancient Rhetoric and Poetic.* pp. 100-101.

74 *The Works of Cornelius Tacitus.* Trans. by Arthur Murphy. London, 1813. II, 421.

75 *Ibid.,* II, 423-424.

76 *Lucian.* Trans. by A. M. Harmon. 1925. The Loeb Classical Library. IV, 137, 143.

77 *Ibid.,* IV, 145-147.

78 *Ibid.*, IV, 151.

79 *Ibid.*, IV, 155.

80 *Ibid.*, IV, 155-159.

81 *Ibid.*, IV, 159.

82 *Ibid.*, IV, 159.

83 *Ibid.*, IV, 161.

84 *Dionysius of Halicarnassus on Literary Composition.* Ed. with trans. by W. Rhys Roberts. London, 1910. p. 67.

85 *Ibid.*, p. 71.

86 *Ibid.*, p. 105.

87 *Ibid.*, p. 121.

88 *Ibid.*, pp. 211-213.

89 *Ibid.*, p. 235.

90 *Longinus on the Sublime.* Trans. by William T. Spurdens. London, 1836. VIII.

91 *Ibid.*, XIII.

92 *Ibid.*, XV.

93 *Ancient Rhetoric and Poetic.* p. 131.

Chapter 4

1 *On Christian Doctrine.* Trans. by J. F. Shaw. In *The Works of Aurelius Augustine, Bishop of Hippo.* Ed. by the Rev. Marcus Dods. Edinburgh, T. and T. Clark, 1873. IX, 5.

2 *Ibid.*, p. 7.

3 *Ibid.*, pp. 72-73.

4 *Ibid.*, pp. 122-123.

5 *Ibid.*, p. 72.

6 *Ibid.*, p. 169.

7 *Ibid.*, p. 139.

8 *Ibid.*, p. 141.

9 Leonard Cox. *The Arte or Crafte of Rhethoryke.* Ed. by Frederic Ives Carpenter. Chicago, 1899. p. 7.

10 *Ibid.*, p. 29.

11 *Ibid.*, p. 36.

12 *Ibid.*, p. 43.

13 *Ibid.*, p. 41.

14 Russell H. Wagner. "Thomas Wilson's Contributions to Rhetoric." In *Papers in Rhetoric.* Donald C. Bryant, ed., St. Louis, 1940. p. 2.

15 Thomas Wilson. *Arte of Rhetorike.* London, 1580 (1567 edition). p. 162.

16 *Op. cit.*, p. 3.

17 1567 edition. London, 1909. pp. 2-4.

18 *Op. cit.*, p. 5.

19 Edition of 1567. p. 123.

20 *Ibid.*, pp. 123-132.

21 *Ibid.*, p. 132.

22 Mair edition. London, 1909. p. 131.

23 Cf. *ibid.*, p. 160.

24 Edition of 1567. pp. 164-172, *passim.*

25 Mair edition. pp. 166-167.

26 *Op. cit.*, p. 7.

27 *Ibid.*

28 Edwin A. Abbott. *Francis Bacon.* London, 1885. p. xviii.

29 *The Works of Francis Bacon.* New ed. Ed. by Basil Montagu. London, 1825. II, 209, 211.

30 *Ibid.*, II, 183.

[31] *Ibid.*, II, 183-185.
[32] *Advancement of Learning.* XVIII, 8.
[33] *Ibid.*, XVIII, 9.
[34] *Ibid.*
[35] *Apothegmes* Nos. 21 and 181.
[36] *Works of Francis Bacon.* I, 231f.
[37] *Ibid.*, II, 212.
[38] Thomas Gibbons. *Rhetoric.* London, 1767. p. 3.
[39] *Ibid.*, pp. 3-4.
[40] *Ibid.*, pp. 4-17, *passim.*
[41] *Ibid.*, pp. 122-124, *passim.*
[42] Joseph Addison. "On Public Speaking."
[43] Thomas Sheridan. *Lectures on Elocution.* London, 1781. p. 6.
[44] *Ibid.*, p. 12.
[45] *Ibid.*, pp. 148-149.
[46] John Walker. *Elements of Elocution.* 3rd ed. London, 1806. p. 1.
[47] *Ibid.*, pp. 1-2.
[48] James McCosh. *The Scottish Philosophy.* New York, 1875. p. 241.
[49] George Campbell. *The Philosophy of Rhetoric.* New ed. New York, 1851. pp. 23-24.
[50] *Ibid.*, pp. 24-27.
[51] William P. Sandford. *English Theories of Public Address, 1530-1828.* Columbus, Ohio, 1931. p. 146.
[52] *Op. cit.*, p. 121.
[53] *Ibid.*, pp. 54-55.
[54] *Ibid.*, p. 65.
[55] *Ibid.*, pp. 84-88, *passim.*
[56] *Ibid.*, p. 94.
[57] *Ibid.*, pp. 103-112, *passim.*
[58] *Ibid.*, p. 162.
[59] *Ibid.*, p. 238.
[60] *Ibid.*, p. 22.
[61] C. W. Edney. *George Campbell's Theory of Public Address.* Ph.D. Thesis State University of Iowa, 1946.
[62] Richard Whately. *Elements of Rhetoric.* New ed. Boston, 1861. p. 21.
[63] *Ibid.*, p. 65.
[64] *Ibid.*, p. 139.
[65] *Ibid.*, p. 140.
[66] *Ibid.*, pp. 141-157, *passim.*
[67] *Ibid.*, pp. 209-210, *passim.*
[68] *Ibid.*, p. 398.
[69] *Ibid.*, p. 404.
[70] *Ibid.*, pp. 442-443.
[71] Wayland Maxfield Parrish, "Whately and His Rhetoric." *Quarterly Journal of Speech,* 15:79 (February, 1929).
[72] Orville L. Pence. *The Concept and Function of Logical Proof in the Rhetorical System of Richard Whately.* Ph.D. Thesis. State University of Iowa, 1946.

CHAPTER 5

[1] J. W. H. Atkins. *Literary Criticism in Antiquity.* London, 1934. I, 66, 69.
[2] *Ibid.*, I, 72.
[3] "Origins of Modern Criticism." *Modern Philology,* 1:1 (April, 1904).
[4] J. F. D'Alton. *Roman Literary Theory and Criticism.* London, 1931, p. 214. (Our analysis of the Atticist controversy and of Cicero's critical theory draws heavily upon the conclusions of J. F. D'Alton.)

[5] *Ibid.*, p. 322.

[6] *Brutus.* Trans. by E. Jones. LXXX.

[7] *Op. cit.*, pp. 225-226.

[8] *De Oratore.* Ed. by J. S. Watson. I, xii.

[9] *Brutus.* LV.

[10] *Ibid.*, LXXXII.

[11] *Ibid.*, LXXXIII.

[12] *Ibid.*

[13] *On The Best Style of Orators.* Trans. by C. D. Yonge. In *The Orations of Marcus Tullius Cicero.* London, 1919. IV, 531.

[14] *Brutus.* IX.

[15] *Op. cit.*, p. 240.

[16] *Orator.* In *The Orations of Marcus Tullius Cicero,* Yonge trans. IV, 410.

[17] *Op cit.*, p. 241.

[18] Torsten Petersson. *Cicero: A Biography.* Berkeley, Calif., 1919. p. 442.

[19] G. L. Hendrickson. "Cicero's Correspondence with Brutus and Calvus on Oratorical Style." *American Journal of Philology,* 47:251. (1926.)

[20] *Brutus.* LXIX.

[21] George Saintsbury. *A History of Criticism and Literary Taste in Europe.* Edinburgh, n.d. I, 355.

[22] *Op. cit.*, II, 41.

[23] *Orator.* pp. 387-388.

[24] *Ibid.*, p. 388.

[25] *Brutus.* XVII.

[26] *Ibid.*, XXIX.

[27] *De Oratore.* II, 29.

[28] *Brutus.* XXXIX.

[29] *Ibid.*, LXXIX-LXXXI.

[30] *Ibid.*, XXXVII-XXXVIII.

[31] *Ibid.*, LXXVIII.

[32] *Ibid.*, XXIX.

[33] *Ibid.*, XX.

[34] *Ibid.*, LXVII.

[35] *Op. cit.*, p. 436.

[36] *The Best Style of the Orators.* p. 527.

[37] John E. Sandys. *M. Tulli Ciceronis ad M. Brutum Orator.* London, 1885. p. lxiv.

[38] *Brutus.* LI.

[39] *Ibid.*

[40] *Ibid.*

[41] *Ibid.*, XLIX.

[42] *Ibid.*, LIV.

[43] J. Wight Duff. *A Literary History of Rome from the Origins to the Close of the Golden Age.* New York, 1928. p. 351.

[44] J. D. Denniston. *Greek Literary Criticism.* London, 1924. p. xxxii.

[45] R. C. Jebb. *The Attic Orators.* London, 1893. I, lxii.

[46] Charles Sears Baldwin. *Ancient Rhetoric and Poetic.* New York, 1924. p. 105.

[47] Jebb. *Op. cit.*, II, 453.

[48] W. Rhys Roberts. "Caecilius of Calacte." *American Journal of Philology,* 18:307, 1897.

[49] *Ibid.*, p. 312.

[50] *Op. cit.*, II, 451.

[51] Atkins, *op. cit.*, II, 104-105.

[52] Jebb, *op. cit.*, II, 109-110.

[53] S. F. Bonner. *The Literary Treatises of Dionysius of Halicarnassus.* London, 1939. pp. 45-46.

[54] *Ibid.,* pp. 48-50.

[55] *Ibid.,* p. 63.

[56] *Ibid.,* p. 64.

[57] *Ibid.,* pp. 65-66.

[58] Roberts edition, p. 46.

[59] *Ibid.,* p. 267.

[60] *Op. cit.,* II, 301.

[61] Atkins, *op. cit.,* II, 354.

[62] *Longinus On The Sublime.* Trans. by W. Rhys Roberts. In *Aristotle's Poetics and Longinus On The Sublime.* Ed. by Charles Sears Baldwin. New York, 1930. p. 87.

[63] *Ibid.,* p. 92.

[64] *Ibid.,* pp. 79-80.

[65] *Ibid.,* pp. 111-113.

[66] *Ibid.,* pp. 82-83.

[67] Tacitus, *A Dialogue Concerning Oratory.* In *The Works of Cornelius Tacitus.* Ed. by Arthur Murphy. London, 1813. II, 436-437.

[68] *Ibid.,* p. 439.

[69] Atkins, *op. cit.,* II, 195-196.

[70] *Demetrius on Style.* Trans. by T. A. Moxon. In *Aristotle's Poetics: Demetrius on Style.* Everyman's Library. New York. p. 210.

[71] *Ibid.,* p. 228.

[72] *Ibid.,* p. 230.

[73] *Ibid.,* p. 250.

[74] *Ibid.*

[75] *Ibid.,* p. 256.

[76] *Op. cit.,* II, 208-209.

[77] *De Oratore.* III, xvii.

[78] *Brutus.* XXXI.

[79] *De Oratore.* III, xvii-xviii.

[80] *Ibid.*

[81] *Ibid.*

[82] John Locke. *An Essay Concerning Human Understanding.* London. p. 411.

[83] *The Works of Lord Bolingbroke.* Philadelphia, 1841. III, 129.

[84] *Ibid.,* p. 130.

[85] *De Oratore.* III, xvii.

[86] *The Rhetoric of Philodemus.* Trans. by Harry M. Hubbell. In *Connecticut Academy of Arts and Sciences,* 23, Sept. 1920. p. 276.

[87] *Ibid.,* pp. 307-308.

[88] *Ibid.,* p. 307.

[89] *Ibid.,* p. 318.

[90] *Ibid.,* p. 301.

[91] *Pliny: Letters.* Trans. by William Melmoth. Rev. by W. M. L. Hutchinson. Loeb Classical Library. 1915. Book VI, 17.

[92] *Ibid.,* IX, 26.

[93] *Ibid.,* I, 19.

[94] *Ibid.,* I, 20.

[95] *Ibid.*

[96] *Ibid.*

[97] *Ibid.*

[98] *Ibid.,* V, 8.

[99] *Ibid.*

[100] *Ibid.,* II, 3.

[101] *Institutes.* II, v, 21-22.

102 *Ibid.*, II, v, 24.
103 *Ibid.*, VIII, v, 34.
104 Cf. J. F. D'Alton, *Roman Literary Theory and Criticism.* London, 1931. pp. 266-353.
105 *Institutes.* XII, x, 10-11.
106 *Ibid.*, XII, x, 12.
107 *Ibid.*, XII, x, 14.
108 *Ibid.*, XII, x, 17.
109 *Ibid.*, XII, x, 35-38.
110 *Ibid.*, XII, x, 43.
111 *Ibid.*, XII, x, 51-54.
112 *Ibid.*, XII, x, 55.
113 *Ibid.*, XII, x, 69, 72.
114 *Ibid.*, XII, x, 80.
115 *Ibid.*, IX, iv, 4-5.
116 *Ibid.*, X, iii, 4.
117 *Ibid.*, XII, xi, 25.
118 *Ibid.*, X, i, 76.
119 *Ibid.*, X, i, 105-112.
120 *Plutarch: The Lives of the Noble Grecians and Romans.* Rev. by Arthur H. Clough. New York. p. 1023.
121 *Ibid.*, p. 1070.
122 *Ibid.*
123 *Ibid.*, p. 1071.
124 *Plutarch's Miscellanies and Essays.* Rev. by W. W. Goodwin. Boston. 1898. I, 445.
125 *Ibid.*, I, 446-447.
126 *Ibid.*, I, 448.
127 *Ibid.*, I, 450.
128 *Ibid.*, I, 451.
129 *Ibid.*
130 *Ibid.*
131 *Plutarch's Essays and Miscellanies.* V, 18.
132 *Ibid.*, V, 31.
133 *Ibid.*, V, 23.
134 *Ibid.*, V, 25-26.
135 *Ibid.*, V, 57.
136 *Ibid.*, V, 58.
137 *Ibid.*, V, 408.
138 *Ibid.*, V, 410.
139 Wilmer Cave Wright, trans. and ed., *The Lives of the Sophists.* Loeb Classical Library. 1922. p. xii.
140 *Ibid.*, p. 5.
141 *Medieval Rhetoric and Poetic.* p. 10.
142 *Ibid.*, p. 17.
143 *Lives of the Sophists.* pp. 17-19.
144 *Ibid.*, pp. 49-51.
145 *Ibid.*, p. 61.
146 *Ibid.*, p. 71.
147 *Ibid.*, p. 29.
148 *Ibid.*, pp. 121, 133.
149 *Ibid.*, pp. 277-279.
150 *Ibid.*, p. 179.
151 *Ibid.*, pp. 187-189.
152 *Ibid.*, p. 209.
153 *Ibid.*, p. 223.

[154] *Institutes*, X, ii, 6-7.
[155] *Ibid.*, X, ii, 24.
[156] *Ibid.*, X, ii, 11-28, *passim*.
[157] *De Oratore*. II, xxii-xxiii.
[158] London, 1759. 410ff.

CHAPTER 6

[1] René Rapin. *Reflexions on Eloquence*. In *The Whole Critical Works of Mon. Rapin*. Trans. by Basil Kennet . . . and others. London, 1731. 2 v.
[2] *Ibid.*, II, i.
[3] *Ibid.*, II, 4-5, 8ff.
[4] *Ibid.*, II, 65.
[5] *Ibid.*, I, Introd., 1-2.
[6] Jonathan Swift. *Works*. Ed. by T. Sheridan. London, 1803. VIII, 14-15.
[7] *The Works of Joseph Addison*. New York, 1850. II, 132-133.
[8] *Ibid.*, II, 133.
[9] *Letters to His Son*, by the Earl of Chesterfield. Washington, 1901. I, 66.
[10] *Ibid.*, I, 83.
[11] *Ibid.*, I, 246-247.
[12] *Ibid.*, I, 253.
[13] *Ibid.*, I, 254.
[14] *Ibid.*
[15] *Ibid.*, I, 257.
[16] Hugh Blair. *Lectures on Rhetoric and Belles Lettres*. London, n.d. p. 3.
[17] *Ibid.*, p. 5.
[18] *Ibid.*, pp. 9-12.
[19] *Ibid.*, p. 14.
[20] *Ibid.*
[21] *Ibid.*, p. 16.
[22] *Ibid.*, p. 17.
[23] *Ibid.*, p. 18.
[24] *Ibid.*, pp. 19-20.
[25] *Ibid.*, p. 277.
[26] *Ibid.*, pp. 286-288.
[27] *Ibid.*, pp. 288-289.
[28] *Ibid.*, p. 289.
[29] *Ibid.*, p. 292.
[30] *Ibid.*, pp. 292-293.
[31] *Ibid.*, p. 294.
[32] *Ibid.*
[33] *Ibid.*, pp. 294-295.
[34] David Hume. *Essays and Treatises on Several Subjects*. Edinburgh, 1817. II, 99.
[35] Blair. *Op. cit.*, p. 303.
[36] *Ibid.*, p. 304.
[37] *Ibid.*, p. 305.
[38] *Ibid.*, p. 307.
[39] *Ibid.*, pp. 310-311.
[40] *Ibid.*, p. 318.
[41] *Ibid.*, pp. 318-319.
[42] *Ibid.*, p. 319.
[43] *Ibid.*, p. 322.
[44] *Ibid.*, p. 333.
[45] *Ibid.*, pp. 335-336.
[46] *Ibid.*, p. 341.

47 *Ibid.*, p. 343.

48 Barron. *Lectures on Belles Lettres and Logic.* London, 1806. I, 478-479.

49 *Ibid.*, I, 479.

50 *Ibid.*, I, 479-480.

51 *The Lives of the Chief Justices of England.* London, 1849. II, 562.

52 *Ibid.*, II, 324*n.*

53 *The Method of Teaching and Studying the Belles Lettres.* 7th ed. London, 1779. II, 223-224.

54 *Ibid.*, II, 229.

55 William Hazlitt, *Table Talk.* In *The Miscellaneous Works of William Haz-litt.* Philadelphia, 1848. II, 170.

56 *Ibid.*, II, 171.

57 *Ibid.*

58 *Ibid.*, II, 174.

59 *Ibid.*

60 *Ibid.*

61 *Ibid.*, II, 175-176.

62 *Ibid.*

63 *Ibid.*, II, 178.

64 *Ibid.*, II, 179.

65 *Ibid.*, II, 180.

66 Thomas De Quincey. *Historical and Critical Essays.* Boston, 1871. II, 183.

67 *Ibid.*, II, 183-184.

68 *Ibid.*, II, 69.

69 *Ibid.*, II, 70.

70 *De Quincey's Literary Criticism.* "Rhetoric." Ed. by H. Darbishire. London, 1909. p. 67.

71 *Ibid.*, pp. 67-68.

72 *Ibid.*, p. 68.

73 Hoyt H. Hudson. "De Quincey on Rhetoric and Public Speaking." In *Studies in Rhetoric and Public Speaking in Honor of James Albert Winans.* New York, 1925. pp. 141-142.

74 *The Works of Henry Lord Brougham.* "Rhetorical and Literary Dissertations and Addresses." London, 1856. VII, 121-122.

75 *Ibid.*, VII, 193-194. Review of French ed. of Demosthenes and Aeschines.

76 *Ibid.*, VII, 5. On "Eloquence of Ancients."

77 *Ibid.*, VII, 6.

78 *Ibid.*, VII, 7.

79 *Ibid.*, VII, 8-9.

80 *Ibid.*, VII, 9.

81 *Ibid.*, VII, 31.

82 *Ibid.*

83 *Ibid.*, VII, 39.

84 *Ibid.*, VII, 41.

85 *Ibid.*, VII, 43.

86 *Ibid.*, VII, 59.

87 *Ibid.*, VII, 58.

88 *Ibid.*, VII, 195.

89 *The Complete Works of Thomas Babington Macaulay.* New York, 1900. VI, 53. University ed.

90 *The Works of Lord Macaulay.* Edinburgh ed. New York, 1897. VII, 378.

91 *Complete Works.* I, 49.

92 *Ibid.*, VI, 50.

93 *Ibid.*, I, 48.

94 *Ibid.*, I, 49.

95 *Ibid.*, I, 50.

96 *Ibid.*, I, 44.
97 *Ibid.*, I, 47.
98 *Ibid.*, VI, 49.
99 *Works of Lord Macaulay.* Edinburgh ed. VII, 380.

<h3 style="text-align:center">CHAPTER 7</h3>

1 *Select British Eloquence.* New York, 1853. Preface, iii.
2 *Ibid.*
3 *Ibid.*, p. iv.
4 *Ibid.*, p. 240.
5 *Ibid.*, pp. 460-461.
6 *Ibid.*, pp. 888-889.
7 *The Attic Orators.* London, 1893. 2 v.
8 *Ibid.*, I, xiii.
9 *Ibid.*
10 *Ibid.*, I, 15-16.
11 *Ibid.*, I, 17.
12 *Ibid.*, I, 59-61.
13 *Ibid.*, I, 124-125.
14 *A History of Classical Greek Literature.* New York, 1880. II, 292-353.
15 London, 1919. pp. 199-267.
16 *Ibid.*, p. 250.
17 *Ibid.*, pp. 250-251.
18 *Ibid.*, p. 240.
19 W. E. H. Lecky. *A History of England in the Eighteenth Century.* New ed. New York, 1892. I, 422-423.
20 *Ibid.*, III, 382.
21 *Ibid.*, III, 390.
22 *Ibid.*
23 *Ibid.*
24 John Morley. *The Life of Richard Cobden.* London, 1881. I, 192-193.
25 *Ibid.*, I, 193.
26 *Ibid.*, I, 195.
27 *Ibid.*, I, 197-198.
28 *Ibid.*, I, 197.
29 *Ibid.*, II, 155.
30 *Ibid.*, II, 159.
31 John Morley. *The Life of William Ewart Gladstone.* New ed. in one vol. New York, 1932. II, 589-594, *passim.*
32 *Ibid.*, II, 590.
33 James Bryce. *William Ewart Gladstone.* New York, 1898. pp. 39-40.
34 *Ibid.*, p. 40.
35 *Ibid.*, p. 41.
36 Morley. *The Life of William Ewart Gladstone.* II, 593.
37 *Ibid.*, III, 312.
38 *Ibid.*, II, 594.
39 George M. Trevelyan, *The Life of John Bright.* Boston, 1913. p. 4.
40 *Ibid.*, pp. 383-384.
41 *Ibid.*, p. 277.
42 11th ed. Chicago, 1891.
43 New York, 1857. 2 v.
44 *Living Orators in America.* New York, 1860. p. 2.
45 *Ibid.*, pp. 30-60, *passim.*
46 Philadelphia, 1854.
47 Trans. from 14th ed. Ed. by G. H. Colton. New York, 1851.

[48] New York, 1896. p. viii.

[49] In *Modern Eloquence*. New York, 1923. IX.

[50] Indianapolis, 1928.

[51] Cf. Edmund Burke's *Conciliation Speech*. Ed. with notes by Albert S. Cook. New York, 1897. Introd.

[52] Henry Cabot Lodge. "Webster." In *The Cambridge History of American Literature*. New York, 1918. II, 94.

[53] *Ibid.*, II, 95.

[54] *Ibid.*, II, 96.

[55] Herbert J. C. Grierson. "Edmund Burke." In *The Cambridge History of English Literature*. New York, 1933. XI, 36.

[56] C. W. Previte-Orton. "Political Writers and Speakers." In *The Cambridge History of English Literature*. New York, 1933. XI, 37-62.

[57] Sir A. W. Ward. "Historians, Biographers and Political Orators." In *The Cambridge History of English Literature*. New York, 1933. XIV, 131-151.

[58] Oliver Elton. *A Survey of English Literature, 1730-1780*. New York, 1928. II, 244-268.

[59] A. C. McLaughlin. "Publicists and Orators, 1800-1850." In *The Cambridge History of American Literature*. II, 70-91.

[60] London, 1913.

[61] *Ibid.*, p. 2.

[62] *Lord Chatham As An Orator*. Oxford, 1912.

[63] Albert von Ruville. *William Pitt, Earl of Chatham*. Trans. by H. J. Chaytor. Introd. by Hugh Egerton. New York, 1907. I, 85-87.

[64] *Ibid.*, I, vii.

[65] *Main Currents in American Thought*. New York, 1930. III, 140-147.

[66] "Hitler, the Orator." *Quarterly Journal of Speech*, 28:123-131 (April, 1942).

[67] New York, 1939.

[68] *Ibid.*, p. 155.

[69] I. A. Richards. *The Philosophy of Rhetoric*. New York, 1936. p. 96.

[70] Irving J. Lee. "Four Ways of Looking at a Speech." *Quarterly Journal of Speech*, 28:151 (April, 1942).

[71] Cf. Stuart Chase. *The Tyranny of Words*. New York, 1938. p. 363.

[72] Cf. such excellent works as S. I. Hayakawa, *Language in Action*, and Hugh Walpole, *Semantics*.

[73] Philadelphia, 1934.

[74] Iowa City, 1932.

[75] New York, 1941.

[76] *University of Missouri Studies*. 14:No. 3, July 1, 1939.

[77] Baton Rouge, 1945.

CHAPTER 8

[1] Thomas Carlyle. *Critical and Miscellaneous Essays*. New York, 1876. III, 11.

[2] *Ibid.*

[3] Ph.D. Thesis. State University of Iowa, 1941.

[4] Ph.D. Thesis. State University of Iowa, 1943.

[5] Ph.D. Thesis. Northwestern University, 1940.

[6] Ph.D. Thesis. Stanford University, 1927.

[7] Ph.D. Thesis. University of Chicago, 1936.

[8] Ph.D. Thesis. Teachers College, Columbia University, 1944.

[9] Columbus, Ohio, 1931.

[10] University of Chicago Press, 1934.

[11] Ph.D. Thesis. State University of Iowa, 1932.

[12] Ph.D. Thesis. State University of Iowa, 1944.

[13] *Speech Monographs*. 3:21-48 (1936).

14 *Ibid.,* 10:68-74 (1943).
15 M.A. Thesis. University of Washington, 1939.
16 *Speech Monographs.* 3:49-74 (1936).
17 *Archives of Speech.* 1:7-98 (September, 1936).
18 Ph.D. Thesis. State University of Iowa, 1940.
19 Ph.D. Thesis. State University of Iowa, 1943.
20 *Speech Monographs.* 5:16-39 (1938).
21 Ph.D. Thesis. State University of Iowa, 1932.
22 Ph.D. Thesis. State University of Iowa, 1936.
23 *Iowa Journal of History and Politics.* 43:209-253 (July, 1945).
24 Ph.D. Thesis. State University of Iowa, 1930.
25 *Speech Monographs.* 5:40-61 (1938).
26 Ph.D. Thesis. State University of Iowa, 1939.
27 Ph.D. Thesis. State University of Iowa, 1942.
28 M.A. Thesis. Cornell University, 1927.
29 M.A. Thesis. Cornell University, 1929.
30 M.A. Thesis. Northwestern University, 1931.
31 M.A. Thesis. State University of Iowa, 1930.
32 Ph.D. Thesis. State University of Iowa, 1945.
33 London, 1867.
34 New York, 1924.
35 New York, 1928.
36 Ph.D. Thesis. State University of Iowa, 1939.
37 Princeton, N. J., 1941.

CHAPTER 9

1 Quoted from Alan F. Herr, *The Elizabethan Sermon.* Philadelphia, 1940. p. 86.
2 *Ibid.,* p. 78.
3 *Select British Eloquence.* New York, 1853. p. 75.
4 *Journalism in the United States, from 1690 to 1872.* New York, 1873. p. 720.
5 *Hansard,* XXIII, 148.
6 *Gentleman's Magazine,* 1737.
7 *Essay on the Life and Genius of Dr. Johnson.*
8 Sir John Hawkins. *Life of Samuel Johnson.* London, 1787. pp. 112-116.
9 Michael Macdonagh. *The Reporters' Gallery.* London, 1913. p. 31.
10 *Ibid.,* p. 298.
11 *Ibid.,* p. 354.
12 *The Lives of the Chief Justices of England.* London, 1849. II, 566-567.
13 Cf. R. W. Postgate. *Dear Robert Emmet.* New York, 1932. pp. 224-241.
14 *History and Criticism of American Public Address.* New York, 1943. II, 631.
15 *Ibid.,* II, 721-726.
16 *Ibid.,* I, 353-356.
17 Cf. "The Stenographic Report of Webster's Reply to Hayne." *The Phonographic Magazine,* 8:22-24 (January 15, 1894).
18 *History and Criticism of American Public Address.* I, 436-437n.
19 Ph.D. Thesis. State University of Iowa, 1944. 225ff.
20 In *Papers in Rhetoric.* Ed. by Donald C. Bryant. St. Louis, 1940. pp. 39-45.
21 Trevelyan. *The Life of John Bright.* Boston, 1913. p. 276.
22 "Are Speeches in Congress Reported Accurately?" *Quarterly Journal of Speech,* 28:12 (February, 1942).
23 United Press report. *New York Times,* Nov. 3. 1942.
24 "Franklin D. Roosevelt's Second Inaugural Address: A Study in Text Authenticity." *Quarterly Journal of Speech.* 23:439-444 (October, 1937).

25 "Four Lincoln Firsts." *Papers of the Bibliographical Society of America,*
36:1-17 (1942).

26 *Ibid.,* p. 12.

27 *Ibid.,* p. 15.

28 *Ibid.,* p. 16.

29 *Speeches on Questions of Public Policy by John Bright, M. P.* London,
1868. 2 v.

30 *The Arguments and Speeches of William M. Evarts.* New York, 1919. 3 v.

31 *Op. cit.,* I, 273-274; 282-283.

32 July 1, 1863.

33 London, 1863. pp. 1830; 1837-1838.

CHAPTER 10

1 Edward W. Emerson and Waldo E. Forbes. *Journal of Ralph Waldo Emerson.* Boston, 1909-1914. III, 256.

2 Edward T. Channing. *Lectures on Rhetoric and Oratory.* Boston, 1856. p. 16.

3 *Ibid.,* p. 14.

4 *The Works of Cornelius Tacitus.* Trans. by Arthur Murphy. London, 1813.
II, 439.

5 *Brutus.* Trans. by J. S. Watson. New York, 1890. XI.

6 James T. Shotwell. *The History of History.* New York, 1939. I, 219.

7 *Selected Essays of J. B. Bury.* Ed. by Harold Temperley. London, 1930. p. 6.

8 *Op. cit.,* I, 220.

9 Frederick J. Teggart. *Theory and Processes of History.* Berkeley, Calif.,
1941. pp. 18-19.

10 *Ibid.,* p. 69.

11 "Vagaries of Historians." Presidential Address to American Historical Association, December 28, 1918.

12 "Scientific Method in Literary Research." *University Review,* 8, 1942.

13 J. B. Bury. *The Ancient Greek Historians.* New York, 1909. p. 250.

14 Preserved Smith. "The Place of History among the Sciences." In *Essays
in Intellectual History.* New York, 1929. p. 212.

15 *Ibid.*

16 *Ancient Greek Historians.* p. 252.

17 *Op. cit.,* p. 15.

18 *Institutes of Oratory.* Trans. by J. S. Watson. London, 1856. IX, iv, 5.

19 Ph.D. Thesis. State University of Iowa, 1938.

20 Loren D. Reid. *Charles James Fox: A Study of the Effectiveness of an
Eighteenth Century Parliamentary Speaker.* Iowa City, 1932. pp. 29-40, *passim.*

CHAPTER 11

1 Cf. section on classical divisions in Chapter 3.

2 *Rhetoric.* Welldon ed. p. 10.

3 *Quarterly Journal of Speech,* 26:667 (December, 1940).

4 *The Function and Forms of Thought.* New York, 1927. p. 359.

5 Compare the views of Cicero and Tacitus on this theme.

6 *The Seven Lamps of Advocacy.* London, 1923. p. 11.

7 *Op. cit.,* p. 359.

8 *De Oratore.* II, 35.

9 *The Working Principles of Rhetoric.* Boston, 1900. pp. 388, 390.

10 *The Nature of Thought.* New York, 1940. II, 66.

11 *How We Think.* Boston, 1910. Ch. 6.

12 Cf. Benedetto Croce, *History.* Trans. by Sylvia Sprigge. New York, 1941.
p. 27.

13 *Burke's Chief American Works:* An Edition with Notes and an Introduction. Ph.D. Thesis. Cornell University, 1929.

14 Ph.D. Thesis. State University of Iowa, 1942.

15 *History and Criticism of American Public Address.* New York, 1943. I, 239-241.

16 Ph.D. Thesis. State University of Iowa, 1942.

17 Chauncey A. Goodrich. *Select British Eloquence.* New York, 1853. p. 270.

18 *Principles and Problems of Right Thinking.* New York, 1928. pp. 315-319.

19 *Op. cit.,* 351ff.

20 *Charles James Fox.* Iowa City, 1932. pp. 89-92.

21 *Op. cit.,* pp. 368-369.

22 *Ibid.,* pp. 369-370.

<h2 style="text-align:center">CHAPTER 12</h2>

1 *A System of Oratory.* 1759. II, 299-300.

2 *Lectures on Oratory and Criticism.* 1777. p. 80.

3 *The Forms of Prose Literature.* New York, 1900. pp. 176-177.

4 "The Literature of Knowledge and the Literature of Power." *North British Review,* August, 1848. Cf. Masson ed. XI, 51.

5 *The Philosophy of Rhetoric.* New ed. New York, 1851. pp. 100-101.

6 *Rhetoric.* Welldon ed. pp. 10-12.

7 *Rhetorica.* Trans. by W. Rhys Roberts. Oxford, 1924. 1354a 12.

8 "Prolegomena to a Political Ethics." In *Essays in Honor of John Dewey.* New York, 1929. p. 334.

9 *Lectures Concerning Oratory.* Dublin, 1760. p. 165.

10 139 :287 (January, 1874).

11 *De Oratore.* II, 42.

12 *The Senses and the Intellect.* 3rd ed. New York, 1888. p. 528.

13 Trans. by Henry Cary. London, 1854. I, 350-351.

14 *De Oratore.* II, 53.

15 *Op. cit.,* 178ff.

16 *Lectures on Rhetoric and Belles Lettres.* New ed. 383ff.

17 *De Oratore.* II, 77.

18 *Institutes of Oratory.* VI, 1, 51.

19 *De Oratore.* II, 45.

20 *Rhetoric.* Welldon ed. p. 31.

21 *Ibid.,* p. 114.

22 *Effective Speaking.* Chicago, 1908. Cf. p. 56, for practical application of Phillips' concept.

23 Chauncey A. Goodrich. *Select British Eloquence.* New York, 1852. pp. 536-537.

24 *The Epic of America.* Boston, 1931. p. 181.

25 *Ibid.,* p. 183.

26 *Principles of Literary Criticism.* 5th ed. New York, 1934. p. 267.

27 Cf. James Burnham and Philip Wheelwright. *Introduction to Philosophical Analysis.* New York, 1932. pp. 71-72.

28 *Semantics.* New York, 1941.

29 *Harper's Magazine,* September, 1934. p. 470.

30 Pamphlet entitled "The Written Word." N. W. Ayer and Son.

31 *De Oratore.* II, 27.

32 *The English Works of Thomas Hobbes.* Ed. by Sir William Molesworth. London, 1839 III, 49.

33 *Op. cit.* pp. 23-24.

34 *Op. cit.* p. 278.

35 *Ibid.*

36 *Ibid.*, pp. 278-279.
37 *Elements of Rhetoric.* New ed. Boston, 1851. p. 55.
38 *Ibid.*, p. 209.
39 *Quarterly Journal of Public Speaking,* 3:109-124 (April, 1917).
40 "Conviction and Persuasion." *Quarterly Journal of Public Speaking,* 3:249-264 (July, 1917).
41 Cf. *Quarterly Journal of Speech Education,* 10:350-362 (November, 1924); 11:319-337 (November, 1925).
42 New York, 1927. p. 110.
43 "The Conviction-Persuasion Duality." *Quarterly Journal of Speech,* 20:482 (November, 1934).
44 *History and Criticism of American Public Address.* New York, 1943. I, 475-476.
45 *Ibid.*, I, 227-228.
46 *Select British Eloquence.* New York, 1853. p. 789.
47 *The Psychology of the Audience.* New York, 1935. p. 110.

CHAPTER 13

1 Edward W. Emerson and Waldo E. Forbes, *Journals of Ralph Waldo Emerson.* Boston, 1909-1914. IX, 342.
2 *Works of Ralph Waldo Emerson.* p. 143.
3 *Lectures Concerning Oratory.* Dublin, 1760. p. 172.
4 *Rhetoric.* Welldon ed. p. 10.
5 *Ibid.*, pp. 10-11.
6 *Ibid.*, p. 113.
7 *Ibid.*
8 *Ibid.*, p. 114.
9 *De Oratore.* II, 43.
10 *Ibid.*
11 *Rhetoric.* Welldon ed. p. 114.
12 "Some Conceptions of Emotional Appeal in Rhetorical Theory." *Speech Monographs.* 6:67 (1939).
13 *Ibid.*, p. 69.
14 *A Critical Analysis of Certain Aspects of Ethical Proof.* Ph.D. Thesis. State University of Iowa, 1942.
15 Chauncey A. Goodrich. *Select British Eloquence.* New York, 1852. p. 638.
16 *Ibid.*, Note, p. 638.
17 Frank Moore. *American Eloquence.* New York, 1857. II, 399.
18 *Charles James Fox.* Iowa City, 1932. pp. 50-51.

CHAPTER 14

1 Examine a recent textbook on speech composition relative to this remark.
2 *The Working Principles of Rhetoric.* Boston, 1900. p. 388.
3 *A Treatise on the Preparation and Delivery of Sermons.* New ed. New York, 1898. p. 260.
4 *A System of Christian Rhetoric.* New York, 1873. p. 332.
5 *Phaedrus.* Trans. by Henry Cary. *The Works of Plato.* London, 1854. I, 342-343.
6 *Rhetoric.* Welldon ed. p. 275.
7 *Ibid.*, p. 301.
8 *Charles James Fox.* Iowa City, 1932. pp. 47-49.
9 *The Art of Oratorical Composition.* New York, 1885. p. 107.
10 *Ibid.*, p. 100.

11 *History and Criticism of American Public Address.* New York, 1943. I, 425-428.

CHAPTER 15

1 *Lectures on Rhetoric and Belles Lettres.* New ed. London, n.d. p. 103.
2 *Institutes of Oratory,* VIII, Introd., 32.
3 *The Practical Elements of Rhetoric.* Boston, 1886. p. 15.
4 *Ibid.,* p. 13.
5 *Ibid.,* p. 15.
6 "Personal Style." In *A Book of English Essays, 1600-1900.* Ed. by S. V. Makower and B. H. Blackwell. Oxford, 1927. pp. 389-390.
7 *De Oratore.* III, 52.
8 *Institutes.* XII, 10, 59.
9 *Ibid.*
10 *Ibid.,* XII, 10, 16.
11 *Ibid.,* XII, 10, 19.
12 New York, 1862. pp. 263-264.
13 *Ibid.,* p. 264.
14 *Ibid.,* pp. 265-266.
15 *Select British Eloquence.* New York, 1853. pp. 636, 789.
16 *Rhetorica.* Trans. by W. Rhys Roberts. 1407a.
17 *De Oratore.* III, 37.
18 *Ibid.,* III, 52.
19 New ed. New York, 1851. 164ff.
20 *Ibid.,* 177ff.
21 *Rhetoric.* Buckley ed. p. 207.
22 *Institutes.* VIII, 2, 22.
23 *Ibid.,* VIII, 2, 24.
24 *Literary Criticism.* New York, 1930. p. 92.
25 *A Treatise on the Preparation and Delivery of Sermons.* New ed. New York, 1898. p. 361.
26 *Op. cit.,* 239ff.
27 *Ibid.,* p. 244.
28 *Ibid.,* p. 249.
29 *Ibid.,* p. 266.
30 *Ibid.,* p. 270.
31 *Practical Elements of Rhetoric.* 1886. p. 21.
32 *Rhetorica.* Roberts ed. 1408a.
33 *De Oratore.* III, 55.
34 *Ibid.,* III, 31.
35 *Institutes.* XII, 10, 69-72.
36 *Op. cit.,* p. 167.
37 *Rhetoric.* Buckley ed. p. 248.
38 *De Oratore.* III, 55.
39 *Ibid.*
40 *Rhetoric.* Buckley ed. p. 246.
41 *Op. cit.,* 122, 133.
42 *Rhetorica.* Roberts ed. 1408b.
43 *Orator.* Trans. by C. D. Yonge. *The Orations of Marcus Tullius Cicero.* London, 1852. IV, 442.
44 Genung, *Op. cit.,* pp. 169-170.
45 Thomas Gibbons. *Rhetoric.* London, 1767. p. 1
46 *Ibid.,* 119f.
47 *Ibid.,* p. 3.
48 *Ibid.,* 22ff.

[49] *Ibid.*, 119ff.

[50] *Works of Ralph Waldo Emerson.* London, 1897. p. 229.

[51] "The Philosophy of Style." *Westminster Review.* New ser. 58:446 (October, 1852).

[52] *Ibid.*, pp. 436-437.

[53] *Aristotle's Poetics: Demetrius on Style.* Trans. by T. A. Moxon. Everyman's Library. New York. p. 207.

[54] *Rhetorica.* Roberts ed. 1413b 9.

[55] *Institutes*, XII, 10, 55-56.

[56] *Ibid.*, XII, 10, 43.

[57] *Select British Eloquence*, pp. 239-240.

[58] Based in part upon the point of view developed in *Speech Preparation and Delivery.* (Chicago, 1942).

CHAPTER 16

[1] *New York World-Telegram.* 1932.

[2] *Lives of the Ten Orators.* In *Plutarch's Essays and Miscellanies.* New York, 1905. V, 52.

[3] *History and Criticism of American Public Address.* New York, 1943. II, 796-797.

[4] *Ibid.*, II, 952.

[5] "Mr. Bright." *Contemporary Review,* 55:654, 657 (May, 1889).

[6] *The Times* (London), Jan. 14, 1878.

[7] *Select British Eloquence.* New York, 1853. p. 71.

[8] *Ibid.*, p. 237.

[9] *Brutus.* LXIII.

[10] *Ibid.*, LX.

[11] *Ibid.*, XXXVIII.

[12] *Select British Eloquence*, p. 404.

[13] *Ibid.*, p. 577.

[14] *Ibid.*, p. 636.

[15] *Ibid.*, p. 789.

[16] *Ibid.*, p. 850.

[17] *Chironomia.* London, 1806. p. 101.

[18] *Life and Times of the Right Hon. John Bright.* London, 1889. p. 558.

[19] *Reminiscences.* New York, 1910. p. 238.

[20] *Op. cit.*, p. 404.

[21] *Ibid.*, p. 577.

[22] *Ibid.*, p. 636.

[23] *Ibid.*, p. 789.

[24] *History and Criticism of American Public Address,* I, 358-360.

CHAPTER 17

[1] *Historical and Political Essays.* London, 1908. pp. 13-14.

[2] Compare several modern textbooks on speech composition relative to this point.

[3] *The Complete Writings of Ralph Waldo Emerson.* New York, 1929. II, 1030.

[4] *Plutarch's Miscellanies and Essays.* 6th ed. Boston, 1898. pp. 450-451.

[5] *Op. cit.*, p. 9.

[6] *History and Criticism of American Public Address.* New York, 1943. II, 821-824.

[7] *Ibid.*, I, 351-353.

[8] *The Religious Uses of Silence.* Doctoral dissertation. Columbia University, 1938. p. 11.

[9] *The Life of John Bright.* Boston, 1913. p. 383.

[10] *Ibid.,* p. 387.

[11] *Modern Parliamentary Eloquence.* London, 1913. p. 22.

[12] *Op. cit.,* pp. 9-14, *passim.*

[13] Quoted from doctoral dissertation.

[14] *Public Addresses of John Bright, M. P.* Ed. by J. E. T. Rogers. London, 1879. p. 366.

[15] *Op. cit.,* p. 4.

[16] *Ibid.*

[17] *The Life of Charles James Fox.* London, 1936. p. 329.

[18] *Edmund Burke.* New York, 1924. p. 45.

CHAPTER 18

[1] Adapted by Holbrook Jackson. *The Anatomy of Bibliomania.* New York, 1932. p. 128.

[2] "A Yardstick for Civilization." In *Essays in Intellectual History.* New York, 1929. p. 359.

[3] George E. C. Catlin. *The Science and Method of Politics.* New York, 1927. p. 306.

[4] *The Politics of Aristotle.* Trans. by J. E. C. Welldon. London, 1897. pp. 128-129.

[5] "Democracy and Language." *Ethics,* 52:221 (January, 1942).

[6] L. T. Hobhouse. *Liberalism.* New York, n.d. p. 23.

[7] *Isocrates.* Trans. by George Norlin. 1928. Loeb Classical Library. II, 327.

[8] *Ibid.,* III, 337-339.

[9] *Literary Essays.* New York, 1878. p. 82.

[10] John Dewey. "Ethical Principles Underlying Education." Reprinted from *Third Yearbook of the National Herbart Society.* Chicago, 1903. p. 30.

[11] *Educating Liberally.* Stanford University, 1945. 10ff.

INDEX

Abernathy, Elton, 293
Academics, 181
Accusation, use in enthymemes, 68
Action, in delivery, 441-443 (See "De-
    livery")
Adams, James Truslow, 11
    on oratory of Sam Adams, 368
Adams, John, Choate on oratory of, 303
Adams, John Quincy, 339
Adams, Sam, J. T. Adams' estimate of, 368
Addison, Joseph,
    on delivery, 128
    on oratorical action, 211-212
Aeschines, 31, 40, 43, 44, 97, 155, 170, 171,
    199, 202, 205, 218, 236, 237, 255, 408
Affectation, Sheridan on elocutionary, 129
Against the Sophists (Isocrates), 46, 48
Alcibiades, Plutarch compares Demosthenes
    with, 200
Alcuin, 51, 110
Alderman, Edwin A., 285
Allegory, defined, 420
Allport, Floyd, and theory of social facili-
    tation, 324
Aly, Bower, 284
Ambrose, 113
American Eloquence (Moore), 271
"American Taxation" (Burke), 397, 458
Ammon, George, 105
Amplification,
    Longinus on, 108
    Wilson on, 118-119
Anacoenosis, defined, 422
Analogy,
    argument from, 349
    use in enthymemes, 67
Analysis,
    emotional, 357-382
    ethical, 383-391
    logical, 331-356
    (See also "Emotional proof," "Ethical
    proof," and "Logical proof")
Analytic criticism, defined, 17-18
Anastrophe, defined, 422
Ancients vs. moderns controversy,
    Brougham on, 233-238
    Cicero on, 152-157
    Quintilian on, 187-195
    (See also "Atticism vs. Asianism")
Anderson, Dorothy, 293
Andocides, 40, 41, 42, 170, 199, 255
    his speech "On the Mysteries," 258-259
    on authenticity of speech "On the Peace,"
    305
Angle, Paul M., on Lincoln's texts, 306, 307
Annual Register, 337
Antidosis (Isocrates), 46, 47, 48
Antimachus, 50
Antiphon, 39, 40, 41, 42, 43, 44, 170, 255,
    301
    Jebb on, 256-257
    Plutarch on, 199
    representative of austere style, 106

Antisthenes, 181
Antitheta (Bacon), 123
Antonius, Marcus, 82, 83, 163, 164, 442,
    444
Aper, Marcus, 102
Apollonius, 97
Apology (Plato), 46
Apophasis, defined, 422
Apophthegmes (Bacon), 123
Aporia, defined, 421
Aposiopesis, defined, 421
Apostrophe, defined, 422
Appropriateness, in style, 414-416
Arcadian Rhetorike (Fraunce), 125
Arcesilas, relation to New Academy, 181
Archidamus, 32
Archidamus (Isocrates), 45
Areas of inquiry, rhetorical, 289-296
Areopagiticus (Isocrates), 45
Argument,
    appraisal of, 341-350
    in Homeric epics, 30
    its part in criticism, 13-14
    (See also "Logical proof")
"Argument from the Point of View of So-
    ciology" (Yost), 376
Aristeides, 203
Aristotle,
    analysis of emotion of envy, 61-62
    as critic, 150
    Bacon's reference to, 124
    Cicero's reliance upon, 90
    comparison of his teaching with Isocrates',
    44
    definition of rhetoric, 6, 58-59
    distinguishes between artistic and inar-
    tistic proof, 59
    emphasis upon deliberative speaking, 58
    emphasis upon invention, 79
    emphasis upon logical proof, 331
    Gibbons' reliance upon, 125
    his point of view, 150
    on audience, 321
    on audience analysis, 60-63
    on delivery, 69, 434
    on disposition, 70, 398, 399, 400
    on emotional proof, 60-63, 358, 359, 362,
    366, 372, 373, 382
    on enthymemes, 65
    on ethical proof, 383, 384, 385, 386
    on examples, 65
    on function of audience, 60
    on function of oratory, 102
    on golden mean, 72-74, 432
    on kinds of proof, 59-60
    on kinds of style, 89
    on logical proof, 60, 63-69
    on memory, 80
    on probability, 35
    on proportion, 72-74
    on relation of philosophy to rhetoric, 180
    on style, 69-70, 412, 415, 416, 419, 426
    on the topics, 60, 63-65

527

Lectures on Rhetoric and Oratory (Adams), 339

Lectures on Systematic Theology and Pulpit Eloquence (Campbell), 139

Lee, Irving J.,
  on difference between ethos and pathos, 386
  on semanticist's way of looking at a speech, 283

Legal Masterpieces (Snyder), 303

"Letter to a Young Clergyman" (Swift), 128, 211

Letters to His Son (Chesterfield), 128, 212-214

Life of John Bright (Trevelyan), 4, 268-271

Life of Richard Cobden (Morley), 263-265

Life of William Ewart Gladstone (Morley), 265-268

Lincoln, Abraham, 285, 313, 334, 351, 436, 471
  effect of his oratory, 450-452
  "textbook" version of Gettysburg Address, 372
  variant texts of Gettysburg Address, 306-307

Lincoln-Douglas debates, 12, 450-452

Lind, John, 325

Listening, as aid to critic, 197-198

"Literary Criticism of Oratory" (Wichelns), 9, 17

Lives (Plutarch), 195-197

Lives of the Sophists (Philostratus), 98, 200-204

Lives of the Ten Orators (Plutarch), 199-200

Living Orators in America (Magoon), 271-272

Livy, 315

Lloyd George, David, 277

Locke, John, 410
  Campbell's agreement with, 136
  on art of rhetoric, 181-182

Lodge, Henry Cabot,
  literary approach to oratory, 274-275
  on difficulty of using rhetorical techniques, 297
  on Webster, 275

"Logic and Public Speaking" (Gilman), 332

Logic, as constituent of rhetorical judgment, 13-14

Logical basis of division, 395, 396-397

Logical proof,
  an analysis of, 352-355
  and appraising refutation, 351
  and appraising usefulness of ideas, 350-351
  and testing argument, 344-350
  and testing evidence, 341-344
  Aristotle on, 60, 63-69
  Campbell on, 135-136
  method of determining integrity of ideas, 334-335
  method of exploring speaker's ideas, 335-341
  nature of, 331-356
  place in rhetoric, 331-334
  relation to emotional proof, 368-378
  ultimate objective of, 355-356
  Whately on, 139-142
  (See also "Audiences" and "Invention")

Longinus,
  compares Cicero with Demosthenes, 175
  compares Demosthenes with Hyperides, 175-176
  his standard of excellence, 174
  on amplification, 108
  on imagery, 108
  on imitation, 176
  on sources of sublimity, 107
  on style, 107-108
  Rapin's reliance upon, 207, 208

Lucian,
  on disposition, 105
  on qualifications of orator, 104
  on rules, 104-105
  satirizes oratorical training, 103-105

Lucretius, 101

Lycurgus, 40, 43, 44, 97, 170, 199, 205, 255

Lysias, 39, 40, 41, 43, 44, 54, 97, 150, 155, 170, 173, 176, 193, 199, 205, 217, 255, 301
  Dionysius on, 171-172
  model of Atticists, 154
  representative of plain style, 42

Macaulay, Thomas Babington, 276, 325, 383, 458, 470
  his appraisals of orators, 241-242
  his standards of judgment, 240-241
  Lodge on, 274
  on Longinus, 176
  on oratory and war, 241
  on parliamentary speaking, 238
  on statesmanship and oratory, 238-240
  views oratory as moulded by the age, 238-239

Machiavelli, Niccolo, 268

Mackenzie, Compton, 33

Mackintosh, James, 241, 249, 251, 442

Macpherson, James, 325

MacCunn, John, on Aristotelian ethics, 70, 72

McBurney, James H., 293

McCall, Roy C., on Parker's invention, 338-339

McCosh, James, 131

McDuffie, George, 272

McLaughlin, A. C., 276

Madden, Richard R., 301

Magoon, E. L., on American orators, 271-272

Mahaffy, J. P., 29, 259, 260

Manningham, John, 298

Mansfield, Lord,
  as writer of speeches, 301
  compares Demosthenes with Cicero, 226-227

Manual of Gesture (Bacon), 127

Marriage of Philology and Mercury (Martianus Capella), 110

Martianus Capella, 110

Mathews, William, 271

Matter vs. manner, theme of, 404, 407

Mean, golden, in rhetoric, 72-74, 432-433

Medieval rhetoric, 110, 114

Melanchthon, 116

Memoria. (See "Memory")